KU-767-261

Foreword

I went on my first and only visit to the United Kingdom in the summer of 1998. I spent some of that time reading Malayan Emergency documents at the Public Record Office, Kew, and subsequently at Rhodes House Library, University of Oxford. It was part of my personal quest to get a broader picture of the war in which between four and five thousand of my comrades were killed.

Discovering what officials in the late 1940s and 1950s London were hatching to further the cause of their anti-insurgency campaign against the Communist Party of Malaya (CPM) was, to say the least, an affirming exercise. Finally, after so many years, I was able to evaluate the propaganda that was fed the world as my men and I trekked through the forbidding jungles of our country.

I have, since those reading sessions at Kew and Oxford, gathered a large collection of relevant declassified reports, not just from the Public Record Office, but also from the Imperial War Museum in London and the Australian War Memorial in Canberra. These have become part of my personal archives. I now see the wisdom in not having rushed to tell my story as I was coaxed to do by several quarters immediately upon signing the peace accords in Haadyai, southern Thailand, on December 2, 1989. I had two reasons. At the time, I volunteered only the patently obvious one. I said I needed time. I had to adjust first to the new schedules and disciplines brought on by the accords. After a lifetime in the wilderness, I had to make sure that the new concept of peace we had worked out with Thailand and Malaysia would work for everyone.

The second reason was not an easy one to explain. I agreed that our side of the Emergency story had to be told. But, not so soon. From where I had been directing our armed struggle, only vague reports reached me of what was being said, decided and ordered in London and Kuala Lumpur corridors of power. I required documented proof to accompany my re-examination of that war. Without it, intrepid detractors would, quickly and conveniently, dismiss my analysis as a summary of unsubstantiated resentments and bits of fiction or, to borrow Gerald Templer's derisive phrase, 'typical of all communist muck'. It was important that I remain as dispassionate as any human being could be in the predicament I had been placed.

Reams of propaganda material had succeeded in categorising me as a 'terrorist leader'. The Emergency was a conflict spurred by the continual onslaught of propaganda. I don't in any way excuse our side and claim we did not indulge in campaigns of persuasion. We certainly tried. But the documents at Kew attest to the paltriness of the CPM propaganda arsenal. This can easily be explained by the fact that we were not shackled to desks housed in grand buildings. My army was constantly moving and reorganising and facing food shortages. You could say idealism was the biggest weapon in our stockpile. We had neither the skill nor the sophistication to phrase columns upon columns of elegant prose meant to mislead. We were raw, hot-tempered and inexperienced. Our pronouncements were largely unadorned and straightforward. What you read was what you got.

In early 2000, Ian Ward, whose name I recalled from his byline in *The Daily Telegraph*, London, contacted me. He was by this stage into the 12th year of his retirement and had become an historian. I knew he had been a war correspondent. I remembered his reports from Vietnam and the 'second Emergency'. He didn't have to tell me that our politics differed. He had, for a quarter of a century, represented a staunchly conservative British newspaper. Ward said the Emergency had long interested him and he had, as a matter of fact, been researching it, on and off, for the past many years. By the very nature of it being a guerrilla war, there were aspects of the Emergency that had yet to be revealed and I held the key to this unexplored territory. He wanted to listen to my story. He added that his politics had not changed.

That started a complex and, at times, fiery collaboration. We were, from the very outset, determined that each would not be a 'stooge' of the other. For instance, it took some painstaking effort on my part to explain to Ward why a comrade would not consider setbacks in the movement as being 'wasted time'. Ward, on the other hand, was adamant that the book should not read like a manifesto.

The presence of the writer and editor Norma Miraflor proved more than beneficial to the project that took much longer than anticipated. It was Miraflor – a 'recalcitrant bourgeois' (her words) married to Ward – who kept her cool and by default became keeper of the peace. But she was more than that. Her contributions to the invariably involved and lengthy discussions led to further insights that were worthy of being analysed and recorded. Like her husband, she knew how to listen and she asked the right questions.

Ward and Miraflor made it plain they were not interested in the history of the Communist Party of Malaya. They were more concerned with the human element of the Emergency story and how large aspects of truth, on both sides of a monumental conflict, could be sacrificed in an avalanche of propaganda. Ward particularly worked at ferreting out episodes that could not have reached the media while the armed struggle raged on. These were discussed and examined. Some he accepted; others he rejected, maintaining it was pointless to chronicle anything based on hearsay or rumours. We concurred.

You may ask, is this book the complete picture, then? It is not, for the obvious reason that it is not the history of the Communist Party of Malaya. Nor do I claim that it represents anywhere near a comprehensive account of the Emergency. It is, simply, the recorded journey of a man who opted to travel along a different road to pursue a dream he had for his country.

Other fears and terrors are now sweeping the world. The Emergency monsters were shaped by the East-West struggle – communism versus capitalism. The world has, of course, changed vastly from the one I opted to challenge. Technological progress transports the art of mass killing to frightening dimensions. But I hold that the smartest of today's 'smart' weapons will still find it impossible to eliminate the human desire for justice and dignity.

I fought in two wars and for many years the jungle was my home. This book is neither a boast nor an apology. It is an invitation to understand how beliefs are formed and how conflicts can start and run unabated. Equally, it is an insight into how peace can be achieved.

Chin Peng 陳平

Chin Peng
July, 2003

Contents

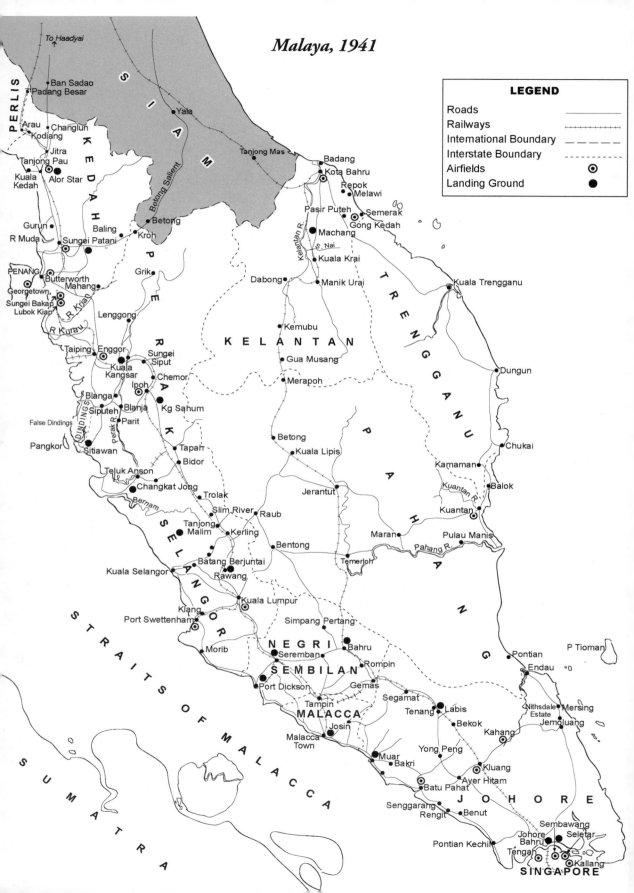

Malaya, 1941

LEGEND

Roads	———
Railways	+++++
International Boundary	– – –
Interstate Boundary	········
Airfields	⊙
Landing Ground	●

To Haadyai

PERLIS

SIAM

Ban Sadao
Padang Besar
Arau
Kodiang
Changlun
Yala
Jitra
Tanjong Pau
Kuala Kedah
Alor Star
KEDAH
Tanjong Mas
Gurun
Baling
R Muda
Sungei Patani
Kroh
Betong Salient
Betong

Badang
Kota Bahru
Repok
Melawi
Pasir Puteh
Semerak
Gong Kedah
Machang
Kelantan R.
S. Nai
Kuala Krai

PENANG
Butterworth
Mahang
Georgetown
Sungei Bakap
Lubok Kiap
R Kran
Grik
Dabong
Manik Urai
TRENGGANU
Kuala Trengganu

Lenggong
Kemubu
R Kurau
Taiping
Enggor
Sungei Siput
KELANTAN
Gua Musang
Dungun
Kuala Kangsar
Chemor
Merapoh
P E R A K
Blanga
Ipoh
Siputeh
Blanja
Kg Sahum
Parit
False Dindings
DINDINGS
Betong
Chukai
Pangkor
Sitiawan
Tapah
Kuala Lipis
PAHANG
Kamaman
Balok
Teluk Anson
Bidor
Jerantut
Kuantan R.
Kuantan
Changkat Jong
Trolak
Bernam
Slim River
Raub
Tanjong Malim
Kerling
Bentong
Maran
Pulau Manis
SELANGOR
Batang Berjuntai
Temerloh
Pahang R.
Rawang
Kuala Selangor
Kuala Lumpur
Simpang Pertang
Klang
Port Swettenham
Pontian
P Tioman
Morib
NEGRI
Bahru
Endau
Seremban
SEMBILAN
Rompin
Port Dickson
Gemas
Segamat
Nithsdale Estate
Mersing
Tampin
MALACCA
Tenang
Labis
Jemoluang
Josin
Bekok
Kahang
Malacca Town
Yong Peng
Muar
Bakri
Kluang
Batu Pahat
Ayer Hitam
JOHORE
Senggarang
Rengit
Benut
Sembawang
Seletar
Johore Bahru
Pontian Kechil
Tengah
Kallang
SINGAPORE

STRAITS OF MALACCA

SUMATRA

Chapter 1

The unlikely alliance

Every generation shapes its dreams. If you yearn to make a difference you become obligated to the clamour of your time. My generation dreamed of doing away with British colonialism in Malaya. I am proud of this fact.

But you pay for your dreams. We certainly paid for ours. So many of us got banished. Under procedures devised by the Colonial Office in London, we were seized, segregated by race and dumped where authorities felt we rightfully belonged. During the years of our armed struggle, we had no counter to the might of the enemy's firepower. Neither did we have the skills, the means or the time to compete with the massive propaganda machinery that portrayed us as nothing more than, first, common bandits, then, as action escalated, communist terrorists . . . CTs. A great number of my comrades perished. Not a day passes that I don't think of them.

Propaganda would have it that I am still unrepentant. To a degree, this is true – but unrepentant of what, I ask. I do not regret having fought for what I considered – and still consider – a just cause. It was time the British quit, stop exploiting Malaya's resources and people to pay off her debts and maintain her Empire status. It was time for us to be independent in the land that belonged to us. I am unrepentant of this belief. Neither do I regret my socialist faith.

Lives were lost as lives get lost in war. Propaganda would also have it that I do not mourn this fact. How could this be possible? Government figures claim six thousand of my army were shot dead. I would more accurately put this figure at between four and five thousand. Some 200 of my followers were hanged, among them a number of women. The British rather conveniently fail to provide statistics for this war category. Nobody has called the British unrepentant killers.

History is the written testimony – or interpretations – of events by those who live it or who inherit its spoils. When it comes to matters of military conflict, history is inevitably portrayed from the point of view of victors whose utterances end up in libraries and archives. Dominant and mightier forces have a way of keeping from prying eyes documents that may depict them in anything but the noble roles for which they would want to be remembered . . . at very least for the duration of their lifetimes. So you have files that remain classified for thirty, fifty, even seventy five years. Some are never released. Such is the protection offered victors against the embarrassment of historical introspection. This is why winners are seldom called names.

So during the Emergency years – for insurance purposes and therefore monetary reasons, the British would not call it a war, which it was – my comrades and I were made to wear the sobriquet of CTs. We were communist terrorists and that's how we were dismissed in the books that touch on that grim and gruesome time. My men died because we wanted to end colonialism and replace it with a political philosophy we believed to be infinitely fairer. The other side lost some 2,000 men – many of them non-British, fighting on behalf of the Empire – because they were defending an idea that had long gone irrelevant.

Colonialism was past its expiry date. The idea of British superiority was dashed the year the Japanese cycled down the roads of Malaya and began a rout that would climax in the battering of Churchill's 'fortress Singapore'. Britannia ruling the waves became a memory when the capital ships, HMS Repulse and HMS Prince of Wales, sank in a one-and-a-half hour South China Sea action, off Kuantan, on December 10, 1941.

But the British would not face up to those realities. After the occupation years, they wanted to return and resurrect *their* glory days as though nothing had happened to alter the course of history. Of course, they would make concessions to achieve this objective. Open their 'for whites only' clubs to a number of privileged natives, for instance. Or assign a few locals to middle-level government jobs; buy them with titles. 'Be nicer'; 'be more congenial' to the brown or yellow person. But they would remain the masters and bullies. So-called agreeable and peaceful negotiations would have taken years and years if nothing had jolted them from their gin and tonic stupor.

That is exactly what my comrades and I achieved. We made the British sit up and acknowledge that they had to listen to the true owners of Malaya. We forced them to the bargaining table long before they were prepared to sit there.

*   *   *   *   *

There is a descriptive phrase in English that talks about eating humble pie. This was a time for the British to gorge on it. Long before the December, 1941, arrival of Japan's 25th Army under the command of Lt General Tomoyuki Yamashita, the colonials had proscribed us, hounded us and either jailed or banished to China every suspected communist ethnic Chinese they could lay their hands on. Our Indian followers also faced the constant threat of being dispatched to India. The fact that you were probably born in Malaya and had never left her shores was incidental. Families were broken up when parents were exiled and children were left with relatives – this was a common punishment.

Then, there we were between 1942 and 1945, against a 'common enemy'. During those years the British actually came to think of us as damn fine fellows. We were their allies. Not once did they suggest that killing a Japanese would make us 'murderers'.

I was acutely aware of Britain's determination to reinstall her colonial supremacy in Malaya once the Pacific War was won. In order to do this she had, of course, to overcome the brutal Japanese. In her commitment to the re-occupation of lost territories and the restoration of lost pride, the British found they had little alternative but to deal with the Communist Party of Malaya (CPM), albeit represented at the time by the Malayan People's Anti-Japanese Army (MPAJA). It was an intensely embarrassing predicament for them. They had to live and sleep with the fact that we were the only functioning resistance movement on the peninsula.

I was never under any illusions about bonding with Britain against the invaders from the land of the rising sun. My allied status was never anything more than a transient arrangement. I knew my old imperialist masters would ultimately be my enemy again. The British were using us because they had no choice. I thought we could use them too. For both sides it was a deal with the devil. I must say I gave my fair share to that affiliation. Two medals and an OBE – you could say I must have done something they had to acknowledge.

Throughout the war, the British thoroughly distrusted us and we were therefore kept in the dark about so much. I have the feeling that, had things worked out the way they had intended, the British, somewhere along the line, might have even dispensed with our close association in the jungle. They would not have severed links completely – we had to be watched, after all – and they would still have used us but from a safe, serviceable distance. This might well have happened if their dreams for the Kuomintang Chinese in Malaya had materialised. I saw for myself how hard the British tried to establish their Kuomintang network, men on side – set up in small businesses, trained as radio operators and attempting to function as spies. But all that came to naught. So they were stuck with the CPM. And they found they had to respect, to the letter, the contents of the December 31, 1943, Agreement.

*　　*　　*　　*　　*

Record of Conference [illegible] 30, 31, DEC. '43. between Messers CHANG HONG, CHEN CHIN SHENG; Messers Broome, Davis, TAN CHOON LIM; Major F. S. Chapman.

App. A.

A. Terms of Cooperation.

1a. Mr Chang Hong (CH) is the elected representative of the Malayan Communist Party, the Anti-Japanese Force and the Anti-Japanese Union, and can put into force any decisions agreed to in these meetings.

b. Major J. L. H. DAVIS, Captain R. N. BROOME and Mr Tan Choon Lim are the Military Representatives (M.R.) of the Allied C in C, South East Asia, and are fully empowered to cooperate with any anti-Japanese party in Malaya.

2. CH agrees that his party will fully cooperate with the Allied Forces while retaking Malaya and for this purpose will follow the instructions of the Allied C-in-C in so far as military operations in Malaya are concerned.

B. Details of Proposals and Decisions.

1. After giving a summary of the numbers and resources of the various Anti-Japanese organisations in Malaya, CH asked in what way these organisations would be expected to cooperate.

The M.R. summarised the military and fifth column activity hoped for and it was agreed that at present, beyond continuing to keep the people anti-Japanese, the only possible action would be to foment labour trouble and carry out sabotage against shipping, naval dockyards, etc. For the rest it was agreed to be a time of preparation for future combined action. CH also undertook to emphasize, in their present propaganda, the need for complete cooperation with Allied invading troops.

Here is the document that transfixed us so at the Blantan camp meeting that December morning in 1943. The original is held at the Public Record Office, Kew, in the United Kingdom.[1]

2. Asked what kind of help was being expected, CH replied (a) Arms and ammunition. (b) Medical supplies including doctors. (c) Military training. (d) Financial assistance.

The MR stated with regard to (a) and (b) that the Allied C-in-C will undertake to despatch to Malaya, by all possible means, the arms and supplies needed for effective cooperation. The introduction of Doctors from outside is difficult at present but the possibility will be investigated.

(C) i The Chinese instructors who are ready in India will be introduced as soon as communications permit. ii Chinese Students will be sent from Malaya for training as instructors and will be returned to Malaya. A party of 6 should be prepared to proceed to India shortly. iii The question of introducing European instructors at a later date will be investigated. (d) The MR have already asked for authority to finance. The reply is expected within a month. CH estimates that 50-70,000 $ per month will meet present requirements.

3. After the MR had stressed the urgency of setting up the wireless installation, the details of para 2 (above) were discussed and an immediate detailed plans for the first shipment of arms and medical supplies was drawn up. Investigation of further specific supply routes was ~~necessary~~ agreed upon.

The above is subject to the ratification of the combined Headquarters of the M.C.P., A-J.F., and A-J.U. And is subject to agreement on the following or similar clause to be added. " That cooperation shall continue during the period in which the army is responsible for the maintenance of peace and Order in Malaya".

J.W.W. Davis Major

R.N. Broome Capt.

Lau Choon Lin

I see it now in my mind's eye. It was a single slip of paper torn carefully from a school exercise book. The meticulous, handwritten English script ran from left-hand margins and appeared to take up every inch of available space on both sides. It looked so innocuous, lying there on the roughly-hewn table in our jungle camp's *atap* conference hut.

It drew us like a magnet. Six grown men sat at the table, riveted by the harmless enough looking document. To a man we saw it determining the future. It did. Though none of us that day – not in the wildest of conjectures – could have foreseen how the terms and conditions set therein, forged through disparate allegiances, would shape such a fearful chapter in British colonial history.

The whole conference hut scene is etched in my memory. A sudden downpour had drenched the jungle surrounds. The sun now burned harshly into the undergrowth and the familiar dank smell of rotting vegetation reached us where we gathered at the long table fashioned by my guerrillas from gnarled rain-forest timber. We sat on two similarly structured wooden benches flanking the table, four men on one side, two on the other.

There was no mistaking it. One thought was paramount in the minds of the three British Army officers across the table: avenge Britain's humiliating capitulation 13 months earlier. Smash Imperial Japan. The CPM guerrillas – for the time being, at least – represented a vital component in the Allies' strategy to drive the invaders from Malaya.

Our short-term agendas meshed. It was the long-term view that was dimmed by dire contradictions. The British were bent on re-gaining priceless colonial territory. Our aim would be to deny them this. Each side knew there would be an inevitable parting of ways.

*   *   *   *   *

It was 33 year-old Major John L. H. Davis, leader of the British trio, who formally read aloud the contents of the document on that humid morning in the hut, perched near the crest of a Malayan mountain. I recall his measured tones contrasting with the continuous buzzing of jungle cicadas in the background. Every so often, Davis paused and turned to a youthful looking Chinese who nodded, then translated the declarations into Mandarin.

Davis sat directly across from me. In the three months or so since we first met, I had formed perhaps the closest association I would ever strike with a European. Physically fit and agile, he spoke both Malay and Cantonese with some fluency. He had been a member of the colonial police before being recruited into Britain's clandestine Special Operations Executive (SOE) only days after the Japanese landing.

To Davis' immediate right was the hunched presence of Captain Richard Broome, a 35 year-old quietly spoken former colonial district officer. For weeks, Broome had been battling a fearful bout of tropical fever. Following lengthy negotiations the previous day, he had, that same evening, managed to summon up enough energy to condense our deliberations onto the double-sided notepaper. But today, wracked in pain, the captain could scarcely utter a comment as he rocked backwards and forwards, sweating, shivering and struggling to follow proceedings. Although I was introduced to Broome during my initial meeting with Davis, our relationship was always conducted at arm's length. Broome, an intellectual, was invariably aloof. Still, I liked the man. He spoke fluent Cantonese and this undoubtedly helped in our exchanges as my knowledge of English, at this time, left much to be desired.

To Broome's right was Major Frederick Spencer Chapman, a British unconventional warfare expert who would, as a result of his anti-Japanese exploits in Malaya, become a legend in his lifetime. Chapman had been establishing guerrilla arms and supply dumps behind Japanese lines for intended 'stay-behind' commando operations when Singapore abruptly fell on the 70th day of the invasion. In Chapman's case, the Japanese advance had been so spectacular that his intended extraction had been thwarted and rather than a 'stay-behind' he had become a 'left-behind'.

Chapman and I had met two months after the British capitulation. Through secret intermediaries, I had learned of his behind-lines activities and invited him to give weapons training to my newly formed and very first guerrilla unit, then encamped in the Perak jungle east of Ulu Slim. Those initial discussions between Chapman and myself marked, perhaps, the first wartime exchanges between the British military and the CPM on how we might together challenge the Japanese military occupation. Each had much to offer the other, though neither of us then possessed the authority to negotiate any formal links between our two operations.

Tan Choon Lim, the bespectacled translator for our December agreement, spoke impeccable Mandarin. He sat with the British, some distance to the left of Davis. It was obvious Tan had enjoyed a privileged upbringing. Seven weeks earlier,

I had played a fairly pivotal role in escorting him through Japanese-patrolled territory to the safety of our mountain camp. I had volunteered to make a high-seas rendezvous in a fishing junk with an Allied submarine bringing in a man described as 'an important Chinese agent'. As soon as the agent introduced himself I knew he was using an alias. I could scarcely complain. So was I. From the outset I took him to be a Kuomintang supporter. Suffice to say that Tan and I viewed each other with considerable skepticism.

*   *   *   *   *

Davis, together with five Chinese agents, had made his first daring 'blind' landing into occupied Malaya on May 24, 1943. After a 10-day journey from Ceylon aboard a Dutch submarine, he had paddled ashore off Tanjong Hantu, four miles north of Pulau Pangkor. His first foray into occupied Malaya had essentially been a reconnaissance and intelligence gathering mission. A month later, Davis was picked up by another submarine and returned to SOE's Malayan Country Section headquarters outside Colombo where he immediately began preparing for a more permanent stay back in the jungles of Malaya.

His initial assignment had established that there was, indeed, a CPM guerrilla network in existence throughout Malaya that was functioning as an anti-Japanese force. The intelligence he gathered suggested there was every reason to believe the communists would look favourably on a joint arrangement with the British targeting the Japanese enemy. It would take delicate negotiations and these would have to be undertaken at the highest possible CPM level – ideally with a member of the Party's Central Committee. In the weeks of preparation that followed, such negotiations became the primary objective of the Malayan Country Section's strategists.

On the night of August 4, 1943, Davis made his second landing on the Perak coast by submarine, this time in the Segari area north of Tanjong Hantu. As on the first occasion he brought with him a substantial stock of supplies. These were duly ferried ashore and temporarily buried in the undergrowth close to the beach fringe.

Broome arrived in similar fashion a month later to join Davis. Connections made with local Chinese fishermen, staunch CPM supporters, resulted in reports of their presence reaching my headquarters in Bidor. At the time I was the CPM's newly appointed acting state secretary for Perak. I had received rapid promotion within the local Party following the arrest by Japanese authorities of both my state leader and his deputy.

The Japanese had substantially increased their security measures throughout Perak's coastal areas following intelligence reports of Allied submarine activity. Still, it was imperative I make contact with the newly arrived British officers as quickly as possible. I chose to cycle to Segari. My route took me via Teluk Anson where I spent the night before setting off early the following morning for the daylong journey through Bagan Datoh and Kampong Koh. Wary of being recognised pedalling through my home town, I decided to by-pass Sitiawan, taking a series of plantation roads through to Lumut and then on to Segari. By late afternoon on September 30, 1943, the CPM, albeit at only the state committee level, was holding its first formal negotiations with the appointed representative of Britain's Ceylon-based, South East Asia Command (SEAC), headed by Admiral Lord Louis Mountbatten.

I introduced myself as Chen Chin Sheng. Davis showed me a letter of authorisation from SEAC empowering him to act on behalf of the High Command. He explained to me how he had been involved in the 101 Special Training School (101 STS) programme. I knew the 101 STS had been responsible for the last-minute preparation and arming of 165 communist recruits to become guerrilla fighters behind Japanese lines. Davis was able to recount details of his association with several of our Perak comrades who had passed through the school. His SEAC letter of authorisation, together with the stories he related, quickly convinced me of his bona fides.

From the outset, Davis and Broome made it patently clear they were anxious to establish, as soon as possible, firm links to the CPM's top leadership. They also asked me for details of the Party's numerical strengths in both the political and military sections. They questioned me about the state of our armaments and the capacities of our guerrilla groups. In turn, I said I could only advise them on matters involving their personal security. However, I assured them I would pass on any messages or requests they might have to the Party's Central Committee.

The three of us then spent time discussing security matters. I ultimately suggested it would be best for them to move from Segari. The entire coastal flatlands were unsafe. I urged they transfer inland to the central ranges where enemy encirclement would be difficult. There the jungle was thick and the terrain most intimidating. I specifically advised them to move to the general mountainous region behind Bidor as this was relatively close to where I was based.

Fortuitously, Davis and Broome were familiar with the topography to which I referred. Prior to the outbreak of hostilities, Davis had been chief of police in

Kampar, a large township north of Bidor on the north-south trunk road. Broome had served as district officer in the Ipoh area.

Both officers listened carefully and after conferring briefly expressed their confidence in my ideas. They asked me to go ahead and pick a suitable campsite for them. These matters settled, our deliberations quickly switched to the best approach for moving them inland. Firstly, we explored the possibility of travelling directly overland from Segari to Bidor, crossing broad stretches of swampland but still passing through populated terrain regularly patrolled by the Japanese. We also reviewed an alternative route involving a boat trip down the coast to the Perak river mouth and from there, up-river to Teluk Anson. I could then meet them for onward passage further up-river to a point where we might cut overland to Bidor.

The two British officers preferred the coastal option. They told me of the availability of a fishing junk owned by one of their Kuomintang contacts. They presented one idea which involved starting their sea voyage from a beach near Tanjong Hantu, a short distance south of Segari. This called for a course well to sea of Pangkor island, which is separated from the Perak coastline by the narrow Dindings Channel. I rejected this idea. I knew Japanese patrol boats were conducting random checks on any suspicious looking vessels in that area. Apart from intelligence indicating Allied submarine activity, vague reports were also circulating about a landing by Europeans. I felt certain a fishing junk taking a circuitous swing around Pangkor would immediately be noticed by Japanese patrols.

I offered another routing choice that took the junk directly through the Dindings Channel, under the very noses of the enemy. Here, I said, we would rely on bravado to carry us through. However, my plan also provided a possible escape route should things go wrong. To negotiate the channel, we would have to stay close inshore. If a Japanese patrol boat should move to intercept, we would have the option – along with the junk's crew – of jumping overboard and swimming in different directions towards the beach. In the darkness most would make it ashore. Afterwards we could re-assemble and resume our getaway through the thick coastal vegetation. Privately, I knew I could count on the particularly strong following the CPM enjoyed among Chinese villages throughout the coastal flatlands.

After mulling over my scheme for some minutes, Davis and Broome agreed with it. We then set about deciding time-frames and future contact arrangements to ensure the move inland was conducted under utmost secrecy and with all possible care to avoid enemy contact.

I returned to Bidor and set about the task of establishing a camp for our newly arrived British associates. It was important that I locate a jungle position at which any future camp could count on emergency support from our guerrilla army's 5th Regiment, then situated in the nearby Cameron Highlands. The site I chose was close to the summit of the 2,200-ft high hill called Blantan, some seven miles north-east of Bidor township. From a security standpoint, Blantan camp offered good protection against Japanese ground encirclement, the surrounding jungle terrain being so thick and so rugged. From the nearest roadway, the position was an exhausting two-hour upwards haul through most inhospitable countryside. The trek proved tough going for even the fittest of our guerrillas.

Although isolated, Blantan provided an extraordinary overview of the coastal plains below and the hinterland mountain range behind. With good visibility, one could scan in a west-nor-westerly direction and spot Pangkor island, 50 miles away, silhouetted against a hazy blue Malacca Straits. To the west lay the Sembilan islands cluster including Pulau Buloh, Pulau Lalang, Pulau Rumbia, Pulau Nipis and Pulau Agas, all easily identifiable given fair weather conditions. From Blantan one gained an almost aerial perspective of the broad Perak River snaking its way southwards, down the centre of the coastal plains before twisting westwards in a series of lurching turns past Teluk Anson, finally to disgorge into the Straits.

I assembled a special platoon to serve as the Blantan camp's security force and issued orders for these men to carry out the required construction work. I chose as camp security commander, Ah Yang, a man I knew to have a good knowledge of English, a relatively rare talent among Party members in those days. Ah Yang was well versed on communist doctrine. But the British would dismiss him as being 'too earnest' to the point of being fanatical. Indeed, it became very obvious in the months to follow that the several Europeans who passed through Blantan camp found Ah Yang quite insufferable. As camp commander, Ah Yang followed security instructions diligently and flatly refused to be drawn into conversations of any substance. He was purposely and adamantly evasive. The European view of Ah Yang, however, was of no significance to me. My man was doing his duty. As far as I was concerned – and even Davis, Broome and Chapman would have admitted as much – Ah Yang was an effective camp commander who had the respect of his men. That no one lost his life as a result of Japanese action against Blantan – or the two later camp locations – stands, I believe, as stout testament to Ah Yang's competence.

Rendezvous Terrain 1943

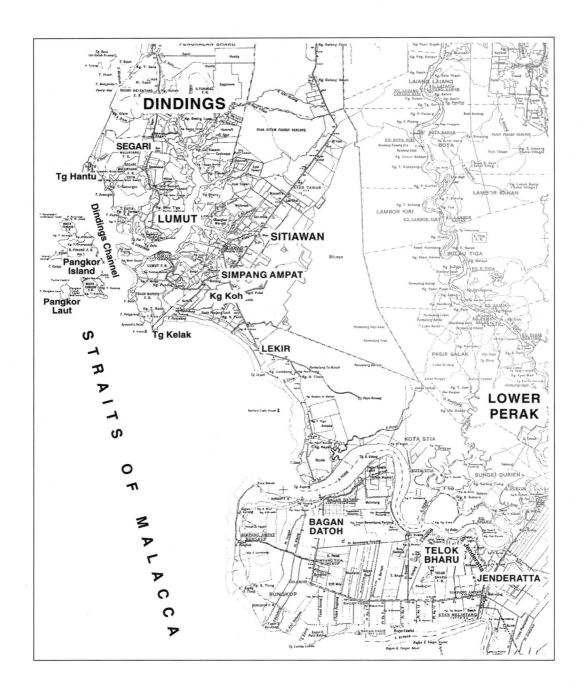

Our Force 136 Campsites

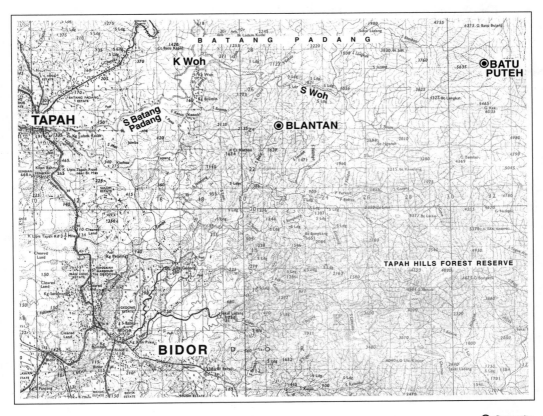

◉ Campsite

When we were ready to welcome the British party, I sent a courier to Segari. His brief was to escort Davis, Broome and their five Chinese agents on the somewhat hazardous sea voyage by junk, through the Dindings Channel to Bagan Datoh, on the southern bank of the Perak River estuary. My calculations proved correct. The junk passed two Japanese patrol craft unchallenged at close quarters as it edged along the shoreline. Meanwhile, I waited in a worker's hut on the Danish-owned Jenderatta estate close by Bagan Datoh. It was daylight when the junk finally arrived. As it would have been suicidal for Europeans to move openly during the day, the British party rested at our rendezvous point and waited for the cover of darkness.

I took this opportunity of briefing Davis and Broome on the 40-mile overland journey that lay ahead. I also introduced them to another of my guerrillas who would be their guide for the two-day-two-night trek. I explained I would have to go ahead by car to arrange their safe passage through the sensitive Bidor area and beyond to Blantan. That night, the two British officers, their Chinese agents and my guide, set out on their circuitous route inland. It took them through rubber plantations, via swamps and coastal jungles. Wide detours had to be made around Malay kampongs and Chinese villages and, of course, Bidor township itself.

Safely in Blantan, Davis took me aside and was effusive in his praise for the camp I had prepared. We talked late into the night and I outlined my earlier contacts with Chapman, relating how he had helped train guerrillas at my first jungle headquarters. Davis asked if I could locate Chapman and have him come to Blantan. I said I would do the best I could. I knew, through our courier system, that Chapman had been moving from camp to camp in central Pahang, carrying out training courses for our men.

The reports I had been receiving suggested he had been very ill with a variety of tropical fevers. I sent a courier message to the Central Committee who then ordered the military commander of our Pahang units to have Chapman escorted to the Bidor area. It took several weeks before the Englishman received the request to move east. For security reasons, we were unable to inform him why he was wanted or where exactly he was going. Because of Chapman's persistent illnesses and the difficulties his guides encountered navigating the forbidding central mountain ridges, it took him almost two months to reach the rendezvous point I had arranged. This happened to be a deserted kongsi house, half a day's trek from Blantan.

On Christmas Day, 1943, I walked into the rambling timber home to greet a pleasantly surprised Chapman. After slogging for hours through jungle drenched by a tropical downpour, he was re-united with his SOE fellows, Davis and Broome. Chapman would later write that the next two weeks he spent at Blantan were among the happiest days of his life.

On every occasion I called by Blantan camp to meet the British officers, they lost no time in impressing on me their urgent need to meet a ranking CPM official who would be able to negotiate terms and sign a military agreement with SEAC. It was the same request Davis had made when we first met at Segari. I had then immediately dispatched a letter to the Secretary General of the CPM himself whom I knew was in Singapore. My message outlined full details of my meeting with Davis and Broome and the various requests they were making. It was a matter of waiting for a reply.

As the days stretched into weeks, the British grew impatient and got the idea into their heads that I was somehow blocking their access to high-ranking communist sources. Nothing could have been further from the truth. Reality was that our lines of communication within the CPM relied exclusively on message-carrying couriers. The Japanese had very early begun targeting our courier links and we were constantly being forced to find innovative ways of circumventing their interceptions. The result was inevitable and infuriating delays.

Finally, I received a reply from the Secretary General informing me he was making arrangements to travel to Perak in late December. The fact that the Secretary General himself would be negotiating with the SEAC men indicated to me the tremendous importance he was placing on the outcome of the meeting. His instructions, however, were that I was not to reveal to Davis and company that he was the CPM's top official. Rather, I was to inform the British that a ranking Central Committee member would arrive in Blantan after Christmas with full powers to conclude an alliance.

At the appointed time, I met our leader north of Bidor. He had driven from Singapore the previous day in his black Austin 10 motorcar. In fact, our rendezvous was at a communist-controlled village close to the approach point for the trek to Blantan. I realised immediately that he was ill. He was emaciated and continually short of breath. The climb to the camp that should have taken us two hours took us more than four. Every 30 minutes or so, we had to stop so he could rest. On reaching the camp, he rested a further hour or so, gathering his strength and composure, before meeting the British.

*   *   *   *   *

As one who had dedicated his life to the communist cause, the gathering I had been instrumental in organising filled me with awe. Although this was my second meeting with the Secretary General and our personal relationship seemed mutually friendly, the Party's rigid hierarchical structure required that I remain very much in his shadow throughout his visit. In the four years I had been a Party member, our leader had remained an enigma. Extraordinarily enough, nobody knew his real name. All, however, were most familiar with his Party alias: Lai Te. An order or directive associated with Lai Te commanded immediate attention, absolute respect and unquestioned adherence. That he was an ethnic Vietnamese commanding an essentially ethnic Chinese movement was undoubtedly a curious contradiction. Amazingly, it never became an issue in the day-to-day running of the Party in those days.

Maintaining the mystique, Lai Te, instructed me to introduce him at Blantan by the alias Chang Hong. I did as I was told. In the conference hut I sat on the right of 'Chang Hong'.

Davis began proceedings by producing his SEAC letter of authority. He went on to confirm that he, Broome and translator Tan, were the military representatives of Admiral Mountbatten, the Allied C-in-C, South East Asia. As such, he said, they were 'fully empowered' to cooperate with any anti-Japanese organisation in Malaya.

For his part, Chang Hong stated he was attending in the role of the elected representative of the CPM, the Anti-Japanese Army, the Party's military arm, and the Anti-Japanese Union, its political movement. There was not even a mention of his being a Central Committee member. However, he made it clear he had arrived with the authority to implement any decisions entered into during the meeting.

It was a truly extraordinary scene. Here sat ostensibly the most wanted man in pre-war Malaya, leader of the communist movement which, itself, had been branded illegal by the former colonial administrators. And there he was, working out terms and conditions for cooperation with the very people who would normally be enforcing our illegal status, incarcerating and banishing us.

Very early in the talks, Davis put forward a general plan calling for our agreement to operate under SEAC orders. In return, the British would provide us with training, arms and ammunition for our guerrillas. In addition, SEAC was prepared to offer running financial funding and, according to Davis, he had already submitted a request to this effect. Chang Hong placed the requirement for funds at between $50,000 and $70,000 (Straits dollars) per month. This estimate in no way seemed to faze the British panel.

As the initial session progressed, I gained the clear impression that these negotiations were critical to our Party's future. We were in a very strong bargaining position at this point. The British badly needed our assistance.

In the event, Davis made it clear, early in the deliberations, that it was to be a meeting on purely military affairs. He, Broome and Tan were not there representing the British Government or any other Allied government, including the Soviet Union. They were there, he said, solely as representatives of Mountbatten's SEAC. Chang Hong did not counter this position and indicated to me that he alone would speak on behalf of the CPM. I sat quietly and listened.

I well recall one point of the discussions in the first session when Chang Hong took issue with the British over the use of the words 're-occupying' and 're-occupation' when defining Britain's eventual return to Malaya. There was much to-ing and fro-ing until a compromise was reached and it was settled that the word 're-taking' should be adopted in the agreement. The semantics of history. 'Re-occupying' had supposed overtones of permanence and legitimacy. On the other hand 're-taking' was seen, at least by Chang Hong, as more of a temporary situation suggesting it shouldn't have been taken in the first place.

By the end of the second two-hour negotiating session on the first day, agreement had largely been reached between the two sides. It was decided a conference record would be drawn up that night. This would be tabled the following morning before being formally signed.

The next day, I listened closely as Davis read aloud the 'Terms of Co-operation' and 'Details of Proposals and Decisions' that the ailing Broome had worked on the previous evening. I noted that the preamble named all six present at the negotiations – the four on the British side and the two communists. When Davis concluded reading the document, he passed it across to the communist side of the table. Chang Hong signed it swiftly and returned it. He considered my signature unnecessary.

Davis promptly affixed his signature. Richard Broome signed next and translator Tan became the last to endorse the agreement. Chapman, not part of the team dispatched from SEAC's Ceylon-based headquarters, was not required to sign.

Handshakes all round relieved, briefly, the unease and tension that had accompanied the deliberations. These completed, I think it is fair to say we all believed the document would become a decisive factor in history.

* * * * *

The seeds of our eventual armed struggle against the British lay embedded in that December agreement. Britain, for her part, would become entrapped by the text's requirements with commitments stretching far beyond their intended scope. Less than three years after the Pacific theatre's guns fell silent, the Malayan Emergency would erupt. Our fight to end colonial domination would drag British and Commonwealth troops back to Malayan battlefields. And this time they would be in combat for 12 gruelling years.

A total of 41 British battalions would be deployed to confront my army. Local police, Royal Malay Regiment forces and various military units from Australia, New Zealand, East Africa and Fiji would also be called upon to fight in Malaya for Imperial Britain. In all, several hundred thousand troops — from army, navy and air forces including a fair proportion of national servicemen — would be committed against our guerrilla strength which at its peak numbered no more than 5,000 men and women and for the most part functioned at around 3,000.

But all that would be in the future.

*   *   *   *   *

I came away from the meeting secretly pleased with its outcome. There was, finally, a formal agreement that, in principle, set down our understanding for co-operation. We had a chance of getting weapons, ammunition, medical supplies, uniforms, financial help — practically everything we needed to equip *our* guerrilla army.

For all the positive aspects of our negotiations, there was no getting away from the fact that there had been a sinister aspect to the dealings. The British read it in us. We read it in them. Neither trusted the other.

That the three Asians present all used aliases was symptomatic of that mutual feeling. Tan Choon Lim was in fact Lim Bo Seng, chief Chinese operative attached to the Malayan Country Section and, as far as I was concerned, a Kuomintang agent. He had been responsible for recruiting suitable agents from the Nationalist Party intelligence headquarters in Chungking for infiltration into occupied Malaya. This was obviously a factor the British were intent on withholding from the communist side.

I had operated underground from the moment I joined the CPM and had no intention of revealing my true identity to the British.

Chapman, for his part, had expertly concealed the fact that he knew exactly who Chang Hong really was. He had been present at a meeting in a dingy second-floor office in Singapore's Geylang area on December 19, 1941, to negotiate with Lai Te – Blantan's 'Chang Hong' – who had then clearly been identified to him as the CPM Secretary General. What was more, the two Special Branch officers accompanying Lai Te on that occasion had earlier briefed Chapman on the staggering circumstances surrounding the communist leader's role for British intelligence. Lai Te, Chapman had been told, had been a British agent from the moment he joined the Party in the early 1930s. He was a plant.

As a loyal Party comrade, I knew nothing of these matters and harboured no suspicions whatever. In truth, by the time Lai Te showed up in Blantan, his duplicity had gone a devastating stage further. He had, by then, been recruited by the Kempeitai and was actively working for Japanese military intelligence as well.

But, even as he turned from a double to a triple agent, Lai Te boasted within the Party of his ever-expanding links to powerful international communist circles. He claimed he personally represented world communism's Comintern organisation. For a long time his deceptions served him admirably. They protected him from the British. They protected him from the Japanese. And for four years beyond Blantan, he would remain immune from even the repudiation of his comrades. Throughout this period he would continue mercilessly to manipulate the Party to his personal advantage.

I said when I began that dreams have a price. I say now that the same goes for betrayals. One ultimately pays for them.

Still standing in Sitiawan is the shophouse – No 36 – where I was born. Sadly, it's the one with the Sports Toto business on the ground floor.

Chapter 2

A Chinese boyhood in colonial Malaya

Several months after my 25th birthday, I discovered that I was, in fact, only 23 years old. The year was 1947. I had been newly proclaimed Secretary General of the Communist Party of Malaya. My appointment to the top Party post was kept a closely guarded secret by our Central Committee for many months. There were very good reasons for this. Lai Te, the man I had replaced, had mysteriously disappeared. Worse still, he had absconded with almost all our Party funds – money and gold amounting to well over $1 million in colonial local currency.

The first major task assigned to me by the Party was to track down Lai Te. We knew our fugitive had fled both Malaya and Singapore. To follow his trail, I needed a passport and, to get one, I required my birth certificate, something I had never set eyes on before. A duplicate was obtained through legitimate government channels. To my astonishment, it showed I, Ong Boon Hua, had been born, not in October, 1922, as I had always been led to believe, but in October, 1924.

In a way, the birth certificate explained, at least to me, why my youthful appearance had always seemed to be an issue in my life. It was thus during my school days; it was similarly so in my early association with the Party and it continued in my dealings with the British through the Japanese occupation. When I became Secretary General of the CPM, many of the comrades were a decade or more older than me. It was difficult to dismiss reservations that I was, perhaps, too young for the job. Looking at the copy of my birth certificate at the time, I felt it better for all concerned that my relegation to an even younger age bracket be kept largely to myself. I shared my feelings with close Party colleagues. Age was not the issue, after all. The issue was conviction and how much I was willing to give up for it.

The confusion over my age came about this way. Under Chinese tradition I was regarded as being one year old a month after my birth. As is the custom, come the following Chinese New Year – three months later, as it was on this occasion – I was given a further year. So, as far as my family was concerned, I was two years old when, by Western reckoning, I was barely four months. We did not have birthday parties in my big family so we only spoke of the sequence of our births – Brother No 1, Sister No 3 and so on. You were only older or younger than the other. My siblings and I were never ones to worry about whether we were born in the Year of the Dragon or some such. The early misplacement of my original birth certificate perpetuated general acceptance of the Chinese calculation.

Quite recently, I came across a declassified 'Top Secret' field document[2] endeavouring to describe me and portray my background for the benefit of various British military authorities planning the re-occupation of Malaya in the days immediately following Japan's surrender. Throughout the Japanese occupation period, I had been careful to conceal my true identity and family connections from British officers with whom I dealt. This was particularly so with John Davis, the same senior Force 136 operative who had been so instrumental in organising the December, 1943, 'Terms of Co-operation' between SEAC and our Anti-Japanese forces. On August 21, 1945, Davis signalled his headquarters:

NAME: CHENG PING. HOKKIEN AGE APPROX 25. EDUCATED CHINESE MIDDLE SCHOOL. ENGLISH MEDIOCRE. UNDER-STANDS MORE ENGLISH THAN SPEAKS. FAMILY UNKNOWN — PROBABLY MIDDLE CLASS, POSSIBLY WELL TO DO. PHYSICALLY ROBUST WITH ROUND BOYISH FACE. COURAGE MARKED AND COMMANDS NATURALLY RESPECT OF MEN WITHOUT FUSS OR FORMALITY. QUIET CHARACTER WITH INCISIVE BRAIN AND UNUSUAL ABILITY. FRANK AND RELIABLE. VERY LIKEABLE. DUE YOUTH AND INEXPERIENCE OF WORLD HE IS OF COURSE NO CONVERSATIONALIST AND NOT A GREAT CHARACTER.

When Davis' message was relayed to London from SEAC HQ in Ceylon on August 23, the line about my 'quiet character with incisive brain and unusual ability' was omitted which only had the effect of underlining my 'youth and inexperience of world'.

All the constant images lingered . . . *round boyish face . . . frank, reliable, likeable* . . . but, in the end, the kid was young and inexperienced. Davis after two years working in close cooperation with the Party through me, was still floundering over my aliases and had no real knowledge of my true identity. Still, I appreciate the compliments he paid me, though his evaluations of my background were way off the mark.

*   *   *   *   *

I was born on October 21, 1924, in an upstairs backroom of No 36 Jalan Kampong Koh, a two-storey shophouse in a long row of similar small business establishments the likes of which still dominate the southern Perak township of Sitiawan, some 50 miles south-west of Ipoh.

My parents had travelled to Peninsular Malaya shortly after their arranged marriage in Singapore in 1918. My father was employed by the Ban Hong Leong company who then had its motorcar and bicycle spare parts business headquartered on the corner of Singapore's Jalan Besar and Mayo street where the building known as the White House Hotel stands today.

My mother was the eldest daughter of the Kwan family who lived in the Rochor area. The family was prominent in the Heng Hua clan. My maternal grandfather rented out two-wheeled rickshaws to rickshaw pullers, most of whom had just arrived from China. All these men were clan members and my grandfather successfully used his clan connections to consolidate the family business.

My father was born in the seaside village of Jiang Dou, halfway between Fuchow, the capital of China's Fukien province and the city of Amoy. His mother died when he was an infant and my grandfather faced a constant struggle to keep his family in the bare essentials of daily living. Father migrated to Singapore as a young boy and came under the protective wing of a family connection, the proprietor of the Ban Hong Leong trading headquarters on the island. Both my father and the Ban Hong Leong businessman came from the same village. Everyone there had the family name 'Ong'.

Proprietor Ong quickly employed my father as a company trainee and he began what was essentially an apprenticeship with the firm. Father was obviously a diligent young man and I attribute this to the challenges of his impoverished boyhood. He attended evening classes where he studied typing and basic English. It was while working at Ban Hong Leong that the match-makers entered his life. Shortly after the marriage, Father moved north to Teluk Anson to work in a Ban Hong Leong franchise operated by an uncle. The young married couple lived there briefly before moving to nearby Sitiawan – No 36 Jalan Kampong Koh – where they, with the help of the Teluk Anson uncle, set up yet another Ban Hong Leong office.

For the better part of the first decade of my parents' arranged union, their marriage appeared happy enough. My earliest memories of my father were of a quiet man who made a lot of sense when he chatted with me. For a first generation Chinese immigrant he had an unusually wide circle of friends across the various racial groupings. I remember two Indian medical doctors, several Malay civil servants and a number of Indian freight-forwarders with whom he mixed socially and engaged in lively discussions. Quite multi-racial in his outlook, he spoke conversational Malay and could read English reasonably well, though had difficulty speaking it. I talked to my mother in the Amoy dialect. But at home, when my paternal grandfather was about, we had to speak in the more formal Eng Hua tongue.

My father had a moderate interest in politics. He had one or two books on Sun Yat Sen. He also had books on the Kuomintang's military exploits. As a small child, I enjoyed accompanying him to the open-air coffee stalls around the corner from our shophouse. There I would sit and listen, quite enthralled, while the adults spoke about the developments going on in China. My father appeared to have a good grasp of what was happening, but avoided personally committing himself when it came to the Chiang Kai Shek – Mao Tse Tung struggle for supremacy. He regarded both men as important figures. But my old man seemed more concerned with the fact of China emerging a great nation than the precise political path taken to this end.

I could not have been more than four years old when I was enrolled in a kindergarten run by the Sitiawan Methodist Church. There I learned my first English words via the song *Twinkle, twinkle, little star* which I sang with gusto. One could say that my interest in learning English was kindled by my brief attendance at this school. For some reason I can no longer remember, I stopped going to the kindergarten after only a few months and stayed home until it was deemed I was big enough to attend 'proper classes'. My formal education began when I enrolled at Hua Chiao Primary School (Sitiawan Overseas Chinese Primary School), a short distance down the road outside my home. Hua Chiao opened as a primary school but was soon expanded to incorporate secondary classes. I liked going to school. I should clarify this claim. As a child, I enjoyed sitting in the classroom and learning new things; I didn't like walking to and from my classes, approximately a mile each way, lugging my books and sweating in my school uniform and regulation socks.

Generally speaking, my childhood in Sitiawan was typical of any Chinese boy growing up in a rural township in colonial Malaya. I had various groups of friends. Games were played to a tropical calendar. There was a season for marbles, a season for football, a season for kites, a season for spinning tops. We had our own bat and ball game – a kind of Sitiawan special – which was a cross between cricket and baseball. I must confess that I was never very good at any of these games but I certainly enjoyed them and made some very good friends through them. Many of them would later join me in the anti-Japanese movement.

The Nan Hwa school where I attended classes is still in the same location down the renamed Kampong Koh road from Sitiawan. The school façade has been modernised but the rear building (bottom photo) with the classrooms where I once sat appears to be intact to this day.

There was a tiny wooden Methodist Church about a mile from our shophouse along the main road leading to Ipoh. From this modest structure, Pastor Shi Yu Shou attempted to spread the Christian gospel among the largely Buddhist Chinese population of Sitiawan. Pastor Shi was active in encouraging sport and recreational activities among the young and, indeed, his only son developed into a champion badminton player.

At Pastor Shi's urging, I, together with a few of my friends, joined the Methodist Church choir. Not because we wanted to sing or be converted, I should emphasise. We were just young lads looking for fun and something different to do. Soon we were singing the appropriate hymns for either Christmas or Easter. There were about ten of us in the all-boy choir. We sang in Hokkien. Practice sessions were held every Sunday morning and the pastor's assistant accompanied us on the organ. If my life depended on it, I could still sing *Yasoh ai gua* – 'Jesus loves me' – in Hokkien and *Onward Christian Soldiers* in English. After practice, we attended the regular service, sang and listened to the lesson for the day. Fundamental to our choir attendance were the after-service tea and biscuits provided by the pastor's wife in her home next door. She was a quiet, modest village woman who was very kind to us. When we had consumed a fair share of our rewards, it would be almost noon. My friends and I would then run across the road to the large grounds beside the local Planters' Club – then an establishment where membership was restricted to Europeans only.

My young friends and I well perceived the club's racial segregation. Still, noon was the hottest period of the day and we knew the Europeans were loath to come out at this time, particularly on a Sunday. Each week we gave ourselves four hours to rummage around the Planters' Club. By late afternoon, however, we understood we should depart. It was then the Europeans' time to play.

From primary school onwards I was always interested to learn about China, her language, her culture, her customs and her history. All our textbooks were printed in China. However, the British colonial authorities censored them heavily. The British didn't want us to read words like 'imperialists' or 'imperialism', 'aggression' or 'invasion'. Sometimes whole pages were ripped from textbooks. From time to time these were replaced by edited text that was pasted in place. When we came to these pages we knew immediately what had happened. Anyway, our teachers were able to tell us exactly what the original text would have been. Although I was only seven or eight years old, I was fascinated and shocked to learn of what was happening in China. I was mesmerised by the Japanese invasion of Manchuria in 1931 and the attack on

Shanghai in early 1932. Although the colonial authorities banned any discussion of these matters in Chinese schools, the same issues were still regularly covered in a subject called 'General Knowledge' and certainly in our Chinese literature classes. Our Chinese language teachers were all China-born. Only the English language teachers were local Chinese.

Apart from classroom lessons, all children from Chinese speaking backgrounds in Malaya at this time were influenced by the gossip indulged in by their adults. Our elders read the reports on China carried by the Chinese language *Sin Chew Jit Poh* and *Nanyang Siang Pau* newspapers published in Singapore. The adults invariably embellished these reports with their own interpretations.

At a very early age I became aware of poverty and the power of money. There were four or five *Chettiar* shops – Indian moneylenders – in the immediate vicinity of our shophouse. As the Great Depression bit, my family became regular clients. My parents were forced, from time to time, to use small land-holdings as collateral for loans. The most difficult years for them were 1930-33. There were six children in the family by this time. The eldest was my brother Boon Eng. I was next in line. After me were two sisters. Then came two more brothers.

My father was nearly bankrupted by the Depression. The Singapore headquarters of Ban Hong Leong had sent accessories valued at over $10,000 to our Sitiawan shop. It was a large amount of money in those days and there was very little demand for what we were selling. The Ford Motor Company had dumped on Ban Hong Leong huge consignments of spare parts for a vehicle model they were soon to discontinue. Ban Hong Leong, unaware of what was taking place, had pushed these spares out to its franchisees. The supplies nobody needed only compounded our financial problems. Fortunately, the Singapore office was understanding and did not press too hard for payment.

In a desperate attempt to make quick money and relieve financial pressures, my father, influenced by a group of local Chinese friends, attempted to establish a middle-man brokerage dealing in small-holding rubber plantations. They planned to buy small-holdings from independent planters and sell these to the bigger rubber estates. My father tried this for about two years. But his efforts came to nothing. If anything, they intensified our financial problems.

As a result of Father's long absences from home, Mother, who up to this point had been a dutiful Chinese housewife, was forced to learn the bicycle and spare parts business. Although she was illiterate, she quickly mastered the 'a-poh suan' – a Hakka phrase roughly translated as 'old lady's calculation' and referring to a system of 'counting by heart'. However, for all her strength in times of crisis, my mother remained true to her Chinese heritage. The feudalism of my parents' backgrounds determined Father remained the head of the household. And an expanding household at that. In the following years more siblings came, crowding an already cramped home. I still remember having to take care of a baby brother while my mother ran the ground floor business. In all, she would have 11 children.

To her great credit, after much perseverance, she managed to resuscitate the bicycle business to a point where it was able to meet the essentials of day-to-day living. The shop became the biggest of its kind in the district. My parents turned it into a semi-wholesale/semi-retail establishment. As their confidence grew we became agents for Dunlop motorcar tyres and tubes. Although our business was the exclusive Dunlop agent in Sitiawan, my parents did not restrict stocks to one brand. They sought business from other suppliers and so we ended up also selling competitive products – Goodyear, Firestone and Michelin. Dunlop, of course, were decidedly unhappy about such conflicts of interest. But they accommodated my parents' straight-from-the-shoulder rationale. In troubling times, it was a matter of survival.

It was the wish of both my parents that Boon Eng and I should take over the family business upon the completion of our schooling. This was why Boon Eng received an English language education at the Sitiawan Anglo-Chinese School while I attended Chinese language institutes. By the time I started middle school, Mother had given up trying to interest me in the mechanical side of the shop's operation. I am afraid I was lazy. I was just not interested in mastering the repairing of bicycles, the mending of punctures and the replacement of worn-out tyres. So a compromise was reached. I would not be required to wrestle with bicycle frames, wheels, spokes, chains, pedals and the like as long as I was prepared to assist in the book-keeping and accounting side of the business.

As trade was conducted throughout the day, takings were dropped into a money-box set of drawers – one slot for coins, another for notes. At the end of each working day the cash was retrieved from the drawers, counted, tallied against receipts and ultimately deposited in a steel safe. There were two sets of keys for the safe. One was held by my mother. The other one was supposedly my father's. But he was away so often that his key was left with me. Anytime I came back from school I could open the safe. I was also responsible for banking functions. When we had accumulated enough funds, I would carry these to the Chartered Bank office, around the corner near the courthouse, and have them credited into our account. The manager in those days was an Englishman. He had two assistants – one Chinese, the other an Indian.

Fortunately my brother Boon Eng had a keen interest in the mechanical side of things. He was a quick learner and showed a decided bent towards hands-on pursuits. Boon Eng mastered the repairing of not only bicycles but also motor vehicles. He became skilled at dismantling complicated mechanisms, restoring their functions and putting them back together again. He could re-wire the most complex dynamo and get it working like new. As it turned out, Boon Eng would ultimately take over the entire business. The trouble was, my older brother was too kind-hearted. He found it difficult to remind people of their debts and thereafter demand payment. Later, some customers took advantage of the fact that I became the most hunted man in South East Asia. It would take a supreme effort on my brother's part to summon up confidence enough to begin collecting outstanding funds. Always, one or two customers would jeer at him: 'If you want your money, tell your communist brother to come and collect it. We'll give it to *him*.'

To the consternation of my mother, I was far more interested in reading. My father and a clerk who worked in our Sitiawan shophouse had jointly accumulated a large collection of Chinese classical literature. At age 11, I discovered and began reading these books and became very familiar with the complicated plots of old Chinese adventure tales. I learned about the dynasties. I devoured battle details, rivalries in the courts and fighting strategies. The story of the Three Kingdoms was a particular favourite of mine then. I had no interest whatever in romantic stories. I read only about warfare. How some dynasties disintegrated and others expanded. The tactics employed by military leaders. How Good and Evil interacted. How Good fought Evil. The poor fighting the tyrants.

My love of old Chinese literature sharpened my mind. I became aware of how much I was lagging behind in my studies. My grades began to improve. So did my Chinese language abilities. It was a very natural transition for me to become deeply concerned with what might happen to China as Japanese aggression escalated.

The subject of my continuing education worried my mother. Boon Eng had passed the critical education age and had done well in his studies. If required, he could readily move into the business at any time. My situation was very different and by the time I was in Primary 6, my mother harboured serious doubts whether family finances would allow me to proceed to middle school.

It so happened that the Catholic priest in Sitiawan, a middle-aged Chinese, rode a bicycle. He occasionally called by our shop to repair punctures or replace tyres. As work was being undertaken on his bicycle, my mother and he would invariably chat away in the Fuchow dialect. Missionaries have a way of sniffing out possible conversions. The plight of a woman trying to eke out a living, surrounded by a brood of children, was obvious operational material. In the weeks that followed, the priest returned to the shop with a formal offer. The Church would send me to a Catholic school in the northern Perak township of Taiping or another on Penang island. My mother discussed the matter with me. She said it was a kind offer, but the choice was mine. Mother was a Buddhist, not a devout one during the time of which I speak; but she ended up very devout in later years. Perhaps she might have had some misgivings had I gone the Catholic route. But I rather think she would have consoled herself with the thought that the issue of my education had diminished by a fraction the mountain of problems she had to scale.

I had absolutely no interest in joining the Catholic Church. In fact, as children in Sitiawan, my friends and I kept well away from that establishment during our games. It all looked too severe and too fearful to us. We preferred playing around the local mosque. In the mosque we knew there was a place for praying where we were forbidden to go. But there was also a pond for washing and there we could splash around without any problems. Childhood images like this tend to stick in the subconscious and it was probably for this reason I made it clear to my mother that I was not interested in the priest's benevolent offer.

With the Catholic Church option gone, my mother scrimped and saved and managed to support me through three years of junior middle-school education. However, my studies were threatened by yet another financial crisis. This time it was the school that ran out of funds. It happened halfway through my senior middle school course. I discussed the problem with my mother and told her that since my school could no longer help me further my education, I would prefer to go to Singapore and live with my maternal grandmother and relatives there. By then my mother's family had sold the rickshaw business but were still living in the Rochor district. I was hoping to attend the newly opened Chung Cheng High School in Kim Yam road.

Some of my old teachers in Sitiawan had already moved to Singapore. I was looking forward to seeing them again. Still, I had mixed feelings about moving away.

It was an emotionally complicated and puzzling time. I was beginning to get involved with Chinese nationalist activities in the Sitiawan area. I was 13 years old although everyone, including myself, thought I was 15. The left wing of politics was of no interest to me at this point. Nor would it be for some time to come.

Looking back over the years, I have always been careful not to fall into the trap of romanticising the past. There has, after all, been very little in my life that would inspire the mendacity of nostalgia. But the fact that I failed to follow through my plan of going to Singapore to further my education would become critical to the direction I would, from then on, chart for myself.

Developments were occurring that would determine the course of my life.

Tan Kah Kee, the influential Singapore-based entrepreneur who headed the China Relief Fund.

Chapter 3

My personal passage to communism

Throughout the 1930s, you could tell the political leanings of the Chinese in Sitiawan – indeed throughout Malaya – by the photographs displayed in their homes and shophouses. This wall-hanging response to events in China began soon after the Mukden Incident in September, 1931, when the Japanese invaded Manchuria and went on to overrun the three north-eastern provinces. The following year, they attacked Shanghai.

In the early part of the decade, some households regarded the Kuomintang's Generalissimo Chiang Kai Shek as the true leader of China. His photograph dominated walls and hallways of these homes. But nearly every shophouse carried a picture of Sun Yat Sen, whom everyone considered the founding father of the Republic of China.

Sitiawan residents, by all appearances, seemed particularly staunch supporters of the Kuomintang. Pictures of prominent Kuomintang war heroes were displayed in households throughout the town. I remember two in particular: that of General Ma Chan Shan, who led the fight against the Japanese in Manchuria, and that of General Chai Ting Kai, the Shanghai area commander. In our home there were no pictures of Nationalist Party leader Chiang. My father's preferences were limited to Sun Yat Sen, General Ma and General Chai.

We wore black armbands on several days during the year set aside to remember occasions considered ones of national humiliation for China. For example, there were two such days in the month of May. The 1928 Japanese attack against Chiang Kai Shek's army in Tsinan, capital of Shantung province, was recalled on May 3. The incident had resulted in the deaths of 3,500 Chinese, many of them civilians. On May 30, our black armbands commemorated the day in 1925 when British police opened fire on protesting Chinese workers and students outside the police station in the British Concession at Shanghai. The resulting massacre triggered waves of strikes across China and evolved into a nation-wide anti-imperialist movement.

In the second half of the decade, developments in the motherland began to produce discernible signs of political polarisation within overseas Chinese communities in Malaya. In the beginning, the division was between the followers of right and left

Singapore Governor, Sir Shenton Thomas, shown here with Lady Thomas before the island fell to the invading Japanese. In order to avoid perceived political embarrassment for the colonial government, Sir Shenton secured Tan Kah Kee's agreement to five important conditions limiting the scope of the China Relief Fund.

wing factions of the Kuomintang operating in Malaya, rather than demonstrations of outright support for the emerging Mao Tse Tung.

The 1936 Xian Incident increased the emotive response we gave to political developments in China. Polarisation was heightened as the communist arguments became more pronounced. The son of a prominent warlord in Manchuria, Marshal Chang Hsueh Liang, followed orders from Chiang Kai Shek not to resist the Japanese aggressors. Furthermore, he was told to withdraw his troops southwards. Chang Hsueh Liang was severely criticised for this move, but concealed the circumstances behind his actions. Subsequently, however, he realised Chiang was manipulating him to crush the communists. Incensed by the double cross, Chang made international headlines when he abducted the Nationalist Party leader. A face-to-face meeting between the prisoner Chiang and the high-ranking communist, Chou En-Lai, reached a form of compromise. A flurry of behind-scenes arrangements consolidated this and China was dragged back from the brink of catastrophic civil war.

Meanwhile, all over Sitiawan, I recall my elders becoming transfixed by these events. Before they could fully digest the implications of Chiang's abduction and ultimate release, the Marco Polo Bridge Incident erupted in July, 1937. Japanese forces launched a coordinated attack on a bridge across the Yunting river near Peking and on a railway bridge a short distance upstream. This aggression would trigger a full-scale Sino-Japanese War.

Mounting calls for national salvation impacted on Chinese communities throughout the Malay peninsula, indeed, throughout South East Asia. The intensifying fervour produced a rash of movements and meetings. Some demanded the boycott of trade with Japan. Many appealed for skilled Chinese to return and help the Kuomintang government in Chungking. A particularly important aspect was the mobilization of fund-raising groups to support China's war effort.

Alarm bells rang along the corridors of colonial power. Fearing the communists would take advantage of the spreading agitation, British authorities manoeuvred to control the groundswell and ensure whatever organisations emerged had government sanction. The China Relief Fund was established in Singapore in August, 1937. It was headed by Tan Kah Kee, a prominent entrepreneur with an impressive following among the local population. He was duly elected the Fund's president after a public rally at the island's Chinese Chamber of Commerce.

Prior to the rally, Tan had met the Singapore Governor, Sir Shenton Thomas. In order to secure the government's sanctioning of the Fund, Tan agreed to five conditions imposed by the governor. These were: (1) All monies raised must be solely for civilian aid; (2) Coercion could never be applied in fund-raising activities; (3) One central organisation only would be responsible for channeling donations; (4) The Fund must not be associated with any provocative anti-Japanese declarations; and (5) Under no circumstances could any aid be directed towards military programmes.

Almost simultaneously – and to the deep consternation of the British authorities – the CPM set up the Anti-Enemy Backing-up Society. It was an identical movement to Tan Kah Kee's Fund. In a matter of weeks, branches of the Backing-up Society had sprouted in townships along the peninsula.

From the outset, the Society announced it was promoting Sino-British friendship. Still, it never emerged more than a semi-official, semi-legal entity. The colonial authorities perpetually blocked it from gaining official registration. To dodge outright government suppression, the Society portrayed itself as a strong supporter of the Relief Fund.

The parallel platforms championed by the Relief Fund and the Backing-up Society sharpened my political consciousness. As a child I had been enamoured of the classics and wished I could have been among the patriots on ancient Chinese battlefields, witnesssing good prevail over evil. As a teenager, I was gripped by the contemporary China story but was lacking in direction on how I could be of some use.

In the latter part of the 1930s, the Chiang Kai Shek government sent military officers to Malaya for the sole purpose of recruiting Chinese youths to help fight the Japanese invaders. The colonial British did not object to this manpower drive; neither did they mind the presence of the Kuomintang recruiting team who wore civilian clothes while they functioned in Malaya. The activities of the recruiters were widely recorded by the Chinese language press. Some of my schoolmates enlisted and went to China. The requirements for military service there were fairly basic. One had to be at least 15 years old, should have completed junior middle school and, of course, had to be reasonably healthy. Once accepted, a recruit was entitled to a three-year training stint at a Junior Military College in Kwangsi. Successful trainees graduated as officers and were qualified to become platoon commanders.

Recruitment of this nature continued until at least 1940. During the Japanese occupation, some of these recruits were sent back to Malaya on orders of the Chiang Kai Shek government to join the clandestine British Force 136.

I was particularly touched and impressed by the decision of an older schoolmate, Fung Shou Yi, who made his way to China by cargo ship and ultimately joined the Chinese Airforce. Fung would later send photographs back to Sitiawan. In these he looked resplendent in his pilot's uniform. I envied him. I enjoyed robust health but simply did not possess the athletic abilities of the likes of Fung. When the recruiting drive began, I was 14 years old and, in reality, only 12. Too young.

Still, I was determined to be useful. Certain things occurred to help me. I had a schoolmate, Du Lung San, who was two years my senior. Lung San had just graduated and become a schoolteacher. One day, he appeared on the Nan Hwa campus with a man he introduced as Jhang Huang Shi. Lung San and Jhang were there on behalf of the Backing-up Society. My friend asked whether Jhang could speak before the school assembly. The school principal, a Chinese nationalist and patriot, nursed liberal attitudes and was more open-minded than most of his colleagues. He decided it was acceptable for Jhang to address the students.

I stood rapt as he spoke on the dramatic turns of history and what might be the fate of China. He urged his young listeners to become involved and participate in the anti-Japanese struggle. He did not, however, encourage us to go to China. He was an excellent speaker and I felt privileged to be among his audience.

The following day, Lung San returned to the school and produced an official registry book for those who were keen to get involved with the Backing-up Society. Nearly 200 teachers and students put their names on the list. My name was among them. Thereafter we organised ourselves into groups according to the requirements of the Society. We held regular meetings and at these discussed the situation in the motherland. As the weeks went by the Society gained a reputation for radicalism and the government began suppressing its activities. Fewer and fewer people attended the meetings. In my particular class, we were left with no more than a dozen or so activists.

I found myself becoming increasingly involved in student affairs at my school. Even prior to signing for Backing-up work, I was part of the school's student union – the Self-Discipline Society – where membership was compulsory. In 1938 I was elected general affairs officer of the student union. In effect I became its secretary general. The president was a girl who was studying to be a teacher. Her deputy was my classmate, a local boy.

The way our student union functioned, the No 3 did most of the work and took responsibility for the day-to-day running of student affairs. I arranged everything

The photograph that impacted so strongly on me. It depicts the dashing Sitiawan teenager, Fung Shou Yi, who had been an older school mate and was then away in China training to be a fighter-pilot. Shou Yi survived the war and went on to become a successful capitalist businessman. Our political outlooks were very different. I last saw Shou Yi in 1938 and only received news of him after I began working on this book. I am happy to report he is now in his eighties, in robust good health and living with his family in Singapore.

from library facilities, to forming a reading club and organising student competitions. During my time as a student leader the reading club became very popular. Members were required to make small donations from time to time. Money raised this way was spent purchasing books which arrived from Ipoh. We bought Chinese books on socialist ideology and nationalist principles. After we had read them, all titles were carefully placed on the library shelves for other students to borrow. It was about this time that I discovered the Chinese translation of *Red Star Over China* by the American author, Edgar Snow.

I found myself straddled across three organisations – the Backing-up Society which fascinated me and which I knew to be semi-legal, the Relief Fund and the student union. School authorities realised the Backing-up Society had political overtones. Thus, the student union was supposedly prohibited from becoming involved with it. I was undeterred by this. In fact, I recognised I was in an ideal position to organise my student union affairs to the advantage of the Backing-up Society.

*　　*　　*　　*　　*

It wasn't until 1939 that I recognised the real motivations behind the nationalist patriotic leanings of the Anti-Enemy Backing-up movement. Schoolteachers had become well aware the government was now clamping down on its activities. The colonial authorities had arrested a number of Society activists in Singapore and banished them to China. All this resulted in a sharp decline of our membership at the Sitiawan branch. However, I saw no reason to leave the movement. From my standpoint, its objectives seemed sound and the British appeared to me to be overly suspicious.

Conversion to communism is as strong as a religious conversion. It provides a faith and belief in a system which, at least to the convert, appears as the incontrovertible true path to what is right and fair among human beings. I had read a great deal of socialist and leftist writings but, looking back, I now realise my personal passage to communism began with the early writings of one man – Mao Tse Tung. I found his booklet *On Protracted War* most convincing. It was essentially a handbook on how to win the war against the Japanese. In it he called for the mobilization of the people and the adoption of guerrilla war tactics. Once I finished reading this study, I lost all longing to join the Kuomintang military college. Instead, I began mulling over the idea of going to China to join Mao. I was supposedly 15 years old. I am sure I was not committed to communism at this point. But I was certainly very fascinated by the philosophy the British colonials found so abhorrent.

The growing illegality of the Backing-up Society did not lessen my enthusiasm. By now I was expanding my reading and becoming greatly influenced by the writings of Chinese military strategists, both Kuomintang and Communist, who, in 1938, were publishing numerous studies on how best to defeat the Japanese invaders. It struck me that those on the Nationalist side simply failed to grasp the threat facing China. Apart from being better informed, the communist strategists seemed to possess greater foresight. I compared the speeches of the Nationalist Party leaders and their communist counterparts. Chiang Kai Shek's speeches, in particular, seemed most unconvincing. He placed too much emphasis on the requirement for Western aid and the knock-on effect this was supposed to have. The Nationalists' war strategy appeared to evolve from the very foundations of Western aid. To my mind this was a very shaky approach. Then, I discovered the pro-communist thoughts of the American writer, Anna Louise Strong, in her book called *Soviet Democracy* which I also read in Chinese. Strong was committed to communism, went to Russia to live and even married a Russian. She later became famous after going to China and interviewing Mao. There the communist leader told her that all imperialists were 'paper tigers' – the origin of the renowned phrase.

The Backing-up Society in Sitiawan was controlled by a district committee. The Society was organised into various groupings depending on membership occupation. There were shop assistants, workers, students and intellectuals. The latter category included teachers and journalists. By 1939, I had been appointed a district committee member in the Backing-up Society. I was also functioning as the Society's local student committee chief.

Group discussions we held within the Society's framework always had strong political overtones. Our primary worry, of course, centred on China and her Japanese aggressors. But we also discussed the privileged position of the white colonial masters around us. We were offended by their innate arrogance and their 'No Asians Allowed' attitude to social intercourse. Our deliberations regularly examined the colonial exploitation of Asia and Asians. We strongly questioned the importation of foreign capitalist principles for local economies. The philosophy seemed only to foster inequality with privileges determined primarily by race.

The Depression years and their aftermath, to our minds, provided ample proof that the inroads of colonialism and its associated capitalist political principles in

South East Asia had to be thwarted. Our elders had watched as the British rounded up indentured Indian labour originally brought in to work the rubber plantations. Now unemployed and sleeping on the five-footways, the Indians, of no further use to their white masters, were promptly loaded onto freighters as deck cargo and deported back to their homeland. Things had to change. But how? At this time I really had no answers and still no commitment to a precise political cause.

In Sitiawan we followed the China school calendar. In the so-called summer holidays of 1938, I had had a month-long break in the July-August period. It was, as always, a particularly humid time of year. Shortly before the vacation began, a teacher took me aside and volunteered to lend me a number of books on Marxist philosophy from the substantial collection he kept in his study. The ones I chose were by Russian and Chinese authors. All were in the Chinese language. They would be my holiday reading.

My mother had recently opened a branch of our shop in nearby Lumut. She had appointed one of her elderly male relatives to run the business there. I asked my mother whether I could go and help out in the newly opened branch. She readily agreed, most probably in the forlorn hope that the son who had shown such scant interest in business thus far might finally have seen the light. Actually, I had little intention of doing anything but read my newly acquired books.

Full-scale warfare in Europe appeared imminent. Germany had occupied Austria in March the previous year. In fact, a month after my holidays, there was the Munich Treaty debacle on September 30, 1938, and Germany's snap occupation of Czechoslovakia's Sudetenland a day later. In our part of the globe, Japanese attacks on China had been gathering momentum. The world was an exciting, if frightening place, and my knowledge of it all seemed so inadequate. The relative whom I was meant to be assisting soon resigned himself to the fact that he remained, to all intents and purposes, pretty much my mother's sole representative in Lumut.

I stayed alone in a room above the shop and read for hours at a stretch right through the heat of each day. For the first time I began to study about communist views on 'materialism' and 'idealism'. Late in the afternoon, still alone, I would stroll down to the nearby river to catch the refreshing evening breeze off the water. It became a ritual. Hours of reading followed by the palliative of cooling contemplation as I sat at the end of a small concrete jetty. I wondered where a Chinese teenager from Sitiawan might fit into the scheme of things at such a tumultuous time. I now recognise that it was during that month-long vacation in Lumut, somewhere between reading on Marxist theories in the humid confines of the first-storey room and the relief of those lazy moments on the jetty, that I became committed to the communist cause.

Towards the end of 1939, my Chinese classical literature teacher, Chen Jin Yun, who came from a scholarly background in China and was a leading member of the local Backing-up Society, arranged a meeting for me with a man called Chen Lu. My teacher described the man as a senior official of the Perak Backing-up movement based in Ipoh. His primary interest was said to be workers' affairs. I did not take the appointment very seriously. I represented the students. Chen Lu was concerned with workers. Except for the Society's overall money gathering functions, we didn't seem to have much in common. So, I failed to show up for the meeting. The next day, when teacher Chen quizzed me, he made it plain I had missed an important opportunity. He was particularly disappointed since his contract with the school had expired and he was about to leave Sitiawan. It was only then that I began to suspect there were moves underway to recruit me into the CPM.

Shortly thereafter my friend Du Lung San came to visit his father. His family owned and operated a grocery store in Kampong Lekir, about six miles south of Sitiawan. Du Lung San asked me to come around to his house and it was there, during a lengthy conversation, that I learned the full story of the communists' role in the Backing-up Society.

First, he told me about Jhang Huang Shi, who had addressed the school assembly at Nan Hwa. Jhang had originally been a communist district committee member in China. He had narrowly escaped arrest by the Chiang Kai Shek police during an anti-communist crackdown a year or two earlier. He had then travelled to Malaya where nobody knew his background. After contacting the local communist movement, Jhang had adopted the party alias 'Huang Chen', a name which would become legendary within the CPM as the years passed. In fact, he would rise to the position of No 2 to Secretary General Lai Te. Lung San explained Jhang had actually begun by working quietly as a paid secretary to the Perak Hokkien Association in Ipoh. Later, he worked as a reporter for a local Chinese language newspaper. While a journalist, he had become a leading member of the Perak Backing-up Society.

Over cups of sweet local coffee, I learned that the CPM was indeed trying to recruit me. Chen Lu, the man whom I had snubbed, was revealed to be a Perak State Committee member. He had travelled to Sitiawan specially to make the initial approach. Lung San confided he himself was a Party member and made it clear he had now assumed responsibility for my recruitment.

He disclosed that my Chinese literature teacher had been the lone CPM representative in Sitiawan. As the teacher had now departed the town, Sitiawan was without Party representation. They wanted me to step into teacher Chen Jin Yun's shoes and head political operations in the district. Lung San further told me that other Party members were due to be transferred to Sitiawan from other states. Before leaving, Lung San promised he would send someone to meet me within the next few weeks.

So it can be said, for the record, I became a probationary member of the CPM in January, 1940. At this point, I was not required to sign any papers or take any oath. My verbal agreement was enough and I willingly immersed myself in Backing-up Society activities and prepared for my first fling at being a clandestine communist activist.

When my school reopened at the end of January, 1940, I discovered there were three CPM members newly enrolled as students at Nan Hwa. Two were youths from Sungei Siput, the third was a girl from Penang. My mother, still irritated by my aborted Singapore move, had hoped I would now switch to the English stream Anglo Chinese School at which my brother Boon Eng had been educated. Students there could not play truant. If they were absent, they needed a note of explanation from their parents.

Such conditions, of course, where highly unsuitable for the life I was now mapping out as a member of the CPM. I needed time for my extra-curricular activities and the prospect of requiring parental notes explaining future school absences was a situation too irksome even to contemplate. To get out of the predicament, I told my mother I was simply over-age for ACS and therefore, regretfully, had to enroll at the Anglo Chinese Continuation School (ACCS). Discipline was indifferent there and I well knew I could use it to my advantage.

My mother did not realise I was taking a decided drop in educational standards in my final year at school. Prior to this I had always been among the top ten students in my class. My contemporaries who went on to the ACS and girls I knew at the nearby Anglo-Chinese Girls School now made fun of my presence at ACCS.

By and large, the teachers at my new school left me alone. They knew who I was and what I had previously been studying. I was therefore able to skip most of my mathematics lessons. On the rare occasions that I attended them, I paid no attention whatever. I just sat in the back row reading my books on socialism.

On one occasion I was in my back row seat, close to the classroom doorway, intently reading the Chinese language edition of *The History of the Communist Party of the Soviet Union.* It was, of course, a banned publication in colonial Malaya. Unnoticed by me, the school principal had entered the room and in a couple of strides was standing by my desk demanding to know what I was doing. He grabbed the book, slapped it on my desktop and then, as if having second thoughts, swept from the room without waiting for my answer. I learned one lesson here. I needed to be more careful when it came to reading banned literature.

I found myself in a curious position. The three students who had transferred to Sitiawan were full Party members. I was only on probation yet was in charge of the Sitiawan cell. Probably the Perak State Committee in Ipoh took into consideration the fact that I was from the area and more familiar with local conditions.

It was a time when the colonial authorities were stepping-up their anti-communist drive. In the March-April period of 1940, several of my former classmates and fellow members of the Backing-up Society were arrested. A local police team had searched their houses and found documents relating to the Society. By then the movement was considered fully illegal. Shortly thereafter my arrested friends were put on trial.

Rumours were rampant that I would be next in line for detention. At the height of the crisis, a senior Party official travelled down from Ipoh to speak to me. I told him I expected to be arrested at any moment. He advised I should leave Sitiawan immediately.

Fortunately for me, my mother, who recognised my radical beliefs but had no idea of my Party connections, had just given birth to a baby girl. It was July 4, 1940, American Independence Day. With my mother confined to the Sitiawan maternity hospital a mile or so away and my father having his usual morning coffee with friends, the coast was clear for me to make an unrestricted departure. I stuffed a few clothes into a small canvas bag and boarded the next bus bound for Parit. Once there, the plan was for me to take a connecting bus to Kuala Kangsar. It was in Kuala Kangsar, according to instructions, that I would be contacted and given an ultimate destination.

I had never left home for any length of time before and on the handful of occasions that I ventured out of Sitiawan it was for comparatively frivolous reasons . . . like a school field trip to Ipoh, or to attend an uncle's wedding at Teluk Anson and a couple of brief trips to Penang. There had been, of course, my month-long reading retreat in Lumut.

My first foray into the underground world of communist activism nearly came to instant grief. Now in my sixteenth year, I no longer considered myself a child. I knew what I was doing. I knew where I was going: I was off to better the world. As the bus lurched along the plantation-rimmed secondary roads leading to the stark tin-mining landscape further north and east, a younger sister, back at the Sitiawan shophouse, noticed some of my clothes were missing from the large cabinet we children shared. When Father returned home later that morning my sister lost no time telling him about my getaway.

Father immediately drew on his network of business associates and soon established that I had left on an Ipoh-bound bus. Another of my father's friends was the bus station manager in the township of Bruas through which I was due to pass. When I reached Bruas, the station manager boarded the bus and spoke to me. He said: 'I'm sorry, son, your father has phoned and asked me to stop you and send you home.' A kindly man, he had been a member of the peasant movement back in China. He added: 'I know what you are doing. When I was young in China I did the same thing.' He made me telephone my father who demanded: 'Why didn't you tell me you were leaving?' I explained it was expedient for me to leave as otherwise I was likely to be arrested. I told him I would be going to a friend's house to lie low for a while. I made no mention of the intended onward journey.

'If you want to hide out,' suggested my father, 'why don't you stay with your uncle in Ipoh? He can then arrange for you to move on to Teluk Anson.' It was impossible for me to say 'no'. So I went to my uncle's shophouse in Ipoh's Hugh Low street. Reluctantly, I stayed with him for three or four days.

Opposite his establishment was a bicycle shop. I knew that the shop assistant there, a former schoolmate of mine in Sitiawan, was a member of the local Backing-up Society. I sought his assistance to get to Kuala Kangsar and he directed me to the railway station. I went there alone, purchased a ticket and boarded the next train.

In Kuala Kangsar, I was approached by a local member of the Backing-up Society. He informed me I had a few weeks to wait before I could move on. I stayed with my contact in his small rented room. He worked in the local Chinese primary school as a purchasing officer. One of his jobs was to operate the school mimeograph machine. In the evenings, after everyone had gone home, I helped him work the copier to print newsletters and pamphlets for the Backing-up Society – a most illegal activity.

A week or two later, I was ordered by the Party to transfer to the outskirts of Taiping where I became the only teacher at a small rural primary school. My pupils were all children of peasant farmers. The classroom was an *atap* hut. Enrolees were required to pay 50c a month. My wage was about $6.00 a month.

Back in Sitiawan, police failed to raid my house partly, I suspect, because it became well known in the town that I had run away and partly because my father was generally respected in the community and they felt obliged to save him further embarrassment.

When the Party ultimately ordered my transfer to Ipoh, it was to work as the secretary of the Backing-up Society there. This was an illegal job in an unlawful pursuit. Finally, I felt I was getting somewhere in the Party. I rented a small room and was glad to discover that my former schoolmate, Lung San, was head of the secretariat for which I would be working.

In Ipoh, I became a full member of the Party. It was a momentous day for me and I remember it vividly. My induction took place in a three-roomed house beside a market gardening area on the Ipoh–Bentong road. The home belonged to the mother of a local Party member. One of our Secretariat members rented the biggest room and there we held our meetings. The owner was quite aware we were doing something radical, but didn't realise we were committed communists. On the day of my swearing-in, I filled in a form, took an oath and chose the cover name 'Ong Ping', or in Mandarin 'Wan Ping'. By rights, all references to me in Party affairs thereafter would be under this alias.

As a full Party member, I was appointed head of all student affairs for the entire state of Perak, operating within the Backing-up Society front. Of course, I couldn't go back to Sitiawan without risking arrest. I left responsibilities there in the hands of local Party members. From then on, I personally took charge of infiltrating middle schools throughout the Chinese population centres of Ipoh and Sungei Siput. At that time Sungei Siput was considered the most heavily concentrated region for communist political activity in the entire Malayan peninsula.

One of my early tasks was to gather financial contributions for the CPM's supposedly ailing Secretary General. A Central Committee directive, headed *Campaign for Aiding Lai Te,* was circulated to all state branches seeking the mobilization of members and sympathisers to donate funds. These were purportedly needed to meet Lai Te's expenses while he convalesced. The directive included a brief career history of our leader and made particular mention that he was a member of the Comintern. I went around collecting money and letters of sympathy and respect addressed to him. Donations came from all sectors. Students, office workers, labourers, farmers – they all contributed. I managed to collect a total of some $50 for the Lai Te preservation fund. This contribution was promptly dispatched to Singapore.

From the day I left home, my mother refused to believe that I would not be returning to Sitiawan. On her release from the maternity hospital, she began her search for her second son. She questioned and pestered my friends. One of them finally contacted Lung San and was then able to inform my agitated parent that I was alive and well in Ipoh. It was not enough that she knew my general whereabouts. Again she repeatedly badgered my friends until one of them – the shop assistant who worked opposite my uncle's establishment in Hugh Low street – finally arranged a meeting. He insisted I should do the right thing and relieve her anxiety. After much hedging, I agreed to a reunion.

This took place in the shop assistant's rented accommodation early one evening. In that cramped and airless room my mother begged me to come home. I told her there was no chance of that. She began to cry and plead. She said she had cried for a whole week after I left Sitiawan. When the weeping did not seem to work, she changed tack and related an extraordinary story. Not long after my departure, she claimed, she had won a lottery prize. With some of the money she had purchased a new car. Starting to cry once more, she implored me to pursue one of two options. Either, I return home and resume my studies as the family could now easily support my education. Or, alternatively, she would purchase a small-holding rubber plantation for me to operate. I reminded her that if I went home I would surely be arrested.

This prompted a third option. She would send me to China where I could attend a university and still pursue my nationalist leanings. After a few years I could return to Malaya and it would then be safe for me to resume my life in Sitiawan. My mother thought that after a few years all would be forgotten. Because of my upbringing and respect for her, I could not talk to her in a confrontational way. I did not wish to offend her. I had to speak carefully, choosing my words. I touched her on the arm, thanked her for the options she had presented, but indicated it was difficult for me to change the course of my life at this time. She looked at me, tears welling in her eyes again and said: 'You have such a hard heart.' After a long silence she used a Chinese phrase in our dialect that speaks of a young bird gradually growing strong wings which eventually become fully developed. I realised what she meant. She had recognised there was no point trying to control me any more. After all the tears, she had accepted whatever direction I had chosen for myself.

Before she left the room she urged me, like all mothers do to their sons, to take care of myself. I promised her I would. She then pressed $300 into my hand and added a further request: 'Don't get yourself arrested.'

I promised her I wouldn't and despite all that's happened I have kept that pledge. Though I readily admit that, over the years, there have been numerous occasions when I thought I would fail my mother one more time.

Chapter 4

From underground activist to anti-Japanese guerrilla fighter

The CPM was barely ten years old when I joined as a probationary member in the first month of 1940. The Party's formal structure can be traced to a congress called in a rubber plantation near the Negri Sembilan township of Kuala Pilah in the final days of April, 1930. Central figure at this gathering was the Comintern representative, Nguyen Ai Quoc, a Vietnamese who would later re-invent himself as the Viet Minh leader, Ho Chi Minh. Also present were leading members of the Nanyang Provisional Committee of the Communist Party of China (CPC). The meeting had resulted from decisions taken sometime earlier by the Shanghai-based Far East Bureau of the Comintern to establish a separate Malayan Communist Party.

Years later, I had the opportunity of discussing this event with Chairman Ho himself during my first visit to Hanoi. Together we tried to pin down the CPM's exact founding date. Ho could not provide the precise day but recalled seeing red banners fluttering in the streets after he emerged from the meeting. These were clearly the May Day banners commemorating Labour Day in Malaya – May 1. In those days, the authorities viewed the display of May Day banners as illegal. Ignoring the law, workers still went ahead and hung these, along with red flags, before the celebrations. They were promptly removed right after the festivities. We in the CPM based our calculations on Ho's recollections and thereafter claimed April 30, 1930, as the Founding Day of the Party.

The Party's initial operations centred, naturally, on Singapore as there was a far greater concentration of union movements on the island than anywhere else on the Malayan peninsula. The Straits Settlements Police (SSP) in Singapore were quick to respond to the Party's inauguration and, backed by what was obviously very accurate intelligence information, targeted it with regular and devastating raids throughout the first half of the 1930s. Reacting to the communist challenge, the police force also carried out some self- re-organisation and re-targeting of its departments. The Special Branch was created in 1933, taking over the responsibilities of what had been known as the Criminal Intelligence Department. The CPM would lose no less than six serving leaders in police raids between 1930 and 1935. Court actions resulted in five of them being banished from the colony and deported to China.

Lai Te had been the Party leader scarcely two years by the time I started my underground activities in Ipoh in 1940. His official title within the party was Secretary of the Central Committee. A number of historians have written about this shadowy character who became as perplexing to us in the Party as he was to the pre-war British, the Japanese occupation authorities and the returning post-war colonials. He curiously chose the party alias 'Wright' which, given the Chinese pronunciation of English words beginning with the letter 'r', soon became distorted to Lai Te. This was further mangled, depending on who was writing or speaking in English, to 'Loi Teck' 'Lai Tak', 'Li Tek' and 'Lighter'. He had other aliases such as 'Chang Hong', 'Wong Kim Gyok' and 'Wong Show Tong'.

Lai Te was not Chinese as some prominent historians have maintained. He was Vietnamese by birth. It is not known precisely when he arrived in Singapore but a special investigation undertaken by the CPM in 1947, which I headed, concluded it was almost certainly in late 1932. It has been suggested he studied as a young man in Russia, returned to China where he became a member of the Communist Shanghai Committee and went with Ho Chi Minh to Indo China in the 1920s to organise the communist movement in Saigon. The findings of our investigations support none of these conjectures.

Prior to his arrival in Singapore, Lai Te had served as a middle-ranking communist official in Saigon. Although his mother tongue was Vietnamese, he spoke heavily accented Cantonese and Mandarin. At the time of our probe, the Vietnamese communists reported to us that Lai Te had been arrested by the French and thereafter disappeared. I believe French intelligence, finding him no longer of any use, arranged, in collaboration with the British, to move Lai Te to Singapore.

He first took a job on the Singapore waterfront as a wharf labourer and became involved in union affairs, thereafter joining the local communist movement. In 1934, all five members of the CPM Singapore Town Committee were arrested in a police sweep. It was a raid that would conveniently provide Lai Te immediate avenues for promotion within the Party structure. He seized the opportunity. Soon he was broadening his influence and manipulating his way among what was left of the leadership.

There were two Town Committees functioning within the CPM organisation at this time; the one in Singapore and the other in Penang. State by state, throughout the rest of Malaya, the Party functioned under 'regional committees'. The geographically large states – Pahang and Johore – had two separate committees each. For Pahang, eastern and western; for Johore, northern and southern.

Official statistics show that, in Singapore alone, police directed 432 raids against the CPM between 1931 and 1935 and arrested 226 suspected members. A large percentage of those detained were later deported to China. For all these exercises in suppression, nothing was quite as dramatic or as disruptive as the 1934 Singapore Town Committee crackdown. With so many of the Party hierarchy jailed or banished, the migrant from Vietnam rapidly rose to become a member of the replacement Town Committee. Then, within a matter of months, he was appointed to the Party's highest policy-making body, the Central Committee. In 1938, he became its highest ranking official.

Just the mention of the name Lai Te was enough to invoke deep loyalty and respect among fledgling communist activists like myself. In 1940, I immersed myself in the allotted task of influencing student organisations in Perak. Working within the Backing-up Society, the main thrust of my effort was in the Ipoh-Sungei Siput region.

I had been operating this way for no more than four or five months when the Central Committee in Singapore, without warning, lowered the boom on the Backing-up Society. The directive explained that the Society's activities were being wound up due to 'the changing situation'.

All was not lost, however. The work I had undertaken had brought me to the notice of senior Party officials and, before the end of 1940, I found myself appointed a member of the four-man Ipoh district committee of the CPM which functioned under the Perak regional committee. I remained in charge of student affairs, but now my responsibilities were broadened to include the less important trade unions such as those for shop assistants, barbers and brick-foundry labourers. The shop assistants' union included restaurant workers, chefs and kitchen hands. For the first time since I had gone underground I found myself eating quite well. One of our regular clandestine meeting points around this time was at a Catholic college in Ipoh. The school principal had a Hainanese chef who specialised in European food. The cook was a Party sympathiser and we enjoyed veritable feasts whenever we met in his kitchen.

Critical unions like those catering for tin mine and plantation labourers and transportation workers were looked after by my older and substantially more experienced fellow committee members. It should be recorded that although my comrades and I were having considerable success in influencing public opinion among the Ipoh Chinese by early 1941, actual CPM membership in the town area then totalled no more than 60. Of this number, virtually all were Chinese. Our main strength, as far as the Perak region was concerned, lay with the tin mining labourers throughout the Kinta Valley to the south. Statewide, our membership was approximately 500. Country-wide, hard-core strength amounted to just over 3,000.

On June 22, 1941, Germany attacked Russia with Operation Barbarossa. As Adolf Hitler predicted would happen, the world held its breath. Russian defences were taken completely by surprise and the Soviet Airforce lost some 1,500 aircraft on the ground. As far as the CPM was concerned, there was an immediate and drastic revision of attitude towards Britain. Lai Te and his fellow Central Committee members in Singapore moved to reposition themselves politically on issues involving the war that was engulfing Europe. The conflict between imperialist powers from which they had been so anxious to dissociate themselves eight months earlier was now regarded as a vital anti-fascist struggle. Support of Britain was not only acceptable within the terms of the Comintern but quite imperative. This was particularly so given the looming prospect of further expansionism into Pacific rim countries by Japan, Germany's Axis partner since the Berlin Pact of September 27, 1940.

Within a matter of days from the launch of Operation Barbarossa, Lai Te had contacted his Special Branch controller in Singapore to offer CPM recruits for military training by the British Army. He suggested they be mobilized into special defence units within Malaya Command and come under the direct orders of the General Officer Commanding Malaya, Lt General Arthur E. Percival. Britain's Governor in Singapore, Sir Shenton Thomas, rejected the proposal outright. Sir Shenton's decision was prominently reported in our Singapore underground newspaper, *Freedom News*, and openly in the local daily, *The Straits Times*. It was a decision the Governor would soon be regretting deeply. Little more than six months later, much to his embarrassment, Sir Shenton would be seeking to reverse his snub.

I found myself in a rather unique position to monitor these events. In early June, I had been transferred to the Party's propaganda effort in Ipoh–Sungei Siput. Part of my task then was to oversee publication of our local underground newspaper, *Humanity News*. It carried regular reports and commentary on local developments as well as on political and military events in Europe and, of course, in China. As the police had placed a high priority on the need to stamp out all communist publications, we were constantly shifting our base of operations to stay one step ahead of an expected raid.

We found it safest to be located in the semi-rural peanut processing Menglembu area, three miles south-west of Ipoh. In the space of a couple of months, we moved from a shed on a Sikh-owned dairy farm to a dilapidated hut on a disused tin mine and then to an isolated *atap* house in Lahat, two miles further south. This third site was hidden by tall *lalang* and located between a Chinese market garden and a Malay kampong. From a security standpoint, Lahat was unquestionably the best of the three situations. Any police who passed by assumed our house was part of the Malay village while the Malay residents, who had nothing to do with us anyway, took it for granted we were connected to the Chinese market garden.

In the end, the health hazards posed by this final location became the dominant factor. The area was infested with mosquitoes and finally I succumbed to a raging form of malaria. For almost a week I lay prone, unable to walk, as my body oscillated between bouts of violent shivering and spasms of soaring temperatures. The word went along the chain of command that I was critically ill and a state committee member who came to visit me ordered I be immediately taken to hospital.

I was lifted onto the luggage carrier of a bicycle and two of my printing staff, giving support on either side, wheeled me down the mile-long track that led past the Chinese market garden to the Ipoh road. There we hailed a taxi which took me to Ipoh General Hospital. I had been in hospital five days and was still very ill, sometimes barely conscious, when the Pacific War erupted. In the early hours of December 8, the Japanese 25th Army under Lt General Tomoyuki Yamashita had landed at Singora and Pattani in southern Siam and at Kota Bahru, high on the north-eastern Malayan peninsula coastline and had begun its thrust southwards to Singapore.

Over the next 24 hours the Indian doctors pumped me with quinine and then ordered that I move out of the hospital as every bed was required for casualties arriving from defending British units fighting on the northern front. For a few days I recuperated with a comrade in his shophouse not far from the hospital. As my condition improved, I re-established contact with the Party and, on orders, moved to Chemor, north of Ipoh, where I was assigned as assistant to the state committee member in charge of propaganda.

*   *   *   *   *

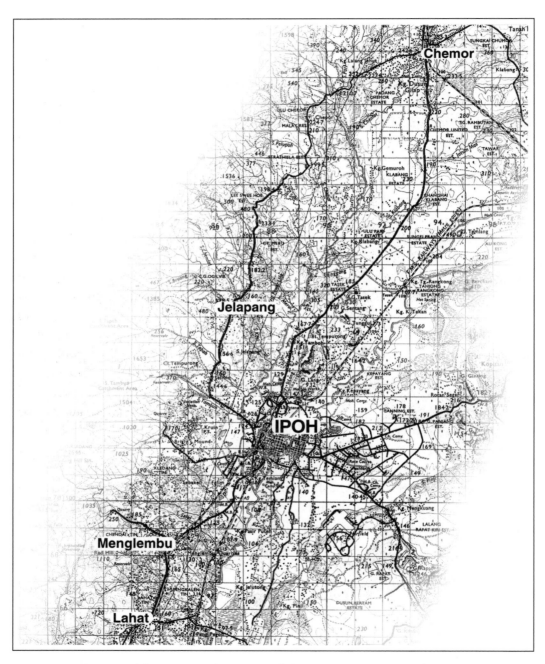

My general location at the outset of the Japanese invasion of Malaya

It was during the course of my duties in Chemor that I first met the girl who would later become my wife. Lee Khoon Wah was from Penang. Her father was Hailam, her mother Cantonese and she spoke both dialects well. She had been influenced by communist philosophy at an unusually early age. By the time she was barely a teenager, she was already active in the movement. When authorities at the Penang girls' school discovered the political leanings of their 13-year-old student, they decided her associations were both unsettling to other pupils and a threat to the smooth operation of their educational establishment. Khoon Wah was asked to leave.

Concerned parents lost no time in arranging her enrolment at a Penang convent. They felt certain their daughter, who already showed an aptitude for languages, would quickly pick up English under the no-nonsense direction of Irish nuns. For about two years, Khoon Wah's studies progressed most favourably. Then she was arrested. At the time the Germans had just invaded Russia. One of her friends in the movement who had moved to Singapore and joined the editorial staff of a CPM pro-Russian, anti-German publication, had mailed her a copy. The police traced this to Khoon Wah's home and seized her for being in possession of banned literature.

A family lawyer argued, quite accurately, that the admittedly illegal underground publication for which the 15 year-old student was being detained was in no way anti-British. To the contrary, it was quite emphatically anti-Hitler. The judge was sympathetic and released the teenager on a year-long good behaviour bond. But the nuns, for their part, took a pretty dim view of the circumstances surrounding Khoon Wah's brush with the law and forthwith gave up on her salvation. For a second time she found herself expelled from a Penang institution of learning.

With her path to educational enlightenment at a crossroads, if not a complete dead end, Khoon Wah went off to stay with an elder sister who was teaching in Kedah. She had only been there a fortnight when the Japanese invaded. The sisters attempted to return home. But the battle for Penang had begun and ferry services to and from the island had ceased. A teaching colleague of the elder sister came to the rescue and escorted both of them south to the then relative safety of Perak. He was a Party member, the son of a wealthy family who operated a tin mine outside Chemor. There he arranged temporary accommodation for his two charges in one of the mine offices.

When the local movement came to hear of the girls' predicament, arrangements were made for them to stay with a peasant squatter family. The CPM controlled all peasants in the area at that time. It was January, 1942. I was still recuperating from that debilitating bout of malaria and my early ejection from Ipoh General Hospital. As I eased myself into my new propaganda role, I came to learn about the sisters recently arrived from Kedah. When our paths eventually crossed, Khoon Wah and I had no difficulty whatever discovering matters of mutual interest. She told me about her father, a strong supporter of the Backing-up Society, who had been banished to China by the British just a few months earlier. She would later learn he had drowned in an attempt to return to Malaya when the *tongkang* in which he was travelling came under Japanese attack. Both of us were totally absorbed in the workings of the CPM and it would be over a year before we even began talking about love.

There was no problem for Party members, male or female, who fell in love. No problem, that is, as long as their chosen partners could not be classified under the accepted definitions of 'reactionary' or 'Kuomintang sympathiser'. It was acceptable if they were politically neutral but, of course, far better if they were sympathetic to the cause and, best of all, if they were committed members. There was, however, one strict rule. If you fell in love, you had to report these circumstances to the Party. Before the matter went any further you needed formal Party approval to carry on the relationship. Once the official assent had been given, the relationship could continue without any hitches. There were, however, numerous cases where love affairs were not reported in the required manner. These frequently led to difficulties. If you were discovered carrying on with an unapproved relationship you would, at very least, be subject to open criticism before your fellow comrades. Meetings were frequently called to discuss such matters.

By the time Khoon Wah and I fell in love, I was acting state secretary in Perak. Abiding strictly by the rules, I contacted Lai Te and made my report. He approved it. I knew he would. My wife-to-be had an unassailable, red ribbon communist track record: two school expulsions for activism, a banished father and current membership status. But it would be another two-and-a half-years before we could marry.

* * * * *

I had been in Chemor less than a week when the Japanese troops arrived. They were fresh from their triumphs on the northern battlefields around Jitra, their seizure of Penang Island and their Perak River-borne outflanking manoeuvres which had sent the British retreating from Kuala Kangsar, north of Ipoh. On Christmas Eve,

British troops of the Indian 6/15th Brigade fought heavily in the Chemor area with the elite Japanese Imperial Guards under the command of Lt General Takuma Nishimura. The action inflicted heavy casualties on both sides as the defenders desperately sought to stem the Japanese advance and buy time for other British units preparing defensive positions around Kampar at the lower extremity of the Kinta Valley.

Events were now moving swiftly. By mid-December, Governor Shenton Thomas had revised his original rejection of the CPM's offer, made through Lai Te, to provide communist volunteers to help the British. The Governor's change of heart actually occurred after he was briefed by General Percival about the complete disintegration of Malaya Command's far northern defences. Front line British Indian Army units were in disarray and General Yamashita had moved his headquarters down to the Kedah state capital of Alor Star where he and his officers held celebrations in the newly abandoned Royal Air Force (RAF) officers' mess.

Down in Singapore there followed a frantic rush to salvage whatever was possible of the CPM offer. Special Branch senior officer, Innes Tremlett, who spoke fluent Cantonese and was the controller of agent Lai Te, arranged the December 19 Geylang rendezvous between the CPM Secretary General and the SOE's, Frederick Spencer Chapman, then a captain. Also present at these crucial deliberations was Special Branch Police Inspector Wong Ching Yok. The meeting took place in a room above a charcoal dispensing shop used as a Party safe-house.

The SOE, operating in Singapore under the cover name Oriental Mission, offered to accept as many communist recruits as its 101 STS on the island could accommodate. Chapman, at that time, was the commanding officer of the school. The British further agreed that those communists under arrest and wishing to volunteer would be promptly released from jail. The first of a series of courses would begin on December 22 at the school's Tanjong Balai headquarters, a commandeered mansion located on a small promontory at the mouth of the Jurong River.

Lai Te promised to have the first 15 volunteers waiting at a pre-determined time on a road junction for transportation to Tanjong Balai. The plan was to train and arm these volunteers to operate in guerrilla units. Where possible, they would be placed in jungle hideouts ahead of the Japanese advance. Chapman delivered the opening lecture to the initial batch of communist recruits and would later report to SOE headquarters that the CPM guerrilla parties who were 'young, fit and full of enthusiasm were the best material we had ever had at the school.' Chapman made a telling observation in the same report. Owing to the friendly relations already established by the police with Lai-Te, he said, liaison with the communists was always most cordial.

Subsequent to the negotiations between Chapman and Lai Te, the CPM Central Committee met in Singapore and issued a directive calling for state and town Party committees throughout Malaya and Singapore to prepare for guerrilla warfare against the Japanese invaders. These orders came through clearly from the Party's Singapore headquarters and the Secretary General himself travelled as far as Malim Nawar, north of Kampar in Perak, just as the Japanese were pushing into the upper reaches of the state. A hasty meeting was called in Malim Nawar where Lai Te sat with senior Perak state committee members. Again, very clear orders were issued for the entire communist movement throughout Malaya to be placed on a guerrilla war footing. In particular, instructions were given to the attendees to supply recruits for special training courses in irregular warfare. These, Lai Te revealed, would soon be starting in Kuala Lumpur.

SOE officers went ahead and made contact with a Kuala Lumpur senior communist underground figure who was only too willing to assist with plans to train 15 separate CPM guerrilla units. These would be infiltrated into various sectors of Perak state where their missions would involve interdiction of Japanese lines of communication, the gathering of military intelligence and rescuing British personnel who were either lost or cut off from their units. The Chinese Chunjin School in the heart of Kuala Lumpur was chosen as the principal training ground. The CPM promptly produced more than 100 keen young recruits from Party ranks.

To say the least, it was an extraordinary time. Police in Ipoh who, a month or so earlier, had been arresting young Chinese and detaining them for being members of the CPM, were now asked to release them from jail and provide them with special transport to take them to Kuala Lumpur. Similarly, CPM members who had been sent down to Kuala Lumpur earlier for further interrogation and eventual incarceration, were now being freed, enrolled in the school, and brought back to the scene of their sins – only this time fully armed and trained to kill. One of the latter group happened to be my mentor in the communist movement, Du Lung San.

Those in the first 20-strong batch that went through the Kuala Lumpur school were mainly Singapore CPM members. Two or three of this initial group had been working with the Party in Penang and had travelled to Singapore to avoid arrest.

Luck had gone against them and they had been arrested in Singapore anyway. At the end of their 101 STS training it was planned they would be released into either Kedah or northern Perak, just below the Japanese front line. But the Japanese pushed southwards so rapidly that, by the time the first trained recruits were ready for deployment, the front line was down somewhere below Tanjong Malim. So the freshly trained communists found themselves being released near Serendah, less than 15 miles north of Kuala Lumpur. Thus, historically, the first detachment of the Malayan Peoples Anti-Japanese Army (MPAJA) is recognised as having been established at Serendah. The date: January 10, 1942. The second batch, or second detachment of the MPAJA, came approximately 10 days later and was infiltrated into the Gemas area of Johore state.

The game plan was to have all the guerrilla units dispersed to jungle base areas and to avoid any contact with the Japanese until the front line had moved well past their various positions. We were the real 'stay-behind' parties. We were to avoid any full-scale action. When we were properly established in our base areas, we were to look at possible sabotage raids against the Japanese logistical support lines. The training given to us by the British was primarily in the use of explosives with rudimentary instruction on rifles and Tommy guns. Each detachment was given two Tommy guns. We were not given Bren guns. Trainees were supplied with a personal pistol and some hand grenades. When it came to explosives, however, the British were very generous. We were given loads of gelignite and TNT.

Those of us organising ourselves behind Japanese lines, but not involved in the British commando courses, followed a necessarily different pattern of activities.

On January 2, 1942, the CPM's Perak state committee met to decide how best it might coordinate with all the anti-Japanese activities now underway with the CPM network further south. Contact had been made with Chapman's party in the Tanjong Malim region. The battle for Kampar was then into its fourth day and at its height. That night the British defenders became spooked by reports that Japanese troops were infiltrating south by sea and threatening vital supply lines to the rear. To the amazement of the exhausted Japanese, who were themselves on the verge of pulling back, the British troops retreated first.

Six weeks later, following a further Perak state committee meeting, I was ordered to Tanjong Tualang, a tin mining area near Batu Gajah, where I was to take over the job of liaison officer between the CPM and Chapman. Simultaneously, I was instructed to lead a guerrilla unit in the Tanjong Malim area.

I remember the day vividly. It was a Monday. I had been told Chapman would be waiting for me at a certain rendezvous point at 3 pm. Due to several bicycle breakdowns en route, I arrived two hours late to discover that the Englishman had departed, leaving behind some of his weapons.

Prior to this, I had been weapon-gathering in the Slim River area. This had been the British forces' next major point of defence along the north-south road following their sudden pull-out from Kampar. A Japanese tank charge and infantry thrust had sent the newly-arrived Slim River defenders reeling back in disarray. There were abandoned British weapons everywhere. Tommy guns, Bren guns, .303 rifles, ammunition and all sorts of military field equipment. There was so much, in fact, I needed a team of local volunteers to help gather it all. In the confused aftermath of the fighting, nobody noticed our activity or, if they did, it failed to register. Hundreds of civilian refugees from the fighting were wandering aimlessly about, trying to get their lives back together. When Japanese reinforcements passed through en route to the southward-heading front line, the weapon gatherers just withdrew into the natural camouflage of the countryside and re-emerged when the danger had moved on.

It was here I gained my first practical insight into the mass of weapons, ammunition and general military equipment abandoned on battlefields by forces engaged in conventional warfare. As the fighting moved further south, local farmers and kampong dwellers re-appeared from their hinterland safe havens to salvage huge stocks of both Japanese and British rifles, mortars, machine guns and side arms along with their respective ammunition requirements. I made a mental note that there would be military supplies aplenty if and when we needed them.

On receiving my instructions to rendezvous with Chapman, I had divided my volunteers into two groups and this way we began cycling down the main road to the appointed location. From time to time we came to batches of Japanese soldiers by the roadside. As we cycled past, they shouted 'banzai!' I was puzzled by this repeated greeting. Later that day, February 16, I discovered the reason for all the roadside jubilation. Singapore had fallen the previous evening. Lt General Percival, Commander-in-Chief of Britain's Malaya Command, had surrendered unconditionally to General Yamashita. The capitulation had taken place in a front office of the Ford Factory, located on a hilly rise at the foot of the western slopes of Bukit Timah.

Eventually, I was able to establish that Chapman, after giving up waiting for me, had pushed on to the Kuala Kubu–Fraser's Hill district where some of his men were camped in the jungle. There were five or six in Chapman's party. One was New

Britain's day of ignominy. The mustachioed Colonel Ichiji Sugita (centre), intelligence chief for the invading Japanese 25th Army, escorts the Commanding officer of Malaya Command, Lt General Arthur E Percival (far right), to surrender negotiations at the Ford factory in Singapore's Bukit Timah sector.

Lt General Arthur E Percival had the dubious distinction of overseeing the greatest defeat in British military history. His signature on the Singapore surrender document – along with that of the victorious Japanese commander, Lt General Tomoyuki Yamashita – effectively spelled the end of the British Empire. From then on colonial Britain ruled on borrowed time.

Zealand mining engineer, Frank Quayle, who had been working in Siam when the Japanese landed. Another was an Englishman, Bob Robinson, and there was a man called Chrystal who had worked for Borneo Motors in Ipoh. I sent a courier to tell Chapman I had arrived and to explain why I had been late. When I eventually contacted him via a courier message, he asked urgently if I could provide a Chinese guide who could speak reasonable English. I found one. The guide was immediately dispatched to Fraser's Hill to assist in bringing back to Tanjong Malim three very ill European men in Chapman's party.

The weapon gathering continued. We explained to the villagers we were organising a guerrilla force and requested they donate what they had recovered from the battlefields. In many instances our approach was enough to secure the weapons. In some cases, though, we had to pay for them. The funds we used came from donations made to our anti-Japanese cause. We made a point of approaching all those who had been involved in the China Relief Fund, the Backing-up Society, the CPM and, in fact, any Chinese at all with money.

While I was waiting at Tanjong Tualang for the envoy to return from Chapman's camp at Tanjong Malim, the acting secretary of the Perak state committee advised me to go back to visit my mother. Perhaps she might part with some more of her lottery winnings. The story of her good fortune and her $300 gift to me – which I had promptly donated to the Party – had spread. Was there more where that came from?

I did as I was told and discovered my mother alive and well. In order to escape marauding Japanese soldiers, the family had evacuated to a village outside Sitiawan township. The awkwardness of our last meeting somehow precluded an immediate and direct request for additional monetary assistance. I arranged to stay for two or three nights and, during that time, my mother let slip she had heard rumours I had a girlfriend in Ipoh. It was just the break I needed. There was, of course, no girlfriend at that time. I had been too busy with underground activities to worry about romance. But I knew mothers always had a soft spot for sons with girlfriends, particularly those sons who might be contemplating matrimony and worrying about lack of funds. We talked. I hinted. When the time came to leave I had $800 stuffed deep in my pocket. Perhaps, as she waved goodbye, my mother had visions of me settling down to a normal routine. She may even have harboured hopes of approaching grand-motherhood.

In Tanjong Tualang, I split the funds 50/50 with the senior CPM cadre who was awaiting my return. It meant we could now go ahead and fund two anti-Japanese guerrilla units for operations in the southern Perak region. He would head one. I would lead the other.

I have often wondered what my mother would have said had she discovered the funds she gave me for a decidedly bogus marriage had been diverted to financing two guerrilla units. As it happened with most of my activities, she never did.

It took us about two weeks to set up my particular guerrilla group. Within a month, there was a network of four similar 'detachments' in Perak. Three were located in north and central Perak and my unit was in the south. We later rather flamboyantly called them 'companies'. Mine was designated the 4th Company.

Generally speaking, these companies operated from jungle fringe bases within striking distances of the north-south road. Each came under the control of the CPM's Perak state committee and, in the initial stages, functioned independently from those units that had been trained by the British and organised by the CPM in Singapore and Kuala Lumpur.

In pre-war colonial days, communicating within our political network, proclaimed illegal by the British, had been hazardous enough. Doing so as an anti-Japanese military force in occupied Malaya was doubly precarious. During those early weeks we were running substantially ahead of Central Committee instructions and had lost reliable contact with Singapore. Although ready to designate our units as part of the MPAJA, we had not received permission to do so. We decided on an interim title for our force: Perak People's Anti-Japanese Army (PPAJA).

I chose a jungle fringe position within fifteen minutes walking distance of a small Chinese village located due east of the Behrang railway station. At that point the north-south road ran parallel and close to the rail line. The village itself was isolated from road traffic by an area of thick scrubland. When it came to building our living quarters, we discovered there was no *atap* in the region from which to fashion roofs. There was, however, an abundance of bamboo and the former farm labourers among us were soon demonstrating how to make solid waterproof shelters by splitting, interlacing and overlapping well-dried bamboo strips.

Early Central Committee directives on how guerrilla forces should be structured had been very precise. Each detachment/company was to be jointly headed by a political commissar and a military commander. While the commander would decide military strategy and certainly be in overall control during action, the political commissar, in effect, would hold the more powerful position. In my camp I was the political commissar. Admittedly, we were all very raw, very inexperienced. However, my military commander proved to be a very daring and determined man. During the Japanese advance in January he had personally knifed to death a collaborator – a traditional Chinese medicine practitioner – in broad daylight. The killing was undertaken in front of a large crowd in the middle of the Tronoh township marketplace.

The deputy military commander of my unit was a former tinsmith in Ipoh. I had the assistance of a onetime Teluk Anson barber as my political affairs officer.

Chapter 5

A succession of betrayals

None of us had a pistol which was what we all wanted at the time. Pistols were small, comparatively light and easy to operate. To small-framed Asians they offered ready protection and enhanced confidence. We had plenty of .303 rifles which, for men of our stature, were really too long and too heavy. Similarly, we were well supplied with Tommy guns. These we learned to master. But the cumbersome Bren guns, with which we were so well stocked, were just too big for us to control without proper instruction. Rather than waste time struggling with the Brens, they were packed away and most were later sent to units further north.

To facilitate the social cohesion of our detachment, we found it best to divide our men into sections determined by dialect group. Initially, one section was Hakka, another Teochew, the third, Hailam. Later, a fourth section was formed from Kwangsi recruits. Still, we all lived in the same quarters and it was during these very early days of trial and error that we learned important lessons on how vital it was for guerrilla forces to have the support of the local people. The Chinese village nearest our first camp had a population of little more than 100 adults. This, it became very obvious, was far too small for the level of back-up required by our 40-strong unit. I discussed the predicament during an inspection visit by a Perak state committee member and it was decided we should push north to Slim River where the Chinese population was larger.

So we decamped and moved to Ulu Slim, well to the east of the north-south link and joined to it by a long, all-weather dirt road. In an earlier reconnaissance of the area, we discovered a large tin-dredging operation some distance from Ulu Slim itself. In the immediate vicinity of the dredge there was a substantial and well-equipped settlement for workers and technicians. Half an hour's walk further east, on the jungle fringe, was a pair of rock caves – a large one capable of accommodating 40-50 people and a smaller one good for 10-15 people. Each had its separate foliage-concealed entrance. The location seemed perfect. I decided the smaller cave would be ideal for the four Hakka girls from Tanjong Tualang who would soon be joining us as trainee nurses. Three of these were the daughters of tin mine workers. The fourth was a student from a well-to-do Chinese business family. The larger cave would be for my men.

A clear, fresh stream ran past the site providing ample water for drinking and cooking. We constructed bathing and toilet facilities downstream. Under the circumstances, there was requirement for only one separate *atap* structure to house our headquarters. This we quickly built close by the entrance to the smaller cave.

Sometime in April, 1942, I received word from the 1st MPAJA detachment, then operating in the Tanjong Malim area, that they were in touch with Chapman. I was informed the British officer and two of his colleagues were on their way to confer with me and that I should try to assist with their requirements. In preparation, we built a separate *atap* hut beside our headquarters for the three European guests.

This was to be an important gathering for both communist guerrillas and the British military. It is perhaps not surprising that my recollections of the events differ in certain key aspects to those that have been recounted by Chapman. Suffice to say the two of us got on well together and when, in early 1947, he started to write his wartime memoirs, he described me as 'a young and attractive Hokkien who was later to become Britain's most trusted guerrilla representative.' Chapman's book, I hasten to point out, was published prior to the outbreak of the Malayan Emergency.

Historians and authors interpreting this segment of history have come primarily from the West. Their bias has been unashamedly pro-West and frequently very racial. If you read Chapman's *The Jungle is Neutral* – unquestionably the best report available of guerrilla life in Japanese-occupied Malaya – you will find his text peppered with slurs against Asians. Interestingly enough, though, Chapman seemed to pride himself on the relationships he established with us. In his and most other western chronicles of these times, Asians during the Japanese occupation, were the sole betrayers – Malay, Chinese and Indians alike. Asians were ignorant, particularly in the art of warfare.

There is another side to this story. However you like to view Tokyo's Malaya campaign, the fact is the British and their Commonwealth allies retreated, scuttled and surrendered. They used us. They abandoned us. When they returned in a clandestine capacity to renew their contacts with us, they expected our undivided loyalty. When they got less they edited history.

Their bias was then taken a step further with an argument which went somewhat like this: *The CPM guerrilla network comprised the one Asian grouping worth cultivating as far as British military interests were concerned. Indeed, it was the only local movement mounting a credible resistance to enemy occupation. We had the bond of a common enemy. But even then, the communists always retained an arms-*

length position from us and never fully confided in us. In short, they didn't deserve to be trusted.

There are some glaring omissions in this train of thought. It overlooks, for one, the carefully structured society that the British colonials had always imposed on Malaya and Singapore, right up to the very last hours before their capitulation to the Japanese. This structure was based on race and the privileges went overwhelmingly to the whites. Examples abound, but one of the more memorable in the general time-frame we are discussing concerned the evacuation orders given by the British authorities on Penang island shortly before the Japanese attacked: *European women and children only.*

The decision to release our men from prison and train them for warfare was not undertaken through any new-found altruism. The British were desperate and found us useful. Conveniently, we both wanted to defeat the Japanese. The fact of a common enemy, however, brought no change to Britain's long-term aim – a return to the colonial *status quo ante*. Neither did this common enemy change *our* agenda which looked to independence from colonial domination and the founding of a Democratic Republic of Malaya.

To this day, I see no reason why we should have worked any closer with the British during the Japanese occupation. Nor do I regard as historically fair the frequently drawn assumption that because we chose to hold back from total commitment to everything British, we were somehow not playing the game. If we were not playing the game, neither were the British. They knew very well that, once back in the colonial saddle, they would have no compunction about returning us to the jails from which we had suddenly been released to help them fight the Japanese. And, indeed, that is precisely what happened.

So it was that I prepared to welcome Chapman and his companions to my camp. I saw nothing wrong with building the British party separate accommodation. Their customs were different from ours. Their food requirements were different. They spoke a different language from the ones we used in our day-to-day camp activities. It was convenient and proper that we should co-exist as separate entities.

Early in our discussions, Chapman explained how he had become isolated by the speed of the Japanese invasion through Malaya and Britain's surrender in Singapore. The original intentions when he and his SOE companions began training CPM volunteers in Singapore and Kuala Lumpur had been to develop a level of irregular warfare sufficient to delay the enemy's advance for two to three weeks.

This, he had reckoned, would have bought enough time for the newly arrived British 18th Division, and the expected Australian 9th Division, to be properly introduced.

Wisely, the SOE men – probably about a dozen in all – had made fall-back contingency plans to evacuate by boat from the fishing village of Trong, in western Perak, up river from the Malacca Straits. From there they had hoped to cross the Straits to Sumatra or, alternatively, sail all the way to India. Chapman's problem was how to get to the west coast of the peninsula without being captured by the Japanese. Could we help?

I told Chapman we would do what we could but that our presence in the state's western coastal areas at that time was weak. I promised to send messages through the PPAJA network to see what assistance might be available. In the meantime, could he help train my men? Some days later another three Europeans attached to Chapman's irregular force arrived. Chapman quickly tasked all three with conducting the training programme I had requested, then departed for another of our guerrilla base areas.

Within a few weeks of imposing military rule in Singapore, the Japanese had targeted the CPM leadership with a series of lightning raids. During these, a number of key Party figures had been arrested and incarcerated. Central Committee propaganda chief, Huang Chen, the man generally recognised as the CPM's top intellectual, was betrayed and eventually executed. Thoughtful and popular, he had been widely considered a most likely successor for the overall Party leadership. I regarded Huang Chen's execution as a serious loss for the Party. It was his eloquent address to Nan Hwa's school assembly four years earlier which had moved me to reflect so seriously on the course of my life. Through stunning good fortune – or so it seemed then – Lai Te had escaped detection. Clearly, the Party hierarchy now needed urgent reorganisation.

Towards the latter part of April, I was promoted to the position of Perak state committee member. By the first week of May, I was attending my first state committee meeting in the jungle near Chemor. The main item on the agenda was a proposal to set up a military wing of the CPM in Perak. By that time we had around 300 volunteers in camps within the state's boundaries. We were planning to expand this number to 500. We had the manpower. We also had the weapons and ammunition. Chapman and his irregulars were training us. What we desperately needed was a proper military structure with clear lines of command and, above all, recognition of our position by the Party's Central Committee.

It so happened that a member of the Central Committee, Siao Chung, was on hand for the Chemor discussions. He openly admitted the Perak guerrillas were among the strongest and most effective CPM armed forces operating anywhere in Malaya. He agreed to support all our recommendations when next he saw Secretary General Lai Te.

Siao Chung briefed us on a cadres gathering Lai Te had called a few weeks earlier in northern Johore. There our leader had spoken to representatives from various parts of Johore, Malacca and Negri Sembilan urging them to enhance Party infrastructure through greater attention to the organisation of industrial labour. More important still, he predicted that a future allied invasion would present ideal conditions for the setting up of a People's Republic of Malaya. The CPM, he said, would welcome the Allied counter-offensive, but oppose the re-establishment of British colonial control.

The Central Committee representative then relayed Lai Te's suggestion that it would be advantageous for some guerrilla units to disband. Their members could hide their weapons and return to the industrial ranks. The Perak state secretary at the time, Ah Nan, argued vehemently that there was very little industrial activity in Perak and therefore the directive was impractical. Finally, Siao Chung agreed that the CPM in Perak could go ahead and tailor military policy to the dictates of local requirements.

Throughout the country, the Chinese population had been increasingly supportive of the CPM's military stance and state leaders were well aware of this fact. Only one state – Negri Sembilan – followed the Lai Te directive at this time and stood down a single guerrilla platoon. Thereupon, the Kempeitai – the Japanese military police that functioned like the German Gestapo – shot many of those who had dutifully hidden their weapons and returned to civilian life. Quickly, the MPAJA in that state resumed its old military programme.

At the same Chemor meeting, Siao Chung passed on a name list of eight renegades allegedly connected to betrayals that had resulted in suppressive operations against the CPM in Singapore. Accompanying instructions were that none of the identified should be pardoned under any circumstances. Furthermore, orders were that each state committee should become actively involved in tracking down the wanted men and ensuring they were summarily executed.

Siao Chung informed us the Secretary General was planning to call together another senior cadres meeting before the end of the year. We took that to mean the Party hierarchy then intended revealing its overall blueprint for the military campaign to be waged against the Japanese occupation. Equally important, efforts would be made to restructure Party leadership in the aftermath of the devastating Singapore crackdown.

The immediate result of the Chemor jungle meeting was a directive from the Central Committee designating the PPAJA as the 5th Regiment of the MPAJA. From hereon, our guerrillas were required to come under the control of the Central Committee. This reorganisation had dire consequences for our operations. It introduced a most cumbersome bureaucratic control system and soon proved a crippling arrangement. Ultimately, we found a way around the problem by forming secret parallel guerrilla groupings in the state. These were termed 'mobile units' and came under the sole direction of the Perak state committee.

The same Central Committee directive that wrested control of our guerrilla units went on to split the Perak state committee into two sections. Two members were placed in charge of military affairs. The remaining three were to direct political matters. I was placed on the political side and given the southern Perak area for my region of operations. This stretched from Teluk Anson and Kampar down to Tanjong Malim. In effect, I then became the No 3 CPM political leader in the state.

My job was three-fold. Firstly, to swell the ranks of the hard-core party membership. Secondly, to attract more sympathisers into the mass movement of supporters then known as the Anti-Japanese Union (AJU) and later to be referred to during the Emergency as the Min Yuen. Finally, I was required to target young men and women and enthuse them with the idea of joining the Party's reserve unit. This was a kind of cadet corps from which we could move manpower into our main force guerrilla units when the need arose. The reserve unit would also have the subsidiary role of a vigilante force providing added security to the smaller outlying villages.

I travelled my assigned area by bicycle, transferring my place of abode as the job required. First I was in Kampar. Then Teluk Anson. I well remember those cycling distances: Kampar to Teluk Anson, 30 miles; Ipoh to Gopeng, 12 miles; Gopeng to Kampar, 12 miles.

I lived in rented rooms. I slept in tin mine offices. I stayed with schoolteachers. For security reasons I used a variety of aliases. Quite quickly, my endeavours gained results. In Kampar, for instance, I was able to engineer a quite dramatic expansion of AJU support. It was a similar situation in Bidor and Teluk Anson.

In order to block the inroads we were making, the Japanese set up their own Chinese organisation known as the *Hwa Chiao Weichi-hui* (Overseas Chinese Law and Order Maintenance Association). But our control in all the main population centres was such that we rapidly learned who were collaborating with the enemy. We took a particularly dim view of collaborators who operated in league with the dreaded Kempeitai.

In order to facilitate operations, it was decided to move the Perak state committee headquarters to Kampar where we felt safer. As my contacts there were strong, I was made responsible for carrying out the move.

*   *   *   *   *

As the weeks passed, directives from the Central Committee and from Lai Te himself made no mention of the vital strengthening of Party leadership. Instead, there came further calls for broad-based restructuring on the industrial front. For those of us involved at the frontline of CPM activity, none of these urgings made sense. There was very little industrial activity underway anywhere in Malaya and Singapore. The war had seen to that. The tin dredges, mines and rubber factories were silent and the associated work forces unemployed. How could anyone start organising labour under these circumstances?

By late July, we had learned Lai Te was planning the all-important senior cadres meeting for sometime in September. The venue and precise time were not immediately disclosed. The MPAJA was ordered to send two of its most senior officers as representatives. Each state committee was instructed to assign one delegate. In most cases this would be the senior committee member or state secretary.

Lai Te himself ultimately issued orders for the meeting. The venue: A jungle-fringe position in the Batu Caves region of Selangor, not far from a village called Shi Shan Jiao in Chinese and Sungei Dua in Malay. The date: September 1, 1942. Forty of the Party's top officials were ordered to attend.

All attendees were armed. The Selangor guerrilla detachment provided a 10-man security guard for the occasion. Four female guerrillas from Selangor were assigned as cooks. Makeshift *atap* accommodation for all had been erected.

Lai Te was expected in time for the main session scheduled for mid-morning on September 1. The other comrades were instructed to thrash out preliminary issues in the afternoon and evening of August 31.

Shortly after midnight on September 1, a Japanese force crept into positions surrounding the meeting venue. A furious firefight erupted as our men attempted to break through the Japanese encirclement. The guerrilla guard unit fought to the last man. Half those in the temporary camp died on the spot. The Japanese also suffered heavy casualties including a Lt Colonel, a major and a captain, all killed in action. Their ranks indicated the importance the Japanese had placed on the Batu Caves attack.

It was the first major action of the Japanese occupation period involving MPAJA forces and what a disaster it had been for the Party. The Central Committee was swift to lay blame on an act of betrayal by a Negri Sembilan delegate who had been arrested by the Japanese en route to the meeting.

Some weeks after the Batu Caves debacle, the Perak state committee received instructions to organise yet another important assembly. Lai Te was again slated to attend. We therefore got the distinct impression that the surviving members of the Central Committee, together with our Secretary General, were anxious to re-convene the discussions so dramatically sabotaged by the Japanese at Batu Caves. Although orders were for the state committee to carry out preparatory arrangements, the responsibility fell on me as I was considered most familiar with the area. Well aware of the devastating failure in security measures at the earlier meeting, I was determined to ensure maximum protection for all attendees this time.

The site I chose was deep in a rubber plantation outside Bidor. More than 20 senior cadres and guerrilla commanders representing the various states were instructed to attend. The extraordinary security precautions I took resulted in a most complex plan for assembling the delegates.

I decided to separate the arrival arrangements for the most senior Party officials involved. This specifically concerned four men: Secretary General Lai Te, senior Party official Chai Ke Ming, Perak state secretary Ah Nan and his deputy. Both Chai and Ah Nan were Batu Caves survivors. The four would gather at Kampar and would be separately escorted to the meeting site at the appropriate hour. All other delegates would approach the meeting point via Bidor. This way I hoped to be able to spot any security leak and protect our top men should the Japanese move against us.

Chai was about 30 years old, a Central Committee member and the Party's most respected ideologue. It was arranged that he would arrive in Kampar by train and there rendezvous in a safe house with Perak's two top communists. Once Chai was safely ensconced, the plan was to bring in Lai Te the following day.

I had gone to great lengths to ensure a precise timetable was followed. Shortly after Chai was due to arrive at the safe-house, the Japanese military police swooped and arrested the two senior Perak communists. Fortunately for Chai, his train had been delayed. Discovering Kampar's streets swarming with Kempeitai, soldiers and police, Chai eventually made contact with a local sympathiser who informed him of the arrests. Quickly, Chai left town and went into hiding in the Chinese village of Kanching, one of our strongholds in the Batu Caves area. At the Batu Caves meeting the previous September, Chai had managed to break through the Japanese encirclement unscathed. Now he had narrowly escaped arrest and almost certain execution in Kampar.

All meeting plans were abandoned. Lai Te was never in danger and delegates managed to disperse safely. Once again the Japanese had thwarted our effort to convene vital policy discussions. More unanswered questions. To make matters worse, both arrested Perak leaders were tortured by the Kempeitai. State secretary Ah Nan was subsequently executed. His deputy turned renegade and worked for the Japanese.

Chai, the Party ideologue, had also clearly been targeted for elimination – before or during the scheduled Bidor gathering. And along with him would presumably have gone another batch of Party leaders.

When one analyses the chain of raids, arrests, tortures and executions carried out against the CPM by the Kempeitai during this early occupation period, it seems quite extraordinary that the finger of suspicion failed to fall on Lai Te much earlier than it finally did. Our natural reaction was to look to other possible betrayers.

Everything, of course, is made much easier with hindsight.

*   *   *   *   *

The Kempeitai's early arrest and subsequent execution of Jhang Huang Shi ('Huang Chen') the No 2 to Lai Te had rocked our movement. Although we did not know it at the time, Jhang's death marked the Kempeitai's opening salvo in the systematic destruction of the CPM's Singapore-based Central Committee. Two months later, more devastating Japanese action against our network on the island had sent reverberations throughout the Party. The Batu Caves debacle then followed and in its wake the over-riding emotion among Party survivors had been one of gratitude. Our Secretary General had been spared! We were told his car had broken down en route!

As astounding as it may seem, we willingly went along with the Party's insistence on complete centralization of control. All matters ended with the Central Committee; the Central Committee exercised absolute command. We all accepted this as a fundamental security requirement. Likewise, we gladly approved extreme secrecy and stringent compartmentalization of Party functions. These conditions, meant to protect the Party, all worked to shield Lai Te.

Many fine revolutionaries would perish before we learned the truth. The truth was this:

On March 26, 1942 – one month and 11 days after the fall of Singapore – the Kempeitai arrested a man assumed to be Chinese in Singapore. They initially identified him as Wong Show Tong. The arresting officer was Major Satorou Onishi, Kempeitai sub-sector commander in charge of screening anti-Japanese Chinese males on the island following the British capitulation. The 41-year-old Onishi was a military police veteran with 18 years' experience and had served in Manchuria prior to the Malayan campaign.

Under interrogation, Wong first revealed to Onishi that he was a member of the CPM Central Committee. Then he claimed his real name was Wong Kim Gyock. After further interrogation, Wong admitted that he was no less than the CPM's Secretary General. As such, he controlled communist affairs throughout Malaya and Singapore and was therefore in a unique position to be of service to the Japanese. A bargain was then struck between the Japanese veteran and Wong, alias 'Lai Te'.

Onishi promptly signed an order detaining Lai Te for more than a month. With the order went specific instructions that the prisoner be well-treated. Upon his release in late April, Lai Te lost no time in meeting his end of the bargain. He proceeded to provide the Kempeitai with a hit list that identified members of the CPM's Singapore Town Committee. The arrangement was for Lai-Te to make twice-weekly reports directly to Onishi. In the months to follow he regularly handed over information on CPM activities in Johore, Negri Sembilan, Malacca and Selangor. As the date for the Batu Caves conference approached, Lai Te provided Onishi with full details of the scheduled time, venue and delegates that would be attending. As a result of this intelligence, Kempeitai officers, disguised as regular soldiers on leave, were moved into the Batu Caves district. There they openly caroused with cabaret girls from Kuala Lumpur, all the time noting movements to and from the selected conference venue. On the night of August 31 Japanese troops were well in place. Early the following morning they attacked.

Lai Te, the man who became Britain's most spectacular spy plant in South East Asia when he emerged Secretary General of the Communist Party of Malaya. An arch opportunist, Lai Te willingly worked with the Japanese during the occupation years, reporting regularly to Major Satorou Onishi, a senior Kempeitai intelligence officer.

Lai Te's Japanese spymaster, Major Satorou Onishi, shown here wearing the No 6 tag during the March, 1947, Chinese Massacre Trial at Singapore's Victoria Memorial Hall. During his debriefing sessions with British war crimes investigators, Onishi revealed full details of his association with Lai Te. Onishi was found guilty of war crimes and sentenced to life imprisonment. After serving five years of his sentence in Singapore, he was repatriated to Japan and later released.

Major Onishi – who would later be sentenced by a British War Crimes Court to life imprisonment – had this to say of his prize agent: 'His first motive was to save his own neck, even at the expense of his comrades. Secondly, he cooperated with me to maintain his position in the Party and to further his own ambitions. It was obvious that the people he sold out were people who challenged his position and authority in the Party. I know now that he held back a great deal of information from me.'

Over the years intelligence agencies and historians have wrestled with the intrigues and mysteries surrounding the sinister and elusive figure of Lai Te. Today, I am the only person still alive who can provide cold, hard facts about the man.

As a result of Japanese interdiction of our lines of communication in the chaotic first months of their occupation, nearly all Party branches throughout the Malayan peninsula became cut off from Singapore where Lai Te was applying his treachery. In effect, his collaboration with the Kempeitai saw the Party's Central Committee methodically dismantled to the point that it became a virtual one-man show – Lai Te himself.

It would be seven years before we saw through the layers of myth and fabrication that allowed him to wreak such havoc within our ranks. He would, however, receive the ultimate repudiation he so justly deserved. I would see to that.

Chapter 6

Face to face with Lai Te

By early 1943, the communist movement in Perak found all links to the Central Committee in Singapore completely severed. We were operating in a vacuum. In terms of Party members, supporters and guerrilla troops in camps, we were undoubtedly the numerically strongest CPM branch of any state in Malaya. Mountbatten's Ceylon-based South East Asia Command was soon to begin the first 'blind' landings of Chinese agents along western Perak's coastline.

Unbeknown to us at the time, of course, we were ideally placed to provide valuable assistance to those coming ashore from Allied submarines. We would give them protection and safe accommodation. More importantly, we could provide them with top-grade intelligence on Japanese military installations. But, for all this, as a movement, we were functioning in isolation. There was an urgent need to be tied into a bigger picture approach.

Party membership within Perak was growing substantially. In Batu Gajah, for instance, we had over 100 members. In Sitiawan we had another 40-50. Among the Kinta Valley mining workers we were soon boasting more than 500 members. Still, against this encouraging expansion of our grass-roots following, I well perceived the frailty of our Party structure at the state level. We lacked cohesion as well as direction. A combination of factors had produced debilitating weaknesses. The Japanese invasion and the battles that followed together with the Kempeitai's anti-CPM action during the early stages of the occupation had disrupted not only our lines of communication but also our lines of command. The confusion was further exacerbated by the jackknife effect of the Central Committee's 1942 directive that gave our guerrillas the designation they were seeking within the MPAJA but, ironically, removed their effective control to the Central Committee in Singapore.

I was determined to sort out the mess. Of special concern to me was the deterioration in links between the political side in the urban areas and the guerrilla forces in the jungle camps. In several cases, these had become non-existent. Military units were simply functioning without any direction whatever. It had got to a stage where the political side could never rely on the guerrillas to take prompt and effective armed action. By now, orders for the assassination of collaborators were being issued by Perak state and district committees. Numerous Chinese, Malays and Indians sought favours with the Japanese authorities, both civilian and military. Our members were under instructions to watch for such activities and report back their findings.

We were gathering lists of suspects and had begun the task of grading them as far as their precise threats to our activities were concerned. Those involved in spying against the CPM, or against the population in general, all became targets for elimination by our forces. From time to time we sought to kill certain Japanese, both military and civilian. Not that there was any lack of enthusiasm for such activities. It was just that in the months following the Japanese occupation, the CPM failed to achieve the level of organisational sophistication essential to a well-directed reprisal campaign.

As anyone who has been involved in this work can attest, it is not a matter of running around with a gun and killing at the first available opportunity. Reprisal eliminations, if they are to have the full required effect against a ruthless occupying military power and those functioning on its behalf, must be astutely selective, daring in concept to the point of being brazen, and always performed with professional precision.

We first tried organising general killing squads within the framework of the Anti-Japanese Army (AJA) – our guerrilla force. The prospective targets here were to have been a number of notorious locals who had chosen to work with the Kempeitai, some local collaborators and informers and a handful of one-time Party members who had seriously betrayed their comrades. As actions were planned and launched, it was painfully obvious just how hopelessly blurred the lines of command had become. The squads supposedly undertaking the killing duties were unhappy receiving orders and directions from those on the political side who, it was felt, had little knowledge of what was entailed in carrying out the orders. Matters went from bad to worse. The AJA finally dug in its heels and, invoking the 1942 directive, insisted the guerrillas only follow commands issued through authorised military channels. They would not follow killing orders from district committees. Neither would they be dictated to by the state committee.

A solution that would circumvent this bureaucratic muddle would take several months of gestation in the back of my mind. It occurred to me that I somehow had to establish a parallel guerrilla force to our main units. This would have to function outside the 1942 directive, return control to the district and state committees and still be acceptable to all concerned. Not an easy task. I would have to wait for the right opportunity to implement my ideas.

As the result of the Kempeitai raid in Kampar and the removal of our state secretary and his deputy, I, by default and at the age of 19 years, found myself appointed acting chief of the CPM in Perak. Worried by the obvious lack of lines of command, I saw no alternative but to try and re-establish contacts with what I believed was the still functioning Central Committee. To this end, I sent a messenger south to Kuala Lumpur to make contact with Chai Ke Ming who was still lying low in Kanching village. Shortly thereafter I travelled south to meet Chai, making my very first visit to Kuala Lumpur on the way.

I waited for Chai in the backroom of a Kanching bicycle repair shop. Two bodyguards came and I assumed they had arrived to escort me to Chai's hideout. Before I knew what was happening, I found myself looking down the barrel of a pistol and being angrily ordered to get my hands above my head. While one of the bodyguards held the weapon inches from my forehead, the other frisked me. I was disarmed. The search over, they both began interrogating me. One of them asked why I was still alive! It didn't take long to realise I was suspected of having caused the Kampar fiasco. They felt I should have at least been arrested by the police and executed by now. That is, of course, if I wasn't guilty of betraying the meeting to the Kempeitai. I protested my innocence and must have argued persuasively as they finally demanded I stay put in the bicycle shop. Then they left.

When they returned after an hour or so, it was to escort me to where Chai was waiting in a village house, 20-minutes away on foot. As I entered the front room, Chai walked up to me smiling, his hand extended in greeting. He apologised for the unconventional welcome provided by the bodyguards. He explained such measures had to be taken in view of the increasing police activity against CPM targets. Quickly he reverted to Party matters.

He revealed that a few weeks earlier, in the final days of March, 1943, Lai Te had travelled from Singapore to Kanching where, on the spur of the moment, the Secretary General had called a Central Committee meeting. Only three people had been present: Lai Te, Chai and Siao Ping, a senior CPM official recognised as being close to our Party chief. With the exception of Ah Chung, the military commander who had been unable to leave Kuantan, all others eligible to attend had either been killed at Batu Caves, executed, or were being held in detention. Siao Chung, the Central Committee representative who had addressed our Chemor meeting the previous May, had been killed at Batu Caves.

Absenteeism notwithstanding, the meeting had proceeded to adopt formally a nine point manifesto[3] which set down plans for an Anti-Japanese programme to be followed by the Party. Chai gave me a copy. It called for:

1. The defeat of Japanese fascists and the establishment of the Malayan Republic.

2. The formation of a national organisation composed of representatives universally elected from the different nationalities to govern and protect our motherland. The practice of people's sovereignty. The improvement of civilian living conditions. The development of industry, agriculture and commerce in order to build up Malaya as a harmonious, free and felicitous country.

3. Freedom of speech, freedom of the press and freedom of assembly. The abolition of oppressive laws and the release of all prisoners and Anti-Japanese captives.

4. The abolition of high and unnecessary taxation and high-interest money-lending.

5. The reorganisation of the Malayan Anti-Japanese guerrillas into the National Army for the defence of Malaya. Assistance for guerrilla veterans and their families and the families of all those who died for the liberation of Malaya. Relief for wounded and disabled veterans.

6. The development of a national culture through free education.

7. Confiscation of all properties owned by German, Italian and Japanese fascists as well as confiscation of properties owned by traitors and collaborators.

8. The establishment of commercial ties with friendly countries.

9. A united effort with Russia and China to support the struggles for independence of the oppressed nations in the Far East.

Chai agreed to work for the re-establishment of links between the Central Committee and Perak. I returned to Kampar with my copy of the manifesto. Shortly thereafter, Lai Te summoned Chai back to Singapore. Back on the island, the Party's top ideologue, the man who had replaced the executed Huang Chen as the most likely contender for the post of CPM leader, went mysteriously missing. Many years later, I discovered what happened to Chai. He was compromised to the Kempeitai by Lai Te when he kept a rendezvous at the Ai Tung Primary School in Singapore. The Japanese subsequently executed him.

In reality, the Central Committee at this point comprised only two functioning members: Lai Te and Ah Chung, the old Pahang warrior. The latter was so far away from the centre of control he was non-functional in his political capacity. The Party had now conveniently slid under the sole control of Lai Te.

I had been back in Kampar scarcely two weeks when Siao Ping arrived from Selangor and announced he had been sent by Lai Te to take over the leadership of the Perak state committee. I had known him from Backing-up Society days. He had once worked in an Ipoh printing firm. He was now in his early 30s. Siao Ping asked me to arrange accommodation for him. This I quickly did and he and his wife were soon installed in a house in nearby Malim Nawar. They were not there long. Hardly a fortnight had passed when, quite suddenly, Siao Ping informed me he had been recalled to a meeting in Singapore with Lai Te. He was on a train somewhere in Selangor, en route from Kuala Lumpur to Singapore, when the Kempeitai boarded and arrested him.

Our later investigations would reveal that Lai Te had supplied the Japanese with Siao Ping's travel details. But as the arresting officers were unable visually to identify the newly assigned Perak Party leader, they used a previously arrested and tortured communist messenger to point him out. The identification was secretly confirmed to the Kempeitai as the train travelled south from Kuala Lumpur.

Following the arrest, the Japanese took their prisoner back to Kempeitai headquarters in Kuala Lumpur and led him directly before the commanding officer, arms bound behind his back. Without waiting for the interrogation process to begin, Siao Ping looked directly at the commander and asked: 'Do you want me to cooperate with you?' Immediately, the senior officer untied the communist's hands and invited him to tea. We came to know these details through double agents we had working with the Japanese at the time.

Siao Ping's first contribution was to identify the CPM's Selangor state committee headquarters which were actually in a rural area just outside Kuala Lumpur. On the day following Siao Ping's arrest, the Kempeitai duly positioned themselves for a raid on the identified location. It was an *atap* hut on the edge of a tapioca plantation. Three leading Selangor communists were there engrossed in a meeting. The Japanese had planned to move through the tapioca and spring a surprise raid. But they made too much noise, were spotted and the three leaders managed to dive through the *lalang* wall on the opposite side of the house and escape. They had known of Siao Ping's arrest but hadn't for a moment thought he would betray them. Siao Ping was a very strong person – both mentally and physically. During the Batu Caves incident, he had led the successful charge that broke through the surrounding Japanese cordon of troops. He survived and succeeded in bringing a group of leading cadres to safety – the only ones to escape unscathed.

Following his release by the Kempeitai, Siao Ping returned to the Party. In existence at the time was the hit list of former Party members considered notorious renegades to our cause. All were to be eliminated. Siao Ping's name was never added to this list. Indeed, no drastic action was called for in his case. Herein lies a most interesting aspect of our wartime operations. The Party fully accepted that every man had his pain threshold when subjected to the brutalities of Kempeitai torture. Respecting this, comrades who broke during interrogation sessions and returned to the Party to reveal details of their capture were essentially forgiven. Quite properly, their return was conditional. Beforehand they were required to bring us worthwhile intelligence information on the enemy. In addition, they should try their best to hunt down and kill one of the top renegades. Though forgiven, returnees were prohibited from resuming full Party membership. Instead, they were from then on recognised as supporters. As such they could never again be let into the inner secrets of the movement.

Siao Ping's case was a curious one. By volunteering to cooperate he neatly sidestepped otherwise certain torture. There were, however, extenuating circumstances. He came back with excellent intelligence. He apologised for not having had the opportunity to kill a top renegade, although he had tried to comply. He brought in a pistol supplied to him by the Japanese who intended employing him as a double agent. Under questioning by the Party, Siao Ping readily admitted he had offered information to the Japanese about the Selangor Party headquarters. When asked why he had betrayed the location, his answer taught us a tough lesson. It had long been accepted emergency drill when a CPM member was arrested and there was risk of compromise, the nearest Party headquarters should be immediately relocated. Siao Ping's defiant explanation for his action was: 'You all knew as well as I did that I had been arrested and that the Party regulations called for the headquarters to be immediately shifted. I merely assumed you had followed the Party's accepted emergency drill. Why did you fail to undertake the required action?'

Siao Ping's admonition forced us to take a close second look at emergency procedures. It also led us to the most secure headquarters arrangement we were ever able to establish in occupied Malaya. Fortunately, the CPM's influence in Selangor was strong, particularly so in the outlying Sungei Buloh district. I don't recall who exactly engineered our move to the Sungei Buloh leper colony, but it occurred shortly after the Siao Ping showdown and would rank as perhaps the wiliest decision on cover ever taken by the comrades. They had done an excellent job of infiltrating the colony's medical staff. This enabled us to occupy two of their smaller staff bungalows. These became our state committee offices. When occasions called for it, our members even took up residence there. For the remaining Japanese occupation period, the Selangor state committee operated uninterrupted from within a colony of a few hundred lepers. All rank-and-file Japanese feared going near the settlement. Their police and troops happily gave the area a wide berth as well.

*   *   *   *   *

In June of 1943, soon after Siao Ping was arrested, Lai Te decided to meet me face to face. I travelled first to Kanching village where it had been arranged for me to contact a female messenger who would, in turn, escort me to the Party's top official. She and I walked for an hour to an *atap* hut owned by a vegetable farmer. I was instructed to spend the night there as my meeting with Lai Te would be the following morning. The hut overlooked a spread of flat vegetable patches. Beyond these, atop a hill, looking down on the main north-south road, stood a substantial two-storey bungalow. The surrounding mountainous area is now known as Templer National Park.

The next day, the female messenger returned and escorted me to the same hilltop house. I arrived ahead of Lai Te who drove up precisely on time at 10 o'clock. I was under the impression he had been staying with a wealthy Chinese businessman. I would learn later he had actually spent the night at the Coliseum Hotel where he normally stayed when visiting the capital. For security reasons I was not allowed to see the car in which he travelled nor even know where it was parked. I remained in the house with a male secretary while the female messenger went outside to greet the Party leader. She ushered Lai Te into the main living room where I was waiting. Situated in the middle of the room were a large table and three chairs. The messenger made the formal introductions and left. Only Lai Te, his secretary and I participated in the meeting which was conducted in Mandarin.

I noted the Secretary General's strong Vietnamese accent. Lai Te was obviously not Chinese. He didn't look Chinese; he didn't sound Chinese. To me he looked almost Eurasian. He was dark and quite small in stature – no more than 1.65 metres. He looked ill. Fleetingly I remembered the *Campaign for Aiding Lai Te* nearly three years earlier for which I had gathered $50 in contributions to help finance his recuperation.

Our meeting began with my report on Party activities throughout Perak. I restricted my remarks to events that had occurred following the departure of Siao Ping on his ill-fated journey south. I had received sketchy news of Siao Ping's detention by the Kempeitai and passed on the little that I knew. Discussions stretched over two days. Each day had two sessions separated by lunch and deliberations had to wind up by 5 pm in order for Lai Te to get back to Kuala Lumpur before the Japanese imposed night-time curfew. Following my briefing, Lai Te went into a detailed resumé of developments taking place throughout the international communist movement. He sounded eloquent and I must confess I was most impressed by his knowledge and grasp of the international scene. Astounding though it sounds today, I came away with the feeling that the Party was in good hands.

Some four or five weeks after this meeting, Lai Te formally appointed me state secretary for Perak. The letter was delivered through a clandestine messenger service. Henceforth, Lai Te and I would manage to establish a two-way correspondence where we sent each other letters in romanised Chinese. There were some parts of his letters which were very difficult to understand. Only much later, on my visits to Vietnam, when I learned a smattering of Vietnamese, did I discover that Lai Te, in those early communications with me, had frequently slipped into Vietnamese – a fully romanised script.

From my viewpoint at the time, this initial meeting with the Secretary General had gone extremely well. He had expressed satisfaction with the way the Party was developing in Perak and commented favourably on my handling of matters as acting state leader during a very difficult period. Those first discussions convinced me I could now operate with a degree of autonomy. Naturally, I was determined to follow Party directives. But Lai Te left me with the clear impression that, as the man on the front line, I was expected to use my initiative.

Furthermore, it didn't seem too far-fetched to hope that my deliberations with our leader had also cleared some of the political logjam. Perhaps we would soon start receiving firm direction from the Central Committee geared to reaching our ultimate goal of an independent Democratic Republic of Malaya.

I returned to the day-to-day problems of administering a committee that had been beset with recent arrests. High on my priority list was the requirement for raising funds for our Perak operations. One important project we were developing involved an enterprise smuggling rice from southern Siam. We dispatched a representative from Sitiawan to the southern Siamese township of Trang. There our man quickly established his bona fides with the local Siamese communist movement and shortly thereafter was able to meet the overall Secretary General of the Communist Party of Siam, Li Chee Shin, normally referred to by his alias, Lao Hey.

As a result of these links, Lao Hey wrote to his CPM opposite number seeking Lai Te's assistance in establishing close working relations between the communist movements of the two neighbouring territories for the overall benefit of the international cause. Our man hand-carried the important correspondence back to Sitiawan where he gave it to the area committee and it eventually landed on my table. I left the letter sealed and on the next meeting with Lai Te, in a village eight miles from Bidor, I personally passed it over to the addressee.

Lai Te broke open the seal, scanned the correspondence blankly then pushed the letter and envelope back to me. 'Read it yourself,' he said with what I regarded as an unusually expansive gesture. He normally played most things very close to his chest – particularly communications with fraternal parties.

Lao Hey had become somewhat of a legend in regional communist circles. Born in Hainan, he had migrated to Singapore as a young man and there joined the CPM. By 1932 he had been appointed personal assistant to the movement's Singapore-based Secretary General and was leader of the Party's Youth League. In that same year he had been detained by the Singapore police and eventually deported. In Hong Kong he had contacted local communists. Within a matter of months he was assigned to work in Bangkok where he ultimately became the Siamese movement's top official.

In his letter to Lai Te, Lao Hey mentioned that, before being banished from Singapore, he had never actually heard Lai Te's name mentioned in Party circles. However, he had since been briefed on the great contribution our leader had made to Malayan communism. His information had come from former CPM Central Committee members, themselves exiles from Singapore, whom he had met in Hong Kong.

After reading the letter I returned it. Then came the remark that jarred. 'This Lao Hey,' said Lai Te expansively. 'A very good man. I've known him for years.'

The CPM's Secretary General could not read Chinese!

If he could, he would certainly have understood Lao Hey was clearly writing to someone with whom he had never been in contact. It was a snippet of information

I decided to tuck away in the back of my mind. Instead I went on to inform Lai Te about the progress of our rice smuggling project. Rice smuggling, I predicted, would be a real money-spinner and would have an important impact on Party finances.

Lai Te's reaction to the Lao Hey letter would also have direct impact on the Party . . . only much later.

Chapter 7

Working with Force 136 . . . launching our mobile squads

Our agreement with South East Asia Command, signed at Blantan camp on December 31, 1943, had been an instant morale booster for both sides. The euphoria would quickly dissipate, however, on the realisation during the following weeks that, unless a radio link between the camp and SEAC headquarters in Colombo was established, the whole exercise of committing ourselves to paper would end up a futile waste of time. From the communist standpoint, both our short and long-term agendas were stymied. There could be no effective planning for integrated operations, no medical provisions, no field supplies, no weapons, no ammunition, no cash and no gold.

During our first discussions at Segari three months earlier, John Davis and Richard Broome had impressed on me the importance of getting their wireless transmitter rigged and operational as quickly as possible. They showed me where they had hidden the radio equipment.

From time to time, British military planners, for all their Sandhurst scholarship, can make monumental blunders. This was definitely a case in point. Deposited in a well-camouflaged, grave-like trench, in a scrub-line just back from the beach, lay a huge crate. It contained a British Army MK 111 receiver/transmitter along with its special generator. Together, the two units weighed well in excess of 400 lbs. Worse, Davis and Broome, after some discussion, sheepishly admitted they shared serious doubts whether the transmitter would be powerful enough to relay signals all the way to Colombo. I questioned why they had bothered to bring along such a doubtful piece of equipment. Surely there was something more portable? More powerful? Their answer: It was the only one available!

The problems involved getting Davis and Broome safely to Blantan were complex enough. So, I flatly scotched any idea they had of carrying their lumbering radio unit along too. After deliberations, agreement was reached to bury the MK 111 in a place where Party sympathisers could keep a watchful eye out until we decided what, if anything, could be done with it.

A little more than a week after Davis and Broome moved into Blantan, they urgently summoned me to the camp. There I was briefed in detail about another incoming Allied submarine. The plan was for Broome to move back to the coast and, employing the same fishing junk they had used previously, rendezvous with the submarine off Pulau Lalang, west of the Perak river mouth. Davis explained three men would be coming ashore: two Europeans and an important Chinese agent. Broome intended to accompany all three back to Blantan. I was asked to supply suitable armed escorts and guides.

I immediately objected to the plans as outlined. In the first place, Broome was ill. Escorting a sick European back to the coast, through Japanese lines, would expose my people to quite unacceptable risks. My arguments convinced both Englishmen that their scheme for the greeting party had to be substantially revised. Eventually it was decided that I would personally undertake the mission of meeting the submarine. I could reasonably expect to travel unimpeded to the coast and back again using the services of a tried and trusted CPM sympathiser who operated a pirate taxicab. We would decide the best travel itineraries for the incoming personnel once they had landed.

Davis gave me a secret report that I was to hand over to the operations head who would identify himself once I had boarded the submarine. My instructions were to pick up an incoming report for delivery back to Davis. Messages carried back and forth by submarine were then the only means of communication available between Davis and SEAC.

The road journey to the junk pick-up point convinced me further of the wisdom of my refusal to escort Broome on this occasion. Roadblocks had mushroomed along the route from Bidor to the coast. Conditions were so precarious that I decided then and there it would be impossible to take Europeans safely back in the opposite direction irrespective of what means was chosen – road, river or cross-country. On the other hand, with careful planning and a portion of good luck, I felt confident of getting one incoming Chinese agent back to Blantan without being compromised.

I met the junk captain as arranged and by midday we had cleared the Perak river mouth and were bound for the high seas rendezvous area. By mid-afternoon we had raised a red blanket on our after deck – a pre-arranged signal that would identify us to the incoming submarine. By late afternoon we had spotted a periscope circling us at a distance of several hundred yards. Then as fast as it had appeared, the periscope was gone.

The rendezvous took place at 2000 hours. It was November 2, 1943. I watched through binoculars as the wallowing steel hull slowly surfaced in the moon-speckled darkness no more than 100 yards from where our junk rode on a gentle swell. I could

My one-time ally of convenience, John L.H. Davis,
pictured here looking very much as I knew him during
the years I was associated with Force 136.

just make out the silhouettes of a folboat being lowered into the water beside the submarine and then the figure of a man slipping into it and paddling our way. Soon the folboat paddler was clambering up the junk's rope ladder. He was a crewman. There was an exchange of passwords and I boarded the folboat for the trip back to the submarine.

Royal Dutch Navy boat No 0-24 was commanded by Lt Commander W. J. DeVries RNLN. Aboard I met the two British SEAC officers who were expecting to go ashore. They were Capt Claude Fenner and Capt F. P. W. Harrison. (Harrison was with the 5th Gurkha Rifles, Indian Army, and Fenner had been with the Colonial Police Force in Malaya before the war. At the end of hostilities, Fenner would return, rejoin the police, rise to the rank of Inspector General of the Force and ultimately be knighted.) I handed the letter from Davis to Fenner who identified himself as the operational officer.

I was also introduced to Tan Choon Lim, identified as a Malayan Country Section agent. Like Fenner and Harrison, he expected to be taken ashore. Both Fenner and Harrison were persistent about landing and attempted to convince me how much their presence was required. As politely as possible, I flatly refused to comply with their requests, explaining how difficult it would be for white faces to make the journey inland.

As it would be decidedly less precarious taking a Chinese face with me, I insisted I could only take Tan if my mission was to have any chance of success. Fenner and Harrison had little option but to concede to my reasoning. So it was Tan Choon Lim alone who returned with me to the junk that night along with his gear which, I was delighted to see, included a substantially improved radio identified as Army model No B.MK 11.

As we stowed the gear transferred from the submarine below decks, the junk began its slow journey back towards the Perak river mouth. Before snatching a few hours' sleep, Tan and I sat on deck and talked as our captain threaded a course through numerous small fishing boats, each illuminated with a single oil lamp. My suspicions that I was escorting a solid Kuomintang supporter were confirmed. Tan spoke earnestly about China and Chiang Kai Shek and roundly praised the Chungking leadership. At times his conversation became a lecture. I kept quiet. It was my policy never to argue with such people. There was just no point. After what seemed a very long time, he appeared to give up trying to convince me. From that point on, he never discussed politics with me again.

Early the following morning, our junk pulled to the southern bank of the river and a shallow river punt was on hand to ferry us up a nearby stream to an isolated fisherman's hut. As it was too dangerous for us to stay in a nearby village on the outskirts of Jenderatta, the hut would be our hiding place for the next 24 hours while arrangements were concluded for our onward journey inland to the comparative safety of Blantan camp.

In Jenderatta, I was again confronted with the problem of what to do with an urgently required wireless. For all its improvements – this one was substantially smaller than its predecessor and was packed in two separate units – Model No B.MK 11 was still a highly tricky load to transport. Rather than run the risk of carrying it in the car and being stopped, inspected and detected at one of the many Japanese roadblocks, we arranged to have Party sympathisers conceal the wireless for us in Jenderatta. I planned to find surer means of getting the precious equipment up to Blantan.

We met our pirate taxi driver at a designated point the following morning and began our run inland. I picked the most direct route but one which skirted all main townships. Before leaving, I explained the difficulties we were likely to encounter and warned of possible roadblocks manned by enemy troops. I requested Tan leave the talking to me and merely smile pleasantly at any Japanese who might stop us. By this stage I had learned a few useful Japanese phrases. My companion had no knowledge of the language whatsoever. Luck was with us and we ran across only one roadblock. This went without incident. We alighted from our taxi at a railway crossing two miles outside Bidor and transferred to bicycles for the remainder of the trip over coastal lowlands. At the foothills of the central highlands we began our two-hour trek up to the camp.

Back at Blantan, I made a rather rash commitment to the effect that I would get the transmitter quickly installed in the camp. I could have kept my word had not one of our local CPM members been arrested by the Kempeitai shortly after Tan and I left Jenderatta. The arrest compromised our entire transportation and movement arrangements in the region. It meant we were forced to abandon our pattern of jungle tracks and plantation back roads. It would take me almost a year to make good my promise to have the transmitter collected and delivered.

The radio would become a thorny issue between Davis and myself. Every time I showed up at the camp he demanded to know what progress I was making. I saw his frustration. He would say to me: 'If you have the contacts you claim you have, surely you can call on their assistance.' As if shaming me would make the exercise any easier. I was doing the best I could and told him so. I sensed he didn't believe me and suspected that somehow I saw advantage in ensuring the British group remained unable to establish radio contact with SEAC. This was, of course, a ludicrous notion. The sooner radio contact was established, the sooner our guerrillas would begin receiving the supplies we had been promised. Moreover, the sooner our guerrillas began receiving their supplies, the sooner we could begin working on our short – and our long-term – agendas.

The sympathisers with whom I had entrusted the second transmitter became too frightened to continue concealing bulky packages in their squatter homes. The Japanese had stepped up their raids and house-to-house searches following reported sightings of landings from submarines. Endeavouring to keep faith with us, the villagers hid the new radio undercover near a swamp.

Just the planning of its transfer to Blantan took several months. We had to cover important contingencies. Ultimately we were able to dismantle the equipment and attach various main parts to bicycle frames. It was a very dangerous operation. There was absolutely no margin for error. One Japanese patrol or roadblock would have demolished the mission. Our couriers had to make countless detours through rubber plantations and jungles. Frequently they had to carry both packages and bikes, poised above their heads, through swamplands.

When the couriers finally reached Blantan, it was discovered water had entered vital sections of the radio. The entire transmitter required re-wiring. Fortunately, the camp's radio operator, a Shanghai-born Kuomintang follower who had been trained in Calcutta by the SOE, was able to undertake the necessary work. Then it was further discovered that the dynamo in the power generator was malfunctioning. I was tasked to obtain a secondhand replacement. The first one I sent to the camp could not be used for one reason or another. The second dynamo I dispatched worked. The operator set about the task of establishing contact with Colombo. But now the batteries were failing and needed replacing. Could I supply? Any old car battery would do. Easy to request. But someone struggling through deep jungle lugging a car battery tends to inspire suspicion. It was a deeply frustrating time for everyone.

Years later, I would learn that a further six submarine missions to the Perak coastline were attempted following the 'Tan Choon Lim' trip. With the exception of one, which accomplished a 'blind' landing of two agents, the rest failed. Indeed, the final mission came under such heavy attack by Japanese Navy patrols that the Malayan

Country Section back in Colombo abandoned any further agent landing operations from submarines along Peninsular Malaya's western coastline.

With the limited message exchange via submarine no longer an option, SEAC's sole chance of communication with Davis rested with the wireless. After several months trying to establish radio contact with his group at pre-arranged hours, the Malayan Country Section assumed Davis and his fellow agents had been wiped out. As a result, the specially assigned watches to monitor transmission from Davis' operation, codenamed 'Gustavus', were dropped.

It was only by chance, I was told, that radio contact was finally achieved. This occurred on February 1, 1945, 14 months after the B.MK 11 was off-loaded at Jenderatta. A trainee female radio operator in Colombo was absentmindedly rolling through a number of unused agent frequencies when she picked up a weak signal. Unable to identify it, she sought the assistance of an instructor to establish the sender's call sign. Within minutes, contact was confirmed and verified.

*   *   *   *   *

To say that the months of radio silence were difficult for the British group would be a gross understatement. They were agonising. Davis and his men had to work hard at avoiding demoralisation. Chapman, a restless loner by nature, took off on jungle forays by himself, making contact with other CPM guerrilla units. He sought out aboriginal tribespeople in the central highlands and endeavoured to familiarise himself with Perak's deep-jungle terrain. On the occasions I visited Blantan during this time, I noticed Davis placing particular emphasis on nurturing their Kuomintang intelligence network. I knew they were setting up cells in selected population centres stretching as far north as Ipoh. They tackled this work through the Chinese agents they had earlier brought with them by submarine and, presumably, others who had been recruited locally. Their senior operative, Tan Choon Lim, emerged an important figure in these operations.

As this clandestine network expanded, Davis and his fellow Europeans became increasingly apprehensive about the location of Blantan camp. They felt it was too close to Bidor which had become the centre of heightened Japanese military patrolling. Additionally, they worried over the camp's lack of adequate jungle canopy to protect it from air reconnaissance. After one of his excursions into the hinterland, Chapman returned with what he pronounced as a far more secure site on the lower slopes of a mountain known as Batu Puteh which was visible from Blantan. It was at a slightly higher altitude than the first camp, close to an aboriginal village and not far from the fork of the Ayer Busok and Woh rivers. In late February, 1944, the occupants of Blantan moved across to their new accommodation, a two-day trek to the north east. Then it was business as usual for the Kuomintang mission.

The most successful of the Kuomintang agents, as far as I could tell, was Ah Ng, a slightly built Hokkien, who opened a rice supply business in Ipoh as a front operation. Within a relatively short period, he was able to negotiate a contract supplying rice to Japanese officials in the town. Unquestionably, Ah Ng produced some excellent intelligence for Davis. The problem was, of course, that Davis, devoid of radio access, was unable to make any use of it.

Information reaching the CPM from our strong grass-roots network in Ipoh and the surrounding region suggested a serious lack of discipline had developed within the Kuomintang ranks. To our way of thinking, Davis' agents in and around Ipoh were in imminent danger of being exposed. Our instincts would be proved right.

By this time, life was getting very hectic for me. On the one hand, I had my organisational responsibility as the Perak state secretary. On the other, as the appointed liaison officer between the Party and the British group and their Kuomintang associates, I was also responsible for camp security. In addition, I was trying my best to meet whatever requirements the British posed. I felt I was becoming overwhelmed as the pressures increased. I sent a message to Lai Te saying it was impossible for me to maintain all roles efficiently. I suggested someone be appointed as my deputy to share my load of Party affairs. Lai Te readily agreed and transferred a man from Selangor to Perak to assist me. I had heard about Ai Ker, my new deputy, but had not met him before. He was about ten years older than I. He had migrated from China to Malaya where he had worked as a clerk in a tin mine. Ai Ker joined the CPM and became tasked with union matters. In 1940, he was transferred to Selangor to become a state committee member.

I discussed the division of our activities with my newly-arrived deputy. I placed most of the areas outside the British supply route from the highlands to the coast directly under his command. Batu Gajah, Ipoh, Sungei Siput and northern Perak were all assigned to the new man. I retained under my control roughly the southern Perak area encompassing Bidor, Tanjong Malim, Teluk Anson and Sitiawan. On reflection, so many years later, the fact that I sought assistance to be relieved of some of my Party burden, yet retained all responsibilities in my liaison with the SOE agents, gives a good indication of the importance I placed on the pragmatic need to expand our cooperation with the British.

As it turned out, my efforts would merit special mention in a top secret war's end summary of Force 136 activities[4] compiled by the head of the Malayan Country Section, Innes Tremlett. The summary dated August 15, 1945 noted:

CTP (by now my Force 136 codename) *who is also head of the AJA Perak group and who has been with Davis on and off for the last two years: An able, sensible and likeable man who has been of the greatest assistance to Davis personally and to our plans in general. It is almost entirely due to him that we have in Malaya today nearly 30 patrols armed and trained ready to strike at Japanese communications and that excellent and friendly relations exist between AJA patrol leaders and the British Liaison Teams attached to them.*

Almost from the outset, Davis and Broome had impressed on me that the CPM's guerrilla army should be conserved and prepared primarily for the intended Allied landings which would mark the beginning of Britain's effort to drive the Japanese from Malaya. There was no doubt this advice had military merit. But it was also a British ploy to ensure we remained controllable in the interim. Mindful of their long-term political agenda, the British were keen to ensure our military capability never exceeded that required for their projected invasion. We were certain these instructions emanated from a SEAC policy directive. Openly we went along with Davis' group and gave them the impression our guerrilla army was being retained for training in deep jungle camps. So it was that the development of our secret mobile squads was pursued away from British notice.

Mobile units functioned in every state of Malaya, with the exception of Pahang. They developed, not as a result of a policy directive from the Central Committee, but rather on the initiative of officials at the state level. Operational control, therefore, came from people on the spot.

In Perak we fielded five mobile squads. I personally commanded one of them. Initially, each one consisted of only three or four specially-picked guerrillas. As the months passed and experience was gained, these ranks swelled. My squad relied on pistols as personal weapons. All squad members carried hand grenades on their belts. Larger squads, in addition to pistols and hand grenades, were equipped with Tommy guns and rifles. The most powerful and feared of the five Perak squads operated in the Ipoh area. As Ipoh was one of the country's largest population centres, it offered a broad variety of targets and our hit-lists were being constantly updated.

Our primary interests remained locals who worked for the Kempeitai, the CID or who were attached to intelligence gathering work against the general public. We in the CPM referred to these as 'special services' people. They were predominantly Chinese. It must be remembered that in Malay areas we hardly had any activities. As far as the Peranakan Straits-born Chinese were concerned, although they were essentially pro-British, they saw value in cooperating with us. They felt our activities were hastening the defeat of Japan which ultimately would ensure the early return of the colonials.

Elimination orders came from the state or area committees where local officials decided on targets. Orders were easily implemented in the outlying villages and rural districts. It was only when an elimination was required in a heavily populated town that careful planning was necessary.

As our Ipoh squad pursued operations, its numbers grew in proportion to its reputation. The armaments of its members included a number of Tommy guns, pistols and a large supply of grenades. This squad's most famous exploit was the raid it staged on the police compound at Jelapang, then located on a side-road between Ipoh and Chemor. Four guerrillas, disguised as uniformed Japanese troops, were dispatched to the post ostensibly on an inspection tour of the premises. The Malay police officer-in-charge, failed to recognise that the raiders were all Chinese and welcomed them to the station. Once inside, the squad leader ordered all staff to line up for inspection with their weapons. One-by-one the arms were taken from the police by the bogus inspection team and carried to a waiting vehicle outside. Then the armoury was emptied. Members of the raiding party drove off, leaving the startled policemen still standing at attention.

This highly successful endeavour secured us substantial supplies of weapons and ammunition. It was necessarily the product of considerable forward planning. Other opportunities for our mobile squads, however, arose spontaneously and demanded swift response. One such occasion I well remember occurred at a small roadside coffee stall north-east of Bidor and close to the approach route to Blantan camp. The stall, operated by CPM sympathisers, was used by our camp security force as a forward look-out position. This particular incident involved a curious reversal of roles to the Jelapang raid I have just related. A Kempeitai intelligence officer arrived at the coffee stall disguised as a local Chinese. Strapped on his hip under his shirt was a German Mauser pistol. When he sat down his shirt parted enough for other coffee drinkers to notice the weapon. He proceeded to speak to some of the local clientele in very broken dialect with a marked Japanese accent. A mobile squad was alerted. Its members descended on the stall and tried to detain the Japanese who made the mistake of resisting. We shot him on the spot, took his Mauser, then buried the body.

I prefer not to use the word 'terror' to describe the work of our mobile squads. We were involved in a free-flowing war. As far as the CPM was concerned it was a two-pronged effort. On the one hand, our guerrillas were independently engaged against the Japanese invaders. On the other, we and the British were mutually involved, under our agreement, fighting the same enemy. In warfare the objective is to eliminate the enemy and those giving assistance to the enemy. That was what was happening. 'Military action' would be a more accurate term to describe our guerrilla activities at this time.

Our mobile squads did not eliminate a lot of innocent people as some historians have suggested. Perhaps from time to time errors were made with identifications. But these were certainly the exceptions rather than the rule. At no time were our squads ever tasked to undertake any mass killing programme. Whenever they went to work they were under very specific and limited instructions.

This all raises a very fundamental and very controversial issue. When the Emergency erupted, the British began by labelling us 'bandits'. Then, because the colonials felt they required a more emotive term, they issued instructions that we should henceforth be termed communist terrorists – CTs. When we worked with the British during the Japanese occupation and killed people – essentially in Britain's interests – we were neither bandits nor terrorists. Indeed, we were applauded, praised and given awards. Thus, you only became a terrorist when you killed against their interests. For the record I can state that throughout the entire Japanese occupation period, our squads eliminated no more than 150 local collaborators in the state of Perak, the majority of them Chinese.

*   *   *   *   *

As we had perceived, problems within the Kuomintang agent network, with its headquarters now at the new camp, began to fester over disciplinary matters. These came to a head in March, 1944. As I recall, there were half a dozen Kuomintang agents that had been brought in by submarine and were living initially in the camp.

I remember them as Ah Han, Ah Ying, Ah Chin, Ah Lung, Ah Chuang and the star operator of the bunch, Ah Ng.

In the course of his networking, Ah Ng, during off-hours from his rice distribution business, came to frequent an Ipoh dance hall. There he became involved with a taxi dancer whom he eventually brought back to live in his rented Ipoh house. According to the Kuomintang code of conduct, agents were not allowed to bring outsiders into their circle and this was particularly so as far as women were concerned. What Ah Ng did was strictly against the movement's rules. You could do anything you liked outside, but you were not permitted to bring that part of your life home. And the movement was your home.

Fellow Kuomintang agents tried to repudiate Ah Ng but he was persistent. In desperation, they sent word to Tan Choon Lim (Lim Bo Seng) and asked him to come down from the camp and resolve the problem. Tan had yet to make his first foray from the camp since arriving at Blantan four months earlier. When he finally left to talk to Ah Ng, he was also under instructions for a separate British mission. The Davis group had requested Tan contact his wealthy upper-class Chinese connections in Singapore to raise badly needed funds for both the Kuomintang network and the CPM security force.

I have read much speculation about the fate that befell Lim Bo Seng – the man I had known as Tan Choon Lim. I regard most of it as wishful thinking by those anxious to enhance the Kuomintang's wartime story in Malaya. It has been claimed that Lai Te had learned of Lim's true identity at the Blantan meeting the previous December and, as a result, was able to identify him to the Kempeitai. As I alone escorted Lim, under his alias, to Blantan, attended all sessions of those negotiations and stayed with Lai Te the entire time he spent at the camp, I know this particular piece of conjecture to be baseless. I personally did not learn of Lim's true identity until immediately after the war. Even then, I did not consider the information important enough to pass on to anybody. Lai Te, therefore, could never have been able to identify Lim for the Kempeitai.

The reality is, Lim Bo Seng was betrayed by one of his own men. Soon after he left the camp, Lim moved into the top floor of Ah Ng's Ipoh house where he posed as a visiting uncle. Ah Ng subsequently departed the premises, leaving a note for Lim to the effect that he was going to Singapore on business. Shortly thereafter, the Kempeitai arrested two agents in a separate section of the network. When word reached the camp, Davis called on my assistance. He asked me to send some of my

Lim Bo Seng who signed the December, 1943,
Blantan Agreement as Tan Choon Lim. This was
the same alias he had given me seven weeks earlier
when I escorted him from a high seas submarine
rendezvous off Pulau Pangkor and took him all
the way inland to Blantan camp.

men to warn Lim about the arrests, to appraise him of the danger of being compromised and to urge him to return to the camp forthwith. Before I could accede to the request, a previously arrested Kuomintang agent who had managed to escape, came back to inform Davis that Lim had been detained.

I believe Ah Ng betrayed the entire network. Davis kept very quiet about the whole affair and refused to divulge anything to me. As the events unfolded, I first formed the belief that it was Lim Bo Seng who triggered the collapse because some weeks after his arrest our new campsite was attacked by the Japanese. As other details came my way, of course, I drastically revised this quite mistaken impression.

At the time of the attack, neither Davis, nor Broome, nor Chapman were in residence. Quayle, the New Zealander, had been left in charge. The Japanese knew the exact location of the new camp and quickly moved to positions on approaches to it. That morning we had sent a group of guerrillas down to the nearest village to collect provisions. On the way they spotted the Japanese manoeuvring into position. A firefight erupted. Our unit withdrew and informed the camp that it was being targeted. It was decided to evacuate immediately. In the rush to pack-up and move out, Quayle forgot the vital radio code-book and other secret documents. A few minutes after we had withdrawn the Japanese surrounded the deserted camp and moved in. There was no fight, no casualties, just the serious loss of vital secret material.

A third campsite was found, this time in the higher reaches of the Telom River at an altitude of 2,500 feet and situated on a ridgeline promontory off Batu Puteh. The camp was frequently mist-covered and it was regularly drenched with rain. So fresh water was plentiful.

With Lim Bo Seng and a number of his agents clearly in detention and undergoing interrogation and torture, the remaining Kuomintang men all had to accept that their identities were now well-documented by the Kempeitai. In effect, they had been neutralised as far as future agent work was concerned. There was no alternative but for them to lie low in this third location and depend on us for their personal safety and everything else. They stopped feeding us their propaganda lines.

For the European contingent at the camp, their Kuomintang operation was clearly over. Fourteen months of painstaking planning, manoeuvring, and stealth – all at very high risk – had been blown apart by indiscipline. A senseless waste. Overnight my guerrillas became the British party's sole operational interest. They asked me if I would try borrowing a vast sum of money from wealthy Chinese, using as a guarantee

Davis' letter of authority from SEAC. They wanted the funds to further their activities. It struck me as a harebrained scheme. But I felt sorry for Davis. He and his colleagues were psychologically down and were obviously clutching at straws. I said I would work on the matter but really had no intention of pursuing it.

The December, 1943, Agreement now became the centerpiece of the Davis group's war effort. Realistically, though, this remained quite inoperable without orders from SEAC and these could not be received until the radio link with Colombo was established. I resolved to do my utmost to help. Spencer Chapman would later write: 'The guerrilla's acceptance of our humiliating position was most gratifying. This was largely due to the very friendly relations we had established with that outstanding character Chen Ping (sic). At no time were we allowed to feel that we were in any way an encumbrance to them, and they gave us every possible assistance.'

Co-existing with the Kuomintang was a decidedly more complex matter to getting along with the British. It demanded that I carefully compartmentalize my mind. We had to live with their agents in the camps. Outside, however, we found ourselves in fierce conflict with bandit groups claiming to represent Kuomintang interests. They were scattered throughout Pahang, Kelantan, Perak and Johore states. In the southern Kelantan area, adjacent to the Cameron Highlands, one bandit force comprised a 300-strong company that operated from a deep-jungle enclave. This particular group directly threatened our control of the Central Highlands and we had to drive them out.

Quite aside from the Kuomintang bandits, the regular Chinese inhabitants in this part of Kelantan were a unique group of people. Their forebears had originally arrived in Malaya some 200 years earlier as immigrants at the time of the Manchu Conquest of China and had been allowed to settle along the shores of the Kelantan river estuary. Later the local Sultan agreed they could move further inland where they started farming. There were few women among these settlers so the men began mixing and intermarrying with the local aboriginal women. As one generation led to another, these Chinese settlers bred darker skinned people but still kept their language which was primarily Hakka. They ended up calling themselves Hakka-hai. With the passing of the years the government lost control over the Hakka-hai. Officialdom only required them to pay nominal rent and tax and stay marginalised.

The area inhabited by these people was ideal for us to set up a permanent base. In this location we could rely on their support and also regular food supplies. Unfortunately, bandit groups had infiltrated the region. The bandits were more recent arrivals from southern China where they had plundered the population in gangs and had been forced out finally by a series of government crackdowns. In Malaya the gangsters began working for both British colonial and Chinese businessmen. They took jobs as contract labourers in tin mines and on plantations. Because of their accustomed lifestyle in China, they preferred a rural existence and tended to live on the edges of the jungle. They retained their local dialects and gradually began moving about the peninsula. Pockets of this group became entrenched in Perak, Pahang, Kelantan and in northern Johore. With law and order generally respected under the colonial British, these gangsters toed the line.

The Japanese invasion changed all that. Law and order deteriorated and the former bandits returned to their old criminal ways. They came down from their homes on the jungle fringes to obtain weapons. Once armed, they began plundering. The CPM took the initiative of contacting them with the aim of forming an alliance. The Party was numerically stronger than the bandits and better organised politically. We recognised that principles were the last considerations on their minds. But we thought we were in a strong enough position to maintain discipline. They agreed to CPM political instructors working with their units and in return we supplied funds and food. This was all done at the state level.

Gradually the bandit elements began rejecting our control and what was being taught them by our political instructors. The men were largely middle-aged and heavily involved in opium smoking. They spent their money freely on drugs and women. When they ran out of funds they began to loot, pillage and rape. At first they tried to hide their criminal ways from us. When we uncovered their activities we openly criticised them and imposed punishments. They escaped to even deeper jungle camps.

As time passed, the various bandit units consolidated their forces into a number of large groups. In Perak, for instance, they merged into one big company and eventually moved to the Grik area, close to the Siamese border. Their activities around Grik grew very disruptive as they began to take advantage of a predominantly Malay population there.

Understandably, the local Malays took strong exception to the presence of these intruders and reported them to the Japanese authorities. In retribution, the bandits swooped on a series of Malay kampong settlements and slaughtered some 400 villagers including children and infants. Additionally they kidnapped numerous women whom they dragged back to their jungle camps. It was an horrific situation. The Japanese claimed the communists' 'Three-Star Army' had perpetrated the massacre and its barbaric aftermath. We promptly issued a denial and identified the true culprits.

The bandits nursed narrow nationalistic attitudes towards China. It was easy for them to dislike us. When we were working at politicising them they would say: 'You are Chinese but you hang portraits of Marx and Lenin beside Sun Yat Sen in your shophouses and homes. We only admire and give respect to Sun Yat Sen, the founding father of the Republic. No bearded and balding foreigners for us!'

To camouflage their criminality and gain some respectability through the projection of a political image, the bandits openly pledged allegiance to the Kuomintang. Thus, our label: 'Kuomintang bandits'. Of course, we considered Lim Bo Seng and his group as totally different entities.

*　　*　　*　　*　　*

Lai Te changed his political attitude to accommodate the progress of the Pacific War. His views became particularly influenced by developments on the Burma front and the general impression that Britain was preparing an Allied invasion of Malaya. In October 1944, he called a meeting of senior cadres in the jungle near the Selangor township of Serendah, just north of Kuala Lumpur. I was there. The commander of the Perak AJA, my close comrade, Liao Wei Chung, commonly referred to by the British and CPM guerrillas alike as Itu, was also there. The two of us had been forced to walk the entire distance from Perak. The journey took two weeks. By this time we had decided, for security reasons, against using any form of regular transport – even bicycles.

Lai Te delivered a most important address to cadres attending from Johore, Pahang, Selangor and Perak. He predicted an imminent Allied seaborne invasion. The Party, he said, would have to be prepared for this. The Secretary General informed the meeting that he had signed a document with the British whereby the Party had agreed to work with the incoming Allied forces. This was clearly a reference to the December, 1943, Blantan Agreement. Lai Te spoke only in general terms. He told the senior cadres he had promised to cooperate with the British and, in return, they would help us. British aid would come, he said, in the form of both military weapons and finance. He then went on to outline a totally new approach to our guerrilla army infrastructure in order to cater to future operations. From then on, we would be required to split our army into two parts. One would be our 'open army'.

This would work with the British and, in effect, function as a British force. The other would comprise the Party's 'clandestine army'. When the time came, this secret force would be in a position to function independently. Lai Te gave us the clear impression our clandestine army would then be taking the fight to the British.

Once the expected landing took place, we would change our designations from Anti-Japanese Army to National Liberation Army and from Anti-Japanese League, to National Liberation League. As the Allied troops splashed ashore our guerrillas should be ready to seize as much territory as possible. Lai Te spoke of the need to capture as many small townships as we could. It was well appreciated we could not hope to hold population centres like Ipoh, Penang, Kuala Lumpur or Singapore. He envisaged our guerrillas taking over banks, post offices and railway stations in the small centres. No mention was made of police stations but in our hearts we felt these, too, were obvious targets for us. We looked to set up our own administrations in the captured towns. Lai Te's address amounted to a rousing call to revolution. Our spirits soared.

The policy for organisation of industrial labour rather than military action had been at the behest of the Japanese, though we were not to know this until three years later. Why the sudden change in policy by the CPM leader? Battlefield developments throughout the Pacific and European theatres were now signalling a defeat in store for the Japanese. Lai Te realised he would have to deal with the British soon and needed to re-position the Party for this eventuality. Then, why the provisions for the secret army? Lai Te was playing all ends against the middle. By the Serendah meeting, he had recognised that the overwhelming feeling among Party rank-and-file – and certainly within the AJA – was for stepped up military activity. As his power base was so slender by this time, he had little option but to appease popular opinion within our membership.

At Serendah, nobody could have predicted the Japanese would capitulate unconditionally. We all thought Tokyo would struggle on to the bitter end. Naturally, we hadn't counted on the impact of a weapon like the atomic bomb.

Lai Te's proposals received solid Party backing. Our discussions then went on to anticipate, quite correctly as it happened, that when the Japanese were defeated, the British would turn to us and demand we hand in our arms and disband. We would ignore such demands and from then on target the colonials. In this instance, Lai Te chose to withhold Party secrets from the Japanese.

So the delegates from the states of Johore, Pahang, Selangor and Perak returned to their respective headquarters and began establishing the clandestine branch of the

CPM army which would soon become known as our Mi Mi Tui (clandestine army) forces. Great care was taken to hide these activities from Davis and company. I am sure they suspected we were up to something but I don't think they ever discovered precisely what.

The incredible February 1, 1945, chance establishment of radio contact with Ceylon enabled Davis to begin relaying to SEAC the wealth of intelligence information he had been hoarding since 1943. The immediate requirement in the wake of these developments was formal talks with the CPM so that implementation of the December, 1943, Agreement could begin. Davis asked me to bring 'Chang Hong' back as soon as possible. It would take two months to arrange this meeting. In the meantime, the radio exchanges enabled RAF Liberators to begin intermittent parachute supply runs.

Davis invited me to witness the initial Perak airdrop which took place at a tin mine area off the Tapah-Bidor road on February 26, 1945. There was intense excitement all round as two European Force 136 officers, two radio operators and two tons of stores landed right on target in the drop zone. Many of the early supply runs were 'blind' drops. Davis coordinated these on his radio. I informed him on the specific areas, particularly in Kedah and Perak, that we had under our control. This information was then radioed back to Ceylon and acted upon.

The vital implementation meeting with 'Chang Hong' took place on April 16. It was held at a temporary guerrilla camp established for the occasion in secondary forest and among foothills close to our original Blantan site. It so happened I was recovering from a bad attack of malaria. Lai Te and Broome were even worse off. Broome, still emaciated by a variety of tropical illnesses, used a cane and had to be supported by Davis and Chapman. 'Chang Hong' was incapable of walking any distance and it was for his sake I had chosen the site close to a road. The result was that we were in serious risk of being spotted by Japanese patrols.

Despite prevailing symptoms of ill-health among the participants, the mood of the meeting was one of accommodation, optimism and cheer, bordering on elation. The British side was represented this time by Davis, Broome, Chapman, a Force 136 officer, Lt Colonel James Hannah and a radio operator, Cpl Humpleman, who brought along his radio transmitter. I had watched Hannah and Humpleman arrive in the first Perak parachute drop seven weeks earlier. 'Chang Hong', Commander Itu and I represented the CPM. The British were now set to prepare their invasion and men of Itu's ilk needed to be appraised of what was to come. At no point during the meeting was mention ever made of the missing 'Tan Choon Lim'.

Davis asked us to expand our army. The SEAC officers examined expansion possibilities state by state. In Perak, for instance, they wanted us to have a total of 800 men. Our Perak guerrilla strength then totalled about 500. The British objective was to set up a guerrilla network along a line corresponding to the main north-south trunk road and the railway that ran parallel to it down the western side of the peninsula. The plan was that our guerrilla force, come the Allied invasion, would be employed attacking both road and rail targets along the length of Japan's two main supply routes from her Singapore logistical base areas. Davis also presented proposals to airdrop weapons to arm our expanded forces and went into details of the types available and their ammunition requirements. He added that the airdrops would include gold bars and fake Japanese currency to enable our units to build up supplies of food. Finances to the tune of £3,000 (Sterling) would be made available to our army on a monthly basis. In addition, extra food supplies would be dropped.

The main condition imposed by the British side was that the CPM accept the liaison officers SEAC intended to parachute into Malaya. Each liaison officer was to be accompanied by a platoon of Gurkhas. We also had to accept the principle that there would be General Liaison Officers (GLOs) with every company-sized guerrilla unit. The GLOs would be in place before the weapons started arriving. They would then be able to oversee the distribution to the guerrillas of weapons, ammunition and various other field supplies.

During a break in the deliberations and away from the hearing of the British, Itu asked 'Chang Hong' whether the presence of Gurkha platoons would pose serious threats to the plans unveiled at the Serendah meeting. 'Chang Hong' was quick to respond. No one need worry on this score. State by state, he explained, the British would only have a single Gurkha platoon on station, whereas our troops in each instance would be in excess of a company.

Suffice to say 'Chang Hong' agreed to all the conditions. The British were jubilant.

Chapter 8

To fight, or not to fight, the returning colonials

With the radio link to Colombo working well and cooperation between our guerrilla army and SEAC imbued with renewed enthusiasm, it became imperative that at least one of Davis' men be extracted from Malaya. The intelligence such an officer could provide would be vital to the final planning stages of Britain's projected seaborne invasion to re-take Malaya and Singapore – Operation Zipper. Even before radio contact was established, it had been decided Richard Broome would make the trip to SEAC headquarters in Ceylon.

When the time came for Broome to leave, Davis thought it best Chapman, who needed urgent medical attention for numerous tropical ailments, should accompany him. Once again I was called in to provide travel arrangements to the coast. These were not easy. Following an exchange of radio messages with Colombo, the Royal Navy agreed to a plan whereby a submarine would make a nighttime rendezvous off the small islet of Pangkor Laut, lying close to the south-western corner of the larger Pangkor island. Pick-up point was to be a sandy inlet called Tanjong Blangah, previously referred to by holidaying expatriates as Emerald Bay. My task was to see that Broome and Chapman arrived safely at Emerald Bay in time for the scheduled appearance of the submarine on the night of May 13.

I divided the journey into three segments. Two involved movement to the coast. The third was the positioning of Broome and Chapman in Emerald Bay. It required a team of guides for various phases of the journey and a well-armed guerrilla escort. I accompanied them for the first couple of days, leaving them in the late afternoon of April 28 near a small village outside the township of Tapah. As I shook hands with the two Europeans with whom I had been so closely associated for more than two years, I had no doubts about the sincerity of their expressions of gratitude. It was an emotional moment, our separate political agendas notwithstanding. They were both fine and brave men and I truly hoped neither would be sent back to defend British interests in Malaya after the defeat of Japan.

The departure of the two Europeans was closely followed by an important airdrop scheduled to take place at a sawmill located in the mountains of central Perak. It required 150 of my ablest guerrillas in order to ensure all supplies arriving

Claude Fenner looking decidedly happier than he did the night
I refused to take him ashore from a submarine rendezvous off
Pulau Pangkor in November, 1943. Fenner, a senior colonial
police officer in Negri Sembilan prior to the war, would have to
wait until July, 1945, before he could return to Malaya, this
time by parachute as a liaison officer working with our guerrillas.
After the war, Fenner rejoined the Malayan police force and rose
to become Inspector General. He was subsequently knighted.

by parachute were quickly gathered and removed from the area before any Japanese search parties arrived on the scene. This the enemy normally did, some two hours after a drop. One of the persistent problems dogging the airdrops was the RAF's repeated use of white parachutes rather than the camouflaged variety. White parachutes were so easily visible from reconnaissance aircraft. Regrettably, the British seemed to have huge stocks of the white variety and very few camouflaged ones.

The safe arrival in Ceylon of Broome and Chapman in late May coincided with the dramatic call by military planners for Operation Zipper's readiness date to be advanced from late November to mid-August. All the old calculations had to be dumped and replaced by new arrangements demanding a massive acceleration of the programme. Supply operations began in earnest from Ceylon on June 6 where three newly arrived squadrons of RAF Liberators became the mainstay of the airlift effort. Records show that Ceylon-based Liberators flying from strips at Minneriya and China Bay were required to fly round trips of between 2,500 and 3,500 miles, under all weather conditions. Very few sorties were cancelled because of weather. Pilots frequently encountered heavy rain and mist over the Malayan drop zones.

With the increased intensity of airdrops came time for the arrival of the British liaison officers and their accompanying Gurkha security platoons. Between July 1 and July 15, a total of 111 men were successfully parachuted into Malaya, an indication of the rate at which operations were then being mounted. Where possible, the British dropped their liaison men into areas with which they were familiar. In Negri Sembilan, for instance, they inserted Claude Fenner, who had served in that state as a senior colonial policeman before the war. Each liaison officer brought in his own radio operator and transmitter and was thus able to establish direct links with Colombo from almost the moment of landing.

The RAF missions were extraordinarily accurate and recovery of the weapons was relatively easy. Pointedly, the Malayan Country Section's resumé of these events notes: 'The percentage of unsuccessful sorties owing to inability to find the drop zones was extremely small and this, in spite of the fact that some of them were described as pocket handkerchiefs tucked into hillsides.'

In some of the drop zones, however, wind gusts did blow parachutes off course making them very difficult to retrieve. In these cases our guerrillas were encouraged to take advantage of the confusion and appropriate weapons for our secret caches.

Much has been made of the fact that the CPM weapons during the Emergency came from these Force 136 airdrops. Some did. But, not many. In fact, it was a very small percentage of our overall post-war stocks. Our early weapons caches consisted mainly of those we picked up from the Malayan battlefields while the Japanese invaders were pushing the British defenders south. During the occupation years, we managed to seize a modest number of arms from the Japanese. We were, however, able to gather a substantial number immediately after Tokyo's surrender. Some were just abandoned by the various Japanese units. Many were acquired after negotiations with senior officers in Japanese garrisons. All in all, our secret army units were able to stash away some 5,000 individual weapon pieces in jungle caches of which no more than 10 per cent were acquired through Force 136 air supplies.

*   *   *   *   *

Amid an atmosphere of fevered expectancy and high morale, I convened the August meeting of the Party's Perak state committee in Ayer Kuning, a small township near Kampar. I was chairing a general discussion of run-of-the-mill Party matters when my secretary burst into the room to announce that Japan had surrendered. He had heard a report of Emperor Hirohito's unconditional capitulation while monitoring the All-India broadcasting network that beamed strongly into Malaya. It was early afternoon on August 16. After the moment's euphoria had dissipated, I promptly switched our meeting's agenda to a review of how best to implement Lai Te's previous October directives. In the interim we had been working, as instructed, on renaming our guerrilla army and our political entity to reflect a revolutionary national liberation movement. In addition, we were well ahead with plans for deploying our secret Mi Mi Tui units and hastening the expansion of our jungle weapons caches. Now it was a matter of tying up loose ends and readying ourselves to take on the returning British.

On the meeting's second day, our Perak courier, a middle-aged Chinese woman, stationed in Kuala Lumpur, arrived with a message from Lai Te. It ordered me to proceed immediately to the capital to see him. All comrades present realised the urgency and it was agreed that we would re-assemble immediately on my return. I caught the first available train and was met at the Kuala Lumpur station by a comrade who escorted me to the Party's new Selangor headquarters. These had just been moved from the Sungei Buloh leper colony to a British-owned estate manager's bungalow nearby. It was August 19.

I missed Lai Te by a few hours. I was informed he had to rush back to Singapore but had left specific instructions which were given to me by my Selangor opposite number, Yeung Kuo.

I originally met Yeung Kuo when I was a young student activist with the Backing-up Society. There was a meeting in Penang for cadres from Perak, Kedah and the island itself. Yeung Kuo attended this meeting presided over by Wee Mon Chen who at that time was the Society's North Malayan Bureau chief. Yeung Kuo was his assistant. (Wee Mon Chen would serve as Singapore's ambassador to Japan from 1973 to 1980.)

Yeung Kuo very early became a full time CPM worker. Bright, energetic and committed, he was soon appointed to the Penang Town Committee. The Party later transferred him to Singapore where he also functioned as a Town Committee member. The British arrested Yeung Kuo in Singapore shortly before the outbreak of the Pacific war. The colonial administration there banished him, packing him off to China by ship with a batch of exiled members and supporters. When the ship was more than half-way to Hong Kong, the Japanese invaded the Crown colony. The vessel promptly returned to its port of departure. Yeung Kuo stepped ashore in Singapore, a free man once again. He immediately went underground before the Japanese advance reached the island.

Our Selangor meeting in 1945 was the first opportunity Yeung Kuo and I had to work together. On this occasion he passed me two separate documents. One comprised an eight point declaration of Party aims for the immediate post-surrender period. The other was an outline of a speech Lai Te had made in Sungei Buloh. With these came written notes of explanation provided by Yeung Kuo.

The Selangor state secretary described to me how Lai Te, in the name of the Central Committee, hastily called together a three-man meeting at the Selangor Party offices the previous day. In attendance were Lai Te himself, Yeung Kuo, and a senior-ranking Selangor official. Lai Te, in addition to addressing the other two, had tabled the eight point programme[5] and secured agreement for its circulation. The CPM would formally release this document on August 25.

As I read the pre-release draft, my heart sank. It instructed the Party to:

1. Support Russia, China, Britain and America in a new organisation for world security;

Yeung Kuo as a young middle school graduate in Penang. This picture was attached to his graduation certificate. Like me, he became an activist very early in life. I first met Yeung Kuo during a gathering in Penang for Backing-up Society cadres.

2. Establish a democratic government in Malaya with an electorate drawn from all races;

3. Abolish the fascist Japanese political structure in Malaya;

4. Enforce freedoms for speech, publications and societies and establish a legal status for the Malayan People's Anti Japanese army;

5. Reform the country's educational and social conditions;

6. Improve living conditions and develop industry and commerce to assist the poor and in doing so increase wages to a standard minimum and impose an eight-hour working day;

7. Stabilize prices and punish traitors, corrupt officials, hoarders and profiteers;

8. Achieve good treatment for the anti-Japanese army and seek compensation for families of those who died in the Allied cause.

I realised the programme amounted to nothing more than a vapid move to appease the incoming British. It was couched in very general terms and made no mention whatever of the CPM's basic goal of self-determination for the nation. It represented a devastating blow to all those who had been involved at the sharp end of Party activities throughout the occupation years. Yeung Kuo's notes and his added verbal explanations deepened my despondency. At the meeting, he related, Lai Te had issued instructions that represented nothing less than a 180-degree turn from those he had given at Serendah ten months earlier. The Secretary General was now firmly arguing against a militant stance by the Party. It would be preferable, he said, to move to a political posture at this time. He was calling for cooperation with the British coupled with a concentrated effort on the organisation of labour and the infiltration of unions. Back to square one. Worse still, he was looking to the transparent disbanding of our open army and the clandestine disbanding of our secret units. The only glimmer of hope was his instructions that all weapons held by units of the secret force were to be retained and stored away in jungle caches. We were to pursue a peaceful struggle.

I was further perplexed by Lai Te's hasty creation at the Sungei Buloh deliberations of what he termed the 'Central Military Committee'. From the outset of my association with Davis, Broome and Chapman, the three Englishmen had repeatedly asked to be put in touch with representatives of the Party's High Command. Except for a very brief period after Britain's surrender to the Japanese, there had been no CPM High Command functioning for the entire occupation. Time and again I had fudged the issue by arguing that communications problems made contacting our High Command officials very difficult. As a Party point of honour, I always felt constrained never to reveal our lack of military coordination. Now I suddenly found, at the end of the war, I had been appointed the No 2 officer of the 'Three Star Army'. Commander in Chief was Lai Te, I was his deputy, then came Liew Yao, Commander of our Selangor troops, known as the 1st Regiment. Armed with my new credentials, I was ordered by Lai Te to meet John Davis at Serendah as a matter of urgency. Once again, nobody questioned the wisdom of our Secretary General's views. He was the Comintern man and this aura had not left him despite the fact we knew the Comintern had been disbanded in 1943.

When I arrived in Serendah and greeted Davis as the guerrilla army's No 2 military commander, he was understandably confused as to exactly what role I had been playing in the CPM. For our first meeting at Segari in September, 1943, shortly after Davis had landed from a submarine, I had identified myself as a representative of the Party's Perak committee. At the important December, 1943, discussions between Davis and 'Chang Hong' which formalised our army's association with SEAC, I was present in the capacity of Central Committee liaison officer and thereafter became Davis' direct link to the Party hierarchy. Now in Serendah, following the Japanese capitulation, I was revealed as a Central Military Committee member. The truth was that I had no real power to decide any military policy. Whether Davis recognised this fact I had no way of knowing.

Davis, himself, was in a very delicate position. He had no idea how the Japanese forces in Malaya would react to their Emperor's order to surrender. He almost certainly would have received information that a number of their units, disgraced by the prospect of becoming prisoners of war, were seriously considering the option of ignoring Hirohito's command and fighting on. Furthermore, Davis was deeply suspicious of the CPM's ultimate intentions. The former colonial police officer had been long enough underground in occupied Malaya and in close association with us to appreciate that the Party's rank-and-file were very serious on the matter of Malaya's independence.

He had been informed by radio that the intended British invasion force – now the re-occupation colonial army – was unlikely to come ashore on Malayan beachheads for at least three weeks. Who would control the territory in the interim? Davis knew the governmental hiatus looming over Malaya and Singapore, at least until the British troops arrived, was fraught with danger. There was every chance that, having just celebrated the Allies' Pacific theatre victory, Britain and her

Commonwealth military partners, particularly Australia and New Zealand, would instantly be thrust into an anti-colonial guerrilla war in Malaya.

Personally, I was totally committed to the idea of continuing the fight but the Sungei Buloh directive from Lai Te had dashed these hopes. Still, I was anxious to get back to Perak as soon as possible. I now faced the unenviable task of conveying to our forces in Perak and Kedah that, for the time being at least, they would be disbanding.

During my conversation with Davis in Serendah on August 22, I, of course, refrained from revealing my frustrations. He informed me he would be moving to Kuala Lumpur immediately where he intended pursuing his efforts at contacting the Japanese governor of Selangor, Lt General Shoura Kakama. He hoped to solidify some form of interim command structure for Malaya and Singapore to carry through until the British forces landed. Davis wanted me to accompany him, then and there, to the capital. He promised all my accommodation would be taken care of by SEAC and indicated he was relying on me to help with the smooth handover from Japanese to British control. That was one way of putting it. I saw his intentions for me more in terms of keeping the lid on likely CPM guerrilla reactions against the incoming British interests. I excused myself from accompanying him forthwith to Kuala Lumpur on the grounds that I had demanding commitments in Perak. Before departing, I promised I would join Davis in the administrative capital as soon as I had completed my missions further north.

It was now August 25. Revolutionary spirit within the Party had never run so high. The greater majority of our guerrilla units had, for seven days, been preparing for continuing armed struggle that would now switch to target the returning colonial power.

Within hours of Emperor Hirohito's Tokyo broadcast on August 16, Japanese military commanders in Malaya began sending out feelers to the CPM seeking negotiations with us. They made it clear they were anxious to ignore the surrender command and were looking to forming an alliance with the Party and our guerrilla army.

They were just as keen as we were to carry the fight to the returning colonial forces. If we decided to do so, they were ready to join us rather than become prisoners of war. Firm proposals along these lines were received from top Japanese commanders in Negri Sembilan, Perak and Kedah. In Johore, where similar but less high-ranking approaches were made, there was heated debate on the issue among

CPM state committee members. It is fair to say the overwhelming desire among the guerrillas then was to swing the action against the colonials and accept the Japanese offers. In that frenetic week during my absence, whole battalions of Japanese had signalled their willingness to come over to our side and bring with them huge supplies of weapons and ammunition.

For example, our military chief in Kedah, Ah Ho, conducted specific negotiations with the top Japanese officer assigned to the state. These were aimed at establishing a unified CPM/Japanese fighting force in that area. In Perak, talks opened at the Japanese military headquarters in Taiping between the senior commander, a major general, and my deputy secretary on the state committee, Ai Ker, who represented me in my absence. The Japanese military headquarters, formerly in Singapore, had, several months earlier, moved to Taiping when their intelligence assessments began predicting the expected British invasion would occur in northern Malaya. So, in effect, my deputy was directly negotiating with the command controlling the entire Japanese military presence in Malaya and Singapore.

In this instance, the Japanese major general told Ai Ker exactly the same message as was being given our commander in Kedah. 'If you choose to fight on, you can rely on our support.' My deputy did not hesitate and immediately promised, in principle, that the CPM would continue the fight. He told the senior Japanese officer he would need a few days to work out the details.

So, when I returned and told Ai Ker everything had changed, he was devastated. The sudden Japanese surrender had provided us with a breathtaking opportunity to manipulate events to our advantage and, rather than seizing it, we were throwing it away! Prospects of a broad alliance with the defeated Japanese vanished before our eyes. However, this would not prevent some 400 individual Japanese being quietly accepted into our ranks. To a man they found their orders to surrender to the incoming British an unbearable disgrace, the antithesis of everything they had been militarily trained to believe. Being naturally racist, they were appalled at the prospect of being subjugated by whites. There were some who, rather than endure the ignominy, chose to commit suicide through the traditional hara-kiri ceremony. Those who joined us obviously were prepared to rationalise their predicament. Teaming up with our guerrillas, they felt, was not a matter of joining the enemy. Rather, it was the formation of an acceptable Asian alliance against the white colonial intruder. These developments, undertaken at the local level in every state and well-hidden from the British, would eventually have a frightful sequel.

Viewed across more than half a century of history, it is perhaps difficult for many to accept how the Party could be so strongly opposed to the Japanese throughout the occupation period and then, within a matter of hours following Tokyo's surrender, be quite prepared to embrace the enemy as possible comrades-in-arms. This seeming anomaly is only intensified by the fact that our mobile squads had, throughout the occupation, sought to eliminate all those collaborating with the Japanese. Surely contemplation of an accommodation with the defeated invaders was tantamount to considering collaboration?

It should first be appreciated that the possible amalgamation of our guerrilla army and the Japanese was an issue that had, for some time, been thoroughly debated and analysed by our senior cadres. The feeling within the Party was that the real war remained in progress. Our objective of independence for Malaya still remained a long way off. Compared with the incoming British, we were numerically weak with our guerrilla army being about 5,000-strong at this point. Our assessments were that the British would inevitably move against us, their war-time allies – as, indeed, they did – and begin re-imposing the sort of repressive measures they had employed against us prior to the outbreak of hostilities. To move against them first was a matter of acceptable tactical expediency. Considerations of honour and morality among wartime allies did not enter the equation. Such notions certainly never impeded British decisions when it came to opposing us in the months and years that followed.

But the rationale went further than this. Hirohito's unconditional surrender had completely changed the picture. Before it, the Japanese were the controlling authority in Malaya and the enemy. They were killing us. We were killing them. Now defeated, they were no longer a threat. If they wanted to join us they would have to submit to our political will and physical control. Without this there could be no alliance and we made this very clear to them in all our negotiations.

As the uncertainty of those immediate post-Tokyo capitulation days intensified, the Party found itself confronting a mounting dilemma. Unless the issue of cooperation between our guerrillas and the Japanese was solved quickly, the CPM would likely split in two. It is my opinion that had this occurred, those in favour of association with the Japanese would have comprised the overwhelmingly larger faction. As it happened, the directive from Lai Te ordering the disbanding of our forces settled the matter and the unquestioning adherence of the comrades to orders from the supreme source ensured Party cohesion.

To retain a balanced perspective, one also has to look briefly at what was happening within the Malay community during this chaotic phase. There were Malay nationalists working with the Japanese throughout the occupation. The Japanese went ahead and helped the Malays set up three basic military organisations. The first of these, the Heiho, was formed in June, 1943, with the aim of supplying labour services to Japanese units. Later that year the Japanese assisted in setting up an all-Malay self-defence force and a reserve. The Giyu Gun or Volunteer Army was conceived as being capable for deployment in coastal defence operations in the event of a British invasion. The volunteer reserves were known as the Giyu Tai. In addition, some Malays were actually accepted into the Japanese Army; but not in combat units. The Malay self-defence and reserve recruits were given military training and were well armed. At the time of Japan's surrender there were some 2,000 of these Malays and they had nowhere to go.

Right up to the very moment of Emperor Hirohito's August 16 broadcast, the Japanese authorities were promising independence for the Malays. Two fundamental proposals were on offer. Independence for Malaya in its own right; or independence for the peninsula within the broader Indonesia Raya concept headed by that territory's nationalist leader, Sukarno. The Japanese had convened a meeting in Kuala Lumpur's Station Hotel to discuss and finalise matters. Among the prominent Malays invited to participate were some conservative nationalists including Johore's Datuk Onn bin Jaafar. The participants at this gathering strongly favoured the idea of joining Indonesia. All along there had been the threat that if there was an opposition to unity with Indonesia, Tokyo could well hand over Malaya to become part of China. Circumstances saved the day. With the conference barely underway, it was announced that Hirohito had surrendered. On this note all bets were off and the participants dispersed.

Outside the northern Johore township of Muar on August 21, a 280-strong unit of the Giyu Gun, moving from Singapore to Kuala Lumpur, came in contact with one of our guerrilla units that had already assumed control of the area. The Malays made their position quite clear. If we were willing to go ahead and continue the fight against the British they were willing to join us. It was this issue that had spurred the heated debate within the Party's North Johore Committee. Perhaps fortuitously, perhaps not, Lai Te's directive settled matters and the anticipated union of Chinese, Malay and Japanese forces against Britain came to naught. The Giyu Gun force had then to dissolve. A number of its leaders, knowing full-well that the

British would haul them before war crimes courts, decided to flee to the Dutch East Indies – Indonesia.

It was an intensely complex time which books, most of them written in the 1960s and 1970s by Caucasian authors, applying neat Western concepts of right and wrong, good and evil, have hopelessly over-simplified to the obvious benefit of the West's position in the region.

The racial clashes in the so-called 'interregnum period', between the hour the Japanese surrendered and when, almost three weeks later, British forces began landing on Malayan beaches to set up temporary military rule, are a case in point. Actually, these clashes had begun even before Tokyo's surrender and I doubt that the Japanese officers even knew that their troops were responsible for igniting tension between Chinese and Malay communities. As early as July – before the first of the two atomic bombs dropped on Japan – Japanese troops, disguised as AJA guerrillas, went to a mosque in Johore and slaughtered a pig. This immediately inflamed Malay sentiments and they turned on the local Chinese villagers.

Datuk Onn was at this time the district officer for Batu Pahat under the Japanese administration. Trouble spread from Batu Pahat to Yong Peng. The Malays were armed with *parang panjang* – the long knife. The Chinese villagers who became their targets were unarmed and desperately called on the AJA for support. We could not ignore their predicament and ordered in units of our army as a protection force. The British liaison officers, who frankly didn't understand the root causes of the problem and were not prepared to listen, tried to prevent us from going. We ignored them. In the end many liaison officers had no option but to move with us. We set up a line and told the Malays not to cross it. The Malays, believing their magic amulets would shield them from bullets, charged our lines. We shot. Some dropped. The rest hesitated then retreated. We chased them into nearby kampongs and arrested the ring-leaders. We also searched the kampong houses and confiscated every *parang panjang* we could find.

This major attack in the Batu Pahat area resulted in our forces actually arresting Datuk Onn and his assistant. In the event, Datuk Onn helped bring the violence to an end by speaking to the Malays. It was a very emotional time and nobody was willing to listen coolly to details of how the racial trouble began. The killing was on a very large scale. At least 1,000 died. Naturally, propaganda had it that the MPAJA was the primary cause. This is patently untrue.

In numerous other racial instances at this time Chinese bandits were the culprits. The CPM, of course, was blamed for their activities as well. Teluk Anson and Ayer Kuning were areas that suffered this way. The history books – most of them written during the West's intensely anti-communist years – invariably point to our guerrillas being the root cause of all trouble. This is also untrue. Of course we were involved. But we reacted to protect. We did not instigate. I have read numerous accounts of these events, the overwhelming number by authors who were certainly not present during the action and had no concept of the issues involved. Of all the material I have analysed, only one report, written by a British Liaison Officer named Alexander and lodged with the Public Record Office at Kew, England, represents what I believe is a fair account of what happened at this very violent time.

When there is talk about Malay units being pro-Japanese, Westerners again invariaby fall into the easy trap of over-simplification. When we, as communist guerrillas worked with the British, none of us, for a single moment, considered ourselves pro-British. We were allies, but we had our own agenda. Likewise, following Japan's capitulation, a different set of circumstances presented themselves to us as far as the defeated army was concerned. I always regard the Malays as having been in similar binds when it came to their relationships with the British and Japanese during the war.

*   *   *   *   *

By this critical point, when responsibility fell upon me to ensure CPM compliance with orders for an about-turn away from an undoubtedly preferred policy of continuing armed struggle, I had never once questioned the motives or wisdom behind Lai Te's directives. I believed these instructions had all along come from a functioning Central Committee.

Even on the specific subject of joining forces with the defeated Japanese against the British, I ultimately rationalised Lai Te's reasoning. He maintained that the Party's influence in Malaya was strong only among the Chinese. It was, on the other hand, weak among the Malays. He referred to the problem as an 'imbalance'. If we were to continue the fight, he said, we could only rely on the support of the Chinese. In fact, we enjoyed considerable support among the rural Malays at that period. We had started recruiting and training Malays in Perak but the Japanese surrender had interrupted this programme.

It fell on me to pass details of Lai Te's latest directive to the various committees in Perak and Kedah. What made things more problematic was the fact that the comrades in Kedah had yet to receive news of the October, 1944, Serendah orders and had thus made no provisions for clandestine forces. Their guerrilla units, therefore, had become fully committed to the British, and had been working in close cooperation with their respective liaison officers. When I explained the implications of the new directive to Kedah Party leaders, they took immediate action. As a result only half of the open army was transparently disbanded when requested.

Some 300-400 guerrillas suddenly disappeared. Ultimately, the Kedah state committee arranged for the vanishing forces to hide their weapons and disband. Only in a few places in Perak and Kedah did guerrilla units put up signboards indicating name changes for our political and military organisations. Along with these went our flags. By the first few days of September, I had completed the task of reversing our Party's preparations for heightened warfare. I had been required to calm and pacify, restrain and arrest. I was mentally and emotionally drained. I consoled myself with the firm impression that although we would not be pursuing an immediate armed struggle against the British, we would, undoubtedly, be so doing five to ten years hence.

It was in this frame of mind that I returned to Kuala Lumpur. Liew Yao, my fellow newly appointed Military Committee member, was already established in the capital. He had moved there with Davis and his British liaison officer, Lt Colonel Douglas Broadhurst, who had parachuted into Selangor to operate with our 1st Regiment. (In 1946 Broadhurst would be appointed Special Branch Director in Singapore.) SEAC had commandeered a number of bungalows in the exclusive Kenny Hill area, near the British High Commissioner's residence. One of these was for CPM senior officials. I moved in with Liew Yao. The two of us were given cars for which we provided our own drivers from the guerrilla ranks.

Soon after I settled into my new quarters, Davis came to the bungalow and invited me to Morib for the landing of British troops on Selangor's south-western coastline. Part of the intended invasion force had departed Colombo and was at sea, en route to Malaya, when Japan surrendered. Rather than halt the movement, the British went ahead with their planned landing and revamped it into a major propaganda exercise. First troops of the re-occupation came ashore at a Penang island beachhead on September 3.

A few days later, Davis and I stood side by side in companionable silence on the Morib shoreline watching what amounted to an anti-climax – a dramatic scene – but an anti-climax nonetheless. At some point, I must have thought: we are letting them back unimpeded to reclaim a territory they have plundered for so long. It was the sentiment that had dominated my days since Yeung Kuo passed on Lai Te's new Sungei Buloh directives. At Morib, I paid little attention to what went on around me. I heard exuberant words of congratulations. Expressions of praise and jubilation were exchanged. Tired, grown men declared how wonderful it was that the war was over and done with.

And what was going on in Davis' mind?

Declassified documents now reveal that, literally hours before the Japanese surrender, SEAC had sent two messages to him via radio. One said in part[6]:

'Victory is now at hand and your contribution has been important and is appreciated.'

The other instructed Davis thus:

'Allied troops will shortly arrive but meanwhile to avoid clashes and unnecessary bloodshed you and those under you should avoid all towns and other districts where Japanese are present.'

Davis must have been livid. On August 19 he sent the following message[7]:

'Your recent telegrams are disturbing. Following must of course be obvious to you. Controlled AJUF are soldiers under command of SACSEA. They expect and await specific orders and not vague directives. I am satisfied they will obey such orders provided they are reasonable. Orders for them to remain half starved in the hills while the Allies leisurely take over the administration from the Japs will not be reasonable. Some arrangement must be made with the Japs for controlled AJUF to emerge during the interim period though they need not interfere with the Japs admin. AJUF must be given full share in the honours of victory. Controlled AJUF should now be limited to those already armed by us plus other armed men who will accept our control. They must be fully equipped rationed and used by us at the earliest opportunity until time for disbandment. Good treatment of controlled AJUF will have an excellent effect on uncontrolled AJUF many of whom may later be absorbed. Do your utmost to preserve and strengthen central control otherwise discipline will collapse. The alternative to all this is chaos and anarchy which may take decingdecades to eradicate. The matter is very urgent. There is serious risk of a disastrous anticlimax.'

Thousands of miles away in London, SOE's Colonel L. F. Sheridan enclosed a 'top secret' covering letter when forwarding a copy of Davis' message to Mr G.E.J. Gent, then a top official in the Colonial Office in London and shortly to become Britain's first post-war High Commissioner to Malaya.[8] Dated 27th August, 1945, Sheridan's letter said:

Dear Gent,

I attach for your personal information only copy of a message received by Force 136 from the senior representative in Malaya.

I would not like you to think that we attach undue importance to Davis' view. He has been in the country for a considerable time living doubtless under conditions of considerable discomfort and suffering all the ill-effects of a trying climate under such conditions.

Our experience is that in cases of this kind the L.O. in course of time becomes rather imbued with the views of the resistance movement to which they are attached.

Nevertheless his message is of interest in that it indicates, I think, what is in the minds of the AJUF leaders.

Yours sincerely
Colonel L.F. Sheridan

As far as London was concerned, Davis had been too long in the tropics and was clearly going native. Sheridan's remarks were a disgrace. His dismissive condescension encapsulated Britain's ignorance of the issues she must face as for a second time she prepared to lower the yoke of colonialism on Malaya and her people.

Gent's response to Sheridan on August 29 read[9]:

Many thanks for your note of 27th August with the message from Davis. His reactions no doubt faithfully represent those of the circle with which he has been living for sometime past and will need to be kept continually in mind by those who in the new circumstances will have the handling of the problem. Nevertheless, I should suppose that those of the AJUF who do not, as a matter of career, prefer banditry to more regular occupations will fairly quickly demobilize themselves as soon as they see a chance of profitable and more comfortable conditions of work. We must expect, however, to have a core who will need sympathetic and careful handling.

Yours sincerely
G. E. J. Gent

Had I enjoyed access to those exchanges then, I would have paid scant attention to their substance. 'Profitable and more comfortable conditions of work' couldn't have been further from my mind. By now I had learned about the superior airs even the most ignorant Englishman tended to affect when discussing Asia from lofty offices on the other side of the world. Sheridan's pretentiousness was just another example and Gent's patronising tone, yet another.

Meanwhile, there were many things on my mind. In a few days I would be travelling to Singapore by train for further consultations with Lai Te who wanted to re-organise the Party's political structure to accommodate the fast changing circumstances.

*   *   *   *   *

I stayed overnight in the MPAJA offices in Selegie road, near the Kandang Kerbau hospital. Attached to our Singapore headquarters at this time were the MPAJA platoons we had sent from Johore to help maintain law and order in the aftermath of the Japanese surrender. On September 10, these platoons were honoured at a Bukit Panjang mass rally where a number of our Chinese female guerrillas, resplendent in their Three Star Army uniforms and caps, became the centre of attraction for the hugely appreciative crowd.

It turned out that Lai Te was planning to form a five-man provisional Central Committee. He was able to push his structuring agenda through the meeting without opposition. Lai Te remained Party leader and Secretary of the provisional

Central Committee. He was joined by Ah Chung, the surviving veteran Central Committee member who had been out of touch for so long in East Pahang, Yeung Kuo, the Selangor state secretary, Chen Yong, the South Johore secretary, and myself.

I had never aspired to such an esteemed position. Despite all that had happened to me within the Party from the outset of hostilities, I never thought of myself assuming a leadership role. I was anything but ambitious. I was not even 21 when the war ended. As a teenager, when I first harboured dreams of going to China and joining the Kuomintang Army, I was quite prepared to die. I knew the attrition rate for young graduate officers who became platoon leaders was about 90 per cent. Later on, when I was influenced by communist doctrine, I planned to go and join Mao's forces to fight a guerrilla war in China. The same sentiments still applied. I was not looking to become an ambitious career soldier. I was intending to die for my motherland, a land I had never even visited.

I was very much convinced by Mao's theories on guerrilla warfare and believed this was the only way of defeating the Japanese invaders in China. China had to engage in a protracted guerrilla struggle. She could not hope to win the war in a short period. Then the face of warfare suddenly changed. The Japanese, who were fighting in China, had invaded Malaya. Now with the Japanese defeated, it was Britain's turn again. If I had been prepared to die in China, why couldn't I die in Malaya? After all, communist doctrine was telling me that I was involved in an international struggle.

Britain's re-occupation of Singapore began on September 5 when, shortly after midday, a Royal Navy convoy, escorted by the cruisers HMS Sussex and HMS Cleopatra, manoeuvred into the island's outer roads. The convoy's arrival had been delayed two or three days while minesweepers cleared passages through Japanese minefields in the Malacca Straits. As the first troops, drawn from the 15th Indian Corps and commanded by Lt General Sir Philip Christison, came ashore, Britain proclaimed a 'temporary form of government' for the Malaya-Singapore region to be known as the British Military Administration (BMA).

In an obvious attempt to appease the CPM, we were invited to provide a total of three Party representatives to serve on BMA advisory councils. In effect, we had a single representative in each of the Singapore, Selangor and Perak councils. This was no magnanimous BMA gesture. It meant we had three voices in a total of 61 others.

At the same time, the British failed to make clear whether the pre-war *Societies and Banishment ordinances*, which they had never repealed, could still be used to threaten CPM activities. As it turned out, the BMA this way intended keeping us in a convenient political nether world where our semi-legal/semi-illegal status could always be manipulated and controlled.

Chapter 9

A cauldron of simmering discontent

I was back in Perak towards the end of September, 1945, working on numerous security problems associated with the unbelievably lacklustre performance of the BMA's first few weeks in office. Its senior administrators, untrained in political matters, displayed a complete absence of understanding of the functions of government.

Its Civil Affairs Department's first move was to declare the Japanese occupation currency valueless. This extraordinarily inept and draconian step exhibited a total lack of fiscal comprehension. It immediately reduced the vast majority of the labouring population to paupers. Their only savings, earned during the previous three-and-a-half years, had been in Japanese notes. As BMA blunder followed blunder, food supplies dwindled and prices soared. Crime rates surged, policing activities floundered and corruption rampaged. Not surprisingly, the people became increasingly embittered towards the returning colonials. Soon, Malaya was a cauldron of simmering discontent.

Against this background, the CPM, at state levels throughout the peninsula, moved to impose a moderating effect and respect for order by encouraging the formation of Peoples Committees, clubs and unions for workers, women and young people. Most of these were directly controlled or influenced by the Party. The CPM was, at the time, the only recognisable political movement functioning throughout the newly reclaimed colonial territory.

There was nothing pointedly revolutionary or unreasonable about the rising public demands. People wanted rice because they were hungry. They wanted jobs because they were destitute. They strongly opposed the other draconian BMA measure that inexplicably restricted the movement of food supplies. Without money, jobs or food, they sought government assistance for free water and electricity over a three-month, immediate post-war period. They hoped, by then, they would be financially re-established. Finally, they asked the BMA to help stabilize the prices of rubber and tin at viable levels to support these two vital industries, so fundamental to the labour market.

After Lai Te's Sungei Buloh directive, we had looked to political progress through accommodations with the BMA. In the light of the tacit recognition the British had given the CPM since the Japanese surrender, we had further hoped the Party might now be granted legal standing. In response to our optimism, Party branch offices were openly established in the bigger towns throughout the peninsula. At the same time, it was thought worthwhile to offer the cooperation of our Peoples Committees to the authorities as possible channels for relief work. Accompanying this move was an expectation that, in turn, the Committees would eventually be assigned a political role.

Around this time, I paid close attention to the way the government was controlling the entire food importation mechanism. The BMA was so incompetent it was incapable of even effectively concealing the free-flowing corruption its decisions were generating. Many of its members were directly involved. I was well aware of the BMA's granting of food distribution monopolies to a handful of chosen firms. The authorities blamed the acute scarcity of rice and other staples on post-war worldwide food shortages. If that was the case, how come there were ample supplies available on the black market? All you needed was money to pay extortionate prices. The dubious 'old boy' networks of pre-war years were being faithfully restored. I fully concurred with the pro-communist *Sin Min Chu* (New Democracy) newspaper of the day that observed:

'If the daily necessities of the people were to be imported by the Government and distributed to the people through wholesale merchants, the public who have already been impoverished will have to suffer because they cannot escape the grip of the imperialistic policy of making profits.'

The returning British had no other political objective than the re-structuring and reinforcement of their old colonial hold on Malaya. And furthest from their thoughts were ideas of sharing power with any local political movement, least of all the CPM. The hope of Party moderates that somehow the colonials could be persuaded to allow the CPM to play a supplementary role was totally misguided.

With public dissatisfaction over the BMA's performance growing by the hour, I was once again summoned from Malaya by Lai Te. This time, my presence was urgently required in Singapore for the formal installation of the five-man interim Central Committee he had named earlier. It was to be a stop-gap measure until a permanent leadership structure, more closely geared to prevailing conditions, could be organised. My old friend, Commander Itu, was also instructed to attend.

For the journey from Bidor to Singapore, we were assigned a large limousine that the MPAJA had confiscated from a senior Japanese military commander. It came replete with an impressive insignia staff positioned on its bonnet. Commander Itu decided he had been presented a unique opportunity for proselytising the cause dearest to his heart. As we were preparing to leave, he produced a large, red, Three Star Army flag with its own wooden pole. Using wire, he attached our military colours to various extrusions at the front of the vehicle, including the car's now dwarfed insignia staff. Commander Itu was scarcely a well-travelled man. But he was never one to shirk duty and he was brave. Over the occupation years he had managed to establish for himself the fearsome reputation of being a blunt, tough guerrilla leader. Let us say Itu was a man you'd rather cajole than cross.

We set off through the faint haze of an early tropical morning, red flag flapping wildly, to attend the first post-war gathering of senior communist cadres. The meeting would be dedicated, we hoped, to one day ejecting the British who had returned to Malayan shores barely four weeks earlier. Close behind our car followed a second vehicle packed with heavily armed bodyguards.

Frankly, I felt most embarrassed by Itu's ostentatious display of Party loyalty, but felt it prudent to withhold comment. From Bidor to Kuala Lumpur, as we threaded down through southern Perak's rubber plantations into the then natural jungle terrain of northern Selangor, we passed numerous fully-manned Japanese road sentry positions. Some enemy units had yet to complete their formal surrender arrangements and were being employed on law and order duties. Fortunately for us, all we received from the sentry posts were rather startled stares. Not a single raised weapon. In several townships through which we passed, we elicited enthusiastic applause and cheers from the locals.

We spent the night in Kuala Lumpur where our convoy was joined by a third car destined for the same Singapore meeting. In this vehicle, which moved into position behind our armed escort, travelled the Pahang veteran Ah Chung, the Selangor state secretary Yeung Kuo and Liew Yao, his army commander.

With red flag still gyrating violently at the front of our convoy, we proceeded to Singapore down the main road. Our journey proved quite uneventful until we came to a point near Senai, barely 15 miles from Johore Bahru. There, a Japanese sentry raised his weapon and ordered us to stop. Apparently there was very bad blood between the Japanese commander at Senai and our guerrilla unit that operated in the area. Our bodyguards tumbled out of their vehicle, rifles, pistols and hand grenades at the ready. Itu vehemently objected to being ordered to stop, shouting his protests in highly descriptive Hakka. The sentry, who was quickly joined by a well-armed group of his fellows, shouted back just as forcibly in Japanese. Neither side really knew what the other was saying and each scanned the other's line-up of weaponry with some apprehension.

Fortunately, reason prevailed. We agreed to lower our red flag in return for the right of onward passage. As our three-vehicle convoy passed over the Causeway linking Johore Bahru to Singapore, Itu and I sat silently in the rear seat of the first car. Itu nursed his beloved red flag on his lap and, I'm sure, a substantial degree of pent-up anger inside. For my part, I nursed a decided feeling of relief that we had been saved from creating a major spectacle with our flag as we drove through the heavily populated streets of Singapore to MPAJA headquarters in Selegie road.

The Singapore streets were very quiet that night. The British forces were in place and so, too, were our Johore-based guerrillas. We spent the night at our Selegie road office, in a building that had housed a YMCA branch before the war. The Japanese had used it as a police post. The following day, we arranged to see Lai Te in the Geylang safe house.

The meeting proved rather anti-climactic, particularly following the exuberance of our trip south during the previous two days. Lai Te concentrated on formally appointing the interim body in which he remained Party leader. No new or innovative policies were presented. The Secretary General seemed content enough to have the eight point programme he had produced in Sungei Buloh accepted as the Party's guidelines.

As a newly appointed Central Committee member, it became advisable for me to vacate my state secretary posting and concentrate on headquarters affairs. There was much to do and every day seemed to get more tumultuous. Local and regional events combined to heighten economic, social and political tensions. After arranging a smooth hand-over to Ai Ker in Perak, I returned to the bungalow in Kuala Lumpur.

Much to the disappointment of Party members who were hopeful the MPAJA could be incorporated into a defence force, our army found itself having to disband by December 1. It was a delicate process. Military parades up and down the peninsula saw uniformed MPAJA guerrillas going through the public motions of demobilization. This, of course, was our 'open' army complying with regulations and dutifully handing in their weapons to the authorities. On all of these occasions, senior BMA officers were on hand to lavish praise on our wartime exploits. Behind scenes, our 'secret' army was quietly dissolving into civilian life. These guerrillas were also giving up their weapons, only this time to the Party. Some 4,000 weapons would be handed across officially to the British. Another 5,000 or so would find their way to our secret jungle caches.

This MPAJA group photo was taken in Ipoh in September, 1945, some three months before our army was ordered to disband.

(Left to right, front row) **Liet Yang**, commander, 5th Regiment, Perak. He joined the Emergency but was killed in early action in Kelantan. **Liew Tse Chung**, company commander during the Japanese occupation. Liew left the Party before the Emergency. Notwithstanding, the British subsequently had him arrested and banished to China.

(Left to right, back row) **Pai Tse Mu**. Commander, 8th Regiment, Kedah. Led the 8th Detachment in Kedah during the Emergency. **Huang Sung**, a company commander during World War 11 but resigned from the Party before the Emergency. He, too, was subsequently arrested by the British. **Lee Tong Lin**, alias Yiang Lin, headquarters member of Perak 5th Regiment and assistant to our Colonel Itu. Lee had studied at the German-run university in Shanghai before the war. After Merdeka he took advantage of the government's amnesty offer and was repatriated to China where he joined his wife and children.

A unit of our 'open' army dutifully complies with the disbandment order in December, 1945.

If the public at large had found the military administration sadly wanting in September, it recognised its performance as decidedly abysmal by the end of the following month. October, 1945, was a turning point for the CPM. The BMA became adamant in its public denials of what clearly was economic inflation engulfing Malaya and Singapore. Every man in the street felt the battering of prices that had soared by several hundred per cent from pre-war days. The authorities' decision to grant wage increases to a maximum of only 33.5 per cent was met by a huge public outcry. Soon after, Singapore's first post-war dock strike began. On October 21, some 7,000 wharf labourers refused to work on ships in the Tanjong Pagar docklands. There were two primary issues – demands for increased pay and protests against handling ships carrying arms for Dutch troops fighting nationalist forces in the neighbouring Dutch East Indies.

The BMA reaction was to create an alternative pool of wharf labour by bringing Japanese prisoners of war and certain British military units onto the docks. Two days later, strikes forced Singapore's main bus operator, the Singapore Traction Company, to abandon services. Workers demanded a 40 per cent wage hike, plus bonuses. The BMA responded by again calling in troops to man the buses. While in both cases the troops ultimately broke strike action, they did nothing to improve the military administration's public image. BMA officials were in for a shock.

On October 25, more than 20,000 workers crammed into the island's Happy World amusement park for the formal inauguration of the Singapore General Labour Union (SGLU). Claiming the SGLU represented a combined union strength of 200,000 workers, the meeting went on to declare solidarity with dockyard labour and sympathy with the freedom movements in the Dutch East Indies and Indo China. Significantly, organisers of the occasion had omitted sending invitations for BMA representation.

Across the Causeway, in Malaya, the threat of civil unrest grew even more ominous. Hunger marches were held. There were mass demonstrations by women pleading for rice and a government handout of $20 to rescue their families from destitution. Tin mine and plantation labourers took to the streets demanding jobs, or, if they had them, higher wages. The numbers of participants in demonstrations and rallies grew alarmingly. Several thousands at a time were angrily massing in towns throughout the peninsula. A nervous and embarrassed BMA now realised that, unless some action was taken, it faced a very serious threat to its authority.

I maintain to this day that the demands at these demonstrations were entirely reasonable. Considering the deprivations suffered by the local population following Britain's 1942 defeat by the Japanese, there was nothing excessive in seeking to survive. The BMA could have satisfactorily and quite simply quelled rising emotions had its officials concentrated on tackling grievances rather than placing their priority on brutal crowd control measures.

Western historians writing the Emergency story frequently begin their accounts with the June, 1948, killings of three British planters at Sungei Siput, as if the violence began there. It is a convenient beginning, but historically quite inaccurate.

The killings began on October 21, 1945, when British troops were called in to disperse large demonstrations involving tens of thousands in Sungei Siput, Ipoh and Batu Gajah, all in the state of Perak. In Sungei Siput and Ipoh, the troops were ordered to fire directly into the crowds. Ten demonstrators were shot dead in Sungei Siput and three more in Ipoh. In Batu Gajah, emotions were so high that the British civil affairs officer was cornered in the Court House and surrounded by 500 furious demonstrators. Troops were ordered to rescue him.

Even the prominent Chinese community leader, Tan Kah Kee, was shocked by the callousness of the British troops. He roundly berated the BMA for its 'brutal action against peaceful, unarmed demonstrators'. He maintained, quite correctly, that the use of tear gas would have been sufficient to subdue the crowds. Undoubtedly, an underlying racial factor was inherent in the killings.

The men who aimed into the crowds, their commanders and, ultimately, the BMA, believed themselves superior and regarded Asian lives as considerably less significant. For British troops to be called out to fire into white unarmed demonstrators demanding better living conditions in, say, Yorkshire or Cornwall, would, of course, have been unthinkable. That they could readily take such action against Asians in far-away Malaya and regard the tactics as not only acceptable, but required, reveals much about the frame of mind of the returning colonials.

In the same turbulent month the BMA, in addition to the shootings, initiated a series of repressive measures, specifically targeting the CPM. It was almost as if they were courting a showdown. Left wing publications sympathetic to our stand were closed down and some of their staff arrested and charged with sedition. Among the newspapers forced to cease operations were the *Shih Tai Jit Pao* in Ipoh, and the *Pai Ma Tao Pao* in Taiping. Two English language newspapers in Ipoh suffered a similar fate – *The North Malaya News* and *The Age*.

If I had to pick a single act that initiated Malaya on the path to inevitable guerrilla warfare, it would have to be the October 12 arrest of senior Selangor communist, Soon Kwong, by the Royal Air Force police. Soon Kwong had worked with me in Ipoh and I knew him well. From his arrest can be traced a series of incidents that served to drag the colony inexorably towards violent rebellion. Soon Kwong was a widely respected CPM figure with an impressive wartime guerrilla record. The RAF provost involved had moved against him without any approval from, or even reference to, the BMA.

Whether or not Soon Kwong was involved, as alleged, in trying to extort a total of $300,000 from a known Chinese collaborator with the Japanese was really of no consequence. The charge referred to activities occurring two days before the BMA-established September 12 time line for prosecutions. Cases involving events prior to this cut-off date were to be regarded as having been justified by military exigency and therefore dropped. This was the basis of the Party's stand on the issue. We stated it publicly. Sanctioning the provost's actions, the BMA insisted it could not interfere in the matter. Only a court of law, it maintained, could decide the issue.

It was alleged Soon Kwong had – between September 4-10 – illegally detained a Chinese merchant named Chan Sau Meng. During this time Soon Kwong was said to have extorted money from the businessman under the threat of death. While a captive, Chan had written a promissory note to the value of $300,000 in exchange for his life. On his release he subsequently paid Soon Kwong $32,000 in cash together with jewellery and other valuables.

The CPM publicly asserted Chan had been employed by the Kempeitai and had amassed considerable wealth as a profiteer with the protection of the Japanese military police. What was more, it had been the MPAJA's duty, as guardian of law and order during the period, to seize and punish Chan and any other collaborators. The profiteering of such men had caused widespread suffering. Chan's punishment – one week's detention and a fine – had been relatively mild.

As a matter of historical record, I am satisfied Soon Kwong detained Chan and extorted money from him as charged. But it is also my view that Chan got away lightly. Had we seized him for his profiteering ways during the occupation we would certainly have eliminated him. The Party, quite justifiably I believe, took the position that the authorities were using the Soon Kwong case to bolster the BMA's flagging authority, intimidate the masses who clearly supported the communist position and dispense selective justice. What made matters worse was the additional evidence we had which showed that Soon Kwong became a target for arrest as a result of prodding by local Kuomintang interests.

Three days after the Soon Kwong affair hit the headlines, a massive demonstration was held on Kuala Lumpur's central padang. The core issues were BMA intimidation and selective justice. The lame attempt by the BMA to sustain its position had been roundly rejected by the people. In the weeks that followed, protest meetings, rallies, strikes and minor skirmishes erupted in towns throughout Malaya.

Soon Kwong's outrageous trial proceedings began on November 1 when he appeared before a court presided over by a BMA official who sat with two local assessors. The two assessors found the defendant innocent. The BMA official disagreed and ordered a re-trial before a new bench. At his second trial, Soon Kwong was again found innocent by the two local assessors and guilty by the BMA court president. A third trial was decreed and this time the British loaded the bench, maintaining that the locals were too scared to impose a guilty verdict. On this third occasion, three BMA officers duly found Soong Kwong guilty as charged and he was sentenced to four years' imprisonment. In an act of final defiance, Soon Kwong hurled his slippers at the bench before being led away. He had been defended by the Kuala Lumpur lawyer, Mr S.M.Yong. The CPM had employed Mr Yong and paid his fees in the belief he was a progressive thinker and sympathetic to the cause. We were mistaken. Lawyer Yong would eventually emerge staunchly pro-British and be rewarded with a seat in the Legislative Council.

The next pivotal incident on the path to rebellion occurred the following month in Kampong Koh, just south of Sitiawan. Prior to the return of the British, we had occupied the Chinese Association Building in the township and there set up an MPAJA office. By November, the local Kuomintang group moved to evict us and take over the Kampong Koh premises. They had the support of the BMA. A showdown ensued. The Kuomintang demanded we leave. The CPM stood its ground. Then, as was fast becoming normal procedure, the British troops were brought in. Their objective: to force us out. They came with their weapons at the ready and an infantryman aimed his rifle at the leader of our local MPAJA unit stationed there. The guerrilla chief drew a hand grenade and, brandishing it above his head, warned the soldier that if he fired they would both be killed. The soldier fired one shot, killing our man before he could release the pin.

The showdown was reported to me and I passed the details on to Lai Te. He ordered me to try and calm public emotions with explanations that it was an isolated incident. I did as I was told. Despite my efforts along these lines, one or two members on the state committee in Perak decided on an act of revenge and contacted a guerrilla unit from our secret army. They had yet to disband and hide their weapons. Hand grenades were lobbed into two groups of British forces at separate garrisons in Perak. I didn't bother to investigate either attack as I fully sympathised with those who had sought revenge. These were the first violent incidents targeted at British forces by the CPM in post-war Malaya. They were in direct retaliation for the unwarranted killing of our guerrilla at Kampong Koh. Neither was reported in the local press. Interestingly enough, Davis, who was then conferring regularly with me, never once raised the subject. It was as though the British, by clamping an information blackout on such matters, were hoping they would just fade away. They were mistaken. Incidents involving violence began to escalate. And as they did, they resulted in accumulating hatred for the British among a large segment of the general public.

In Kuala Lumpur, I was now overseeing the operation of three parallel offices. One was for the Party and another was for our AJA ex-servicemen which we called the MPAJA Old Comrades' Association. The third was for the AJU. The Old Comrades' Association was the brainchild of Lai Te. I interpreted his enthusiasm for this project as a ploy to appease or console the Party rank-and-file after our guerrilla army had been ordered to disband and hand in weapons. We might not have an army any more but at least we had a club. This was Lai Te's – and obviously the British – point of view. The rest of the CPM leadership thought differently. We saw the veterans' association as having great potential for the cause. It could be a ready-made vehicle for retaining essential ongoing contact with the former guerrillas while at the same time maintaining their enthusiasm and fighting spirit. The Selangor branch of the Old Comrades' Association had its headquarters in a three-storey building on Klyne street, opposite the Hokkien Association establishment. I was determined to see our Old Comrades' Association flourish.

The inter-related problems of poverty and food shortages that intensified throughout the final months of 1945 would impact seriously on many Party projects, but none more tragically than on our newly acquired Japanese volunteers who had joined our ranks rather than surrender to the British. When it became obvious the CPM would not be continuing the war, many of these men just disappeared. They didn't return to their units. I got the impression most were hoping to move north across the frontier and perhaps try to get home overland through Siam, Laos and southern China. The odd one or two were certainly caught and interned by the British. A number probably died in the jungles. But a hard-core remained with us.

While the group's military expertise and enthusiasm were undoubtedly of benefit to our cause, their presence with us at a time of mounting economic hardship posed critical complications. When it was first decided to accept the Japanese, measures had been devised to disguise their presence. They were scattered among our supporters in squatter villages in the hope that, as Chinese and Japanese generally looked alike to the British, they would go unnoticed during cursory inspections. These were temporary measures. When the time came, the Japanese would join us in the jungles.

In most areas, the unusual billeting arrangements went off smoothly. The numbers of Japanese were mostly small and the job of blending them into our racial surroundings and supporting them was comparatively easy. This was not the case, however, in the Kuala Kangsar area where a particularly large group of some 100 had initially come across. The matter presented a major predicament for the Perak state committee. When more than half that number departed, convinced there would be no further fighting, we still had to create social camouflage for some 20 to 30 Japanese around Kuala Kangsar, none of whom spoke Chinese, Malay or English.

Quite obviously, we couldn't hand this group over to the British because we would be implicating ourselves in a most dubious activity. But neither could we continue to support the foreigners in our midst. Our peasant squatters were experiencing hardship enough finding food for their families, let alone additional supplies for their uninvited guests. Then there was the constant requirement to keep the Japanese secluded which, in turn, involved a whole range of awkward social manoeuvrings.

Ultimately, the Perak state secretary, Ai Ker, was forced to take up the issue directly with Lai Te. He explained that local communists were running the risk of being discovered harbouring the Japanese. Lai Te promised to get back promptly with an answer to the dilemma. A week or so later the order came through: Eliminate the Kuala Kangsar Japanese. It was, of course, a ghastly command. The Japanese had pledged their loyalty to us. We had accepted their offer of help and had worked to keep secret their presence among us. In turn, the Japanese, to a man, had behaved extremely well while living with our supporters.

Ai Ker went ahead and instructed several of our armed squads to remove the Japanese from the squatter villages in small groups of no more than two or three at a time so as not to raise suspicions. The order made clear that the Japanese, on the pretext of training exercises, were to be led to isolated jungle positions for their executions.

It should be remembered that Lai Te, by now, had most certainly re-established his connections with British intelligence and was operating as their agent as he had done before the war. The massacre of our Japanese would-be recruits occurred in either the final days of 1945 or the first days of 1946. At the time, the BMA was firmly established as the controlling authority.

Without question, Lai Te would never have issued these orders at such a sensitive and volatile time had he not first discussed the matter thoroughly with his British spymaster. To have done so would have courted most serious repercussions. I remain convinced that someone in the BMA gave the official nod to Lai Te's solution to the Japanese deserter problem. After all, it was one way of settling an issue quickly and without fuss at a time when the pressure of events was enormous. It is furthermore most unlikely that British intelligence in the Sungei Siput–Kuala Kangsar area failed to pick up reports of the mass execution. The fact that no attempt was ever made to investigate the matter, to my mind, is additional evidence of British complicity.

I was stunned by the callousness of Lai Te's order.

As far as the other Japanese who joined us were concerned, there were some 20 in Kedah and another Perak group of about 10. In addition, there were a small number in Johore. In the immediate post-war peace they remained secluded in squatter villages. These Japanese were saved by the fact that they were in smaller numbers and thus had not become a burden. There was no need for state committees to bring them to the attention of Lai Te. When the Emergency began they joined our guerrillas and became fighters once again, only this time not for their Emperor but for world communism.

As the years passed, some got killed. Some couldn't stand the hardship and surrendered to the British. Those whom the British identified as operating with our guerrillas became targets for heavy psy-war operations. In such cases, their wives, sisters, parents and friends in Japan were contacted and induced to write letters imploring them to surrender and return to their families. These letters were then printed into leaflets and dropped over sections of jungle where our Japanese guerrillas were believed to be operating. Similarly, friends and family members, on instructions, made tape recordings of personal messages. These, in turn, were used on loud-speaker planes that flew low over the jungles blaring out the psy-war messages. The leaflets, tapes, and messages secured a handful of Japanese surrenders. But for all the money and effort spent in this pursuit, I am certain the results did not justify the expenditure. The majority of the Japanese who came with us died in action.

Only two of our Japanese recruits survived the entire Emergency. Hashimoto Shigeyuki and Tanaka Kiyoaki retreated with us to the safety of southern Siam and, in 1989, finally returned quietly to Japan. Back home, they were regarded as anything but returning heroes. Both were looked after by their families and lived into their 90s. They have since died. The last one survived the 1995 Kyoto/Osaka earthquake but succumbed to old age shortly thereafter.

*   *   *   *   *

Immediately after the formal disbandment of the MPAJA, Khoon Wah and I got married. We had to inform her mother who was then living in Tanjong Tokong, Penang. Following tradition, my mother-in-law organised a small wedding dinner for relatives and close family friends. Unfortunately, I was too busy with Party matters to attend. My mother was introduced to Khoon Wah in Ipoh much later when my wife and I happened to be travelling through the town. Mother came up from Sitiawan especially for the occasion. My father, who was never one for social niceties, didn't.

Yeung Kuo helped me find accommodation in Kuala Lumpur. Khoon Wah and I moved into a bungalow on Kuala Lumpur's Ampang road which became our first marital home. We lived there for more than two years. Yeung Kuo stayed in a nearby house on the same road.

Our home came complete with a piano that had originally been confiscated from a Japanese household. The Party placed it there despite my protestations about the impropriety of being surrounded by bourgeois accoutrements. The Party overrode my objections, insisting that I needed the trappings of a middle-class lifestyle if my cover of an up-and-coming businessman was to be effective.

Chapter 10

Awards . . . a letter of apology . . . and accelerating political confrontation

In the first week of January, 1946, I was one of eight Three Star Army representatives who travelled from Kuala Lumpur to Singapore to attend a special campaign medals ceremony presided over by the Supreme Allied Commander, South East Asia Command, Admiral Mountbatten. Each of us was scheduled to receive two medals – the Burma Star and the 1939/45 Star – in recognition of our contribution to the war effort.

The BMA booked us into lavish accommodation at the famed Raffles Hotel. On January 6, escorted by motorcycle outriders, we were driven a short distance down the road, past St Andrew's Cathedral, to the Municipal Building, now the City Hall. There, the Royal Marine Band was already playing. In our military uniforms, we were ushered to a position on the padang immediately in front of the Municipal Building steps. A British flag-draped podium had been placed in the centre of a landing halfway up the flight of steps that led to the building's main doors. To the left of the podium stood a small table on which rested a cushion. On top of the cushion lay our medals.

Why, you might ask, had the British gone to so much expense and trouble to honour us so publicly, nearly five months after Japan's surrender? After all, on September 12, 1945, 16 of our guerrillas had already participated – prominently positioned – in the official victory celebrations staged at the same venue. Furthermore, arrangements had been finalised for a special MPAJA contingent to participate in the June 8, 1946, Victory Parade in London. Was this January 6 display another propaganda exercise? Was it aimed at smothering us with attention in the hopes our resolve to pursue an anti-colonial stand would be undermined? If so, Admiral Mountbatten and his High Command had been badly advised.

On hand with us outside the Municipal Building that morning were two Kuomintang Chinese, three Malays and a single Chinese Dalforce representative in separate groupings. They were to receive decorations identical to ours. Was this some kind of misguided gesture demonstrating Britain's willingness to treat all political persuasions equally? Or get things racially correct? Declassified documents now

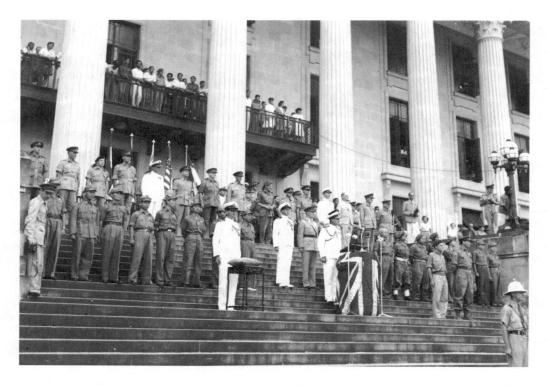

January 6, 1946 – the day we received our war medals from Supreme Allied Commander, South East Asia, Admiral Mountbatten. Our eight-man contingent to this occasion can be seen standing in line before Singapore's then Municipal Building, now the City Hall. That's our group eight steps up to the left of the photo. I'm fourth in from the left.

Mountbatten pins the two medals on MPAJA's **Liew Yao**. This prominent guerrilla commander was the third man of the hastily convened MPAJA Central Military Committee (High Command) proclaimed by Lai Te in August, 1945. The CPM's armed struggle would suffer a major set-back when Liew Yao was betrayed by his own bodyguard and killed in a police raid near Kajang, barely a month into the Emergency.

I get my awards: the Burma Star and the 1939/45 Star.

Mountbatten congratulates **Deng Fuk Lung** who commanded our 2nd Regiment in Negri Sembilan during the Japanese period. Deng went on to command our 2nd Regiment in the same state during the Emergency. This brave guerrilla leader died in action in the mid-1950s.

reveal that it was John Davis who had pressed for CPM operatives to be given awards immediately after the cessation of hostilities. But it had taken the system a long time to become convinced about the merits of Davis' suggestion. His idea was not popular when first presented. In all probability it would have been shelved had civil disturbances throughout Malaya not been on the increase. Some quarters must have decided matters would improve if *we* got placated.

Mountbatten spoke of our contribution to the great Allied victory over Japan. After the glowing speech, he left the podium, descended the steps and approached our line. He stopped and spoke to each CPM guerrilla, shaking his hand and personally thanking him for his selflessness and courage. Then the Supreme Commander walked back up the steps to where the medals lay. One by one we were called to the table so he could pin on our awards individually. Each of us recognised Mountbatten with our salute – a clenched fist raised to cap peak. In turn, the SEAC Supremo acknowledged us with the normal Royal Naval salute.

That evening we were all required to appear in our uniforms at a gala cocktail party held in Singapore's Government House, now the Istana. Mountbatten was in attendance. We all noticed he was wearing, among his various decorations, the special Star he had been given by Generalissimo Chiang Kai Shek. He made a point of again shaking hands with every member of the CPM contingent and thanking each personally, this time with a few phrases in Mandarin he had specially learned for the occasion. I was able to mingle with numerous British generals and admirals and chatted briefly with the former Commander of the 14th Army, Lt General Miles Dempsey, who would have led Britain's invasion of Malaya had the Japanese capitulation not rendered the invasion plan obsolete. Instead, General Dempsey commanded the re-occupying forces, some of whom I had seen coming ashore at Morib. He was now Commander-in-Chief, Allied Land Forces, South East Asia (ALFSEA).

On returning to Raffles Hotel after the cocktail party, we learned the BMA had arranged an extensive military programme for us the following day. The plan was for the CPM contingent, along with the Kuomintang and Malay representatives, to visit British military bases on the island. The grand tour we were being asked to take was obviously another propaganda exercise. BMA intentions, from the CPM viewpoint, were to demonstrate what surely faced us should we choose to challenge Britain's post-war right of return to Malaya and Singapore. The schedule said we were to visit the Royal Navy's Far East headquarters at the Sembawang Naval Base, the Royal Airforce's Tengah Air Base and the Army headquarters at Alexandra Barracks, in that order. At each stopover, the respective Base Commander would be on hand to receive us with the full official trappings the British normally accorded VIPs.

The CPM contingent talked late into the night and reached the conclusion that we had just been presented with a unique opportunity to demonstrate the Party's displeasure at the way comrade Soon Kwong had been treated by the BMA. When John Davis and our official escorts came early the following morning, we flatly refused to leave our hotel rooms. I explained to Davis why we were boycotting the excursion. Our position seemed to anger him immensely. He tried hard to persuade us to change our minds. I could sense him controlling his frustration as I had seen him do on numerous occasions in our Perak jungle camps. But we were determined not to budge and informed Lai Te of our firm intentions at short notice, leaving him little opportunity to reject the idea. We stood our ground. The Kuomintang Chinese and Malay groups duly went through the schedule.

John Davis could not let the matter rest. Back in Kuala Lumpur, he soon instigated a meeting with Lai Te, Liew Yao and myself at our headquarters. As far as Davis was concerned, he had the entire former CPM military committee in one room. He intended making the most of it. Following some very brief and tempered preliminary remarks, Davis suggested that in view of our guerrilla delegation's snub to all three British Service Commanders in Singapore, a letter of apology would be appropriate. Such a letter, he went on, would best be addressed directly to no less a personage than Mountbatten himself.

I was taken aback by this extraordinary request. Adding to my amazement, Davis produced a neatly typed letter of apology duly addressed to the Supremo and containing everything the British wanted us to say. At the bottom of the single page document were the appropriate spaces awaiting our signatures. My astonishment turned to anger. Both Liew Yao and I looked across to Lai Te for a lead on what to do next. The highest-ranking official of the CPM sat in his chair, head bowed, and said nothing.

To my mind, the British had conspired to demonstrate their might by treating us like naughty schoolboys. It was insulting. Again I looked at Lai Te. Still there was no response. Liew Yao and I had no option but to sign. We did so, grudgingly. Through our boycott we had intended demonstrating the Party's bitter resentment towards selective justice and its related intimidation being dispensed in Malaya by

Britain. The colonial authorities were smarting under these tactics. Nothing short of our humiliation was acceptable in the circumstances. Hence, the demeaning letter of apology. As far as I know, the letter was regarded as highly classified by the British, was thereafter never even publicly hinted at, much less released. Here was yet another key incident in the series determining the path to armed struggle.

Securing those signatures on the prepared letter of apology was Davis' last official function with us. Shortly thereafter he came round to bid us farewell. He was returning to London. He said he was going home to demobilize from the military but indicated he intended returning to Malaya in a civilian capacity.

Exactly two weeks after the galling letter of apology episode, Lai Te called what he termed the 'Eighth Enlarged Plenum of the Central Committee'. It was held in Kuala Lumpur. He invited representatives from all states. Each one sent several senior cadres. The upshot was the election of a 12-strong Central Committee which, in turn, elected the five members of the four-month old interim body as a Standing Committee to serve as the Party's political nucleus. This five-man grouping later became known as the Politburo. Shortly thereafter, the CPM's tactical area of operations was divided into three parts. Chen Yong, the senior communist official from southern Johore was placed in charge of what we called our Southern Region which included Singapore and the two sectors of Johore state – south and north. Our Central Region – Malacca, Negri Sembilan, Pahang and Selangor – came under Yeung Kuo. I was assigned the Northern Region: Perak, Penang and Kedah.

At the same January gathering, Lai Te introduced his new policy line for the Party. He termed it the 'Malayan Democratic United Front'. Essentially it sought a broad alliance with other political parties. In addition, it aimed to expand our front operations. It dovetailed with steps taken a few weeks earlier when the CPM backed the setting up of two political organisations: the Malay Nationalist Party (MNP) and the Malayan Democratic Union (MDU). Lai Te sought to pacify those of us in the Party who remained convinced that the policy of accommodation and cooperation with the British was getting us nowhere.

He suggested we should look at our struggle from two perspectives. We could follow the examples of Indo China and the Dutch East Indies where, by this stage, nationalist movements had mounted armed rebellions against the returning French and Dutch colonial authorities respectively. The price of this option, he said, would be immediate and excessive bloodshed. Or we could wait. Lai Te admitted the BMA's repressive measures were worsening. Rather than confronting these head-on, he argued, we should instead manipulate the politics of the situation through his united front approach to achieve what he termed a 'revolutionary high tide'.

Clearly sensing the restive mood of the Party at large which was tallying the mounting death toll among demonstrators and the many other repressive actions of the BMA, Lai Te conceded the inevitability of armed struggle. However, he tied this to a long-term objective without specifying any time-frame.

My disenchantment with Lai Te, which had started with the sudden change in policy direction the previous August and grew when he acceded to the letter of apology to Mountbatten, really began to trouble me at the Kuala Lumpur meeting. In a private conversation with one of the delegates, I learned that two of the men, just installed as Central Committee members at Lai Te's instigation, were not even full members of the CPM any more. They were the onetime Negri Sembilan state secretary, known under the alias Lo Shi Mo, and his deputy, Ah San.

Lo and Ah San had both been arrested by the Japanese and revealed Party information under severe torture. They were released on the understanding that they were to serve as Japanese agents. The Kempeitai issued each a pistol for personal security. Following Party policy for dealing with members tortured by the Japanese, Lo and Ah San were eventually accepted back to the fold, but as sympathisers only.

Lai Te was able to engineer their Central Committee appointments by taking advantage of the Party's rigid approach to organisation. Security precautions determined that no CPM member should ever probe for details on matters beyond their immediate functions. State committees operated similarly and never intruded into the affairs of their opposite organisations in other states. Nobody, therefore, had heard about the time Lo and Ah San spent with the Japanese and thus two men who had collaborated with the enemy and who should have been banned from Party membership for life became elected to the CPM's top secret policy-making body. Each appointment amounted to a serious breach of security. How could the Secretary General, of all comrades, who certainly knew the full circumstances of each case, flout Party regulations so wantonly? The presence of Lo and Ah San on the Central Committee – and the fact that they were now obviously indebted to Lai Te – concerned me deeply.

The Eighth Plenum coincided with a general 24-hour colony-wide strike we had organised for January 29. This was to protest Soong Kwong's conviction and sentence along with other convictions and sentences meted out to union officials in Perak. In Singapore, where Mountbatten now held office, we estimated some 200,000 followers observed our stop-work call. With that impressive show of support, the BMA became convinced of our powers to paralyse the island if provoked to do so. In a report on the event, Mountbatten himself recognised the level of efficiency and widespread influence the CPM was able to muster on the island. In Malaya it was much the same scenario. There, however, heavy-handed police and military patrols coerced some shops and businesses in several population centres to remain open.

Quite unexpectedly, five days after our general strike, the BMA released Soon Kwong who still had three years and nine months of his four-year sentence to serve. Most people felt this was a direct result of our January 29 action. They, of course, had no knowledge of the letter of apology to Mountbatten. I have always suspected that Lai Te struck a secret deal with the British. If he was successful in securing a letter of apology, he could be sure Soon Kwong would be released at the first opportune moment. Soon Kwong's freedom was short-lived. During the Emergency, he was re-arrested for being a communist and banished to China. He died there in the mid-1990s.

In the midst of the escalating labour unrest I had an unexpected visit from a most important South East Asian communist figure - the Secretary General of the Siamese party, Li Chee Shin. He had contacted us during the Japanese occupation. Li was, of course, the 'Lao Hey' who had written to Lai Te via my office two years previously. He was also the man our Secretary General claimed he knew so well. On his brief stopover in Kuala Lumpur this time, Li was accompanied by another regional communist figure, Alimin, formerly one of three prominent leaders in the Indonesian Communist Party (PKI). Alimin had worked with the Comintern's Far Eastern Bureau in Shanghai and later moved to Moscow where he had been attached to the Comintern headquarters.

Li and Alimin had travelled overland together from Bangkok for discussions with the Party hierarchy in Malaya. They were looking to establish greater coordination of effort between the communist parties of Malaya, the Dutch East Indies and Siam. I had the job of getting them together with Lai Te who was also in town. The meeting took place in Liew Yao's expansive bungalow. When it came time for me to make the formal introductions, it was very clear that Li had never before set eyes on Lai Te. I silently recalled Lai Te's puzzling remarks in Bidor two years earlier . . . how he had known 'Lao Hey' for so long . . . and how accomplished the man was.

I then introduced Alimin who happened to have been an elected Orient member of the Comintern executive attached to both Shanghai and Moscow offices. It was now very obvious that Alimin had never before encountered Lai Te either. At this point my curiosity prickled. After Lai Te departed I couldn't resist asking my two guests whether they'd ever met our leader before. Both assured me this was the first time they had had the pleasure. Why should our leader have lied?

As I had done in Bidor, I decided not to dwell on distracting contradictions. Perhaps there was an explanation. Perhaps there was none. I again would file the observation at the back of my mind and concentrate on more urgent Party matters.

*   *   *   *   *

If the British were shaken by the precision and the energy that fuelled the January 29 strikes, they were not prepared for the more wounding impact of the second general strike called for February 15. The choice of date stung the British to the core. It coincided with the fourth anniversary of Percival's surrender to General Yamashita. Clearly, the returning colonials hated having their noses rubbed in the commemoration of their defeat – the humiliation, after all, was monumental – and they must have despaired of being made to remember how long their abandonment of 'fortress Singapore' had been.

Official British records tell of how, on February 9, Mountbatten met with his men – among them ALFSEA Commander-in-Chief Dempsey and SEAC Chief of Staff, Lt General Sir Frederick Browning – to discuss the issue. The ban imposed on the February 15 action was arrived at apparently only after exhaustive deliberations marked with obvious differences of opinion. In the end – and this does not surprise me at all – Mountbatten had to protect British interests and was therefore persuaded that if their grip on peninsular Malaya and Singapore was to be maintained, the BMA had to attack the problem at its source, namely the CPM and its troublesome leaders. To his credit, Mountbatten ruled against preventive arrests. He personally believed that banishment to China would not help the British cause. He concurred with indications from London that banishment should not be an ongoing policy.

Still, two days before the strike, the SEAC Supremo, pressed to take a firm stand, issued a public decree banning processions and meetings on February 15. He threatened anyone challenging the authorities would be liable to deportation. Yet, within hours of Mountbatten's official statement – and despite his opposition to 'preventative arrests' – the BMA rounded up 24 communists allegedly involved in the strike plot.

The venue of the Party's main anti-British demonstration was the open ground opposite St Joseph's Institution along Bras Basah road. It was conveniently close to our Singapore headquarters which had now moved to Queen street. The rally's primary aim was to draw public attention to the need for territorial self-reliance. If we wanted to defend our interests and our territory we had to be in a position to do so ourselves. This meant we had to be ready to fight. It also meant we must seek self-government. The public had to be reminded how we managed on our own, albeit with some difficulties, during the occupation years. Now, in a time of peace, we would be able to manage better.

The decision to push ahead with the demonstration had anything but unanimous support among the members of the CPM Singapore Town Committee who were the sole organisers. Wu Tien Wang, head of the Singapore office, strongly disagreed with the idea of challenging Mountbatten's order. At a preparatory meeting he argued that the Party would be courting unnecessary confrontation and bloodshed if it ignored the prohibition decree. An intra-Party disagreement followed. Wu withdrew and his deputy, Lim Ah Liang, took over organisational responsibilities.

The protest went ahead. I have never been able to establish whether this was done with, or without, Lai Te's personal approval. I only know the British called in the Army and once again the troops opened fire on the people. This time they killed two and wounded 19. The British would claim much later that people came armed with bottles and crowbars. Significantly, there was no mention of the event or the casualties by *The Straits Times* the following day or any day thereafter.

The response to our February 15 strike call was even more dramatic on the peninsula. In Labis, 20 miles south of Segamat, in the state of Johore, a large crowd gathered to listen to speeches delivered by two former MPAJA members, Ong Koon Sam and Chong Swee. Once again the British army, called in to disperse the rally, fired into the crowds. Fifteen people were killed. At the trial of Ong and Chong, three months later, the presiding magistrate, a Mr J.U. Webb, handed down punishments of six months' jail and fines of $200 each. In passing sentence, Webb made the incredible observation: 'The loss of life which occurred must be taken into consideration.' One would have thought, from this remark, that it was Ong and Chong who had fired into the crowd! A few days later, five more fatalities, this time in Mersing, were added to the list when troops were ordered to fire on a group demonstrating against the slaughter at Labis. The fact that water hoses were adequate enough to disperse crowds at a February 15 rally in Penang without fatalities apparently failed to make any impact on the BMA.

While the BMA was hell-bent on reinforcing power through the gun in Malaya and Singapore, the politicians in London were frantically putting together a hopelessly inept programme. In their ignorance, they believed it would somehow introduce political reform to these territories. The proposal, called the Malayan Union, was presented as a panacea to the mounting problems. It was first announced in the House of Commons, Westminster, on October 11, 1945, by Britain's Colonial Secretary, Mr George Hall.

The Union idea envisaged a grouping of the nine states in Peninsular Malaya together with the two Straits Settlements of Penang and Malacca. Singapore island, the trading hub, would be conveniently retained as a separate colony. The island's economic potential and its strategic importance as a location for military bases were clearly the primary considerations behind Britain's desire to keep it neatly separated – and thereby more easily manageable - from the mainland. The British proclamation noted: 'His Majesty's Government are, however, well aware of the many ties between Singapore and the mainland, and that these ties may well work towards ultimate union. This will be a matter of the Governments of the Malayan Union and Singapore to consider in due course.'

The Malayan Union proposal, with its more liberal attitudes towards granting citizenship across the racial spectrum, had been gestating in the Colonial Office since the early days of 1944. Mountbatten, who had been fully appraised of the project, started urging the Colonial Office to release its details publicly from as early as July of the same year. He thought it would be an encouragement to the MPAJA guerrillas with whom his men were working. The politicians resisted. In a following letter to the then Secretary of State for the Colonies, Mr Oliver Stanley, Mountbatten observed: 'Presumably, we have not previously found Colonial Subjects rising to fight on our behalf when we were about to occupy their territory, and the fact that they are doing so today seems to me a wonderful opportunity for propaganda to the world in general, and to the Americans in particular, at a time when we are being accused of re-conquering colonial peoples in order to re-subjugate them.'

A key to the Malayan Union proposal's launch lay in its requirement for acquiescence on the part of the various Malay sultans to significant constitutional changes which involved re-negotiating their separate treaties with Britain. The sultans protested vehemently, not only about the changes themselves, but also about the outrageous high-handedness of the British representative, Sir Harold MacMichael. MacMichael travelled to Malaya and thought he could ramrod the ideas past the sultans with all sorts of veiled – and not so veiled – threats. Once word of the sultans' displeasure became public, Malays thronged to the support of their rulers. Led by Datuk Onn bin Jaafar, they began forming what later became defined as the United Malays National Organisation (UMNO), an amalgamation of 41 Malay associations. Britain could never have foreseen such Malay unity of purpose.

The CPM, for its part, also took strong exception to the Malayan Union idea. We attacked, in particular, its citizenship proposals. They were too restrictive to the Chinese. We opposed its provisions for legislative and executive councils. In a special press statement we declared the councils 'would be entirely under the supervision and control of the British Government and those bodies would not have the slightest tinge of democracy.' We added: 'Our Party is of the opinion that the political framework of Malaya should be decided in full compliance with the Atlantic Charter and the United Nations Charter.'

Undeterred by the anti-Union clamour, Britain stubbornly went ahead with her plans to replace the BMA with the Malayan Union civilian authority and the separate colonial status for Singapore on April 1, 1946. Mr Malcolm MacDonald, son of the former British Prime Minister, Mr Ramsey MacDonald, flew in to become the first Governor of Singapore and simultaneously Commissioner General overseeing the Malayan Union and Singapore.

In Kuala Lumpur, the newly knighted Sir Edward Gent was installed as Governor of the Malayan Union before a half-empty Legislative Council. UMNO had boycotted the entire replacement administration and the Governor's induction ceremony was snubbed by the sultans. The UMNO boycott would remain in force until the Malayan Union was dissolved and replaced by the Federation of Malaya on February 1, 1948.

*   *   *   *   *

A string of workers' strikes were called in 1946. All, of course, were organised by the Party – not by the Central Committee but by individual state committees. The Central Committee could never have handled such a pace of activity. Contrary to BMA assertions, we did not go around merely instigating trouble. In every case we brought to a focus existing and genuine demands from workers' ranks. It was the workers themselves who pressed for agitation to improve their lot. Their economic plight was truly desperate. It was this desperation that formed the foundation of the dramatic responses achieved by the various state committees. The spontaneity of the public rallies could never have materialised without it.

As the strikes mounted, the BMA began making its calculations. Projections by senior colonial experts soon revealed that unless something was done to quell the strike action and accompanying violence, the economies of Malaya and Singapore would quickly slip into chaos. They certainly factored in the likelihood of the CPM turning the chaos to its advantage.

From our viewpoint, the BMA had no interest whatever in the fair distribution of wealth. It was an intensely corrupt operation. Only recently have historians begun discovering the extent to which graft, exploitation, fraud and general malfeasance dominated every aspect of British colonial control at this time. The courts were corrupt. The civil service was corrupt. The military was corrupt. The police were corrupt. The troops and their commanders were trigger-happy.

As estate violence expanded across Malaya and crept into Singapore's industrial scene, Lai Te, I noted, kept a very low profile indeed. He vigorously maintained his anonymity and the protection it gave him. But by now he was undoubtedly feeling the heat generated by his clandestine role for British intelligence. When the comrades had wanted to press for an enhanced military posture during the Japanese occupation, he had insisted we concentrate more on organising labour. Now organised labour had taken the bit and was running with it. Lai Te's long-term policies were proving uncannily prophetic. He should have been well-satisfied. Except that he was obviously a troubled man. His British controlling officer must have been heavily pressuring him to quell the strike action.

In Central Committee meetings, Lai Te raised the subject of strike activity on only one or two occasions. He chose not to confront us, realising he could scarcely reverse the policy he had so controversially introduced in the first place and was now so dramatically successful. To do so, he knew, would have sparked a revolt against his leadership. To avoid this, he paid lip service to the ongoing action and certainly never expressed any negative views about it.

Sensing his flagging popularity within the Party, the Secretary General decided to play the international card that had proved so effective for him in the past. Much of his glowing reputation, after all, had been based on his claims of high-ranking contacts in world communist circles and, of course, his supposed membership of the Comintern. To travel, he needed documents. During one of our Kuala Lumpur meetings in mid-1946, he asked me to secure him a Chinese passport and gave me a recent photograph taken in a Kuala Lumpur studio.

There was a hotel in Kuala Lumpur's Sultan street owned by the family of the financially and politically well-connected Mr H.S. Lee who would later become Finance Minister in the Merdeka government of Tunku Abdul Rahman. Mr Lee's grandfather had made his fortune importing indentured labour — we called it slave labour — to Malaya and Singapore. The family had then gone into tin mining. They became even richer. By 1946, the Sultan street hotel was catering for businessmen shuttling between Malaya and China. In this respect it had special arrangements with the local Chinese Kuomintang consulate. It so happened that one of our comrades had a contact with one of the hotel executives. We were able to go to the hotel with a photo of Lai Te, together with a certain amount of money and, very shortly thereafter, receive a Chinese passport for him in the name of C.H. Chang — or, in Chinese, Chang Chan Hong. Not quite legal but very useful.

In the party hierarchy at this time, Lai Te was No 1, Chen Yong was recognised as No 2, and I was regarded as No 3. This pecking order had been established by Lai Te himself during the Plenum meeting in Singapore the previous September. His travel plan was to leave Singapore for Hong Kong and ultimately make direct contact with the Communist Party of China (CPC) in Shanghai. Lai Te announced Chen Yong would also be going along on the mission. In their absence, he appointed me 'Acting Secretary General'.

I now believe Lai Te became worried about having to maintain his regular meetings with British intelligence. These would, of course, have to continue in Hong Kong and probably Shanghai as well. How could this be managed without arousing the suspicions of his travelling companion, Chen Yong? He therefore arranged that the two of them travel by separate routes. He went by passenger ship directly to Hong Kong. Chen Yong, on another passenger vessel, was told to travel to the British colony via Bangkok. Lai Te insisted the separated journeys were required for security reasons.

In the event, Chen Yong's vessel was delayed in Bangkok. He was then unable to make contact with Lai Te and returned to Singapore by rail. We suspected nothing at the time but clearly this was part of an overall picture of deception created by Lai Te.

Indeed, the Secretary General went to Hong Kong and on to Shanghai as planned. But on his return he said nothing about the discussions he had held while abroad. He made no mention – even to his Politburo colleagues – of what advice, if any, the Chinese Party had given him. We got the impression – and he certainly didn't correct it – that he had met Chou En Lai in Shanghai. I would later establish that this was untrue. In fact, he spoke with the elderly Tung Pi Uu, one of Chou's deputies.

On Lai Te's return, the CPM's overall philosophy and approach to the masses underwent a significant change. We were henceforth not to portray ourselves as Overseas Chinese. Rather, we should regard ourselves as local Malayan Chinese. We were an ethnic group belonging to Malaya. Our loyalties were to Malaya, not China.

We began writing articles in our newsletters and newspapers along these lines and immediately ran into opposition from the older Party members. The Chinese communists who had left China for Malaya after the outbreak of the anti-Japanese war all complained. They objected strongly to throwing in their lot with Malaya to the exclusion of their China ties. They wrote articles emphasising that they were Chinese, the interests of the motherland were paramount and the concentration of effort should be towards helping China. They were determined to remain Overseas Chinese.

Another important change was ushered into Party affairs by Lai Te on his return from Shanghai. He told us that Central Committee functions needed to be more efficient. On this pretext, he proceeded to streamline its operations by splitting the Central Committee into two parallel groups. The five-man Standing Committee, the Party's highest authority, would henceforth cease dealing with organisational matters. It was directed, instead, to concentrate purely on political decisions as a Politburo. We were assigned propaganda duties. We were henceforth to oversee the development of the new united front policy and its furtherance through front operations.

Non-Politburo members of the Central Committee were appointed to the Party's Organisational Bureau. Both Politburo and the Organisational Bureau came under Lai Te's direct control. He deemed that contact between Politburo and state committees had to be restricted, if not entirely avoided. Only the Organisational Bureau would now deal at the state committee level. All these new arrangements had the immediate effect of restricting the Politburo's power and authority and cutting its links to the Party's grass-roots. It proved a neat form of divide and rule.

However, Lai Te's manipulations could not contain the gathering momentum of strike action throughout the rest of 1946 and into 1947. With the passing months it became very obvious that British and Chinese businessmen, estate owners and mine operators were all discriminating against former CPM guerrillas when it came to hiring workers. They regarded – understandably enough, I suppose – the once communist jungle fighters as potential troublemakers. Reports reaching the Central Committee told of deep dissatisfaction on this issue among the rank-and-file of our membership. Mounting demands called for strong action to be taken by the Party and pressures intensified on the Central Committee to find a solution.

Once again, Lai Te took matters into his own hands, singling out the Selangor state leadership for particular criticism and blame. Despite the fact that agitation was coming from every corner of Malaya and Singapore, Lai Te picked on Selangor alone and, specifically its secretary, Yeung Kuo, one of the five-man Politburo. In a Central Committee meeting held in Kuala Lumpur, Lai Te bluntly accused Yeung Kuo of being incompetent and allowing his state's Party organisation to become chaotic.

Yeung Kuo was incensed. He knew the accusations were baseless. Still, he declined to defend himself before his colleagues in the hierarchy. Lai Te went on say Yeung Kuo must be held responsible for the intra-Party problems which he termed an 'organisational crisis'. Yeung Kuo should therefore be punished. The suggestion was that the Selangor secretary be demoted and removed from all his Central Committee responsibilities. In Party terms this was a truly shameful prospect.

Lai Te called on committee members to give their views. Some eagerly agreed with him. Others just kept quiet. I rose and defended Yeung Kuo, though I admit I did it in a very cautious way. I started by making the point that it seemed to me the Party crisis under discussion existed throughout Malaya and Singapore. It was not just limited to Selangor. I argued that the Central Committee – including myself – should be held responsible for the problem. Unspoken was my insinuation that, this being the case, Lai Te himself should also be punished.

All waited for an expected outburst from our leader. It failed to manifest. Whether it was my words or a general feeling that Lai Te was having second thoughts, I wouldn't know. But after having vented his dissatisfaction in front of the entire Central Committee, the Party leader decided Yeung Kuo should be saved the disgrace of demotion and given a stern warning instead. Yeung Kuo would have none of it. Then and there he offered his resignation from the Central Committee and Politburo, asking to be relegated to the state level.

There followed an awkward silence. One-by-one the other members present rose to dissuade Yeung Kuo from leaving the Central Committee. Even Lai Te himself moderated his criticism. It was therefore decided that Yeung Kuo would remain on the Central Committee and in the Politburo, but would be allowed to move back to his hometown in Penang as he wished. Clearly, Lai Te recognised a strong body of opinion behind Yeung Kuo. Rather than challenging it, he took the option of delivering the Selangor state secretary a token reprimand.

Shortly thereafter, Yeung Kuo left Selangor and moved back to Georgetown. His return to Penang, in fact, served as a useful 'cooling off' period. But it would also spark a chain of events that would finally demolish any Party ideas of accommodating British colonialism.

Chapter 11

Plotting the betrayer's overthrow

With the Party under intensifying pressure from the BMA, Lai Te could not have chosen a worse time to drive a wedge in Central Committee cohesion. He failed to arm himself with sufficient information about Yeung Kuo. He needed a target to deflect attention from the organisational mess. But zeroing in on Yeung Kuo was a serious miscalculation.

What had spurred Lai Te's outburst against such a long-serving Party comrade? I was attempting to analyse the Secretary General's motivations while carrying out my somewhat restricted duties as a Politburo member when I received a call from my father. He was travelling to Penang via Kuala Lumpur and asked whether I would like to accompany him on the journey north. It was mid-October, 1946, a period between monsoons when the sky is heavy with tropical rainclouds. The thought of spending a few days on an island was most enticing. Added to this, Khoon Wah and our newly-born daughter had recently moved to Penang to be with her mother for a while. My father asked me to drive him there. At that time, the Party had provided me with a small Austin 8 motorcar that had been confiscated from the Japanese.

I stayed at my mother-in law's house. Shortly after we arrived, Yeung Kuo called and we agreed to meet for breakfast two days later. The two of us took a bus to Tanjong Bunga, on the island's north-eastern coast. Being mid-week, the place was virtually empty. The multi-coloured, high-prowed boats lay beached where the fishermen had earlier moored them on an outgoing tide. We each ordered a plate of *char mee* and a glass of iced coffee and sat down at an eating-stall table.

At first, our conversation meandered around subjects of little consequence. Then, quite abruptly, Yeung Kuo looked directly at me and enquired: 'What do you really make of Ah Le?' He used the familiar Party alias for Lai Te, a shortening of the name 'Lenin'.

I pondered my response then replied carefully: 'As usual, I regard him as our leader.'

I realised my friend was still very angry with Lai Te. I had no idea where he intended going with the conversation. By Party standards this seemed very dangerous talk, indeed.

Camera angles can be deceptive. The top photo shows Tanjong Bungah beach much as I remember it as Yeung Kuo and I, in October 1946, sat down over coffee there to discuss the treachery of Lai Te and how he might be removed from control of the CPM. With a different angle on the same subject, the bottom photo depicts the same beach with its dramatically altered backdrop.

Ignoring my hesitancy, Yeung Kuo said, quite bluntly: 'He's an international spy.'

I looked into my glass and slowly stirred the cool liquid as I searched for a response. I could sense Yeung Kuo's tension. I asked: 'What proof do you have?'

'I'm certain he's a spy,' he said, in a tone that left little room for dissension. He added: 'He worked for the British before the war. He was a Japanese agent during the occupation. I know that. Now he's back working with the British again.'

The magnitude of what was being said struck home with me as Yeung Kuo went on to enumerate occasions in the pre-war period when Lai Te had escaped arrest by being conveniently absent from meetings at the time of police raids. It had happened too often to be coincidental. On one occasion, when Lai Te was actually present during a police swoop, they mysteriously released him without so much as asking him questions, let alone putting him through interrogation sessions. Interrogation was then standard procedure for all suspected communists detained by the colonial police.

I admitted I had heard references to such events. As my functions had been restricted to Perak, however, any information reaching me from beyond my state boundaries had usually been out of date and very vague. I recalled that Lai Te's apparent ability to avoid detention around that time was generally attributed to his extraordinary shrewdness. It seemed all part of his mystique.

Yeung Kuo shook his head in frustration. 'Look what happened in Singapore under the Japanese,' he continued. 'Central Committee members were arrested one after another. Then there was the Batu Caves massacre. Lai Te was supposed to have been there. Again he was mysteriously detained. Japanese troops attacked, killing so many of our senior cadres. Another coincidence?' my friend asked, mockingly.

After listening carefully and weighing my thoughts, I decided to share my concerns about Lai Te's supposed involvement with senior international communist circles. These appeared to be fabrications. I recalled the circumstances of my Bidor meeting with the Secretary General and his reactions to Lao Hey's letter. I followed up with details of the Lao Hey – Alimin visit to Kuala Lumpur earlier in the year when both told me they had never before met Lai Te. Things didn't add up. Was he embellishing stories about his international communist connections to solidify his position as Party leader?

For a while Yeung Kuo and I fell silent.

I broke the silence. 'We have to expose the man,' I told my comrade, reaching deep inside for fortitude enough to sound convincing. By now the morning sun had crept midway into a cloudless sky. Barely a ripple disturbed the surface of the sea. The air was oppressively still. The fishermen who had earlier been idling in the distance had now gone into their huts. The beach remained deserted but for the two of us.

Looking seaward and across to the mainland, I followed the jagged blue silhouette of prominent Kedah Peak. In the rising humidity it seemed so inviting, so deceptively cool. My eyes wandered further east where I knew lay the northern reaches of the central range that stretched from the border region of southern Siam all the way south down the spine of peninsular Malaya. In those mountainous, sweating triple-canopied jungles our guerrillas had died protecting malarial-infested camps. Carefully hidden in caves and underground caches, along the length of the same range, were the weapons of war we had so painstakingly salvaged. To what extent had Lai Te informed the British about such matters?

Yeung Kuo and I well understood the inherent danger in what we were contemplating. Whatever action we took would have to be swift and decisive or else we simply wouldn't be alive to see the results. That was how the Party dealt with plotters against top leadership.

The two of us agreed to place our Secretary General's activities under close surveillance and wait for the right opportunity to strike. Meanwhile, we would continue normally in our Party functions.

Before we left Tanjong Bungah, we assessed, in minute detail, each of our fellow Central Committee members. We came to the conclusion that all, with the exception of the two renegades Lai Te had propelled onto the Committee against Party rules, were good men. Motivated purely by the best interests of the movement, each could be relied upon to support us once they had been given the facts. It remained a matter of seizing the moment.

This would present itself much sooner than we anticipated. Barely two months after Yeung Kuo and I conferred at the beachside, Lai Te called a Central Committee meeting in Kuala Lumpur. This time he behaved very strangely.

The meeting took place in the ground floor dining room of a two-storey wooden bungalow situated behind a huge Ampang road home originally built by the late tin mining millionaire, Loke Yu. The Central Committee sat at a long dining table. Immediately after opening the proceedings, Lai Te announced he had other pressing matters and excused himself. He instructed us to go ahead with preliminary discussions and draw up the main agenda without him. This was curious. He had always insisted on preparing the agenda himself.

Following our leader's abrupt departure from the room, we hastily sought to select an alternative chairman for the occasion. Someone proposed Chen Yong from Johore – a Politburo member, our Southern Region chief and well recognised as the No 2 man in the Party hierarchy. The nomination was seconded and the meeting got underway. Whatever Lai Te was doing took a long time because our preliminary discussions rambled on without him for two days.

During lunch break on the first day, Yeung Kuo walked with me to my Ampang road home no more than ten minutes away. My wife and I were then living in a compound of six houses where our immediate neighbour happened to be a middle-ranking Rubber Research Institute officer, married to a Malay woman. He had been a prisoner of the Japanese.

As we strolled, I could sense Yeung Kuo was excited. Hardly had I closed the front door when he blurted: 'The entire Party leadership is gathered in session without Lai Te. This is just the opportunity we need.'

We discussed tactics over lunch. Since Tanjong Bungah, both of us had taken every available opportunity to examine the way Lai Te had been conducting Party affairs. Separately we had arrived at one very definite conclusion – he was most vulnerable on matters of finance. Since the Japanese surrender, Lai Te had never once submitted a report on the state of Party funds. Nor, I discovered, had he done so during the occupation days. That meant he had controlled the Party coffers for over four years without ever being held accountable.

It was agreed that I would raise the question of Party finances immediately the afternoon session began. I would make the point that it was necessary, in the interests of accurate accounting, for every state to prepare a general rundown of its financial situation during the post-war period. This accounting would, of course, include details of funds dispatched to Party headquarters. No one could legitimately complain about such a request as it was accepted that state committees were required to make regular contributions to the Party's central operations. Indeed, considerable kudos went to states providing the highest remittances.

Once we had set the groundwork and secured solid support for the financial requirements on the agenda, we felt we would be in a strong position to challenge Lai Te. My broad calculations indicated around $1 million to $2 million dollars had been passed by the CPM's state branches through to Lai Te since the Japanese surrender.

Having established the basis for legitimate enquires into finances, we planned for Yeung Kuo to bring up the touchy subject of leadership style. He had to be careful. We both recognised this track could easily trigger sympathy support for Lai Te. Central Committee members awaiting conclusions on the financial issues could be wary of exploring the leadership question. Leadership style encompassed a very broad spectrum of subjects and gave us the opportunity of opening up discussions on issues never before raised by the Central Committee.

Our plotting completed, Yeung Kuo and I returned for the resumption of the afternoon session and proceeded to put our scheme into action. Discussions on the matters we raised went through until late on the second day. Presiding chairman Chen Yong was then required to sum up and settle the agenda.

The first agreed point for discussion sought clarificatiion as to why the political analysis of the international situation presented by Lai Te at the CPM's January Plenum was in such variance to the analysis of the same subject by the propaganda chief of the Chinese Communist Party. It appeared Lai Te was not up to date with international developments and this, in turn, threw a large question mark over his supposed international credentials.

The second point on the agenda was directed at leadership style. The suggestion had been made during preliminary discussions that a feudal style of authority was prevailing within the Party. Other points for discussion were added. The final one sought a state-by-state preparation of party accounts along the exact lines that I had suggested.

Lai Te duly appeared on the third day for the start of the main meeting. He began by asking for the prepared agenda. He read it without obvious reaction. For a while he attempted to justify his political analysis until he realised he was failing to win over his audience. He then abruptly changed tack and insinuated that the comrade who had presided over the drafting of the agenda was involved in a plot. Chen Yong, merely the instrument through whom we channeled our machinations, denied the accusation vehemently. Eventually he lost his temper and offered his resignation.

Taken aback by Chen Yong's outburst, Lai Te abruptly revised his approach again. 'I'm getting old and you all know I've been unwell for a long time,' he announced. 'I would like your permission to take a holiday. Perhaps I could use the time to improve my Chinese language skills.' This remark struck home as, once more, I was reminded of the Bidor meeting and the letter from Lao Hey. We knew

Lai Te was unwell. We also knew he needed to improve his command of Chinese. But we were certainly taken aback by his suggestion to go on leave.

Our Secretary General sat at the top of the long rectangular table. I sat at the opposite end looking directly down the table towards him. Chen Yong, still smarting from Lai Te's accusations and insults, was seated directly to my right.

Lai Te then singled me out, claiming he regarded me as a most capable comrade. He remarked I had worked diligently and well for the party for almost a decade. 'Comrade Chin Peng will make a worthy future leader, so I feel confident in leaving the Party in his capable hands while I'm away on vacation.'

He continued to heap praise on me. It was, of course, all calculated to belittle Chen Yong who was understood to be his deputy. Not regarded as a man with a short fuse, I sat patiently through the false praise until I could stand it no more. Now it was my turn to lose my temper. As Lai Te droned on, I suddenly banged the table and, leaping to my feet, I shouted: 'That's enough. Stop praising me. I don't measure up to those words.'

Chen Yong was a close friend. At one time he had been my immediate superior and I had worked under his direction in the CPM's Perak propaganda section. He was then a state committee member. I was cutting stencils for the copying machine although I had the glorified title of 'editor' of our newsletter. The two of us went back a long way.

Before I had finished my outburst, Lai Te, to the total amazement of everybody, burst into tears. He sat weeping silently at the head of the table, his head cradled in his hands. Through his sobs he repeatedly murmured: 'You have misunderstood me . . . you have misunderstood me.' If his theatrics had been calculated to win sympathy, they were an instant and stunning success. Disapproving grumbles over my attack rippled around the table. Siao Chang, a Batu Caves survivor and renowned west Pahang guerrilla leader, delivered a vehement defence of the sobbing Lai Te. He indirectly accused me of causing wilful disunity within CPM ranks at a time when unity had never been more vital to the Party's goals. 'Our leader is a sick man,' Siao Chang thundered. 'He must go on vacation and regain his health. We should give him our support.'

An anti-leadership plot had been exposed. What a blunder! Still, I saw no reason to apologise. I remained silent. So, too, did Yeung Kuo and Chen Yong. The meeting dissolved in an atmosphere of high tension but with a decision, nevertheless, to resume at 8 o'clock the following morning.

That evening, Yeung Kuo came to my bungalow and berated me for my foolishness. 'We agreed not to expose ourselves. Now look what you've done,' he lamented. 'The two of us are now clear targets for assassination. You'd better take precautions. I've already started mine,' he added.

The meeting re-convened promptly as scheduled. Yeung Kuo was there but the seat beside mine was vacant. Chen Yong, obviously a frightened man, had chosen to stay away. A messenger who was dispatched to where he was staying nearby returned with his signed letter of resignation. It was read aloud, then passed around the table. Our No 2 man said he had lost heart and saw no point carrying on as a committee member. It was as though he was awaiting the inevitable.

Lai Te brushed aside the issue, directing discussions to other matters quite unrelated to the prepared agenda. Towards the end of the day, he announced he had further urgent business awaiting him, this time in Singapore. As usual, no one probed for details and the gathering was promptly adjourned on the understanding that the next meeting would be held at the same location three months hence.

It was late January, 1947, when the top CPM officials again descended on Kuala Lumpur. Because of the problems encountered on the previous occasion, there was an air of uneasy anticipation as we filed to our seats around the same long table in the same bungalow off Ampang road. Still, no one could have envisaged the massive ramifications the day's events would have for the South East Asian region as a whole and, indeed, for Britain and her Commonwealth of nations worldwide.

Once again, Chen Yong failed to appear. Personally, I was not surprised. What did surprise me, though – and surprised everyone else in attendance – was the vacant seat at the head of the table where Lai Te should have been sitting. The Party provided Lai Te with a permanent place to stay on his visits to Kuala Lumpur. It was a small, single storey brick and cement bungalow in Setapak-Gombak. The Secretary General had the reputation of being a very punctual man. He would meticulously time his arrival for appointments so as to be neither late nor early. I think he took a leaf out of Lenin's book. Meetings at which Lai Te presided always started at 8 o'clock each morning, recessed for the lunch break at 12 midday, resumed at 2 pm and adjourned for the day at 5 pm. Lai Te would leave home exactly 10 minutes before each session.

At this January meeting, we waited for fifteen minutes . . . half an hour . . . an hour. At 9 o'clock it was finally suggested someone should go to Lai Te's home in Gombak road and retrace the drive en route just in case he had been involved in an accident. Ah Dian, a Johore state committee member, was deputised to carry out the search mission but he could not drive. I offered to take him in my Austin 8.

In Chen Yong's absence, Ah Dian was then functioning as the Johore state secretary. He was the most trusted lieutenant of Chen Yong but still very loyal to Lai Te. We drove slowly along the ten-minute route to Lai Te's house, scanning the road and sideroads for any signs of an accident. There were none. As we progressed, Ah Dian mildly advised me not to confront the leader this time as I had done previously.

We finally arrived at Lai Te's house. There we met his pregnant Chinese wife, Jang Sueh Yong, herself a CPM member. She had been the female messenger who escorted me to my first meeting with Lai Te in the hilltop bungalow four-and-a-half-years earlier. I enquired as to her husband's whereabouts. She appeared genuinely taken aback and insisted he had left home by car in time to arrive at the Ampang road address for the start of the meeting. By now, Ah Dian and I had become very worried and persuaded Lai Te's wife to accompany us and talk to the gathered members.

Back at the meeting, she related what time her husband had taken his breakfast and when he had driven off. She then left us. There followed a concerned conversation among committee members. What had happened to Lai Te? One member suggested he had probably been kidnapped by the British. I thought this unlikely but chose not to speak and certainly not to explain my reasons for holding opposing views.

Yeung Kuo and I were both convinced something very serious had happened. Before we dispersed late that afternoon, it was agreed to appoint an investigating team to get to the bottom of the mystery. Three men were selected. With Chen Yong self-imposed on the sidelines, it fell to me to head the team. The other two investigators appointed were Ah Dian and Yeung Kuo.

That night, Yeung Kuo turned up at my place again and we discussed the full implications of Lai Te's disappearance. We were at a loss as to how to begin our investigations. We had no contacts in the Special Branch. Furthermore, we could scarcely go up to the local police station and report the clandestine leader of the dreaded CPM as 'missing, believed kidnapped by the Special Branch'.

Yeung Kuo and I became apprehensive. We felt certain Lai Te and his Special Branch controller would launch a counter-plot against us. We could have already been lined up for elimination. Following our demise, Lai Te would re-appear as the restored unopposed CPM chief. The two of us decided we would also disappear for a while and allow the dust to settle. More importantly, we wanted to establish if anyone was seeking us out. Before leaving home, I confided the problem to my wife and advised it might be best for her to return to her mother's house in Penang. She decided to remain in Kuala Lumpur.

Late that night, Yeung Kuo and I knocked on the door of a house in the Kampong Bahru section of Kuala Lumpur. It was occupied by two mutual friends who were Party members. Both worked in the editorial section of the CPM's bi-monthly newspaper, *The Combatant*, circulated among members of our MPAJA Old Comrades' Association. We asked to stay and swore them to secrecy. For a few days we hid there at night and roamed the capital's bookshops and movie theatres during the day, making the odd check with our homes to see if anyone had been trying to contact or follow us. They hadn't. Eventually we realised our evasive measures were getting us nowhere. If anything, they might well be making us easier targets. So, we decided to come out of hiding and return to our regular Party functions.

By now, other members of the Central Committee were clamouring for action to be taken and explanations to be given. Confusion, tension and latent anger hung in the air. Underlying all was the basic fear that unless the mystery of Lai Te's disappearance was quickly solved, the Central Committee could become paralysed.

The job I was given was two-fold. I must first solve the mystery of what had happened to Lai Te. Secondly, I needed to gather all evidence associated with his disappearance and present this to the Central Committee. It would then be up to the Committee to decide what action to take.

Equally important, I felt, was the need to shatter a personality cult that had been nurtured within the Party for almost a decade and a half. Lai Te had deliberately cultivated this as a means of sustaining control. It became his most powerful weapon. Historical circumstances abetted him and afforded him the opportunity of championing particular popular causes. When he first joined the CPM the Party was in disarray. He managed to bring order. Then, when the Japanese invaded China, Lai Te worked at mobilizing aid for the motherland. With the outbreak of World War 11 the cost of living rose. Now Lai Te swung the concentration of his effort towards improving the pay of workers and under conditions of the day it was a simple matter to organise strikes. Through this chain reaction of high-profile causes, the local communist movement expanded rapidly and Lai Te accrued substantial credit at the grass-roots level.

Our missing Secretary General had given the Party hierarchy the impression he had worked with communist movements in France, Russia, China and Indo China.

His story was that, after working on the Shanghai Town Committee of the Communist Party of China, he had been assigned back to France and had made a stopover in Singapore. While in Singapore, he had assessed the highly disorganised state of the CPM. Plans for him then changed, so his story went, and he stayed on to bring direction and order to the local revolution as the Comintern's 'man on the spot'. He exhibited considerable skill in organising undergound activities. His credentials seemed impeccable. His Vietnamese background and French-language education only added to his aura. He became accepted without question by members throughout the Party and was regarded as a most influential figure.

By now Yeung Kuo and I knew in our hearts that the Lai Te story was a massive fraud. But how do you destroy an illusion? What pieces of proof, under these circumstances, can be salvaged for presentation to a disheartened Central Committee?

Our first break came some weeks later from, of all sources, the Vietnamese. A group of Vietnamese communists, who had travelled overland from their Bangkok base, arrived in Kuala Lumpur on a pre-arranged visit. They were seeking our assistance, as they had done on previous occasions, for the war effort in Indo China. Since the outbreak of revolutionary action there, immediately following Japan's surrender, the CPM had gladly given the Vietnamese comrades financial support and retained close relations with their Viet Minh movement. Every time a clandestine group of Vietnamese visited us, they would get together with their fellow-countryman, Lai Te.

More recently, Lai Te had been the driving force behind the mobilization of some 600 volunteers in Singapore to help the Viet Minh on the battlefields. Only the intervention of the British authorities at the last moment had prevented this volunteer force from moving to Vietnam.

On this particular visit, our Vietnamese comrades intended taking up an earlier offer by Lai Te to supply weapons to the Viet Minh. The CPM had earmarked some 400 pieces for them. These had been stored away in three secret caches along the east coast of Johore between Mersing and Kota Tinggi. We had also readied a *tongkang* and crew to pick up the weapons and sail them across the South China Sea to Vietnam's southernmost Ca Mau Peninsula.

The Vietnamese finalised their arrangements. They would board the *tongkang* in Mersing. However, while waiting in Kuala Lumpur, they received news from their Bangkok headquarters that the intended landing point for the weapons had come under heavy attack by the French Army. The supply mission had to be aborted.

As on all previous visits, the Vietnamese asked to see Lai Te. Initially I told them our leader was out of town. They accepted my answer and moved south to Singapore for a few days. On their return they again requested me to arrange a meeting with Lai Te. It took some days before I felt I knew the visitors well enough to admit that, much to our embarrassment, our Secretary General had vanished. I added that there was a popular belief he had been kidnapped by the British.

To my surprise, the visiting group then went ahead to appraise me of a few facts they had learned about Lai Te's activities in Singapore. They felt quite certain the British were not holding him. Before they left they gave me the name and Singapore address of a Vietnamese man. They advised me this contact could greatly assist me in providing information about Lai Te.

I hurried to Singapore and there met the man in question, a middle class intellectual in his late 30s. During the war, he had worked with All India Radio's overseas broadcasting network translating news bulletins from English into Vietnamese. He had also been an announcer. When his broadcast unit closed down after the war he had moved to Singapore. He was a nationalist and intended returning to Vietnam to fight the French. With this background, he was considered reliable by the Bangkok-based Vietnamese communists.

My new contact confirmed the stories I had been told earlier about Lai Te's association with the Japanese during the occupation years. He said the Vietnamese community in Singapore had long suspected Lai Te was operating for both the Japanese and the British. The Vietnamese business community on the island at this time was some 300-strong. In a matter of weeks I was able to amass a huge file of evidence detailing our absent leader's various activities. At one point, apparently, he had even boasted among the local Vietnamese that the British wanted to award him a special war service medal. He had turned down the offer.

I also uncovered disturbing information about Lai Te's private life which, remarkably enough, had remained concealed from the rest of us. Miss Jang, a Hakka from Penang, the woman who had addressed the Central Committee the morning Lai Te went missing in Kuala Lumpur, turned out to be the Secretary General's fourth wife. In Singapore I learned that his first wife, a Vietnamese, was the daughter of a government contractor who had purchased a beachside bungalow in Katong for the family. There was also another beautiful Vietnamese mistress who had lost a hand in an accident. She lived in a flat in the Hill street area of Singapore paid for by Lai Te. Our Secretary General had also provided the capital behind the bar and restaurant she ran in the same district. A third woman, a Cantonese, also lived in quarters maintained by Lai Te. He had married our comrade, Miss Jang, soon after the Japanese surrender.

Much of these details were written down for me in the Vietnamese language which I then arranged to have translated into Chinese. While this work was being done, I received firm documentary evidence that Lai Te had indeed absconded with more than a million dollars worth of Party funds. Armed with my file, I called a meeting of the CPM's Central Committee for March 6, 1947. At this I would present my findings.

The picture that caused years of confusion. Taken when I was recovering from a heavy bout of malaria, it was subsequently confiscated from the photographer's Kuala Lumpur studio by Special Branch. I had rejected it as bearing little likeness to the young businessman which was to be my cover during overseas missions. Subsequently Special Branch used it to identify me publicly.

Chapter 12

Eliminating Britain's spy . . . then an OBE!

In the days leading to our scheduled March 6, 1947, Central Committee meeting, I began receiving alarming reports of orders Lai Te had issued seeking details of the Party's secret weapons caches. These demands had been surreptitiously coursed through the recently created Organisational Bureau. Activities here were unknown to the Politburo where I had been working since the Secretary General's streamlining of Central Committee functions six months earlier.

All state committees, I discovered, had been asked to provide lists of weapon numbers, details of ammunition stocks and, most alarmingly, the locations of our various jungle caches. For good measure, Lai Te also wanted to know the identities of the senior cadres charged with controlling each cache.

Such requests were, of course, in direct contravention of our basic security provisions. I now fully appreciated the motivation behind Lai Te's division of Central Committee functions. Under these arrangements, all information on questionable orders remained exclusively on the organisational side and we in the Politburo could be kept in complete ignorance of them. It was an ideal ploy for manipulating the Party. At the same time, it ensured that those with both authority and confidence to question directives were kept shut off from day-to-day developments.

As it happened, our main weapons storage areas were in Johore, Perak and Selangor. Fortunately, on this occasion, the Party branches in these states and elsewhere all baulked at supplying the requested details. Their lack of action was not prompted by any suspicion that Lai Te was working for the British. Rather, the comrades judged that compliance with such incredibly inappropriate instructions would likely yield disastrous results. Accepted practice at state and district levels ensured that classified information of this nature was never committed to paper. Numbers and details of weapons and ammunition stocks, in particular, were committed only to memory.

I became convinced then – and remain so today – that Lai Te's attempt to extract, in one hit, a mass of vital intelligence on our weapon supplies, so fundamental to the Party's existence, could only have been directed under extreme pressure from his British spymasters. I interpreted it as a plan to nip our armed struggle in the bud.

But the British had failed to think through their moves. They pushed Lai Te too hard. Adhering to their instructions, he was forced into taking measures that immediately raised eyebrows. Had it worked, had the British been more subtle in their pursuit of intelligence on our weapons caches, the information might well have been forthcoming and the CPM would probably have fallen apart within a matter of months. Even if the Party had survived, there certainly would never have been a guerrilla war. You can't fight without weapons.

All these latest reports detailing Lai Te's extraordinary quest for specifics on our secret arms dumps added to the body of evidence I was able to present to the Central Committee at our March 6 gathering in Kuala Lumpur. With the exception of Chen Yong, every Central Committee member was present. Although well aware the CPM was facing its deepest crisis ever, my other committee comrades had no idea of the extent to which Lai Te had betrayed the movement.

After speaking at length on the documentation I had accumulated, I sat down to an eerie silence. It was obviously difficult for those present to absorb the gravity of the activities perpetrated by our absconding leader. Which of these had been the most damaging? How far had they undermined our ability to function as a revolutionary movement? What sort of damage control measures would be most appropriate? After a while the silence broke and we began to share these thoughts. The decisions taken on Lai Te at this meeting were three-fold. First, we recognised his spying activities for the Japanese. Then we expelled him from the Party. Finally, we confirmed that he must be dealt the most extreme form of punishment – death.

At the conclusion of this meeting, I was formally appointed leader of the CPM. I then spoke on the need to consolidate our efforts at Party rejuvenation and restructuring. To this end it was decided that an enlarged Plenum should be called.

Afterwards, I felt it was incumbent upon us to inform Lai Te's Malayan Chinese wife, our comrade Miss Jang, about the evidence against her husband and the decisions we had taken. We held Miss Jang in high esteem. Shortly after Lai Te's disappearance from Kuala Lumpur, she had departed for her parents' home in Penang and there given birth to a daughter. Yeung Kuo and I discussed how best to break the news to her.

As Miss Jang had known Yeung Kuo since their student days, it was thought preferable that he see her personally. I was rather relieved at this arrangement. I had spent weeks gathering incriminating information against her husband and was too close to the subject to be of assistance to a fellow comrade who would undoubtedly be grief-stricken. Miss Jang's father ran a tailor's shop in Georgetown, just off Penang road. There Yeung Kuo met her and explained what we had uncovered. He went on to describe the length and breadth of her husband's betrayal – through the pre-war British colonial period, the Japanese occupation years and finally the post-war British re-occupation. He informed her how fellow Vietnamese communists had helped uncover Lai Te's duplicity and how there could be no doubt of his guilt.

Yeung Kuo had expected a distraught outburst and frantic pleas for clemency. Instead, Miss Jang accepted quietly everything she was told and raised not a single question. After a long silence she murmured flatly: 'Then I suppose you must kill him.'

'We must,' agreed Yeung Kuo, adding, 'we are now looking for him.' A year later, the British authorities would arrest Miss Jang and deport her to China. There she died of kidney failure in the 1970s.

Having cleared the decks with Lai Te's Chinese wife, we were now in a position to launch the hunt for our betrayer. We knew exactly the location of his father-in-law's Katong seaside villa and we placed an extensive watch on it hoping he might return.

Ma Ting, chief of the Singapore Town Committee, led the hunt. He had been trained at 101 STS, and was well known to Chapman during the occupation. Ma Ting was instructed to form a special killer squad to wipe out Lai Te at the first available opportunity. Each squad member was furnished with a photograph of the quarry. Our Katong villa stake-out lasted more than two weeks. We followed numerous vehicles that entered and departed the compound. No results. Eventually Ma Ting reported that all efforts to locate Lai Te in Singapore had failed and we surmised the man had most probably fled the immediate region.

As we pondered the next steps of our manhunt and adopted damage control measures, we began receiving, state by state, more accurate estimates of the extent of Party funds Lai Te had misappropriated. From this latest flow of information we were able to calculate the precise contributions each state had forwarded to the Singapore Party headquarters during the time Lai Te was in control. Additionally, we found out the exact amount of funds the CPM had made available to fraternal communist movements in Siam and Indo China during the same period. We were also able to determine the actual running costs of the Singapore office. By simple subtraction, we arrived at a bottom line for misappropriated funds that was far more substantial than originally thought. The new figure was closer to $2 million and further investigations revealed Lai Te had channeled CPM money into personal investments not only for himself, but for his various women as well. By financial yardsticks of the time, the sums involved in his double-dealings were quite staggering.

Here I should explain how the CPM managed to amass such wealth in the first place. It occurred in the immediate aftermath of the Japanese surrender before our guerrilla army demobilized. A spontaneous single act of seizing rubber-stocks triggered a rush of similar raids by CPM branches throughout the peninsula. These were certainly not ordered but were nonetheless welcomed by the Party leadership. Our comrades found themselves in a perfect configuration to confiscate rubber from the Japanese who had usurped stocks from the British as war booty in the first place.

After the victorious Japanese had commandeered the piles of rubber abandoned by the departing British, they had encountered great difficulty taking them back safely to Japan. There was a shortage of merchant shipping and those vessels operating were subject to regular attacks by Allied submarines and aircraft. Attempts were made to build big wooden *tongkangs* in Penang and, in these, ship the rubber to Japan via routes closely following the Chinese coastline. The whole laborious process of constructing the *tongkangs* and then sailing them to Japan by such a circuitous course proved ineffectual. The result was that huge stockpiles of rubber remained in occupied Malaya and were there when the Japanese surrendered.

In the frantic weeks following the capitulation, Chinese capitalists tried to corner the rubber stockpile market, making surreptitious deals with the Japanese. We didn't deal. We just seized. We seized from the Japanese. We seized from the capitalists. Then we moved our stocks to warehouses we controlled. We had the manpower to do it. We had the weapons to protect our interests. The capitalists weren't in the race. Incoming BMA officials were too preoccupied re-imposing colonial control to appreciate our guerrillas were equally busy carting off the country's rubber. With our rubber stocks secured, we then waited for the post-war market to evolve. Then we sold. Well over $2 million was quickly raised this way.

We knew with some degree of accuracy that $1 million of the income from our rubber haul alone was passed through to Lai Te. The remaining rubber funds were largely wasted at the state level. Senior Party cadres wanted to make more money in the post-surrender confusion. Most of their efforts, though, failed. They were good underground operators. They were better than average guerrillas. But they were not businessmen.

As the weeks of grappling with the Lai Te crisis passed, I decided the enlarged Plenum I had alluded to at the March 6 meeting would now have to be assembled in June. By this time I had become very concerned about threats to Party security posed by three Central Committee members. There was the disillusioned Chen Yong. Then there were the two renegades, Ah San and Loh Shi Moh.

Chen Yong, it appeared, remained determined to dissociate himself from the CPM. But he realised, as well as we did, that it was far from a simple matter for him to just walk away. As a Central Committee member he had been privy to a wealth of Party secrets. There was also another matter. It had come to our attention that Chen Yong owed us some $50,000 which he had withdrawn from the Johore branch funds soon after the Japanese capitulation. He had supposedly invested this money in personal enterprises which were now failing. One was a guava plantation, another a printing press in Taiping. He had paid back a very small percentage of the 'borrowed' sum.

Chen Yong's case confronted us with very critical decisions. As far as we were concerned, the money he had taken would have to be paid back. The Party would insist on that. In the event that we ultimately committed ourselves to armed struggle, the prospect of taking such an obstinate man to the jungles would appear to be courting security risks. Similarly, he would remain a continuing threat if he was allowed to leave the Party and become a businessman outside our ranks. We decided to give Chen Yong a chance. He was kept as an ordinary member without any executive rank. By this means we hoped to be able to maintain a close watch on him. We also extracted from him the promise that he would pay back the Party funds he owed. This lenient approach would have very serious consequences for us all in the months and years ahead.

As far as Ah San and Loh Shi Moh were concerned we found it extremely difficult to establish their true loyalties. They had both attended the March 6 meeting at which we had examined the evidence against Lai Te. If they remained loyal to him and still retained contacts to him they, too, would pose very serious security risks. Further complicating matters was the undeniable fact that we had no evidence whatever to connect them directly or indirectly to any acts of disloyalty or even minor misdemeanours. We had no valid reason to take action against them. We decided we would monitor both closely and keep them isolated from what went on within the Party's inner circle.

Faced with these security problems, we drew up highly unusual precautions for the June enlarged Plenum. These consisted of holding the gathering in two separate venues simultaneously. I presided at one in Ipoh. Approximately half the Plenum attendees were there. Yeung Kuo conducted the second meeting in Kuala Lumpur. We did this so that if one group was compromised, half of the Central Committee would survive. Ah San and Loh attended the Ipoh gathering. Neither had knowledge of the Kuala Lumpur assembly.

The overall aim of the split-venue Plenum was to explain the leadership crisis to the leading cadres and inform them about the corrective steps being taken. Yeung Kuo and I worked from identical agendas and presented identical resolutions for adoption. Essentially, the resolutions were very similar to those previously adopted by the Central Committee. They acknowledged Lai Te's spying activities, confirmed his expulsion and reaffirmed the punishment should be death.

One resolution saw the promotion of two new Central Committee members to take the place of the expelled Lai Te and the resigned Chen Yong. The Plenum also appointed the new Politburo which consisted of myself, Yeung Kuo, Ah Chung, Ah Dian, and Siao Chang.

This newly elected Politburo then held a further meeting at which I was empowered to travel abroad for the purpose of getting in touch with fraternal parties in the region. Yeung Kuo would be acting Secretary General in my absence. Specifically, I was given the task of formally contacting the Siamese, Indo Chinese and Chinese communist movements. I was to brief these organisations on our crisis situation, explain the remedial measures we had undertaken, and seek their assistance in tracking down our former leader. At the same time, I was to solicit their help in ensuring Lai Te was eliminated.

I hurriedly obtained a passport through the identical channels I had used a year earlier to secure a travel document for Lai Te. I called by a studio close to the H. S. Lee family-owned hotel in Kuala Lumpur's Sultan street to have my passport photograph taken. A day or two after collecting the prints, I decided they were really unusable for my purposes. I had recently recovered from a bad attack of malaria and appeared exhausted and gaunt in the prints, far from the young Chinese merchant which was to be my cover during my trip abroad. I decided to wait a fortnight, rest and feed well. Then I had another set of photographs taken. The second batch proved more appropriate.

I mention this episode because it would have a curious twist in the years to come. Quite obviously I was followed on my first visit to the studio. It would appear a Special Branch agent called on the photographer and demanded duplicates of the negatives. Satisfied his assignment was accomplished, the agent had then passed the duplicates to the authorities without bothering to establish whether there were any other photographs taken of me. The frail, malaria-wracked image, which I had rejected as unsuitable for my passport, would become the sole photo-identification emblazoned over all the posters, leaflets and newspaper stories seeking my apprehension, dead or alive, during the Emergency years. The fact that it bore such scant resemblance to me was, I always felt, an unexpected bonus.

The healthier looking likeness of Ong Boon Hua supported my travel document's description of the holder's occupation. With this I set off on my first overseas trip by taking a train north to Butterworth where I changed to another bound for Bangkok. Arriving in the Siamese capital in early July, I checked into a cheap downtown hotel and then set about contacting both the Vietnamese and Siamese communist movements operating in the city. I gave both a full run-down on Lai Te and the decisions we had taken in the affair.

The Vietnamese had been forewarned by members of their delegation who had come to collect weapons from us earlier in the year. I formally asked both the Vietnamese and Siamese communist parties for their assistance in tracking down our former leader. My schedule envisaged a two-week stopover in Bangkok at the end of which I was anxious to secure a firm booking on a Hong Kong-bound flight. The Siamese comrades kindly offered to help me get my ticket. Towards the end of my stay, a senior Siamese communist official escorted me by trishaw from their party headquarters, a wooden building located on Si Phaya road, to the Cathay Pacific Airways office then situated on Suriwong road.

During the trishaw-ride back from the airline office, we were travelling along a main thoroughfare with our driver pedalling in a rather leisurely fashion, well to the left. More relaxed with my air ticket now secured, I observed the passing scene, my eyes wandering beyond the oncoming traffic line to the footpath on the opposite side. My attention was suddenly caught by the outline of what seemed a very familiar figure. Surely it couldn't be Lai Te! When I first spotted the man, he was standing with his back to us and seemingly in the middle of a transaction with a cigarette vendor. There was something about the body language. As we moved with the traffic I couldn't take my eyes off the figure. We then came to a position where

I was looking directly back at the man's face. It was Lai Te, all right. He was taking a first puff on a freshly-lit cigarette. He raised his head and appeared to look in my direction. I ducked back behind the trishaw canopy and frantically shouted to my Thai companion: 'Stop, stop, stop. Tell the driver to turn back. I've just spotted the renegade.' As the instructions were relayed and we negotiated the traffic, I saw Lai Te board a motorised tuk-tuk and take-off in a cloud of blue-black smoke. Pedal power was no match for the motor and soon my quarry had vanished into the high-noon traffic.

After dropping my Siamese comrade at his office, I rushed to the Vietnamese communist party headquarters located on Sukhumvit, a mile or so beyond the sprawling British Embassy compound. There I informed my contact about sighting Lai Te. He told me not to worry. His office, he said, had the means of determining the whereabouts of any Vietnamese on the run in Bangkok. He assured me it was just a matter of time. I understood what he was saying. I knew the Vietnamese communists were then operating a large para-military undergound force in the capital city area. They would start by sending their men to check on all hotels, middle-class establishments down to the cheap ones. I was leaving Bangkok within the next 48 hours. The Vietnamese promised me they would follow up immediately and would probably have the mission wrapped up by the time I returned.

I flew to Hong Kong aboard a Cathay Pacific four-engined Skymaster, considered one of the best aircraft of the day. In Hong Kong I first moved into a quite luxurious, newly built hotel in Causeway Bay, situated next door to another hotel where Bao-Dai, the last Vietnamese emperor and recognised Japanese collaborator, had been staying since the reinstatement of French colonial rule throughout Indo China in March, 1946. My hotel proved too expensive. Eventually, I transferred to cheaper accommodation in Nathan road, Kowloon. By then I was in touch with the colony's communist movement. Once more I made a full report on the Lai Te saga which was duly sent through to the Chinese Party's Central Committee headquarters in Shanghai. I then prepared to wait for a reply, knowing it would take some time. I remained in Hong Kong for five weeks.

Much of this time I spent reading newspapers and visiting cinemas. Some days I would take the Star Ferry over to Hong Kong just for that wonderful trip. I'd walk around the Wanchai and Central areas for a while, ride the ferry back and then retire to my room to resume reading the English and Chinese language press. It was on just such an occasion that I was glancing through the day's edition of the *South*

China Morning Post when my eyes fell on the page detailing passenger arrivals and departures by sea and air. In those days, the paper regularly published passenger lists for the previous day's movements. The names were arranged alphabetically, ship by ship, airline by airline.

Somewhat mechanically, I was scanning the arrival schedules from Singapore, Tokyo, Calcutta and Bangkok when, there under the 'c's' in a flight from the Siamese capital, I spotted the name 'Chang Chan Hong'. Now, there was a name I recognised! It was as bogus as the man who bore it. I ought to know. I secured him the Chinese passport in the bogus name that enabled him to travel.

So the Vietnamese had missed him in Bangkok and he had made it to Hong Kong after all. The following day, I reported this to my local contact who held office at the Chinese Business Daily, *Hwa Sung*. The newspaper premises were acknowledged as the unofficial Hong Kong meeting point for the Communist Party of China (CPC). A few days later, my contact informed me that Lai Te had called by the *Hwa Sung* office and spoken to one of his colleagues. To this man he had related an incredible tale of how the British had seized him in Kuala Lumpur and deposited him in Bangkok.

I knew the Chinese communists in Hong Kong would shy away from any involvement with what amounted to an assassination within the colony's precincts. They had to maintain a deft balancing act with the British and avoided any unnecessary confrontation, particularly violence of this nature. However, my contact provided me with some valuable information. He said Lai Te had, in fact, submitted a report to the Chinese Party indicating he intended returning to Bangkok. He then planned to make his way back to Singapore and rejoin the movement there. Lai Te had received a sum of money for his expenses and was preparing to depart Hong Kong. Although my contact would not provide me the precise departure details, I was able to gather, more or less, when Lai Te was proposing to fly off. I gave him a day or two to get away, then took a return BOAC flight back to the Siamese capital where I quickly spoke to the Vietnamese. They initiated a second manhunt, again starting with a check on hotels.

Two days later the Vietnamese search bore fruit. They established Lai Te was booked into a middle-ranking hotel. He was not in his room when they called. As it happened, our man on the run had contacted the Siamese communists the previous day. Shortly before the Vietnamese search party arrived, he had left the hotel to keep a rendezvous in a shophouse with his Siamese communist contact.

Acting on my earlier request, the Siamese comrades had sent a three-man squad to meet Lai Te. Its members were obviously young and inexperienced. Instead of moving in quietly and engaging their target in conversation, they pounced as soon as Lai Te entered the premises. One grabbed him in a headlock. Another lunged for his throat. The man gripping him around the neck applied increased pressure. The struggling form began writhing and contorting. Then he frothed at the mouth, went limp and stopped breathing. At the back of the shophouse, the men conveniently discovered some lengths of hessian used for making sacks. They wrapped the body in these and waited for darkness. Late that night, the deposed and disposed leader of the CPM — surely one of Britain's greatest spying triumphs — was unceremoniously dumped into the swift flowing waters of Bangkok's Chao Praya river.

I knew nothing about these events and the following morning called by the Vietnamese office to be told they had located Lai Te's hotel, had staked it out over night, but he had failed to return. 'He's probably found some company,' it was laughingly suggested.

A few days before my scheduled departure for Malaya, I called to see my opposite number in Siam, Secretary General Li Chee Shin, to bid farewell. When I raised the Lai Te issue, Li quietly responded in Mandarin: 'He's no more.' I pressed for details but Li politely refused. It would be three years before I learned the full facts of Lai Te's demise. In 1950, a CPM delegation was in Peking and met some senior cadres from the Siamese party. One of the Siamese had been in the youthful unit sent to rendezvous with Lai Te at the safe house that morning.

Many years later I was also to learn that soon after the assassination, British intelligence was reporting how a very senior Special Branch officer flew from Singapore to Bangkok to keep a pre-arranged meeting with Lai Te. The officer was acting on information suggesting his agent was in imminent danger and was being tailed around South East Asia by a high-ranking member of the CPM. The intelligence was good. Obviously, the British were close to the action. But not quite close enough. The officer returned to Singapore and reported Lai Te had failed to show up for the rendezvous.

Frankly, I was disappointed with the way Lai Te had been handled. As I was on the spot in Bangkok I would have preferred to confront him personally before he got eliminated. There was so much he could have told me. Normally, when we detained our renegades, we held them alive in order to get them talking. In the case of Lai Te, a gag across the mouth would have silenced him. Too much physical pressure was applied to a frail man. And that is probably why the Siamese communists initially avoided providing details about the matter. Their botched mission had been an embarrassment.

After Lai Te's assassination, I rode the train back to Penang and spent overnight at my mother-in-law's home. From there I telephoned Sitiawan where my wife was staying at my mother's house. In August, during my absence, Khoon Wah had given birth to our son. I was so looking forward to seeing them both. My brother, Boon Eng, happened to answer the phone and immediately on hearing my voice exclaimed excitedly: 'You have been given a very high British honour. The King has granted you an OBE.'

'The King has given me what?' I blurted, believing my brother was surely joking. I had no idea what an OBE – Order of the British Empire – might be. Neither, it seemed, did Boon Eng.

I then spoke to my wife, enquired after our son and put down the phone to think. I had just returned home from ensuring the neutralisation of perhaps the most daringly successful espionage operation ever undertaken in the Far East by His Britannic Majesty's Government. I had ensured the elimination of their principal spy. Now the British had chosen to bestow on me a particularly high award. None of this added up.

The following day, I took a train to Ipoh and was met at the station by a beaming Boon Eng. That evening an uncle took me to dinner at an Ipoh restaurant serving western food. Strangely he said nothing about the OBE, but his choice of venue had made the point. My award had given the family something special, something to counter the controversies that had for so long surrounded my persona.

The next day Boon Eng and I drove to Sitiawan where I was reunited with my wife, son and parents. I was just in time to participate in the customary distribution of red eggs to mark my son's first month since birth.

From Sitiawan I wrote informing Yeung Kuo I would be staying a few days with my family. He wrote back acknowledging the arrangements and making a point of congratulating me on my award. I spent a week or so with my family, then drove to Kuala Lumpur and reported to the Party on my trip to Bangkok and Hong Kong. I met Yeung Kuo and personally informed him Lai Te had been dispatched. I provided my friend with as much information as I could.

Awaiting my arrival in Kuala Lumpur was a letter from the British authorities informing me of my OBE. It had been opened in my absence and everyone in the office knew of its contents. I had received a similar communication not long after the Japanese surrender when the War Office in London wrote to say that, as a result of my operations on behalf of SEAC in occupied Malaya, I had been mentioned in despatches.

I was in two minds about how to handle the OBE communication. At the time, we had two English-speaking intellectuals working with us in the Party. Their primary job was to produce the bi-monthly newspaper called *The Democrat*. One of them was a Eurasian of Portuguese ancestry, Gerald de Cruz. I approached de Cruz for guidance as to what I should do about my OBE.

A local man, de Cruz had an interesting, if unusual, background. During the occupation, he was taken to Saigon and became an announcer on Japanese radio. After the surrender, he returned to Singapore and there made approaches to our headquarters. He said he wanted to work with us. We had a shortage of men who spoke good English. He was very open with us about his collaboration activities and told us exactly how he had been employed by the Japanese. It was Lai Te who accepted him into the Party at the end of 1945. At the beginning of the Emergency, de Cruz disappeared and found his way to Czechoslovakia. He must have been disillusioned by what he saw in Prague. He later moved to Britain and subsequently returned to Singapore and worked for the People's Action Party government.

I told de Cruz that my inclination was to reply accepting the award. He advised me to wait and let the British make a follow-up move. He said the High Commission would inform me when the award ceremony was to take place. I followed his counsel and let matters rest. The British clearly got the impression that I was snubbing their gesture. To the contrary, had I meant to reject it, I would have promptly sent a letter to this effect. It wouldn't be long, however, before the bestowers would change their minds. They were placed in the curious position of having to take back an honour which I had never formally accepted in the first place.

Leaving the OBE matter aside, I turned my attention to the decidedly more pressing problem of restoring order and morale to the CPM. Fundamental to my task was the urgent need to convey and explain the whole Lai Te saga to the Party rank-and-file.

The Politburo decided on a step-by-step approach. First, we informed the state committees. From there the information was presented to the district committees who, in turn, were tasked with filtering it through to the general Party members. It became a process that took months as we were also looking for important feed-back to what we had to say. It took us until December, 1947, to consolidate the feed-back, an almost four-month period during which we worked at devising CPM policies tailored to the requirements of the times.

Almost to a man, Western historians exploring this segment of Malayan history have asserted that I used this four-month stretch to agitate resolutely for armed struggle. This is a complete distortion of the picture. Their misinterpretations appear to have stemmed from intelligence reports that sought to portray the CPM as being divided into what today would be termed camps of 'hawks' and 'doves'. I, of course, have been readily portrayed by the historians as the bloodthirsty head hawk.

In stepping into the Party's top position on my return from Bangkok, I found myself the undisputed leader of the CPM. I could have issued any reasonable directive at this juncture, including a call for armed struggle, and have been confident of the response. I freely admit I was personally devastated by Lai Te's policy switch to cooperation with the returning British in August, 1945. However, as I have already indicated, I rationalised the issue and knuckled down to making organisation of the masses and peaceful political agitation the cornerstones of our effort.

Now that I was Secretary General, neither I nor any member of my Politburo saw a need, at this critical moment, to transfer the emphasis of our approach. Indeed, the political direction established by the August, 1945 manifesto, instituted by Lai Te, had proven very successful, whether intended or not. The CPM controlled labour unions throughout Malaya and Singapore. Our political influence and following had never been stronger. Far from seeking to push the idea of armed struggle, I resolved, along with my fellow Politburo members and the Central Committee, merely to enhance the political format we were following. As I saw it, the requirement was for subtle re-adjustments.

That is not to say we were rejecting armed struggle. We regarded it as inevitable. That is precisely why we were maintaining our jungle caches. But in the final weeks of 1947, we were envisaging an eight to ten year time-frame before we would be forced to launch guerrilla warfare. Plans of rushing into armed struggle couldn't have been further from our minds.

A poignant signpost to history – to be lost forever in the name of urban redevelopment. Archibald 'Archie' Nicolson's neglected gravestone at Singapore's Bidadari Cemetery. In October, 1947, it became such an anti-communist rallying point for Malaya's expatriate planting community. Gathered at this graveside on the day of his funeral the planters swore vengeance against the CPM. But, if the truth were known, Nicolson died as a result of common bandit activities – not those of communist guerrillas.

The inscription reads:

In ever loving memory
of
my beloved husband
Archibald 'Archie' Nicolson
who was killed in Johore
on 6 October 1947
aged 42
so loved – so mourned

Chapter 13

Committing to armed revolution

On the night of Monday, October 6, 1947, 42 year-old Archibald 'Archie' Nicolson, manager of the Gunong Pulai Rubber Estate, was driving home with his wife in their Hilman Minx car along the Skudai-Pontian road in south-western Johore. The couple had been dining in Johore Bahru with the chairman of the South Johore District Planters Association, Mr A.J. Boyd and his wife. At about 10 pm, just as Nicolson swung his car through a double bend at the 14˘ milestone, his headlights illuminated a crudely constructed roadbock 50 yards ahead. Rubber trees flanked both sides of the road. A rubber tree log and three planks spanned the roadway itself but left narrow gaps on either side where the grassy verges ran.

Nicolson well understood the danger. Banditry across the state of Johore had been rising steeply throughout the year and gangsters were operating with increasing ruthlessness and near impunity. Police action to curb the alarming crime wave was proving ineffective, to say the least. In a split second, Nicolson had to decide on the best option he and his wife faced in their sudden predicament. He chose to charge the roadblock and make for the gap at the left hand end of the log. He failed. His off-side front wheel caught the soft embankment and he lost control. The Hilman was hurled to the right side of the road where its tyres gripped the surface, flinging the vehicle violently back to the left again. There it skidded, rolled onto its right side, and ended up in a shallow road-side ditch.

The crash killed Nicolson. He died instantly when his head slammed against an inside section of the cabin during the car's wild gyrations. Four masked men descended on the overturned car and one of them wrenched a gold watch from the wrist of the dead planter's wife, May, who lay stunned in the wreck but otherwise unscathed. When a second bandit, armed with a Sten gun, demanded Mrs Nicolson's diamond solitaire wedding ring, she refused to give it up. Her defiance resulted in a crack over the head with the butt of the Sten. She would survive the ordeal.

Thirty minutes earlier, two Chinese taxi drivers who chose to stop rather than charge their vehicles through the same roadblock were able to drive away unharmed after parting with small sums of money. The first taxi had no passengers. In the second, the bandits seized $20 from an Indian man and $70 from a Malay Regiment ex-soldier. A Chinese woman and her child, also travelling as passengers in the second vehicle, lost nothing. The mother was able to hide $100 in the taxi's seat. Like the drivers, all passengers were released unharmed.

In the circumstances, it would appear Nicolson, a Scotsman from the Isle of Skye, who had been a planter in Malaya since the late 1920s, had been a prisoner in Changi and had served and survived on the infamous Siam-Burma death railway, took the wrong option that night on the Skudai-Pontian road. Viewed one way, it was perhaps a senseless death that might well have been avoided. But in the following weeks, Nicolson's untimely demise would become an emotional rallying point for the European planting community. It would also serve to hasten political polarisation between expatriate planting, mining and business circles, on the one hand, and the colonial administrations in Singapore and Malaya, on the other.

Seen from the CPM perspective, it was the pressures this polarisation imposed on colonial government frameworks that triggered an onrush of militancy in all quarters during the final weeks of 1947 and into the first half of 1948. Curiously enough, though, the Party would be among the slowest of those directly affected to react to these developments.

Of course, we well understood the intensifying climate of industrial unrest throughout 1947 that saw more than 300 separate strikes erupt in Malaya and Singapore. We fully recognised that the loss of nearly 700,000 man-days to strike action during the period had caused extensive disruption to rubber plantations and tin mines on the peninsula and to merchant shipping traffic through the ports. After all, we were the primary organisers and supporters of these activities. There had been, during this time, repeated representations to government heads by expatriate business leaders demanding urgent remedial action.

None of the top administrative officials, in particular the Governor of the Malayan Union, Sir Edward Gent, had responded with too much sympathy to these mounting approaches. The official line, from the Governor down, was that arbitrary power should be exercised with decided caution lest violent reactions follow from workers who, under the conditions, had little to lose. Furthermore, Gent appeared to harbour a degree of distaste for what he regarded as an expatriate community, hell-bent on returning to the pampered lifestyle of pre-war colonial days. Expatriate suspicion of the Governor's competence soon grew into outright hostility which, in turn, would ultimately seal his fate in a most tragic manner less than three weeks after he proclaimed the State of Emergency.

We only had to read the local press to be aware of the problems the Governor faced with the expatriates. Unbeknown to us then was another widening rift, this time between the Special Branch in Malaya and the regular police force led by Commissioner H. Langworthy. The Special Branch, for its part, was urging the mass arrest of known communists operating in towns and cities throughout the peninsula. This advice was predicated on its estimates that the CPM could muster 5,000 armed guerrillas and the support of 250,000 Min Yuen. Commissioner Langworthy regarded these figures as vastly overstated and advised the Governor accordingly. At least for the greater part of 1947, it seemed, Gent tended to accept the guidance of the less alarmist of his police advisers.

Even before Nicolson's coffin was lowered into its grave at Singapore's Bidadari Cemetery, his planting colleagues were plotting grim agitation. Mr Boyd, the association official with whom Nicolson and his wife dined on the night of the accident, leapt to the cause. 'Don't you worry,' he told reporters, 'there'll be action.' His group had immediately lodged a complaint with the Malayan Union Government demanding immediate steps be taken to stem crime and banditry in Johore. Even at the graveside, talk on Nicolson's life and the loss of a friend was sparse. Rather, the 50 or so supposedly mourning planters seemed more concerned with what Nicolson's death might mean for their personal futures in the Malayan planting industry.

'Things will start moving now,' predicted one.' 'I don't feel like having my wife in this part of the world any longer,' observed another. Threatened a third man: 'One more example of this sort of thing and I'm off.' And a fourth: 'We haven't even got arms to defend ourselves. And if we had, we'd be liable to imprisonment at least.' All these graveside comments were reported prominently on the October 8 front page of *The Straits Times*.

Nine days later, the Governor met representatives of the United Planting Association of Malaya and the Incorporated Society of Planters. He promised all planters living in remote areas would be granted licences to bare arms. Gent also promised that military patrols, working with police in dangerous areas, would be stepped up. Pressure on the Government continued.

On October 20, a hartal – a general strike concept borrowed from India which aimed to close down all businesses for a 24-hour period – proved monumentally successful. Called to protest the proposed constitutions of the Malayan Federation and Singapore, its organisers were identified as the Chinese Chambers of Commerce, the Federation of Trade Unions and the All-Malayan Council of Joint Action.

We in the CPM gave the hartal our firm support and worked hard behind scenes to ensure a good result. On the eve of the 24-hour shut-down, Commissioner General Malcolm MacDonald ridiculed the idea in a special broadcast over Radio Malaya. 'However small or great the public response . . . do not let anyone be misled into supposing that they represent a large and united body of opinion on the constitutional issue. They represent nothing of the kind,' the Commissioner General told the two territories only hours before the hartal was due to get underway.

In the event, hartal day saw Singapore's commercial life at a standstill. Non-European business houses remained closed across the island and streets in the downtown area were empty. It was a similar picture in all the main Malayan cities and towns. Virtually all estates and mines were idle. Malaya's principal port, Port Swettenham – now Port Klang – saw an absence of all shore labour and stevedores. Scheduled work on five merchant ships in the harbour failed to materialise. On the country's main coalfield at Batu Arang, all 2,000 labourers declared a holiday.

The Straits Times front page news report the following day maintained that fear had dominated the hartal. Those participating had done so, claimed the news account, under threat of retribution. Curiously, the same issue's editorial commented: 'Singapore presented an impressive spectacle, with its miles of shuttered shops and its streets almost empty of traffic. The organisers of the hartal certainly made a proper job of it.' In the same commentary the paper noted that 'there was little or no outward intimidation in Singapore yesterday and certainly no hooliganism calling for police intervention. The streets were quiet; the people were peaceful.'

MacDonald, who had warned of the day's dangers, was made to look somewhat out of touch and the two governments had to make serious reassessments of the issues at the core of the peaceful defiance. Still, after the reviews, it was clear there would be no British concessions on the citizenship issue or anything else.

There is an interesting historical sidelight to the hartal story. The All-Malayan Council of Joint Action (AMCJA), a key promoter of the protest, had been originally established as the Council of Joint Action (CJA) in December, 1946. It was intended as a united front movement against the Malayan Federation constitution proposals that the British were trying to impose following the dismal failure of their Malayan Union concept. Although sympathetic to the Council, we in the CPM decided not to become directly involved. The Chinese Chambers of Commerce, while supporting the Council's objectives, also preferred not to join formally. The Malayan Indian Congress (MIC) joined as a party. So did the Malayan Democratic Union (MDU) composed of left-wing non-Malays based in Singapore. The prominent millionaire Chinese politician/businessman, Tan Cheng Lock, joined as an individual. The left-wing Malay Nationalist Party (MNP) baulked at joining for fear of being branded pro-Chinese by the United Malay National Organisation (UMNO). Like-minded Malay organisations set up a parallel grouping called the Putera Pusat Tenaga Rakyat (PUTRA). The PUTRA, in turn, cooperated with the AMCJA and drafted a people's constitution as an alternative to Britain's Federation proposals. In August, 1947, in the lead-up to the hartal, the Council and its affiliates emerged under the revised AMCJA-PUTRA banner with Tan Cheng Lock and a Dr Burhanudin as its recognised co-leaders.

The AMCJA was not exactly a communist front but it would be fair to say that it was firmly under our influence. Gerald de Cruz, once a prominent member of the MDU but now a CPM member, was assigned to work on a hedging Tan Cheng Lock before the latter became the movement's joint head. After lengthy discussions, de Cruz managed to persuade Tan to fight openly for and with the AMCJA-PUTRA. In return, de Cruz guaranteed that he could swing all left-wing opinion behind Tan. I am sure it was never in Tan Cheng Lock's mind to become a CPM stooge. But that is exactly what happened.

With British intransigence established for all to see, local public attention began to focus on the CPM as the only indigenous political movement in Malaya and Singapore capable of offering a challenge to the imperialists. The colonial establishment began to view us with even deeper suspicions and certainly now as the major threat to their well-being. *The Straits Times* newspaper led the process by repeated innuendoes in its news columns suggesting that all violence associated with strikes and demonstrations was traceable to a communist source. Right from the outset of the BMA period, those strikes and demonstrations organised by the CPM had, as their foundations, the genuine grievances of workers who were being appallingly exploited by the returning colonial masters.

As our successes grew on the labour front, so did the strike-breaking efforts across our picket lines. Labour was supplied through special contractors who, in turn, hired gangsters to intimidate and crush our demonstrations. By taking no action against the contractors or the gangsters, most of whom were drawn from Chinese secret societies, the colonial British signalled their tacit approval of strong-armed tactics against our unions. The incompetent and understaffed police were thankful to go along with this situation.

Hired gangster intimidation had long been a festering problem for us and, as 1947 drew to a close, it became a major issue – so prevalent had become the stand-over measures on the part of the various employers and their labour suppliers. Up to this point, we had postponed confronting the gangsters head-on with similar methods. We feared walking into a British trap. The CPM leadership was convinced, and I think rightly so, that any move on our part to confront gangsterism with gangsterism would only provide Government with the tailor-made excuse necessary to suppress and ultimately ban the Party. When, in March 1948, we did decide to counter with our own version of heavy tactics, it would be a decision with momentus implications for us.

In the meantime, the hartal had demonstrated, at all levels of society and across the racial board, a widespread frustration with what the British were promoting as their gradual democratisation of the territories. As far as the masses were concerned, the process was too gradual, far from democratic enough and deviously calculated to benefit colonial interests. The Nicolson incident had galvanized the planting community into a combative mood which easily overflowed to the mining and general business sectors. Then there was the gathering violence. Why such turmoil? The simple way out was to blame the communists. The administrators did it with alacrity. So did the pro-government politicians. *The Straits Times* had been doing it for some time. We were the perfect scapegoats.

An overriding consideration for the Party, going back to the Lai Te days, had been the need to throw off the cloak of semi-illegality which the British had forced on us. As far as I, the new Party leader, was concerned, official recognition as a legal entity was a fundamental goal of the CPM. We discussed how best to pursue this objective. One of the first steps we took was to abandon our practice of having secret residences. We would maintain open offices, our officials would be readily identifiable and it would thus be more convenient for us to contact the people. At one stage I was actually living in the Singapore office. It was when we were trying to set up the Central Committee headquarters in our Queen street premises which were located next door to the Catholic Chinese school.

The move to Singapore proved more arduous than we had anticipated and, in February, 1948, our headquarters remained at the old MPAJA offices in Klyne street, Kuala Lumpur. Despite all the negative attention the Establishment was heaping on us, including the propaganda line that we were being lavishly financed from Moscow, the truth was that the Central Committee was by now in serious financial difficulties.

To help out, I arranged to vacate the Ampang road bungalow where Khoon Wah and I had been living since late 1945. A Royal Air Force squadron leader and his wife moved in and paid me $800 'tea money'. I was pleased with the arrangement and so, it seemed, was the squadron leader. I remember his wife was especially glad that we left the piano originally assigned to the bungalow by the Party. I placed the $800 in the Central Committee coffers, not a tidy sum, but it provided us a brief breathing space.

*　　*　　*　　*　　*

The Federation of Malaya came into being on Monday, February 1, 1948. On the eve of the official celebrations, we began a scheduled Politburo meeting at our Klyne street headquarters to draw up a Party position towards the new government process. A High Commission would now administer Malaya. Gent's title of Governor would be changed to High Commissioner. On Federation Day, our meeting was still in progress when we heard the booming of British artillery accompanying the formal installation of Gent as the first British High Commissioner to Malaya.

As the artillery rounds fired off, Ah Dian, the trusted lieutenant and now Politburo replacement of Chen Yong, addressed his fellow members: 'I feel we have tried our best. We have used every peaceful means to further the cause of the masses. We have set up united front organisations. We have, in effect, the entire plantation workforce of the country under our control. It is the same situation in the mines. It is the same situation on the wharves, in the public transportation companies and with all the essential services. Yet we have had no impact whatever on even a single clause in the Constitution which is coming into force at this very minute. If we continue like this, what future lies ahead for the movement?'

Ah Dian couldn't have picked a more dramatic moment to present the dilemma facing the CPM. Indeed, what was the point of a peaceful and constitutional struggle? I was chairing the meeting at the time and said: 'Well, since you have raised the subject, go ahead and discuss it. Let's see what everyone present here has to say.' At that point I remained totally uncommitted to any specific course of action. I was certainly quietly infuriated over what I felt was Britain's railroading of Federation. It was obviously imperative for the Party to devise a policy to fit the circumstances. But I was keen to hear what the body of opinion was within the Politburo.

The subject of armed struggle was then introduced. There followed a lengthy but inconclusive discussion. One firm understanding though came out of our deliberations. Our Party was in no shape, financial or otherwise, to launch a guerrilla war at this juncture. Shortly thereafter I moved to Singapore where I joined our Queen street office.

Within a few days of my arrival, the Communist Party of Australia's Secretary General, Mr Laurence Sharkey, made a stopover in Singapore on his way to Calcutta to attend the Communist Party of India's Second Congress. Sharkey's itinerary called for him to change ships in Singapore and he found he had two days up his sleeve. He dropped by our Queen street office to establish fraternal contacts.

Sharkey came with substantial credentials. The son of a small landholding farmer in the central New South Wales district of Orange, he had joined the CPA in 1922 and risen quickly to become a member of its Central Committee. In Moscow, in 1935, he had been elected to the executive committee of the Comintern.

I spoke with Sharkey for several hours on matters of general interest. When he was about to leave for his Raffles Hotel room, I asked him whether, on his return passage through Singapore en route home to Australia, he could take time to brief us on the Calcutta meeting. I explained we had not been invited to the gathering, probably because, by international communist standards, we were still a young party. Sharkey said he would be pleased to comply.

I had the feeling Calcutta might produce some dramatic results. I had recently read that a Pravda commentator had openly attacked the policies of Indian leader Pandit Nehru. Nehru and his Congress Party were accused of compromising with the British. I was sure the Pravda attack might spur a new direction by the Indian communists. In March, I convened a meeting of our Central Committee to decide, once and for all, whether we should continue peaceful and constitutional politics or whether we should revert to armed struggle. This was underway when the Australian communist leader arrived back from India. On my invitation he attended one of our sessions.

Sharkey reported on the Calcutta congress and it was quite obvious that the gathering had, indeed, been very decisive. Henceforth the CPI would attack Nehru's Congress Party for betraying Indian nationalist interests and compromising with the British. But this came with the strict proviso that no mention would be made publicly of armed struggle. I interpreted it as implying that while they may not want to talk about it openly, armed struggle was now definitely on the CPI's agenda. My interpretation on this occasion was fairly accurate. The Indian communists went on to stage a rebellion in Hyderabad that was ultimately put down by the army. Would the developments in India influence our decisions? I thought so. However, some of the Central Committee failed to see the significance I read into what was happening there.

Concluding his report, Sharkey asked whether there were any questions. There followed one or two seeking clarifications of Sharkey's reading of international communist developments in the light of the Calcutta meeting. His answers were direct, if not matter of fact, but produced nothing startling. Then a Central Committee member in charge of trade union affairs asked our guest the critical question for which we had been seeking answers for months. 'Comrade,' he requested, 'how do you Australians deal with strikebreakers?'

We had long been following news reports of protracted union action taken in Australia and had marvelled at the way boycotting labour 'down under' had been able to hold out for months on end. Of special interest to us had been the extraordinary successes notched up by Australian waterside workers who flatly refused to load cargo for the Dutch East Indies and repeatedly tied up, in endless strike action, all ships linked to this trade.

Earlier in the month, *The Straits Times* had carried a front page lead story headed 'Reds have invaded Queensland'. The state premier in Brisbane had declared a 'state of emergency' and had gazetted 'regulations to impose strict censorship on strike news in the press and on the radio'. Twenty-three thousand railway men had refused to work and the powerful Waterside Workers' and Seamen's Union had ordered their members to strike in sympathy. The report continued: 'The port of Brisbane is now immobilized with 19 ships idle and a complete paralysis of all other Queensland ports seems certain.' Adding to the clamour, the premier, Mr Hanlon, alleged that 'the High Command of the communist party has invaded Queensland'.

Now, here, about to give us the benefit of his knowledge and experience, was the man directly responsible for all the spectacular developments that had been dazzling us so. His genius for organisation had preceded him. We all recognised that the CPA had been declared illegal from 1940 to 1942. Sharkey had not only managed to retain control of the outlawed movement but had actually led it back to legality with an increased membership. We felt privileged to have such a guest.

The meeting eagerly awaited Sharkey's views on strikebreakers and how his party handled them. Our visitor leaned back in his chair as the question, originally posed in Chinese, was translated into English. Pausing for a moment, Sharkey glanced along the row of Asian faces at the table and said bluntly: 'We get rid of them.'

Someone who spoke English followed up. He thought he might have misheard the response which had been delivered in such a thick, slow Australian drawl. 'You mean you eliminate strikebreakers, Comrade . . . kill?'

Sharkey considered the question carefully. Then he said: 'But not in the cities. Only in the outlying areas. The rural areas. The mining areas.'

Translated, Sharkey's words sent a rush of reinforced fervour through our gathering.

I should make it clear that at no point during his address to the Central Committee did Sharkey urge us specifically to take up arms against the British. What he said, however, was pivotal in its overall effect.

When Sharkey left to walk back to Raffles Hotel our meeting continued. The same man who had questioned the Australian communist leader went on to present a copy of a draft law which was being proposed by the Malayan Federation in order to restrict the powers of our unions. An Indian worker at the Government printing press had stolen a copy of the projected law and passed it along to a union official. The union official, a CPM member, had in turn forwarded it to our Central Committee man. It was printed in Kuala Lumpur and was proposed for discussion and ultimate adoption by the Federated Legislative Council.

We well understood the British colonial approach. Drafted legislation slated for discussion was almost always for adoption as well. In a few cases, vested interests, like plantation owners' organisations or tin miners' groups, were able to influence deliberations and thereby alter legislation. The local man or woman in the street had no influence at all.

The stolen document was duly read to the meeting. It became very obvious to all present that not only would such a piece of legislation restrict union powers, it would also deprive the CPM of the right to lead the trade union movement. With this in the pipeline we saw as the inevitable next step the outright banning of our party. We would have to be prepared. If the banning took place we would have no other option but to fight. Subsequently, the law as outlined in the stolen document was passed without any alteration from its drafted form.

Had we not known in advance about that piece of draft legislation, we would have been in total disarray when it was announced. We could never have managed to convene a spur-of-the-moment policy meeting to take countermeasures. And even if these had been introduced, it would have been too late anyway. It should be understood that at this time we were inexperienced. We recognised this fact. We accepted that we were new to the movement. We looked to leads from outside our party. We looked to Australia, to India, to the Dutch East Indies, to Indo China and to China where there were communist parties with far greater knowledge than we had been able to amass. The news of the developments within the CPI certainly had its impact. Laurence Sharkey's visit was inspiring. But more important still was the stolen document revealing the piece of draft legislation.

It was within this context and in this mood that we went on to accept we had no option now but to wage war for our principles. The subject was debated and everyone present had his say. Everyone seemed in agreement to the principle of taking to the jungles. But it was seen only as a decision 'in principle'. The complex details of timing and implementation would have to come later. From the chair I asked whether there was any dissenting voice to the motion. Nobody disagreed. We all took this to mean we had arrived at a unanimous decision.

Then our discussions naturally gravitated to estimates on how long our war against the British would last. One or two suggested two or three years. Another felt it would be longer. My prediction was that it would last at least ten years.

This led to a very general exploration of how the war might be fought. There was general agreement that action would take similar lines to those pursued during the Japanese occupation. It would thus be rather haphazard in direction – at least for the first year or so – and would be waged on a state-by-state basis. State committees, in collaboration with their military commanders, would call the day-to-day action, issuing the required orders and functioning independently just as we had done during the Japanese period. I voiced the opinion that I did not believe we should, at this stage, adhere to the classical guerrilla warfare tactics of base areas and liberated zones as espoused by Mao. To this there was no objection.

Laurence Sharkey's words had inspired us to the point that, as the meeting progressed to its final stages, there emerged total commitment among those present for a toughening of our policy line towards strikebreakers. Of particular concern were the hired thugs brought in by the labour contractors intent on smashing our union work throughout the peninsula's plantations and mines.

Accordingly, we went ahead and approved the issuing of a directive targeting for elimination all strikebreakers and all contractors using thugs for this purpose in

Malayan rural areas. It was, of course, a move directly influenced by the measures we had been told were being employed by our Australian comrades. Because of the very serious repercussions of this directive I am compelled to explain what I believe happened to it along the line. The Central Committee was the authorising and drafting body. The document then was addressed to the various state secretaries for attention to their committees. Our intention was that the directive would be passed down to the district levels and there explained fully.

I believe we made a serious blunder in the drafting of the directive and in it failed to define precisely the intended targets for elimination. But there were other mistakes as well, which suggested a bad lapse in monitoring. As the directive went down the line, individual interpretations were made of it and, based on these, actions were taken that should never have occurred.

When this most decisive meeting finally wrapped-up on March 21, 1948, I remember walking to my office in the same Queen street building in Singapore feeling most encouraged by the unanimity of sentiment expressed by my comrades. I had hardly settled in my chair when Yeung Kuo walked in the door. He appeared troubled. I could detect anxiety in his face. When I asked what worried him, he replied: 'I'm still doubtful. Are we really prepared for this? Perhaps we should reconsider our position.' He went on to express misgivings on whether the conditions in Malaya and Singapore were ripe for armed struggle. It was not the strategy per se that disturbed him, rather our likely timing of its introduction.

This rankled and for a moment I lost my patience. I said: 'Why didn't you raise your doubts during the discussion? Why come to me now when it's all decided?' Yeung Kuo didn't press his objections and in the conversation that followed he indicated he was content to let matters rest. However, I was shortly to learn there was a second Central Committee member who also nursed doubts; again, not on the armed struggle commitment as such but on its timing. Both men finally accepted my position that full agreement had been reached at the Queen street meeting and there was no point going back and diluting the Party's position.

Shortly after the Singapore deliberations wound up, we brought together all state secretaries in Kuala Lumpur to sound out their individual reactions to the idea of armed struggle. Their opinions were supportive and unanimous. Ah Dian and I were there on behalf of the Central Committee. I remember being taken very ill during the preliminary proceedings. I could only stay a few hours and had to leave. Ah Dian presided over the discussions in my place. I was suffering crippling stomach cramps. I could not sit. I could not lie. I didn't know how to place myself. I didn't know then, but it was the beginnings of a long bout with ulcers that would plague me throughout the Emergency.

As the momentum for armed struggle gathered, I became worried that British intelligence had probably infiltrated our ranks to a degree that a number of our decisions had become known to the authorities. This consideration, in itself, tended to accelerate our activities. I reconvened the Central Committee on May 5, this time in northern Johore. Attendees were basically the same line-up as had been at the previous Singapore meeting. The aim now was to discuss the implementation of armed struggle.

We decided on setting up, state-by-state, guerrilla force nuclei. We went on to analyse the best means of inserting them into jungle camps. We discussed how best to retrieve weapons and ammunition from the jungle caches we had established – or, at least, from those still undiscovered by the British – and how to get their contents into the hands of our guerrillas. We worked out directions for military training in the camps and looked to the problem of sustaining our men for lengthy periods in jungle terrain.

As a general rule of thumb, each state would start its own nucleus of one or two guerrilla platoons. Whether they would field one or two units, and the size of the units, depended essentially on the financial standing of the respective state committees. In essence, each state committee would be required to fund the operation of its own guerrilla force. Platoon strengths would vary between 20 and 30 men, depending on the tasks they were required to perform. The Johore, Selangor, and Perak state committees were each financially capable of fielding two platoons. The other states started with one guerrilla unit each.

At the same time, we had to work out how we would withdraw our civilian cadres from the towns and cities to the rural areas. During the Japanese occupation we managed to exert complete control over all jungle fringe squatter areas. While the cadres worked for the Party in the squatter villages, they would also function as farm labourers which provided cover for their real activities and assistance to the villagers. This was the environment where the bulk of our civilian operatives would lie low.

Where we were operating open front organisations in population centres, as well as newspapers, printing presses and the like, we arranged to retain skeleton office staff. Our instructions were for offices to function with one or two people while the remainder withdrew from view and went underground to await any suppressive action by the government.

Erroneously, as it happened, we estimated we still had several months up our sleeves before the British made their move. Without completing deliberations on the preparatory steps for warfare, we scheduled another gathering in August, this time in Johore Bahru. This would be to finalise matters. We anticipated that if the British were going to launch a concerted suppression effort against the CPM, the earliest this would materialise would be September.

We devised one fall-back position should our calculations on British action be in error. If they were to launch full-scale repressive measures against us in the interim, the next meeting would be at my headquarters rather than in Johore Bahru. We considered the state of Pahang as offering the best conditions for this requirement. Not only did it have vast jungle areas devoid of population, but geographically it was ideally positioned in the heart of the Malayan peninsula. I was given the task of moving to Pahang and overseeing the setting up of our key jungle base.

Chapter 14

Sungei Siput, the Emergency declaration and 20 seconds that saved me

The task of establishing a permanent jungle headquarters forced me to take urgent stock of Central Committee funding. The various state committees seemed financially strong enough to support the guerrilla actions we envisaged. But Central Committee resources had dropped to around $10,000. This was hopelessly inadequate for setting up a focal point for operations. We needed a place where our top political and military planners could function and inter-relate. This, we hoped, would ensure close coordination of Party policies. It was a measure of our naivete that we had gone so far down the preparation track without first resolving vital issues associated with creating a continuing line of funds to sustain a headquarters.

In the immediate aftermath of our planning meeting in Johore, it occurred to me that a quick way of raising money might be to resurrect a tin mining joint-venture the CPM had entered into two years earlier with a well-known Chinese capitalist. I was obviously grasping at straws when I decided to call in the particularly big favour owing us by the businessman concerned. I figured a quick injection of, say, $20,000, would help enormously.

The mine was located about four miles north of Kampar. The miner was Lee Tong Ching. He had inherited the Tong Fatt Tin Mine from his father before the outbreak of the Pacific War and had run it quite successfully until the Japanese invasion. Thereafter, as the local economy came to a standstill, Tong Ching went broke. After the Japanese surrender, the family desperately needed cash to resume business. It coincided with the time our state committees, flush with sudden wealth from rubber dealings, were looking to investments.

I had come into close contact with Tong Ching's family during the occupation years. His elder brother, who was studying engineering in Shanghai when the Japanese invaded Manchuria, had quickly joined the Communist Party in China and become a guerrilla fighter there. When the Chinese communists learned he was the eldest son of a wealthy tin-mining family, he was sent back to Malaya to raise funds for the motherland party. He arrived in Kampar a few weeks before the Japanese invasion and was unable to escape back to China. Instead, he joined our movement and became one of our guerrilla commanders.

Tong Ching was the younger brother and, unlike his sibling, was English-educated. Following his local schooling, his father had arranged his marriage, then sent him packing to China to further his education. His new bride was made to remain behind in Kampar. There she would complain endlessly to anyone who would listen. Meanwhile, in China, Tong Ching paid little attention to his studies but clearly had a good time. He fancied himself a playboy. For all this, I knew him to be a physically brave man. During the Japanese invasion, he had been a member of the local ARP. When most of the other capitalists were high-tailing it out of Kampar as British troops endeavoured to establish a major defence position there against the Japanese advance, Tong Ching opted to stand firm. He placed himself at great risk and did his best to aid the defenders. Tong Ching was an ardent capitalist and I, a committed communist – still, we became quite good friends.

As a result of my representations on Tong Ching's behalf in 1946, the Perak state committee agreed to a joint venture between the Party and the mining company. The CPM would fund the restoration of his mine to the tune of $50,000 in return for a percentage of the profits thereafter. With the Party's generous infusion of capital, engineers and mine workers quickly had the machinery operating again. As luck would have it, within weeks of resuming work, they struck a particularly rich tin deposit. My Party comrades, who subsequently learned of this story, would inevitably rib me that I should have, on the spot, dropped politics and gone into the tin business! There was never a chance of that.

With our cash injection, Tong Ching became enormously wealthy once again, this time almost overnight. However, he failed to share the mine's profits with the Party as he had originally agreed to do. As we were engaged with more immediate problems amid the post-war chaos, the job of securing our rightful returns became shelved for the time being. We did, however, keep track of the mine's progress – an easy matter as several of our members were workers on site. The comrades regularly fed us information on the business activities and so we had very precise knowledge of the mine's financial situation.

When confronted with the facts as we knew them, Tong Chin denied the mine was making profits. He even showed a senior CPM official a set of financial records to support his claims that the mine was yet to break even. These were, of course, bogus records. We had information on how, when and why they had been drawn up. After some pressure by the Party, Tong Ching agreed to have two party officials attached to the mine's executive staff. Our representatives had hardly begun work when we learned that the capitalist was attempting to isolate them from the important day-to-day routine of the company.

Eventually, a full report on Tong Ching's intransigence reached me. I must say I was most surprised to learn of his attitude towards those who had helped him so trustingly in his hour of need. I decided it was time for a personal showdown. I went up to Sitiawan for the 1948 Chinese New Year celebrations with my parents and family. As these drew to a close, I headed for Kampar and the confrontation the Party had arranged for me with my supposed tin-miner partner. In the company of Ai Ker and another leading Perak CPM official, Ah Hai, I visited Tong Ching who continued insisting the company was not profitable. He showed me the doctored accounts to substantiate his claims.

After some persuasion, the capitalist saw reason and admitted that, in fact, the mine was now making money and could afford to pay the Party at a rate of 50 per cent of net profits from mid-year onwards. It seemed like a fair solution and, before departing, I arranged to return in June to collect the first installment of the profit split.

*   *   *   *   *

As arranged, and again in the company of comrades Ai Ker and Ah Hai, I arrived in Kampar on the weekend of June 12-13. For security reasons, Ai Ker and Ah Hai were billeted at the mine workers' quarters some distance away from Tong Ching's residence.

I was a reluctant guest at Tong Ching's house which was a sprawling hilltop bungalow outside Kampar. Party needs forced me to bide my time amid capitalist opulence as the money was not immediately available. I stayed in the bungalow's guest quarters while the funds were supposedly being gathered. I was uneasy about these arrangements. Time was pressing. I had no intention of remaining in Perak. My primary objective was to rendezvous in northern Johore with some of my Central Committee comrades – among them Siao Chang – and with them head off to Pahang to establish our headquarters. But the funds were essential to the task at hand and I felt quite certain Tong Ching would, this time, produce them as promised.

With a deep and nagging impatience I contemplated my host's swimming pool. I sat reading in the capacious lounge area as an army of servants padded about attending to their seemingly endless chores. Stifled by inactivity, I would every now and then wander about the immaculate grounds which included a private rose garden. A driveway swept in a broad arc from the roadway behind the bungalow, past the pool, between neat lawn landscapes and around to the main front entrance.

Still, the creature comforts surrounding me could not lull me into complacency. The CPM underground life I had chosen to lead, along with my experiences as a guerrilla, ensured that my sense for the unfamiliar or threatening remained sharp.

Wednesday, June 16, was an eventless day at the Lee bungalow. Over morning coffee I read the latest editions of the *Sin Chew Jit Poh* and *The Straits Times*. News columns told of Commissioner General Malcolm MacDonald's return to Singapore from China the previous day. In Nanking he had held discussions with Generalissimo Chiang Kai Shek.

The Straits Times' front page lead story spoke of Britain's 'grave concern' over reports from Rangoon that Burma was considering swinging towards Soviet-led communism. An eight-line news filler from its Bangkok correspondent reported: *'The first press bulletin issued by the Soviet Legation here appeared today. Daily publication of the eight-page bulletin is expected. Russian films will be shown here soon.'*

I read both papers from cover to cover. There was nothing else to do. Once again I had been left alone in the huge home with the servants. Before departing that morning, Tong Ching assured me that the Party's share of profits would soon be in my hands. In fact, he said, that very evening he had arranged an important meeting and would probably return with the money. Throughout the day I looked forward to my exit from the hilltop residence. And what an exit it would turn out to be!

In expectation of being able to wrap-up my finance-gathering mission within 24 hours, I also mulled over my delayed move to Pahang and the best way of allocating the funds once we got there. The task ahead was clear. I was required to activate a jungle point from where all our movement's plans and decisions of the past three months could be orchestrated into a sustainable, countrywide armed revolution.

*   *   *   *   *

Quite unbeknown to me, as I deliberated from the comfort of a rattan lounge chair on Tong Ching's verandah, the very worst possible scenario I could have envisaged was being enacted by Party elements barely 40 miles north of where I sat.

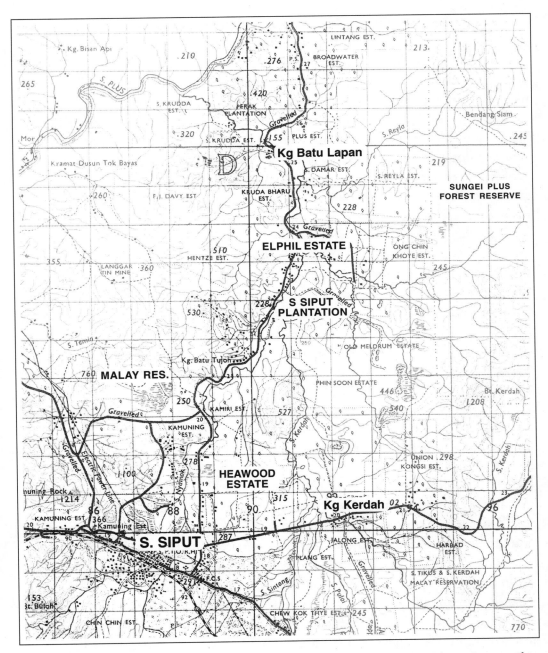

A map of the period showing the locations of the Elphil and Sungei Siput plantations on the Lintang road, north of Sungei Siput township.

At 8.30 am, three comrades cycled up to the main gate of the Elphil Estate, on the Lintang road, some seven miles from Sungei Siput township. There, the 50 year-old English estate manager, Arthur Walker, who had spent the occupation years incarcerated in Changi Jail, was engrossed in last-minute paperwork. He and his wife were scheduled to depart for the United Kingdom on home leave the following week. The three comrades, all Chinese, pushed open the door leading to Walker's room. One greeted him in Malay: 'Tabek Tuan' (Good day, sir). As Walker's dog barked in protest at the intrusion, the estate manager returned the greeting: 'Good morning.' Moments later, the comrades fired at point-blank range, shooting Walker through the head and chest. As swiftly as they had arrived, the men departed on their bicycles, leaving the estate manager slumped and dying on the floor, his safe keys beside him. Curiously, the estate safe remained untouched.

Thirty minutes later, at the Sungei Siput Estate, less than two miles back down the Lintang road, a separate guerrilla unit, this time comprising 12 comrades, one armed with a Tommy gun, besieged the main plantation office. The manager, 55 year-old John Allison and his 21 year-old assistant, Ian Christian, had just begun the day's work. Christian, a former Gurkha officer, was newly arrived in Malaya and due to be transferred the next day to the Kantan Estate, several miles to the south near Ipoh. It was to be a promotion to acting estate manager for the fledgling planter.

This second attack, obviously coordinated with the Elphil raid, was better planned and more deliberate. Allison and Christian were quickly immobilized with their hands tied behind their backs. One of the comrades discovered a set of keys on Allison. The two estate safes were opened and $1,000 in cash was taken. With their hands still bound, the two planters, in full view of office staff, were frog-marched to a nearby bungalow as the guerrillas searched for weapons. Both were then led back to the verandah. There, again in full view of workers, they were bound to separate chairs and executed with repeated bursts from the Tommy gun.

Rather than dispersing hurriedly, the invading force found time to ransack a plantation store for kerosene. This they liberally splashed throughout a smokehouse stocked with 56,000 pounds of rubber packed and ready for shipment. In addition, the smokehouse contained a further two tons of loose rubber. The comrades torched the rubber stocks which burned fiercely, sending up dense black smoke. Before cycling off, the Malay-speaking leader of the raiding party calmly told the estate's chief clerk: 'We are out only for European strikebreakers.'

Local newspapers reported that remnants of the rubber stock were still smouldering 36 hours later.

On the same day as the Sungei Siput raids, other CPM killer squads were in action. They executed a Kuomintang foreman on the Senai Estate, 15 miles north of Johore Bahru and a Chinese contractor on a plantation near Taiping. These additional actions were, of course, fully in line with the Central Committee directive we had issued in Singapore on dealing with strikebreakers.

Personally, I have always felt very sorry for the young assistant estate manager, Ian Christian. Only on probation and new in the country, he could never have been considered someone with a history of activities harmful to our movement. Walker and Allison, were in a different category altogether. They had histories of imposing harsh and bullying treatment on the workers who had no legal redress and no way of achieving any form of justice other than through strike action. As long as the two senior planters had the support of the colonial administration and all the corrupt departments that functioned therein, and as long as their use of thugs to break-up strike action was ignored by the authorities, they would have maintained their highhanded ways. From a revolutionary's point of view at the time, I saw no validity in the killing of Christian. The deaths of the other two were acceptable.

* * * * *

Although I was only 40 miles away from the Sungei Siput raids, I knew nothing about them as I settled back that day to await the return of Tong Ching. This was 1948 – long before CNN, Channel News Asia, the internet and instant information. If Radio Malaya had mentioned the events during the day, I had missed the broadcasts. Tong Ching came home for an early evening meal and mentioned nothing. At around 6.30 pm, he left purportedly for the meeting he had spoken about earlier in the day.

It was half-light and a still tropical evening. I was in the front room of the bungalow when I first heard the rumbling of approaching vehicles negotiating the steep rise along the road to the rear of the property. I listened closely to the revving engines. There were two vehicles. Both lorries. I sensed they could only be military or police. They couldn't be from the mine. It had closed for the day. Danger. In a flash I considered gathering my belongings from the guest room. My passport. Some important Party documents. Two suits I had brought back from Hong Kong and had

The entrance to the Elphil Plantation today is little changed from June 16, 1948, when three armed comrades cycled up to launch their fateful raid which resulted in the death of English estate manager, Arthur Walker. A plaque proclaims it an historical site.

A new administrative unit stands on the site of Walker's old office and can be seen in this photo, remarkably close to the roadway, beyond the company signboard. Quite clearly this raid, which began at 8.30 am, was coordinated with the Sungei Siput plantation attack some 30 minutes later and only a mile and a half away back down the Lintang road.

Like the Elphil entrance, the dirt road leading into the modern Sungei Siput plantation has been left almost unchanged by the passage of years. It was down this track that 12 determined comrades, one armed with a Tommy gun, rode their bicycles to settle what they believed was their score with the plantation's strike breaking management.

(Left) The old Sungei Siput office building and verandah where expatriate English plantation manager, John Allison, and his newly arrived 21-year-old assistant, Ian Christian, were trussed up and executed with bursts of Tommy gun fire.

(Right) The old timber and corrugated iron office building has been demolished but its concrete foundations remain and today provide handy parking for staff motorbikes. Beyond the foundations is the plantation's new administrative unit. Pictured behind the mini-bus is the replacement smokehouse constructed on the site of the one torched by the 1948 raiding party.

meant to leave in Sitiawan, but had forgotten. There was no time. The switch in engine noise told me the two lorries had reached the crest of the hill behind and were approaching the bungalow's main gate.

I ran through the front entrance, across the verandah, over the driveway and into a section of shrubbery immediately opposite. From there I glanced back along the driveway to see two pairs of dimmed headlights swing in through the front gate. Police. Still hidden by the shrubbery, I watched the lorries pull up outside the main door. Two European police officers alighted from the cabins as a number of Malay constables tumbled from each of the canvas-covered rear sections. To a man, all rushed inside the bungalow.

Behind me lay the rose garden. Beyond this was a decorative stone wall. I threaded my way through the rose bushes and in the dim light spotted a jambu tree conveniently abutting the wall. I saw my chance and went for it. I climbed the tree, negotiated the wall and dropped down to the safety of the other side. I was in rough terrain. Rolling mounds of tin-tailings offered little cover beyond the wall. I moved some distance away and by now the blackness of the night had settled protectively around me. In the distance I could hear orders being shouted to the police party rummaging through the bungalow.

I decided to wait until early morning light before making my next move. I knew an old retired servant woman from the Tong Ching household lived in a wooden hut some distance down the road. If I could get there, I would be safe. I could rely on her assistance.

Through the old lady, whose son worked in the mine, I soon learned that my host, Tong Ching, had been arrested. I was also able to establish that Ai Ker and Ah Hai, had, like myself, narrowly escaped a police raid on the mine workers' quarters. Ah Hai's younger sister, a washer in the mine, came to inform me that her brother was hiding out in Ipoh with another brother. Ah Hai had left word that I should try and join him there. While still in the old lady's hut the following day, I was able to read copies of the *Nanyang Siang Pau* and *Sin Chew Jit Poh* newspapers carrying accounts of the government's swift reaction to the Sungei Siput raids. Within hours the colonials had declared a 'State of Emergency' in several districts of Perak and Johore states.

Quite clearly, I was in a most precarious position. The newspapers would say the Sungei Siput attacks had been the CPM's open declaration of war against the British. That was ridiculous and my position at this time fully attested to the fact.

If I, as leader of the CPM, had sanctioned the Party's declaration of war against Britain on June 16, 1948, what was I doing, 24 hours later, stuck in an old woman's hut? A raid from which I had barely escaped had resulted in my passport being seized. I was totally isolated from any connection with the Party apparatus. I was alone, devoid of security escort and in an area over which a state of emergency had been clamped.

My one chance of survival was to get to Ipoh and re-establish connection with the comrades. It was my good fortune to have Ah Hai's brave sister volunteer to accompany me. We posed as a young Chinese couple visiting relatives. But how were we to travel without drawing attention to ourselves? There seemed to be no other way than taking public transport. We boarded the Kampar to Ipoh bus for the 25-mile journey north.

It was during this trip that I saw for myself the degree to which the British authorities were imposing their restrictions. Two-thirds of the way along the route, as the bus neared Gopeng, we lurched to a sudden stop. Looking out the window I saw a police roadblock. Uniformed armed men boarded the bus and walked slowly back and forth down the aisle looking at faces. I remembered my passport tucked into the inner pocket of one of my Hong Kong suits and was convinced my number was up.

The scrutiny felt interminable while my companion and I struggled to be convincing as a young couple en route to a family reunion. To our immense relief the police, satisfied the bus was clean, ordered the driver to move on. Clearly, my passport, with its comparatively recent photograph of Ong Boon Hua, had yet to be linked to its owner's alias, Chin Peng.

In the days to come I had mental images of a bright young constable, on his day off, proudly strutting down the main street of Kampar in one of my only two suits. Along with these images went the hope that in order to appropriate the suit for himself, the young constable had quietly disposed of my passport. I have never been able to establish the truth of what happened to my belongings seized that night at the tin miner's bungalow. I have certainly tried. During our 'peace talks' negotiations in the late 1980s, I asked Malaysian Special Branch representatives if the authorities had recognised how close they had come to sealing my fate in the very first hours of the Emergency. I also enquired whether anyone had recognised my passport and what might have become of it. No one could provide any answers. The significance of these events appeared to escape them. I reminded myself that I was speaking with second generation officers.

Immediately following the State of Emergency declaration, colonial security authorities moved to close down all CPM offices and related operations throughout both Malaya and Singapore. The above photographs were taken during the police raid to close down our Queen street office in Singapore. This happened to be the location of my last formal 'open' headquarters. The top photo shows a senior officer instructing a young constable to deface our street-side noticeboard that carried details of what we termed the CPM's Democratic Programme. The bottom photo shows the gathering crowd outside the Queen street building shortly after it had been sealed.

At Ipoh, Ah Hai's sister helped me contact her two brothers and, in turn, they assisted me to re-establish myself within the Party proper. I settled in a hide-out in an undeveloped area on the edge of town. There, for the first time since I fled Tong Ching's bungalow, I was able to analyse the momentous developments triggered by the Sungei Siput killings.

Local daily newspapers comprised my primary source of information although comrades visited me from time to time bringing added details and interpretations from the local Party committee. The initially limited State of Emergency had been expanded to cover all areas of Perak and Johore and then clamped, within the following 24 hours, over the entire peninsula.

Our various Party offices, together with the Kuala Lumpur premises of our daily newspaper, the *Min Sheng Pau* (Voice of the People), had been raided and sealed. Special police reinforcements had been rushed to strategic locations throughout Perak. Authorities were pinning the murders of the three Sungei Siput planters on a specific CPM 'killer squad' led by a man identified as Lui Tong Tai. Measures were underway to ensure special escorts for all European estate managers across Perak. At the same time, all local leave for police had been cancelled and European police officers vacationing in the United Kingdom had been ordered to return immediately by air to their Malayan postings.

At 2 am on Monday, June 21, police launched a peninsula-wide coordinated swoop on houses, estates, mines and offices suspected of harbouring CPM members. Among the targets were the offices of our MPAJA Old Comrades' Association in Osborne road, Ipoh, not far from where I was hiding. For all the publicity received by this concerted police action, the results seemed most limited and reports reaching me confirmed this. On the other hand, there were accounts of serious disruption of plantation activities, the resignation of terrified planters, estates left without managers and deserted bungalows. The Station Hotel in Ipoh was packed to capacity with plantation managers and their families.

The Straits Times, in a story from a Special Staff Correspondent in Ipoh, claimed the CPM had won the opening rounds of what it termed the 'Perak battle'. It had, the correspondent said, become a war of nerves. The newspaper credited the successes thus far to 'communist murder gangs'.

I would like to recall, as an historical footnote, a story which appeared alongside *The Straits Times'* front page account of the Sungei Siput killings. Headed 'Victims of the gunmen', it listed the names and occupations of those who had been killed in industrial or political murders by Chinese gunmen on estates in Malaya from the beginning of May, 1948, up to June 16. With the exception of an estate worker mistaken for his contractor brother, all nine other liquidations on the list would have fallen under the Party's directive issued from Singapore targeting strikebreakers and, in particular, strikebreaking contractors.

I do this, not in any way to seek justification, but rather to establish that, at this stage of the struggle, neither I, nor the Central Committee, had ordered the killing of European planters. Despite speculation at the time and since, the CPM at no point in the Emergency ever drew up a planters' hit list. Indeed, if I had had my way, the killings at Sungei Siput would never have taken place. They resulted from over-enthusiasm for revenge at the local level coupled with a serious lack of command control at the state level.

Over the years, academics and historians have suggested that the killings gained us the initial advantage. In reality, the events at Sungei Siput amounted to a serious mistake on our part. The executions pre-empted our plans and undermined our efforts to withdraw our cadres into a well-organised underground network and our guerrilla army to secret jungle bases. In addition, they disrupted our moves to consolidate essential links with our Min Yuen civilian supporters. Basic to our projections was the need to create a large element of self-sufficiency for both civilian and military arms of the revolutionary movement before the armed rebellion began. We had fully expected it would be the British who triggered the action by launching a full-scale suppression of our movement. But Sungei Siput dashed any hope of us achieving a level of self-sufficiency within our ranks before the war began. We were forced at the outset onto the defensive and it would take some time before we could seize the initiative.

Warfare, like life itself, is full of might-have-beens. I have sometimes reflected on how things would have turned out had I not been 20 seconds ahead of the raiding party at the Kampar bungalow. Unquestionably, I would have had a very brief Emergency indeed. Quite certainly, the British would have sent me to the gallows. Many might speculate that this turn of events would have seen the CPM crumble and the rapid end of the Emergency. I disagree. It would have just been the end of Ong Boon Hua, alias Chin Peng. My deputy, Yeung Kuo, would have taken over. With weapons in hand, the movement would have lived. The struggle would have gone on.

Chapter 15

The Batang Kali massacre and British propaganda

We gave the matter of locating our CPM base headquarters a great deal of thought for obvious reasons. At first we considered locating somewhere in southern Johore so that we might be near the population centre of Singapore. However, we eventually rejected this idea after reviewing the security risks it would involve. We then thought of situating ourselves in the Labis-Segamat area of northern Johore with the ultimate aim of moving into central Pahang which offered such conveniently isolated jungle prospects. In the end, it was the rush of events at the outset of the Emergency that would determine the details of our strategy and the position of the nerve centre for our campaign.

The original plan had been for me, after collecting our tin-mining profits from the Kampar capitalist, to move back to Labis and call a final meeting of the Central Committee. There we had hoped to conclude arrangements and directives for the switch to armed struggle. In fact, some of our key men, in expectation of these developments, had already moved to a temporary base in Johore.

As it turned out, Yeung Kuo, had a similar narrow escape from capture to mine and at around the same time. Although he had moved permanently to Selangor by this stage, he had gone back to Penang in mid-June to visit his wife and newly-born daughter. As soon as he heard the State of Emergency had been declared in Sungei Siput, he felt it best to leave his in-laws' Georgetown house and go into hiding nearby. The police raided his in-laws' residence and arrested Yeung Kuo's wife. She was subsequently banished to China.

Yeung Kuo decided to make for Selangor by train. He reached Kuala Lumpur safely and headed for the Ampang area of the capital to re-establish connections with the local comrades. As he had spent so much time in Kuala Lumpur during the Japanese occupation and in the months leading to the Emergency, he was a well-recognised figure there, particularly as far as the Special Branch was concerned. But, in the confusion, he found he could move quite freely at this tense time.

For all their early ineptitude, the police, in the first few days of the Emergency, managed to organise two arrests that we considered potentially very damaging to our revolutionary prospects. The first we quickly neutralised. The second would present consequences with which we would have to live for nearly a decade.

On the very eve of the Emergency, 30 year-old Wang Li, a Pahang state committee member, was secretly detained and began collaborating with the British. When we were discussing preparations for armed struggle he had requested a transfer to Perak. Wang Li had been an AJA leader in the state's Pusing tin mining region during the Japanese occupation. It was his loyal service with our forces that had earned him promotion to the state body. Wang Li claimed his knowledge of the Pusing area would be valuable to the Party once our guerrilla activities against the British got underway.

We granted his wish and posted him to a jungle camp near Pusing. Soon after he arrived, camp comrades noticed Wang Li behaving rather strangely. Everywhere he went he seemed to be drawing maps, taking notes and gathering information to the understandable consternation of his subordinates. Eventually, the comrades reported their suspicions to the Central Committee member assigned to that area. Wang Li was placed under surveillance and eventually a message he was sending from the camp, hidden in clothing, was intercepted. He was quickly arrested and placed on trial. In the face of firm evidence of his collaboration with the enemy, Wang Li admitted his guilt.

The Central Committee member heading the jungle court, the same man who had received the original complaints against the accused, returned a verdict of guilty and a sentence of death. Wang Li was immediately taken away and shot. The matter was considered closed.

The second early arrest by the British proved far more problematic for the CPM. Soon after the declaration of Emergency, Chen Yong, the one-time senior CPM official to whom we had given a second chance, was taken into custody by Special Branch investigators. He quickly collaborated with them. For several years Chen Yong would represent the most senior member of the CPM the British had under their control. After all, he had been a state committee member, then a Central Committee member, even a member of the five-man Politburo. Now he was assisting in the interrogation of captured comrades. So useful did he become that the British arranged to pay him a regular wage. In addition to his interrogation work, he was also utilised in persuading detained comrades to collaborate with, and become agents for, the government.

Chen Yong's defection – for that is what it soon became – was a very bad situation for us. Far beyond his help with interrogations and the turning of captives into hired informers, he was able to provide the British with vital psychological profiles of all those in the CPM hierarchy. Furthermore, his insight into our separate personalities would have enabled the enemy to make valuable assessments of our likely policies and reactions. These could then be used as the basis of contingency planning.

Our former Politburo member functioned for the Special Branch for almost 10 years. I had misread Chen Yong's character. I placed too much importance on the fact that I had once served as his junior. I was convinced a basic loyalty had developed between us. I understood his commitment to direct involvement with the CPM had waned. But still I counted on his self-respect and moral fortitude.

Time would gradually diminish Chen Yong's usefulness to the Special Branch. Then, suddenly, he disappeared. We eventually learned, through our contacts, that the authorities had arranged for the renegade and his family to migrate to Australia. He settled there along with his wife, son and daughter. He's still alive and living under an assumed name in a Melbourne suburb.

*   *   *   *   *

The planning that had taken place at the May meeting in northern Johore envisaged that our guerrillas would start launching major attacks against British targets in September of 1948. Under these circumstances we predicted an Emergency-like situation would be enforced immediately thereafter. Specifically, we were counting on the three extra months – July to September – to prepare the withdrawal of our cadres and the dispersal of our guerrillas to jungle camps. This preparatory period was an important aspect of the general logic behind our idea of creating jungle guerrilla nuclei.

We had predicted strong British military responses to our opening salvos. But, with adequate preparation, we felt confident we would be capable of out-manoeuvring the enemy counter-attack. All our experience confirmed revolutionary warfare theory that guerrilla forces held supreme battlefield advantages when it came to determining the time and location of attacks and the intensity of following actions. Where the enemy was weakest, the guerrillas would strike. When the enemy massed in strength, the guerrillas would withdraw to the jungle terrain they had long mastered. We were therefore confident we would not only control the initial fighting, but also be able to expand the jungle areas we had claimed.

We had about 3,000 weapons ready for dispersal when we were making our plans. We had to take into account the fact that several of our main dumps had been discovered by the British in the three years since the Japanese surrender. We lost these dumps, not because of Lai Te's treachery at the top, but because of betrayals by guerrilla guards entrusted with arms dump security. We saw major caches seized in Trengganu, north Kedah, the Rawang and Batu Caves regions of Selangor and in the Sitiawan area of Perak.

As our intentions were to operate the early phase of armed struggle on a state-by-state basis, we had to think in terms of nine separate insurgencies all running at the same time. We believed that in the confusion to follow, we would be able to secure important initial battlefield advantages. The next phase, as we saw it, would require our army to revert to an overall strategy in which two jungle base areas would play critical roles. But the details of this switch in tactics had still to be finalised when the British declared the Emergency.

Pre-empted by our own actions at Sungei Siput, the plans we had carefully laid were thrown into disarray. Still, I felt it was unreasonable to start repudiating my comrades. To begin with, I had to rely primarily on enemy newspaper reports for my battlefield assessments. These arrived daily and were generally slanted in the Government's favour. Our own reports were taking up to a month to reach me. There was no point in demanding self-criticism from my troops based mainly on enemy information. Rather than dwell on what had happened, I thought it best to try and make sense of the chaos and from there establish fresh perspectives recognising that we had been caught severely wrong-footed.

For all my early efforts to re-establish order, however, the tumult persisted through the rest of 1948. Individual state committees and their military commanders, seemingly emboldened by the spectacular newspaper headlines they were creating, and undoubtedly provoked by the increasing intensity of British suppressive measures, couldn't resist pressing the attacks. All this was underway without any reference whatever to me or the Central Committee.

Of course, the turmoil brought some successes. At dawn on July 2, a 50-strong guerrilla force launched the biggest communist attack of the then two-week old Emergency when they invaded Kulai village, just 20 miles out of Johore Bahru at the start of the main road to Kuala Lumpur. Three Chinese civilians were accidentally caught in indiscriminate firing of Tommy and Sten guns, rifles and pistols. A few signs declaring 'Down with British Imperialism' were pasted about village walls. This earned prominent headlines undoubtedly favourable to our cause. Little else of substance was achieved, however. No weapons or ammunition were seized and these were our main requirements. From my point of view, the Kulai raid, for all its daring, amounted to wasted adventurism. No guerrilla unit, at this stage of the war, should have been attempting action of this nature so close to the enemy's military strong-points in Singapore.

Ten days later, at Batu Arang, in Selangor, our local commander demonstrated the sort of result we could expect if we followed recognised guerrilla tactics and chose our targets carefully, planned the action meticulously and attacked and withdrew with the element of surprise always on our side.

We had gathered a force of some 100 guerrillas for the Batu Arang initiative. The principal target was Malaya's only coal mine located there. At 7.00 am on July 12, coordinated raids were directed against the mine itself, associated buildings, the local police station and the nearby railway station. We isolated Batu Arang by severing all telephone lines. We employed road ambushes against the possible introduction of counter attacking government forces. We even managed to seize a train. In addition, an accompanying assassination squad sought out five local Chinese, identified as strikebreakers, and summarily executed them all.

More than two weeks later, the British Army in Kuala Lumpur claimed a great military success at Batu Arang. It had taken the anti-insurgency forces 18 days to discover the nearby jungle camp from which we had made our original attack on the mine. The army claimed to have killed 22 insurgents and captured another 47, many of whom were said to be badly wounded.

A week earlier, however, Sir Alec Newboult, then deputising for High Commissioner Gent who had been recalled to London, made a more realistic evaluation of our Batu Arang raid. During an evening broadcast over Radio Malaya, he observed: 'We have learned many lessons from Batu Arang and have taken what steps we can to avoid a repetition, but let us face the fact that in this particular type of warfare we are very much open to attack.' Admitting that the coal mine had been insufficiently protected, Newboult said that a disturbing feature of the event was that 'such an attack could be planned and organised without one breath of information coming to the ears of the police.' Future targets, he predicted, would not be well-defended places as the CPM's immediate purpose was to discredit and disorganise the government machine rather than inflict material losses.

The Deputy High Commissioner asserted that our plan of attack was becoming clear. We had launched our campaign under the guise of industrial unrest and had failed. We had then switched tactics and started targeting the lives of management and estate employees, both European and Chinese. Now, according to Newboult, we were entering the third phase and directing our attacks on police stations and important industrial sites like Batu Arang. If the insurgents succeeded at this stage, he predicted, public morale would weaken. 'Where it will next be directed, we do not know, but we can be sure that it will be directed with ruthlessness and cunning.'

As it happened, I did not hear this particular broadcast and only saw press reports about it several days later. It was as though I was reading about another war. The cunning, foresight and planning abilities attributed to us by the highest British colonial official in the land were embarrassingly complimentary. I only wished they were true! If Newboult didn't know where the guerrillas would strike next he would undoubtedly have been immensely relieved to learn that neither did I.

As insurgency leader, I was, at this point, still hiding out in Ipoh, isolated from my senior colleagues and devoid of any central headquarters. The daily press was my main, if not only, source of battle reports. To issue day-to-day orders was an impossibility. It would be another two months before we were able to establish a secret courier network and even then it would take weeks for messages to be delivered.

A month to the day after the British declared the Emergency, I lost Liew Yao, unquestionably one of my best military commanders. He was killed in a police raid on a jungle fringe hideout a mile north of the Selangor township of Kajang. Liew Yao had been the third man in the MPAJA's High Command, the Central Military Committee proclaimed at the last minute by Lai Te in August, 1945. The following June, he had led the MPAJA contingent in the Victory Parade through London.

Compounding the loss of Liew Yao was my continuing struggle to establish reliable contact with fellow Central Committee members – particularly Yeung Kuo – and with them develop a fundamental strategic approach determined by battlefield realities. Clearly, our original intention to prosecute the war on a state-by-state basis would not work, even for a short period. The concept of having state committees responsible for military planning in their specific areas and local commanders given wide authority to pick targets, was far too unwieldy to be workable. It was intended to cause confusion to our enemy. Regrettably, it was causing just as much to ourselves. We needed to introduce much stronger lines of command control and there had to be a recognised element of centralised authority if we were to re-establish direction.

Aware of my requirements to leave Ipoh as soon as possible, the Perak state committee made arrangements for my onward journey to Ayer Kuning, south of Kampar. This meant I had to travel through the area where I had narrowly escaped

Part of the MPAJA contingent to London's Victory Parade celebrations in 1946, photographed outside their tent accommodations in Kensington Gardens.

(Front row, left to right.) **Chou Yang Pin**, commander 1st Regiment. Chou became a Special Branch agent during the Emergency; **Chen Tien**, commander 4th Regiment, South Johore.

(Back row, left to right.) **Wang Ching**, commander 6th Regiment, West Pahang; **Sun Wen Chin**, commander 7th Regiment, East Pahang/Kuantan area; **Liao Wei Chung**, alias Colonel Itu, commander 5th Regiment, Perak, arrested at the beginning of the Emergency and banished to China where he died in the late 1980s; **Liew Yao**, third member of the CPM's 3-man Central Military Committee and also a state committee member for Selangor; **Deng Fuk Lung**, commander 2nd Regiment, Negri Sembilan.

the police raid at Lee Tong Ching's residence two months earlier. The plan was for me to join our 60-strong guerrilla force around Ayer Kuning. These jungle fighters would then become my personal security unit. Ayer Kuning and the whole surrounding rural area had been one of our most reliable strongholds since the Japanese occupation days. Unlike my unceremonious departure from Kampar, I would not be taking public transport this time. Instead, I would ride to war from Ipoh hidden in the back of a biscuit delivery van. The driver was a Party member.

At Ayer Kuning, my guerrilla group had already set up a camp for themselves in swampy ground close to the Sungei Manik where, in pre-war days, the British had introduced a padi planting scheme with an extensive irrigation system. An irrigation ditch separated Malay rice farmers from a Chinese squatter community. Members of the Perak state committee were now living among these squatters. Our camp abutted the squatter shacks. Soon after my arrival, I decided to hold a meeting of the state body as any gathering of my Central comrades was clearly out of the question.

At the earlier southern Johore discussions, general plans had us locating one of our two main military base areas in the northern half of the peninsula and the other in the south. Our intended war headquarters would be close to, but separate from, the southern main base. The overall concept, discussed and approved by the Central Committee, was based loosely on our anti-Japanese war experiences. At this point we were still discussing a military programme with its focus in Perak. Still undecided were the exact geographical sites for our two general base areas. Nor had we reached any conclusions on the numbers of guerrillas to be attached to each. I was hoping the Ayer Kuning deliberations would at least firm up details for the northern base which I anticipated would involve a battalion-sized force of some 500 men.

It was mid-August. By now we had received from Ah Dian an analysis of future battle strategy based on Mao's theories of guerrilla warfare. This had already been endorsed by Yeung Kuo. We chose for our meeting venue a squatter's hut well concealed in high *lalang* and bush country and located near the rear of the Ayer Kuning camp. The obvious approach route for any attacking force was from the main north-south trunk road close to the front of the camp. Sentries had been posted between the camp and the road as a precaution against British troops carrying out search operations.

I am now sure the anti-insurgent forces had been informed of my presence because in the middle of our meeting, RAF Spitfires swooped out of the morning sky and began strafing runs. Intermittently, the strafing would stop and a lumbering

Dakota would drone overhead, flying in circles until the Spitfires returned. While the target was obviously the camp, cannon fire also tore into the squatter huts, killing three civilians and wounding several others.

Five of us were involved in the meeting and each was accompanied by a personal bodyguard. The main guerrilla force remained some distance away in the camp proper. We had mistakenly felt the security arrangements were sufficient. As soon as the first strafing runs began, all five of us, along with our bodyguards, dashed out of the meeting hut and took up defensive positions, hidden by the bushes and *lalang*. To our dismay, our combined weapons strength amounted to only two Tommy guns and a few pistols. Within minutes we were stunned to see a British Army patrol advancing stealthily towards us from the rear. We lay there breathing slowly and as quietly as humanly possible.

A number of the British troops crept to within a few paces of my position. I could see their faces clearly. They were very white and very young. I am sure they were newly arrived in Malaya and terribly inexperienced. They would have been among the first batch of what later became known, aptly, as the 'virgin soldiers'. One of them appeared to be looking directly at me and for several heart-stopping seconds we seemed to be eyeballing each other. I felt he had surely spotted me. But then he looked away. Shortly thereafter the British withdrew some distance and began setting the brittle *lalang* alight. Briefly, there was the promise of a raging fire and the reduction of our cover to ashes. Through hand signals, we prepared for a withdrawal to the only alternative cover open to us – the nearby swamp. It was a desperate option. We would have been literally sitting-duck targets there. But, astonishingly, the sky suddenly darkened and unleashed a tropical rainstorm. This quickly doused, not only the flames, but apparently the enthusiasm of the young enemy as well. They soon moved off.

Straightaway, we abandoned that camp and by the following day had moved to a jungle redoubt. We continued reviewing Ah Dian's proposals for a new strategic approach and Yeung Kuo's supporting notes. These called for the establishment of liberated areas, whereas previously we had been thinking in terms of main base areas. We would have to revise drastically our earlier plans for Perak. Now we began exploring how best to extract the most experienced guerrillas from our Perak units and thereby form the northern main force. These men, all of them veterans of the Japanese occupation years, were to be assembled in the Cameron Highlands. They would then be moved to the position we had chosen in Kelantan.

Our meeting spanned the next 48 hours, by which time we had agreed on the best means of getting our Kelantan base operational and introducing the new guerrilla strength. I sent news of our decisions to Yeung Kuo in Selangor and gave him the responsibility of selecting the men and location for the southern liberated area. In order to achieve this, I suggested he convene a Central Committee meeting which I would try to attend. At the Ayer Kuning gathering's conclusion, I moved to the Cameron Highlands.

When first mooted, the liberated areas strategy had sparked considerable enthusiasm among senior comrades for the idea of launching a heavy attack on Gua Musang, in central Kelantan. So much so that Gua Musang, as a priority target, took on a life of its own in our minds. I came to view it as presenting undoubtedly the best opportunity for a major lunge at the British which, I hoped, might eventuate in our first liberated zone. My intention was to use guerrillas from our northern main force.

Yet another grand plan was to be pre-empted. Fierce fighting erupted in Gua Musang itself.

Situated some 100 miles south of Kuala Krai, the township had been a Party stronghold since the Japanese days. Our guerrilla unit there was well-armed, well-motivated and enthusiastically led by a commander who had established formidable credentials for himself in actions against the Japanese. The local comrades were seething when they received reports of peninsula-wide police raids and the large numbers of arrests of suspected communists. Without any official orders, the local Party committee decided to launch a major attack against the British.

Some 100 comrades, all experienced in jungle warfare and led by Commander Kim Siong, massed for the attack on Saturday, July 17. The primary target was the Gua Musang police station where the entire police staff was taken hostage. In effect, at this point, the guerrillas held the town. A five-day battle ensued as the British threw in reinforcements and counter-attacked. At the height of the action the comrades declared Gua Musang liberated. At the end of the fighting, the township reverted to government control. As such, it became the first and only liberated area we ever declared throughout the Emergency.

For all the immediate psychological advantages of this episode, the five-day liberation did nothing for our long-term cause.

*   *   *   *   *

Gua Musang, the only liberated zone claimed by the CPM throughout the Emergency years. The top photo shows the town's police compound which fell rapidly to our attacking force on Saturday, July 17, 1948. At this location our guerrilla forces held hostage the entire police staff and in effect the town fell under our control. This lasted five days. The lower photo depicts Gua Musang township as it is today.

At this point the British in colonial Malaya had their own pile of problems to sort out. Heading this was a grave leadership crisis. I genuinely felt sorry for the Federation's first High Commissioner, Sir Edward Gent. It was some days after the events before I heard about his abrupt recall to the United Kingdom and his untimely death on the afternoon of July 4 in a mid-air collision over Northolt Airport on the outskirts of London. The RAF York Transport taking him home had collided with a Swedish Skymaster passenger plane. Removed on the urgings of Commissioner General MacDonald, Gent was being made a scapegoat for the rising CPM activity in Malaya and the perceived failure of British countermeasures.[10]

More recently, I read declassified papers which reveal how a clearly guilt-ridden MacDonald moved to protect his position by distancing himself from any blame for the manner in which Gent was recalled.[11] However, his copious letters to London after Gent's death look decidedly hollow in the light of an earlier submission to Cabinet by the Colonial Secretary, Mr Arthur Creech-Jones. On July 1, 1948, while Gent was flying home, Creech-Jones told the Cabinet:

'In the last few days, the Commissioner General, Mr Malcolm MacDonald, has represented to me that the High Commissioner for the Federation of Malaya, Sir Edward Gent, has lost the confidence of the public in the Federation and the heads of other Services. He reported that in consequence, it was essential, in his view, to recall Sir Edward Gent to England at once and that he should not return to Malaya. His recommendation was made in such terms that I had no alternative but to agree to it at once, and Sir Edward Gent is now flying home. He is due in England on 3rd July. The Chief Secretary of the Federation of Malaya, Sir Alexander Newboult, is now acting as High Commissioner pending another appointment.'

My opinion of Gent differed greatly from the popular feelings of the day. I believe he was a very subtle colonial administrator. He bided his time and allowed us to expose ourselves. He had an acute sense for political manoeuvring. All along he knew that an Emergency would have to be imposed. But he wanted to be sure that when the clampdown came, it would be in answer to a perceived declaration of war against Britain by us. This, indeed, is exactly how it happened and we were the ones caught off balance.

Gent had, for months, suffered the jibes of European planters and mining executives who demanded a show of British force to confront our increasing activities within the unions. To them, Gent was weak and indecisive. I disagree. If the planters and miners had had their way, Britain would very early have been declaring open war

The nattily attired Malcolm MacDonald (right), arrives at Singapore's Changi military airstrip on the evening of May 21, 1946, to take up his posting as Commissioner General of Malaya. He is to be Singapore-based. He is shown here exchanging pleasantries with the Governor of the Malayan Union, Sir Edward Gent (left) who has flown in from Kuala Lumpur for the occasion. It will not take long before the manoeuvring, manipulative MacDonald is plotting to undermine the authority of Gent.

against the CPM. In the propaganda struggle we would have then immediately become the victims in the eyes of the masses. Conversely, Britain would have been the villain. For all our alleged excesses, we were solidly identified as struggling to better the lot of the exploited workers. Gent appreciated these political subtleties. These were beyond the comprehension of the planters and miners with their narrow colonial mentalities and innate racism. Unprovoked suppression would have played right into our hands and gained us valuable sympathy right across Malaya's racial spectrum. The political spin-off from this situation could well have been disastrous for Britain.

It should not be forgotten that, at the height of the Emergency, the planters and miners were demanding the authorities revert to military rule, measures similar to those employed by Britain in the previous century to suppress the Indian uprising. Unfortunately for us, the authorities ignored these demands. Had they acceded to them they would have walked into our trap.

Gent was replaced by Sir Henry Gurney, a 50 year-old highly experienced administrator who had previously served as the Chief Secretary of the Palestine Government.

*   *   *   *   *

From my temporary camp in the Cameron Highlands, I organised a North Malayan Bureau to control the northern states of Perak, Kedah and Penang. As the weeks passed, I pressed ahead with a campaign reassessment. Despite the events at Gua Musang – and perhaps because the ramifications of our ill-timed early attack there had yet to sink in – I still favoured the establishment of a liberated zone in Kelantan. Meanwhile, following the instructions I sent in August, Yeung Kuo had gone ahead and scheduled a Central Committee meeting for December. He had duly notified all participants.

As the meeting time approached, it became obvious I would be unable to reach the intended location – a jungle camp near the small Negri Sembilan village of Titi, situated in the tri-border region shared with Selangor and Pahang. By this time security precautions dictated that senior Party officials could not move in vehicles along public roads. The journey from Cameron Highlands to Negri Sembilan was too far to undertake on foot within the specified time. So I sent word to Yeung Kuo that he would have to step into the breach and proceed without me.

Sir Henry and Lady Gurney arrive in Kuala Lumpur on an RAF Dakota flight from Singapore. Sir Henry is to take up his appointment as High Commissioner in Malaya, replacing Sir Edward Gent who was killed in an aircraft collision outside London. Sir Edward was returning to England following Malcolm MacDonald's behind-scenes representations to cabinet for his recall. MacDonald would soon be finding fault with the newly appointed Gurney's handling of Malayan affairs and, as he had moved to undermine London's confidence in Gent, so, too, would he start plotting the removal of Gurney.

The tri-border December gathering reached two major decisions. From the military standpoint it confirmed we would stick to our intentions of setting up liberated areas in both the northern and southern regions of the peninsula. The meeting's second resolution directed that, from then on, our guerrilla army would follow Mao's blueprint for revolutionary warfare to the letter. We also clarified our position at the political level. From that point onwards our ultimate aim would be the establishment of the People's Democratic Republic of Malaya.

In hindsight, I think we made another critical mistake here. What we should have done was to announce our aim of fighting for the broad concept of independence. This approach should have gone on to emphasise independence for all political persuasions and all races. Our battle cry should have been: Independence for Malaya and all Malayans who want independence.

But had I been at that meeting I am quite sure I would also have strongly supported the directions then favoured by my Central Committee comrades. We were all hot-headed in those days. In our minds we were convinced that our cause was just and our struggle would succeed.

At the time the Central Committee comrades were having their December meeting, I was involved in parallel discussions with the Perak state committee in the Cameron Highlands. Guerrilla groups from throughout Perak had been brought to a nearby area to join the battalion-sized force I was amassing. At our gathering it was decided who among our senior commanders would join the main force there and who would return to their former posts in Perak. Through our couriers I kept in touch with the deliberations taking place under Yeung Kuo. It was a less than satisfactory situation trying to consolidate a single strategic approach from separate discussions. But it was the sort of problem we were to confront regularly. We simply had to muster as much logic as possible, lean on the counsel of senior comrades and, in the final analysis, rely on a sizable input of intelligent guesswork.

Resulting from the review of strategy over which I presided, orders were given dispatching our northern main guerrilla force from the Cameron Highlands to jungle bases in the central Kelantan region around Gua Musang. Under the overall command of the Perak state secretary, Ai Ker, this force was divided into three separate units – two comprising 200 fighters each, the third 100-strong. As originally intended, I would transfer to a position in southern Pahang and there establish the Party's war headquarters.

*　　*　　*　　*　　*

Before I could move on, I began receiving initial reports of an action that had taken place in a small rubber tappers' village near Batang Kali, some 20 miles north of Kuala Lumpur. It appeared a platoon of the 2nd Battalion Scots Guards had inflicted a crushing defeat on one of our armed units. News accounts trumpeted the encounter as the 'biggest success in any one day's operation in one area' since the declaration of the Emergency. Twenty-six Chinese 'bandits' had been captured and held overnight in jungle huts. One man who attempted to escape had been shot dead. The remaining 25 had tried to flee the following morning and had also been killed. A police officer was quoted as saying: 'The Scots Guards were well placed, and the bandits just ran into their guns. Everyone was killed.' A few weeks later, doubtless uneasy about the clinical slaying of so many 'bandits' without so much as a scratch suffered by the Scots Guards, colonial authorities decided an enquiry of sorts was warranted. On January 2, 1949, the Federal Government issued an official statement suggesting the Batang Kali killings were justified and no action would therefore be taken.

The government version of what went on in the village read: 'Information from interrogation was that armed bandits were in the habit of visiting the area and used it for obtaining supplies, which were brought in every morning by the lorry which brought food for the tappers and others who occupied the clearing. If attacked, the clearing was a death trap, and the sergeant therefore posted three groups to cover the entrances. These groups were out of sight of persons in the clearing and were posted on the afternoon of December 11.' The government account stated that the men, detained for the night under guard, had made a break to escape in three groups. As they ran past the security force positions, the soldiers had called out in Malay for them to halt. When nobody obeyed, the Scots Guards gave chase and opened fire.

It was some months before I began hearing our side of the Batang Kali story. But it would be decades before I could piece together the truth of what really happened on that December night among those tapper huts and along the banks of a nearby stream.

According to our underground, Batang Kali had been a calculated massacre. Those gunned down had been neither armed nor, indeed, even CPM members. They were civilian village workers – some were rubber tappers, others were tin mine labourers. The Scots Guards had seized and held them overnight in a hut. During their hours of incarceration, one had been led off and shot in the back to terrify the rest. The following morning all were led outside, separated into three groups and, on a given order, executed. Unbeknown to the enemy, one worker had escaped to tell the horrific tale. Apparently unnoticed, or forgotten by the Scots Guards, a number of female villagers had also witnessed the slaughter.

Ironically, in London at precisely this time, propaganda experts were busily searching for the most emotive terminology to be employed in government bulletins referring to our revolution. To be avoided at all costs was any suggestion that the comrades might be true nationalists, enjoying mass support and fighting for a just anti-colonial cause. Colonial Secretary Creech-Jones was in the middle of preparing a major international propaganda offensive justifying Britain's military role in Malaya when details of what had occurred in Batang Kali landed on Cabinet desks. Up to this point various epithets had been used to describe us. The official line had been that care should be taken to avoid any phrase that might 'unduly dignify' the CPM. The 'bandit' label had served its purpose. But now, as the Batang Kali slaughtered civilians were buried and as Kuala Lumpur went into damage control mode, British propaganda experts tabled another preference. Henceforth it would be more advisable to refer to all armed communists in Malaya as terrorists – communist terrorists, CTs.

It would take a Vietnam conflict massacre more than 19 years later before the carefully concealed truth about Batang Kali began to surface. The mass killing of civilians by US servicemen at My Lai on March 16, 1968, had attracted world-wide publicity. Reporters on the mass-circulation UK Sunday newspaper, *The People*, received a tip-off that a similar incident involving British troops had occurred early in the Malayan Emergency. The paper launched an investigation and its reporters conducted numerous interviews with ex-servicemen who had served at the time. The result was a front-page exposé in the February 1, 1970 edition. It flatly charged that on December 12, 1948, the Scots Guards platoon had perpetrated a cold-blooded massacre of unarmed civilian workers at Batang Kali.

Two days later, reporters in Malaysia tracked down Inche Jaffar bin Taib. He had been a Special Constable stationed at Batang Kali and had acted as a guide for the Scots Guards. Inche Jaffar said: 'The Scots Guards told me not to look at the male detainees. I turned my back towards them and suddenly there was a terrific burst of gunfire. Women and children screamed. I turned around. There were dead bodies everywhere.' The former constable claimed he counted 25 victims after the shooting.

Rethink on 1948 Malaya killings

By Our Foreign Staff

BRITAIN has agreed to consider holding an inquiry into a "massacre" of 24 unarmed villagers during the Malayan Emergency in 1948.

The decision was taken three months after the Government turned down a request from Malaysian activists to investigate the killings, which took place during anticommunist operations.

The "Batang Kali massacre" occurred in a village in Selangor state on Dec 12, 1948, when 14 members of the Scots Guards allegedly killed 24 ethnic Chinese.

"The [British Government has] decided to reconsider the decision… that no inquiry would be established or other investigation undertaken into the incident at Batang Kali in 1948," said a letter sent to activists in Malaysia.

The British High Commission in Kuala Lumpur confirmed the contents of the letter, but said there was no guarantee that an inquiry would be ordered.

A spokesman for the activists urged a speedy resolution to the issue. "The British Government must act quickly instead of simply dragging their feet until the surviving witnesses, who are very old, are no more," said Quek Ngee Meng, adding that one of the witnesses died last week.

Mr Quek said that his group had traced nine former British soldiers and four Malaysians who were witnesses.

TELEGRAPH 30/4/09

was commuted to life without parole but in 1952 he escaped from jail and fled to Germany. He became a German citizen and could not be extradited.

the direction of the Talkatora Stadium and it was spotted by a sentry who sounded the alarm after it landed inside," a security official said.

pe'

America. The 'mules' would pass themselves off as tourists to try to elude police controls," said a police statement. It is the first time this method had been used to introduce cocaine into Spain, the statement added.

Sex strike could end Kenya deadlock

Thousands of Kenyan women are to go on a week-long sex strike in an attempt to force an end to the ongoing political bickering.

The deadlock is threatening to plunge the country into another explosive crisis. The Women's Development

Organisation plans to ask the wives of both President Mwai Kibaki and Raila Odinga, the prime minister, to take part.

GUARDS KILL
28 BANDITS

PATROL ACTION IN
MALAYA JUNGLE

FROM OUR OWN CORRESPONDENT
SINGAPORE, Sunday.

Operating in the Batang Kali and Rawang areas of Selangor, Scots Guards and police have killed 28 bandits in the last 24 hours. In one operation a patrol of 14 men killed 26 Chinese, the biggest success in any one day's operation in one area since the declaration of an emergency.

In addition a Chinese bandit leader has been seriously wounded and five bandits have been captured. The security forces opened an offensive round Rawang, in the tin fields north of Kuala Lumpur, at the week-end.

The 26 Chinese who were killed had been surprised and captured yesterday in a jungle hut in the Batang Kali area. One who attempted to escape was shot dead.

Learning that food was expected to arrive, the patrol waited, and a lorry was escorted to the hut, from which the captured bandits could see only three sentries.

The remaining 25 men made a sudden break, running in all directions. The police officer said: "The Scots Guards had been well placed, and the bandits just ran into their guns. Everyone was killed."

While local newspapers in Malaya and Singapore gave front page prominence to the Batang Kali action, portraying it as the biggest one-day operational success of the Emergency thus far, UK newspapers chose to play the story on inside pages. The short account (above) was all that was initially carried by *The Daily Telegraph* in London. Just on a month later *The Times* (right) dutifully carried the colonial government's carefully worded whitewash of the Batang Kali killings.

SCOTS GUARDS AND
SHOT CHINESE
T4 JAN 1949
MALAYAN INQUIRY

FROM OUR CORRESPONDENT

SINGAPORE, JAN. 3

The Government of the Malayan Federation has decided to take no action after investigation into the shooting near Rawang, Selangor, on December 12 of 24 Chinese by Scots Guards and a police patrol.

An official statement issued at Kuala Lumpur to-day says that the Guards section concerned was commanded by a sergeant under general orders that if any detained person tried to escape he was to be chased and recaptured, but in no circumstances was he to be allowed to escape. The section patrolled an area which included rubber estates and jungle, and bandits were seen and fired on. The sergeant feared that these bandits would carry the news to others and decided to press on. He eventually arrived at a clearing of *kongsi* (communal living) houses, huts, and shacks, in one of which ammunition was discovered. The statement continues: "·Information from interrogation was that armed bandits were in the habit of visiting the area and used it for obtaining supplies, which were brought in every morning by the lorry which brought food for the tappers and others who occupied the clearing. If attacked the clearing was a death-trap, and the sergeant therefore posted three groups to cover the entrances. These groups were out of sight of persons in the clearing and were posted on the afternoon of December 11."

PREARRANGED PLAN

The interrogated men were placed in a *kongsi* house for the night under guard, and in the morning, seeing only the sergeant and two sentries, they made a break in three parties in accordance with what was obviously a pre-arranged plan. The sentries and the sergeant called upon the men to stop, but could not use their arms because their hidden comrades were in the line of fire. These three groups heard shouting, but did not know what was happening until they saw Chinese running through the jungle past their posts. The soldiers called in the Malay language upon the fleeing men to halt, gave chase, and finally opened fire.

From June 16, when a state of emergency was declared, until the end of the year 409 bandits have been killed and 268 captured. Police, service, and civilian casualties were 482 killed and 404 wounded. Civilian casualties, of which more than two-thirds were Chinese, were 330 killed and 194 injured.

Twenty four hours after Inche Jaffar gave his account, Batang Kali's lone survivor, Chong Hong, then aged 45, described how he had fainted when the British soldiers fired on his group. When he regained consciousness he found himself lying among the dead. Chong Hong recalled: 'The soldiers gestured to us to turn our backs. We were all standing still, too frightened to move. Then the shooting began and I fell to the ground. I think I fainted from fright.' He then ran to his village, where he hid, too terrified to speak to anyone. Local police later arrested him and he spent three days in jail. Chong Hong said he was never informed why he had been arrested and was adamant that none of the dead had tried to escape.

Public reaction was such that, two weeks later, Labour's Defence Secretary, Mr Denis Healey, called in the Director of Public Prosecutions. In turn, Scotland Yard became involved and a top police team led by Chief Superintendent Frank Williams began investigations. Williams and his men worked out a plan of action calling for three months interviewing work in Britain followed by a period of on-the-spot evidence gathering. In Malaysia they planned to get statements from Batang Kali's lone survivor, from the Malay Special Constable who had worked with the Scots Guards and from various other witnesses. They also intended allocating time for forensic testing on the victims' remains.

With their UK enquiries completed the Scotland Yard team began packing for their flight to Kuala Lumpur. In the same week Britain went to the polls for the June, 1970, general election which saw Mr Harold Wilson's Labour government voted out of office and replaced by the Conservatives headed by Mr Edward Heath. Williams and his investigators felt confident the change in political leadership would have no impact on their travel plans. They were wrong. On July 9, 1970, the newly appointed British Attorney General, Sir Peter Rawlinson, in answer to a Parliamentary question, told the House of Commons that there was no reasonable likelihood of obtaining sufficient evidence to warrant criminal proceedings in the Batang Kali affair. He indicated Parliament and Britain at large should be satisfied that a full investigation had been carried out.

Another 22 years later, the British Broadcasting Corporation's TV documentary series, *Inside Story*, took three former Scots Guardsmen back to Batang Kali to retrace the story. None of the three were involved in the killing of the workers but had been in a follow-up patrol sent to the scene. In addition to their personal observations, the programme highlighted interviews with the lone survivor and various eye-witnesses, including the widow of one of the victims. It also revealed testimony made to the Scotland Yard investigators by Guardsmen who had participated in the massacre. Some time before the event they had been told by a sergeant there was to be a mass killing and were given an opportunity to withdraw from the exercise. All had stayed. Their statements made it clear that none of the Chinese shot that day were armed, neither had they attempted to escape.

Batang Kali had been a massacre by an enemy whose political leaders on the other side of the world had simultaneously decided it would be more advantageous to their colonial cause to describe *us* as terrorists. That the December 12, 1948 executions remain a British secret is a measure of the advantage held in warfare by the side that dominates propaganda. The UK Ministry of Defence has remained tight-lipped. All police files on Batang Kali are classified to this day. At the outset of my book I referred to the way victors edit history. This is certainly a case in point.

*　　*　　*　　*　　*

I set out from the Cameron Highlands with a party of five bodyguards in the latter part of December, 1948. My jungle trek took me south-east to Kuala Lipis, a railway town on the Sungei Jelai waterway which forks with the Sungei Tembeling. Together, these two rivers flow on to form the upper reaches of the Sungei Pahang. As the crow flies it would be a journey of some 60 miles. By the time I reached the Kuala Lipis region, a section of guerrillas had been dispatched to act as my security force for the remainder of the journey. My intention was then to move south to the Raub area but I was warned that British patrolling made that route impassable.

At each stop I was able to contact comrades who arranged safe jungle camps for me. In these we held wide-ranging discussions as I continued to work on strategy. Thwarted from moving to Raub, I decided to push eastwards and then in a broad arc move south to reach Jerantut. From there we continued due south to Kerdau, a small railway township where we faced the unavoidable prospect of crossing a well patrolled secondary road now known as Route 98. Then we plunged back into triple canopied jungle for another cross-country trek to the Sungei Semantan and then down to a Chinese village, ten miles east of Mentekab on the Mentekab to Bentong road. This village, very appropriately, was known as the Ten Milestone Village.

I arrived there in May. It had taken me five months to reach there from the Cameron Highlands, walking all the way through deep jungle. Half an hour's trek from the road, the Pahang guerrillas had our headquarters camp waiting for us.

The expected forces moving up from Johore had yet to arrive. However, my close friend Yeung Kuo was in place and came out to welcome me and escort me to my new jungle home. Ah Dian was due shortly from Johore. By the end of June, 1949, the entire five-man membership of the Politburo was in residence: Yeung Kuo, Lee An Tung, Siao Chang, Ah Dian and myself. We proceeded immediately to hold the first Politburo meeting of the year-old Emergency.

Chapter 16

Second thoughts about Australian involvement

Two weeks after Britain proclaimed the State of Emergency in Malaya, Colonial Secretary Creech-Jones presented a special paper to his Cabinet colleagues in London, outlining the crisis as the incumbent Attlee Labour Government saw it. His preamble began with the curious comparison of the Malayan peninsula being about the same size as England without Wales. Malaya had a population, he said, of approximately 5,800,000 people of whom 2,200,000 were Malays, another 2,600,000 were Chinese and a further 600,000 were Indians.

Since the war, pursued the Colonial Secretary, the whole of South East Asia had been a disturbed area. 'The Japanese occupation which overthrew European and colonial governments and deeply upset the whole social structure of the occupied countries released a surge of nationalist movements whose force is by no means spent today,' said Creech-Jones. 'Furthermore, during the time of occupation it was, of course, greatly to our own interests that subversive movements against the Japanese occupation should be encouraged and supplied with arms. It is no wonder that some of the resistance groups which sprang up at that time should – as happened also in Europe – prove after liberation an embarrassment to their own Governments.'

If I had been privy to these particular observations, I would have had little cause for dissent thus far. Perhaps the usefulness of presenting the size of Malaya as Creech-Jones did might be questioned, but his round-figure population statistics were accurate enough. Even more accurate was his observation of the effects on South East Asia of Japan's occupation. By implication, he was suggesting that the CPM was one of those nationalist movements that had 'surged'. No argument here. Neither could there be disagreement about us being an 'embarrassment' to the British.

In the fifth paragraph of his report to Cabinet, the Colonial Secretary spoke of the post-war crime-wave that had engulfed Malaya. Later in the same document, he specifically noted: 'There is no concrete evidence that the Malayan Communist Party is directly responsible for the present lawlessness but extreme political factions and certain trade unions have been infiltrated by communism.' Once again I would have agreed wholeheartedly with Creech-Jones' assessments. We had certainly infiltrated the unions. Indeed, we controlled virtually all of them. And the reason why there had been no evidence of us being responsible for the lawlessness was simple enough. We weren't. Independent gangsters, secret society members, strikebreaking labour contractors, planters, miners and the like all took advantage of the colonial authority's inability to impose law and order.

Prior to the lawlessness, the Cabinet was told, Malaya had been the most peaceful territory in South East Asia and had taken long strides towards the 're-establishment of stable, prosperous conditions'. Creech-Jones' choice of words here is telling. No talk of long strides towards independence or even self-government. 'Stable, prosperous conditions' were the requirement. And why should this be so?

The Colonial Secretary's next two sentences provided the answer for his Cabinet colleagues: 'During 1947 the total value of the exports of Singapore and the Federation together was £151 million, of which dollar exports accounted for £56 million. It is by far the most important source of dollars in the Colonial Empire and it would gravely worsen the whole dollar balance of the Sterling area if there were serious interference with Malayan exports.'

This was the reality of Britain's position at the outset of the Emergency. These were the issues that dominated the British Cabinet's deliberations. The thought of granting independence or self-government did not enter the picture. Preserving Britain's access to the exploitable wealth of her prize South East Asian colonies in order to meet debts on the home front was the paramount consideration.

To do this and sustain credibility, domestically and internationally, in the immediate period following World War 11, demanded a skilfully geared propaganda effort. The United States, Britain's closest wartime ally, had granted independence to the Philippines on July 4, 1946, clearly acknowledging that the idea of maintaining post-war colonialism in the region had become indefensible. At the same time, there was no altruism involved when Britain herself granted independence to India and Pakistan in 1947. She left the sub-continent because she had to. Meanwhile, the Dutch East Indies were well on the way to being granted self-rule by the Netherlands, an event which would take place the following year – 1949 – with the formation of Indonesia. If Malaya and Singapore were to be special cases for retention based solely on their relevance to Britain's financial well-being how, then, could London camouflage and justify this in public pronouncements?

When it came to formulating the necessary propaganda campaign, the British found it expedient, initially, to portray our armed struggle as part of an international communist conspiracy plotted in Moscow. Such a scenario, totally contrived, sat well with the political problems Britain was facing in Europe. For opportunistic politicians, cosseted senior civil servants and pampered diplomats charged with disseminating propaganda, the conspiracy line was far easier to sell than the reality of a group of Asian nationalists blocked from the political process but still determined to put an end to British exploitation.

The facts of our supposed links to the Soviet Union are these. I frequently toyed with the idea of developing contacts with the Communist Party of the Soviet Union (CPSU) around this time. I was interested in discovering what the Comintern's Far Eastern Bureau in Shanghai had been doing and whether this could be of any assistance to our cause. But at no point, either prior to the Emergency or during it, did I have contact of any nature whatsoever with the Soviet Union. I never sought Russian aid and no Russian, or agent of Moscow, ever approached me personally, or my Party, with offers.

As Britain pieced together its propaganda programme, early direction for Government public statements came from the Colonial Office's Assistant Secretary of State, Mr J. D. Higham who demanded: 'On no account should the term 'insurgent', which might suggest a genuine popular uprising, be used.' By August, 1948, Creech-Jones was writing to Commissioner General MacDonald in Singapore revealing that the Attlee government intended conducting a 'vigorous counter-attack on communist propaganda both at home and abroad' to disprove the argument that 'present troubles in Malaya arise from a genuine nationalist movement of the people of the country.' What also worried the Colonial Office was the possibility that, given an extended Emergency, our CPM guerrillas might start to acquire what it privately described as 'a certain glamour'. Thus, orders were given that terminology describing my jungle fighters should never dignify them.

Commissioner General MacDonald had been quick to anticipate the British propaganda drive. In a broadcast over Radio Malaya on June 6,[12] less than two weeks before the Emergency declaration, he characterised the CPM leadership as being like senior officials of communist satellite states in Europe. The people should be wary of those who had to toe the Russian line, he said, 'like dolls in a Malay shadow play, where the stage manager dictated every move from the Kremlin in Moscow.' MacDonald's words certainly impacted on the expatriate community but, in reality, had little effect on the mass of workers throughout the peninsula and Singapore who comprised our supporters. I eventually came to regard MacDonald as the epitome of the high-ranking British colonial administrator whose personality and style actually inspired the inroads of communism.

*   *   *   *   *

According to a War Office assessment[13] dated August 18, 1948, exactly two months following the Emergency declaration, Britain's available ground forces in Malaya and Singapore then comprised:

- Four British infantry battalions
- One British field regiment
- Seven Gurkha infantry battalions – all seven considered under strength
- Two Malay Regiment battalions
- One Squadron RAF Regiment (Malaya)
- Some 4,000 Gurkha recruits from regimental centres

Scheduled to arrive in Malaya within two months were the 4th Hussars and three infantry battalions of the 2nd Guards Brigade.

Aside from providing 'a measure of protection of the civil population against terrorists', Britain's basic military plan, the War Office document reveals, called for the deployment of ground forces in such a way that my guerrillas would be driven into the jungles of Central Malaya and there destroyed. The strength of our fighting units in July, the previous month, was placed at some 2,500 and official predictions were that the CPM proposed increasing this strength to 5,000 by mid-September.

The assessment went on to list the tasks of the anti-guerrilla ground forces thus:

(a) guarding of vulnerable points
(b) offensive patrolling to locate and destroy bandit hideouts
(c) attacks on located bandit hideouts
(d) patrolling of the Siamese border in an attempt to prevent communist elements in Siam crossing the border and reinforcing the bandits in Malaya

The War Office experts noted: 'Militarily, it is of the utmost importance that we get the upper hand as soon as possible. Delay in doing this adversely affects the situation in other Far Eastern countries faced with the same communist problem. Further, the longer the communists retain the initiative in Malaya, the more difficult it will be to regain and the lower will sink the morale of the civil population, especially of those who are the objects of attack and on whom the economic life of the country depends.'

Commonwealth Relations Office correspondence, originally marked 'top secret and personal', accompanying the War Office file from which I have quoted, claimed there was 'convincing evidence' the campaign of terrorism in Malaya did not 'at present' represent a genuine nationalist movement. But, the longer terrorism remained unchecked, 'the greater the danger that its communist supporters will be able to represent the terrorists as national heroes. Once this idea gained ground, the effects on the strategic position in the whole of South East Asia might be incalculable.'

These two inter-related documents, as it happens, should also shatter popular acceptance among Australian military historians that Britain delayed requesting direct involvement by Canberra in Malaya until as late as April,1950. In fact, British Secretary of State for Commonwealth Relations, Mr Philip Noel-Baker, made just such a request during talks he had in London with visiting Australian Minister for External Affairs, Dr Herbert Evatt, on August 17, 1948 – just 62 days after the Emergency declaration. According to the official extract from the record of conversation between the two men,[14] the Australian minister enquired about the general situation in Malaya. Thereupon, Noel-Baker proceeded to provide a briefing at the end of which Evatt remarked that it was 'a matter of great concern to Australia'.

In Noel-Baker's own words: 'This gave me an opening to enquire whether he thought Australia and New Zealand could give any help. The Australian minister had replied he thought they could.' However, according to the British minister, Evatt specifically requested no formal telegram on the subject be sent direct to Canberra. Instead, he suggested he be provided a comprehensive statement on the Malaya situation. From this he would draft his own telegram.

The British Secretary of State wrote: 'He wanted this paper to include a full factual statement of the present situation of the forces which we have there, and of the forces which we propose to send; together with a statement of the kinds of help we thought that the Australian Government might be able to give.

'I asked him if this should include a reference to military help. He said that he did not exclude the possibility of military help, but thought that it would be unwise to suggest it in our paper. We should cover it by speaking of help in training police, provisions of wireless operators, provision of technical equipment and perhaps also other more extensive help. He thought this would enable him to make tentative suggestions to his government and see how they were received.'

It took the British less than 24 hours to prepare both War Office and Commonwealth Relations Office documents for the Australian minister. The following day, August 18, Noel-Baker signed the following 'top secret and personal' letter to the Australian Minister for External Affairs:

My dear Bert,

As promised at our talk the other day, I enclose a memorandum about the situation in Malaya, together with an annex containing a military appreciation by our service authorities, made at my request.

As you will see, the situation is one of considerable urgency, and I should be most grateful if you could let me know the result of any approach you may be able to make to your Government on this matter. Best wishes for your journeys.

Yours ever,
Philip Noel-Baker

Speculation on the possibility of an Australian military commitment to Malaya was clearly generating much controversy in top British circles even before the Noel-Baker-Evatt meeting. Indeed, on August 14 a high-ranking ministerial official submitted a memorandum advising Noel-Baker to think again on the idea of having Australian troops trudging through Malayan jungles.[15]

'Before Japan entered the war,' the advice noted, 'Australia was asked to send troops to Malaya. The Australian Government did warn us that Australian troops were not suitable for garrison duties, but under pressure from us they eventually sent a division. I am afraid that before the outbreak of war with Japan this division had, on the whole, created a bad name for itself, and subsequently, when Singapore fell there were some disgraceful scenes at the wharves. Again, at the end of the war, when the Australian prisoners of war were released from their internment camps, there was some bad behaviour.'

The memorandum concluded: 'There seems to me, therefore, to be considerable danger in sending Australian ground forces to Malaya again. This is naturally a very delicate subject, and clearly, once we have committed ourselves by asking the Australian government for troops, it will be difficult, if not impossible, for us to withdraw the invitation. I served with the Australian Imperial Force in the 1914-18 War, and there is no doubt that Australians have splendid fighting qualities. But unless they are kept under the strictest discipline (which they do not like) they are too high-spirited to be really suitable for the kind of work for which they are likely to be required in Malaya and are liable to be at their worst off parade.'

Other senior ministerial advisers, appearing to support the memorandum's views, added recommendations suggesting additional British forces for Malaya were surely available in Egypt and urged the various matters raised be brought to the Defence Minister's attention.

Two months later, as British contingency planning for military operations in Malaya intensified, the War Office, looking at the threat of expanding world hostilities, began seriously considering her South East Asian colonial peninsula be divided into specific areas of strategic responsibility. A map had actually been prepared depicting at least one of these areas as territory to fall under the responsibility of Australia. The Foreign Office reacted with undisguised disdain. In a formal appreciation of the proposals dated October 14, 1948, the ministry revealed that far more than the possibility of antipodean high-spiritedness lay at the nub of their apprehension over Australian involvement.

As this document[16] provides a wealth of insight into official British strategic thinking in the late 1940s and the views formulated by her political leaders when it came to defining national interests and requirements, it deserves to be quoted in full.

Headed 'Australian Defence Cooperation' it read:

'It is the view of the Foreign Office that it is premature to consider the allotment of an area of strategic responsibility to Australia as defined on the map attached to this paper in view of the very serious political considerations involved. While it is true that the decision need not be regarded as final, once the idea has been communicated to Australia that the United Kingdom are prepared, in the event of war, to allot this area of strategic responsibility to Australia, it is going to be very difficult to bring about any change. Past experience has shown that once lines are drawn on maps defining areas of strategic responsibility, they lead to the assumption that the Supreme Command in those areas is allotted to the power responsible. This, in turn, involves political complications which, in the case of this paper, do not appear to have been taken into consideration at all.

'Chief of these considerations, from the Foreign Office point of view, is the political position of the United Kingdom in Asia generally, and in South East Asia in particular. This position was greatly weakened as a result of the last war, and though efforts have not been by any means unsuccessful in restoring a considerable measure of our prestige in that area, much remains to be done if our influence is to be maintained and if we are to be enabled to play our part in consolidating the position, politically and economically, against Soviet attempts to undermine it.

'There is no doubt whatsoever that in Asia today it is the United Kingdom, and not Australia or New Zealand, which alone enjoys a measure of influence and prestige with the Asiatic races involved (not excepting India, Pakistan and Ceylon). We have already had the experience of surrendering our position to Australia in Japan, and unfortunately it is a fact that politically this has not been a success. Were we to surrender our position in any respect, either in the period of uneasy peace, or in the event of war, to Australia in a wider field, it is no exaggeration to say that this would be likely to lead to the final extinction of United Kingdom influence in the area involved. It would not be clear to the Asiatic mind why the United Kingdom, which still enjoys considerable power and prestige in world affairs, should be in any way prepared to cede its position to another member of the Commonwealth which in no way enjoys the same degree of influence and prestige. The Asiatic understands that old people retire from active life and hand over to their juniors, and it would be disastrous to give the impression that is what is happening to the United Kingdom.

'The Foreign Office recognise that, in the event of war, United Kingdom resources may not permit of our contributing much to the Far Eastern theatre and also that, as a matter of necessity, Australia may have to be invited to extend her sphere of strategic responsibility in an emergency. But it is clear that, at any rate for some years to come, the threat to the Commonwealth and in particular to the United Kingdom from the Soviet Union, will be political rather than military. It is therefore of primary and vital importance that the political capacity of the United Kingdom to influence the situation should in no way be weakened by pledging in advance to Australia a position which, in the event, she may not even be called upon to occupy. We may, when the time comes, have to discard from weakness, but if we have to do so we must be prepared to contemplate the final extinction of United Kingdom influence over a vast area where even now it contributes materially to the stability and prosperity of the region and draws a very necessary dividend in hard currency.

'Finally, and this is also of importance, we have no right to allot areas of strategic responsibility to Australia which include foreign territories without seeking the prior consent of those territories. In the case of Indonesia, it is quite impossible to say now how the political structure will develop. It would certainly be premature to raise the matter either with the Dutch at present, or for some time to come with the United States of Indonesia, if and when it comes into being.'

As things turned out, it would be another two years before the first Australian defence forces arrived to join the British-led war against the CPM army. Six Lincolns from the Royal Australian Air Force (RAAF) No 1 Bomber Squadron flew into Singapore's Tengah airbase in late June, 1950. Around the same time, a flight of Dakotas from the RAAF's No 38 Transport Squadron was stationed at Changi airbase. But it would be a further five years before the 'high-spirited' Australian ground forces began operations in Malaya.

Naturally, none of the behind-scenes activities that I have cited here from declassified documents were known to us as we settled down to our first wartime Politburo meeting near the Ten Milestone Village in June, 1949. But through intelligent guesswork once more we were able to arrive at fairly accurate assessments of Britain's intentions. For all the propaganda effort the enemy was directing, both locally and internationally, to justify their side of the war, we remained convinced that well-targeted guerrilla attacks would see us triumphant. As we couldn't hope to compete in the propaganda contest, our deliberations quickly moved to an emphasis on military matters, specifically the organisation of our southern main guerrilla force and its introduction as a fighting formation.

There was much on the international scene to boost our morale and convince us that we were on the right track. We were greatly emboldened by the developments in China which, since the beginning of the year, had seen Mao's army cross the Yangtze river and capture Shanghai. By the time our meeting got underway, Chiang Kai Shek had fled to Formosa and we were reading newspaper reports of a further decisive battle going in favour of the communists. All these matters were discussed at length and we reached the conclusion it would be only a matter of weeks before Mao controlled all of mainland China. Not surprisingly, this had the effect of encouraging us to press ahead even harder with our military programme.

*   *   *   *   *

There was, however, one political consideration, prompted by the fast-changing China scene, that demanded we divert our attention from military matters, at least for a while. During my visit to Hong Kong in 1947, I was able to establish, via a senior CPC official in the colony, a series of code names and safe postal addresses through which our Parties could correspond. Up to mid-1949, communications via these ordinary mail channels had only been intermittent and of no major consequence to the CPM.

I received the first substantial letter through our secret mail system soon after arriving at the southern Pahang camp. It came from a CPC official inviting me to visit Hong Kong. I detected in the text a tone of puzzlement over what might be happening in Malaya. I assumed the invitation was sent in order for me to explain personally to the Chinese communists the intended course of our campaign. Pressure of events prevented me from taking up the invitation and I dispatched a reply in this vein. It was a tough decision. In view of our predictions that China would be communist within weeks, I regarded direct links to the CPC as nothing short of imperative. I resolved, then and there, to try and establish these connections via other means.

In the latter part of 1948, I had persuaded the Central Committee to allow eight senior cadres at the state level, all suffering from tuberculosis, to travel to China for medical treatment. Neither our political wing nor our guerrilla army had any effective way for tackling TB. Quite obviously, none of the eight could check into a government hospital without immediately being identified and arrested. At the same time, word from our unit commanders was that they were loath to have TB sufferers with the troops for fear of contamination. From the sufferers' point of view, they worried they would become isolated from their comrades and that their effectiveness would be undermined. It was a serious problem and something had to be done. With events going so favourably for Mao's army, there were now doctors and medical facilities functioning in communist-held mainland areas capable of caring for TB patients. My aim was for the CPM's ill comrades, once cured, to undergo special skills training useful to our side before their return to Malaya.

In the closing weeks of 1948, I utilised our secret postal arrangements to organise the departure of our first TB patient. The man I chose was Ah Hai, one of the two senior cadres who became separated from me during the Kampar bungalow raid and whose young sister had helped me rejoin the communist network in Ipoh. He travelled by ship to Hong Kong where he received initial treatment through courtesy of the CPC. Subsequently, the CPC arranged for Ah Hai to move to Peking. Thus Ah Hai became our first official contact with the Chinese communists. As we discussed these and related issues at our first wartime Politburo meeting, my hope was that Ah Hai, together with one or two of his fellow TB sufferers, would develop into Peking-based conduits to high-ranking CPC circles.

In the meantime, we transferred the other seven TB patients from state committees in Pahang, Johore, Selangor and Malacca. At the outset the newly established communist regime in Peking agreed to cure our senior cadres, enrol them in their Party's training schools, and once their studies were completed, send them home. The training course, involving tuition in all aspects of communist theory and practice, military and political, was spread over three years.

By the time the Korean War broke out in June, 1950, all our senior cadres in China were TB-free and were deep into their course studies. As the Korean conflict intensified, Peking began devising contingency plans that envisaged fighting overflowing the Korean peninsula onto Chinese territory. One counter-strategy in this eventuality proposed the Chinese People's Army thrusting down into South East Asia as the entire Asian continent became enveloped in what would have amounted to World War 111. Against the backdrop of a threatening dramatic escalation of the Asian land war, our eight CPM men, instead of being sent home, were asked to stay and complete their studies. They were still in China when the Panmunjom Armistice Agreements were signed in July, 1953.

April, 1955, saw the Bandung conference in Indonesia. There, China's Prime Minister, Chou En Lai, played a pivotal role in gaining unanimous consensus for a 10-point declaration on world peace and cooperation. We thought perhaps now Peking would send our senior cadres home. After all, they had then been in China for some five years. This was not to be the case. The Chinese then went ahead and arranged for our men to gain further experience in the practical application of communist theory. It was not until 1959 that they eventually returned to Malaya.

*   *   *   *   *

As our Politburo discussions in south Pahang continued, batches of guerrilla reinforcements arrived at our camp from Johore. These had been ordered as there were insufficient numbers in local state units to create our intended southern main force. Within several weeks we had amassed a strength of around 300 men.

Our camp had a small parade ground. Surrounding this were *atap*-roofed huts that accommodated about ten men each. We had sentry posts at the entrance to the camp. At the rear was the headquarters area with the administration and lecture huts. The five Politburo members had separate accommodation behind the headquarters.

We were situated halfway up the side of a jungle-covered hill. To build the camp, the jungle had first to be cleared. Of course, from a defence standpont, the ideal place would have been on the hill's crest. But this would have made access to water very difficult. One always had to make compromises. If the enemy came from behind they would occupy the higher ground and would hold an immediate battlefield advantage. To compensate, we established defensive positions with trenches and logs on the rear approaches, very much like a mini-stockade arrangement.

The layout of our camps was not based on any special theories handed down by experts. It came from trial and error during the Japanese period. Where mistakes were made, we modified and improved. During the occupation we were not really troubled by Japanese air reconnaissance. So the preparatory clearing of jungle at campsites became routine. This persisted in the early stages of the Emergency, but as the British established air reconnaissance as an important aspect of their war against us, we quickly adapted our techniques. Rather than remove jungle foliage we retained it as a defence precaution.

Our immersion in complex strategic matters did not isolate the five Politburo members from responsibilities for the day-to-day running of Party affairs. A case in point involved a serious crisis of loyalty involving our Malacca state secretary, Siew Lau, long regarded as one of our most experienced senior officials. During the Japanese period, he had commanded the 3rd Regiment which operated with considerable success in the north Johore – Malacca area. From 1946 to 1948, he had gone back to being a school master.

It was brought to the attention of our Politburo discussions that Siew Lau was now insisting on diverging from agreed Party policy on the delicate subject of land distribution. The Party line called for the broad nationalisation of the rubber industry. Siew Lau was demanding we announce publicly that the CPM, when it came to power, would seize all plantation land, irrespective of ownership, and redistribute it to Malay peasants. To make matters worse, he had already begun to propagate these thoughts by distributing a badly written booklet expanding on his theories.

Siew Lau's ideas were preposterous. They would never work and could only spawn horrendous communal problems. On the British plantations, most of the workers were Indians. The next largest racial group was Chinese and the remainder were Indonesian Malays. As an exercise in damage control, we dispatched Ah Koek, a member of the Central Malayan Bureau, to Malacca with orders to pull Siew Lau back to the Party line and dissuade any of those he may have influenced.

Ah Koek had no problems with the rank-and-file but Siew Lau proved recalcitrant. Reports we received from our Central Bureau man intimated that the top communist in Malacca was on the verge of forming a splinter group. The Politburo demoted Siew Lau thus isolating him from the rest of his state committee. As our orders impacted, Siew Lau planned a dash for Sumatra. His intended escape route was revealed and together with his wife, also a Party member, and two bodyguards, he was found hiding in a coastal village. A fishing boat had been ordered to take the group across the Malacca Straits. All four were immediately detained, sentenced to death as military deserters and executed on May 15, 1950. The execution order was issued by Ah Koek. The Malacca problems then dissipated, but the overall incident would have a shocking backlash several months later.

Extra-curricular demands notwithstanding, our Politburo's wide-ranging review of the Party's performance thus far concluded that we still enjoyed strong support among the Chinese workers in both urban and rural areas. Plantation and mine labourers were well under our control. Britain's banning of our unions and various front organisations had failed to undermine the widespread sympathy we had long attracted. Indeed, our influence as an underground political movement seemed even to have gained in stature over the previous 12-month period. We interpreted this as a direct result of our guerilla actions.

As far as battlefield strategy was concerned, we remained committed to the overall two-base/liberated zones objectives and much time was spent exploring how best to develop these. Our hit-and-run tactics, though more often than not devoid of centralised control, had been successful to the point that public morale on the enemy side had clearly deteriorated. In order to maintain this trend we resolved to hit the British even harder with the specific aim of racking up a higher killing rate among government security forces. In order to achieve this we concluded that a switch to larger unit attacks was necessary. Where platoon-sized groups involving ten or twenty guerrillas at a time had been the mainstay of our approach thus far, we now saw the need to launch company-sized attacks involving strike forces 100-strong and more. These were to be coordinated within our two-base programme.

In line with this, we selected, as an experimental target to test our theories, an isolated hilltop police station south of Mentekab. Dispatching 100 of our newly arrived Johore guerrillas, whom we regarded as experienced jungle fighters, we aimed to attack, capture and then hold the position for a number of days. We reckoned we would be able to seize a sizable supply of weapons and ammunition. In addition, startling headlines would demoralise the British further and only enhance our standing with the local population throughout Malaya.

In hindsight, it was a foolish endeavour which could not be justified, even had we fully succeeded. We were soon to discover that what we judged as experienced guerrillas were, in fact, sorely lacking in the techniques we now required. During the Japanese period these men had become skilled in defensive warfare. When the Japanese came into the jungle to search for our bases, the guerrillas had a system of firing from fixed defences and then leading the enemy into ambushes. Entirely different tactics were now needed.

Our raid on the police station proved a failure. The police held the superior hill-top position and defended from well-prepared trenches. We even tried human-wave tactics and twice charged the police compound, thereby suffering a substantial number of wounded each time. Our commander ultimately gave the order to withdraw to avoid huge casualties.

Our June meeting was still underway when the results of the misconceived raid reached us. We reasoned that not only were our tactics in error but our enhanced strike force was still too small. At once we held a post-mortem. Discussions I chaired devised a plan for the formation of what we referred to as our 26 Independent Company. We envisaged fielding this force to launch raids involving at least 200 guerrillas each time. Rather than focusing on isolated police compounds, we began thinking in terms of targeting small towns. Foremost in our minds was the psychological impact such attacks would likely produce.

All five members of the Politburo were still in residence at our war heaquarters when the British launched an attack. On this occasion, however, our Min Yuen supporters were able to provide prior warning. Quickly we packed our few belongings and all our important documents. Together with our camp security guerrillas, we withdrew deeper into the jungle before the first aircraft began bombing and strafing runs and the enemy ground troops started defusing the booby-traps we had inserted along the approach to our position. When the British troops finally reached the cluster of bamboo huts that had formed our camp, they found nothing. All they could do was set the structures alight and withdraw.

My intention had been to have all five Politburo members permanently attached to Headquarters. I wanted to ensure that our armed struggle phase was always directed by policies reached through consensus at least within the Politburo. As it turned out, developments worked solidly against my hopes for a cohesive leadership able to meet at a moment's notice to decide policy.

In the aftermath of our hilltop police station debacle, we were faced with a crisis within the Politburo itself. A regional committee member, Lam Swee, who operated in the western Pahang area, accused Politburo member, Ah Dian, of cowardice for refusing to carry a weapon as expected of all senior comrades. Under the Emergency regulations in force at the time, any communist caught with a weapon faced mandatory death on conviction. Those unarmed, were charged under laws demanding only jail as punishment. News spread of the allegations against the man who was widely regarded as an important guerrilla warfare strategist. We were forced to take action.

Ah Dian, so well-read on Mao's writings, and the very person who had set us on the path to achieving liberated zones, denied he was a coward, arguing it was unnecessary for him to carry a weapon as his bodyguards were fully armed. I did not find his defence very convincing as I myself certainly carried a pistol all the time. Similarly, the other three Politburo members carried weapons and all our bodyguards were armed. We had no choice but to demote Ah Dian back to the state committee level. He took his punishment and, after a re-education session, went off to work in his new posting without comment. He remained true to the cause and continued to function in Pahang until he was killed in action in 1956.

We also demoted Lam Swee whom we felt had exaggerated the whole issue in an effort to gain personal kudos. After he, too, completed a period of re-education, we assigned him to a western Pahang unit to become its political commissar. He went off deeply resentful and on June 27, 1950, defected to the police, along with his bodyguard. To the British, Lam Swee, who claimed he had escaped from the CPM after we targeted him for execution – a ludicrous allegation as he had just been given a new posting – proved to be a propagandist's dream. They produced a psywar booklet ostensibly written by Lam Swee. It was entitled *I Accuse*. Through it, the British were able to launch a classical smear campaign against us. The booklet claimed all members of the Central Committee were cheats and liars who had squandered Party funds meant for urban revolutionary work. Lam Swee was later used to insinuate that I had been the man responsible for the 1942 devastating Kempeitai raid at the Batu Caves that killed so many senior comrades. All effective propaganda, but baseless from beginning to end.

Our extended first meeting pushed ahead with Politburo ranks reduced to four. Then, within a short period, Yeung Kuo was requesting to return to Selangor to conclude outstanding Party matters requiring his personal attention. He promised to return in a matter of weeks. I gave him permission to leave upon the adjournment of our discussions. I was there when he set off through the jungle. That was the last time I would see my old and trusted friend. Yeung Kuo would try several times to rejoin us. But it never worked out. On some occasions British military patrolling prevented him returning. On others, couriers carrying reports to me of his intended movements were captured. Straightaway, his schedules had to be abandoned.

* * * * *

Setting up 26 Independent Company and getting it trained and battle-ready took time. As we undertook these tasks we remained in the general Mentekab area. It was not until mid-1950 that we were able to dispatch 26 Independent Company north with orders to put our revised strategy to the test. It was to seek out targets of opportunity. The first of these was the township of Kuala Kerau. On September 11, led by Commander Chin Nam (the Ah Yang of Blantan camp days), the company launched coordinated attacks on the town's railway and police stations. The guerrillas burned down the railway building and two nearby dwellings, killing two British railway engineers. In addition, they managed to derail an armoured train sent to reinforce the Kuala Kerau defenders. Continuing the momentum of increased activity, 26 Independent Company went further north again. They hit small townships and plantations and looked to ambush substantial military convoys. We wanted our men to gain as much battle experience as they could in the shortest possible time. In fact, we had issued general orders along these lines to all units peninsula-wide from as early as October, 1949.

By sheer coincidence, these orders had run parallel with British preparations to launch what they termed 'Anti-Bandit Month' spanning late February to late March, 1950. The main aim of this was for security forces to kill as many of our comrades as possible. But there was a secondary objective. This had significant psychological implications. By manoeuvring to involve as many civilians as possible in voluntary anti-insurgency work alongside security forces, the colonial administration was endeavouring to inculcate a sense of broadened responsibility for tackling the Emergency. Our intensified military programme was just gaining momentum when the 'Anti-Bandit Month' kicked off. The result became a disaster for the Government. Official statistics for major guerrilla incidents for the period showed a remarkable rise in our activities during these weeks. There was also a substantial increase in security force casualties over the same reporting period. The press, planters and miners loudly berated the authorities and pronounced the much heralded government programme a dismal failure.

Interestingly enough, a report made by the Commander-in-Chief, Far East Land Forces, General John Harding, on April 11, 1950 interpreted the Anti-Bandit Month as having delivered a temporary fillip to civilian morale and confidence. But Harding went on to emphasise these results had been more than offset by the increased bandit activity and the pressure of external events. The external events to which he referred were, of course, China's fall to communism in October, 1949, and Britain's recognition of the Chinese People's Republic on January 6, 1950.

The Harding assessment pointed to a public 'fear' of the possible arrival in Malaya of Chinese Communist consuls. He noted: 'In spite of all precautions on our part, such consulates will inevitably operate as intelligence, inter-communication and direction centres for the bandits, and thereby constitute a substantial reinforcement for the enemy.'

The General drew attention to press reports, locally and in the UK, and defeatist statements by individuals believed by the public to be well-informed. These, he declared, had all contributed to a slip in public confidence. He warned that the slide would continue 'out of all proportion to the facts' unless and until further measures were taken to check the downward trend.

'Moreover,' added Harding, 'further Communist successes such as the capture of Hainan and Formosa would give a further fillip to the bandits' morale and increase their supporters. The possibility of other Communist successes in French Indo China, Siam, Burma and Indonesia, must also be taken into account in estimating the course of events in Malaya and Singapore.' Harding went on to recommend that Britain beef up its military commitment to Malaya by transferring from the Hong Kong garrison the Royal Marine Commando Brigade. He also asked that armoured car reinforcements be dispatched as a matter of urgency.

Coming as they did so soon after Britain's commitment of the 28th Gurkha Brigade to the Malayan theatre, Harding's recommendations obviously jolted the Ministry of Defence in London. Within 18 days, the Cabinet's Defence Committee had discussed Harding's evaluations and submitted proposals based on them for

Prime Minister Clement Attlee's approval. Harding would be getting the Commando Brigade he asked for and, in addition, the 13th/18th Hussars armoured car regiment would be transferred to his command from the Middle East.

By May, as the British were contemplating how best to deploy their soon-to-arrive reinforcements, we were preparing to move our headquarters north and get closer to the activities of 26 Independent Company. If I had to pick a high point in our military campaign I suppose it would be around this time. But it would be a high point without euphoria and it would be so short-lived.

Chapter 17

The Briggs Plan bites

Despite all the consternation we were fermenting among the enemy, I knew by the time we were moving 26 Independent Company north that our strategic approach of setting up major jungle base areas and eventual liberated zones was running into very serious problems. The trial-and-error attempts we had undertaken around Mentekab had produced sufficient evidence that our guerrilla tactics needed to be drastically refined. Reports I was receiving from our main northern force that had moved into the Gua Musang region with the aim of establishing a liberated zone there were anything but encouraging.

Divided into three separate units under the overall command of Perak state secretary, Ai Ker, our men in Kelantan had begun operations earlier than we had in Pahang. From the outset they had run into heavy enemy counter-action. British field intelligence promptly discovered a substantial guerrilla presence had moved in. Enemy reinforcements were thus deployed and began operating in company strength. Instead of identifying targets, preparing attacks and launching raids, guerrillas from our northern main forces found themselves spending most of their time avoiding British patrols. Six gruelling months yielded little of substance and our field commanders were compelled to undertake a major review of tactics. They decided the only option open to them was withdrawal from Kelantan and a radical reorganisation of their jungle fighters into smaller units. This was quickly put into effect once they were back in the more familiar terrain of Perak.

Reports detailing our military activities in the north made our task of finding the right format in Pahang decidedly more complex. One measure I had hoped would avoid the pitfalls being encountered in Kelantan was the deployment of our all-Malay unit we identified as the 10th Regiment. To my mind it had always been a critical requirement that we be able to attract substantial numbers of Malays to our ranks. The political implications were immense. As early as 1948, I had looked to creating a prominent Malay unit. We began recruiting from kampongs around Temerloh. History, I thought, would be on our side. A rebellion had been launched the previous century against the British in this general area and we could sense latent radicalism and residual anti-British feelings among the villagers.

Our drive proved highly successful. In a six-month period from late 1949 to early 1950, we were able to attract more than 500 Malay recruits. These we immediately introduced to an intensive training programme under Malay officers. Their overall commander was our colourful and experienced Abdullah Che Dat known throughout the movement as Abdullah C.D. Our overall objective was to split the 10th Regiment into two sections and with these establish two separate jungle bases in Pahang – one in the north, bordering Trengganu and Kelantan, the other in the south, bordering Johore and Negri Sembilan. When the time came to move the first 300 Malays north to a temporary base near Jerantut, Abdullah C.D. was away from our headquarters with his personal security platoon. He sent word he would join his men once they reached Jerantut.

Awaiting the arrival of Abdullah C.D., the Malay section had barely established its camp north of Jerantut when they were attacked by, of all people, a special force of Kuomintang bandits controlled and operated by the enemy High Command. These were pillaging outlaws who had operated with Britain's Force 136 during the Japanese occupation. They had been regrouped, trained and now came under the control of the Special Branch. No more than 50 or 60 of the bandits, well equipped and battle tested, struck our 300 raw Malay recruits. The result was demoralising. Our temporary leader failed to order a counter-attack and just withdrew. As the Kuomintang charged towards the camp they drew fire from our perimeter defence sentries, but no additional support came from the bulk of the main force behind.

We didn't lose a single Malay guerrilla. They just left. The sentries who had fired the first defensive shots decided to depart the battlefield once they realised they were getting no support. In the chaotic withdrawal, the rank-and-file were unable to locate their leaders. More than half of the retreating Malays moved down to the nearby Pahang river, found a number of fishing sampans, some of which they paid for, some of which they stole, and in them paddled downstream back to their home kampongs. Once the British realised they had a rout on their hands they organised a large-scale search operation with the aim of getting as many as possible of our retreating men to surrender. They coordinated this with a heavy propaganda effort. One by one the Malays turned themselves in. Some 200 of the original 300 surrendered in this manner. They were sent to a detention camp where their period of captivity was brief. After receiving strong reprimands, they were ordered to go home and never again get involved with the communists.

Our colourful Abdullah C.D. as a young guerrilla commander in 1949.

Abdullah C.D. headed for Temerloh in a forlorn effort to collect stragglers. He managed to gather about one platoon – some 50 men – and re-formed them into a new unit. But word of the Jerantut debacle soon spread and we had to face the reality that our prospects for attracting a hard-core, all-Malay fighting force were doomed for all time. It was a thoroughly humiliating episode. I should make it clear that we never considered the Malay guerrillas involved as cowards. They were just terribly inexperienced. The fault lay entirely with us in the war headquarters.

*   *   *   *   *

It was around this time that Britain's Secretary of State for War, Mr John Strachey, was finalising an important report[17] for circulation among members of the Cabinet's Malaya Committee. I include here an excerpt of his remarks, tabled on May 12, 1950, to reinforce two points. Firstly, that Britain's policy in Malaya was being solely determined by the requirement to retain the territory because it represented the colonial power's most important dollar earner. Secondly, that Britain knew all about the outrageous gap between rich and poor that lay at the very core of the CPM's argument.

Strachey wrote: 'We emphasise, and rightly, the most indispensable character of Malaya to us as a dollar earner. Should we not therefore be willing to expend considerable resources in Sterling on Malaya, in order to develop her both economically and socially at the most rapid pace physically possible? Some of these resources will have to come from the United Kingdom, but some ought to come from Malaya itself by way of a better distribution of income. It is suggested that one of the most significant facts of which the Malaya Committee has been informed is that only about one quarter of the proper revenue is derived from the present rate of income tax in the colony. I take it that this means that it has hitherto been found impossible to collect anything like the taxes due from the rich Chinese and European merchants and employers of Malaya. This must mean that there are extreme inequalities in the distribution of income in Malaya.'

*   *   *   *   *

After Mentekab, I chose to establish my next camp in the Kerdau region. The local population there were among our staunchest supporters. We arrived at our intended campsite on June 24, 1950, a day before war broke out on the Korean peninsula. I never intended Kerdau to be a permanent base as its remoteness would obviously make communications with state committees difficult. This proved particularly so when it came to keeping in touch with Yeung Kuo in Selangor. The isolation of my new camp had the effect of bringing into sharp focus a whole range of problems now confronting me two years into the insurgency. Topping the list was the critical requirement of food supplies for my jungle fighters.

A year earlier, during deliberations at our first headquarters camp, Yeung Kuo had approached me privately and made what would turn out to be a most prophetic observation. He registered his concern that the British authorities in Malaya might well adopt a policy similar to that initiated by the Japanese in Manchuria in the 1930s where the people were concentrated in camps to keep them from contacting the local guerrillas. This way, the Japanese managed to deprive the communists of vital supply lines.

I must confess that I regarded the chances of Britain adopting tactics originated some years before by the subsequently defeated Japanese as rather far-fetched. Indeed, I told Yeung Kuo, in no uncertain terms, that I thought such an outcome was most unlikely. I argued that the Japanese had themselves introduced the very same policy into Malaya to counter our guerrilla activities during the occupation period. They called it their 'fortress villages' policy. It had failed to have any effect on us and the British would surely have full information on this. Why introduce a proven failure?

When I examine my process of reasoning then, I can see how far off the mark I was. To impose such a policy would have required an element of ruthlessness that the Japanese certainly had but, I felt, the British character lacked. More important still was the whole question of whether a guerrilla army of our size would be so reliant on the population for sustenance. I thought of the vast uninhabited jungles of Malaya. Surely they could nourish us? Once again I was wrong. Unfortunately, Yeung Kuo had chosen not to argue with me.

Within a very short space of time I was to learn to my cost that even a small group of, say, 30 guerrillas, was unable to sustain itself for much longer than two weeks in any one place on natural nutrients available in the jungle. Beyond this time limit, if they were to be expected to fight, their diet had to be supplemented by food provided from outside. If, when Yeung Kuo first raised the subject, I had fully appreciated the manifold problems associated with sustaining guerrillas in jungle camps, we might well have reduced the size of our units and developed appropriate food supply techniques. We might then have circumvented the severe problems later imposed on us.

Two months before I moved to Kerdau, Lt General Sir Harold Briggs (rtd) arrived in Kuala Lumpur to take up his appointment as the colonial government's Director of Operations in the anti-communist campaign. He had agreed to accept the position on the understanding that his term would not extend beyond 18 months. Briggs came with an impressive war record which included service in the Western Desert, Iraq and in Burma where, in 1946, he became General Officer, Commander-in-Chief, Burma Command. Within days of stepping into his Kuala Lumpur offices, he set out on an extensive tour of Malaya. Six weeks later he submitted a blueprint to the British Defence Coordination Committee, Far East, calling for the elimination of my army across the peninsula 'step by step, from south to north'. It amounted to a four-point approach that would eventually be referred to as 'The Briggs Plan'.

Firstly, it recommended that the whole process of intelligence gathering, both police and military, be completely overhauled. Secondly, it urged a programme be launched to smash our Min Yuen support network in the squatter areas. Thirdly, and most devastatingly as it would turn out for the CPM, he advised that precise measures be taken to sever our food supply lines. Finally, he proposed that a strategy be adopted that would ultimately force us into fighting government security forces on their own terrain.

The Briggs Plan – with its 'new villages', so similar to Japan's 'fortress villages' idea – was introduced in the latter part of 1950 and began directly affecting our food supplies by the first half of 1951. In the early stages of the Briggs Plan I still felt we could survive on the support we enjoyed from the masses. We had devoted much effort to cultivating the Min Yuen in the squatter communities and the supply lines we created were effective. However, as more and more people were herded into the new villages with their high cyclone wire fencing, their barbed wire, flood lights, police guards, constant searches, frequent interrogations and general restrictions on movement, we realised we were facing nothing less than a crisis of survival.

As the months passed and the British fine-tuned the Briggs Plan, the authorities became very adroit at improvisation. It was not enough for them to control the passage of food in and out of the villages. They introduced central cooking systems in each. This ensured all food would be monitored to the point of consumption.

(Top) Lt General Sir Harold Briggs (centre) came reluctantly to Malaya on condition he would remain Director of Operations against my guerrillas for no more than 18 months. He arrived with an impeccable war record covering tours of duty in the Western Desert, Iraq and Burma. It was Briggs who drew up the original blueprint calling for the elimination of my army 'step by step, from south to north'. His approach became widely known as the 'Briggs Plan'.

(Bottom) The Briggs Plan called for the establishment of so-called 'new villages' throughout the squatter areas of Malaya. These fenced, patrolled and fortified centres, illuminated by night and continually monitored throughout the day, eventually succeeded in severing our food supply lines from the Min Yuen. Movements to and from the villages came under constant surveillance and checks by the security forces and police.

From then on villagers had no further reason to move back and forth gathering supplies. When the Briggs Plan later became our Achilles' heel I would have plenty of time to ponder the rashness of my response to Comrade Yeung Kuo.

So it was that my men and I were forced to sit down and analyse our food predicament very carefully. Malaya, we realised, was not a food-growing country. Much of the country's rice was imported as was a substantial proportion of its meat requirements. There was, of course, an abundance of rubber trees. Our situation became so desperate at one point that I even looked into the possibility of making the rubber seed edible. If this could be achieved, our food supply problem would be solved and the Briggs Plan greatly undermined. We heard from some of our Malay comrades that there were traditional stories relating how grandfathers had discovered ways of making the rubber seed palatable and nutritious. So convinced were the Malays these were genuine accounts, I even sought Peking's assistance in researching the question. When the answer came back, it was to inform us that rubber seeds contained a basic toxin. There was no way of removing this poison to make the seeds edible.

The problems were endless but there always seemed to be enough encouraging episodes within the armed struggle to sustain our resolve. The results achieved in the early attacks by 26 Independent Company, for instance, were reassuring enough for me to withhold our intended move from Kerdau while we tested both tactics and the mettle of our men. Then the British countered and moved six battalions of reinforcements – three of them Gurkhas – into the Jerantut area to block our push northwards. At times the fighting became very heavy indeed. Just as had happened with our northern guerrillas, 26 Independent Company found itself losing the battlefield initiative and concentrating its efforts on avoiding the increased enemy jungle patrols. These conditions sustained for three months and heightened enemy pressure eventually forced us to move our headquarters, first to the west and then south to the jungles around the township of Bentung. By then I had given orders for 26 Independent Company guerrillas to break contact and withdraw to deep jungle positions for recuperation. There I intended they should stay until we had completed a meticulous tactical review.

Our post-mortem recognised that we had been taught some very hard lessons. When we first launched our Kelantan and Pahang forays we were confident we could occupy sections of the two states and hold them against whatever counter-measures the British chose to introduce. Then, as the weeks turned into months, we realised we had undertaken objectives beyond our capabilities. At that point, the two operations had become practical exercises in gaining battle experience and developing skills. We needed to arrive at a new strategic blueprint that could be followed by all guerrilla units throughout our movement.

The logistical supply lesson was equally daunting. Keeping 200 guerrillas functioning in a single unit required a logistics commitment beyond the capacities of our supply lines. Food alone presented huge problems. Everywhere we had travelled it was the same situation: serious food shortages. You can't expect a village, no matter how loyal to the cause, to supply food for two hundred ravenous fighters for several days on end. Nor can any single stretch of jungle produce natural sustenance of readily edible fruit and wild animals for such numbers.

As the British introduced their reinforcements the whole fighting pattern moved to our disadvantage. We had begun by picking the time and place for raids where we could dominate the action until such time as it was expedient for us to withdraw. Classic guerrilla tactics. Now our forces were losing the fundamental requirement of being able to dictate when, where and for how long the action would last.

Continual moving, fighting, withdrawing, regrouping and fighting again took its toll on unit morale as our guerrillas became physically exhausted. Interestingly enough, our casualties were low. We lost men, but not in significant numbers. As the British increased their pressure, we chose to avoid fighting if we could. We had mastered some useful tactics. We took care to withdraw to favourable overnight jungle positions that made surprise attacks difficult. We had gained valuable experience in the art of luring the enemy into ambushes. Still, we had much to learn. We had been keen to stamp our mark on the fighting by annihilating British patrols. This objective largely eluded us. We achieved a limited number of kills but we were never in a position to sweep the battlefield after the action and seize weapons and ammunition. And to have been able to do this was vital to our continuing operation.

Above all else, though, the experiments we had undertaken with our 200 guerrillas operating as a single unit taught us that we must re-evaluate our intentions of setting up liberated zones and holding them with what we termed company-sized forces. Such tactics, we recognised, would be suicidal against the already demonstrated British ability to respond.

Immediately after the review, we reorganised our 200-strong main force, into smaller-sized guerrilla groups. Furthermore, we issued instructions to the effect we would henceforth abandon all ideas of large-scale attacks.

*　　*　　*　　*　　*

In Bentung, our camp was located in dense jungle. By this time a number of new villages were already up and running under the Briggs Plan. There were some relatively close to our position. We had two platoons – about 60 men – of our main force Pahang guerrillas attached to Headquarters. Basically we relied on two villages for support. Then, one after another, there occurred a string of disturbing police swoops on our Min Yuen supporters.

Suddenly, we found ourselves without food supplies. The prospects of re-establishing smuggling routes from the villages seemed very remote. We had to take emergency measures. We dispersed the bulk of our headquarters force, broken down into small units, to other areas. That left us primarily with a security platoon of about 30 men, the Politburo members, their individual bodyguards and a small armed work unit camped nearby. In all there were about 80 of us left. Even then we were unable to supply ourselves with enough food.

We tried rationing. Everyone got one Milk Maid brand condensed milk can of rice per day as the basic staple. In a very short time we were reduced to a state of semi-hunger and it was too much to ask our guerrillas to be ready for battle under these circumstances.

Security arrangements at the new villages were organised jointly by the police and military. The British troops involved in our area were based in Bentung, some ten miles away by road but probably no more than three as the crow flies. The police supervised the villages. Special Branch officers functioned inside each fenced-off community and it was their task to provide intelligence on the links between our sympathisers and forces. The military provided the jungle patrols and there were an enormous number of these. Remarkably, though, our headquarters position in the Bentung area was never discovered, probably because our security force was under strict orders to avoid all contact with British patrols.

There was a small river near our headquarters. It was a tributary of the Sungei Semantan. As the food crisis intensified we began sending daily parties to the river to collect grass-like reeds that grew along the banks. These were poisonous and caused severe skin irritations. However, they were edible if left to soak for 24 hours in water and afterwards washed thoroughly. We then cooked the reeds which became supplementary food to our rice rations. After eating a helping of reeds and rice you felt full. But the feeling lasted barely two hours. You then became extremely hungry again. We hunted wild boar and monkeys for meat. We persisted this way for months. The Briggs Plan was working.

I have seen it stated by people who have written about the Emergency that we constantly used brutal tactics to ensure the support of the Min Yuen. Such accusations are grossly distorted and the result of very effective government propaganda. Without question we employed controlling measures. Lectures were given to the Min Yuen by our political commissars. From time to time threats were made as we worked to secure our supply lines. Undoubtedly there were excesses. In this sort of situation there always will be. But that was certainly not the general rule. Government propaganda, of course, played up such aspects and distortions became solid beliefs, in just the way it was intended they should. We exerted harsh punishments on those who wilfully set out to betray us; that is true. I make no apology for that. It was war. But the overwhelming percentage of the urban and rural work forces were solidly behind us and had been so since the Japanese occupation days. It would have been totally counter-productive for us to brutalise roundly those on whom we were so dependent.

*　　*　　*　　*　　*

Towards the end of our lengthy Bentung reappraisal sessions, the colonial government publicly identified me for the first time as leader of the CPM. A special government announcement on September 5, 1951, promised rewards of $80,000 for my capture alive and $60,000 if I was brought in dead. Pointedly, only my Party alias – Chin Peng – was revealed.

In December, 1950, Sir Harold Briggs, as Director of Operations, had issued orders for a series of rewards to be paid for information leading to the apprehension of a whole range of CPM functionaries. Topping the list then was a bounty of $30,000 on my head. However, my identity then was not disclosed. I was merely referred to as 'Secretary General of the Central Executive Committee'.

I think the British, very early in the Emergency, possessed firm intelligence on my position in the Party and on much of my personal background. If they hadn't

மலாயர் கம்யூனிஸ்ட் கட்சி, எம். ஆர். எல். ஏ., மின் யூன் சங்கம்
ஆகியவைகளின் அங்கத்தினர் அனைவருக்கும்

அறிவிப்பு.

மலாயன் கம்யூனிஸ்ட் கட்சி, எம். ஆர். எல். ஏ., மின் யூன் சங்கம், இன்னும் இதர கம்யூனிஸ்ட் ஸ்டாப் னங்களின் கீழ்க்கண்ட உத்தியோகஸ்தர்களையும் அங்கத்தினர்களையும்
(அ) பிடிந்து வரும் அல்லது
(ஆ) பாதுகாப்புப் படைகள் பிடிப்பதற்கான அல்லது கொல்லுவதற்கான தகவல்களைக்கொடுக்கும் மேற்படி ஸ்தாபனங்களின் அங்கத்தினர்களுக்கு இதனடியில் குறிப்பிட்டுள்ள இரும் தொகை கொடுக்கப்படும்:—

நபர்கள்

மத்திய நிர்வாக சபிட்டியின் பொது காரியதரிசி. (Secretary-General of the Central Executive Committee)	இலவசப் பிடிப்பதற்கு	$ 30,000 இரும் கொடுக்கப்படும்.
பாலிட்பியூரோ என்னும் அரசியல் கழகத்தின் அங்கத்தினர். (Members of the Politburo)	"	$ 25,000 "
மத்திய அல்லது வட மலாயன் (பியூரோ) கழக அங்கத்தினர் அல்லது மத்திய அல்லது தென் மலாயன் (பியூரோ) கழக அங்கத்தினர். (Members of the Central or, North, Central or South Malayan Bureau)	"	$ 20,000 "
சமஸ்தான கமிட்டி காரியதரிசிகள், டவுன் கமிட்டி காரியதரிசிகள், பிரதேச கமிட்டி காரியதரிசிகள். (State Committee Secretaries, Town Committee Secretaries, Regional Committee Secretaries)	"	$ 15,000 "
கமஸ்தான கமிட்டி அங்கத்தினர், டவுன் கமிட்டி அங்கத்தினர், பிரதேச கமிட்டி அங்கத்தினர், சமஸ்தான இராணுவ அதிகாரத்துவத்தின் அங்கத்தினர். (State Committee Members, Town Committee Members, Regional Committee Members, Members of State Military Commands).	"	$10,000 "
ஜில்லா கமிட்டி காரியதரிசிகள். (District Committee Secretaries)	"	$ 7,000 "
ஜில்லா கமிட்டி அங்கத்தினர், கம்பெனி அதிகாரத்துவத்தின் அங்கத்தினர். (District Committee Members, Members of Company Commands)	"	$ 5,000 "
வழிநடத்த உத்தரவாதமுள்ள கமிட்டி அங்கத்தினர், பிளாட்டூன் (படைப் பகுதி) அதிகாரத்துவத்தின் அங்கத்தினர். (Directing Committee Members, Members of Platoon Commands)	"	$ 3,000 "
கிளை கமிட்டியின் அங்கத்தினர், படை "செக்ஷன்" அதிகாரிகள், மின் யூன் இராணுவ வேலை படைப்பின் தலைவர்கள், பாதுகாப்பு அணியைச் சேர்ந்த தலைவர்கள், விசேஷ சேவை படைகளின் தலைவர்கள். (Members of Branch Committees, Section Commanders, Leaders of Min Yuen Military Work Forces, Leaders of Protection Corps, Leaders of Special Services Squads)	"	$ 2,500 "
கட்சி "செல்"களின் தலைவர்கள். (Leaders of Party Cells)	"	$ 1,500 "
கட்சியின் சாதாரண அங்கத்தினர், படையைச் சேர்ந்த தனி நபர்கள், விசேஷ சேவை படைகளின் அங்கத்தினர், இராணுவ வேலை படைகளின் அங்கத்தினர், பாதுகாப்பு அணியைச் சேர்ந்த அங்கத்தினர். (Ordinary Party Members, Combatant Members, Members of Special Service Squads, Members of Military Work Forces, Members of Protection Corps)	"	$ 1,000 "

உங்கள் சொர்த ஆயுதத்தைக் கொண்டுவந்து கொடுத்தால் அதற்காகக் கொடுக்கப்படும் இரும் தொகை நீங்கள, இதை தப்பாவிட், தொட்டா முதலான ஆயுதங்களுக்கு மேலும் அதிப்படையான இரும் கொடுக்கப்படும்.
உங்கள் குடும்பத்தை ஆதரிப்பதற்கு இப் பணத்தை நீங்கள் உபயோகித்துக்கொள்ளலாம்.
சில சொன்னபர்களின் பெயர் அதிவிக்கப்பட்ட அவுள்கோப் பிடிப்பதற்கான விசேஷ இரும் தொகையும் கொடுப்பதாக அதிவிக்கப்பட்டுள்ளது. அத் தொகை இந்த நூபிதாவில் உள்ளதைவிட அதிப்மான தாபிருந்தால் அந்த அதிப்மான தொகையே கொடுக்கப்படும்.
நீங்கள் ஒரு கட்டாக இருந்து வேலே தெய்தால் இரும் தொகை உங்களுக்கு பகிர்ந்து கொடுக்கப்படும்.

மூக்கிய குறிப்பு:

பிடிபட்டவர் அல்லது கொல்லப்பட்டவரின் சரியான அடையாளங்கோப் பற்றி திர்க்கமாக விசாரித்த பிறகே இரும் தொகை கொடுக்கப்படும்.

Harold Briggs.

An early offer of monetary rewards by the colonial authorities for providing information leading to the apprehension of a whole range of CPM members. This particular notice was signed by Director of Operations Harold Briggs. At this point the authorities appeared anxious to withhold any identification of the CPM leader as being Chin Peng, the same man they had decorated for military service to Britain three years earlier. You will note my value at this point was placed at $30,000 (Straits dollars) – still a tidy sum if calculated at today's rates.

Finally, Britain's anti-insurgency experts arrive at the conclusion they have no alternative but to reveal my identity. They get around the propaganda dilemma that has held back this decision by briefing journalists about the man Britain once 'trusted'. The implication being, of course, that I had somehow run off the rails since Force 136 days and for this I was now being proclaimed Public Enemy No 1.

uncovered this information on day one when police raided the tin miner's bungalow outside Kampar, they would certainly have learned much about me when they interrogated Chen Yong in the weeks thereafter.

We in the CPM leadership speculated on why the British chose to maintain my anonymity so long. Undoubtedly, it was for propaganda reasons. One theory was that the government, by unmasking me, would immediately be faced with the problem of explaining, both locally and internationally, how it was that the character heading the 'terrorist' organisation they were so feverishly portraying as bloodthirsty and ruthless, had been worthy of two military medals and an OBE for services to Britain? Yet another theory argued that by maintaining my anonymity the British were hoping I would become complacent and less security-conscious which, in turn, would lead to better opportunities for killing me. As it happened, more pubic attention was paid at the time to accompanying exhortations by High Commissioner Gurney for the Emergency to be wound up by the following year.

But in September, 1951, with my Chin Peng alias disclosed, local reports in both English and Asian language newspapers endeavoured to delve into my background from whatever sources were available. The result was scarcely what the authorities were looking for. *The Straits Times*, for instance, in a report on September 6, 1951, went back to Spencer Chapman's post-war book, *The Jungle is Neutral*, from which they extracted the quote about me having been 'Britain's most trusted guerrilla'. The story was headed 'Chin Peng – the man Britain 'trusted' is now a dangerous foe'.

The same account noted that there were several Federation residents – John Davis, Richard Broome and Claude Fenner, among them – who described me as soft-spoken, quiet and with a gentle manner. 'Chin Peng,' the story continued, 'is a man who will keep his word to the letter. The British army found that in the days immediately after the reoccupation when they were immersed with the problems of disarming the MPAJA and satisfying their post-war needs.'

Perhaps, in revealing my identity in the 1951 rewards notices, the authorities were hoping they would spur the process of betrayal. If so, they were wrong. At no time during the Emergency did I ever feel in danger of being compromised by those around me.

My wife, Khoon Wah, was transferred back to Headquarters while we were still in Bentung. She had been working as an area committee member in the Tras region of Perak which, in fact, was not far away from our camp position. She had left our Mentekab camp at the end of 1949, when it was decided we must reduce the numbers of non-combatants attached to Headquarters. My wife and some other female comrades all departed at the same time. It had become necessary to ensure that a touchy problem of wives and families in camp situations be contained. I knew it was often difficult for rank-and-file guerrillas to come to terms with the presence of senior CPM officials living what would appear to be normal family lives in the otherwise harsh confines of a jungle environment.

Much was made of this by British propaganda following the defection of Lam Swee who obviously used the issue to ingratiate himself with the enemy. In reality the matter never got out of hand because we acted on it. But the result was that Khoon Wah and other wives had to leave Mentekab and the enemy undoubtedly scored some propaganda points. Khoon Wah and another female comrade were called to Bentung to look after complex administrative matters. They arrived in late September, 1951.

*　　*　　*　　*　　*

While the post-war fiscal recovery in Britain dragged on, politicians in Westminster – the Emergency aside – remained encouraged by the developing economies in Malaya and Singapore. They felt certain that, together, the two territories would return to their full pre-war roles of being Britain's fountain of 'dollar' riches. The speed by which the debt-laden mother country would emerge from her post-war financial crisis depended on her success in maintaining colonial dominance. By as early as June, 1949, official statistics were showing that rubber, rice and tin production figures were all exceeding pre-war record years. In an editorial on June 16, the influential British newspaper, *The Daily Telegraph*, noted that a Colonial Office report on these record results had paid generous tribute to the men on the spot 'whose energy and ingenuity have played so large a part in these achievements.'

The paper commented: 'These would have been greater still but for the evil hand stretched out from Moscow to thwart progress. Ideological banditry in Malaya, whose war and post-war record is on all fours with its practices elsewhere, has been partially scotched, but the communist hydra now threatens Hong Kong. The Far Eastern peoples enjoying the proved benefits of British administration must, at all costs, be protected from this new enemy whose depredations otherwise promise to outmatch the Japanese themselves.' The propaganda men in London must have been delighted.

With the Korean War came further wealth to Malaya and Singapore way beyond the wildest imaginings of the greediest colonials. It was super prosperity that had an extraordinary overflowing effect on our movement. Even small landholders among the Min Yuen prospered as rubber and tin prices skyrocketed. Donations to the Party similarly soared to the point that, as a movement, we became financially wealthy. But, for all our wealth, we still lacked food. The Briggs Plan had determined that we couldn't go shopping, nor could it be done for us. The nation's sudden affluence then impacted on our recruiting efforts. These plunged. As villages prospered, far fewer people were swayed by political philosophy. Even fewer were those who could be convinced of the glory of laying their lives on the line for a cause.

Still, we persisted. By the end of 1950, nearly every major unit had its own portable radio receiver but none of us had transmitting equipment. We could receive news from Radio Peking, Radio Moscow, the Far East relay network of the BBC and Radio Malaya for local news. We gathered around our radio sets. Regularly, we recorded the bulletins, transcribed them, and then circulated through leaflets the relevant points as we saw them.

*   *   *   *   *

In 1951, the Singapore Police directed a series of lightning raids against the CPM's infrastructure on the island. Communication links with Singapore and my Pahang headquarters were operating effectively at the time and I was getting updated reports of the actions being taken by the colonial authorities against English-educated local intellectuals. Most of the victims of this period of suppression had joined our ranks after the Emergency declaration. Some had come to our fold via the Anti-British League. Some, considered reliable by our Singapore underground, had been inducted into Party membership without reference to Headquarters. I was puzzled why the British were moving against these people. All had been rather open in their public statements and would always have been regarded by us as likely to be exposed. Consequently, there was no possibility of them being moved into sensitive positions within the Party framework.

I followed carefully the reports I was receiving from our Singapore underground. As the crackdown escalated I issued instructions for all those we categorised as 'open figures' – meaning members who had been publicly exposed – to withdraw to any convenient safe destination. Some left for Indonesia. Others went to China. It was decided that crossing the Causeway into Malaya could not be an option. Fighting there was far too intense and widespread.

One of the evacuees was Eu Chooi Yip, a senior Party member who had secretly run *Freedom News*, our Singapore underground newspaper. An economics graduate from Raffles College, he had been more openly associated with the Tan Kah Kee owned *Nan Chiau Jit Pao*, a pro-CPC publication. Eu and his departing colleagues were to lie low in neighbouring Indonesia. Their intention was to return to Singapore only when the political situation on this island turned favourable to the communist cause. A highly experienced propagandist, Eu was one of very few comrades leaving Singapore then who would remain fully active in exile. He established himself in the Rhiau Islands south of Singapore and there continued his clandestine Party activities. It would be a decade before I got to meet him personally and then, in Peking, we would together begin planning yet another major evacuation of our members – again from Singapore.

Against the background of all that has been written about us by people who have never met us or communicated with us in any way, it is probably difficult for a modern student of these events to accept that we were truly convinced of the morality of our position. There was no question in our minds about the injustices of the colonial system. The greed of the colonial 'masters' in our midst was obvious to all who chose to view the world beyond the sanctuaries of the 'whites only' clubs. Exploitation of working men and women who barely scratched at survival on the wages paid them by the wealthy plantations and mines on which they worked was an undeniable fact of life. The corruption of the administrative and legal trappings that inevitably worked to the colonials' advantage was there to experience on a daily basis. Furthermore, the determination of the real power behind the scenes in London to continue extracting Malaya's natural wealth for its own purposes was as clear as the cloudless tropical nights we knew so well.

*   *   *   *   *

The realisation that our military approach from late 1948 through to 1951 had been utterly inappropriate was a bitter pill to swallow. The review of our armed struggle strategies dominated a two-month period from August to September, 1951. Disheartening though our findings were at times, there was never a suggestion of giving up the campaign. Based on our experience during the Japanese time, we remained confident we could continue guerrilla warfare for many years.

While in Bentung we were receiving reports from Kedah which indicated our guerrillas there had been successful operating in platoon-sized formations. In a period of only a few months they had notched up a string of lightning ambushes across a broad stretch of countryside. We distributed details of these noteworthy platoon actions to all sections of our army and made a point of awarding Party commendations to the Kedah forces involved. In addition we issued orders for all units to follow the Kedah example.

Unfortunately, the now quite legendary October 1, 1951, Resolution – the main document emerging from our broad-based tactical review – failed to come to grips with the military problems and their solutions as we had perceived them during our deliberations. Worse still, our field commanders concentrated, not on the accompanying orders, but on the resolution itself. As so much has been written about this episode, I am once again compelled to set the record straight. Resolution and all accompanying directives, were completed probably a month before their release date. They were the products of Politburo discussions between myself, Lee An Tung and Siao Chang. Fortuitously, Ah Chung happened to arrive in Bentung from east Pahang during our deliberations and joined them. Special Branch assertions attributing authorship of the resolution to Yeung Kuo are baseless as are similar claims repeated by various historians. Yeung Kuo had long left us for Selangor.

The document had resulted from lengthy soul searching. It placed primary emphasis on the politics of our predicament rather than on required military strategy. We considered military matters had been adequately covered in the accompanying orders. The resolution itself underlined the importance of guerrillas taking remedial actions to demonstrate greater support and sympathy with the masses. This was, of course, a reflection of the undeniably successful Briggs Plan implementation and the difficulties it was imposing on us. We admitted to many mistakes which had jeopardised our close relationship with the people, particularly the middle classes. We instructed our rank-and-file to cease slashing rubber trees, confiscating identity cards, burning buses and attacking civilian trains.

I have heard it argued that such excesses might not have developed in the 1950-51 period had I been able to exert better control over our guerrillas nationwide. There is a great deal of truth in this. Quite categorically I can state that apart from the confiscation of identity cards, neither the Politburo nor the Central Committee

The photographs on these two pages record the sort of incidents that were at the source of my concern when Politburo discussions resulted in our issuing the October 1, 1951, Resolution. The wanton slashing of rubber trees, as illustrated above, was quite counter-productive to our cause.

The Aik Hoe factory blaze in Singapore in July, 1950, was also a case in point. The colonial administration on the island at the time claimed they had documents to prove the fire was the work of communist agents. I would not dispute this charge.

In early 1950, comrades derailed a Day Mail train outside the Johore township of Gemas. The above photo shows three of the seven coaches that left the track that day. This was scarcely an isolated incident. It was the fourth train derailment in a 24-hour period.

issued orders for the destruction of rubber trees or the violent disruption of public transportation. But these things did happen on a large scale and they appear to have resulted from individually issued orders. From the propaganda standpoint, they cost us dearly.

Almost a year after the resolution was distributed within the Party, the government revealed it had secured a copy but conveniently omitted indicating when this had happened. Not only had the document given the enemy valuable insight into the best counter-tactics to impose, but, more importantly, it revealed the beginnings of our struggle with flagging morale. Certainly it indicated, very explicitly, that I was anxious to avoid excesses and was perturbed by the impact these were having on our Min Yuen. The document should have provided the British with an immediate propaganda bonanza.

By neglecting to drive home military requirements in the October 1 Resolution, we most assuredly lost the initiative on the battlefield at the precise moment the enemy were deeply concerned with what we might be planning to do next. While drafting it we, of course, had no inkling of the leadership wrangling then underway in Kuala Lumpur's corridors of power. Director of Operations Briggs was on the cusp of resignation, demoralised by what he regarded as crippling restrictions to his authority. Deep personal differences had developed between the Director of Intelligence, Sir William Jenkin, and Commissioner of Police, Mr Nicol Gray. Both these men were also on the verge of resigning.

As it had been with Sir Edward Gent, Commissioner General MacDonald was at odds with High Commissioner Gurney. Again MacDonald in Singapore was busy behind scenes plotting and manoeuvring to undermine the confidence with which London viewed its senior representative in Malaya. Such was the deterioration in relationships between Gurney and MacDonald that the High Commissioner, in a hand-written letter to the Colonial Office dated March 19, 1951,[18] submitted an offer of resignation based on the backroom manipulations that had taken place. The offer was turned down. Gurney was assured that the Colonial Office retained full confidence in his ability.[19]

Rather than get mired in the propaganda politics of the time, we in the CPM should have launched ever increasing classic guerrilla raids on targets of choice. We were well capable of doing this. The greater the difficulties we encountered as a result of the Briggs Plan, the more dramatic and determined should have been our small unit military responses. I believe this would have maintained our initiative.

<u>Secretary of State.</u>

The attached manuscript letter from
Sir Henry Gurney is disturbing. You will see
from its last paragraph that he asks that,
apart from showing the letter to you, I should
keep its contents to myself. He also there
says that the letter requires no reply but I
should much dislike leaving it unanswered, and
I hope that you will feel able to agree that
I may reply to him in sympathetic and reassuring
terms.

Looking back now I am sorry that, when I
heard that Mr.Malcolm MacDonald was bringing
Sir John Harding with him, I did not advise
you to ask that Sir H.Gurney also should be
included in the party. He is, of course,
responsible only to you and in no sense to
Mr.MacDonald for general administration in
Malaya and it is only natural that he should
feel (as this letter shows he does) that there
is a loss of confidence in him when others
from South East Asia are given the opportunity
to criticise the conduct of affairs which are
primarily his responsibility. It was with
these considerations in mind that, in my last
talk with Mr.MacDonald, I expressed to him the
strong hope that when he told Sir H.Gurney what
had passed at the Ministerial talks, he would
make it very plain to him that both he
(Mr.MacDonald) and you during those talks had
expressed complete confidence in Sir Henry's
administration. I fear from Sir Henry's letter
that Mr.MacDonald cannot have done this as
effectively as you would, I am sure, have
wished.

I have tried my hand at the draft of a
reply to Sir Henry. You may wish to discuss
this, and his letter, with me.

[signature]

2.4.51.

[handwritten note] We can discuss — I
had your reply is
on the right lines *[initials]* 3/4/51

When the Colonial Office receives Gurney's hand-written letter offering
to resign following behind-scenes politicking by Commissioner General
MacDonald, there is immediate reaction. Here a high-ranking official
– in diplomatic double-speak – advises the Secretary of State for the
Colonies that MacDonald is behind the trouble.[20]

But we had miscalculated and bungled. A critical moment was lost, never to be regained.

For all my problems of control at this time, I still met people. Together with my Politburo colleagues I could move and re-assign field commanders. We could promote and demote both political and military officers. Indeed, we were continually readjusting the Party political and military frameworks to meet ever-changing exigencies. As the Emergency proceeded, the need to plan specific, spectacular attacks purely for their political impact in the colonial motherland escaped me. By the time the Viet Minh had demonstrated these tactics so brilliantly during the 56-day Dien Bien Phu battle culminating in the defeat of the French on May 7, 1954, any lesson we could have learned would have come too late.

Curiously enough, though, within days of our October 1 Resolution we did succeed with one extraordinarily spectacular small-scale action which had a shattering effect on British morale both in Malaya and the United Kingdom.

Chapter 18

Assassination on the Gap road . . . enter the hectoring Templer

Comrade Siew Ma and the 36 guerrillas in his independent platoon had been lying in ambush for almost two days along the winding Gap road leading to the popular expatriate highland retreat of Fraser's Hill, some 60 miles north of Kuala Lumpur. Our most celebrated commander – whose name in Mandarin translates to 'Little Horse' – had chosen the roadside position carefully.

His mission called for split-second timing. The danger element he and his men faced was high. It was not just a matter of wiping out the enemy in a prepared ambush 'killing box'. This time he was hoping to attack a large armed convoy. The aim: To seize as many weapons and as much ammunition as the comrades could carry away.

Siew Ma, son of a working class family, was short and very fit. He had joined the CPM before the Japanese invasion and was one of the last students to pass through the 101 STS training course in Singapore. So he well understood how much a guerrilla raid's success depended on precision.

One particular 300-yard segment of steeply inclining roadway running to a sharp bend had caught Siew Ma's attention in the early hours of Friday, October 5, 1951. Located just before the 57th milestone, the bend was so severe that drivers of all forms of transport were forced to drop to a crawl. Our commander placed his guerrillas in lush undergrowth on the hill side of the road. Their arms included rifles, two Bren guns and a Sten gun. Siew Ma decided on three separate firing positions. In addition, he organised three charging squads whose task was to rush and plunder the convoy once it came to a standstill with heavy casualties. He had earlier instructed two men to keep notes on passing traffic which they duly started doing once they got into position.

By midday the following day, Saturday, Siew Ma was becoming restive. Food rations were almost exhausted. He had expected a far heavier flow of weekend traffic past his ambush point. He knew police convoys regularly used the Gap road and by now there should have been at least one group of military vehicles carrying supplies to the nearby operational area of the Royal West Kent Regiment. He decided he would hold the ambush for another two hours. If a substantial convoy target had not appeared by then, he would break off and withdraw to his deep jungle camp.

Shortly before 1 pm, Siew Ma's spirits were lifted by the familiar revving sounds of what he guessed was a Land Rover dropping through gears as it negotiated twists and turns further back down the road. Then round a lower sharp bend leading to the start of the ambush zone came the vehicle. It was a Land Rover, sure enough, packed with at least half a dozen local police – all carrying arms. A hundred yards or so behind it followed a shiny black limousine. Lead vehicles of a convoy? Siew Ma was uncertain. Seconds of high expectation passed as the first vehicle was given time to move into the 'killing box' and the limousine, a Rolls Royce, followed up unsuspectingly. Attack! A volley of rifle, Bren and Sten gun fire rent the humid stillness of the early afternoon, tearing into the Land Rover and wounding all except one policeman aboard. The Land Rover swerved to a halt on the left hand verge. Its passengers, wounded or not, scrambled into the nearby undergrowth and were soon shooting back.

It took some moments before the driver of the limousine reacted. He had also swerved to the left, skidding to a stop 40 yards back from the Land Rover as bullets began peppering his vehicle. Wounded, the Rolls Royce driver edged open his door, rolled onto the roadway and there lay motionless. As the initial burst of firing subsided, quite inexplicably the rear off-side door of the limousine opened and a slim European man in light tropical clothes stepped out. He began walking calmly and directly towards our high bank ambush positions. He had taken no more than three or four steps before he fell, face down, in a clatter of rifle fire.

With the police party still active in the undergrowth, Siew Ma was unable to order his charging squads to retrieve weapons. Then, round the bottom bend came a scout car its Bren gun blazing as it approached the first of the two stationary vehicles. A very disheartened Siew Ma, discouraged by his failure to gather weapons and quite oblivious to what he had accomplished, ordered his platoon bugler to sound the retreat. With no casualties on our side, the withdrawal was completed rapidly. It would be an hour before police and military reinforcements reached the scene. They would discover the European lying sprawled near a drain on the hill side of the road. It was His Excellency, Sir Henry Gurney, British High Commissioner in Malaya, the most senior colonial official in the land. Dead.

I was about 35 miles away across the highlands in my Bentung headquarters when the Gurney assassination took place. It was not until the next day, while tuned to the early morning news on Radio Malaya, that I first learned we had killed the High Commissioner. Lee An Tung, Siao Chang, Ah Chung and I were gathered around the camp radio when the report was read. I recall very clearly the silence of amazement that briefly followed. It then dissipated to shouts of incredulity. I knew it must have been the work of Siew Ma. The radio report was brief and it was not until later in the day that a courier arrived with the newspapers that provided greater details. As we sat around reading these, we could hear British aircraft directing heavy bombing runs onto jungles around the ambush location. Enemy gunners were also firing off barrages of artillery. There was no gloating on our part. But we did exchange light remarks about the enemy kindly providing celebratory explosions for us to mark the occasion. It was agreed we would issue a special headquarters proclamation commending all guerrillas involved in the Gurney ambush.

Personally, I could not help but reflect on the irony of the situation. There we were, having just completed a tortuous reassessment of our campaign with its recognition of our countless regrettable errors. We were being increasingly isolated from the Min Yuen by the Briggs Plan, suffering debilitating food shortages and continually undertaking measures to avoid enemy military patrols. Indeed, so serious was our predicament that we had begun contemplating yet another major move of our headquarters. Not the best of times. Then, on a weekend that had appeared to promise nothing of consequence, a small band of hungry, dedicated comrades, concealed in the undergrowth, had unwittingly eliminated no less than the High Commissioner himself. I was stunned. I was elated. So, too, was every comrade – man or woman – at my Bentung camp.

The British descended on the nearby township of Tras in a follow-up action to the assassination and interrogated anyone they could lay their hands on. That was how they discovered that Chin Peng's wife, Khoon Wah, had, until recently, been functioning in the area's communist underground. In a rather blatant, if feeble attempt at further blackening the public enemy No 1 image of the CPM's Secretary General, British propaganda linked Khoon Wah to the plot behind Gurney's assassination. Unfortunately, no such plot had ever been hatched and as the conspiracy theory could obviously not be sustained, the claim of my wife's involvement was allowed to evaporate.

Our emotional high following the assassination would soon have to give way to Party routine. While preparing the October 1 Resolution we had received a letter from the now well-entrenched communist authorities in Peking. The letter requested

(Right) Pageantry and pomp were important elements of British colonial control. Here High Commissioner Sir Henry Gurney, who supposedly aimed to get closer to the people, demonstrates that rubbing shoulders with the masses was, perhaps, not his primary consideration after all.

(Bottom) The bullet-riddled Rolls Royce in which Gurney was travelling when he and his party ran into the Gap road ambush prepared by Siew Ma.

This patrol from A Company, 1ˢᵗ Bat., Royal Australian Regiment, claimed to have killed three of the guerrillas who assassinated Gurney. As Gurney was shot on October 6, 1951 and Australian ground forces did not begin operations in Malaya until late 1955, I hold deep reservations about these claims. Apparently the photo was first published in the Sunday Times on November 23, 1958 – nearly seven years after the events on the Gap road.

Almost forgotten in a display of old vehicles at the Penang Museum, the Rolls Royce in which Gurney travelled to his death is today in a decrepit state with peeling, rusting paintwork and disintegrating upholstery.

that a senior member of the CPM be sent to China for important discussions. I had no idea what lay behind the Chinese overture. I was sure, however, that Peking would not have gone to such lengths to contact us had there not been a good reason. I chose Siao Chang to go as he was, without doubt, the most experienced of us all. He moved north to Bangkok where our Siamese communist contacts smuggled him, after interminable delays, aboard a China-bound freighter. He reached Peking in the early weeks of 1953.

The combined effect of heightened British military patrolling and tightened controls in the two new villages providing us with supplies left us little option but to depart Bentung. We moved north to the Raub area where we knew police supervision of the resettled Chinese was less vigilant. In Raub the new village residents consisted of small-holder rubber planters. Most of them grew bananas as a secondary cash crop. Bananas were good for us and we had lots of them.

Within a short period we had put in place effective food channels. But, given our experience in Bentung, we were determined to create alternative food sources independent from the Min Yuen. One project involved cultivating our own crops. We sent members of our armed workforce on a three-hour walk into the jungle to clear an area for vegetable growing. We started by planting several acres of rice and maize. But before we could begin harvesting, the British attacked our base headquarters. I was an hour's walk away, at the time, engaged in discussions with some local cadres. Tactics for this enemy strike were identical to those used on previous occasions against my headquarters. First they bombed and strafed heavily. Then they launched ground assaults.

In my absence, Lee An Tung was in charge of the camp. Under his direction our people withdrew to the *lalang* and I lost all contact with them for more than two weeks. I had three bodyguards with me. The cadres with whom I was meeting were the important Malay leaders – Abdullah C.D. and Rashid Maidin – each accompanied by his personal bodyguards. News of the raids reached me as our discussions were concluding. I instructed Abdullah and Rashid to return to their respective camps and I, together with my bodyguards, moved to a jungle fringe position near a banana plantation which was owned by a member of the Min Yuen. For ten days we ate little else but bananas. Re-establishing links to my headquarters was a matter of waiting for camp comrades to emerge from the jungle on food supply missions. At very least they had to send in a single runner to pick up salt and sugar. One finally arrived and my group returned with him to the new headquarters location.

*   *   *   *   *

The epitaph tends to support the theory that Sir Henry walked alone from his Rolls Royce towards our ambush position that afternoon in an heroic bid to draw fire away from his companions. Both his wife and secretary remained in the car and survived the ordeal.

The grave of the late Sir Henry Gurney is probably the most prominent of all in Kuala Lumpur's Cheras cemetery. The British authorities ensure it is well tended.

It took the British four months to find a replacement for Gurney. Throughout this period we repeatedly attempted to analyse the extent of the psychological damage Siew Ma and his guerrillas had managed to inflict on the enemy. Everything we read in newspapers or heard on radio broadcasts convinced us that, administratively, Kuala Lumpur was in turmoil. What was more, London appeared, from our jungle position, to be stunned into inactivity. The boost to morale that surged through our ranks resulted in a spontaneous increase in both the number and intensity of guerrilla attacks.

It is fair to say that we in the Politburo never allowed ourselves to be carried away by the euphoria. We had been at war for three-and-a-half years. We were seasoned enough to understand about the psychological ups and downs of conflict. Equally, there was no hiding the reality that we had lost the battle initiative well before Siew Ma and his men killed Gurney. If we were to prevail it would take far more than a transitory heightening of morale. We needed that tactical blueprint for battlefield success which had eluded us from the outset of hostilities.

*　　*　　*　　*　　*

Hand-wringing on the enemy side persisted for weeks after the Gurney assassination. Had there been a breach of security? Had the CPM received prior warning of the High Commissioner's movements that day? Who ordered the ambush? Why had follow-up patrols failed to track down the ambush gang? The public was repeatedly reassured that everything was under control.

As usual, the planters and miners were complaining loudest of all. There were insinuations in official releases that perhaps Gurney himself was partly to blame. They noted he had always refused to travel in armoured cars. They pointed out he had persistently rejected large armed escorts because he wanted to get closer to the people. Closer to the people in a Rolls Royce! To our mind that made no sense at all. Why had he walked away from the car? The suggestion was that he was trying to protect the remaining two occupants – his wife, Lady Gurney, who was sitting in the back seat and his private secretary, Mr D. J. Staples, who occupied the front passenger position. Both had stayed in the vehicle throughout the ordeal. Both had survived.

British newspapers responded in typical knee-jerk fashion. Reports referred to the 'grave deterioration' of security in Malaya. The underlying message was that the communists now had the upper hand. Parliamentary questions were tabled. Faced with this pressure, the Churchill Conservative government, just installed on October 21, reacted by dispatching the new Colonial Secretary, Mr Oliver Lyttelton, for a first-hand assessment. A former soldier and hardened politician, Lyttleton happened to have served on the boards of London Tin and Anglo Oriental, two substantial mining companies with large interests in Malaya.

When he returned to London in December after a two-week tour of the colony, Lyttelton privately reported on the administrative mess he had encountered during his travels. He highlighted, in particular, the appalling lack of coordination and cooperation between civil and military functions in Malaya, the dearth of reliable police intelligence and the generally poor standard of police work. Collaboration between the Chinese in Malaya and the communists, he told his Cabinet colleagues, was widespread. Lyttelton's principal recommendation was that one man alone should be in charge of both civil and military affairs in Malaya. Whoever was appointed, he advised, should be a general.

In the late afternoon of February 7, 1952, Lt General Sir Gerald Templer flew into Kuala Lumpur to take up his posting as 'Supremo' of the revamped anti-insurgency effort. King George V1 had died the previous day and the colonial administration was officially in mourning. Within a week the new High Commissioner was telling a meeting of senior government officers that he had come as a soldier and would run the anti-communist campaign as a soldier would. If he could only rely on the full support of the entire population, he boasted to his audience, he could 'lick' the Emergency in three months.

In the next breath, however, he recognised the unlikelihood of this scenario and went on to predict the general situation would actually deteriorate in the coming months. Communist imperialism, he claimed, was transferring its attention to South East Asia to embarrass the European colonial powers, undermine their economic position and pin down as many troops as possible. As I read newspaper reports of his early remarks I imagined how heartened the expatriate planters, miners, traders and local capitalists would be.

I first heard of Templer's appointment over Radio Malaya. By this time we were really feeling the heat of the new villages. I was not surprised that the Churchill government saw value in appointing a military man to head their colonial administration after our assassination of Gurney. Even making allowances for the British electoral process in October, 1951, which brought Mr Winston Churchill back to office, I was still amazed that it had taken the enemy so long to find a replacement.

The Singapore-based Commissioner General MacDonald (left) didn't like Gent, didn't like Gurney and from all I can establish didn't like Templer (right) too much either. But in the latter case he recognised power, as the body language in this photo seems to be suggesting.

At Headquarters, we refrained from issuing any special propaganda announcement to coincide with Templer's arrival. Our propaganda line as far as he was concerned was handled at the state level and set out to expose the cruelties of the tactics he was quick to put in place. We termed his approach 'barbaric' and perhaps for the first time we found an element of sympathy within the ranks of the colonial administrators and the British press.

On Thursday, March 22, 1952, General Templer stormed into the township of Tanjong Malim, 51 miles north of Kuala Lumpur on the Perak-Selangor border. He was there to punish, personally and severely, a widespread civilian population for failing to warn of our guerrilla activities in the area. Two days earlier we had ambushed a Public Works Department party, killing a total of 12 men including an assistant district officer and an engineer, both Europeans. We had also frequently been clashing with local police patrols resulting in the deaths of eight officers over the previous three months. Government intelligence apparently pointed to no less than 16 guerrilla camps in the surrounding jungles.

For over an hour Templer harangued 350 community leaders who had been herded, especially for the occasion and much against their wishes, into a training college assembly hall. The mixed audience of Chinese, Malays and Indians listened in silence as his words were translated, sentence by sentence, into all three languages. He lambasted and threatened and said he had come to announce the punishment he intended imposing for everyone's cowardly silence. The General told them: 'Communism is the most evil thing in the world. Do you think that under a communist regime you will be able to live a happy family life? Don't you realise that even your children will be set to spy on you? Are any of you communists in this room? Put your hands up!'

Not surprisingly, nobody did.

'All right,' he resumed, 'then I shall have to take extremely unpleasant steps.' He proceeded to enumerate some of them. Until further notice there would be a 22-hour curfew imposed on an area stretching from Tanjong Malim north to Trolak in Perak, a distance of some 18 miles. No one could leave the region. Shops would be open for only two hours daily. Schools would be closed. Bus services suspended. Most draconian of all, the population would be reduced to half rice rations.

With the restrictions and curfews beginning to bite ten days after his Tanjong Malim appearance, the High Commissioner sent letters to every affected household seeking secret information on CPM activities. In the letter Templer wrote: 'If you are

The all powerful High Commissioner and Director of Operations, Sir Gerald Templer, was photographed here opening one of the earlier boxes collected during Operation Question Box. This operation followed closely on the punitive measures he slapped on the people of Tanjong Malim in March, 1952. It was reported that as he opened the container for the benefit of photographers he remarked: 'There'd better be something good in this.'

a communist, I do not expect you to reply. If you are not, I want you to give on this sheet of paper as much information as you can to help my forces catch the communist terrorists in your area.'

It was the beginning of a pattern of behaviour that would characterise the General's entire two-year stint as Britain's High Commissioner in Malaya. It would win him much praise. In London on April 3, Colonial Secretary Lyttelton told a Royal Empire Society gathering that 'there is a new spirit abroad in Malaya. And it has been inspired by Sir Gerald Templer . . . you may be assured that Sir Gerald has all the powers necessary to carry out his job. There is nobody who can interfere with him either on the civil, military or police sides. And, of course, he has the whole support of the Colonial Office.' However, the harshness of his approach would ensure Templer also quickly earned many detractors.

On May 1, less than three months after he first arrived in Malaya, Templer more than trebled the price on my head. A reward of $250,000 was promised to anyone bringing me in alive. If I was brought in dead the cash settlement would drop to $120,000. The High Commissioner was clearly banking on somebody close to me being lured into a major act of betrayal. He must have envisaged widespread disaffection within our leadership ranks and among those in physical proximity to us. Templer obviously regarded the CPM leadership as little more than a bunch of cutthroats who, given financial incentive, would eagerly set about destroying one another. He and his advisers apparently had come to believe their own propaganda.

Several notables at Headquarters including Wu Tien Wang, Chen Tien, and Lee An Tung all had rewards for their capture or assassination substantially increased at the same time the High Commissioner raised mine. None of our Headquarters group ever faced an attempt at assassination or betrayal. Nor did we ever feel threatened in this way. We only took special precautions when we were required to leave our camp to meet with local communist leaders or cadres personally unknown to us. Templer was operating on the principle that if loyalties couldn't be won they could most assuredly be bought. The fact that I am still around and able to make these observations suggests the limit to his logic.

For all the kudos given to Templer as the dominant military figure of Britain's Malayan Emergency campaign, he was not, in my estimation, the man who determined the CPM's defeat on the battlefield. It was the Briggs Plan that began isolating us so dramatically from our mass support. Britain was very fortunate that Briggs received his appointment to Malaya when he did. I well appreciated at the time that our

The Straits Times

MALAYA'S NATIONAL NEWSPAPER: ESTABLISHED 1845

TWELVE PAGES   SINGAPORE, THURSDAY, MAY 1, 1952.

Engagement & Wedding Rings
VISIT
U.S. de. SILVA JEWELLERS
100, ORCHARD ROAD · TEL: 22466

NOW IT'S $250,000 FOR PUBLIC ENEMY No. 1

—if brought in alive

KUALA LUMPUR, Wednesday.

THE FEDERATION GOVERNMENT today announced a reward of $250,000 for "bringing in alive" or giving information leading to the capture of the leading Malayan Communist terrorist, Chin Peng.

The new reward is three times the reward of $80,000 offered for Chin Peng in June last year.

Chin Peng, 31-year-old secretary-general of the Central Executive Committee of the Malayan Communist Party, is the man responsible for directing the armed Communist revolt in Malaya.

A sum of $125,000 will be paid for information leading to Chin Peng's killing. In June, 1951, $60,000 was offered for his death.

An indication that the new rewards might be directed at the "bringing in alive" of the leading Communist figures in the Federation is given in the Government statement announcing the rewards.

"BRINGING IN ALIVE," THE STATEMENT SAYS, "INCLUDES THE POSITIVE ARRANGING WITH THE AUTHORITIES OF THE SURRENDER OF A KNOWN TERRORIST NOW IN THE JUNGLE."

It is known that many of the leading Communists have relatives living in new villages and towns in the Federation.

Other rewards

Other rewards increased today were for the capture or killing of all Communist leaders above district committee level.

that the Commissioner of Police had already sanctioned and paid the full scale of enhanced reward of $35,000 to the persons who gave information which led to the recent successful ambush of Long Pin in North Selangor.

Long Pin was a member of the Selangor state committee of the Malayan Communist Party and commander of the Selangor regiment of the Malayan Communist Party's armed terrorist organisation.

The Government also issued a warning to bandits who might have deserted their comrades in the jungle but had not given themselves up.

Any terrorist who deserts from the jungle and fails to surrender himself to the police, if later arrested, will be classified as "captured." If such persons report themselves voluntarily to the police forthwith they will be classified as "surrendered."

The new scale of rewards announced today are (first reward for "bringing in alive or for information leading to the capture of", figure in bracket for information leading to the killing of"):

$250,000 ($125,000); Secretary of the Central Executive Committee members.
$200,000 ($100,000); Members of the central politburo;
$150,000 ($75,000); Central committee members, and members of the central committee.

★ See Page Seven

THIS IS CHIN PENG. The brains behind the terrorism in Malaya, he is worth $250,000 to anyone who has information which will lead to his capture.

GEN. TEMPLER MAKES THE CLERKS JUMP

SEREMBAN, Wednesday.

STARTLED clerks jumped to their feet in Negri Sembilan State Secretariat in Seremban today as the High Commissioner, Gen. Gerald Templer, paying a surprise visit, walked through their offices.

AS LABOURERS WORK ROUND THE CLOCK—

When General Templer hikes the bounty on my head to a staggering $250,000 – equivalent to millions at today's currency levels – the decision is taken to put a face to the name Chin Peng. The image is that of the malaria-wracked young man photographed at a Kuala Lumpur studio five years earlier.

military programme began faltering the moment Briggs' initiative had the new villages operating. Up to that point the chaos we were able to instil across our chosen battle zones had the numerically superior government security forces confused and off balance. This confusion only exacerbated the widespread ineptitudes, racism and corruption inherent in the civil administration.

A review of any historical struggle invariably leads to the introduction of 'what might have beens'. Hypothetical questions always pose dangers but I think it is valid, in this case, to consider the likely course of the Emergency had a programme like the Briggs Plan not been imposed when it was. I feel quite confident that our insurgency would have quickly gained an unstoppable momentum, given the degree of popular support we enjoyed throughout both Malaya and Singapore. The counter argument to this, of course, is that someone else, if not Templer himself, would have devised similar methods. I do not subscribe to these views in any measure.

Templer, for all the glory that has been bestowed upon him, was a most controversial man. He faced heavy criticism even among the ranks of loyal colonials. If anyone employed terrorist measures, he did. His techniques of brow beating and threatening peasant villagers – well beyond Tanjong Malim – are documented. Combine all this with British military ruthlessness and its accompanying brutality and you have a particularly abhorrent anti-insurgency campaign. If Britain had gone ahead and posted Templer, without the Briggs plan being in place, I am quite certain his leadership style would have worked substantially to our advantage, swiftly compounding problems for the authorities and only adding further to our mass support.

Having said that, however, I recognise Templer's efforts in establishing a focal point for overall control and introducing coordination between the military and civilian administrations. All ultimately worked to enhance the impact of the Briggs Plan. He introduced centralised cooking facilities in the new villages. Mundane though it may seem, this measure gave the authorities tighter management of food stocks and, in turn, greatly restricted the Min Yuen's ability to carry supplies, destined for the comrades, through village main gates.

I have also seen comment by historians to the effect that Templer greatly improved the collection and application of intelligence and was instrumental in attaching military intelligence officers to a number of Special Branch sections to great effect. I would not dispute that the enemy's intelligence efforts improved under Templer's direction. But here I feel students of history should appreciate two salient points. Firstly, the idea for combining the military and civilian efforts under a 'supremo' leader was not Templer's. Credit here must go to Colonial Secretary Lyttleton. Secondly, Templer's approach to the mission he had been given was anything but an overnight success. This is why I maintain that Templer without Briggs would have provided us valuable months for manoeuvring – both politically and militarily.

I have read that Briggs, who retired to Cyprus and passed away there in October, 1952, died convinced he had been a failure in Malaya. As I see it, Briggs, the soldier, devised the programme and implemented it with little concern for marketing the man behind the Plan. This was a very different approach to that taken by Templer. The latter was a supreme egoist who wallowed in the limelight.

I suppose, following the extraordinary impact of the Gurney assassination, we should have seized on the idea of targeting Templer for early assassination. Regrettably, neither I nor any of my close associates in the CPM leadership came even close to envisaging such a scheme.

*   *   *   *   *

Right on the heels of the Tanjong Malim affair came the greatest challenge British propaganda experts would be required to face throughout the entire Emergency. On April 28, 1952, the London communist morning newspaper, *The Daily Worker*, ran a front page photograph across four columns showing a Royal Marine commando posing for the camera and holding the severed head of one of my guerrilla fighters. The British soldier stood outside a hut which bore the sign '40 Commando RM'. To his right were two Dyak recruits wearing Royal Marine berets, one of whom was pointing a rifle at the severed head. In the background other British troops appeared to be walking about unconcerned. The headline above the photograph read: 'This is the War in Malaya.'

The following day an Admiralty spokesman in London claimed the photograph was a fake. Other British newspapers dismissed it as a 'communist trick'. However, a question was tabled in the House of Commons seeking a full statement on the matter by Colonial Secretary Lyttelton. His answer was deferred a week as officials scurried to find an acceptable public stance. A telegram was sent seeking Templer's reactions. The Admiralty launched an independent investigation to trace the marine depicted in the photograph. Finally, the Colonial Office Information Department

One of the horrifying souvenir photos that should have shocked Britain but didn't.[21]

The *Daily Worker* newspaper published this photo on May 10, 1952, with an accompanying report pleading that Britain save her honour by ending the war in Malaya. In the political climate of the time, the newspaper's series of shocking reports and harrowing pictures was regarded as mere communist propaganda and ignored by the British public at large – much to the relief of the Colonial Office.

was instructed to coordinate closely with the Public Relations Office of the Admiralty. The stage was set for a propaganda showdown with the communist newspaper.

As this whirl of civil service activity built up, *The Daily Worker*, on April 30, countered the charge of 'fake,' by publishing a second horror photograph from Malaya. With this came a story challenging the wisdom of fielding Dyak headhunters with British anti-insurgency troops.

As requested information began feeding back into Whitehall, it became patently clear that the issues being dealt with were major. To the dismay of the government, the marine depicted on *The Daily Worker's* front page was swiftly identified and discovered to have returned to Britain. He readily admitted the photograph was genuine. Furthermore, it had been established there were many other similar photographic 'trophies' in existence, brought home by servicemen returning from Malaya. Legal advice to the Admiralty warned 'there is no doubt that under International Law a similar case in wartime would be a war crime.'

The Penal Code of Malaya also had a section dealing with offences involving the desecration of human corpses. A newly retired senior Malayan police officer, invited to the Admiralty, confirmed that 'it is not an uncommon practice, in the Malayan Police, to bring in the heads of killed bandits for identification.' Those involved in the enquiry were now looking at the possibility of an accepted decapitation policy in Malaya going back months, if not years. Troop deployment figures indicated that 264 Dyaks were operating as trackers for locally deployed British forces.

To make matters even worse for both the Colonial Office and the Admiralty, Templer's response was anything but conciliatory. In a telegram to Lyttleton[22] he said: 'War in the jungle is not a nice thing but we cannot forego the necessity for exact identification of communist dead.' In short, he was not only justifying decapitation as a battlefield procedure in the fight against my army, but was making the strongest possible representation for its continuing application.

At no time as a liberation commander – first against the Japanese and then against the British – did I ever order the mutilation of enemy bodies for any reason whatever. Nor did I quietly condone such excesses. I have often pondered what the colonial propagandists would have said had intelligence reports indicated I was seeking from, say, my Politburo colleagues, the same sort of permission Templer sought from his superiors in London to enable an ongoing headhunting programme.

Finally, on May 7, Colonial Secretary Lyttleton rose in the House of Commons to deliver his delayed reply on *The Daily Worker's* April 28 picture and story. ' Yes,' he confirmed, 'it is a genuine photograph.' He went on to provide background information on the action that had led to this particular decapitation. Lyttelton said a jungle patrol had been ambushed by bandits in April, 1951. In the action that followed a Royal Marine Commando officer and a corporal had been killed. Two other marines had been seriously wounded. One communist had died in the clash. Lyttelton was quick to point out that a Dyak tribesman, not a Royal Marine, had severed the head of the dead communist. This had been undertaken to enable identification. The Colonial Secretary added: 'The photograph was not authorised and should not have been taken. Instructions have been given to the High Commissioner that bodies should not be decapitated for identification which should be secured by photographs and fingerprints.'

A senior civil service expert advising the Colonial Office on the best propaganda approach wrote: ' . . . the most dignified way of dealing with this matter would be to ignore the articles in *The Daily Worker* and to deal with the matter in Parliament if it is raised there. Moreover, to issue a statement would be to draw much wider attention to this matter and might well provoke further discussion in the press.'

If that advice failed to supply a clear picture of the colonial attitude towards prosecuting the Malayan Emergency, the same expert's next statement admirably filled in the gaps. 'To my mind,' he went on, 'the really revolting aspects of this case are not the mere fact that, occasionally, a dead bandit is decapitated for purposes of identification, but the behaviour of the individuals in posing for such photographs as those which have appeared in *The Daily Worker.*'

From my standpoint, the ranking civil servant advising the Colonial Office's top echelons in this instance was far more concerned with British decorum than the horror of a severed head. He missed, completely, or conveniently, the moral position on the mutilation issue.

On May 10, the communist newspaper devoted its entire front page to appalling photographs brought back from Malaya. One showed a smiling Royal Marine holding two severed heads – that of a female in his right hand, and a male in his left. Quite obviously the female's front teeth had been knocked out. Other pictures featured a Dyak headhunter with human body parts.

Amazingly, Lyttelton's words in the House and the joint public relations effort of the Admiralty and Colonial Office seemed to satisfy Fleet Street. All other national dailies in the UK ignored the decapitation issue as a major story. No mention was ever made of Templer's attempt to justify and retain the hideous measure as a required

INWARD TELEGRAM

TO THE SECRETARY OF STATE FOR THE COLONIES

COPY FOR REGISTRATION

FROM FEDERATION OF MALAYA (Gen. Sir G. Templer)

Cypher (O.T.P.)

D. 6th May, 1952.
R. 6th "   "   08.30 hrs.

EMERGENCY
SECRET
No. 559

Addressed to S. of S.
Repeated to Chiefs of Staff Headquarters Malaya,
Chiefs of Staff G.H.Q. FARELF.

13. Your personal telegram No. 82.

Daily Worker Photograph.

It is absolutely essential that communist dead should be identified. If a communist is killed in deep jungle it is sometimes impossible to bring back the body for a variety of reasons. Cameras have therefore been issued, though sometimes a camera is not available when such instances occur. Where distance is too great, or terrain too difficult, or a camera is not available, it may accordingly be very occasionally necessary to remove the head of a dead communist. (It should be remembered that if a member of a patrol is killed and his body cannot be carried back to the base, he is buried where he is and subsequent recovery of his body, perhaps a year later, may be the subject of a special military operation).

2. Photography of such a rare instance obviously undesirable from every point of view. Strict orders have been issued on this and negatives are held by the police for record purposes.

3. The incident in question, which is the only one of its kind which can be traced, took place over a year ago. It is unfortunate that the Daily Worker has now made use of it for its own purposes.

4. War in the jungle is not a nice thing, but we cannot forego the necessity for exact identification of communist dead. The view point of the Daily Worker in this matter is easily understandable. The viewpoint of others who may criticise, and who have no possible inkling of an understanding of conditions or terrain or physical exhaustion of operations, is not understandable to the Security Forces who have the task of tracking down armed communists/murderers and producing evidence for necessary identification.

5. Two police contingents of Selangor and Malacca have issued instructions on photographing and finger printing of killed terrorists for identification purposes. None has mentioned severing heads. Subject to checking when photograph is received, it is believed that photograph in the Daily Worker was taken in Perak.

This is the full text of General Templer's far from conciliatory response to the Secretary of State for the Colonies on the matter of beheading for identification purposes.

tactic of war. Within a matter of weeks, what today can only be judged as the most ghastly visual images of the Emergency were relegated to bottom drawers in ministerial back offices.

There was an embarrassing, if brief, phase for the British in late May that same year when it was recognised in Kuala Lumpur that the colonial administration could not produce photographs of communist atrocities to match those showing acts perpetrated by security forces. This was skilfully sidestepped, however, with the explanation that it had been considered undesirable to publicise details of terrorist atrocities. It was claimed such details were always excluded from official reports. A scan of the *The Straits Times'* front pages for the years 1948-60 – not to mention official military assessments of the period – thoroughly disproves the assertion that somehow the British wished to play down reports of alleged excesses by my army. That these numerous reports lacked supporting pictorial evidence must weigh strongly in the CPM's favour when it comes to evaluating the role of propaganda in the Malayan Emergency.

Six weeks later, the killing of one of our most successful guerrilla leaders by a patrol of the 1st Battalion, The Suffolk Regiment, drew attention for the first time to yet another commonly employed terror tactic on the part of the security forces. Unlike the decapitation issue, though, this one would actually cause reverberations of public concern and be examined by the British press. After ambushing and killing Liew Kon Kim, widely referred to as 'The Bearded Terror of Kajang,' the colonial authorities arranged to parade his body on the back of a lorry around new villages in southern Selangor. With the lorry went a motorcade of vehicles including loudspeaker vans providing a running commentary on the dead guerrilla's past and how he met his end. The grisly parade lasted three days. Perhaps because initial press reports followed so closely on the decapitation story, UK newspapers took a more critical view of the security forces' long established practice of publicly displaying the corpses of slain communists. Usual display points were in front of police stations in outlying towns. But it would still be a long time before this contemptible activity, geared specifically to terrifying the rural population into compliance, was outlawed.

Apparently compelled by the mounting unsavoury reports of security force measures being applied in Malaya during 1952, the *Daily Mirror* in London launched a campaign that year against the military's system of 'league table' tallies for dead and wounded communists. The practice itself was more geared to achieving impact via local headlines – particularly in the English language press and on Radio Malaya –

Liew Kon Kim, the so-called 'bearded terror of Kajang' with a comrade.

than courting the support of the British at home. Colonial spirits, after all, had to be kept high.

The CPM could have looked to operating our own body-count 'scoreboard'. We could have kept monthly comparative lists of running 'kill' totals for fallen British forces – the ones who wouldn't be going home. There might well have been subsidiary categories for 'wounded' and 'missing'. From all these figures we could have established grand record months and challenged units to compete for the accolade of 'kill-rate champions'. This might have given the British second thoughts about celebrating body counts. As it happened, we, the supposed terrorists, left all that behaviour to the British.

I wonder whether the passage of years has been long enough for those who lived through the Emergency to glean the difference between what is historical fact and what was propagandist fiction. The following is historical fact: Throughout the Emergency years, all our units were instructed to treat captured enemy forces humanely. On this issue we followed the Mao Tse Tung guerrilla warfare principles on the treatment of prisoners and our High Command issued specific directives on this matter. On occasion we actually treated enemy wounded. But, in reality, we were never in a position to take on the responsibility of holding prisoners. It was difficult enough meeting our own needs. The accepted practice was to seize the weapon and release the enemy soldier. I know much has been made by British propaganda of our supposed maltreatment of prisoners. I reject these claims. On no occasion during the Emergency did I ever receive a report indicating my troops had maltreated, tortured or executed enemy personnel. As far as I know, there are no official files offering proof that they did. Certainly, I have yet to see any photographic evidence supporting such claims. On the other hand British authorities regularly executed captured armed members of my army. This sort of action is specifically prohibited under Article 13 of the 1949 Geneva Convention covering the general protection of prisoners of war. Britain neatly sidestepped the war crimes dilemma these activities posed by maintaining, just as she did for insurance reasons, that the military action underway in Malaya was an Emergency, not a war.

This is not to say that I was undisturbed by certain episodes perpetrated by our guerrillas. Two incidents, apart from the Ian Christian execution at Sungei Siput, trouble me to this day.

The first is the 1952 assassination of 51 year-old David Chen Chung En, the popular principal of the Chung Ling High School in Penang. A student activist had

School principal, David Chen, was undoubtedly loyal to the Kuomintang and worked to undermine CPM inroads at Chung Ling High. But his assassination was counter-productive to the CPM cause.

reported to our area committee that headmaster Chen, loyal to the Kuomintang, was also functioning as a police informer. The decision to eliminate Chen was taken at the district level. Over the years I have endeavoured to find hard evidence and documentation that would confirm the specific charge levelled against him by the activist. I have not found any.

The second incident involved an acid attack on the headmistress of a girls' school in Singapore. It occurred at a time when acid attacks were far from uncommon, many of them crimes of passion or acts of personal revenge. But this particular case was blamed on us and, like the Chen affair, I have simply been unable to find any valid reason whatever for the attack.

Both these incidents I consider to have been utterly unwarranted and quite counter-productive to our cause.

*   *   *   *   *

While our headquarters were still in the Bentung area, Yeung Kuo decided to combine the CPM's Central and Southern bureaux in an effort to decentralise control and thereby streamline decision-making. With the concurrence of my comrades I placed this new unified grouping under the overall leadership of Ah Koek, the guerrilla commander who had proved so able in averting a disintegration of the Party in Malacca.

Ah Koek knew the region well as he had been born and raised in Raub where his father had worked in an Australian-owned gold mine. Educated in Kajang to Chinese middle school standard, he was my age. After resolving the Malacca problems he had been scheduled to report personally back to me in Bentung. At this proposed meeting he was to be informed of his new appointment. Because of stepped-up British military activities following Templer's arrival in Malaya, Ah Koek met countless delays. As I awaited his arrival, security pressures on my headquarters also began to intensify. With yet another camp move imminent, I dispatched a courier to inform Ah Koek that he was being tasked to establish a deep jungle base.

By the time the courier and Ah Koek met, my headquarters had undertaken the transfer north to jungle outside Raub. On his way to take up his new appointment, Ah Koek was murdered, allegedly by one of his three bodyguards – two men and a woman. I am convinced this killing resulted from a well-orchestrated Special Branch operation.

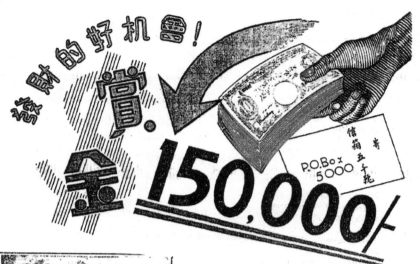

發財的好机會！

賞

金 150,000/

P.O.Box 5000

信箱五千號

這個人是馬共所謂"柔甲邊區委員會"的負責人，兼"馬共中委"亞谷，又名房金全，呆仔方，房方及蓉。

他是客家人，大約廿九歲，身高只有四呎九吋，所以人人都叫他做矮仔谷！

凡是供給情報，使保安隊伍把他生擒，或是設法協助政府使他來投誠的公眾人士，可以獲得賞金：—

凡是供給情報，使保安隊伍把他擊斃的公眾人士，可以獲得賞金：

壹十五萬元！ 十萬五千元！

The colonial administration's poster offering a special $150,000 reward for Ah Koek.

Much earlier, on September 24, 1952, *The Straits Times* had run a prominent news story on its front page headlined: 'The Man Who Is Worth $150,000.' It reported that the Federation Government had, the previous day, posted a $150,000 reward for anyone providing information leading to Ah Koek's capture alive. A sum of $75,000 would be paid if the informant's tip resulted in Ah Koek's death. The newspaper account, accompanied by a photograph, said thousands of posters had been circulated in new villages and kampongs in order to snare the man it identified as 'Shorty'. *The Straits Times* went on to calculate that at 4 feet 9 inches, Shorty Koek would be worth $3,000 an inch – 'probably the most expensive bandit sought.' I regarded this observation as most bizarre.

Reports reaching me indicated that a few weeks after the story appeared, Ah Koek was murdered. Inexplicably, the killing was not reported in the press until May 2, 1953. No mention was then made as to when it took place. If the first story's calculations were bizarre, the second story's details were equally so. It told how a driver of the Gemas to Jerantut train had spotted two armed communist guerrillas and a female comrade – one of the trio clutching a freshly severed head – standing by the tracks and waving for him to stop. Apparently unconcerned for his own safety, let alone the rest of the train, the driver duly pulled to a halt and enquired how he could help. In the ensuing conversation the driver learned – no doubt to his intense relief – that all the trio wanted was a lift to the Mentekab police station further down the line so they could surrender. The three communists explained that the head they were carrying had belonged to their 'chief'. It was suggested they should place the head in a haversack and remain in the train's armoured carriage for the onward journey. All three were detained at the Mentekab police station. The train driver had been awarded $500 for his trouble. No mention was made as to whether the $75,000 reward due was paid out.

To this day I am rendered incredulous by the story. But there is one interesting aspect that I have long considered. The colonial authorities, still smarting under London's reprimand over the 'decapitation for identification' policy and unable to counter with proof of similar communist activities, finally had a case of a guerrilla-initiated beheading.

That it was contrived was beside the point. What mattered was public perception and the propagandists, with their almost limitless aids, could be sure of nailing this in place.

*   *   *   *   *

From the moment Templer began functioning as High Commissioner, misinformation campaigns flew thick and fast in Malaya. Some were successful. Others were farcical failures. Over morning coffee in my Raub headquarters sometime in December, 1952, I was astonished to read that I had been dislodged as Secretary General of the CPM by a woman. More amazing still, my replacement was a 40 year-old 'master spy from Red China'. Her name: Hsia Hsueh Hung.

The first account of my overthrow by Miss Hsia was published in the local *Chung Hsing Jit Pao* and subsequently developed into a front page lead story by *The Straits Times*. The English language daily ran a seven-column headline: 'Woman Is New Red Boss.' Beneath this, a subhead proclaimed: 'Master spy of China will take over from Chin Peng, says report.' In the body of the story I learned that my dismissal was a decision reached by no less than the Cominform. My successor was apparently still in China and it was hinted she would be travelling overland to Malaya assisted by the Siamese communists. Mention was made that the CPM was receiving aid from the neighbouring comrades. The suggestion was that the source of the story could be traced to a radio broadcast in Kuomintang-dominated Taiwan. It was a plant aimed at undermining my authority at the rank-and-file level. That didn't happen.

*　　*　　*　　*　　*

In the first few weeks of 1952, while still in Bentung, Headquarters received information that one of our courier networks had been compromised. Details at first were sketchy but it seemed almost certain that a copy of our October 1, 1951, Resolution, had fallen into enemy hands. It represented a serious security breach but there was little we could do about it. As the days passed, subsequent reports only reinforced our concerns that British military intelligence was now privy to the contents of this pivotal document.

We waited for the reaction. We scanned both the Chinese and English language dailies for the launch of a propaganda campaign based on my most recent instructions to field commanders throughout Malaya. Silence. Nothing. As we moved north to Raub, Templer began stamping the imprint of his authority onto the anti-communist campaign. Government pronouncements increased in number as did the prominence of Emergency-linked stories carried by the various local newspapers. As February gave way to March, the dailies were packed with pronouncements and activities of the new High Commissioner. 'Templer Gives His Blueprint for United Malaya' . . .

'Sir Gerald Punishes Town of 20,000 Cowards' . . . 'Sir Gerald Backs The Trade Unions.' Not a word on our resolution. An extraordinary propaganda opportunity had dropped in the enemy's lap. This time, however, they had chosen to hold back. Why?

Once again it would be years before I could fit the pieces together. In October, 1952, exactly 12 months after we began circulating our resolution and perhaps nine months after enemy intelligence first saw it, a story leaked in the London press revealing that the British indeed held a copy. The revelation caused a flurry of anxiety at Far East Land Forces (FARELF) as a furious Templer demanded to know how and why a serious breach of security had occurred. It had been on security grounds that my document was given the highest possible classification and specifically ordered to be withheld from the public domain. Templer and his top advisers felt it would be most counter-productive to release information indicating the CPM was seeking heightened discipline within its guerrilla ranks. The resolution was very clear in its instructions to avoid activities that might be construed as terrorist tactics targeting the Min Yuen or the masses.

Although I have already provided a general description of the October 1 Resolution in the previous chapter, there are a few extra points I should make about the document now if the incident involving its sudden and unexpected release into the public domain is to be fully appreciated. It amounted to a particularly lengthy study of guerrilla tactics undertaken by us to that point in the war. The English language translation, I understand, ran to over 30,000 words. Having been issued by the Politburo, the directives our document contained represented orders from the movement's highest source. There was no question but that they had to be obeyed. And they were. British military statistics on CPM initiated incidents showed very clearly that these dropped dramatically during the period from late 1951 to the end of 1953.

The resolution was quite specific in its instructions that acts of wanton terrorism should be avoided. It even went as far as defining, within a substantial list, the sort of activities our guerrillas should specifically avoid.

The High Commissioner's dilemma over our resolution was multi-layered. So much of the British propaganda emphasis had been directed at depicting us as mindless killers with terrorism as our sole objective. If a publicised Politburo document had disclosed the CPM seemed considerably more concerned about excesses than the British side, what would have been the local population's perception of the government's lurid portrayal of our party over the previous four years? What would have been the reaction in Britain where the Government was looking at substantially increased defence spending in order to defeat dreaded terrorism in Malaya? Of more immediate concern to Templer, of course, was how he could then justify 22-hour curfews, sweeping accusations of cowardice, reduction of food rations, forced confessions and threats of even harsher penalties to come if we were seen to be on a decidedly softer track.

Furthermore, between February 7, 1952, the day he arrived in Malaya to take up his posting, and exactly three months later when he was ordered by London to stop decapitation for identification, Templer well appreciated that while we had issued orders banning mutilation of corpses, he approved such activity as legitimate and required policy for his army. By the same token he recognised as acceptable the regular displaying of slain guerrilla corpses outside police stations.

As long as our Politburo orders remained blanketed by security, Templer was safe.

But on December 1, 1952, *The Times* of London ran a prominent news dispatch from its Singapore-based correspondent that amounted to a devastating scoop. This revealed publicly for the first time the existence of the October 1 document that had been held under rigid security classifications for over a year. The story was headed: *Changed Policy of Terrorists*. The newspaper's correspondent, Louis Heren, noted early in his account that our directive had been issued before the assassination of Sir Henry Gurney. Pointedly, he went on to observe that since there was now an almost complete absence of terrorist activity in every state and settlement, with the exception of Johore, Perak and Pahang, the suggestion was that the CPM was adapting to a new party line.

Templer was livid that security provisions should have been treated with such indifference. What the Supremo didn't know at the time was that the highly classified document had been leaked to Heren by none other than General Sir Rob Lockhart. At the time, Lockhart was Deputy Director of Operations, Templer's immediate No 2. Nearly three decades later Heren, writing in his book '*Growing up on The Times*', revealed how he had promised Lockhart he would always protect the source of this story.

In Heren's words, the search for the leak by Templer was 'as extensive as anything attempted by President Nixon's plumbers many years later'. The journalist recalled that from then on Templer regarded him as 'one of the enemy'. Heren's scoop only

CHANGED POLICY OF TERRORISTS

MORE DISCRIMINATION IN CHOOSING MALAYAN VICTIMS

From Our Own Correspondent

SINGAPORE, Nov. 30

The significance of the changes in tactics of the Malayan Communist Party briefly reported last month can be seen in a "directive on the execution of most urgent and important duties of the party" issued on October 1 last year by the Politburo, details of which have been obtained by your Correspondent.

Although the directive was agreed on before the assassination of Sir Henry Gurney, the late High Commissioner, its full effect is not yet evident, but the almost complete absence of terrorist activity in every state and settlement with the exception of Johore, Perak, and Pahang suggests that most state committees are now adapting themselves to new party line.

PAST ERRORS

According to the preamble, serious errors have been committed in the past by state organizations, and many working methods have been diametrically opposed to accepted principles. Party members are reminded that their primary duty is to expand and consolidate the organization of the masses, which is to take precedence over the purely military objective of destroying the enemy. This is to be attained by creating a united front of all communities and classes by acquiring the support of the bourgeoisie and capitalists and avoiding violent tactics which have antagonized peasants and workers. Attempts are to be made to penetrate into the police, Home Guard, the Malay Regiment, and the Civil service.

To win the masses the party must (i) stop seizing identity and ration cards; (ii) stop burning new villages and coolie lines; (iii) stop attacking post offices, reservoirs, power stations, and other public services; (iv) refrain from derailing civilian trains with high explosives; (v) stop throwing grenades and

to be exploited rather than attacked. No new villages are to be destroyed, but reasonable and acceptable conditions to protect the interests of resettled Chinese squatters are to be put forward, and whenever possible their demands are to be fulfilled by lawful means. The formation of Home Guard units is to be delayed, obstructed, disabled, or made use of. Stubborn reactionaries are to be killed, but others are to be persuaded to help the party or remain neutral.

If the masses are conscribed, propaganda must point out that they have been enlisted to fight in China and Burma as well as Malaya, and others should avoid conscription by escaping to China or India. Should they decide to join the Communist bands, they must first save food; "otherwise a sudden rush of recruits will create an insoluble food shortage."

The "self-protection corps," in which the young recruit serves before graduating to armed units, is to infiltrate new villages and collect food instead of committing acts of terrorism. Stricter security is to be enforced, and cell-leaders are to restrict their activities and attendances at party meetings to avoid suspicion.

Political activity and education is to be increased in large towns. The international and Malayan situations must be analysed to strengthen confidence in revolution, and morale must be raised by instilling class-hatred against the British and the capitalist system. Grievance meetings, at which people will describe their sufferings, are to be encouraged, and the widespread belief that the Chinese peasant is worse off than the Malayan must be "corrected." More "Know more words" classes are to be held, and the military and civilian reader published by the Press of the Malayan races liberation army" will be used.

WARNING ATTACKS

Yellow (legal) trade unions are to be penetrated, and their leaders and members may be assassinated if the masses can be made to recognise their treachery to the class struggle. Where there is access to estate workers, secret

Fleet Street journalist, Louis Heren was the Singapore-based South East Asian correspondent for *The Times* of London when General Templer arrived in Kuala Lumpur to take up the post of British High Commissioner in Malaya. Their relationship was prickly at the outset and became progressively more hostile after Heren filed his scoop on our October 1, 1951, Resolution. (See cutting on the right.)

Subsequently, *The Times'* representative joined a brigade-sized British military operation targeted with searching for and destroying my headquarters. His daily reports detailing the operation's failure would, a few days later, trigger a highly embarrassing scene in Kuala Lumpur's Legislative Council building. The journalist was talking quietly in the council lobby to a group of Malayan politicians when Templer, accompanied by ADCs, rushed up waving an airmail edition of *The Times*. 'What do you know about warfare?' shouted the general, 'you, you ! . .' Heren would later write: 'I thought he was going to strike me, but after a moment which seemed an eternity he stalked away followed by his gaping ADCs.'

magnified the already strained relations between the widely respected representative of Britain's most influential daily and the soldier on whom Churchill had bestowed almost unrestricted powers to quell our anti-colonial insurgency. Heren, it is said, soon became referred to by the volatile Templer as 'typical of all communist muck'. It became worse. A member of the Malayan War Council privately confided to Heren that Templer had actually labelled him a communist. *The Times'* man, of course, was as much a communist as I was a capitalist.

The High Commissioner would go on and badger Colonial Secretary Lyttleton until representations in London were finally made to Heren's editor, Sir William Haley, to have his correspondent removed from the Malaya/Singapore theatre. After hearing both sides of the argument, Haley, newly appointed to the editorship, stood behind Heren and rebuffed Templer's demands. Heren would later write, clearly with some amusement, that as far as Haley was concerned 'Templer could scream until he was blue in the face, but I would remain the South East Asian correspondent of *The Times* until the editor decided to post me elsewhere.'

Had the leak of our resolution been ignored by Heren, Britain and her colonial representatives in Kuala Lumpur would most surely have retained the document's tight security clamps. These may never have been lifted. I have often wondered what the result might have been had the propaganda teams not been prevented from working on our document and, in the course of their work, its contents had been divulged early in 1952. Or, indeed, had the leak occurred just prior to Templer's arrival, for instance.

Chapter 19

Pushing north as Britain plans to invade southern Siam

Our decision to move north from Raub was taken in late 1952. Central to this was the desire to retain our headquarters intact. But it was a decision that had followed immense soul-searching.

After the third major air attack against us in Pahang, I felt it imperative we institute measures that would work towards a continuing prosecution of the struggle should the headquarters be wiped out the next time. I also had to take into consideration the similar precarious situation facing Yeung Kuo in Selangor.

As early as Bentung, Siao Chang, Lee An Tung, Ah Chung and I had discussed a special contingency arrangement that would come into force in the event of a major communications breakdown between us. As Siao Chang was soon to depart for China, we felt he would be in a good position in Peking to issue communiqués and statements in the name of the CPM Central Committee should a communication emergency arise. Before he departed, the Politburo gave him the authority to do so.

Siao Chang would, naturally, have to consult with Ah Hai, our first representative in China who had gone there as a TB patient in early 1949. Ah Hai, by now, was involved in extensive training programmes run by the CPC. My rationale for these instructions went further. If we were all killed, or for some other reason ceased to function, Siao Chang and Ah Hai would effectively take over the Party leadership.

It was early 1953 before we actually began our trek back to the Cameron Highlands, to the very area where, in December 1948, we had plotted our basic strategic approach to armed struggle with high expectation of success. From there we had departed with such confidence to establish liberated zones – Kelantan in the north and southern Pahang in the south. In the final days of 1948, our dreams were of establishing our own revolutionary government apparatus across the regions we would hold. Now, on our return, more than four years later, it was very obvious we held no territory, no liberated zones.

Throughout our return journey to the Cameron Highlands, I was in very limited contact with the rest of the Party and certainly not issuing orders of any consequence from Headquarters. I had become quite isolated from the revolutionary activity that was being maintained at the state committee level with small-scale actions throughout the country. At one point, I was receiving no reports whatever. The courier system between Yeung Kuo and myself had completely broken down. Yeung Kuo was then effectively running the revolution from a jungle camp near Kajang.

As I recall these desperate days, I am quite amazed by the resilience demonstrated by my fellow comrades at all levels of the Party apparatus. Despite the hardships we faced – the mandatory death sentences, mass deportations, mind-bending jail sentences, and overwhelming enemy firepower – early 1953 still saw our commitment to a continuing struggle. From my standpoint then, and I know it was the same for all my Politburo colleagues, we were not looking for a means of ending the struggle but rather seeking a way out of our predicament so we might continue with our campaign. We saw the extreme difficulties we faced as temporary aspects of the course we had embarked upon.

It is my understanding that around this time the British received very accurate intelligence reports of a large group of guerrillas on the move north towards the Cameron Highlands. Through the defections of the demoted Lam Swee and the bodyguard who murdered Ah Koek, the enemy were obviously confident I was operating in the general Pahang area. News of a sizable communist force trekking north in western Pahang, would have immediately led to assessments that I was probably somewhere thereabouts.

Our Cameron Highlands campsite was situated north of the Sungei Telom. Once we had moved into place I sent word that I should get together with the new Perak state secretary, Chen Hong, who was located in the Gopeng area. We had to wait for nearly two weeks before he arrived. I needed to establish with him the best permanent location for my headquarters. I was out of touch with Perak. I'd been away for so long. It was a matter of renewing contacts with the movement there all over again. I would have to put a jungle courier network in place. We also wanted to create an open courier network so that I could resume regular contacts with Yeung Kuo. I had sent a message informing him of my departure from Pahang but had no knowledge whether he had received it. My attempts to re-build our headquarters' courier network and re-establish communications with Yeung Kuo would result in quite unintended and spectacular international headlines which I will discuss in the following chapter.

Our initial camp was makeshift and had been earlier abandoned by a local guerrilla unit. As such it was not sufficiently covered by tree foliage and jungle canopy and thus became a fairly easy target for detection by air reconnaissance. Our intentions were to move quickly to a deeper jungle location. We had expected the arrival of the Perak state secretary within a few days and that our new camp location would be quickly settled. At the time, our headquarters unit was approximately 50-strong, including our security force.

Our campsite was located halfway up the slope of a hill which formed one side of a narrow valley. Defensive trenches had been dug along approaches to the area. Some distance behind these were huts for our main force guerrillas together with a command centre and parade ground. At the rear of the camp was a large tropical tree that provided a wide area of shade. Here was located our headquarters unit with separate huts to accommodate each senior official.

It was an extremely steep, ten-minute walk from the campsite down to a small stream on the valley floor below. To climb back up took anything from 20 to 30 minutes. The stream provided our water supply for drinking, cooking and bathing. It was very cold so we normally bathed at around noon, the hottest time of the day. From the elevation of our camp, an equivalent position on the opposite side of the valley would be less than 100 metres away.

Not long after we had established our temporary Highlands camp, the Soviet leader, Josef Stalin, died. He passed away on the night of March 5. We learned of his death from local newspapers delivered to the camp some two days later. It was definitely an historic milestone for world communism. On a personal level, however, Stalin's death will always remain my means of pinpointing in time a most hair-raising attack by the Royal Australian Air Force (RAAF).

The air raid, which occurred four days into the Kremlin wake, began early in the morning as we were finishing breakfast. An Auster reconnaissance plane suddenly appeared flying down the valley, just above treetop level. Once the pilot spotted our camp, he fired a flare into the air above us. Within a few minutes the sky was buzzing with aircraft. Because of the narrowness of the gap between the two hillsides, the attacking pilots had very little room for error. From my position squatting in a shallow trench beneath the large tree I could watch as the planes swung around to begin their attack runs down the centre of the valley. Some opened up with machine guns. Others dropped bombs.

Two of my bodyguards crouching a short distance away received direct hits. Both died; one from shrapnel wounds to the head, the other from a machine gun round in the back. They were our only fatalities. Three others were wounded, one seriously with a broken leg. The other two escaped with superficial injuries. Curiously, though, the damage to our camp was minimal.

But on the other side of the valley, not a single tree remained standing. Strafing and bombing runs had lasted three hours and we estimated that about 70 sorties were flown against us that day. The Australian attack had flattened an area of vegetation directly opposite and parallel to our position. The levelled area had the same dimensions as our camp.

As we were obviously so visible from the air, why did the pilots hit the other side of the valley? Had they been given target coordinates that erroneously placed us on the other slope? Or, was it because the contours of the high country in this specific area prohibited targeting our side? I have never been able to discover the answer.

But I know what would have happened had the Australians been on target. Nobody in the area of the raid that day could have possibly survived – such was its destructive power. The neutralisation of our headquarters in March, 1953, would have been a catastrophic blow to the revolution. My earlier instructions for the creation of a fall-back, Peking-based leadership alternative to assume control at just such a critical moment could never have snapped into place. Siao Chang and Ah Hai would not have had time to become organised. Furthermore, it was obvious to me that the morale problem throughout our guerrilla ranks was now far more serious than it had been during the attack on our Raub Headquarters the previous year, or on the Mentekab base camp two years before that.

The raid put us in a particularly vulnerable position. It was imperative that I talk to the Perak state secretary and quickly settle where our new headquarters were to be located. I estimated he could not be more than two days' walk from our position. If we moved, we would almost certainly miss him and to organise another meeting could take months. Alternatively, if we failed to move we would be in serious danger of being ensnared in a British Army follow-up ground operation to the Australian air raid. In attacks on remote areas such as this, the enemy frequently introduced special troops on damage assessment missions. One of these could have been quickly expanded into a major assault force once suspicions had been raised that the Politburo's base camp could be in the area.

I decided to give the Perak state secretary another 24 hours to reach me. My military commander inserted look-outs at strategic jungle positions throughout the surrounding hills to give early warning of any approaching enemy force. The hours passed very slowly that day and every sound from the jungle around us seemed to heighten the tension. We buried the dead and arranged for the injured to make their way to a nearby camp of mass workers. Then, late that evening, the man I had been waiting for, along with three of his bodyguards, arrived. Hastily we held our meeting as others in the camp continued packing and readying for a quick departure the following day.

What Chen Hong conveyed to me that evening was unquestionably the most disturbing report I had received since the start of the Emergency. Calmly, he ran through a general appraisal of guerrilla activities throughout Malaya for the months I had been out of touch. Then he switched to a more specific review of what had been happening in Perak, his home territory, which he naturally knew intimately. The situation had deteriorated beyond my worst imaginings.

He explained how he had scoured the state's central region, from Sungei Siput down to Bidor, and had failed to discover a single area that could come anywhere near supporting a group the size of my headquarters unit – 50 people. I was stunned. Perak in the days I remembered was packed with our supporters. I had helped to organise them at the grass-roots level prior to the war. Our AJA had enjoyed the overwhelming support of the population during the occupation. Post-war, the CPM's following across Perak had even expanded.

I knew the Briggs Plan was having a substantial impact on our food supply lines in Pahang. I had rationalised that problem by making mental allowances for the fact that Pahang was sparsely populated compared to its neighbouring states to the west and south. It would, I felt, be extremely difficult for new villages to be effective in the more heavily populated states like Perak, Selangor, Negri Sembilan, Malacca and Johore. But my calculations were definitely flawed and the Perak secretary spared no detail in putting me right.

'So, how do we operate our headquarters?' I asked. 'It's essential we maintain one. Right from the start we've been struggling with the problem of control. Without headquarters there is chaos.' I went on to give my comrade a breakdown of the way we saw our guerrilla activities henceforth reverting to small unit actions. Could we maintain this level of attacks with the food problems being imposed in Perak by the presence of the new villages?

Chen Hong sat silently for some time, pondering the two-pronged dilemma. When his answer finally came, he dealt with the second prong first. Small-scale guerrilla attacks, he noted, could be maintained. But the intensity of these would have to be lowered. General supplies had become extremely scarce owing to the prevalence of new villages. Turning to the problem of locating the headquarters, he advised solemnly that I had no alternative but to move further north to the Grik area. Even if supplies from the Min Yuen became difficult to obtain there, he argued, I could send special food forays over the border into southern Siam. Movement back and forth across the frontier, despite British patrolling, was still relatively simple.

I had to take this advice. Intensely worried, I slept fitfully in the jungle that night. Early the next morning we received word that an enemy ground patrol was approaching. Packed and ready, we departed within minutes.

It took us about two months slogging through the world's thickest jungles to reach Grik. Once there, I immediately held discussions with the local area Party leader. All was not well in this region, either. For over a year, the Grik comrades had recognised there was a traitor in their midst but could not identify him. Intended guerrilla operations had been thwarted by the British before they could be launched. Weapons, ammunition and food supplies had been revealed to the enemy and seized. Key Party officials had been betrayed and arrested. Whoever it was working for the British was obviously well-placed and well-informed.

When I arrived in the Grik area with my headquarters, the drama of the Grik traitor was at its height. It was mid-1953 – a year since the betrayals had begun – and the finger of suspicion had finally fallen on a middle-aged area committee secretary by the name of Lian Sung.

At my suggestion, the suspect was detained and brought in for questioning. We were camped in deep jungle about two days' walk east of Grik. Lian Sung was brought to a point near my camp. The first thing the comrades did was to body-search him. In a shirt pocket they discovered a government cheque in his name. It was for the amount of $50,000. The cheque, of course, was part of the reward given him by the authorities for his year-long service spying against the Grik comrades. Under interrogation he admitted he had been working for the Special Branch. He further admitted that the $50,000 cheque was only part of his reward. Other funds were being held for him by the Special Branch. He was, of course, executed immediately. On this occasion, our actions saved the government a considerable amount of money. Lian Sung would never be in a position to withdraw the funds the authorities were holding in his name. The $50,000 cheque discovered on him would go uncashed.

We had eliminated a spy in our operation and very quickly came to realise the damage he had inflicted. Nearly every food supply line so painstakingly opened to

Shen Tien, the northern Perak state committee man who exposed the spying activities of Grik area committee member, Lian Sung. This picture was taken in 1964 when Shen Tien was en route to China for medical treatment.

I first sent Ah Hai to China as a TB patient in early 1949. After his treatment, he completed a series of extensive training programmes run by the CPC. His arrival at our jungle headquarters in southern Thailand in 1960 would eventually allow me to depart for Peking.

new villages in the area had been blocked by government countermeasures. There were one or two small supply outlets still operating. However, we became convinced these were purposely left that way by the Special Branch to enhance future surveillance opportunities.

We were also convinced that Special Branch officers had used their unique connection to the local Party hierarchy over the previous year, to expand their intelligence network. If they had not, they had not been doing their job. Our headquarters, once again, had no option but to move on. This time, our destination was deep jungle across the frontier in southern Siam.

*   *   *   *   *

At the beginning of the Emergency one unit of our Kedah guerrilla force had been attacked by the British and had withdrawn north across the frontier into southern Siam's Betong Salient. Another group, this time in Perlis, had also been engaged and similarly escaped across the frontier, further to the west, into the Sadao area. The Perlis withdrawal resulted from a very heavy British counter-attack following a most successful guerrilla ambush of a Gurkha platoon. Half the platoon were either killed or wounded. Both these actions took place in the first two weeks of the Emergency and resulted in British troops pursuing us onto Siamese territory in each case.

In the Perlis attack, we were greatly assisted by renegade Japanese who had joined our guerrilla ranks. They happened to have been trained by the Japanese Army in the techniques of constructing, laying and operating land mines. There were numerous tin mines in the Perlis area and we were able to obtain substantial supplies of explosives from them. Our Japanese guerrillas devised a detonating system using a flashlight bulb. They drilled a small hole in the bulb's glass and filled the inside with a flammable substance. Sometimes the tops of matches were removed, gently crushed and the powder inserted into the bulb. Great care had to be taken not to break the tiny wire filament inside. Thus constructed, the device was then connected to 50 or 100 yards of wire and then a battery provided the current necessary to set off the explosive mechanism.

Our guerrillas had carried out surveillance of a section of road often travelled by the Gurkhas. Under cover of darkness the land mines were laid beneath the road's dirt surface at a point where foliage was dense on both sides and provided ideal concealment for ambush positions. Very skilfully, the Japanese camouflaged the wire lead and our guerrillas moved in to await their quarry. The mines were command-detonated as the Gurkha vehicles passed over them. This action took British commanders completely by surprise. They had not suspected we had the capacity to employ land mines.

At that time the control exerted by Bangkok over her four southern provinces in the Kras Isthmus was tenuous. As long as we stayed in the hinterland and caused no trouble, the Siamese police and troops left us alone. If they didn't see us, as far as the Siamese authorities were concerned, we weren't there. There was also a *quid pro quo* in it for them. At the time they were experiencing a rash of gangster attacks throughout their frontier provinces. We took on a number of the bandit gangs in the Sadao region and wiped them out, saving the local police considerable trouble and greatly helping to restore law and order for the population. All round, we became most welcome.

To the east in the Betong Salient, our men found themselves confronting Kuomintang bandits who had been terrorising the locals since around the time of the Japanese surrender. The bandits were organised into two platoons and numbered around 70 men in all. Within a few days of the arrival of our guerrillas, approaches were made to us by the Siamese. Could we get rid of the other Chinese group as they were causing too much trouble?

The Kuomintang bandits put up little resistance and ran off, leaving untouched their supply of weapons and ammunition. Unable to re-group, the remnants of the two platoons made their way north to the tri-border 'golden triangle' region where the frontiers of Burma, Siam and Laos converge. There they joined forces with the infamous General Lee's 93rd Kuomintang Division which had been driven out of southern China in 1949 by Mao's army. They quickly became part of the general's production line, assisting his troops in poppy cultivation for the opium trade.

The Kuomintang guerrilla base in the Betong Salient, which had taken several years to develop, then became our territory. It was well situated north of Betong and straddled the main road leading from the Malayan frontier.

Once we had installed ourselves in both the Betong Salient and Sadao regions, we endeavoured to establish firm local contacts. To some extent we were successful. But the central authority in Bangkok was military, pro-American and therefore strongly anti-communist. So our position in southern Siam was never cut-and-dried safe. It continually rested on the degree of cooperation we could forge with the authorities. This, not unexpectedly, ebbed and flowed depending on a whole range of factors: new administrative and police appointments, day-to-day events in the region, our ability to smooth over any problems arising from our presence and the like.

*   *   *   *   *

When I moved into the Betong Salient in the final weeks of 1953, our resident CPM guerrilla network there was in company strength. Our comrades occupied positions on both sides of the main Betong road. The terrain to the east of the road was far preferable. This offered us a whole range of probable campsites across a wide expanse of jungle. From a security point of view, the area was also far enough north of Malaya's Kelantan border.

To the west, however, the Kedah frontier was disturbingly close and consequently restricted our movements. We could very easily be attacked from the western side over the Kedah border if and when the British chose to implement the internationally recognised rights of hot pursuit which, early on, allowed them to penetrate Siamese territory to a depth of five miles. This was later extended to ten miles and eventually to 25 kilometres sometime after the metric system was adopted.

Circumstances were such that I had no time to inform my units in the Salient of our impending arrival. We just turned up. Following discussions with the locally based comrades, we set up our headquarters to the east of the road. The relationship of the terrain we chose to the Malayan frontier made it extremely difficult for the enemy to encircle us there. Conveniently, we were not in very deep jungle. To get to our camp we had to pass through rubber estates which made carrying supplies comparatively easy. Our first camp was within five miles of the border, but we were not troubled by the threat of hot pursuit. The jungle between us and the frontier was so dense that it was almost impossible for the British to plough through it. If they tried, we would be up and away long before they came anywhere near our position. We would establish three camps in the same general area in the years to follow.

*   *   *   *   *

In the early stages of the hot pursuit arrangements, the British were required to seek formal approval before entering Siamese territory. This demanded they supply to the Siamese details of troop numbers and intended target areas for the proposed cross-border operation against the CPM. More often than not the local Siamese officials rejected the British applications. On the occasions that they approved them, the Siamese insisted on a group of their officers accompanying the intruding force. Our Siamese contacts would invariably tell us when, where and in what strength the British would be arriving. This was clearly a useless system from the enemy's viewpoint.

The colonials in Malaya tried to get around the problem by sending primarily Malay police across the frontier in hot pursuit. This also failed to produce worthwhile results. They then attempted to enlist Siamese military involvement in joint exercises with Malayan units in the frontier regions. Kuala Lumpur agreed to provide full logistic support plus, as I understand it, there was a financial arrangement that saw funds set aside to pay for the involvement of Siamese troops. This likewise produced problems. The Malayan force was seen to get better rations and the Siamese complained, saying there was discrimination.

Having lived as long as I have, I am now able to enjoy what I can only describe as a levitated view of history. I was instrumental in playing out one side of the Emergency story. Access to declassified documents today gives me the ability to look back and down on the other side and see the broad picture. In the grim days of 1953, my comrades and I were struggling to hold our headquarters together. We plotted and manoeuvred to outfox security force ground patrols and outwit not only enemy jungle tactics but overall strategy as well. Sometimes we succeeded. Sometimes we failed.

A British intelligence summary for the period October 15 to November 15, 1953,[23] reported that the Politburo 'is not now thought to have moved far from its old headquarters in Western Pahang'. By this stage I had spent months trudging across the thickest jungle-covered mountains imaginable to reach the Siamese frontier regions of northern Perak. At least in this instance the enemy were lagging badly in their intelligence gathering. So I believe it is accurate to state that when I moved into the Betong Salient, the British had no knowledge of my whereabouts and would remain in the dark for some months to come.

Interestingly, the same document reveals that intelligence information had recently reached the British suggesting the Communist Chinese had asked the CPM to send an emissary to Peking. Here again, enemy intelligence reporting seems to have been particularly slow. It was late 1953. I had sent Ah Hai off to China in early 1949 and similarly dispatched Siao Chang shortly after the completion of our October, 1951,

Resolution. One way or another, this information appears to have taken either five or two years to land before British eyes.

The document continues: 'There is also evidence of a difference of opinion at top level in the CPM. Yeung Kuo, the Vice Secretary General of the Party and a close friend and mentor of the Secretary General, Chang Peng (sic), is reported to have told the Secretary General that he has serious doubts about the Politburo's directive of October, 1951 by which the Party was to concentrate on a more selective terrorism of a type calculated not to alienate 'the masses'.'

The assessment went on: 'Yeung Kuo appears to think that the directive does not go far enough. He advocates 'a revolutionary policy of duplicity' and the combination of all anti-imperialist groups into a 'racial independence united front'. The most important task of the party must be to organise the masses and all terrorist military activity should be entirely subordinated to that end.' It concluded with the observation that there was no evidence Yeung Kuo's view had influenced communist policy.

There was, of course, no truth in the suggestion of a rift between myself and Yeung Kuo. As the courier network between us had been smashed shortly after I issued the October, 1951, directive, my long-time friend had then no means whatever of communicating with me, even had he disagreed with the substance of the resolution.

However, I readily concede that the enemy, by 1953, had gained a keen sense of assessing battlefield developments and predicting likely patterns for conflict thereafter. This is illustrated most graphically by the minutes of a meeting which took place at King's House, Kuala Lumpur, on April 10, 1953.[24] Participants were General Sir Gerald Templer, representing Malaya, and Lt General Pao Sriyanond, Siam's Director General of Police. Also present were Mr J. P. Morton, Director of Intelligence, Malaya, and a Major Thana, an aide to General Pao. A reading of the minutes reveals that Templer was anticipating a growing CPM guerrilla presence in southern Siam and was already predicting that the emphasis of continuing warfare on the peninsula would concentrate northwards.

Pressed by the British High Commissioner, General Pao suggested that the Siamese authorities had revised their views about the CPM in the Kingdom's southern provinces. Previously, the attitude towards our intrusion had been one of indifference. The neighbouring communist movement was largely inactive when north of the frontier and caused no harm to local communities. Still, General Pao was not prepared to acknowledge to the meeting that the CPM now constituted a considerable threat and should be treated accordingly.

Templer then demonstrated on a map the order of battle of my army as enemy intelligence believed we were deployed in the frontier regions. He went on to hand General Pao a detailed statement explaining strengths and dispositions and at the same time requested that the collaboration under the Siam-Malaya border agreement be extended to more effective joint operations against us. Before the meeting concluded, Templer also asked General Pao to repatriate to Malaya, instead of China, any surrendered or captured Malayan communist guerrillas.

From my background research into this period I have come to the conclusion that Templer had, by this stage, been fully briefed on the latest top secret contingency planning British military strategists in London were undertaking for an invasion of southern Thailand. Codenamed Operation Warrior, it was to be launched with or without the Bangkok government's approval.

The plan, which bore a striking resemblance to Britain's appallingly bungled Operation Matador blueprint to thwart the predicted World War 11 Japanese invasion via the Kras Isthmus, called for the occupation of what was referred to as the 'Songkhla position'. In effect, it would have meant the seizure, by Britain, of Siam's four southern border provinces. At a meeting of the Chiefs of Staff in Whitehall on January 20, 1953, a full memorandum on the plan was approved for submission to the Cabinet Defence Committee which, in turn, directed that the Australian and New Zealand Chiefs of Staff be informed of its contents.

The preamble of the memorandum entitled *Defence of Malaya*[25] stated: 'Her Majesty's Government have noted previously that the occupation of the Songkhla position would be essential for the successful defence of Malaya against an increased threat. This threat might be either – (a) the infiltration threat; or (b) the threat of invasion by Chinese forces through Siam.

Instructions from the Commonwealth Relations Office to United Kingdom High Commissioners in Canberra and Wellington underlined the 'exceptionally secret nature' of the memorandum. They directed that special precautions be taken to ensure 'complete security of the information'.

It was also pointed out: 'Nothing has been disclosed about these plans to the Americans or to the French and this should be made clear. Australian and New Zealand military authorities will no doubt ensure that their representatives make no reference to this information in discussions in proposed Five Power Staff Agency or in ANZUS.'

TOP SECRET

196¹³

13

Copies to: Gen. Brownjohn

OFFICE OF THE LORD PRESIDENT
OF THE COUNCIL

PRIME MINISTER.

Your minute M.133/53 of the 2nd May.

You will remember that you decided it was premature
to talk to the Americans about our plans for the
occupation of the Songkhla position.

I have had a most interesting talk with General
Templer. He emphasized that, if Siam succumbed to
Communism, it would have very serious effects on morale
in Malaya; and that, if the Songkhla position had to
be occupied, it would be essential to occupy it in
plenty of time, so as to avoid any chance of Siamese
opposition. He did not foresee the situation arising
in the immediate future, but stressed that, when it did,
it would be necessary to take the decision quickly. He
was strongly of the opinion that, before taking action,
we must enlist American support.

I appreciate the great need for secrecy in this
matter and the undesirability of our plans becoming
widely known in the State Department or the Pentagon.
It occurred to me, however, that while you are in
Bermuda, you will be discussing the situation in South-
East Asia with the President and that you might think
it opportune to tell him personally of our plans.

I am sending a copy of this minute to the Minister
of Defence.

(SGD) SALISBURY

<u>28th May, 1953</u>

As far as Britain's Operation Warrior plan to occupy southern Siam (now Thailand)
was concerned, London in May, 1953, wanted their American allies to be kept
largely in the dark. In this top secret message to Prime Minister Winston Churchill,
Lord Salisbury reports on recent discussions he had held with General Templer
and, in the fourth paragraph, suggests a discreet approach on Operation Warrior
might be made to the American president.

A month after his meeting with General Pao, Templer flew to London and on May 19 attended a session of the Chiefs of Staff Committee. Here he was brought up to date on the full implications of Operation Warrior and was asked to provide a review of the South East Asian situation.

Templer began his review by assuring the gathered top brass that the Emergency was 'at last well in hand'. However, the anti-insurgency effort was proving a slow process and, as he saw it, the only way to end it was 'to kill its leaders, in particular the members of the Central Politburo and the Propaganda Bureau'. Such measures, he indicated, were easier said than done. The CPM leaders met infrequently and their clandestine communications were, he said, 'excellent'. If Templer's latter claim had only been true! Pointedly, he went on to indicate a 'particularly vital operation' would be initiated against the Party leadership. When the time came, he told the Chiefs of Staff, he would ask for temporary air reinforcements.

On the subject of occupying the Songkhla position, Templer emphasised that such an operation should be undertaken long before Siam succumbed to communism. If the timing was right, the commitment of one brigade would be sufficient to achieve the objective. The loss of this brigade from his command could be accepted temporarily, he argued, by re-disposing forces already available. However the British general appeared to differ with policy when it came to keeping the Americans in the dark about Operation Warrior. He told the service chiefs he considered it vital that the situation on the Siamese border with Malaya be discussed with the United States since there was a large American military mission in Siam.

Four months later, the British ambassador in Bangkok, obviously under instructions to gauge closely Siamese sentiments on southern frontier issues, was reporting back to London on discussions he had held with the same General Pao.[26] Minutes of this meeting disclose that the British Ambassador informed the Siamese police chief how the centre of bandit pressure was 'beginning to move towards the north'. The ambassador emphasised the last thing Sir Gerald Templer would wish would be to 'land the Siamese with the Emergency baby'.

General Pao reportedly smiled at this somewhat colourful declaration, obviously calculated to alarm. Perhaps taken aback by the coolness of the smile, the senior British diplomat insisted that what he was referring to was 'a most serious development'. He re-emphasised Sir Gerald Templer was 'extremely worried' about possible developments in southern Siam. The minutes say that General Pao continued to smile.

The meeting between ambassador and police chief went on to examine further British requests for an expansion of cross-border cooperation under the Siam-Malaya agreement. The recorded minutes state flatly that the Siamese general remained non-committal. It was the ambassador's impression that General Pao would have preferred to invite the Malayan police 'for further joint operations rather than formally extend the operational area'.

I would have heartily agreed with this idea.

Meanwhile, the most pressing issues I had to tackle once settled into our new Betong Salient headquarters in the final days of 1953 involved communications. It was vital that I rapidly establish contact with Siao Chang in Peking. I needed to bring him up to date with my new location and with the latest sombre appraisals I had been receiving of our armed revolution's progress. Likewise, I had to contact Yeung Kuo. To do this meant another restructuring of our ever fragile 'open' and 'jungle' courier networks, a branch of which had been attracting so much international attention during the year.

Chapter 20

The Lee Meng saga

Months before Britain imposed the Emergency regulations, the CPM's senior leadership was well aware of the difficulties entailed in establishing secure and reliable communication networks. The Japanese occupation years had taught us much. Ideally, we needed radio receivers and transmitters. We also required skilled operators and relevant codes. Should these be unavailable, we would be forced to rely on improvisation and the further development of our couriers.

During our preparations for armed struggle, I authorised Ah Dian, our ideologue, to purchase ten sets of portable military radio equipment on the Singapore black market. They were of British manufacture and had obviously floated through the side door of some colonial army installation on the island. The intention was to smuggle these sets, one by one, into Malaya over a period of weeks for distribution to key guerrilla units. Events overtook us. Within a week or so of securing the radios, the Emergency was proclaimed and stepped-up security measures thwarted all our attempts to get them across the Straits of Johore.

This major hiccup meant we were forced to rely on three cumbersome B-11 receiver/transmitters we had been able to appropriate from misdirected British airdrops to Force 136 contingents in 1945. Two of these were kept in Johore. The third was in Negri Sembilan. Officially designated 'portable', the B-11s were far from it – particularly if there was a requirement to lug them through jungles, swamps and paddy fields or across rivers as, in our case, there always would be.

During the war against the Japanese, Force 136 had been reluctant to train any of the MPAJA comrades in radio operating skills although they had given similar tuition in Colombo to several of the Kuomintang agents they later introduced to Malaya. Eventually, the British relented and agreed to train three of our members, one of them a female comrade called Lee Jhen. Lessons were restricted to basic reception/transmission theory, Morse code and equipment maintenance. The tuition was undertaken prior to the establishment of radio links between Malaya and the SEAC headquarters in Ceylon. So our students were never able to gain practical experience. Of the three trainees, only Lee Jhen survived the occupation.

As she represented the CPM's sole 'radio expert', I arranged for her to join our Mentekab headquarters in mid-1949 and endeavoured to bring in the three B-11s. It proved a convenient arrangement as she had, for some time, been Chen Tien's lover. While awaiting the arrival of the radios, she ran a class for three would-be operators. It was a futile exercise. None of Lee Jhen's pupils had ever sighted a receiver/transmitter – a severe handicap compounded further by the failure to have the equipment delivered before we were forced to move camp. As we transferred from one temporary headquarters position to another, Lee Jhen travelled with us. During a re-location in late 1950, she was part of a forward unit that ran into a Gurkha patrol in central Pahang. A burst of fire from an enemy automatic weapon sent our guerrillas scattering. All escaped injury with the exception of Lee Jhen. One round struck and killed her instantly.

By 1952, we learned that smugglers operating in the Kras Isthmus region of southern Siam had illegal radio networks linking them directly to Hong Kong and Shanghai. These were essentially capitalist businessmen functioning illegally. If they could get radio links going, why shouldn't we? I then instructed our North Malayan Bureau to establish contacts in the black market to see if we could secure radio sets suitable for our requirements. We were able, eventually, to purchase eight units. Each was about the size of a shoebox and came with a power pack and transformer. They were for reception/transmission of Morse code only.

As we struggled to sort out the radio side of our communications requirements, we realised, against the background of our Japanese occupation experience, that – radios or no radios – we would still have to rely heavily on couriers to keep message traffic moving. We knew the British would have the means of electronically intercepting our radio traffic if and when it was established. In other words, our war headquarters would simply be unable to function without regular incoming reports and outgoing orders carried by couriers. As I had become personally involved in setting up the courier network initially, I thought it wise to remain as close as possible to its ongoing operation.

One of my best couriers, Jhen Yin Fen, was a middle-aged schoolteacher from a Chinese primary school in Ipoh. I had known Yin Fen's family for some years. She was the coordinator of a courier group comprising several older women. When I left Perak for Pahang, her network began expanding. Within a relatively short period it was linking various camps in Perak and Selangor to my Mentekab headquarters. Such were our security arrangements that the couriers never learned of the exact location

One of our best-ever couriers, Jhen Yin Fen. I sent her to China after she was compromised in Ipoh. Unable to return to Malaya, Yin Fen eventually settled in China and there married one of our veterans.

of the camps nor met guerrilla leaders. They worked through safe houses and dead letter boxes that normally functioned in isolated areas. My key lady courier was the one exception to these rules.

Unfortunately, Yin Fen's network became compromised in early 1950. Her primary school headmaster and two teachers, all ignorant of her already established links to the Party, tried to involve her in distributing communist leaflets. The police swooped, arrested the headmaster and his two teacher helpers. Yin Fen was also detained. She was held for two days, subjected to various threats and finally released on condition she report regularly to the authorities. Her value as a courier immediately ceased. Indeed, her entire network was crippled. She managed, however, to slip into Mentekab where we reviewed her situation. She accepted my offer to send her to China for a cypher course. The plan was for her to be away from Malaya for approximately two years. On her return she would have to avoid going back to Ipoh. She would need to choose another population centre and assume a different identity. Once resettled, she could then contact us again.

Regrettably, Yin Fen was unable to return. Like the TB sufferers, she found herself stranded in Peking when the Chinese clamped down on all travel abroad. The Peking authorities, while deeply involved with the Korean War talks underway at Panmunjom in 1952, were determined not to be discovered with links to Asian subversive activities. She would never again live in Malaya.

As I moved my headquarters from Kerdau to Bentung, then to Raub, and further north back to the Cameron Highlands from mid-1950 to 1953, I was constantly working at restructuring my courier network. No sooner would we get an alternative group in place than the police would discover its existence and detain those involved.

*   *   *   *   *

On July 24, 1952, Special Branch police raided a house in Lahat road, Ipoh, and detained two women whom they suspected were linked to the CPM. Searches of the premises failed to uncover any trace of Party connections. Both women were held in custody and underwent rigorous interrogation. So harsh was the police questioning that one of the women, Cheow Yin, committed suicide while in custody – or so the authorities claimed. The other, identified as 24 year-old Lee Ten Tai, remained in detention for several weeks as enquiries into her background were pursued. Police claimed she had been raised in the Ipoh area by an uncle. Her mother had been banished to China in the late 1940s as a suspected communist. The mother's history obviously further incriminated the daughter in the eyes of investigators.

When brought before the Ipoh Magistrates Court on August 6, a barefooted Miss Lee was formally arraigned on three charges under the Emergency regulations. It was alleged: 1. That between August, 1948, and September, 1951, in the Kepayang area of Ipoh, she had carried a pistol; 2. That during the same time-frame and in the same area she had carried a hand grenade; 3. That she had consorted with persons who had arms and ammunition in circumstances that raised a reasonable presumption she had been acting in a manner prejudicial to the maintenance of public order. All three charges carried the death penalty.

The prosecution alleged Miss Lee was better known to CPM members by her Party alias, Lee Meng. The following day's local press reports spoke of the pretty 24 year-old prisoner, dressed in smart navy blue slacks and checked blouse. Despite being shoeless, it was reported she had walked 'nonchalantly' into the dock to hear the capital charges read out and explained. The combination of oriental youth, beauty and defiance sat well with Western expectations of the mysterious East. Police suspicions that Lee Meng ordered the killings of at least two Europeans only added to her aura. The stage was set for a trial guaranteed to grab international headlines.

When brought before the Perak Assize Court to face trial exactly a week later, Miss Lee, now dressed in a 'neat navy blue and red spotted sumfoo' discovered she faced a fourth charge. The latest allegation had her carrying a Browning automatic pistol during a two-month period prior to her arrest. After having levelled the fourth charge, the Deputy Police Prosecutor, Mr M.G. Neal, promptly announced to the court that he would only be calling evidence on the second charge. This related to possession of the hand grenade. Speaking clearly and forcefully in Cantonese, Lee Meng told the court: 'The charges are unfounded and I want to know the names of the persons who accuse me of these crimes.' The trial then got underway before the presiding judge, Justice J. Thomson, sitting with two assessors as required under the Emergency's criminal law procedure. One assessor was Chinese; the other was Indian.

In his preliminary remarks, Mr Neal explained that the raid on the Lahat road residence and the arrest of Lee Meng had been prompted by information gleaned during interrogation of a 'suspected bandit courier'. As there had been no incriminating

Lee Ten Tai, alias 'Lee Meng'

material seized during the raid, the case against the accused rested on evidence to be presented by nine 'former bandits'. Mr Neal added that the prosecution would be submitting photographic evidence showing the accused armed and in uniform.

Prominent Ipoh barrister, Mr S. P. Seenevasagam, acting for Lee Meng, was quick to latch onto the status of the nine prosecution witnesses. He pointed out they were 'owing their lives to the mercy of the government'. The defence counsel's information was accurate. Only one of the nine had received an official pardon. The rest were awaiting confirmation of theirs. As a result of Mr Seenevasagam's remarks, the judge went on to rule that the nine prosecution witnesses should be treated as accomplices and that their evidence needed corroboration before they could be believed.

The prosecution called on its nine witnesses. One claimed to have been a member of the communists' 'mobile corps' and to have met Lee Meng on several occasions when she visited his jungle camp near Kepayang. On every visit, he maintained, the accused had arrived with a hand grenade strapped to her waist. Later, she showed up at a camp near Gunong Rapat where he had been transferred. She was again wearing a hand grenade. Completing his evidence, the witness described Lee Meng as a ranking Party official who had issued orders for the killing of several Europeans in the Ipoh district.

An Indian witness told the court that Lee Meng had once visited his camp in the Sungei Siput area and taken several photographs of the guerrilla force in residence. He said she had also had herself photographed with a number of the guerrillas on the same occasion. A third prosecution witness, a female, claimed she had worked for Lee Meng as a courier for ten months. Whenever they met, she said, Lee Meng wore a hand grenade. The remaining six witnesses had similar stories to relate.

The photographs submitted in evidence to the court had been discovered in a cave near Gopeng. What was not made clear during the trial was the fact that they had been found by a former communist guerrilla-turned-policeman. In the event, the photographs were accepted as corroborative evidence.

In a ten-minute statement from the dock, Lee Meng emphatically stated she knew none of the police informers testifying against her. She vehemently denied being the woman in the photographs. She insisted she was not 'Lee Meng' the ranking CPM official, but Lee Ten Tai as shown in her identity card. Refuting suggestions she had been a functioning communist in Ipoh as early as 1948, she informed the court that was the year she left for Singapore and lived with her married sister for the next 24 months.

An awkward moment followed Lee Meng's declaration that, whenever she visited Ipoh, she stayed with her friend Cheow Yin. She told the court she had wanted to call Cheow Yin as a witness as they had both been arrested together. This was not possible, she said, as her friend had supposedly committed suicide in prison.

After a three-day hearing, the Court delivered its findings. The two Asian assessors pronounced her innocent. The European judge found her guilty. Clearly piqued at the response of the assessors, Justice Thomson declared to his court: 'How, as reasonable men, they came to that opinion, I have no means of knowing. I disagree with their opinions and order a retrial.'

Justice Thomson's demand for a re-trial, though unusual, was acceptable under Emergency law. In cases involving Europeans when joint opinions of assessors contradicted 'guilty' pronouncements, the charges had usually been dropped. The conflict in legal opinion was an added dimension to the already enticing Lee Meng saga. By this stage it was beginning to command column inches in newspapers throughout the British Empire.

The re-trial began 10 days later at the same venue, this time before Justice J. Pretheroe and two different assessors. A significant departure from accepted procedure was employed in the appointments of the second pair of assessors. For the first time on record, a European was chosen to serve as an assessor in a Perak trial of an Asian under the Emergency regulations. Lee Meng understandably objected and voiced her opinions in Cantonese to the court interpreter. The judge queried what Lee Meng was saying. When told she was objecting to the presence of the European assessor, Justice Pretheroe, without considering Lee Meng's remarks, replied curtly: 'Tell her that her objection is overruled.'

Undeterred, Lee Meng continued to voice her complaint. She argued that, as she was being accused of associating with people who had allegedly killed Europeans, she feared a European assessor would be prejudiced against her. Again ignoring what the accused was saying, Justice Pretheroe directed the interpreter to order Lee Meng to 'stop talking' as she was only prejudicing her case.

The trial was now playing to a packed courtroom. Journalists were taking notes. So, too, were interested observers, several of them lawyers, sitting in the public gallery. The same parade of witnesses appeared. The same photographs were submitted. Essentially the same objections and arguments were directed by the defence against the prosecution case. When the trial proceedings concluded, the assessors were first asked to give their separate verdicts. The Chinese assessor, a Mr Tan, found Lee

Showing signs of the pressure imposed by the trial procedure, Lee Meng is escorted to the Ipoh court complex for her retrial ten days after a British judge, at the original hearing, had ridiculed two Asian assessors for pronouncing her innocent.

Meng innocent. The European assessor, a Mr Wolfenden, maintained she was guilty. Quite predictably, Justice Pretheroe agreed with Mr Wolfenden's view, declared Lee Meng guilty as charged and went on to sentence her to death.

The cumulative result of the two trials delivered a legal conundrum that would subject the whole process of British Emergency justice to widespread international ridicule. Two judges and one assessor, all Europeans, had pronounced Lee Meng guilty. But three assessors, all Asians, had, at the same time, declared her innocent. Taken collectively, it amounted to a 3-3 split decision. Only the presence of the European assessor, introduced specially for the occasion, had secured conviction and the death penalty. If justice must be seen to be done, this was clearly not the way to do it. Escorted by women constables and guarded by heavily armed police, Lee Meng was taken in a covered van to Taiping prison, an hour and a half's drive north of Ipoh, and there placed in a condemned cell on death row.

Thereafter began a flurry of legal moves to save the beautiful Lee Meng from the gallows. Her lawyers lodged an appeal with the Federation's Court of Appeal sitting in Kuala Lumpur. As part of a three-judge panel, the Chief Justice of Singapore, Justice Murray-Aynsley, found that he would allow the appeal on the ground that the charge against Lee Meng was defective in law. He was outvoted, however, by his two judicial colleagues – The Chief Justice of Malaya, Justice Mathew, and Justice Whitton. The third trial only made murky waters murkier. Three separate trials had all arrived at split decisions.

As a pauper, Lee Meng petitioned the Judicial Committee of the Privy Council in London for special permission to appeal against her death sentence. She was represented by one of Britain's most respected legal figures, Mr Dingle Foot, assisted by Mrs Wee Phaik Gan, then the only Chinese woman called to the English Bar. The petition was heard by Lords Porter, Tucker and Asquith of Bishopstone. They dismissed it on Monday, February 16, 1953. Reasons for decisions on such petitions are not usually provided and none was given in Lee Meng's case.

A firm of London solicitors then took up the cudgels on behalf of the controversially condemned woman. Briefed by Mr Seenevasagam's Ipoh law firm and waiving their legal fees, the London solicitors organised a special petition to the Sultan of Perak signed by 50 leading members of the House of Commons. Among the signatories were well-regarded politicians like Michael Foot, Jennie Lee, Tom Driberg, Richard Crossman, Marcus Lipton and a future British Prime Minister, Harold Wilson. In a parallel move, the solicitors sent cables giving details of the petition and the signatories to the Malayan Attorney General, the British High Commissioner in Kuala Lumpur, and the personal adviser to the Sultan of Perak.

The London solicitors, in what was regarded as a highly unusual step, called a press conference to bring to public notice the puzzling circumstances leading to Lee Meng's death sentence. They drew attention to the way the assessors had been appointed for her re-trial: 'The usual practice is for three Asian assessors to be summoned from whom the judge selects two. In this case two Europeans and only one Asian were summoned by the Registrar of the Supreme Court, thereby ensuring that at least one assessor would be European.'

In a separate London move, another leading parliamentarian, Sir Leslie Plummer, headed a four-man political deputation to the Colonial Secretary questioning the legality of Lee Meng's conviction and advising that her death sentence be commuted.

Back in Kuala Lumpur, the Chairman of the Malayan Chinese Association (MCA), Tan Cheng Lock, also drew up a petition to the Sultan of Perak seeking clemency. Given the climate of the times and the determination of the colonials to demonstrate tough anti-communist measures, Tan's work on his petition indicated considerable political fortitude. He argued that Lee Meng had been denied the right of a fair trial under the assessor system. Had she been a European, two European assessors would have been on the judicial panel. The inference was, of course, that Malayan law functioned one way for white colonials and quite another for Asians.

Tan also pursued an important argument put forward in the London petition. Had Lee Meng been charged and tried in the settlements of Penang or Malacca, or the colony of Singapore, she would have been tried by a judge and jury. In these circumstances, her case would have come under the criminal procedure code of the Straits Settlements. Had the jury then arrived at the same opinion as the assesssors in Lee Meng's first trial, she would have been acquitted forthwith.

Within hours of the two petitions being dispatched to the Sultan of Perak in the final days of February, the already dramatic Lee Meng story took a quite sensational turn. Hungary, a Soviet satellite, offered to exchange the girl on Taiping prison's death row for 49 year-old British businessman, Edgar Sanders. The Briton had been incarcerated in Budapest by the communist authorities since his arrest on spying charges in November, 1949. The British press at once interpreted the Hungarian offer as evidence of monolithic communism in action. Reports suggested that Budapest, Moscow, Peking and the CPM had somehow all been involved in brokering the deal that extended across two continents. International communism, they said, had placed a high value on Lee Meng. For the first time, European communists had openly come to the aid of comrades in the Asian theatre.

Newspapers discovered Sanders' wife, Winifred, working as a waitress at Frinton-on-Sea, Essex, to help support the couple's three daughters. In the summer she ran a beachside refreshment kiosk in order to earn extra cash. They learned how Sanders himself had been a wartime captain in the British Army and had been on a three-year contract as an accountant with the Standard Electric Company's Budapest office when he was arrested. Lee Meng's death row dilemma, as far as Western journalists were concerned, paled in comparison to the plight of the loyal British housewife struggling to make ends meet while her unjustly convicted husband languished in a communist prison. It was icing on the cake when it was revealed Edgar Sanders was the cousin of debonair British film star, George Sanders.

Should Britain take up the Budapest offer? Some argued yes. Others said no. It was seen as a tussle between humanity and distrust. At the core of the issue was whether an agreement to swap would set a precedent for communist governments around the world to start snatching innocent hostages anytime they required a barter arrangement. Those favouring the exchange pointed to how the United States handled the release of American businessman, Robert Vogeler, who had been arrested with Sanders. Vogeler had been given 15 years' jail for espionage at the same time the British businessman was handed down a sentence of 13 years. Both men had pleaded guilty to being spies.

Vogeler was released after 17 months. To achieve his freedom, Washington agreed to the re-opening of Hungarian consulates in the United States. American tourists would also be allowed to travel to Hungary. Furthermore, Washington promised to aid the recovery of Hungarian assets looted by the Nazis. London had attempted similar negotiations for Sanders, offering to release Hungarian property located in West Germany. This had failed. If you could negotiate thus, why couldn't you consider the Budapest offer?

British Prime Minister, Mr Winston Churchill, reacted swifly. Three days after Budapest's proposal was made public, he rose in the House of Commons. 'There can be no question of bartering a human life or deflecting the course of justice or mercy in Malaya for the sake of securing the release of a British subject unjustly imprisoned in Hungary,' he thundered. 'Every effort will continue to be made by Her Majesty's government to induce the Hungarian Communist government to release Mr Sanders with whose family and friends we express our deepest sympathy.'

A week later on the other side of the world, Mr W. J. Burton, Superintendent of Taiping Prison, summoned Lee Meng to his office and informed her the Sultan of Perak had commuted her death sentence to life imprisonment. Superintendent Burton would later reveal that his prisoner had exhibited 'no emotional reaction whatsoever' to the good news he had relayed.

Before the year was out, Edgar Sanders would be pardoned by the Hungarian government and released to return to England. Shunning the high-flying international business world, he strangely became a £12-a-week bus driver for seaside holiday-makers at Clacton. 'After being in the limelight for so many years, I really enjoy bus-driving,' he told a journalist three years after his homecoming. 'Anyway I have to earn a living. There seems to be no demand for 50-year-old businessmen; not even for one who has been the centre of international incidents.' Commenting on the validity of his conviction, Sanders volunteered: 'I was never a paid spy. But I certainly passed information to the British military attaché in Budapest.'

Paid or unpaid, Edgar Sanders unquestionably was a spy.

*   *   *   *   *

Nothing more would be heard of Lee Meng for the next 11 years. In 1964, the Malaysian government quietly announced she was being released and exiled to China. Before her departure, Lee Meng requested Mr Seenivasagam buy her a sewing machine, two bicycles and some clothes. The lawyer met her requests. His now 36 year-old client promised to keep in touch by post. Until the time of his death, several years later, Mr Seenivasagam had received no mail from Lee Meng. I feel this was not the result of ingratitude on the part of Lee Meng. Rather it came about because of the strict censorship of the day imposed at the Malaysian end.

A pawn in daunting East-West power play, Lee Meng has remained an enigma to this day. Was she guilty of the charge of carrying a hand grenade? Was she even a member of the CPM? She never backed down from her emphatic denial of the arms charge. Nor did she waver from her rejection of being Lee Meng, the hard-core communist. All along she insisted her name was Lee Ten Tai and, indeed, that is the name under which she was deported to China. She still insisted she was framed by the nine former communist guerrillas seeking leniency from the authorities. She liked to refer to them as 'dead surrendered devils'. Furthermore, she stuck to her denial of being the woman in the photographs presented in court. It had been, she said, a matter of mistaken identity.

I have no idea whether Lee Meng was guilty of carrying a hand grenade as charged. I do know, however, that Lee Ten Tai was certainly Lee Meng, the dedicated communist. During the 1950-52 period when I was working on consolidating my Ipoh-based 'open' courier operation, I had asked the Perak secretary at the time, to find a suitable head courier. Once secured, this person was to replace the compromised Yin Fen whom I had sent to China. The state secretary promptly appointed Lee Meng and I was subsequently informed she had begun working.

To my way of thinking, Lee Meng had always lacked caution. There was a recklessness in her operational style. I first noticed her during the Japanese occupation when she worked for one of my fellow Perak state committee members. She was certainly dedicated, active and brave. But I remember then being glad she was not functioning for me. I was naturally perturbed when she was seconded to my personal courier network. With hindsight I should have made it very clear that Lee Meng be made to undertake only one specific task at a time. Either she should operate only as a courier under the direction of the Central Committee, or, she should be restricted to guerrilla activities under the state committee. Without clear direction, Lee Meng started mixing her work as a courier with her guerrilla duties.

Revolutionary couriers, like all good clandestine operators or espionage agents, must be capable of performing individually. They should never allow their various activities for the Party to overlap. In short, they must be skilled at compartmentalizing their lives. Otherwise, if one segment of their work becomes compromised it is only a matter of time before their other clandestine activities get detected.

It would not be long before Lee Meng started mixing her work as a courier with her duties for the state committee. She used one of her couriers within my personal network for a task linked to other Party matters. Special Branch police uncovered the subordinate courier working on the secondary task and, through her, were able to trace back to Lee Meng who was then living in the house on Lahat road.

The international spectacle caused by the Lee Meng case had little impact on the day-to-day workings of the CPM. We followed the case carefully in the daily newspapers and on radio news bulletins. For security reasons, we avoided all contact with her lawyers and certainly never contributed to her legal fees. To have commented in our propaganda on her trials would have been tantamount to giving her the kiss of death. Frequently we were left incredulous at British suggestions tying us to an international conspiracy involving Budapest, Moscow and Peking. How anyone in their right mind could have seriously disseminated such groundless information is difficult to

My trusted friend and comrade Chen Tien who later became
Lee Meng's husband.

perceive. What was even more baffling was the fact that virtually the entire British press fell for the ruse.

I am glad to record that Lee Meng's story has had its bright patches. Upon her arrival in China, she was reunited with the mother she had longed to see. She looked after her mother during the old lady's dying years.

Love also entered the picture and while she may have married late in life, Lee Meng had the very good fortune of marrying one of the finest men a woman could hope to spend the rest of her years with – Chen Tien, my able comrade and trusted friend. A widow now, she is still living in China. I'm sure the memories of Lahat road and the prison cell in Taiping are buried deep, superseded by the remembrances of a mother and a husband who shared her views about the value of human life and justice.

As a footnote to the Lee Meng saga, I would personally like to place on record my gratitude to all those British politicians, lawyers and concerned individuals in Europe and Asia who recognised the injustice of the colonial legal process during the Emergency and saved my courier's life. Credit must also go to the then Sultan of Perak and Dato Tan Cheng Lock for the humanitarian stands they took at a time in history when only those with great courage were prepared to challenge the system.

Chapter 21

Initial peace overtures

The instructions we gave Siao Chang authorising him to issue communiqués from Peking in the name of the CPM Central Committee would produce entirely unexpected results. The Politburo had devised this fall-back transfer of control as an emergency measure. It was to be used if Party communications on the peninsula collapsed, or, if Yeung Kuo and I were both killed in action.

Within a few months of concluding these arrangements, we suffered a calamitous communications breakdown throughout Malaya. The vital courier network between my headquarters in western Pahang and Yeung Kuo in the Kajang area of Selangor was smashed by joint British military and Special Branch operations. At the same time, other courier systems linking me to the rest of the CPM guerrilla army were also demolished by enemy interception.

From Siao Chang's isolated position in the Chinese capital, the very crisis for which I had prepared my latest guidelines appeared suddenly to have taken effect. Naturally, he felt constrained to assume responsibility. Since arriving in the Chinese capital in the early weeks of 1953, he had gained considerable experience dealing at very senior levels with not only Chinese leaders but Russians as well. Siao Chang had travelled to Moscow where he conferred at length with top Kremlin men. Back in Peking, he enjoyed easy and regular access to decision-making levels of the CPC. Despite these contacts, I must emphasise that the CPM, up to this point, had received no direct assistance, financial or otherwise, from either the Russian or Chinese communists as British propaganda – and the UK press – were regularly proclaiming.

As a result of the international links he had cultivated, Siao Chang had spent some time preparing a special strategic study of the CPM's ongoing armed revolution and its relationship to the overall world communist picture. He and Ah Hai were hard at work on this project when they found themselves abruptly cut off from both my headquarters and Yeung Kuo's camp. The silence would last several months.

This communications black-out coincided with the build-up to an important conference of delegates from British Empire communist parties scheduled for London in early 1954. The CPM was expected to present a position paper at the gathering.

With both Yeung Kuo and myself incommunicado, our two men in China went ahead and drafted the required document. Not unexpectedly, their work had become strongly influenced by the advice they had been receiving from both Peking and Moscow. Again I should underscore that this was fraternal advice only, not orders.

The text our Peking-based duo prepared gave an appraisal of the situation in Malaya and went on to hint that the Party was perhaps ready to look favourably at negotiations to resolve the conflict. As such, it would be the very first overture for peace talks to be made by either side involved in the Emergency.

The position paper was ultimately presented to the London conference by our United Kingdom representative, the journalist Lim Hong Bee, who functioned there as spokesman for the All Malaya Council of Joint Action (AMCJA). Strangely, for all the work he did on our behalf in London, including his editorship of the cyclostyled *Malayan Monitor* newsletter, Lim was only ever a Party sympathiser, never a Party member. British political analysts and the press were quick to seize on what became roundly interpreted as the CPM's offer to begin peace negotiations.

I had just arrived in Betong and, in fact, had not seen a copy of our document before it was read to the London meeting. Where we had all along been demanding the establishment of a People's Democratic Republic of Malaya, we now spoke in terms of a united fight with all parties for the country's independence. Dropped from our platform was the earlier emphasis on the leading role to be played by the communist party. We called for an end to the Emergency and a repeal of the Emergency regulations. We talked in terms of human rights but left open how these were to be achieved. The document appeared to imply that the CPM was looking for a new strategy to fight for independence other than through armed struggle. The 1954 London position paper therefore heralded a significant directional switch.

There was a curious sidelight to all this. The document was, of course, written first in Chinese and then translated into English in Peking before being sent to London. After presentation in London the English language version was then translated back into Chinese for the CPM leadership in Malaya. Our connections with Siao Chang and Ah Hai were still down. The multi-translated text landed first at Yeung Kuo's jungle camp. By this time he and I were in intermittent contact via a new and still tentative courier network. After considerable difficulty, Yeung Kuo eventually passed the document on to me in Betong and in an accompanying message noted that the Party had appeared to have substantially changed its policy. Pointedly, thus far, neither he nor I – the CPM's two most senior figures – had had any say whatever in the fundamental strategic redirection. Still, we found ourselves faced with the urgent requirement of devising how best to implement the Party's new approach.

In the same message Yeung Kuo indicated we should develop an underground organisation that demonstrated no allegiance, overt or covert, to armed struggle. This movement would be concentrated in the main towns, not the rural areas where the armed struggle approach would continue.

Before we had a chance to exchange views, communications between us were again broken. But Yeung Kuo, knowing we would fully agree with his proposal, began setting up the mass organisation he had envisaged. This effort was aimed primarily at shifting mass support in the towns away from armed struggle to the new call for a negotiated settlement.

Not long after the London conference, a copy of the CPM paper landed in the hands of MCA President, Tan Cheng Lock, who, like everybody else, concluded that we had shifted our political ground. He decided to become personally involved in an initiative to kick-start peace talks. These developments were playing out against grand expectations of, if not world peace, at least peaceful co-existence promised by the preparations underway for two international gatherings. The first of these involved the Geneva talks on Indo China that took place from May to July, 1954, and which concluded with accords covering an end to fighting in Vietnam, Laos and Cambodia. Somewhat later came the Bandung conference in Indonesia in April, 1955, where the dominant theme was peaceful co-existence as championed by China's Premier, Chou En Lai. Making matters more complicated for the CPM were growing indications that Malaya might soon be seriously considering general elections to usher in a form of semi-representational government through a Federal Council firmly under colonial control.

Sensing the changing political nuances, both domestically and internationally, Tan announced he was prepared to go into the jungle and meet me for initial discussions. Unfortunately, we were cut off from all communications when this news broke. Thus, Tan's offer was considerably delayed reaching me. Had we known about the MCA leader's offer, we would have quickly issued statements to the effect that he was welcome to see us in the jungle or anywhere else providing our safety was guaranteed. It would have amounted to a magnificent propaganda opportunity for the CPM. If the British had blocked it, so much the better.

As it happened, the British government very quickly and very vocally opposed the MCA leader's idea on the grounds that it was impossible to guarantee the safety of those taking part in the sort of meeting Tan was proposing. For all its good intentions, the idea just frittered away and this, of course, was exactly what the British had intended. They saw distinct advantages in the maintenance of a contained communist threat in Malaya. Against the broad perception of a continuing Emergency, London could readily justify, both locally and internationally, an ongoing British military presence in Singapore and on the Malayan peninsula. To the skeptics, Britain would insist she was there to 'protect, not to re-subjugate' her colonial peoples, just as Mountbatten had advised eight years earlier.

Back in our Betong base camp Lee An Tung, Ah Chung and I immersed ourselves in an extensive review of the new political position that had been imposed on us. What did it mean for our overall campaign? From all the interpretations we were receiving, it was very clear neither Moscow nor Peking saw value in an armed struggle dragging on in Malaya. A military victory for the CPM, it had been decided for us, was out of the question. This was by far the toughest of the tough realities we had had to confront since the onset of the Emergency.

I waited in the hope that I could get reliable communications re-estabished to Yeung Kuo. Intense British military patrolling would ensure this did not happen. While I waited, the political situation in Malaya was fast changing. Now there was rising political fervour for the type of Federal elections that had been quietly discussed for months in the Kuala Lumpur back rooms. Local political leaders had been voicing their preferences for time-frames. Concerned by the clamour, Britain had begun to dig in her heels against what she feared might emerge as a premature concerted push for power by the Malay-dominated parties. Colonial officials preferred to talk in terms of progressive steps towards independence with the determining factor always being Malaya's ability to achieve a non-racially based political framework. To my mind, then and now, the British were quite convinced that the racial divides would sustain and that some form of colonial control could be kept in place for many years to come.

The broad political review we had undertaken at our Betong headquarters began to focus more acutely on the fast evolving political trends in Malaya and how we might influence these to our advantage. So much had changed in the political arena since our planned move out of it to armed struggle had been pre-empted by the June 16, 1948, Emergency proclamation. UMNO had grown from a 1946 amalgamation of 41 Malay associations, opposed to the Malayan Union idea, to become a significant political entity. Its founder, Datuk Onn bin Jaafar, had departed from the organisation in August, 1951, to form a rival non-communal movement called the Independence of Malaya Party (IMP) through which he promised to win independence by 1958. After a closely fought election, the UMNO leadership vacuum was filled by the charismatic presence of Tunku Abdul Rahman. The Tunku had won by a single vote over the radical nationalist Mustapha Hussein. Then 51 years old, the Tunku was the younger brother of the reigning Sultan of Kedah. An almost reluctant politician, he eventually gained solid support throughout UMNO by rejecting the non-communal urgings of Datuk Onn bin Jaafar, adopting a fervently Malay nationalist line and declaring that Malaya would emerge a Malay nation.

But the Tunku was a realist. It was not long before he, too, recognised Britain's determination to gear the pace of progress towards independence to the degree of racial accommodation achieved by local politicians. Thus, he consented to an alliance with Tan Cheng Lock's MCA, to contest the February, 1952, Kuala Lumpur Municipal Council elections. These resulted in a resounding victory for the UMNO-MCA camp which secured nine of the 12 seats up for decision. The UMNO-MCA link had then transformed into the Alliance Group and eventually became known as the Alliance Party in early 1953. In April that year the Tunku, by this time confident in the mandate of his followers, had begun openly endorsing a non-communal approach to politics. This represented a 180-degree turn from his unrelenting Malay nationalist programme proclaimed barely two years earlier.

As if on cue, an all-party committee appointed by the government soon began studying the requirements for holding Federal elections. I was certainly not surprised by the revelation that a majority of the appointed members on this important body would be selected from the IMP ranks. We in the Politburo felt then that the British strongly favoured Datuk Onn over the Tunku as the IMP leader had long demonstrated a far greater willingness to support a protracted granting of independence.

After lengthy debates within the all-party committee it became obvious there was a wide rift in opinions between the IMP and Alliance groupings. The IMP representatives were opting for a 92-member Federal Council of whom a minority of 44 would be elected. The Alliance members, on the other hand, proposed a 100-strong Council. They then demanded a majority of 60 be elected. What rankled with the British even more was the Alliance's insistence that the projected elections be held by November 1954 – a time-frame providing scarcely nine months for implementation.

Fuelled by popular support, the Alliance attempted to fast-track the elections issue by dispatching to London a three-man delegation headed by the Tunku. This

SECRET

INWARD SAVING TELEGRAM

FROM SINGAPORE TO FOREIGN OFFICE

2146A

Dep. Sec. ....
Sec. B ....
G. Its ....
S. I C ....

(Commissioner General for the United Kingdom .
in South East Asia)

167

By Bag

FOREIGN OFFICE SECRET AND
WHITEHALL SECRET DISTRIBUTION

Mr. MacDonald

No. 8 Saving
March 23, 1954   R. March 27, 1954.

SECRET

Addressed to Foreign Office telegram No. 8 Saving of
March 23.
Repeated for information Saving to   Washington   Paris
                                        Peking   Moscow.

GENEVA CONFERENCE AND MALAYA

At the High Commissioner's invitation Dudley has visited
Kuala Lumpur to discuss the possible implications of any mention
of Malaya being made at the Geneva Conference. The following
conclusions, which I endorse, were reached.

(a) It would be greatly to our disadvantage if the subject of
     Malaya was discussed or even raised, since this could easily
     be misinterpreted as an indication that the Malayan Communists
     constituted a real nationalist movement in revolt against a
     Colonial régime rather than a Communist conspiracy of alien
     inspiration. It would therefore be best to refuse all
     discussion of the subject.

(b) If it proves impossible to prevent the Communists raising
     the subject in such a way that attention has to be paid to
     their statements, the objective should be to turn the tables
     on them by saying that their insistence is evidence that they
     accept responsibility for Communist terrorism in Malaya.
     The United Kingdom Delegation should affirm that the Malayan
     insurgents are primarily an alien force acting under alien
     instructions. It should be made plain that no one can be
     allowed to depict the Malayan war as a spontaneous
     Nationalist uprising.

Singapore (Commissioner General) telegram No. 8 Saving
to Foreign Office

- 2 -

(c) It is obviously undesirable to prejudice the case on Indo-China by making any unnecessary admissions about the indigenous character of Ho Chi Minh's rebellion, and it is important to lay as much stress as possible on its alien inspiration and support. Nevertheless any comparison between Vietminh and the Malayan terrorists is likely to be disadvantageous from the Malayan point of view, since undoubtedly there is an opinion in many countries that Ho is a true patriot.

(d) If, though this seems extremely unlikely, the Communists were to put out feelers for an end to the shooting war in Malaya, it still seems undesirable to engage in discussion at the Geneva Conference itself, much as it would be to our advantage to bring the war to an end. In these circumstances the only answer we could give would be to refer to our existing Surrender Policy. If specific proposals for surrender should be put forward we should show willingness to examine them, especially if they involved repatriation to China. There might, perhaps, be an opportunity to steer any suggestions the Communists might have to make round to repatriation.

De-classified documents now reveal Britain harboured distinct fears in the run-up to the 1954 Geneva Conference that the proposed gathering might seriously undermine her international posture on Malaya and the continuing prosecution of the colony's Emergency. The document reproduced here[27] consists of advice Commissioner General Malcolm MacDonald placed before the Foreign Office in London two months before the Geneva talks got underway. Above all Britain must preserve the baseless position that the communist movement in Malaya resulted from a foreign conspiracy and was therefore not a genuine nationalist movement.

had a two-pronged aim. Firstly, to gain support from British Labour opposition ranks for the Alliance's overall position on time-frames and numbers in the Council's elected majority. Secondly, to secure a face-to-face showdown with the serving Colonial Secretary, Mr Oliver Lyttleton, before Britain made public its final word on the election proposal. But if the Tunku thought the momentum he was creating was unstoppable, he had badly miscalculated the British capacity for deft behind-scenes manoeuvring. On April 27, 1954, with the Alliance delegation still meeting parliamentarians in Westminster, the Colonial Office released a White Paper on the subject of private agreements already reached on the elections question between Templer and the Malay sultans. It showed that the rulers had concurred with British proposals for a 98-strong Legislative Council of which 52 seats would be elected and the remaining 46 nominated. By releasing the White Paper the British were implying that all points of relevance had been settled and it would be unacceptable protocol to tamper with conclusions already reached by the rulers. This, indeed, was the general message conveyed to the Alliance men when they eventually met Lyttleton.

By the time the Tunku returned to Malaya he was threatening that Alliance members would resign their positions from all Federal and State institutions, including the numerous government committees, unless Britain agreed to increase the number of elected seats in the proposed Federal Council to a three-fifths majority. The impasse had no effect on Templer's scheduled return home on June 1, at which time Sir Donald MacGillivray, his deputy, was promoted High Commissioner.

Templer spoke at a pre-departure news conference and declared the Emergency 'contained'. But he admitted that a hard-core guerrilla force still operated from deep jungle redoubts and that he had failed to dislodge these activities. More interestingly, from the CPM's point of view, he was unable to give pressmen any assurances on when the hard-core, many of them armed with machine guns, would be defeated. In other words, the Emergency might be contained but certainly was not at an end. Those who understood jungle warfare realised it could drag on interminably.

Political impasse and Templer's parting words notwithstanding, Britain remained convinced the Emergency was sufficiently under control that responsibility for colonial affairs in Malaya could be safely returned to civilian hands. The military position of Director of Operations which Templer had held jointly with his civilian duties as High Commissioner, thereafter became a separate function once more. It was filled by Lt General Sir Geoffrey Bourne.

Two weeks after MacGillivray assumed control, the Alliance made good its threat to boycott all government institutions. Once again Britain resorted to some deft manoeuvring, this time with a touch of characteristic colonial pomp and ceremony. On the evening of July 2, MacGillivray received the Tunku and two other Alliance leaders aboard the Royal Navy frigate, HMS Alert, then docked at Singapore's Sembawang Naval Base. During two hours of negotiations in the captain's cabin, the basis of a compromise settlement was reached. A bloc of seven Federal Council seats, which had been exclusively reserved for personal appointees of the High Commissioner, provided the breakthrough. MacGillivray agreed that nominations to five of the seven seats would only be concluded after discussions with representatives of the majority party. Two seats – those of Economic Affairs and Defence – would remain the High Commissioner's sole prerogative. Five days later, Alliance leaders lifted their boycott. In August, the Legislative Council amended the Federation Agreement to permit the holding of general elections. By March, 1955, election day had been proclaimed. Polling would take place on July 27, 1955.

Throughout 1954, the Tunku, for all the time he spent jousting with the colonials, was quietly and skilfully manipulating his main-force Malay followers away from their traditional communal outlook on politics. Before the year was out, he had been roundly proclaimed leader by both UMNO and MCA groupings. By early 1955, the Malayan Indian Congress (MIC) had also joined the Alliance. Meanwhile, Datuk Onn had dissolved the IMP and replaced it with a new non-communal entity called Parti Negara.

Viewed from our Betong headquarters it seemed to me that Britain was playing favourites in the power struggle between the Tunku and Datuk Onn. Scrutinising political developments throughout the peninsula, I became increasingly convinced the colonial authorities were preparing to support the aspirations of the openly pro-British Parti Negara leader. Datuk Onn was then a government minister holding the Home Affairs portfolio. Within his Ministry operated a rural development agency known as RISDA. Early in the election year, the government chose to channel substantial additional funds to RISDA, ostensibly for expanding rural projects. We were highly suspicious of this stepped-up budget allocation in an election year and read it as an attempt to subsidise Datuk Onn's political endeavours.

In the run up to the 1955 polls, we concentrated our analysis on the differing platforms between the Alliance and Parti Negara. In particular we reviewed how each handled two specific issues directly relevant to our struggle: independence and the

Emergency. Parti Negara still favoured the British preference for a protracted route to independence. As far as the Emergency was concerned, Datuk Onn and his colleagues remained non-committal. We took all this to mean that Parti Negara, should it win, would toe the British line, give lip-service to the idea of independence sometime in the future and continue the jungle war, ignoring any opportunities for peace.

The Alliance, on the other hand, exhibited a far more radical approach to the electorate. They promised both self-government and independence within four years of becoming the ruling party. On the matter of the Emergency, the Alliance platform had made the dramatic campaign offer to end the fighting via a general amnesty.

Our Betong deliberations fully recognised that the CPM's position was getting extremely tight. Albeit in varying measures, both Datuk Onn and the Tunku would be perceived by the electorate as being committed to independence. The top card in our hand since the outbreak of the Emergency had been our commitment to fight for independence. This was now in danger of being snatched away. We were left with two options. We could fight on and try militarily to win independence within the Tunku's promised four-year time-frame – an impossible goal. Or we could seek some form of negotiated settlement.

With armed struggle we had sought power through force, having been blocked from the political route by the colonials. We had calculated that within an eight-to-ten-year period force would have predominated. Britain, we believed, would then have had no option but to recognise our control. Our calculations had been misplaced. Reality now was that Britain, whichever way the elections went, would be handing over control – and this would be independence – to what would essentially be a Malay power bloc.

If we could achieve a reasonable peace settlement with the incoming party, following the elections, perhaps we would face five or ten years in the political wilderness. That would be acceptable. During this time we would lie low and re-group. After that, we would re-emerge to fight again – this time not with arms but within the constitutional framework – for the creation of a socialist state. This was precisely what I was envisaging then. Had the scenario worked out, I would never have contemplated returning to armed struggle.

As the two main Malay-led political groupings shaped up for the election, we felt sure the colonials had no real desire to hand over early independence. They would go to great lengths to hang on. The British in the late 40s and early 50s had enjoyed dangling the enticement of so-called self-government in front of the people. Self-government, as we saw it, was certainly not independence. And I am quite sure the British definition of self-government, throughout that period, was pretty much as we would have defined it. Through it they intended to retain control behind scenes and thereby continue their economic dominance. Malaya promised a continuing valuable source of revenue. Only if Britain was forced by a combination of domestic and international circumstances would she fully relinquish the reigns of colonial control.

As my Politburo colleagues read the fast emerging Malayan political scene in late 1954 – early 1955, the CPM had really no alternative but to signal support for the Tunku. To do this meant an initial overture on our part. So, I came up with the idea of creating a high ranking communist official who would have the title of 'spokesman' for General Headquarters. Identified thus, it was clear he would not be speaking for either the Central Committee or the Politburo. This way we would have an 'out' if the exercise went sour. We gave our fictitious spokesman the Mandarin name Wu Xing, a pseudonym that the press would transpose to its Cantonese equivalent, Ng Heng.

With the concurrence of my Politburo colleagues, I set about drafting a letter to be signed by Wu Xing. It was my intention to display, for all to see, the CPM's determination to press for what we regarded as a just resolution of the conflict.

Reacting to the Tunku's amnesty offer, we dispatched this letter in May, 1955, to the government in Kuala Lumpur making it clear that the Party wanted talks to end the fighting. We believed the timing was right. The election date had been announced. Dissolution of the Legislative Council had been scheduled for June 2. What was more, our peace initiative would be coming in the immediate aftermath of the Bandung Conference. Peaceful co-existence had become an international catchphrase.

Our letter called for a 'fair' approach to the proposed discussions. It suggested a round-table conference of all political parties be convened. Furthermore, it hinted that the CPM would accept an amnesty, but not quite as the Tunku was suggesting. The Alliance leader had stipulated that amnesty would be granted only after our surrender. I countered that we should talk things over first and this way negotiate the amnesty arrangements. 'In spite of the thousands of methods adopted by the British Government to liquidate us,' I wrote, 'it has failed to do so. Neither has it defeated

馬來亞民族解放軍總部代表的聲明

——本人根據總部的命令，對首間以談判方式結束戰爭及實現馬來亞獨立的問題發表聲明如下：

——(一)我們的鬥爭目標是，而且一直是：和平、民主、獨立的馬來亞。只要有可能，我們都表示願以和平方式爭取實現上述目標，不言而喻，和平實現馬來亞獨立，不僅對馬來亞人民，而且也對英國政府及英國人民是有利的。

——但是，不能不指出，直到目前英國政府還在各種藉口下繼續其殖民統治，對要求舉行會議與關於人權相自決、關於附屬國人民問題的決策則採取拖延態度。目前在新加坡與聯合邦實施的憲制，有一個共同的基本特點：英國政府控制了國防、外交財政軍大權，英人總督或欽差大臣有權否決立法機關通過的法令，外國軍隊有權繼續駐紮在馬來亞全境，並且有權在馬來亞各地建立和擴建只是為外國利益服務的軍事基地。只要上述情況一天不改變，馬來亞就一天也沒有解放或獲得獨立，人民的民主自由權利就一天也沒有得到可靠的保障，馬來亞也就很可能被拖入為外國利益而進行的一場亞洲人殺亞洲人的戰爭——人民已無權過問又毫無干係合其切身利益的戰爭，要人民付出鮮血代價的戰爭，立法議員的年俸俸薪再高馬來全部民選，都不能掩蓋這些鐵的事實。

——(二)為了爭取和平實現馬來亞獨立，必須首先結束戰爭，廢除緊急條例，保障人民的民主自由權利，以便在和平、民主的氣氛中舉行全國大選。

——馬來亞的各政黨，例如任何人，只要真正要爭取獨立的，不論其屬於甚麼階層，不論其對獨立持有甚麼見解，也不論其過去的行為如何，都可以而且應該為爭取實現共同目標的觀點下團結起來，為爭取結束戰爭，和平實現馬來亞獨立而努力。

——因此我們呼籲各黨派、團體及各界代表人士，應爭取儘早舉行圓桌會議，對有關結束戰爭、和平實現馬來亞獨立問題進行充分討論，以求達成符合馬來亞實際情況的一致協議。這樣一個協議，必將對促成早日結束戰爭，和平實現馬來亞獨立的事業——符合全國各民族、各階層人民的切身利益的事業作出重大貢獻。我們將對這個會議採取積極合作的態度，毫無疑問由於各民族各有其特別關心的一些問題由於各種政治見解的不同黨會之間的意見，必然會很大的效果。但是由於大家具有共同目標，只要大家採取互相諒解，互相尊重的態度，以求達共同願望而又允許保存不同觀

(1)

First page of the Wu Xing (Ng Heng) letter that I wrote from our Betong Salient headquarters.

us in war because we are supported by masses of people and hence we will never be defeated.'

A copy of the letter was dispatched to Chief Minister David Marshall in Singapore along with a request that its contents be shared with the local Labour Front party. A further copy was addressed to the United Planters Association of Malaya.

As soon as the government received our letter, they called an emergency meeting to discuss how best to deal with our approach. High Commissioner MacGillivray then flew to London for consultations. On his return, the Malayan Government quickly issued a statement flatly rejecting our proposals. Shortly thereafter, MacGillivray spoke over Radio Malaya laying down conditions for talks with the CPM. His message was curt. If we wanted talks we had first to surrender. It was as simple as that. The communists, he said, were seeking peace because they were being defeated.

In truth, I never for a moment thought that the defiant tone of the Wu Xing letter would go unchallenged. Perhaps we were at a military disadvantage. But that was only one aspect of our peace overture. By the very nature of the conflict that had been waged for the past seven years, a resolution could never be neat or simplistic.

As the election campaign gathered momentum, the British chose to stonewall on the peace talks issue. The Tunku, on the other hand, gained considerable political mileage by repeatedly referring in public rallies to his previous amnesty offer and the prospects, given an Alliance victory, of peaceful negotiations to end the war.

The Tunku's astounding triumph over Datuk Onn at the July 27 polls stunned the British. Indeed, no one had predicted such a sweeping win. Out of the 52 seats contested, the Alliance won 51. The remaining seat went to an independent. Datuk Onn had been dismissed as irrelevant. The Tunku had emerged all-powerful. It was now pointless for the colonial British to try and play divide and rule between the two Malay camps because there was now only one camp and the Tunku led it.

Still, the British tried to rein him in when it came to the issue of opening talks with us. Brushing aside this pressure, the Tunku made it clear he was determined to get discussions going. Finally, the British relented on the understanding that any meeting with me would be only exploratory. Two months after the elections, the Tunku issued a statement indicating a willingness to meet me. Radio Malaya carried an announcement which stipulated: 'There will be no preliminary meeting with any representatives or anybody else. The meeting will take place at a suitable place in North Malaya. An official, who is known to Chin Peng, will be nominated as the conducting officer. He will hold himself in readiness to meet Chin Peng at a rendezvous in a safe area, in which a local ceasefire will be arranged.'

The statement went on: 'He will conduct Chin Peng safely to the meeting place. If Chin Peng wishes to attend such a meeting he should address a private letter to the Tunku naming the rendezvous time and date where the conducting officer will meet him and bring him to the meeting place. The rendezvous selected must not be in the jungle, but preferably close to a village.'

I responded with two letters, one dated October 2 and addressed to the Tunku, the other dated October 4 and addressed to David Marshall. I arranged, through our underground network, to have both posted in Penang. I took care in drafting my replies in courteous English – a point noted by Marshall when he spoke to the press some days later. British officials were quick to repeat the colonial position that neither the Tunku, Marshall, nor Dato Tan Cheng Lok, the three-man panel of local political leaders slated for the talks, should enter into any negotiations with Chin Peng. All three were there purely to explain the terms of amnesty and must refrain from any discussions on the matter of recognising the CPM as a legitimate political party.

For all the earlier insistence that there would be no preliminary talks, these soon got underway and, in fact, involved no fewer than three separate sessions. The first of these took place on October 17 at the northern Perak tin-mining village of Klian Intan, close to the Siamese border. I was quite happy with this chosen venue as we had long regarded the 2000-strong population there as solidly pro-CPM. The Tunku sent his Assistant Education Minister, Too Joon Hing. He was accompanied by the Acting Police Commissioner, Mr I. S. Wylie. During the final days of the Japanese occupation, Wylie had parachuted into Johore to become a Force 136 liaison officer with our guerrillas. Following his demobilization he had returned to Malaya and joined the police force where he received rapid promotion. We well recognised that the man we had to deal with during these discussions was Wylie, not the Assistant Education Minister.

Our representative at these talks was Chen Tien. I chose him because, during the Japanese period, he had been the AJA chief in Johore and as such had worked with Wylie. What was more, Chen Tien had been with our headquarters since the beginning of the Emergency and was very familiar with my political views. The local newspapers referred to him as the CPM's 'propaganda chief'. This was wrong but we did not trouble to correct the error. Lee An Tung had, from the outset of the Emergency, always headed our propaganda section. Chen Tien was his deputy.

During the initial session, held in the Klian Intan community hall, there was rapid accord on the establishment of a ceasefire arrangement to enable Chen Tien to travel to and from the talks in safety. The only sticking point was an objection on the British side to our demands that the CPM be allowed to hold a press conference during the main talks between myself and the Tunku. There were some very heated arguments made on this point by Wylie, but no conclusion was reached by the end of the first session.

The second round of preliminary talks took place exactly a month later, again in the Klian Intan community hall. This lasted a whole weekend. I had written a letter to the Tunku and given it to Chen Tien with instructions to pass it to Assistant Education Minister Too. At the same time the Politburo had prepared a statement and leaflets for Chen Tien to give out to press reporters covering the event. If the British were going to prohibit us from holding a press conference at the main talks, we simply had to find other avenues to be heard. Chen Tien duly carried out his instructions and the reporters received our statement. It said, in part: 'The masses hope both sides at the peace talks will treat the matter with sincerity, conciliation and compromise. Any attempt to induce members of the liberation army to surrender will only create an adverse atmosphere for the peace talks and therefore be against the people.'

Our attempt to place the CPM case before the public at large received a stinging rebuke from the Tunku. On November 18, he declared: 'If the communists ever again issue statements to the Press and indulge in propaganda tactics, as they did yesterday, I will not meet Chin Peng or anyone else. I am not going to negotiate with or treat Chin Peng as my equal. I am going to explain the amnesty. I will listen if he proposes something to me and will consider it. I represent the Malayan government and we have all the resources to fight and beat the communists. I want peace and I want to end the Emergency. I will end the Emergency in any case, but I do not want any more bloodshed if I can help it.'

The third and final round of preliminary discussions took place in a tent on a temporary airfield outside the border township of Kroh, some nine miles north-west of Klian Intan. By this stage Assistant Minister Too remained silent during the discussions which were dominated by Wylie. Whether that was part of a planned scenario, I have no idea. But what happened during this third round of talks was very significant. At one point there was a break in the exchanges when Wylie excused himself and went to the toilet. Suddenly, Too found his voice. He said: 'I have a personal message from the Tunku for you to pass to Chin Peng. The Tunku told me to tell you that, no matter what happens, he hopes Chin Peng will come and talk with him. If the first round of the talks fail to settle the problem, when he returns from London, the Tunku will continue the discussions.' It was a clear undertaking made verbally, a promise that would ultimately trap me.

I personally took this approach as indicative of a genuine gesture on the part of the Tunku. At the time, my reading of the Tunku's offer was as follows: He doesn't believe he can come to a meeting of minds at our first round of discussions. However, he feels confident he will be able to act far more independently on his return from his scheduled UK talks in January. Not for a moment did it cross my mind that the CPM would emerge an important bargaining chip for the Tunku during his London negotiations and that thereafter his plans for dealing with the Emergency problem would undergo a radical review.

During the Klian Intan and Kroh meetings, the British were aware that our headquarters had been in southern Siam for some months. I, of course, recognised this but still felt it much better for us to be seen emerging from a Malayan jungle. Thus, a major point of issue was naturally my right of free passage to and from the talks venue. This, it had been agreed, would be at the northern Kedah township of Baling. A ceasefire would have to be imposed over a specific stretch of Malayan border territory. Chen Tien initiated the discussions by suggesting the ceasefire last for a week before, a week after, and, of course, during the proposed talks. We had wanted the widest possible stretch of jungle for this arrangement in order to disguise the routes we would take in and out of Malaya. The government argued about the size of the ceasefire area but we reached a compromise fairly readily.

The Kroh meeting settled the problem of food rations for my accompanying security force. The British agreed to supply these and I instructed Chen Tien to inform Wylie I would be bringing out a guard of some 60 guerrillas. My guard would eat well. Actually I brought only a 20-strong security platoon with me. It was agreed that the British troops would not move close to the jungle fringe. For our part, we would not leave the fringe. Details of where and when I would emerge from the jungle at the Rahman Hydraulic Tin Mine in the Gunong Paku area were finalised, as were our accommodation arrangements at the conference venue.

When Chen Tien returned to Betong from Kroh bearing the Tunku's private message, I was greatly encouraged. I resolved then and there to proceed with the proposed Baling meeting and make the best of it.

Chapter 22

The Baling talks

About a month before the Baling talks were scheduled to begin, a special emissary from Siao Chang arrived at my Betong headquarters after an overland journey from China. He had travelled for many weeks on a two-fold mission. Having completed a radio technician's course in Peking, part of his task was to get our wireless operational so we could begin communicating directly with Siao Chang in the run-up to the peace talks. More importantly, he had been instructed to pass on to me personally the contents of unquestionably the most critical document ever addressed to the CPM by the two most powerful parties in world communism. So sensitive was the 1,000-word communiqué, known as the *Joint Written Opinion of the CPSU and the CPC,* that Siao Chang, who had first received it in Moscow on our behalf, decided it must not be physically carried.

Instead, the messenger was required to commit the full translated Chinese text to memory. This took several days after which he duly set off south for our headquarters. By the time the comrade reached my camp, his memory on certain segments of the text had begun to fade. He was able to provide whole slabs of it without trouble. But on some important aspects the precise phrases escaped him. And these proved critical to my comprehension.

From the messenger's recollection I was able to establish that the purpose of the memorandum was to convey four main points to me. Firstly, that Malaya had no common frontier with a socialist state. Secondly, that the CPM's struggle had failed to form a broad united front across all races. Thirdly, that as there was an extreme imbalance in military strength between the CPM and the enemy, there was no hope of having any negotiations. Finally, there was the clear suggestion that we should wind up our armed struggle and concentrate on political endeavours from then on.

I instructed the emissary, as a matter of urgency, to get the radio link functioning and was soon requesting Siao Chang transmit the full text of the Sino/Soviet advice in code. This never arrived. To my utter amazement, his reply was a curt declaration: the document's contents were no longer valid.

It was only when I went to China six years later that Siao Chang gave me the full text. It was a Chinese translation. He explained the original, written in Russian, was the result of discussions he had held with Soviet ideologue, Mikhail Suslov, at the time one of the prominent secretaries in the Soviet Party. Only then did I fully appreciate the reason behind Siao Chang's abrupt reply to my request for the text years earlier. The emissary's message had been overtaken by the intensification of the Sino/Soviet split.

*   *   *   *   *

We had calculated that our overnight jungle campsite in the southern Betong Salient, close to the Malayan frontier, was no more than a two-hour trek from the agreed rendezvous point with the British officer who would escort me to Baling. If we were to reach the outskirts of the disused Gunong Paku tin mine by the appointed time – 10.00 o'clock the following morning – we would have to de-camp and be moving by 8.00 o'clock at the latest. The sun had set before I could begin a last-minute review of the strategy we would adopt the next day. My two fellow 'peace talk' delegates, Chen Tien and Rashid Maidin, were on hand to help me. Cocooned in the jungle blackness, the three of us talked in hushed tones until well past midnight while our security force maintained constant vigil. If the British were going to break their word on guaranteeing my safe passage to and from the meeting venue, this, we felt, would be the time to do it. Strike now. Wipe out the CPM leadership. There would then be no need for peace talks.

Eight thousand miles away, in London's Fleet Street, editorial and feature writers were making final adjustments to copy that would form 'scene setters' to the Baling discussions for Britain's December 28 morning newspapers. An unnamed leader writer on the *Daily Mail* kicked off his column with the somewhat melodramatic paragraph: 'A tiger will emerge from his lair in the Malayan jungle today to talk of peace.' The tiger, the journalist pursued, was Chin Peng, head of the communist terrorists 'who for more than seven years have spread death, destruction and misery in a vain attempt to gain political power by force of arms.' With obvious relish he added: 'This man is notorious for his ruthlessness and calculated ferocity. It was at his command that more than two thousand Asians, women and children among them, were butchered with the bestial savagery equalled only by the Mau Mau in Kenya.'

A more sober approach was taken by the distinguished columnist, James Cameron, who chose to link the last days of Britain's Christmas season to the prospect of peace offered by the scheduled gathering in a Baling schoolroom. Renowned for his lyrical opening paragraphs, Cameron began: 'To soften today's numbing scene – those wilting evergreens, those empty bottles, those gaunt ornithic skeletons, that petrified goodwill – is the surprising fact that the world has been going on like anything all the time, in spite of us.' He continued: 'Other things, even tougher than Christmas, are coming to an end. Today, on the other side of the earth, it is just possible that we may be seeing the finish of a war. At least it comes in sight.' Cameron went on to refer to me as '. . . the man whom we once honoured for his patriotism and have ever since been trying to kill, the man who could decide today to give Malaya the first true peace it has known since 1941.' Later in the column he delivered me one of his characteristic backhanders. 'Chin Peng is the most extraordinary of men, symbolic in a bitter way of much that has corrupted human values since the war. . . .When did his personal crisis come, his values change, his loyalties become ingrown? If we knew that we would know more of the Chinese than we do, and perhaps more of ourselves.'

There had, of course, been no personal crisis; nor an altering of my value system. But, I would have agreed wholeheartedly with Cameron's latter assertion that a better understanding of other races and other views would have done the British a power of good back in the 1940s and 1950s. They might have accepted, as countries like the United States and the Netherlands did, that colonialism was abhorrent, as were the white supremacists who propelled it and the exploitative greed that sustained it. Had that been the case, there might never have been an Emergency.

The strategy we proposed to adopt during the Baling talks had evolved from the months of close scrutiny our Politburo had been giving to political changes taking place in both Malaya and Singapore. As prospects for the talks firmed, I made a point of reading everything I could lay my hands on dealing with the individual personalities of the Tunku, Dato Tan Cheng Lock and David Marshall.

I gathered from my background reading that perhaps the Tunku could be harbouring latent anti-colonial feelings. For all his simplistic utterances, the UMNO leader was quite a complex man. His unaffected candour was always well considered. In some public announcements he had made it clear he was going into the Baling talks with the sole aim of explaining to me the terms of the amnesty offer and to listen to what I had to say. But when he was criticised by newspapers and some political figures of the day, he made contradictory pronouncements on what his attitude towards me might be. Sometimes I was to be at the conference table on equal terms. Sometimes, he indicated, I would be there in a decidedly inferior capacity.

On at least one occasion he referred to me as being a former friend though, in truth, I had never had any previous meetings with him. I surmised that all this was well calculated to meet the varying demands of the electorate.

As for Dato Tan, I felt comfortable that I could read the machinations of a fellow Chinese. I was certainly unfazed by his privileged background. Indeed, I probably knew as much about his political involvements as he himself. As I have previously cited, Dato Tan had, in the past, maintained a close association with our onetime comrade, Gerald de Cruz. Over the years I had also been receiving, through our underground network, regular reports on Dato Tan's activities as MCA leader.

Thus, I felt confident I had a good grasp of the politics and personas of both the Tunku and Dato Tan. I was less certain of David Marshall. I had, of course, read the views he had expressed publicly on various issues as Singapore's Chief Minister. I recognised his legal prowess. I noted, however, there was an obvious theatrical side to his make-up. This caused me some concern. His flair for drama probably assisted him in courtroom representations on behalf of clients. It doubtless aided him at the hustings. But I wondered to what extent he would employ it during peace negotiations and the effect this might have, if he did.

By this stage, my headquarters' radio communications had marginally improved and I had brought along a transmitter/receiver for the Baling exercise together with an operator trained in coding and decoding messages. Via the Betong-Peking direct radio link, Siao Chang and I had together analysed how best the CPM might present our case face-to-face with the Tunku and his two associates. We arrived at two basic sets of peace conditions. These represented our maximum and minimum positions. Having defined these two categories, we then went ahead and worked on our negotiating strategy. It was then up to me to make on-the-spot decisions as to the best means of manoeuvring between the two.

At the core of our maximum position was recognition of the CPM as a legitimate political organisation. Our maximum position also sought guarantees of freedom of movement for Party leadership and rank-and-file as they set aside their arms. It asked for assurances that we would not be dragged into courts or incarcerated in camps or cells. Finally, it demanded an agreement on both sides that full independence must be granted at the earliest possible date.

Contrasting with this was our minimum position. This accepted the non-recognition of the CPM but saw us participating in Malaya's ongoing political life. We would have the freedom to join any established party or the right to form a new entity which, specifically, would not be termed a communist party. As with our maximum position, our minimum demands also sought assurances on freedom of movement for former comrades along with understandings that they would not face legal harassment or detention in any form. The most important minimum condition, as we saw it, was that we should not have to capitulate to the government or comply with any requirement that implied surrender.

A week before the talks were due, UMNO convened a General Assembly in Kuala Lumpur. At that time all the big meetings were held in Kampong Bahru. The gathering filed a resolution demanding full independence for Malaya by August 31, 1957. The Tunku happened to be present on this occasion and insisted two words be inserted into the draft – 'if possible'. The resolution was adopted unanimously.

In our preparatory discussions back at Headquarters and in our radio communications with Siao Chang in Peking, not for a moment did we believe that the British would be prepared to grant independence within the 18 months being suggested by the Malays. When we learned of the 'if possible' aspect we interpreted it as a carefully manipulated 'out' for Britain. We remained convinced she would use it to retain her colonial presence.

While Chen Tien, Rashid Maidin and I were discussing strategy, I received a last-minute message from Siao Chang. He said I must try my best to reach an agreement for peace at Baling. The pressure then was really on me. That night we settled back in our hammocks to rest. My companions slept soundly. I didn't. In fact, my mind worked overtime all night.

We set out for the Gunong Paku rendezvous point even earlier than our agreed 8 am start. I sent Chen Tien ahead, along with our Klian Intan courier guide, Lee Chin Hee, to explain that my arrival would be delayed for half an hour or so. Both comrades emerged from the jungle at Gunong Paku shortly before the agreed time – 10 am. It was only then that Chen Tien learned our conducting officer was to be none other than my old wartime associate and onetime ally, John Davis. He had been brought across from his Butterworth posting where he was now serving as district officer.

I met Davis just outside the jungle fringe among old mine tailings. It had been ten years since we last saw each other. To me he looked unchanged. Still as fit as ever. Tough. Seemingly not a day older. Davis, dressed in light cream shirt and shorts, held out his hand and as I moved forward to shake it, he said to me in Cantonese: 'Long time, no see.'

En route to the Baling talks. This photo was taken moments after my arrival at the Gunung Paku rendezvous point. Behind me to my right is Chen Tien, and to my left, Rashid Maidin. The partly shown colonial representative to my immediate left is, of course, my old associate John Davis, on hand as our conducting officer.

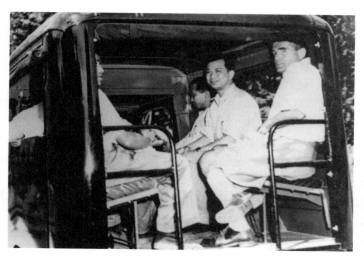

John Davis accompanies us in a police Land Rover, the first in a series of vehicles laid on for our transportation into Baling.

From where I stood in a small clearing I must admit I had been momentarily taken aback by the first sight of my old associate. I had not expected him to be there. I surmised the British were hoping our wartime relationship could be exploited to some advantage. In less than 48 hours I would discover my intuition was quite accurate. Still, I was very glad to see the man. Memories flooded back and there was much I wanted to ask him. But it was not the time for reminiscing. For now protocol took over. Mr John L.H.Davis, our appointed conducting officer, methodically took us through the transportation and security details that had been arranged to ensure we got safely to and from the conference venue. He explained that our three-man delegation, together with our personal bodyguards and a cook would all be billeted in a small brick bungalow within the Baling English School's grounds, less than a minute's brisk walk from the meeting room.

The briefing over, we boarded police Land Rovers and were driven a short distance to the vacated mine workshop. Here I got an initial glimpse of the extensive security measures put in place for my arrival. On the fringes of the mine compound I spotted no less than 100 British troops, fully armed and battle ready. They stood impassive beside a neat row of newly pitched tents. Transferring to a military truck, we were then driven down the dusty mine track to the main Baling road for yet another switch in mode of transport. Now we rode to the venue in police vans, part of a 14-vehicle convoy, escorted by two armoured scout cars.

At around 12.30 pm our convoy swept through the school's main gates obviously to ensure that the large crowd gathered there would get the very briefest view of us possible. Within minutes Davis was showing us to our quarters. In a neat row on each bed were placed a tube of toothpaste, a toothbrush, a bar of bath soap and a towel. Davis asked me whether I was satisfied with the accommodation. I said I was but asked if we could purchase some cigarettes and tobacco. Maidin smoked a pipe; Chen Tien and the rest preferred cigarettes. Davis left us and our cook hastily prepared a meal of bread and vegetables. There was no time to cook rice as the first conference session was due to start at 2.30 pm.

Davis came back to the bungalow at 2.20 pm sharp and, after a brief exchange of pleasantries, led us out past the rolled barbed wire surrounding our billet and up a slight bank to the end section of a row of classrooms. On the hillside of the school, a broad swathe of tropical forest had been levelled as a security measure. Police had imposed a 1,000-square yard 'protected area' around the premises and posted marksmen with orders to shoot on sight any intruders. The two Chief Ministers and

The Baling school's former staff accommodation bungalow where Chen Tien, Rashid Maidin and I, together with our cook and bodyguards, were billeted during the Baling talks. Since this photo was taken I understand the school has painted and renovated the bungalow in the name of tourism.

The Baling talks were held in the first classroom of this block. We were escorted up the concrete steps by Davis and entered the doorway beyond the chair.

Dato Tan Cheng Lock had arrived before us and were already seated when we entered the room.

Two long tables, covered in white cloth and placed parallel to one another, dominated the conference room. Along the outer side of each table were three straight-backed chairs. Set against the surrounding walls were positions for secretaries and stenographers. Davis indicated which was to be the CPM table. I took the centre seat. Chen Tien was to my left and Rashid settled on my right. The Tunku sat directly opposite me on the other table with Marshall to his right and Dato Tan to his left. Once we were all seated, a signal was given, a door was opened and a barrage of local and international press photographers, reporters and movie cameramen stormed into the room. For five minutes the press went about their frenetic business; clicking, whirring cameras, flashing bulbs, stumbling, tripping and intermittently taking notes. None of the newsmen spoke to us. They had been prohibited from trying.

On another signal the press were herded out.

Moments before the talks got underway, I noticed microphones placed at the centre of each conference table. Wiring from both trailed off somewhat suspiciously to an adjoining room. There had been no mention of such equipment at any of the preliminary discussions. It seemed counterproductive to raise questions at the outset of the meeting, so I made a mental note that I would enquire at a more opportune moment about the obvious electronic recording measures being used.

The Tunku asked if I would like to speak first. Before I could start putting down my case for peace I needed to understand more clearly and hear more about the call for independence 'if possible' by August 31, 1957. So I requested the Tunku take the lead.

His opening remarks were moderate to the point of being mild. They were also conciliatory. He thanked us for the confidence we had demonstrated in coming out to meet him. He emphasised he had not travelled to Baling to judge us. Rather, he had come to talk and explain things to us. Then, very quickly, he focused on the July, 1955, election results that had so dramatically consolidated his power.

Looking directly at me he said: 'Our victory was based on one big promise we made to the people; that one big promise made to the people was responsible for our victory and perhaps our victory is without parallel in any free elections in the world. That one big promise which we made was that colonialism must end and that this country must be given freedom – that was the promise we made.' The

Tunku went on to explain how the UMNO Assembly, which had concluded only two days earlier, had arrived at the independence resolution. He maintained he had introduced the words 'if possible' to facilitate a smooth handover of power from the outgoing British to his government. Time was needed, he argued, to prepare a constitution specifically tailored to the needs of the country. 'I am leaving on the 1st of January, 1956, for England, to take part in round-table talks with the British Government. I have no doubt that the talks will produce results and I will be successful,' he said confidently.

With the Tunku's re-confirmation of his departure for London in four days' time, I recognised that the other side had pre-determined that the Baling talks would be of decidedly limited duration. Two days, at the most. I had thought, given the complexities of the issues to be reviewed and the fact that we had been at war for over seven years, our discussions would continue for several days. I worried that we had been lured into an exercise in political grandstanding for both local and international consumption.

Then the Tunku talked of peace and the search for an end to the Emergency. He assured me he had meant every word he had been saying on these matters during the pre-election campaign. 'But in my opinion there is no way of bringing about peace other than to offer suitable terms for the surrender of the Communist Party against whom the Government is fighting today.' With these words the atmosphere in the room tightened several notches and the Tunku proceeded, as we had predicted he probably would, to present the Government's legal case against the Party. The CPM had been fighting the lawful authority of the land – the Government of the Federation of Malaya. That was why laws had been passed whereby any armed communist captured could be sentenced to death for treason. The Emergency Regulations also allowed for the death penalty for those caught supplying food to communist guerrillas and incarceration for anyone deemed to be in sympathy with the insurgent movement. We hardly needed to be reminded of these facts but, as it was the Tunku's opening gambit, I held my tongue.

He then switched to the subject of the latest amnesty offer. Those who accepted it would be pardoned. Under its terms all would be guaranteed safety. As if with a sudden burst of inspiration he added: 'I guarantee that with my own life.' It was an offer I regarded more geared to making headlines than to be taken seriously. There would be no general ceasefire and security forces would remain on alert to help those wanting to surrender. Furthermore, the Government insisted on investigating all those who surrendered. Restrictions on the movement of surrendered personnel would remain in force for some time. The requests of surrendering insurgents wishing to go to China, or any other country to which they belonged, would be given due consideration.

David Marshall, the lawyer who had become Singapore's first Chief Minister only eight months earlier, spoke next. From his opening words, the already tense atmosphere turned decidedly sour. 'Well, as far as I am concerned,' he began in his best courtroom voice, several decibels above the Tunku's, ' it has been a campaign of hate that has corroded our civic life, a campaign of violence, brutality and atrocities that has achieved nothing except misery of the people.' He alluded to the CPM being a stooge of a 'foreign ideology' and then, sneeringly, with a flamboyant sweep of his hands, he declared: 'We will forgive your past delusions and errors, if you yourselves are now conscious that along that path only misery for the people lies . . .'

Sensing that Marshall's initial approach was threatening to unravel the meeting before it had scarcely started, the Tunku interjected. Pouncing on his fellow delegate's stooge reference, the Malay leader remarked he himself was not a stooge or running dog of colonialism. Then, in an almost kindly gesture, he assured me: 'I wish to make it clear that you are free to say what you like, we will not mind.' Order was restored.

Now it was my turn to speak. Despite Marshall's outburst I felt the best strategy was to try and lay down our maximum position and from there work back to a reasonable compromise. I had to think fast. If the talks were to continue at a constructive level, I would have to avoid heavy debate with Marshall at all costs. I seized on the Tunku's interjection and replied to him personally: 'I wish to say that it is precisely because we realise that you are not the spokesman of the British government and are not the running dog of the British government, the stooge of the British government, that we have come out to meet you at the risk of our lives.' In an oblique rejection of the line just taken by Marshall, I emphasised I had not arrived at Baling to debate the question of ideology, but to discuss peace. 'We also hope that peace will be realised early so that the misery of the people can be reduced.'

My suggestion that the CPM be recognised as a legal political entity, free to fight for reforms through constitutional means, was roundly rebuked by both the Tunku and Marshall. I had, of course, fully expected this. I then moved to discuss

The brief photo opportunity at the outset of the Baling discussions catches the three-man Malayan delegation led by Tunku Abdul Rahman (centre). To his left sat Dato Tan Chen Lok, and to his right the Singapore Chief Minister, David Marshall.

The CPM delegation at Baling (left to right): Rashid Maidin, myself, and Chen Tien.

the confusion arising from differing versions of the amnesty offer. Looking straight across the two tables I said: 'In the past the Tunku mentioned that if we stopped the armed struggle our Party could then enjoy equal status so that we could fight for independence by constitutional means. But the present amnesty terms do not contain such a point. That is all I want to say. If I have said it wrongly, impolitely, I wish Tunku to point it out.' It was a good argument, and the Tunku knew it.

He admitted he had talked about equal terms in campaign speeches but clarified that equality in status could only be earned. 'First you have got to convince us that you will be loyal to Malaya. To be just anti-British does not suffice to indicate that one is loyal to Malaya.' He had countered well. Shortly thereafter the Tunku deftly called a ten-minute break and the two sides adjourned to separate rooms for refreshments.

Dato Tan had failed to make a single comment throughout the first session and I wondered why. It appeared the Tunku was wondering as well because immediately the second session began he coaxed the MCA leader to join in.

Referring to the overwhelming Chinese aspect of the problems being discussed, the Dato observed that it was the country's Chinese population which had suffered most during the Emergency. Injecting a decidedly materialistic viewpoint into the historic proceedings, he added: 'Why waste money unnecessarily on the Emergency, there is no point in that. The vast majority of the people of this country are not in favour of the communists because they are not working for a prosperous Malaya . . .'

I felt the Dato's contribution was taking the discussions nowhere and it appeared the Tunku was of the same mind. Ignoring the monetary content of the MCA leader's opening salvo, the Tunku changed direction completely and began discussing the CPM manifesto which I had sent him via Chen Tien during the preliminary meetings at Klian Intan. He described our document as 'quite good' and went on the say: 'You mention in the manifesto fundamental freedoms – freedom of speech, freedom of movement, human rights. We have accepted that, too, and we are carrying all that out.' He admitted he could see little difference between the CPM and government manifestoes. Once more the Tunku had been able to nudge the talks back onto a positive footing.

Again he pursued the amnesty issue and asked for my opinions. I responded by asking him to explain what loyalty to Malaya meant. There followed a long discussion of his definition which touched on responsibilities, duties and attitudes towards authority. At one point the wealthy Prince said, somewhat defensively: 'One cannot help being born into a class. One cannot help being born rich. One cannot help being born lucky in business and making money. But I admit that people born rich, or who have made money in business, should have part of their money distributed for the welfare of the country.'

I gathered the very strong impression, as the Tunku droned on, that the other side was seeking ultimately to force all returning CPM members into making political confessions via the process of interrogation. This, from their point of view, would be a most effective way of demonstrating the fact of our total defeat. By establishing loyalty according to its definition, the government also sought justification, through us, of its banishment ordinances. The official proclamation of 'unloyal' elements would continue and those falling within the definition would still be banished to their perceived countries of origin – either China or India.

The Tunku talked on and finally Dato Tan chipped in with the bland and rather obvious comment: 'If a man wants to live in Malaya he should assume the responsibilities and duties of a good citizen.'

The past few minutes had infuriated Marshall. Pompously, he pronounced: 'It seems to me that this is a rather sterile discussion. We are really here to find out to what extent we can achieve an end to the violence which they themselves admit has led to misery for the people.' Back we went to discussing the amnesty and related issues. Again the Tunku and Marshall insisted the CPM had to be dissolved. I offered the example of Australia, where the communist party was functioning legally, to support my contention that we could set aside our arms readily if we were allowed to operate similarly. This, too, was roundly dismissed as unrealistic. The communists were not pressing armed struggle in Australia, I was told. I retaliated by saying that, in the past, the CPM had been fighting a colonial and un-elected government where the voices of the people had not been heard.

Quickly I was appraised of the changed political circumstances in both Singapore and Malaya.

About half way through the second session I made the declaration: 'We will never allow ourselves to be forced by others to give up our ideology, but wish to put our ideology to the people to decide, if that is possible.' I readily admitted that citizens of nations had obligations but at the same time they must have freedom of thought.

The Tunku concluded his reply to my argument with the response: 'Now, speaking for myself, I have no doubt whatsoever, that if they were allowed to take part in free elections, the people would choose our system.'

I agreed with the Tunku and said so. Yes, the people would likely vote against us. That was not so much my concern. The principles of freedom of thought and choice were the fundamental issues I wanted recognised. If there was a moment in the Baling talks when some form of agreement was possible, it was now. But it dissipated as quickly as it had surfaced. Direction became fuzzy. The Tunku wandered off into a vague dissertation on the Malayan way of life. Marshall waded in with more tough talk and it took all my patience to abide by my resolve not to be trapped in aimless verbal jousting with the pugnacious politician from Singapore.

Moments before the second session broke up for a 45-minute adjournment, Marshall turned to me and said: 'It has been made clear to you that the Governments of the Federation and of Singapore are not prepared to recognise the communist party. Now, is there any purpose of continuing these discussions? It is a fair question. Please reply with frankness.'

I read this as a manoeuvre by Marshall to scuttle the talks on what was essentially our maximum demand. I was clearly being pushed into a corner and needed more time to work towards our minimum position. I decided to let the question pass and instead turned to the Tunku to change the subject completely. I asked whether the matters we were discussing would ultimately have to be vetted by the British government. The Tunku replied: 'If I decide, and Mr Marshall agrees with me, that will be all.' Added Marshall: 'The British government may disagree with the course of action, but as far as we are concerned, we take our own decisions.'

It was still light when the third and final session of the day began and during the intermission I had decided there was no option but to begin the process of compromise. But before I did so, I felt an urgent need to block Marshall's steamrolling tactics. If he used these while I was negotiating a fall-back position there would be a grave danger of our minimum demands being rendered meaningless. I sensed the Tunku had also become disturbed by the Singapore leader's constant antagonism. So I reverted to the query Marshall had fired at me – and which I had side-stepped – just before the break. Addressing myself to the Tunku, I asked if Marshall's questioning of there being any purpose to continuing the talks was, in effect, an ultimatum for ending them. I was encouraged when both the Tunku and Marshall fudged their replies and urged progress to other matters.

From there I sought clarification of Britain's true attitude towards Malayan independence. The Tunku affirmed that the British had already given assurances of independence to the Legislative Council. When I asked about the likelihood of Britain transferring power of internal security to the elected government, the Alliance chief said this was precisely why he was going to England. 'That I will get first, before independence,' he added firmly.

In the midst of our discussion about the colonials and their intentions I thought it now valid to question the purpose of the two microphones I had noted at the outset. I said: 'We want to find out whether there is someone listening in at this meeting. If that is the case, I wish you to invite them also to attend the meeting and discuss it openly.' I was, of course, referring to the likelihood of a British official monitoring proceedings from the classroom next door.

The Tunku assured me that my fears were groundless and arranged for Chen Tien to inspect the ante-room where the recording machines were located. My fellow delegate returned to report that all was in order as far as he could see. I was compelled to apologise. 'I want to beg your pardon,' I told the Tunku, ' but it seems to me that everywhere the British are listening to me.' I have since learned that there was, indeed, a British monitor on duty in the ante-room when I first raised the matter. As arrangements were being made, very vocally, for Chen Tien to verify the Tunku's assurances, the British monitor withdrew, to return immediately the furore had subsided.

Perhaps the most important aspect of the third session was the examination made of government restrictions to be imposed on CPM members once peace was secured. The Tunku revealed we would all be kept in camps while investigations were undertaken. He argued that this did not amount to incarceration but rather was a process essential to establishing the genuineness of our loyalties to the elected government of Malaya. The detention in camps, he suggested, would not last more than a few months. I objected strongly on the grounds that this violated the dignity of man and was tantamount to surrendering which we had no intention of doing. We were there to negotiate a peace agreement, not a surrender.

Marshall could not resist leaping on the subject of man's dignity. 'Where is the dignity of man? You're making yourselves suffer indignities and miseries in the jungle with its disease and its lack of a lot of the essentials of human life.' Marshall was defining the dignity of man in terms of creature comforts. He simply didn't understand. It would have been a complete waste of time trying to point out the shallowness of his opinion.

But Marshall would not let up. The methods chosen by the CPM, he taunted, had been proved wrong. I replied: 'I am not prepared to argue on this question. But since you continue to mention it, I have to point out quite frankly that we know our struggle has produced certain effects. For example, the British now have to make certain concessions to the people of Malaya.'

Marshall: 'You really believe that?'

I responded: 'It is not, of course, our struggle which has been the only cause for these concessions.'

Marshall: 'You really believe that your struggle contributed to these concessions?'

I said: 'Yes.'

Before we concluded for the day we tackled the issue of whether CPM members, following the declaration of peace, would be allowed to join any political party, or, for that matter, form a party of their own which would not espouse communist ideologies. The idea of a follow-up party to the CPM was roundly rejected. I had anticipated as much. At the end of nearly five hours of negotiations we had gained only one concession. The Tunku and Marshall had both agreed that CPM members, once they had returned to society, could join existing political parties. It was not much. I realised that. But as we went back to our quarters for the night I was not totally despondent. I still had one card to play. Predictably, though, *The Straits Times* reported the following morning that I looked like a thoroughly dejected man and that the shoulders of my colleagues were 'bent almost in despair'.

In fact, I slept soundly that night. So did my two fellow delegates. We went to bed early after a review of strategy for the next day's session.

The final round of the Baling talks began with the Tunku providing a summary of the deliberations thus far. The communist party would not be recognised. There was no way of avoiding detention and investigation of CPM members. The governments of Malaya and Singapore would be willing to assist all Party followers who opted to be exiled to either China or India. Only those who chose to remain in Malaya would be subjected to investigation.

The Tunku then turned to me and said: 'I appreciate that you have got to obtain the best possible terms before you can agree to surrender, and I understand that attitude. So, I would like to hear what you have to say.'

My reply was plain. 'If the conditions as laid down cannot be changed, then I am not empowered to accept them.'

Shortly thereafter I decided to play my one remaining card. I argued that although popularly elected, the present Malayan and Singapore governments were still not truly independent. Marshall, to my amazement, interrupted to support my point. I continued: 'If these popularly elected governments of the Federation and Singapore have self-determination in matters concerning internal security and national defence, then all problems could be solved easily. As soon as these two governments have self-determination in internal security and national defence matters, then we can stop the war immediately.'

An air of optimism filled the room. A noticeably buoyed Tunku leaned forward and said: 'Is that a promise? When I come back from England that is the thing I am bringing with me.'

I followed up: 'That being the case, we can straightaway stop our hostilities and also disband our armed units.'

They enquired what exactly did I mean by 'self-determination' in matters of internal security and national defence? I clarified this as 'full power to control'.

The Tunku seized on a problem area arising from the fact that Malaya and Singapore, as the British had intentionally divided them, remained separate territories with independent political frameworks. What would happen, asked the UMNO leader, if Malaya got control of internal security and Singapore didn't?

Marshall's hackles rose instantly. 'Don't assume that, Tunku,' he said with marked irritation. 'Forgive me, Tunku, my government will not remain in power if we don't get control of internal security.'

The Tunku was not prepared to drop the issue. 'I have got to make my point because I am going to London before you,' he said to his Singapore opposite number. Then turning to me he further queried: 'Assuming the Federation gets control of internal security and national defence and Singapore doesn't, would you give up the struggle, or would you want both territories to get it before you give up?'

There followed an acrimonious exchange between Marshall and the Tunku as they placed their separate situations before me. Finally, I answered: 'If Tunku obtained control in matters concerning internal security in February – and national defence – then we will stop our hostilities at once and we will not wait for the result of Mr Marshall's mission.'

I expanded on my position by adding: 'Our armed forces are called 'National Liberation Army'. When we have attained our object, in other words, when this country is already liberated, then there is no point in continuing the existence of this army.'

Marshall: 'I agree.'

I then asked: 'But by that time, will we still be subject to investigation?'

The Tunku replied: 'Would you ask for any terms before you throw down your arms?'

I responded: 'This question is very simple. The answer is very simple. If the CPM is recognised, if members of the CPM are not subject to detention and investigation, they can throw down their arms at once. The question of weapons can be solved easily.'

The official interpreter informed the meeting that he did not understand what I meant by the term 'throw down their arms'. In fact, I used the Chinese term which describes the 'setting aside of weapons'. This is not equivalent to the English phrase 'surrendering arms'.

All sense of optimism dissipated immediately and from then on the talks unravelled. The chance for peace had gone. Exchanges between the Tunku and myself also became acrimonious. At one point he declared the CPM was a very powerful organisation receiving support from within and aid from outside Malaya. 'In fact, we would be powerless to control your movement, if you were to come out of the jungle and put yourselves on the same level and same status as we are. Therefore, if you do not come out to surrender, we would rather not accept you in our society.'

The Tunku continued: 'If you want to have peace in this country, one side must give in – either we give in to you, or you give in to us. The two ideologies, yours and ours, can never work side by side.'

I responded: 'But if Tunku's opinion is that after he has obtained power he is afraid of subversion as has been reported in the editorial of *The Straits Times* of yesterday's date, I think this question is not difficult to solve.' Looking back on the discussions at this point I know this was a last-ditch effort on my part to save the Baling talks from total collapse. I was indicating that if we were not forced to face the humiliation of surrender, incarceration and interrogation, we would be more than willing to pledge loyalty and thus remove any threat of subversion.

The Tunku quickly rejected my suggestion that a solution might not be so difficult. 'To me I think it is quite difficult,' he told me. He cited the example of political developments in China where Chiang Kai Shek's Nationalist government had been driven from the mainland.

'If I accept you on equal status, I have no doubt that I and my party will similarly be driven out of Malaya before long because our ideologies are widely different. That is plain language. Therefore you either give in to us on certain terms which we consider fair, or else this struggle will have to go on, much to my regret.' It is my recollection – a matter not covered in the transcripts of the meeting[28] – that the Tunku then made the point that Malaya was a small country and that he, unlike Chiang Kai Shek, would have no island to which he could go.

Ultimately, I told the Tunku that capitulation would subject the comrades to a level of humiliation too great to bear. 'If you demand our surrender, we would prefer to fight to the last man.'

As the failed talks wrapped up, the Tunku returned to his friendly and gracious demeanour. He told me he had not expected very much when he came to Baling. But he was nevertheless glad we had had the opportunity to meet. He said to me: 'I hope you are comfortable, that you had everything you wanted. Please let me know whether you want anything before I go away.'

Marshall cut in to say he thought we wanted a fan. To this day I don't know what he meant by that remark. Perhaps it was intended as a last jibe at me.

I said we required nothing and certainly not a fan. 'The question is, how are we going back?' I asked.

The Tunku replied flatly: 'In the same way that you came. You will be escorted.'

Chapter 23

An offer from Davis, a triumphant Tunku and a still hopeful Politburo

In the late afternoon of December 29, John Davis returned with me to the jungle fringe at Gunong Paku. As it was too late for us to move off, I prepared to spend the night there with the local security force and push north at first light the next morning. I felt drained and saw no need to rush. Under the Klian Intan arrangements, the declared ceasefire in the Baling area would be in place for ten days. The British had kept their word thus far on my rights of safe passage. I could only hope they would continue abiding by the agreed terms.

Davis asked me if he could remain in my temporary camp for the night. He wanted to talk. He said he would return to Baling the next day when I left with my men. Naturally, I had no objection. I had always liked Davis, indeed, admired him. We could talk over the good old days when we at least played at being on the same side.

As it turned out, the Butterworth district officer was interested in far more than just swapping wartime recollections. Davis asked me why we had failed to reach an agreement. I told him it was because the Tunku and Marshall had insisted we surrender. The demand to surrender, I added, had been at Britain's instigation.

'Why can't you?' he prodded. 'You can't keep fighting like this, Chin Peng. It's getting you nowhere.'

After four very frustrating sessions at Baling, I was in no mood to argue. The sun was setting as we talked. I sat cross-legged on one poncho. Davis lay sprawled on another. Around us the evening sounds of the jungle began to rise.

'It's a matter of principle. . . .' I started to reply, then gave up the effort. There was a long pause. Davis remained silent. I tried again: 'Surely, you understand, John.' The last rays of the sunset were visible through the foliage. 'If you can make the sun rise from the West,' I told the Englishman with whom I had been through so many dangerous times, 'then I can order my army to suffer the indignity of surrender.'

Davis understood what I was saying and changed the direction of our conversation. 'Look, there is not a vast gap between your position and the

'HE SAID HE HAD NO AUTHORITY, HE FEARED TO MAKE DECISIONS'

Marshall: I don't believe Chin Peng leads Malaya's Reds

30 DEC 1955   30·12·1955 S.T.

WHEN the Chief Minister, Mr. David Marshall, returned to Singapore last night from the talks at Baling he said he believed that Chin Peng is not the leader of the Communists in Malaya.

He said he gained this impression from the manner in which Chin Peng conducted negotiations and his fear of making on-the-spot decisions.

Chin Peng, he said, did not deny that the M.C.P. ideology was "a foreign one."

He kept on repeating that he had no mandate, no authority.

Mr. Marshall, who looked tired, said he would not describe the outcome of the talks as a failure.

He said that at least the people now knew that a genuine attempt had been made to knock sense into the heads of the Reds.

We are alert

He said Tengku Abdul Rahman felt that the Communists would come back in February and ask for peace talks to be re-opened.

Stating that Singapore would suffer from the continuance of the Emergency, Mr. Marshall added: "Let us be frank. Our Government has always been very conscious of this threat. We have always been on the alert.

"We will take counter-measures if there are any fresh outbreaks of violence."

THE COMMUNISTS' LINE: PARTY BEFORE WELFARE OF PEOPLE

Describing Chin Peng as "soft" and "baby-faced," Mr. Marshall said: "He looked like a chap who has been mollycoddled in his office."

Mr. Marshall added: "When I offered him some coffee, he said 'No thanks: I am not used to this heat.'"

The Chief Minister quipped: "I wondered then if Chin Peng had just come from Switzerland."

Mr. Marshall said that reports of Chin Peng being ill must have arisen from the fact that he could not walk as fast as Chin Tien.

Hock Lee strike

The Chief Minister said that when he asked Chin Peng if he was in control of Singapore Communists, the reply was: "Of course; but not all who call themselves Communists are in fact so."

Chin Peng then referred to the Hock Lee bus strike last April and said: "Some leaders of that strike claimed to be Communists. But I say they are not true Communists. True Communists do not want

chaos in that fashion."

Mr. Marshall said Chin Peng was angry over the April disturbances and because people were misrepresenting the Communists.

No answer

30 DEC 1955

But at the same time, Mr. Marshall said, Chin Peng stressed that the M.C.P. would continue the struggle to the last man.

Mr. Marshall added: "When I asked him what they were struggling for, he replied: 'We will not discuss that question.'"

This is how Mr. Marshall summed up his two days with the Communists:

"To them it is to Hell with the welfare of the people — the Communist Party comes first. They say they cannot disband the Communist Party and that it will last for ever in Malaya.

"We did not seem to be able to talk the same language."

Still playing to the gallery, David Marshall arrives back in Singapore from the Baling talks and announces to the press that he didn't believe I was leader of the Malayan communists. *The Straits Times* report (above) dated December 30, 1955, quotes Marshall as saying that at least the people now knew that a genuine attempt had been made to 'knock sense into the heads of the Reds'. It concludes with the quote from Marshall: 'We did not seem to be able to talk the same language.' At least he got that right.

government's. Surely, there must be a way to breach it.' Our talk went back and forth over the issues raised during my discussions with the Tunku. I had to admit that on at least two occasions there had appeared to be chances for a breakthrough. Davis reacted quickly. 'Let me go with you into the jungle and see if the two of us can't settle this matter. After all, we won very convincingly the last time we cooperated.'

I asked him to explain further. Davis was prepared for my reaction. 'I have brought a small patrol with me. They are equipped with a radio. We can keep in direct touch with Kuala Lumpur.'

I thought the proposal through carefully. Trusting the British to keep their word on the ceasefire was one thing. Entering a new round of jungle negotiations to end the Emergency through, of all people, John Davis, was quite another. When I had first seen him 32 hours earlier, I instinctively felt he had been introduced for a purpose quite aside from his role as conducting officer. In my heart I now felt sure the British wanted to talk with me behind the back of the Tunku. If they could twist some concessions out of me, through Davis, they would be in a much stronger position to deal with the Tunku at the London talks.

The Tunku's failure to get an agreement with me would be world news within 12 hours. It would make the front page of every major morning newspaper in the British Commonwealth. If, 48 hours thereafter or sometime before the London talks, the British, on their own, were seen to snatch the chestnut from the fire and conclude a peace agreement with me, what kudos it would mean for the white colonials.

I was sure then, and remain so today, that Davis' offer to move into the jungle for further talks, was not part of a trap to seize or assassinate me. I like to think Davis would never have been a party to something like that. Moreover, the patrol Davis was suggesting accompany us was small, no more than five or six-strong. We well outnumbered them.

It was very obvious Davis' men were prepared and ready to move. I could see the British had given their ploy considerable thought. So I concluded the aim was for Britain to continue the peace talks with me using Davis as a conduit or middleman – a sort of peace talks on-the-trot as we threaded our way through the jungle.

I felt uneasy about the offer. 'It is very difficult for me to guarantee the safety of you and your patrol under these conditions,' I told my one-time collaborator. 'We have been fighting you people for so long. It's not a good idea.'

We talked on into the night and about other things. It was like the old Japanese occupation days all over again. We ate British military rations and drank hot coffee made by my bodyguards on an open fire. I asked about the British agents I had worked with and assisted during the war years. He asked about those he had encountered as members of the MPAJA. Where were they now? What were they doing? Who had survived? Who had died? Most of the agents I mentioned were alive and well. Most of the comrades Davis asked after had died in the Emergency.

It was a very friendly conversation even though I had always found Davis to be a somewhat remote individual. Still, he was brave and energetic; perfect for the extraordinarily dangerous job he did in Malaya during the war. Ideal for what he was doing now.

The next morning the Butterworth district officer once more suggested he accompany me into the jungle. Again I rejected the idea and he recognised it was pointless pressing the issue further. Instead, he proposed a secret message system for use should either want to contact the other. I agreed to this and we worked out a 'dead letter box' arrangement somewhere on the jungle fringe in the Gunong Paku region. I cannot recall the exact details but I know the box was never activated by either side. We checked it out on several occasions.

*   *   *   *   *

Why did the Baling talks fail? Unquestionably the dogmatic outbursts by the grandstanding Marshall made the search for that elusive formula extraordinarily difficult. Any glimmer of rapport between myself and the Tunku was repeatedly snuffed out by the Singapore Chief Minister. I felt constantly under attack by him. It was as though he regarded the talks as a fairground sideshow at which I was there as a target for his political pot-shots.

Had the British not been lurking behind the scenes and had it been left to the Tunku and myself, and perhaps Tan Cheng Lock, the promise of an honourable resolution might have been reached at Baling. From my side's point of view we were surely seeking a settlement. I went to the talks because I believed the Tunku's private message to me was a genuine statement of intent and that he, too, was committed to reaching a fair conclusion. It was never a matter of the CPM seeking special privileges on the basis of our willingness to end the fighting. Rather, after so many years of struggle and deprivation and after so many deaths and casualties, we sought a peace agreement whereby we could at least retain our dignity. At what point would the humiliation cease? Unquestionably it would continue just as long as it was deemed politically useful. In this context, it is valid to note that the communist bogey has been kept alive and well by both Malaysia and Singapore to this day.

In the years to follow I noted the Tunku took flak for the failure at Baling. Finally, he came out and openly placed the blame on Marshall. Marshall, of course, strongly denied the accusation. During Party discussions the CPM thoroughly traversed this ground. On numerous occasions our underground people asked me whether it was true Marshall had sabotaged the talks. My response was always the same. In a sense this was true. Marshall poisoned the atmosphere.

But there was another fundamental reason for the failure. The British were determined that a negotiated peace could only be concluded on the basis of our unconditional surrender and continuing humiliation. London was well aware of the international impact such a settlement would have on a world dominated by the East-West struggle. Baling, it should be remembered, came in the wake of far from satisfactory outcomes for the West both in North East and South East Asia.

For Westerners with staunch Cold War outlooks and persistent imperialist tendencies, the armistice signed at Panmunjom at 10 am on July 27, 1953, might well have silenced the guns on the Korean peninsula. But the result was anything but the crushing communist defeat they desired. In three languages – English, Korean and Chinese – Article 62 of the armistice document stated: 'The Articles and Paragraphs of this Armistice shall remain in effect until expressly superseded either by mutually acceptable amendments and additions or by provision in an appropriate agreement for a peaceful settlement at a political level between both sides.' Pointedly, those 'mutually acceptable amendments and additions' have, to this day, never materialised. Just as elusive has been the hoped-for appropriate peace agreement at the political level. The Korean issue was then, and has ever since remained, at a stalemate.

On the heels of the inconclusive Panmunjom armistice came the ignominious defeat of the French colonial army at Dien Bien Phu on May 7, 1954. The French debacle, as it happened, occurred the day before participants at the Geneva Conference were scheduled to start deliberating how best to restore peace in Indo China and guarantee ongoing independence for Cambodia, Laos and Vietnam. The final Geneva declaration on Indo China that year, which was never signed, did little more than formally split Vietnam at the 17th parallel of latitude and thereby clearly define a set of opposing Cold War frontiers and regional political alignments. In the climate of the time this was all tantamount to laying firm foundations for the second Indo China conflict – an interpretation well-appreciated then by regional communist leaders, including myself.

So, having claimed, quite erroneously but for so long, that the Malayan Emergency was a product of monolithic communism – first the Moscow variety, then the Peking version – total victory over the CPM was seen by London as essential. Britain could then trumpet the results through the world's corridors of power. Such an outcome would do much to redress the degrading defeat the British had suffered over the exact same terrain 13 years earlier at the hands of the invading Japanese.

With hindsight, I have considered that my very presence at Baling probably created an impasse. During the bitter fighting that had gone before, an aura of intense mystery had developed around my persona. No British or local government official had, in fact, seen me since the outbreak of the Emergency. Indeed, very few had met me before the June 17, 1948, declaration, such was the underground life I had followed from the time I first joined the Party as a young teenager. Of course, there were several so-called anti-terrorist experts whose employment by the authorities rested on their bogus claims of having known me personally in the past. Not one of those I am referring to, though, had ever encountered me.

Notwithstanding, Chin Peng was perhaps the most hunted man in the world at that time. He was No 1 on the British wanted list. He also topped wanted lists as far as Malaya and Singapore were concerned. He was similarly regarded by Commonwealth nations like Australia and New Zealand who had committed troops to the conflict. It was one thing to come to an amnesty arrangement involving faceless guerrillas. But what was to be done with somebody like Chin Peng? My public image had been transformed into a fearsome legend by a combination of carefully concocted propaganda and the world press' natural inclination for exploitation of crisis situations. Suddenly, this man was sitting opposite the Tunku, Marshall and Tan in a Baling schoolroom. It would take a very dispassionate observer indeed to separate the man seeking peace, from Chin Peng the widely portrayed callous terrorist which, of course, I have never been. We had neither the propaganda expertise nor media access to counter any of this most telling psywar activity on the part of our enemy. So, to a large extent Britain, at Baling, became hoisted by its own propaganda petard. As long as Chin Peng was there, peace was impossible.

For the return journey to our jungle headquarters in southern Siam, I was careful to choose a different route from the one we followed when we came out to meet the Tunku. My way back was a more hazardous trek which took us directly through rubber plantations where we might well have been easy targets for the British had they decided to renege on their assurances. Once over the frontier we reverted quickly to the safer deep jungle tracks. By nightfall I had reached my headquarters.

The very next day, I convened a Politburo meeting to review what was unquestionably the setback we had suffered at Baling. We endeavoured to bolster our flagging spirits by looking towards the likely outcome of the Tunku's trip to London. Politburo members reassured one another that all was not lost. After all, the Tunku had promised that a second round of peace talks – no matter what the outcome at Baling – would take place in the aftermath of his negotiations in Britain.

But it was one thing to clutch at wild straws of optimism, quite another to come to grips with the reality of our ongoing armed struggle while we awaited the next opportunity for peace. The most important decision taken at this post-Baling conference concerned the military stance we should adopt from that point onwards. We studied three options. We could lower the intensity of our attacks. We could increase them. Or we could generally maintain the war at its then current level. Each was examined for the impact it would likely have on the CPM's long-term prospects – both military and political.

There was little enthusiasm for decreasing our military activity. To do so would be read as our acknowledgement of defeat at Baling. But if we wanted to raise our military impact it was accepted we had to elevate to company-sized attacks. These did not have to occur regularly. Indeed, we were in no position even to contemplate such a scenario. But the odd large unit attack against targets of choice would serve notice to Kuala Lumpur that the CPM must still be considered a serious threat and that peace negotiations were a preferred option.

The Politburo members present understood that a programme of company-sized attacks, even on an intermittent basis, could only be attempted in the northern border regions of Peninsular Malaya. Operating from sanctuary bases in southern Siam, our CPM guerrillas could have staged fierce thrusts south across the border against government military outposts, police stations and other likely targets of opportunity. Each strike would be followed by a rapid withdrawal back to the relative safety of our sanctuaries – very similar to the tactics later used by the Viet Cong and their northern mentors from bases in eastern Cambodia.

Certainly, such a programme would have necessitated heightened costs and we would undoubtedly have been faced with increased casualties. The Malayan Emergency would then have reverted to a form of frontier warfare and it would have been anyone's guess as to how long we could have sustained it before the Siamese came under heavy political and diplomatic pressure to move purposefully against our activities. These were the issues that moulded my perceptions during that vital post-Baling meeting. Ultimately, these considerations had me arguing for maintaining the same level of our guerrilla war activities.

The other Politburo members present tended to follow my lead and were probably swayed from their own instincts and judgements by my insistence. After lengthy discussions the prevailing view was to maintain the level of attacks and, in this way, keep moderate pressure on the government until such time as the Tunku sought to reopen peace talks with us. Looking back, I recognise that I probably dominated that occasion. This was a serious error on my part and I should have been far more astute in my assessment of our overall position at that critical time.

The border was unquestionably long enough for us to have the choice of a wide variety of targets. Tactics of that nature tend to open up new opportunities as they become applied and, I believe, would certainly have done so in this case. Coordinated with a solid political stance demonstrating a real desire on the CPM's part for peace talks, we could probably have pressured the Tunku back to the negotiating table. I am not suggesting here that we could have turned defeat into victory or even restored full cohesion to our fighting units. I am merely arguing that the war might have been brought to a conclusion earlier and large numbers of lives might well have been saved.

It became clear to us, when the Tunku returned, that the London meetings had yielded results beyond his most ambitious expectations. The British had granted every concession the Malayan leader had sought and more. Britain was obviously prepared to grant Malaya independence on August 31, 1957. The 'if possible' tag had become quite incidental. Furthermore, the colonials had acceded to the Tunku's request that full powers over internal security and defence be transferred to him as head of the Alliance government on the granting of independence.

Marshall, on the other hand, failed to get self-government for his island colony under the terms he required and as a result resigned in June, 1956. I have the impression he used Baling in a bid to affirm his democratic and anti-communist commitments. He had hoped his performance there would convince the colonial authorities that he alone in Singapore should be trusted with self-government. As I read it, the British, at this time, were in a quandary. They had little confidence in Marshall's ability as Chief Minister. They must have been deeply suspicious of the upcoming young Lee Kuan Yew who, in their view, exhibited political affiliations with the comrades. British fears became further fuelled by Lee's stoic legal representations on behalf of CPM members.

Clearly, the Tunku had bargained heavily with the British on the basis of my Baling promise to ensure our guerrilla army set aside its weapons once the Malayan government were granted fundamental powers of internal security and defence. In effect, the Tunku capitalised on my pledge and gained considerably by this. My Baling pledge had been given in good faith and on the understanding that there would be a second round of peace negotiations from where we could proceed further.

Perhaps it was, once again, political naivete on my part that had me accept the Tunku's assurances of an all-important follow-up meeting. Certainly, it was in this spirit that we phrased our letter to the Malayan leader on his return from London in February, 1956. We sought a resumption of the peace talks. Far from replying to it, the Tunku's response was to release our letter to the press with comments to the effect that he had no intention of meeting with me again unless I agreed to what amounted to unconditional surrender. This was, of course, unacceptable.

With the assurance of Malayan independence in 18 months, the core of our armed struggle had been abruptly extracted. We were in a political limbo and the Tunku's public snub to our letter had ensured that the fighting would never conclude through reasonable negotiations. It is for the passage of history to determine whether Britain, Malaya and, indeed, Singapore, might have benefited more had the Emergency ceased on firm principles of agreement five years earlier than the proclamation of its end in July, 1960. For my part I state categorically that I was ready to bring the conflict to a close at Baling.

The battlefield outlook for our forces by this time was indeed gloomy. The Briggs Plan with its objective of starving us out of the jungle had been the foundation of a devastatingly effective programme. It had increasingly denied us access to our Min Yuen supporters and lines of supply. Compounding this was the effective British and, later, Australian patrolling of deep jungle areas. This made permanent base camps impossible to maintain. Further adding to our problems was the fact that, by now, our lines of communication south to both our military and underground political functions had all been severed. We had lost contact with Yueng Kuo in Selangor as early as 1953. In fact, he operated quite independently of Headquarters, from 1953 right through until the time of his 1956 death in action. Yeung Kuo, although in a desperate situation, had managed to maintain a certain level of contact with our Southern Malaya commander, Hor Lung, whom I had appointed as the replacement for the murdered Ah Koek in 1951. Hor Lung operated in the Yong Peng area.

Yet, for all the problems, our military activities, though smaller in scale, remained functioning. We could still hit targets of opportunity and withdraw in classic guerrilla fashion to avoid enemy contact. Of course, we were disheartened by events in the aftermath of Baling. But we were certain we could still inflict significant damage and casualties and that our guerrilla army could be maintained at a level of activity which would make the British and the Tunku's government regret they had not been prepared to negotiate with us more fairly.

While Headquarters' links to the battlefields of Malaya and our underground activists to the south were severely impaired at this time, the same cannot be said for Siao Chang's operation in Peking. He was able to maintain quite regular contact with our operatives in Singapore and throughout the main population centres in Malaya. Much of this traffic was directed through comrades who had withdrawn to Indonesia and there established themselves in clandestine networks working together with local Chinese communists.

Throughout our post-Baling deliberations we had kept in touch by radio with Siao Chang in the Chinese capital. He, like us, nursed the hope that, after independence in August, 1957, there would be a chance of resuming the peace talks. After all, that was only a year-and-a-half away. What was this compared with the seven years we had devoted to armed struggle? Until that time the CPM's political stance would maintain that the independence being granted by the British was not genuine. For it to be genuine, all British and Commonwealth troops had to be withdrawn and their military installations throughout Malaya and Singapore closed down.

And so the Emergency continued.

Chapter 24

A strategic reversal

The rot did not set in within the CPM immediately after the Baling talks. Initially, our guerrilla fighters, though tempted by the government's amnesty offer, seemed prepared to wait out the 18-month period leading to independence. They remained hopeful that the Tunku, in the excitement of the nation's birth, would make good his promise to negotiate peace with us.

However, as the months passed, it became obvious our guerrilla activities were fast stagnating. The Politburo's post-Baling resolve merely to maintain the military status quo had smacked of indecision from the outset. Now it was seriously compounding the morale problem in our ranks.

On the eve of Malayan independence, the Politburo met to formulate a policy statement geared to reminding the Tunku that, nationhood or not, the CPM remained an outstanding problem he still had to tackle. The ensuing debate at our Betong headquarters was lengthy and difficult. It is fair to say there were two schools of thought among those present. One faction wanted to take a strong line against the Tunku and openly criticise both Kuala Lumpur and the British. The other wanted to play the issue far more softly and avoid any direct denunciation of the Malay leader. In the end, it was this latter approach that prevailed. Our statement was issued shortly before the August 31, 1957, independence celebrations and was published by *Hsin Hwa*, the official Peking news outlet.

So, we looked to Merdeka (independence) to provide renewed hope for the revival of peace talks. We were certain, and I think we were right on this issue, that public opinion throughout both Malaya and Singapore earnestly wanted to bring the Emergency to a formal conclusion. We opposed the continuing military arrangements with Britain and indicated that these rendered independence flawed. The suggestion was that Merdeka, under these conditions, could not be described as true independence. We categorised it in Malay as 'stengah masa' – half-cooked. This is a term often used for rice. If it's half-cooked it can't be eaten. Not unexpectedly, we were hotly censured by the UMNO leadership for this stand.

Around this time, sporadic guerrilla attacks were still taking place against limited targets. But, pointedly, none of these were on orders from my headquarters. Our jungle courier system had broken down completely. We had a certain amount of message traffic moving via open couriers.

Finances were no problem at my Betong camp. We had strong support in southern Siam among the Chinese and the local Siamese. We encountered serious problems, though, when it came to sending assistance south of the border. Indeed, by this stage, all field units in Peninsular Malaya were forced to rely exclusively on local Min Yuen in their particular areas of operation.

We were never able to maintain accurate statistics of our military strength. But around this time the British released figures indicating CPM ranks consisted of approximately 2,000 surviving hard-core fighters. I would not argue with this figure. I would also add that these guerrillas were, by now, in particularly difficult straits.

Our comrades had the prospect of surrendering, but little else. If they dissolved units and sought to infiltrate back into civilian life, seeking jobs on plantations, tin mines and the like, they faced the prospect of the death penalty if discovered as unsurrendered communists.

As CPM leaders, we found ourselves in an appalling predicament. We could not urge our fighters to break ranks because if they were to do so they should surrender first. Without surrendering, they would be courting death on the gallows. To surrender was to desert the cause. In exceptional cases we sought to send them to Sumatra. Indeed, by early 1957, we were contemplating dispatching our entire remaining guerrilla force to Indonesia. We actually began smuggling some as unarmed individuals in boats across the Straits of Malacca.

After Independence we issued a formal statement saying we wanted talks with the government. Again the Tunku was swift to reject our overture. Within the Politburo and the general hierarchy of the Party there lingered a feeling our campaign could be maintained for quite some time, albeit at a much reduced level. I, for one, believed we could retain the military pressure at least for the rest of the decade. However, at the cadre level, opinions were faltering and I know now that the isolation of our headquarters from the battle zone prevented me from being able to assess true feelings among those on the front line. I failed to realise how demoralised our guerrillas had become.

Following Merdeka, the government devised a programme whereby security measures were concentrated against us area by area, one at a time. Codenamed *Operation Harimau,* these tactics, which centred on the deployment of Malay Home Guard units, were first applied in southern Perak. Reports I received suggested there

A Home Guard unit check point in the Tanjong Malim district. The sign on the left reads in four languges: 'Drivers and pedestrians are liable to be shot if they do not obey Home Guard orders in this district.'

were as many as 10,000 men mobilized this way by the government. Official claims at the time were somewhat less.

Essentially, Home Guard recruits were deployed along the jungle fringe areas. They were not well armed. Most of them only had shotguns. But they were strategically placed and operated at night when they knew we would be moving down from deep jungle camps to forage for food. From Jelatan up to Sungei Siput, government forces were particularly successful in applying coordinated tactics. When a Home Guard unit intercepted one of our patrols, another was able to move into position and block our retreat. On already disheartened guerrilla units these tactics proved most effective. A large number of our men were ambushed and killed. Some surrendered because they simply had nothing to eat.

The real disintegration of our guerrilla army began here in southern Perak. The trigger was the surrender of a key district committee member. He was based in the Bidor area and could boast a long and loyal association with the CPM. He had been a trusted messenger for our army during the Japanese occupation years. Indeed, when we set up the special security force to protect Davis and his Force 136 unit, this man was one of those chosen for the task. Thereafter he quickly became a section leader. When Japan surrendered he was a platoon commander and came into the open. After the Emergency began he rejoined us and was promoted gradually to become a district committee member. Had it not been for our requirement to break down into small units, he would have been installed as company commander. As it happened, he surrendered and took with him our entire southern Perak military strength of more than 100 guerrillas.

Immediately, the police and military combined to lay traps for various CPM political activists identified by the surrendered CPM official and those he had taken over to the government side. Our Perak state secretary became trapped in an ambush, refused to surrender and was killed. Collectively, these operations wiped out the CPM presence in southern Perak. The betrayals spread very rapidly to Malaya's southernmost state of Johore. This period would become known as our 'mass surrenders' phase and would continue for the next two years.

Following the southern Perak debacle, we tried to consolidate and withdraw units totalling some 300 guerrillas to the central and northern Perak hinterland. But, once again, we were thwarted. The orders I issued for this change of strategy failed to reach our deep jungle bases. The documents containing them were captured by government forces and countermeasures quickly imposed. From then on our Perak units were reduced to defensive manoeuvres only. It became a seemingly endless exercise in avoiding contact with British or government patrols. Our offensive impetus in this important northern state was gone forever.

The CPM's disintegration as a fighting force in Johore stemmed from one man's massive act of betrayal. When our southern area commander, Hor Lung, defected in 1958 and was reported to have brought out 150 guerrilla fighters, he personally pocketed no less than $120,000 – a veritable fortune in those days – and earned himself a blanket pardon. The British claimed, at the time, that this extraordinary incident was one of mass voluntary surrender. That was a vast distortion of the truth.

The facts are these: Hor Lung and his bodyguards surrendered to the government side in April, 1958. Food shortages had earlier required him to disperse his men in groups of two's and three's. Special Branch officers clamped an information black-out on his capitulation and, offering huge financial rewards, persuaded our southern area commander to arrange two separate jungle meetings with his men. Hor Lung regrouped his guerrillas on the pretext that he needed to inform them about latest directives from the Central Committee which, of course, I headed. As a point of historical fact, I should record here that I had sent Hor Lung no instructions whatever. Actually, we had not communicated since the day I appointed him Southern Area Commander replacement for Ah Koek.

On each regrouping occasion he organised, Hor Lung was accompanied back to the jungle by Special Branch officers posing as bodyguards. These events were choreographed in such a way that attendees were required to place their arms in clumps, teepee-fashion, on the edge of the jungle clearing where our southern commander was scheduled to address them. At an appointed time in Hor Lung's remarks, his 'bodyguards' whipped out small arms and government troops emerged from the surrounding jungle to seize the unsuspecting followers.

Well after both operations had wound up, the authorities proudly announced, on August 27, 1958, that Hor Lung had led a mass surrender of his troops. Various figures – between 150 and 160 – were subsequently given for supposedly surrendering communists involved in this overall operation. In fact, it had not been a mass surrender. More accurately it was a case of a commanding officer betraying his men and being instrumental in arranging a mass capture. The Tunku revealed rewards to the tune of $496,000 had been paid out. Commented the Tunku at the time: 'On principle, Hor Lung should be hanged for what he has done. But we have to get results; and if money can buy the end of the Emergency – we will buy it.'

The Hor Lung operation encompassed our entire Southern Area Command from the Johore border with Negri Sembilan through northern Johore to southern Johore. In the aftermath, all that was then left of our southern army were a few small pockets of guerrillas operating in the Kulai-Skudai region. They fought to the last. One of these units was led by a woman from Pontian. The government claimed she was killed in an ambush. As far as the Party is concerned, this has never been verified. We have conflicting reports that she was wounded and taken prisoner. Whatever her fate, the British maintained she was the last woman guerrilla leader in Johore.

The other surviving group in the state, was led by the southern Johore state secretary, Yang Tze Ching, and his wife, Cheah Swee Seng, a Penang girl who had been active in the Party's Women's League on the island. Their unit comprised about 10 guerrillas. Contact was maintained with our Party underground and food supplies continued to be made available. One fateful day, though, the state secretary sent a trusted bodyguard on a scheduled three-day special mission. Instead of following orders, the bodyguard went straight to the authorities to surrender and thereafter attended a training session with the Special Branch. This, of course, delayed him and he was late for his scheduled return to his unit. By this stage he was under police instructions to assassinate the couple. Naturally, the husband and wife had become suspicious and demanded a full explanation of his late return. In the middle of giving this, the bodyguard suddenly drew out his pistol, aimed at the husband and fired a fatal shot. A split-second later, the wife reached for her pistol and fired at the betrayer. Sadly, her aim was off target and the bullet sped past the man's head. Wheeling around, the bodyguard shot the wife, killing her instantly.

It was later officially reported that the husband and wife guerrilla duo were killed in an ambush. We believed this version at the time. Subsequently, a survivor of the guerrilla unit escaped, found his way across the border to southern Siam where he told us exactly what had happened. But the fact remained, once the husband and wife team was wiped out, we had not a single guerrilla operating throughout the state of Johore.

By now, the government side was functioning most effectively at several anti-insurgency levels. Military actions were notching up impressive kill-rates. Psy-war dirty-tricks were being applied via the infiltration of government agents into guerrilla units. As we were forced to contract into small groups, the opportunities for individual guerrillas to surrender greatly expanded. No longer under the watchful eyes of unit leaders, they were left to their own devices and were rendered vulnerable targets for enemy enticements via leaflets, loudspeaker aircraft and rumours.

An all-encompassing leaflet programme that had been operating for some years, now began producing quite dramatic results. A particular leaflet, specially designed for guerrillas to carry on their person as a safety pass, was extremely effective. There was really no way we could prevent the comrades holding onto one of these for use in emergencies. Caught without them, they would be executed. Caught with them, they could surrender. In addition, the government was offering most generous monetary rewards to trigger large-scale betrayals. Hor Lung's contrived 'mass-surrender' illustrates the success of this programme.

To summarise, our guerrilla strength in northern Pahang had been crushed by early 1955. By 1956, southern Pahang's contact with Perak had been severed through British military action and subversion by Special Branch. Our guerrilla presence in southern Perak had been wiped out by late 1958 as had our forces throughout the states of Johore, Negri Sembilan and Malacca.

By the end of 1958, what remained of our main-force army was primarily spread across deep jungle camps in northern Perak, Kedah and Perlis. Numbers here probably totalled no more than 350 hard-core fighters. There were some 10 to 20 stragglers grouped as a single unit in Pahang. This was led by a state committee member and Siao Chang's wife who was a district committee member. In Kelantan, we had a few small groups in very remote camps working among the *orang asli*. Finally, there was our 30-strong unit that had operated since early Emergency days from the central mountain jungles of Penang island. So small had been their operational area that, by this time, they had run out of places to hide.

The political side of our activities also took a battering in 1958. With battlefield statistics so obviously in the government's favour, our political underground found the business of spreading communist doctrine a thankless task. Indeed, our activists could do little more than concentrate on maintaining personal security and avoiding arrest. At the same time the government was notching up successes in infiltrating Party political ranks with agents who were reporting back regularly to Special Branch.

Extraordinarily, British propaganda experts, skirting around the fact of Britain's recognition of China a decade earlier, continued actively feeding misinformation to the effect that the Communist Party of China was manipulating, supporting and even controlling the CPM. Local and foreign media readily snapped at this bait as avidly as they had done at the Soviet Union's supposed involvement with us in the

SAFE CONDUCT.

THE BEARER OF THIS PASS WISHES TO SURRENDER. HE IS TO BE GIVEN GOOD TREATMENT, FOOD, CIGARETTES AND MEDICAL ATTENTION IF REQUIRED. HE IS TO BE TAKEN AS SOON AS POSSIBLE TO THE NEAREST SENIOR POLICE OFFICER.

سورت اكوان

اورڠ ڤمباوا سورت اكوان اين هندق ممباليق. هندقله اي دبري دڠن باٴيق
دري مكانن دان روكوه سرت دراواتن جك مستحق. هندقله اي داٴباوا كڤد
ڤڬاواي ڤوليس ڠ كانن جب دكت كالي دڠن سبوليه مسڬيل.

通行証

此証之持有人投誠意欲予以供給寬待予以煙香並於
需要時以予上藥及儘速往見近之高級警官.

சேமச் சீட்டு

இந்த சீட்டை வைத்துள்ளவர் சரணடைய விரும்புகிறார்.
இவர் நல்லவிதமாக நடத்தப்படவேண்டும். இவருக்கு உணவும்,
சிகரெட்டும், தேவையாயின் வைத்திய சிகிச்சையும், அளிக்
கப்படவேண்டும். இவர் கூடிய சீக்கிரம் அருகிலுள்ள
ஸீனியர் போலீஸ் அதிகாரியிடம் அழைத்துச் செல்லப்பட
வேண்டும்.

HATH UTHAE KO MANCHHE KO PASS

YEO PASS BHAYE KO MANCHHE HATH UTHAUNU MANGCHHA. WUH SITA
RAMRO GARI KANA BARTAO GARLA, ANI KHANA AUR CIGARETTES PANI
DELA. AGAR USLE DOCTOR KO ILAZ MANG CHHA BHANI TEYO PANI
BANDOBAST GARLA. AUR USLAI JATI CHHITO HUNU SAKCHHA POLICE
STATION MA LAI JAULA.

No. 471

A sample of the safe conduct leaflets that were dropped by the millions into jungle areas we occupied. Rather than attempt to prohibit our guerrillas retaining one of these on their person, our High Command actually permitted them to be held as ultimate life-saving tools.

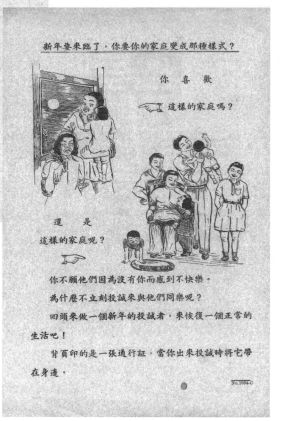

新年要來臨了，你要你的家庭變成那種樣式？

你 喜 歡

這樣的家庭嗎？

還 是

這樣的家庭呢？

你不願他們因為沒有你而感到不快樂。

為什麼不立刻投誠來與他們同樂呢？

回頭來做一個新年的投誠者，來恢復一個正常的

生活吧！

背頁印的是一張通行証，當你出來投誠時將它帶

在身邊。

No. 1004-C

404

early stages of the Emergency. Nobody wondered: If the CPM, since 1948, had been getting all this direct assistance from both Moscow and Peking in terms of weapons, equipment, finance and political direction, how come its armed struggle was in such a shambles ten years later?

Britain's calculated propaganda hoodwink that portrayed us as tools of foreign powers, proved eminently successful. It enabled her to continue colonial domination and exploitation. Eventually, it facilitated her extraction from Malaya with perceived dignity when her continuing presence became politically unsustainable. That the propaganda line, so fundamental to Britain's justification of her position internationally and to the defeat of my army, was baseless in fact, must surely cast doubts on the validity of her pursuit of hostilities – military action she preferred to define as an Emergency rather than the war that it was.

*　　*　　*　　*　　*

Before 1958 was out, the Politburo had completed a broad revision of battlefield strategy. If we were to have any chance of survival we would have to direct future military activities from bases outside Peninsular Malaya. I then issued orders to disband completely certain highly vulnerable units and disburse their numbers. We felt sections of Sumatra, along with Singapore, provided the best prospective destinations for these comrades. The 350 guerrillas in Perak, Kedah and Perlis were instructed to break down into even smaller groups and withdraw north over the Siamese frontier, there to establish new base camps.

As far as those ordered to disburse abroad were concerned, our intention was to place them in civilian environments where, hopefully, they could mingle without detection. At this critical time for us, Penang provided special problems. We realised the 30 or so guerrillas hiding in the central mountainous jungles of the island had no hope whatever of avoiding government patrols in the months ahead.

We recognised the Penang guerrillas had to withdraw and disperse. Singapore was the first choice for their relocation. The island had never become a fully-fledged Emergency battlefield. Our Penang underground contacted their Singapore counterparts and our guerrillas went south disguised as eager students. In this manner we managed to move approximately ten of the total Penang force down south. Once there, they took care to live separately with families in what was then rural sections of the island. They felt relatively safe until the time of Lee Kuan Yew's PAP victory in the 1959 General Elections.

We succeeded in smuggling the remainder of the Penang guerrilla unit to Sumatra by fishing vessels. The Indonesian island was regarded as a good prospect as it was geographically close – a relatively short sea voyage across the Straits of Malacca. Furthermore, immigration and security measures there were extremely lax. Half of the 20 or so remaining troops went to Medan. The rest sailed to Aceh after we had arranged their passages through our connections with the Aceh rebels with whom we believed we had retained good working relationships. I should point out it was not a matter of calling in favours to get our men extracted. We paid hard currency to the neighbouring rebel group for places on vessels they employed on regular smuggling runs between Penang and Sumatra.

By late 1959, we began receiving reports at Headquarters suggesting life was getting very difficult for the Penang guerrillas we believed had successfully re-settled in Indonesia. We discovered that, upon landing in Aceh, our comrades had been placed immediately under what amounted to house arrest by the rebels. They had been detained this way for several months. One by one, though, they managed to escape. Security in Aceh was really very loose. From that point, the comrades became people on the run once more and this time they were in a foreign land. Very obviously they were anxious to return to where they felt they belonged – Malaya, Singapore or even our new camps in southern Siam. But conditions had deteriorated so much that we were unable to give them assistance from Headquarters. Regrettably, they were left to fend for themselves. I know five or six of the Penang guerrillas who escaped to Indonesia were eventually able to get themselves smuggled onwards to Singapore where they obtained false identity cards and began working as farmers in the Ulu Sembawang and Kranji regions.

Earlier in the year, security precautions had dictated that we move our general headquarters from the Betong Salient west to deep jungle some ten miles in from the frontier with Perlis. Fortunately, the Siamese authorities were insisting that all British military patrols remain on the Malaya side. Under a border agreement negotiated between Bangkok and Kuala Lumpur, the Malay Police and military were granted limited pursuit into Siamese border territory. We could cope with this. However, I know some British SAS detachments were infiltrated into the Kingdom from time to time to gather intelligence on our various camps. To what extent they were successful, I cannot say. From the psychological standpoint, however, the threat thus posed was significant.

As our move from Betong approached, two females comrades – one of them my wife, Khoon Wah – fell seriously ill with raging tropical fevers. Our limited medical people were unable to make precise diagnoses and both patients soon became stretcher cases. I arranged to have them taken to a local Chinese village where they could secretly be given better medical aid. It would be an arduous overland trip to the site we had selected for Headquarters in the Sadao area. Neither woman would have survived it. So, I organised for them, once strong enough, to be smuggled to Bangkok where, by undercover means, we would secure them passages on a freighter bound for China. There they would receive further treatment.

*　　*　　*　　*　　*

Our new Sadao base represented a contraction in numbers over our previous camp in Betong. We now had only two security platoons totalling some 60 guerrillas. Within weeks of our relocation I called a Central Committee meeting to review Malayan battlefield prospects in the light of our overall physical withdrawal. Present at this crucial gathering were seven other Central Committee members – five Chinese and two Malays.

Given the low level of guerrilla activities to which we had been reduced, the prospect of scaling down even further lacked any strategic purpose. In addition we fully recognised we had lost a large number of men in combat. Although we still enjoyed a flow of finance from the Min Yuen, this was certainly insufficient for large-scale actions. Also, the perpetual problem of securing food supplies could never be solved.

Finally, we came to the realisation that the only option open to us was to phase out our armed struggle programme and revert, via our underground, to a clandestine political campaign. We envisaged a lengthy period of political preparation, perhaps as long as a decade. Thereafter, if the climate proved suitable, we might take up arms again. For now we would attempt to re-integrate back to mainstream societies in Malaya and Singapore those guerrillas we considered reliable and capable enough to work in underground roles.

The rest we would bring out of our southern Siam jungle bases and try to relocate in the towns and rural areas north of the frontier. At this time, Bangkok's control over the southern provinces remained loose, and the whole area somewhat freewheeling. As it was an easy matter for us to secure genuine identity cards for these ex-guerrillas, there was no requirement for forging documents. We also decided to send some of our guerrilla army to China, others to Vietnam.

Having arrived at this momentous conclusion, we went on to discuss the mechanics of winding down our military posture. We would have to hide our weapons in the jungle once again. In short, it was a return to square one, just like the immediate aftermath of the Japanese occupation. It was a most disheartening period. Still, we consoled ourselves that time probably remained on our side. We surmised Ho Chi Minh was about to launch his push against South Vietnam. We calculated Vietnam would evolve into a major theatre of conflict with western power participation. Mao was clearly solidifying communism's control of mainland China. The Korean peninsula remained stalemated. The Indonesian Communist Party, led by Comrade D.N. Aidit, appeared to be expanding impressively within the rampant corruption of the regime headed by the strutting Sukarno.

Throughout the meeting, Siao Chang in Peking was kept up to date with our deliberations through our radio link. In fact, he was able to participate in our discussions through this means. His opinions were sought on many subjects up for settlement. His input, always considered highly significant, came in coded messages and we termed these our 'wireless exchange of opinion'. We looked to Siao Chang for direction. After all, he had been so long in Peking and had established extremely good contacts there with the CPC hierarchy. What was more, he was sounding out top CPC officials and interpreting their opinions on our intended return to political struggle. On the other hand, the eight of us had been in the jungle for 11 years and were so out of touch with day-to-day developments in the communist world.

As the CPM Central Committee grappled with the problem of phasing out its army through 1959, we were forced to leave our senior political cadres in both Malaya and Singapore very much to their own devices. What little Party direction they received came from Siao Chang in Peking who was able to maintain an effective, albeit slow, message dispatching and receiving system. In southern Siam we kept abreast of political developments in both territories as best we could. We had correctly anticipated that Britain might well seek the severance of her remaining colonial links in the region through the creation of an expanded Malaya to include Singapore, British North Borneo and Sarawak. We read this as a likely ploy to pre-empt Indonesia's Sukarno who, it was generally felt, would be unable to resist the temptation of igniting his own anti-colonial struggles in Britain's remaining Borneo territories.

In Singapore, 1959 was a crucial election year. Historically, our Town Committee there had always functioned with a high level of autonomy. Throughout the Emergency I had been unable to exert any reasonable degree of control over the CPM's operations on the island. One committee grouping after another had been smashed by British-directed police action in the early stages. Thereafter our island-wide political network was continually being compromised by betrayals and defections. Still, the Party had been able to amass and maintain a huge following among the working classes. Historians and self-appointed political pundits have frequently claimed that we in the Central Committee were dismissive of the Singapore Town Council and regarded them as a bogus operation. Such claims are groundless.

From our Sadao headquarters we naturally observed the run-up to the Singapore polls in May, 1959, with considerable interest. We had concurred with our Town Committee on the island that the CPM should solidly throw its support behind lawyer Lee Kuan Yew and his People's Action Party (PAP). A leading PAP election agent who worked closely with Lee was our man. He was a card-carrying member and reported regularly to his Town Committee. I am sure Lee didn't realise the electoral agent was a hard-core communist at the time. He certainly knew the man had close and useful communist contacts. I always felt that Lee's attitude towards our underground activist in his camp was purely pragmatic. The young PAP leader would use him as much as he could and use his 'contacts with the devil'. We regarded the arrangement in very much the same light.

I cannot, with any degree of accuracy, place a figure on the numbers of people we controlled among the Singapore voting public in 1959. But I can certainly say that most of the island's workers sympathised with the left-wing trade unions and members of these unions well appreciated they were under the control of the CPM. The pro-government unions then functioned in name only. Our supporters, sympathisers and fellow travellers went on to provide Lee's grass-roots electoral support. Without them he would never have achieved his stunning 43-seat victory in the 51 constituencies up for decision at the May 30 polls.

In our review of the Singapore election results, the Central Committee rightly predicted that the victorious Lee would one day move against the CPM to consolidate his power. We appraised our cadres accordingly but could do little more. Meanwhile, the wind-down of our armed struggle continued with complication after complication having to be resolved. One particular thorny problem concerned my personal security during the Party's continuing delicate transitional phase. Linked to this was a perceived need for a convenient safe haven from which I could maintain my leadership role. Because of my public exposure at Baling four years earlier, I was now readily identifiable by regional security organisations.

Irrespective of where we eventually decided to base our safe-haven operations, it was going to be a tricky job arranging my extraction and onward passage from the jungle. The committee fully appreciated that we now faced the high-probability threat of a British SAS or commando-led raid across the border aimed at either assassinating or capturing me. Indeed, we felt that as long as we maintained our jungle headquarters in southern Siam the threat of such a raid would increase almost in proportion to the speed of our demobilization. At the same time it was acknowledged that other senior CPM leaders were in similar danger.

With Siao Chang's continuing participation in our deliberations via radio, we went on to draft a demobilization plan. This also embodied the mechanics of moving to a purely political struggle directed from a Peking-based headquarters. Pointedly, Siao Chang agreed with all aspects of our thinking. But nothing could move ahead without China's consent. Accordingly, Siao Chang began lobbying the Chinese leaders. Several months passed before the Peking authorities finally signalled their willingness to host our revised programme.

It was decided that three of us – Chen Tien, Lee An Tung and myself – would move to Peking. Lee An Tung was an important figure in our organisation. He had been a newspaperman and his earlier writings in the Chinese language press had gathered him a following throughout Malaya. He headed our propaganda department and all felt it important he get to Peking in the first batch. In fact, the transfer to China by the three of us would comprise the first phase of our wind-down process. Before we could move, however, it was essential we revamp our presence in southern Siam. Initially, it was decided Siao Chang would replace me as acting Secretary General in Sadao. He had been Peking-based for more than six years and it was felt he would not be easily identified. However, this arrangement was held in abeyance. It would take months to clear his commitments in China. Instead, he proposed sending Ah Hai to serve as acting Secretary General in the interim. All readily agreed to this proposal as Ah Hai had not been exposed. Very few renegades from our cause had ever met him and those who had were considered unlikely to have appreciated his importance to the CPM.

Ah Hai arrived in Sadao in early 1960, some months before my departure. He had travelled overland via Vietnam, and southern Laos. It was good to see my old comrade again after so many years. Quite obviously, he was totally rid of the TB infection which had prompted me to send him to China back in early 1949. His stay in Peking had sharpened him enormously. He now sounded very politically astute. I briefed him about the demobilization measures we were taking on the local front. In turn, he informed me of the latest steps he and Siao Chang had taken in Peking to complement our efforts.

He said that following our decision to abandon armed struggle, he and Siao Chang had approached the Chinese with a proposal for the CPM to set up two separate business operations in Bangkok. These, it was suggested, would serve as covers for the furtherance of our clandestine political activities. One was to be a general import/export trading company; the other a motor vehicle repair centre. They were to be pure capitalist ventures. Through them, we would be able to move finances, both internationally and within Siam, without raising suspicions. Furthermore, if successful, the companies would be able to provide us with regular and reliable funding.

Ah Hai related how they had approached the Chinese with considerable diffidence. They were concerned, like I had always been, about appearing to go cap-in-hand to Peking. Understandably, they were unsure what the Chinese reaction would be to the idea of the CPM developing capitalist covers to facilitate and fund a communist movement. They feared their ideas might be regarded as a serious break with the strict Marxist-Leninist principles of party self-support from the masses. They needn't have worried. The Chinese liked the idea and made available some four million Siamese baht for the overall project.

Before the year was out, the two companies were up and running with several of our members in each posing as Siamese nationals and functioning as capitalist company executives. Also holding executive positions were a number of legitimate local nationals – except they were all members of the Communist Party of Siam. Both our companies remained profitable for almost six years. Indeed, they would probably still be in business had it not been for an unfortunate police raid. All our communist entrepreneurs were arrested, thrown in jail and charged on various counts including – as far as CPM members were concerned – living in the Kingdom on false identity papers. They were subjected to numerous interrogation sessions. In each, an American official sat in taking notes. As the months passed, the police sent investigators to Kuala Lumpur to check Special Branch records. The Malayan Special Branch, in turn, sent officers to Bangkok in an effort to have the CPM men extradited. But here they struck a hurdle. The CPM members in custody had never registered for Malayan citizenship. Being stateless, they could not be extradited. Still, all those charged served long prison sentences.

I continued to oversee the initial stages of our military wind-down in Sadao as Ah Hai eased himself into his new responsibilities. Meanwhile, intricate arrangements had to be concluded with a series of fraternal communist party networks to ensure my safety during the overland journey that would take me to Peking. The whole process took over a year to finalise.

Chapter 25

Off to China

My retreat north began in December, 1960, the month that Hanoi's ruling Lao Dong (Workers' Party) established the National Liberation Front of South Vietnam and launched a series of armed insurgent attacks against Saigon government rural targets. Very quickly, the North Vietnamese comrades would establish infiltration routes to support their insurgency. These would thread through Laos and Cambodia. Of course, I had no knowledge of these developments as I set out on what, for me, was a journey heavy with uncertainties and disappointments.

But it would be only a matter of months before, militarily defeated and clinging to hope for a political resurgence of my party, I would discover what was transpiring in Hanoi. This news would sustain me during the tough trip ahead. I would be able to reflect on what it might all mean for South East Asia, for world communism and, in particular, for the CPM to which I had dedicated my life. I began to think that all was not lost. Perhaps there really was a time to attack and a time to retreat and that the eventual winner was the one who mastered these manoeuvres best.

Travelling with me – but initially by another route for reasons of security – was my fellow Central Committee member Chen Tien, together with a bodyguard.

The first phase of my withdrawal would take me to Bangkok with the help of the Communist Party of Siam. We had first established contact with our Siamese counterparts during the Japanese occupation and had managed to sustain good working relations ever since. These had included a number of joint cross-frontier activities.

To help disguise my features for the trip I donned dark glasses, a false moustache and sloppy civilian clothes. The local communists assisting me sent a special courier on motorbike and the plan was for me to ride pillion for the entire 800 kilometres to the Siamese capital. A rendezvous was arranged for me and my courier at a roadside house situated at the edge of a rubber plantation near a small village north of Sadao. Chen Tien and the bodyguard would travel on another route via motorcar.

My departure was set for 4 pm to ensure that the bulk of the plantation workers had cleared the area. We rode a circuitous route, bypassing the nearby population centre of Haadyai. Before we reached the provincial capital of Phatthalung, the motorbike, to my dismay, sputtered and stalled, refusing to start again. It was dusk and rapidly getting dark. A motorised trishaw man, after much verbal persuasion – and the passage of some funds – eventually agreed to carry me, my courier and his immobilized motorbike altogether on his tuk-tuk to Phatthalung. Here preparations had been made for me to stay the night.

We arrived at our destination near midnight, some four hours later than expected, much to the relief of our worried hosts who suspected we had been intercepted. They had feared it was only a matter of time before they themselves would be apprehended. We rested overnight in the house of a comrade and awoke to find that the local communists had fortunately arranged alternative transport. Our bike, it seemed, would take some time to repair. The replacement vehicle was a comfortable station wagon. As an added precaution, a middle-ranking cadre from the local communist movement, together with his wife, came along for the ride. Unable to speak Thai at that time, I sat in the front seat between the husband, who drove, and his wife who sat next to the off-side window. Should we be stopped for any reason, either husband or wife would handle the questions on my behalf.

Our journey that day took us west through Trang near the coast, north to Krabi, and on to Phang-Nga, close to Phuket. We then swung north again to the Burmese river frontier at Ranong where we spent the second night in a small hotel. It was New Year's Eve and celebrations were underway. From my point of view, there seemed little to celebrate. But, as it happened, the merrymaking around us would prove to our advantage the next day when we were required to take a back road into Burmese territory and return via both Burmese and Siamese immigration checkpoints. The occupants of both establishments were all suffering hangovers that morning and were clearly uninterested in the close scrutiny of travel documents. The back roads on which we travelled were untarred and the bridges across rivers and streams little more than felled tree trunks lashed into place to prevent them parting under the weight of rolling wheels.

Once back inside Siamese territory, we headed east for Chumphon on the Gulf of Siam and then swung north on the main highway to Bangkok. We reached the capital late on New Year's night, January 1, 1961. The local comrades quickly installed me in a safe house in the heart of the city. There I was informed that I would probably have to wait some days before my journey could proceed. Undoubtedly, the most hazardous sections of the trip lay ahead and these could only be undertaken with the close cooperation of Siamese, Lao, Vietnamese and Chinese communist parties.

I was informed I would be met by a special Vietnamese military courier at the southern Lao panhandle township of Thakhek on the Mekong River frontier with Siam's north-eastern sector. Before this rendezvous could be arranged, a relatively safe passage had to be confirmed so that I could travel from Bangkok right across Siam to the township of Nakorn Phnom, which lies across the river from Thakhek. Word also had to be sent to Pathet Lao communist guerrilla forces operating in the Thakhek area. They were to provide a series of security patrols for my journey across Laos via the land-locked Kingdom's southern highlands, to the safety of communist North Vietnam's lower provinces. My exact arrival point in North Vietnam would not be revealed until a last-minute decision was made on the best available landing zone for a helicopter that would ultimately fly me to Vietnam.

Chen Tien, his bodyguard, and Lee An Tung, joined me at the Bangkok safehouse. Here we had a two-month wait while the various segments of our complicated travel schedule were pulled together. Then, late one morning in mid-March, the four of us set off in two vehicles bound for Nakorn Phnom. As my car, driven by a special courier supplied by the Siamese communists, lurched along a rural highway leading to Korat, I felt suddenly very ill. I was wracked by intense stomach pains and it soon became obvious I was bleeding internally. At Korat we debated whether to press ahead to Udorn, where we knew there was a hospital, or return to Bangkok. To abandon the schedule now would mean further delays and it could have taken weeks, if not months, to reassemble the cooperation of the various fraternal communist links absolutely essential to our retreat.

So I opted to proceed to Udorn. My driver had to make countless stops to accommodate my nausea and wrenching stomach pains. We arrived at our scheduled hotel around 9 pm. It was a small establishment owned by a local comrade who took one look at me and insisted I move immediately to hospital, despite the security problems this might entail. I strongly opposed this view but felt so unwell that I simply could not sustain a counter argument. When our host assured me he knew of a private clinic where I could be safely treated, I gave in.

My companions hailed a trishaw and I was lifted into the seat. En route to the hospital I lost consciousness. I came to just as medical staff were lifting me onto a stretcher. I could not move. When I looked up I saw one of the Siamese comrades crying. I asked: 'Why are you crying?'

He replied: 'You fainted. I was so scared.'

By the time I was examined, I had a raging fever. The doctor diagnosed amoebic dysentery and immediately admitted me to the clinic for medication, tests and observation. It now seemed certain I would be confined to hospital for some days. Since I had no choice, I instructed Lee An Tung to go ahead and inform all those involved with our onward passage that there was now a hitch. It was imperative that the meticulously arranged meeting points ahead be kept open. Chen Tien would stay behind with me and, once I recovered, the two of us would resume our journey along the intended route.

After seven days, although still feeling frail, I decided my journey must resume. Chen Tien and I, together with a bodyguard, were driven on to Nakorn Phnom. There we booked into another small hotel for a few hours while contact was established with Vietnamese communists. These were operating in a nearby Mekong River fishing village populated by refugees from the French Indo China war battlefields. We were eventually handed into their care. In a fishing boat provided by the village, we crossed the Mekong and on the other side were met by our appointed five-man security force. All members of our escort – three Pathet Lao guerrillas led by two Lao-speaking North Vietnamese Army officers – were armed with Russian-made AK-47 assault rifles.

The point at which we had landed on the Lao side of the river frontier in the half-light of late evening was considered to be in strongly held government territory. Indeed, in that particular area, all land between the river and the main road linking the national capital of Vientiane in the north to the Mekong River townships of Thakhek, Savannakhet and Pakse was regarded as being under the firm control of the then Souvannah Phouma government. However, the mountainous hinterland east of the road was a no-man's land. Here the Pathet Lao and North Vietnamese forces roamed virtually unmolested. It was to our decided advantage to clear the narrow government-controlled riverfront strip of territory as quickly as possible and disappear into the no-man's land. The objective seemed simple enough. Reaching it proved an entirely different matter.

Whether as a result of allowances made for my state of health, or tardy planning on the Vietnamese officers' part – I was never able to confirm – the decision was taken that we should rest that night on the government-held side of the road. Our dash across the highway to the relative safety of the terrain beyond would be made pre-dawn the next day.

After nightfall, we kept moving for some two hours through scrub country and light jungle to a position within easy walk of the critical roadway. There our Vietnamese escorts decided to make camp. The chosen position was deemed a safe distance back from regular paths patrolled by government troops charged with keeping the road open.

In their calculations the Vietnamese had failed to make allowances for one important factor: the extraordinary amount of noise created during breakfast preparations by the three very raw Pathet Lao guerrillas seconded to us. Chen Tien and I were aghast at the racket the trio created as they cooked their rice, prepared their fish and barked encouraging instructions at one another as they did so. Aluminium dishes and pots were scraped and banged. Smoke from poorly chosen firewood billowed high into the early morning stillness so that even the deaf could have discovered our exact whereabouts. Unbeknown to us, our campsite was located within shouting distance of a Lao village. Obviously the villagers heard the early morning cacophony, spotted the smoke and promptly lodged a report. Before our party could start tasting the results of the decidedly unnerving Pathet Lao breakfast ritual, a burst of automatic fire signalled we had been surrounded by government forces.

If ever we needed a lucky break it was now. Extraordinarily, it came to us in the guise of the troops surrounding us. Our attackers demonstrated they were as inept and as casual as our Pathet Lao defenders. We returned fire. Silence followed. We expected an attempt to overrun our position. It failed to materialise. The government side was clearly unwilling to risk casualties in a free-for-all fire-fight. Seizing the opportunity, our Vietnamese patrol leaders organised a quick withdrawal under fire. We broke through the encirclement unscathed, thanks to the obvious desire of the government side to depart the area with as little combat involvement as possible. We scrambled over the road to the comparative safety of the hinterland. It was dawn. From then on our Pathet Lao escorts were left in no doubt as to what might happen to them if they continued their noisy ways.

We soon learned that the two North Vietnamese with us were under the direct control of Hanoi's Liaison Department, an office overseeing all associations with fraternal parties. From the Mekong River onwards, our group would be relying entirely on arrangements put in place by this department. But language difficulties with the two Vietnamese, who spoke neither Chinese nor English, precluded much discussion as we moved on foot as quickly as we could towards recognised liberated areas further east. We pressed ahead all day, at first through a fringe area of cultivated fields, then intermittent clusters of thatch-roofed huts. It was not until we reached the interior jungle that we felt reasonably safe. After trudging for hours I must have looked totally exhausted. Remembering I was still convalescing, Chen Tien requested the Vietnamese halt for the night. Our escorts were not altogether amenable to the idea. They indicated we were still a few hours short of the real liberated areas. However, they acceded to our wishes on the understanding that we move off eastwards again before first light the following morning.

Very early the next day, we were climbing into the jungled foothills of the southern Laos highlands. Just before midday, we broke into a clearing atop one of the hills. There, in curious contrast to the matted surrounding foliage, stood a lumbering Russian helicopter. It was unarmed as was its all-Russian three-man crew consisting of pilot, co-pilot and loadmaster.

The more senior of the two Vietnamese with us made it clear we should get aboard without delay as we were already running late. Chen Tien, the bodyguard and I clambered up. The senior Vietnamese joined us, leaving his companion with the three Pathet Lao who all waved farewell. We rose, clattering into the midday humidity, hovered briefly over the landing zone and finally swept away towards the east. An hour or so later, we were descending to the airstrip at Dong Hoi, a provincial capital on the shores of the Tonkin Gulf, north of the Demilitarized Zone that separated North from South Vietnam.

On hand to greet us was a delegation of high-ranking provincial officials and military officers from units based nearby. We were taken to the VIP guesthouse where the local party secretary hosted a somewhat delayed welcoming lunch. The next day, Communist Vietnam's Central Committee dispatched a two-engine PS-84 transport aircraft, Russia's version of the DC-3, to fly us on to Hanoi. Shortly before midday, we landed at Hanoi's Gia Lam airport, north of the capital. It was the final week of April, 1961.

Le Van Luong, a Lao Dong Central Committee member, was on the tarmac ready to shake my hand and welcome me to a truly communist heartland. Beside him stood my old comrade Siao Chang. Almost a decade had passed since we last saw each other.

We were driven to a large house in central Hanoi that had, until a few weeks earlier, been the official residence of no less a figure than the powerful Le Duan. He had been appointed Secretary General of the North Vietnamese communist party the previous September. Next to Chairman Ho Chi Minh himself, Le Duan was the man who called the shots in Hanoi. He had temporarily moved out of the expansive home on the broad city boulevard in expectation of my arrival. It was indeed a great

The final week of April, 1961, sees Lee An Tung and I safely in Hanoi after the tough overland journey from our southern Thailand headquarters. There to greet us was our man in Peking, Siao Chang. This photo shows me on the left with Siao Chang in the middle and Lee An Tung on the right standing on the steps of the government residence put at our disposal during the stop-over.

As we were in Hanoi, I was keen to visit the scene of the Vietnamese triumphant siege of French troops at Dien Bien Phu from March 13 to May 7, 1954. The 56-day action proved the most decisive battle of the First Indo China conflict and resulted in the final snapping of France's political will to continue her colonial struggle. The photo shows me, one foot on an abandoned French cannon, and surrounded by the large Vietnamese party which accompanied us that day.

honour. It was a private gesture that recognised me as leader of a fraternal communist movement and specifically was made despite the major military setbacks we had suffered in our struggle. I believe it was also the Vietnamese way of thanking us for the assistance we gave them in the period immediately following World War 11.

The day after our arrival, the Vietnamese hosted a formal banquet in our honour. It was held at the residence in which I was staying and a number of high-ranking government officials attended. I was quietly told that it would be preferable if I wore civilian clothes rather than my formal military uniform as CPM chief. Though puzzled, I readily acceded to this request. It would not be long before I discovered the reason behind this and other subtle adjustments I would be required to make during my stop-over.

Hanoi's May Day celebrations were to be staged the following week. We learned the capital, on this occasion, was to be the venue for a massive rally and highly organised political demonstrations. We felt, erroneously as it happened, we might well be invited to witness these. After all, May 1 had long been regarded as a fundamental date on the socialist calendar. However, it was soon made clear to us we would be unable to watch either rally or demonstrations and should remain indoors in the official residence.

We consoled ourselves with the thought that, as the CPM was regarded a secret party, it would be better that I not be openly involved in these particular celebrations. Still, from our central location we could hear the progress of events. Halfway through the festivities thousands of young Vietnamese women in farming peasant attire marched past our residence, their wooden clogs thundering in rhythmic unison. We rushed to windows for our only glimpse of Hanoi's 1961 May Day March.

There was, indeed, a valid reason for keeping the CPM's presence in Hanoi inconspicuous. Only seven months earlier, both Ho Chi Minh and Le Duan had attended a conference in the Russian capital at which the leadership split between world communism's pro-Moscow and pro-Peking elements had openly surfaced for the first time. It had proved to be a most acrimonious occasion and one with deep significance for Hanoi's leaders who were poised to launch their guerrilla war campaign to regain the pro-Western territory of South Vietnam created by the 1954 Geneva Agreements.

No less than 81 senior international representatives from communist or affiliated parties had been present at the Moscow meeting. As the assembly progressed, it became obvious that Russia's Nikita Khrushchev, proponent of the new 'peaceful co-existence' principle for relations with the West, now regarded the Chinese as conservative and blinkered by dogma. Those on the side of Mao quickly retaliated by accusing Khrushchev and the pro-Moscow faction of being revisionist and betrayers of basic Marxist-Leninist doctrine.

Clearly, by May Day, 1961, Hanoi had a vested interest in avoiding any form of alignment in the Moscow-Peking leadership struggle. In order to prosecute the war in the south, the Vietnamese communist leaders had to retain the simultaneous active support of the Soviet Union and China. The huge financial costs and massive requirements in military materiel required for the campaign ahead could only be secured by structured impartiality. To have had a line-up of Chinese guests on the official May Day viewing dais or at some other prominent location – albeit Chinese from Malaya – would certainly have signalled the wrong message and endangered Hanoi's cultivated neutrality. This was particularly so given the fact that, as leader of the Chinese party concerned, I was on my way to establish my new headquarters in Peking.

Siao Chang had not travelled to Hanoi on my account. He was there supervising a ten-strong group that we had sent to North Vietnam for training both in the theory of guerrilla warfare and, more specifically, in the establishment and maintenance of underground political networks. The Vietnamese had gained much valuable experience in their operations against the colonial French and we were anxious to learn from this. Hopefully, we could pinpoint the areas where we had made our mistakes. Given the CPM's decision to revert to a political posture, the courses being conducted at Hoa Binh by the Vietnamese experts were considered vital to our rejuvenation programme.

Our trainees in Hanoi were senior CPM cadres. We had hand-picked them from various districts in Malaya and then dispatched them to the North Vietnamese capital for specialist political instruction. Following their training, a number of cadres went to Bangkok, on staggered schedules, to establish an independent clandestine communications network for the CPM. At the time, we wanted to ensure we could maintain an independent supply network leading south through Siam without having to rely on local communist party assistance.

We were planning to infiltrate the bulk of our trainees back to Malaya after their Hanoi studies. Both clandestine communications through Siam and preparations for infiltration of trained political cadres were judged essential to the success of our long-term plans. Clearly it was important that I take the opportunity of my presence in

Hanoi to forge personal links with those cadres whose future activities appeared so fundamental to the CPM's survival. I therefore made several visits to Hoa Binh and became very familiar with the work they were undertaking.

While still in Vietnam, I received a number of invitations from the country's communist hierarchy to tour various sections of the country. Siao Chang, Chen Tien and I were taken on several forays. Initially, we went to the Dien Bien Phu valley, in the north-western sector of the country, scene of the Viet Minh's stunning victory over French colonial forces. It had been seven years, yet we still had to move with considerable caution. Vast areas of the surrounding terrain remained peppered with French land mines, un-detonated bombs and live artillery shells. They lay there, a lingering, lethal testimony to the intensity of the extraordinary siege which had provided world communism with such a brilliant psychological boost.

Concerned over my state of health, the Vietnamese insisted I take a few days' rest and recuperation at Halong Bay, their fabled retreat, 170 kilometers east of Hanoi and close to the port city of Haiphong. Spread throughout the bay are some 3,000 islets and limestone rocks. The surrounding coastline is honeycombed with caves and grottoes featuring breath-taking creations by centuries-old stalagmite and stalactite action. The Vietnamese proudly claim the area has inspired some of their nation's greatest literary works. For several days, I stayed in a sprawling waterside bungalow that served as a government rest house. Two years earlier, Indonesia's President Sukarno had been similarly feted by the Vietnamese and had enjoyed the same facilities.

*   *   *   *   *

Ho Chi Minh was due to depart for Peking shortly after the May Day celebrations. There he would participate in crucial discussions with Mao, Chou En Lai, Deng Xiao Ping and other Chinese leaders. Problems associated with the Moscow-Peking split must certainly have been high on the agendas and Ho was obviously under considerable pressure at the time to assure Mao of his intended neutrality on the issue. I had been informed that Ho was anxious to see me prior to his departure and that it was just a matter of arranging a convenient time to suit his heavy schedule.

When the invitation finally came for me to meet the Vietnamese leader, it arrived, very correctly, through the government Liaison Department. Ho had two residences. The official one was a rather lavish mansion, a remnant of the French colonial era. There he attended to party business, held conferences and met visiting dignitaries and foreign guests. In stark contrast, Ho's real home, situated a short distance away, was simple to the point of being austere. He lived day-to-day in a small single-storey structure which contained his private quarters, a dining area and a modest reception room.

Together with Chen Tien and Siao Chang, I met the legendary 'Uncle Ho' in his sparsely furnished home. We were ushered into the reception room and there he was, seated in a plain wooden chair. A single Vietnamese interpreter stood nearby. The 72 year-old wispy-bearded man wore a thin cotton tunic matched with a pair of his now famous sandals cut from old rubber tyres for the soles and held in place by strips of discarded inner tubing. During the course of our conversation there was a glint of humour when Ho urged us not to be influenced by his attire. He had worn identical clothes and footwear when he visited both China and the Soviet Union. 'Don't follow my example,' he advised us, a smile flickering across his face. 'This is just the way I like to dress. But when *you* go out to meet people you should be properly attired.'

Ho's first question to me was: 'Do you speak Malay?' I assured him I did. Then we talked in very general terms for over an hour. Once our informal discussions were over, the three of us enjoyed a simple luncheon with Ho. We shared rice, a single meat dish and some vegetables.

The meeting with the Vietnamese leader on this occasion was essentially a courtesy call on our part. The real business between ourselves and the Vietnamese had occurred some days earlier at a formal party-to-party meeting. I had led the CPM side. Le Duan had led the Vietnamese. These talks had taken place at the Vietnamese Lao Dong party headquarters.

Le Duan was unquestionably a southern communist and as such the only one in the Hanoi hierarchy at that time. He had been born in a village near the old Imperial capital of Hue and had the reputation of being both powerful and egotistical. Self-educated, he had worked for a time on the Vietnamese railways and on two occasions had been arrested by the French colonials. While in prison, he had taken the opportunity of studying political philosophy. Two lengthy periods of incarceration, together with his refusal to bend to French pressures, had helped solidify his power base and, ultimately, greatly assisted his rise to political prominence.

At the party-to-party talks, we introduced our situation and our policy. The Vietnamese did likewise. Both sides spoke in broad concepts. Hanoi promised a range of assistance within their capacity. The Vietnamese didn't seem to be particularly interested in how the British anti-guerrilla tactics functioned. I think they felt that, given all their experience with the French, they knew decidedly more about guerrilla warfare than we did.

With the Sino/Soviet split now in the open, I was careful to avoid any subject matter that could come within the parameters of this issue and cause embarrassment to our hosts. Le Duan delivered a dissertation on his government's determination to fight for Vietnamese unification. Following the Geneva Agreements, he had returned to South Vietnam to work for the communist cause. He spoke to us of his experiences there, of the repressive regime of Ngo Dinh Diem and the large numbers of Vietnamese communist activists who had been arrested, tortured and killed by the Western-backed Saigon government.

Le Duan explained that despite the sizable repatriation of pro-communists north of the 17th parallel immediately after the Geneva Agreements, the clandestine movement in the south had remained actively intact. Hanoi, he said, had expected elections to be called in July, 1956, as required by the Agreements. He went on to argue that as the Diem regime had failed to comply with this aspect of the accords and as it had led a military crackdown against the communist movement in the south, the north had no other option but to recover the southern territory militarily. He left us in no doubt that the move to foster revolution in South Vietnam had already begun and that small-scale actions were being directed at government targets there. These would be stepped up as the campaign expanded.

Le Duan went on to emphasise that the final decision for this policy, tantamount to the launching of armed struggle, had not come until after North Vietnam's ruling Lao Dong party held its Congress in September 1960, the same gathering that had confirmed his personal position as Secretary General.

I explained to Le Duan the problems we had faced fighting the combined British Commonwealth troops and the reason why we had decided, at least for the forseeable future, to abandon our armed struggle and revert to underground political activities. I made the point that, as we had received no form of outside military or financial assistance, it would be many years before we could take up arms again.

It was a curious position in which I found myself. A mere eight months after the Vietnamese had committed themselves to full-scale armed struggle, I was arguing strongly the opposite case for the CPM. Le Duan, on the other side of the table, was insisting that a political struggle in South Vietnam could simply not be sustained because the enemy kept hunting down, arresting and killing the political activists. I'm sure Peking had failed to inform the Vietnamese of the CPM's 1959 policy-switch. Le Duan and his group looked decidedly surprised at what I had to say. It seemed obvious this was the first they had heard of our resolve to give up armed revolution in favour of political struggle.

The next day, the influential Le Duc Tho, then head of the politburo's Organisation Department, made a special point of contacting me. Regarded as the No 2 man in the Lao Dong party's affairs, Tho was clearly troubled by what I had told the party-to-party meeting and wanted clarification. He had not been at the meeting and I surmised he had been appraised of my remarks by Le Duan. Tho went to some pains to indicate Hanoi would much prefer we remain on an armed struggle footing. However, if we felt that the conditions precluded this, then it was no disgrace for us to change tactics and the Vietnamese would respect our decision.

At the same time, Tho reviewed the Vietnamese assistance that had been promised us during the previous day's meeting. He began by emphasising that the support would necessarily be limited as Hanoi itself depended so heavily on aid from the Soviet Union and China. However, they would be prepared to assist in any way possible with cross-country travel between Malaya and China undertaken by CPM members in the course of our activities. Furthermore, they were willing to continue hosting training programmes for our selected cadres. In addition, they would also look favourably on the CPM stationing long-term students in North Vietnam where they could reside and become involved in all aspects of revolutionary studies. He pointed out that some 1,000 Cambodian resistance forces were already there under these arrangements and that they would be trained and ready to return to their homeland when the time was right. I was gratified by the Vietnamese offers and immediately began planning how we might avail ourselves of them.

It was widely known in top communist circles, at the time, that Ho Chi Minh was deeply concerned at the threat posed to the revolution in South Vietnam by the Sino/Soviet split. It was also appreciated that Ho was involved in a personal effort to mediate between the Chinese and Soviet leaders. In this role he made numerous trips north to China. Tentative commercial airline bookings had already been made for our onward passage to Peking when we were informed that the Chinese aircraft that had just brought Ho back from Peking was about to return empty. Would we like to take advantage of the VIP flight and travel that way? We accepted with enthusiasm. We had been some six weeks in Hanoi and I was anxious to get to the

Chinese capital, settle in and begin what I felt would be the enormous task of rejuvenating my party.

Ideologically, Siao Chang and I had always been strong supporters of the Mao line and the CPC. But there were many aspects of the China story that still puzzled me. I couldn't understand, for one thing, how there could possibly be famine in a country with such vast areas under agricultural production. China was a closed country and very little of what went on there appeared in the Western media to which I had had access over the years. In Hanoi, Siao Chang and I, on many occasions, had talked about these and related issues long into the night. For the first time I heard that the Great Leap Forward had been a total disaster.

Siao Chang had been very blunt about the mistakes being made by Mao. As a result of these discussions we concluded that the CPM must remain linked to the Mao/CPC ideology, but would have to be more flexible with its practical application. Siao Chang argued we should not become categorised by the Sino/Soviet split. We should make a point of retaining our relations with Moscow. After all the Chinese themselves were doing just this. On the surface, at least, the two communist giants were then being quite friendly towards each other. Unless there was an open break, we should try to maintain the balance. If an open break came we would then, naturally, align ourselves with China. I thought this was all very sound advice.

We flew into Peking's international airport one morning in the first week of June, 1961. I was met by the then CPC Liaison chief, Liew Ning Nyi, a close associate and loyal follower of the then head of state, Liu Shao Chi. Accompanying Liew were leading figures in the Liaison Department which, like the one in Vietnam, was charged with handling all matters concerning fraternal communist parties.

I was given a substantial bungalow next to Peking's highly secret Liaison Department headquarters. Close by was the Chinese Military Museum and the Railway Department building. The Liaison headquarters then comprised such a secret operation that it hid behind a high stone wall and there were no signs announcing its functions. Within the Liaison compound was a separate mini-compound of houses, enclosed behind yet another wall, for the families of those working for the department. Strict regulations forbade any family members strolling into the office section. All matters in the Liaison offices were handled on an appointment-only basis.

My bungalow formed part of an accommodation section set aside to house officials of fraternal communist parties operating in Peking. It was located on a broad boulevard leading straight into Tienanmen Square in the heart of the Chinese capital.

It is June, 1961. I am freshly arrived in Peking and standing in historical Tienanmen Square in my newly tailored Mao suit.

December, 1961 – Peking. Siao Chang and I are pictured here near the Summer Palace.

Khoon Wah, who had been in China since 1959 and was now fully recovered, rejoined me. Since her arrival, she had lived among the bulk of our Peking-based cadre-force in a general accommodation area elsewhere in the city.

There were two other fraternal South East Asian communist parties in residence in our compound – the Burmese and the Siamese. The Burmese formed the largest contingent at that time. All were ethnic Burmese and eventually most moved back to Burma. The permanent Siamese staff was relatively small although there was a large group of them in residence attending a lengthy training course.

Soon after we had settled into our new home, I was visited by a number of senior officials from the Liaison Department. We held long discussions during which I further explained the CPM's intentions of reverting back to a political struggle in Malaya. The Liaison men listened carefully to all I had to say and obviously went back and reported to the Central Committee where, I think, all decisions concerning our affairs were being made by the Secretariat. At that time, Deng Xiao Ping was Secretary General of the CPC.

Two welcoming dinners were given in my honour. The first was hosted by the Liaison Department. The bigger reception was organised by the Central Committee. I was accompanied on both occasions by Siao Chang, Chen Tien and our then Chairman, Musa Ahmad. The Chinese were obviously anxious to boost our morale at a time when our spirits were low. They praised our fortitude. They lauded our struggle. Listening to them, you would hardly think we'd been militarily defeated. In the days to follow, we had lengthy discussions as to what might be behind the extraordinary compliments being heaped on us by China's leading communists.

We got our answer in July, 1961, when we were invited to formal discussions with Deng Xiao Ping. Siao Chang and Musa Ahmad attended this session with me. We met in Deng's office at the government's administrative headquarters at Chung Nan Hai. Three other senior Chinese officials were present along with a secretary who took notes.

Deng opened the deliberations. South East Asia, he informed us, was about to undergo monumental changes. We knew he was fresh from discussions with Ho Chi Minh. What he was telling us, I surmised, was based on his knowledge of Hanoi's intentions towards South Vietnam and the extent to which Ho was prepared to go to ensure the unification of the fatherland. Additionally, Deng knew the minds and plans of the Burmese, Siamese, Lao, Cambodian and Indonesian comrades who all maintained important training facilities in China at this time.

Strategically, the whole region, Deng insisted, would become ripe for the sort of struggle we had been pursuing in Malaya for so long. The CPM must not, he urged, switch policies at this point. We must take advantage of the opportunities that would soon be presenting themselves throughout South East Asia. I was momentarily taken aback. 'I can't decide this matter on the spot,' I told the Chinese leader. 'This question must be determined by our Central Committee.'

Gathering my thoughts I hastily added: 'If we were to revert back to armed struggle, what sort of assistance might we expect from China?' This, I explained to Deng, would be the very first question that would be posed by my Central Committee comrades.

Deng was obviously well prepared for my reaction. Their Liaison Department had been closely monitoring the CPM's position for several years. It had been Siao Chang's task to keep in regular contact with the Peking hierarchy. Since the establishment of our radio link, he had provided the Chinese with very accurate progress reports on the various political and military events in Malaya. At that time, the CPM's total finances amounted to a cash fund of around US$100, 000. We had calculated this would be sufficient to cover our much-reduced operations for no more than 12 months.

Deng was probably encouraged by the fact that I had raised the subject of finance. He doubtless interpreted this as a hopeful sign we would ultimately fall into line with China's wishes. We concluded our discussions on the understanding that I would present his proposal to my Central Committee. Deng assured me China would support us if a general agreement was forthcoming. Details of the arrangement would be handled by the Liaison Department. This office, the Secretary General explained, was also empowered to conclude budgeting arrangements. Our talks lasted through two sessions – one in the morning, one in the afternoon – on the same day.

Psychologically, we now found ourselves in an even tougher position. In Sadao, we had suffered months of mental torment before finally coming to the conclusion that our one remaining hope of survival lay in a return to political struggle – despite the immediate pain this might mean.

In private, I went over every detail of Deng's argument. For these deliberations I brought in Siao Chang, Chen Tien and Lee An Tung. By radio we also made contact with Ah Hai back in Sadao. After all, our newly appointed acting Secretary General – if we were to follow China's advice – would be the one facing the daunting task of returning to war. There could be no question Deng had been most persuasive. Prior to this I had always felt awkward whenever the suggestion of seeking direct financial assistance from China had been raised. But after my first few weeks in Peking, I realised the Chinese communists were well down the track of funding the other South East Asian fraternal parties. All had representatives in residence and large batches of people under varying training schemes.

*　　*　　*　　*　　*

Three months after my talks with Deng, I was invited to Moscow. The intention was for me to attend the Soviet Congress. It turned out that I was also asked to watch the Red Square parade celebrating the 44th anniversary of the 1917 Bolshevik Revolution. The Congress was the one used by Soviet Premier, Nikita Khrushchev, to denounce Stalin publicly for the first time. He chose to castigate the Communist Party of Albania on the same occasion. I also visited Leningrad for a week during this trip.

I had known about Khrushchev's criticisms of Stalin and his policies. These had surfaced in 1956 and 1959 during secret assemblies of the Soviet Party. Personally, I strongly disagreed with the new attitudes emerging in Moscow. I was ready to admit that Josef Stalin had made some serious mistakes and his regime was responsible for excesses. Still, he had been an extraordinary leader at an extraordinary time. He had taken the USSR out of the wilderness and made it into a super power. Without Stalin, Russia could never have resisted the Third Reich.

Khrushchev and Deng both regarded themselves as reformers and worked at opening up their respective communist nations to the modern world. Khrushchev resorted to an absolute condemnation of the past regime as he manoeuvred to secure his power base. As I listened to him address the assembly that year, I felt such demagoguery had its serious pitfalls. I worried what effect the Soviet Union's new view of politics would have on Sino/Soviet relations. As things turned out, my concerns were well founded.

Deng, on the other hand, never denigraded Mao. To do so would have meant denouncing himself. Over the years I would have my disagreements with Deng and would doubt the wisdom of some of his policies. However, I reviewed my position on his leadership after the Tienanmen episode in June, 1989. I now accept that the only form of communism left is the one he moulded. I believe China today is

November 7, 1961–Moscow. I am a guest in the Soviet Union to attend the 22nd Congress and celebrations of the 44th Anniversary of the 1917 Russian Revolution. With me here in Red Square is a Russian Army Colonel from the International Department.

moving in the right direction but for some time yet she must retain a large element of centralised control. Otherwise, she will travel the same route as the Soviet Union did in 1990-91. I tell people now not to be hasty about predicting China's political submission to the forces of capitalism. It will take a lot longer than most people think.

Chapter 26

Back to armed struggle

Ironically, it was Musa Ahmad, the man we had elevated to the Party chairmanship before Baling – and who would ultimately betray us – who proved the most optimistic of all when it came to discussing Deng's proposal.

'With China's backing we can take over Malaya in five years,' he confidently predicted. I thought Musa was getting carried away. His assessment seemed most improbable. I suggested an eight-to-ten year time-frame might be more realistic. Even then, I still harboured doubts and said so.

After my recent conversations with Le Duan and Le Duc Tho in Hanoi, I had come away firmly convinced that it was only a matter of time before South Vietnam, Cambodia and Laos were liberated. But I was decidedly less confident about Siam. The Kingdom, to my way of thinking, presented an entirely different case. If, I reasoned, it would take eight to ten years to liberate Indo China – in fact it took nearly 15 – what would our position in Malaya be during that time? We desperately needed a common border with a national territory controlled by a fraternal party – a requirement even the liberation of the three Indo Chinese territories would fail to meet.

To my mind, a communist Siam was little more than a pipe dream. I well recall how anxiously I monitored Siamese politics from 1945 to 1960. I was searching for a glimmer of neutrality from whatever government was in power – military or civilian. A neutral Siam would have afforded us critical advantages. Our movements would have been decidedly less hampered and we could have been sure the Siamese would never join hands with the British to fight us. The latter was a constant threat we faced during our stay in the southern reaches of the Kingdom.

These were among the major issues that had decided our 1959 abandonment of armed struggle. Now, in Peking, barely 18 months later, we were examining them all over again. Only this time, there was the promise of financial backing from China. Would that be enough to sway the argument?

Ah Hai in Sadao thought it was and lost no time in signalling back his willingness to lead a re-ignited armed revolt. Musa Ahmad was highly enthusiastic about the idea. Siao Chang was also supportive. I fell in line, as did the rest. But, in truth, behind our affirmative decision lay a degree of reluctance. After all, our 1959 Sadao resolution had not been a passing whim. We had arrived at it following much analysis and self-criticism.

So, when we went back to the Chinese, the nub of our position was that success or failure for the CPM's return to armed struggle rested on the degree of assistance Peking was willing to extend. Deng had delegated the CPM policy issue. We were now dealing with top Liaison Department officials. Pointedly, we refrained from asking for arms and ammunition. We realised all too well the problems associated with the delivery of such equipment to Malaya. Hard currency was the key.

Our negotiations with Liaison officials straddled several weeks and were most successful. For the first time since I joined the CPM, the Party's finances were secure. Meanwhile, Ah Hai was given the responsibility of presiding over a Sadao headquarters meeting at which the resumption of armed struggle was the main subject for discussion. He was tasked with devising a blueprint for factoring in China's financial support. His input would be incorporated in the overall Central Committee planning going on in Peking.

Firstly, we would have to remobilize and reorganise the masses and substantially rejuvenate our position in the Siam–Malaya border areas. We would once again have to target the Kuomintang influence and the bandit gangs that passed themselves off as Kuomintang. As we were winding down our military posture from 1959, the gangs had begun trickling back to fill what they viewed as a power vacuum. The thugs we had driven to the Golden Triangle in the early 1950s were also reappearing on the scene.

To re-establish our presence with appropriate impact, it was decided we would need to eliminate a certain number of these re-infiltrating criminal elements. The kill rate would make it very clear to the gangster fraternity that, if they intended staying around, they would surely have to contend with us. In this context, Ah Hai introduced a quite brilliant piece of strategy aimed at neutralising Siamese reaction to our hardline stance against the bandits.

He devised a special leaflet in the Siamese language for distribution throughout the border provinces. It addressed itself to the population at large as well as the civilian and military authorities. In it the CPM explained that we were in the area for the sole purpose of securing supplies. These would be purchased from local markets in local currency. We assured the population that we respected Siamese sovereignty. We set out a series of scenarios that, we felt, would be helpful in establishing what we were about. We started by suggesting that the Siamese should avoid attempting to locate us in the jungles. However, if they did come and merely fired into the air, we would reciprocate by also firing into the air. On the other hand, if they fired directly at us we would return fire in similar fashion. We assured the police and army we had no desire to fight local authorities. If they patrolled away from the jungle we would never bother them in any way.

As the leaflet was being distributed, we made it compulsory for all our guerrilla forces to understand its implications and follow the measures outlined to the letter. It turned out to be a most effective exercise. It sought to preserve the jungles as our territory and worked that way. Copies quickly reached top police, military and political offices. Almost overnight we were not bothered again.

Another important requirement for our return to armed struggle was the reconsolidation of our entire organisation through political education. We resumed a heavy programme of lectures. By this time our headquarters had moved from Sadao and eventually settled back in the Betong area. As order and purpose got restored, we looked to recruitment drives for our political underground throughout both Malaya and Singapore and our guerrilla force then concentrated in southern Siamese border jungles.

The demobilization programme we were now reversing had begun well before my departure for Peking. A substantial number of our guerrillas, who opted not to go to China, had left the jungle and joined local Chinese communities north of the Malayan frontier. To have moved south would have risked the death penalty. As demobilization proceeded, our numbers had begun shrinking rapidly. Our hard-core guerrilla strength had dropped to little more than 300 when the reversal of policy was decreed. This was our lowest military strength ever. With our new programme and access to funds, we launched the first recruitment drive in mid-1961. By 1964, our guerrilla strength had grown to around 800. These particular recruits all came from north of the frontier. This time we had considerable success winning over and recruiting local Muslims.

Our army was now spread across four main jungle bases. One camp was in the Sadao jungles to the west. Another was in the central Betong jungles. The remaining two were located further east along the frontier section of Siam's – by now generally called Thailand's – Narathiwat province. Pointedly, our guerrillas received no regular wages, only what we termed pocket money. It was enough to buy cigarettes, soap, toothbrushes, and other small personal items they might require.

With the overall expansion, morale returned to our ranks and the flow of finances became fundamental to smooth operations. Our two front businesses in Bangkok, while important conduits for funds, were, by themselves, incapable of handling our ever-mounting requirements. Transferring money became a perpetual problem that only intensified when both ventures were forced to close down. Often we had to carry cash. This was always risky. If the courier was apprehended and searched for any reason at all, you could be certain the funds got confiscated on the spot whether or not a formal arrest was effected. When it came to carrying cash we had a definite preference for British currency. The £100 note provided us with the most value in a single note and was always easy to exchange for local currencies.

Of course, we were continually on the look-out for enhanced fund-moving facilities and were able to develop numerous and varied international options. I don't wish to go into the exact details of how our secret financial channels came about. Suffice to say we operated them in very respectable circumstances for 20 years and were never disturbed. The CPM always functioned within strict budgetary constraints and even tougher controls were applied the moment Peking started funding us in 1961. Each year our requests, based on US dollar calculations, were lodged with the Chinese. But we could draw funds in practically any currency we liked. As requirements presented themselves, our budget was expanded accordingly by the Peking authorities. These general arrangements remained in place until the financial assistance dried up in 1989.

Although nominally I remained Secretary General of the party from 1961 onwards, the day-to-day functions of this position really lay in the hands of Ah Hai. In Peking my job became more one of coordination at the highest levels. As requirements came to me from the field I endeavoured to deal with the various intricacies these entailed. At the same time I became involved in interpreting Malayan political developments for the Chinese hierarchy. What I was providing was a depth of understanding and interpretation not available from the daily press. I submitted regular reports. From time to time, when there were major developments, the Chinese would seek my opinions on specific subjects.

*　　*　　*　　*　　*

Senior Singapore communist leader, Eu Chooi Yip – or ECY as we called him – travelled to China from his headquarters in exile in the Rhiau Islands shortly after my arrival in Peking. Siao Chang and I received him and together the three of us worked on a plan to disperse all exposed underground activists remaining in Singapore. ECY was able to brief me first hand about the problems other exiled comrades were facing in various parts of Indonesia. In this context, he confirmed numerous reports we had been receiving since 1959. Our deliberations also touched on the best means of preserving intact what was left of our Singapore underground. Two years earlier the CPM Central Committee had warned that Lee Kuan Yew, having secured such a resounding electoral victory in May, 1959, was likely to move heavily against the Party's island-wide infrastructure. Our predictions had been premature. However, in 1961, we remained more convinced than ever that the crackdown we had long feared was just around the corner.

Our Peking meeting also examined in detail the Malaysia Plan that was being hatched between London and Kuala Lumpur. The three of us came to the conclusion that it would be in the best interest of our Party if we plotted to sabotage this. If we couldn't derail it, at least we might substantially delay its implementation. We took the position that Singapore should be kept a separate entity from Malaysia, despite the fact that, right from the outset of our struggle, we had envisaged unity between the island and its peninsular neighbour.

We interpreted Lee Kuan Yew's keenness for the Malaysia concept as due in part to his perception of the advantages it provided him in moving against the CPM. We were convinced Lee was planning to manoeuvre behind the Tunku and, through manipulation, smash us not only in Singapore but throughout Malaya. Our interpretation was wrong. Ultimately it was the Tunku who determined the timetable for Lee's move against the CPM.

During the consultations with ECY, we lacked firm information on the Malaysia idea. There had been little open and authoritative discussion about the so-called Malaysia Plan since it was first mentioned publicly by the Tunku earlier in the year. I missed these remarks as I was then travelling to Peking. Although I agreed with the political aim of working to sabotage the plan, I had reservations about the workability of such strategy.

ECY argued strongly that there was an ever widening split between the PAP's right-wing faction, led by Lee Kuan Yew, and a middle-of-the-road group, seemingly headed by Sinnathamby Rajaratnam, a Malayan-born Tamil and former associate editor of the anti-colonial *Singapore Standard*. There was also a third faction ECY identified as the 'Chinese communal group'. In a bid to convince us of Rajaratnam's political leanings, ECY related how, at one time during the very early days of the Emergency, his tuberculosis infection had flared up. He needed urgent medical attention and, for reasons of security, he decided to go and see a left-wing doctor who, at the time, happened to be staying in Rajaratnam's house.

I doubted the depth of difference between Lee's faction and the other two – particularly when it came to the association between the PAP leader and Rajaratnam. My two comrades were convinced that the rift was present and would worsen. I was outvoted and went along with their opinion. We then decided to instruct our Singapore underground to work on winning over the Rajaratnam faction to an anti-Malaysia stand and at the same time do everything possible to undermine Lee's determination to press for the formation of the new Federation incorporating Singapore. I was decidedly uneasy about these decisions and managed to convince my two enthusiastic comrades that, from then on, our political strategy would be to plan for the best but prepare for the worst. As it turned out, my skepticism was on target. Rajaratnam was, from the very beginning, undoubtedly Lee Kuan Yew's man. My idea of planning for the worst was likewise valid but, to our cost, would never be followed through.

As the public debate on the Malaysia concept gained momentum, Lee devoted considerable time and effort to winning over Chinese middle-class businessmen. He promised to decide the question of whether Singapore should join Malaysia via a plebiscite. We stood strongly against the plebiscite proposal. Singapore, we maintained, would be entering Malaysia on terms that would be unequal to the other territories. Malaya's legislation, we said, strongly favoured the Malays to the disadvantage of the Chinese and this situation would remain in force within the new Malaysian concept. We knew the Chinese of Singapore would be deeply worried by the prospects for education in general and Chinese schools in particular under a Malaysia controlled from Kuala Lumpur.

The plebiscite was Lee's bid to legitimise his policy of joining Malaysia. The opposition Barisan Socialis Party stood firm against the idea. Contrary to the countless allegations made over the years by Singapore leaders, academics and the Western press, we never controlled the Barisan Socialis. We certainly influenced them. But neither Dr Lee Siew Choh, the Party chief, nor, as I understand it, other prominent opposition figures like the Puthucheary brothers – James and Dominic – had ever been CPM members. Nor had we ever been able to control them. Unquestionably we tried, as we did with many other aspiring politicians of the time.

After he won the plebiscite in September, 1962, Lee noticeably gained confidence and began an energetic programme of explaining Malaysia to the Singapore electorate. He made speeches, and continued to expand the influence of the People's Association community centres as a cornerstone of his political strategy. Up to this point, these centres were still being considerably influenced by us.

Then on February 2, 1963, confident in the consolidation of his power base and with Malaysia barely seven months away, Lee lowered the boom on the CPM. In a pre-dawn thrust he launched Operation Cold Store which saw a combined force of local and Malayan police conduct an island-wide round-up of alleged communist activists. Working from prepared name lists, the raiding parties managed to seize 115 suspects. Among them was James Puthucheary. The Singapore crackdown we had been expecting for almost four years had, in fact, only materialised after strong pressure on Lee from both the Tunku and the British. Our deliberations with ECY two years earlier had correctly forecast the event, but had failed to visualise putting in place any form of effective countermeasures. My plea to 'prepare for the worst' had been to no avail. Operation Cold Store shattered our underground network throughout the island. Those who escaped the police net went into hiding. Many fled to Indonesia.

In Peking, Operation Cold Store notwithstanding, I continued to work at how best we might raise the impact level of our activities on the front line in Malaya. Very early in the piece, I had wanted to establish our own broadcasting network but hesitated in presenting such a large-budget project for financing by China. The Peking authorities were being more than generous as it was.

Shortly before the Tonkin Gulf incident in August, 1964, the Vietnamese Central Committee sent me an invitation, via the Chinese, to visit Hanoi. I answered, through the same channel, expressing my pleasure in accepting. Before I could leave Peking, the Tonkin Gulf incident erupted and there was general expectation in all communist circles that Washington would start bombing North Vietnam. The invitation still stood and I duly flew into Gia Lam airport one evening in late August. There to meet me was no less than Le Duan. For the first few days I was taken on a tour of various points of interest in the immediate Hanoi area.

Thereafter Le Duan and I met to discuss matters of mutual interest. Since I last saw him when I was on my way to Peking in 1961, the CPM had reversed policy and returned to armed struggle. He was interested to hear the progress we were making. He also briefed me on how the war was going in southern Vietnam. Le

Duan, who had just returned from Peking, confided in me that only a few days earlier Mao had personally told him that revolution would soon spread across South East Asian countries, one after another. The Chinese leader had predicted Vietnam, Cambodia, Thailand and Malaysia would all fall.

In the middle of our talks, Le Duan was interrupted. A secretary entered the room and whispered urgently in his ear. As the secretary left, my host switched our subject of conversation and informed me he had just received word that a flotilla of US warships was manoeuvring very close to the North Vietnamese coastline. His intelligence analysts were predicting the Americans would begin a naval bombardment at any time. Hanoi, he said, was considered a likely target for attack. In the light of this assessment, Le Duan pursued, he would make arrangements for me to move to Son La, the former French colonial mountain resort northwest of the capital.

I travelled by road and, at Son La, spent a few expectant days awaiting the predicted attacks. Then came notification that the US flotilla had veered away. A driver was sent to escort me back to Hanoi and within a day of my arrival I was back again talking with Le Duan. During the ensuing discussions, where we were sometimes joined by Le Duc Tho, I mentioned that I understood the Thai communists had, for the past two years, been operating a clandestine radio station from somewhere in North Vietnam.

'Could the CPM be given similar facilities?' I asked.

I had originally hesitated over requesting this of the Vietnamese as I felt, given our recent history and the fact that we were still in the throes of reviving our party, we might not be considered a prominent enough entity for association in this manner. I needn't have worried. Le Duan immediately agreed to my proposal. He was quick to add that the CPM would, of course, have to provide the broadcasting staff. That would be no problem, I assured him. The Vietnamese, for their part, he said, would be happy to provide the technical staff to keep the station operating. Furthermore, they would provide us with a full list of all the electronic equipment necessary for such a project. There was just one problem. Vietnam, he informed me, was not in a position to provide the necessary transmitting equipment. Le Duan suggested there were two possible sources: China and East Germany. I realised right away that both sources might well be available to the Vietnamese. But as far as the CPM was concerned, at this stage of the Sino/Soviet split, we would have to requisition from China. To have turned to East Germany would have created all sorts of problems for us in Peking.

The Vietnamese were about to take me on another inspection tour outside the capital when I received a note from the Chinese ambassador to Hanoi suggesting I should return to Peking in time for the National Day celebrations on October 1. There was an element of urgency about his request. The note indicated October 1 that year would be a particularly important occasion as it would be the 15th anniversary of communism's defeat of Chiang Kai Shek's Kuomintang regime.

The ambassador's approach caught me completely unprepared and I found myself in a most awkward position. The Vietnamese were eager to extend our discussions and clearly had further suggestions to put to me. On the other hand, I was keen not to offend the Chinese whose facilities in Peking, not to mention financial support, were now vital to the CPM's continuing existence.

Before leaving for Hanoi I had paid a courtesy call on the deputy head of the Liaison Department, a Central Committee member, to inform him of my intentions and, specifically, to clear with him if it was convenient for me to be away during the October 1 arrangements. He had urged me to go ahead with my travel plans. The government's intentions, he assured, were for relatively low profile National Day celebrations that year. Obviously, these plans had drastically changed in the interim. Much later I learned the reason. Mao, faced with major economic problems, had decided at the last moment to stage a National Day spectacular.

After careful consideration of the dilemma I faced, I decided to write a polite note direct to the Liaison Chief in Peking explaining my predicament and regretting that I simply would have to carry on with the extensive programme the Vietnamese had arranged for me. I pointed out that I had previously cleared my departure with Liaison and had secured their agreement to my plans.

Because we were considered a 'secret party' I knew there would be no invitation for me to attend the official October 1 embassy reception in Hanoi hosted by the Chinese ambassador. On the eve of the gathering I went to the embassy armed with a large bouquet of flowers to pay my compliments to the ambassador and wish him well on his National Day.

The Vietnamese learned of the manner in which I had set about solving my problem. They regarded my actions as highly respectful to Vietnam. Before I returned to Peking several days later, they hosted a very private and very secret send-off dinner party for me at their Hô Tây (West Lake) government centre. There were less than 20 names on the guest list. But practically all the senior politburo members including Le Duan, Le Duc Tho, Truong Chinh, General Vo

Nguyen Giap, even Ho Chi Minh himself, were in attendance. In fact, the only leader missing was Pham Van Dong.

Early the next morning, shortly before I was due to leave to catch the plane back to Peking, Ho Chi Minh turned up at the front door of the Hô Tây bungalow where I had been staying. He had come to bid me a personal farewell.

When I arrived back in Peking I told the Chinese that the CPM had received Hanoi's agreement for the establishment of a clandestine broadcasting station in North Vietnam, just like the one the Thais were running. Could they possibly supply the transmitting equipment? At the same time I was able to hand over the complete electronic requirements list provided me by the Vietnamese. I noted at the time that my request seemed to fall flat and I was told I would have to await a decision from the Central Committee.

When the answer finally came a few weeks later, it was a rejection. It was explained to me that the Tonkin Gulf incident had created a precarious military situation in North Vietnam. North Vietnamese airforce aircraft had already been transferred to the southern Chinese province of Kwangsi. Plans were now underway to move the Thai broadcasting station out of North Vietnam and onto Chinese territory. If I went ahead and established our station in North Vietnam at this juncture, I would inevitably be forced to move it to a safe position somewhere within China's borders. Thus my idea for starting up our own revolutionary radio network had run into a substantial brick wall. I was disappointed at the time but the situation would turn positive for us in the long run.

In the meantime, a major international development demanded my close scrutiny: the overthrow of Khrushchev in October, 1964. Where did this leave the CPM in the shifting world communist picture? Quite clearly, Peking leaders were absorbed by the Kremlin's changing scene. There was lack of unity among policy makers as to the most appropriate stand for China to adopt towards the Soviet Union. A handful of influential Caucasian communists, residing in China, all regarded as close to Mao, became sounding boards for policy. But the Chinese were soon to discover there were as many disagreements on these matters among the Peking-based Caucasians as there were among local policy makers.

One set of advice urged an entirely new policy line towards the CPSU. Another, which appeared to be in agreement with Mao and the bulk of the Central Committee, wanted to pursue the old criticisms of Moscow's revisionism under Khrushchev. Among the more vocal Caucasians were Americans – Israel Epstein whose Jewish

It is March 19, 1965, and I am being received by Chairman Mao Tse Tung at his Wuhan official guest house. In the background, partially hidden by the Chairman, is Lee An Tung, wearing spectacles.

parents had fled to the United States in 1949, Anna Louise Strong and Frank Coe. Strong, as I understood it, was urging China to find a compromise so relations with the Kremlin could improve. The CPC Politburo appeared to favour an opposite view. Personally I remained doubtful that the Russians would abandon their revisionist trends just because Khrushchev had fallen.

With the differing policy suggestions appearing to result in an impasse, Mao sought opinions from a cross-section of fraternal parties. Lee An Tung, Musa Ahmad and I, grouped with Epstein and Coe, found ourselves summoned to meet Mao at his official Wuhan residence. Anna Louise Strong was not invited. I presumed this was because she held rather strident opposing views to Mao on the issue.

A special aircraft flew us from Peking to Hubei's provincial capital. We gathered first in a large reception room and then went to lunch with the Chairman. At the Wuhan discussions, Mao appeared alert and on top of the situation. He asked questions, listened intently and critically to our answers, then expounded on his views. It was easy to believe that the Chinese party was, by now, unified on the Moscow relations question and that Mao was in full control. We came away from Wuhan convinced that the Chinese leadership would remain censorious of Moscow.

*   *   *   *   *

Even before I visited Hanoi in 1964, a difference of opinion had already erupted over the best means of directing our renewed armed struggle programme. Essentially the crisis evolved in 1963 from a majority opinion of those in Peking regarded as 'in the rear'. Our Central Committee people in the Chinese capital became critical of our 'front line' policy. They claimed Ah Hai was too conservative. They regarded our move towards armed struggle as requiring more vigour and more initiative. They called for an immediate resumption of direct military attacks south across the border into what was now Malaysian territory. They even began urging that attacks be launched against Thai targets. Pointedly, they had begun to regard the Kingdom as part of the enemy camp. It was no coincidence that this hardening of opinion within the CPM leadership in Peking developed in parallel with the initial rumblings of what would later evolve as the Cultural Revolution. The word was about: revisionists were surreptitiously undermining the purity of Marxist-Leninist doctrine.

Ah Hai and the comrades at the front disagreed with the Peking assessment which had manifested itself from hardline leftist positions adopted by Chen Tien, Lee An Tung and Musa Ahmad. My personal sentiments in this difference of opinion lay firmly with Ah Hai. I felt we should give more thought to those in the field. Surely their reading of the situation was more valid than ours made at such a distance.

In Peking we tried to sort out the problems through extended discussions and via our radio link with Ah Hai's headquarters. Both means failed us. The hardliners, heavily influenced by the rising tide of extremism across China, would not budge. At the same time the requirement to convert radio messages into brief, coded extracts undermined all efforts at seeking common ground and mutual understanding with our guerrilla bases.

Finally I suggested we bring Ah Hai back to Peking. We could then thrash out the problem once and for all. I felt that if he came and personally briefed us on the detailed realities at the front, the policy block paralysing our leadership could be overcome. This was accepted and Ah Hai, whose wife in Peking had been stricken with heart problems, was ordered to return for consultations.

Siao Chang left China for the Thai-Malaysia border in 1963 to assume the leadership at the front line. It took him more than a year to reach Headquarters. He became stuck in Bangkok because of communication difficulties with the south and it was 1964 before he completed his journey. As Ah Hai could not depart before his replacement's arrival, it was 1965 before he appeared in the Chinese capital.

For a while things settled down. Then the Cultural Revolution erupted with full force in 1966 with Red Guard demonstrations throughout the country. At this point the unresolved rift over the CPM's armed struggle policy manifested itself once more. Most of those who had opposed heightened military action on both sides of the Thai-Malaysia frontier now fell into line with the widespread clamourings for a return to the basics of revolution. From the CPM's point of view, this meant re-invigorated pressure for a far more militaristic approach.

Musa Ahmad was influenced by speculation that China would soon start differentiating between fraternal parties that were 'revisionist' and those who followed the pure Maoist line. Because of problems we were having with the Liaison Department, Musa came to the conclusion that we might soon be on the outer and labelled 'revisionists'. He started distancing himself from us. He even left our premises and went to stay with others who held similar views. Eventually, of course,

Musa decided to defect. He went back to Malaysia and in November, 1980, made a public confession.

In late 1969, I decided that the two other most vocal militants within our Peking-based community – Lee An Tung and his wife – should travel to the border camps and see things for themselves. Together they duly departed overland and within a few months had reached our Betong headquarters. From then on I heard nothing from them. Their continuing silence ensured that our original policy for the front line remained intact, albeit temporarily. Husband and wife stayed on in the border camps. Their decision to do so would have dire consequences.

As the months passed, I myself became caught up in the Cultural Revolution's fervour. I felt obliged to become directly involved in what I then regarded as an important milestone in the evolution of world communism. Ah Hai wanted none of that and was strongly opposed to my participation in any way. He took an entirely neutral stand. With the hardliner's argument defused as far as our guerrilla army's policy was concerned, he wanted us to restrict our attentions to the requirements of our front line.

Chapter 27

Banishees, broadcasting and bargaining

As I watched the Red Guards gain centre-stage, I felt the time was surely approaching for the CPM to come clean with Peking authorities over our long held concerns about the way the Chinese party had been treating our exiled members and supporters over the years. In private discussions limited only to CPM leaders, we referred to this as our 'historical problem'. It concerned the thousands who had been exiled to China by the British.

The colonial power chose to use the appalling term 'banishees' when categorising these people. They were all ethnic Chinese. Essentially they believed in the principles of the Chinese revolution. They spoke Mandarin and various dialects as their mother tongues. They accepted without question the teachings of Mao, the man who had shaped contemporary China. Yet, once on Chinese soil, they were constantly being reminded of their overseas status. They were regarded as second-class citizens. The tumult of the Cultural Revolution seemed to offer ideal conditions to bring into the open and resolve this 'historical problem'.

Towards the end of 1966, as the Red Guards rampaged through the streets of Peking and invaded government offices, we approached a contact in the Liaison Department and outlined our views on how we felt our CPM comrades ought to be accepted when they came to China. Prior to the 1949 liberation of the mainland, our members exiled there were freely allowed to transfer their membership to the Communist Party of China. Why couldn't they be treated similarly now?

Word of our grievances reached the topmost echelons of power. As I understand it, both Mao and Chou En Lai got to hear about them. Soon we were told that party-to-party talks were being scheduled early in the new year. In an obvious demonstration of goodwill, Chou En Lai himself hosted a dinner in our honour on December 31, 1966. Four of us, Chen Tien, Musa Ahmad, Lee An Tung and myself, together with our respective wives, attended this function which was held at the Diao Yu Tai State Guest House in the western section of Peking. Our host, the Premier, had arranged a special cultural evening to which representatives of other fraternal parties were invited. I am not sure whether the Chinese leader was aware that one of the guests sitting at his dinner table – Lee Meng – had, 14 years earlier, been languishing on Taiping Prison's death row.

Feted thus, we were now buoyed by prospects of the scheduled party-to-party talks. When these eventually began in mid-January, we found that the CPC panel was headed by none other than our long-standing contact in the Liaison Department, Kang Sheng. By this time he had become a particularly powerful figure. Not only did he guide the operations of important departments like Liaison and Propaganda; he was also the sole adviser to the Cultural Revolution Group which, at the height of the political turmoil, ended up superseding the Central Committee Secretariat.

Our proposed radio station project became a significant part of the agenda for the party-to-party meeting. This time the powers in Peking were prepared to view our clandestine broadcasting proposals most favourably. Not only would China provide the site and equipment, she was also amenable to supplying the technical staff to operate it. Our task would be to provide and train the broadcasting and production people. As it turned out, it would take two years before our network was up and running.

We were less fortunate when the issue of the 'banishees' was raised. A great number of them were Malaya and Singapore born. According to Chinese statistics, more than 5,000 of our members had been banished to China since the outbreak of the Emergency in 1948. If we were to take statistics covering exiled supporters and family members into consideration, the number by 1966 was over 20,000. In the pre-Emergency years, the colonials generally banished small groups. Once the Emergency was declared, the 'banishees' were transported in large shiploads, sometimes numbering in the hundreds per batch. British statistics show that in the two-month period alone between November 16, 1950 and January 15, 1951, some 2,812 Chinese 'persons and dependants' were ordered to leave Malaya and transported to Swatow on a Norwegian-owned vessel.[29]

We proposed that any CPM member deported in this manner be eligible to rejoin our armed struggle. We knew the numbers would be substantial. Our plan was to collect all willing recruits from the ranks of the exiled and relocate them to an area close to the southern Chinese border with Laos. There we would set up one or two collective farms on which we would not only produce our own food requirements but also train the recruits in guerrilla war tactics. Cultural Revolution emotions were running high and consequently much emphasis was being placed on world revolution. We felt sure our idea of providing the comrades with intensified military training on the farms, then sending them overland in batches to our frontline operations, would be well-received.

Kang Sheng rejected these ideas outright. We then switched tack. We pressed for our banished people to be granted membership in the CPC. But even this was dismissed. The same explanation Kang Sheng had given me during an earlier one-on-one meeting at his bungalow was repeated – the CPC had changed its policy toward banished fraternal party members since the dissolution of the Comintern in 1943.

I was told that at the end of each party-to-party session, Kang Sheng and his people worked into the small hours to prepare summaries of our discussions. These were forwarded to Mao himself. With the party-to-party talks completed, arrangements were made for us to meet Mao for substantial discussions. These occurred in late January 1967. I was accompanied by Lee An Tung, Musa Ahmad and Chen Tien. The Cultural Revolution was at its height. A rebel group had taken over the leadership of Shanghai city.

We were summoned to Peking's Great Hall of the People on Tienanmen Square. As a secret party we were not afforded the privilege of moving into the Great Hall through the front entrance located on the main boulevard. Instead, we were taken via a side door.

Kang Sheng was in attendance with two leading officials from his department. Chen Tien was there to record the minutes. The CPC Chairman began by asking us how the party-to-party talks had gone. But, significantly, Mao wanted to talk to us about the Cultural Revolution. I quickly gained the impression Mao had become quite isolated from his party's leadership. This meeting was in such contrast to our spirited exchanges in Wuhan two years earlier. As the desultory conversation progressed, I wondered whether Chen Tien would be allowed to continue with his notes. Amazingly, he was.

This lengthy get-together was, I believe, Kang Sheng's way of demonstrating to Mao and the CPC leadership his ability at solving problems among the fraternal parties. The message now was that we should abide by the dictates of the Liaison Department. We had made our representations at the party-to-party gatherings. We had seen Mao. We were to be given the radio station facilities we had been seeking for three years. The next word would come from Liaison Department representatives.

*   *   *   *   *

Circumstances were such that when the order came for us to move our entire CPM offices south to Hunan in 1969, I was deeply involved extricating myself from the political quagmire created for us by the Cultural Revolution. Ah Hai initially had to go in my place.

In Hunan, the CPM was allotted facilities in the middle of a heavily restricted military area bearing the codename Project 691. It took a 12-hour overnight train journey from Peking to reach our new complex. Project 691 encompassed what appeared to have been a recently vacated village located in hilly terrain. Our broadcasting station was underground, dug into the side of a hill. Nearby was a bungalow assigned to us as an administrative building.

Our broadcasts commenced from Hunan in November, 1969. We decided on the call-sign 'Suara Revolusi Malaya' – Voice of the Malayan Revolution. Programmes were beamed across the region via a powerful 20-kilowatt transmitter. We had two wave-lengths and as far as I know, nobody ever tried to jam us. From the feedback we received, our members and sympathisers all tuned in eagerly throughout Malaysia and Singapore.

Our announcers, production and clerical staff were also housed in Project 691 quarters. The Chinese technicans stayed in a separate section, but within the same project area. In the years we operated from Hunan we had little communication with the population outside our perimeter fence. Day-to-day supplies were provided by the Chinese authorities. Although some distance from Peking, the location of our radio station still enabled us to get regular and prompt deliveries of all the newspapers we requested. The Chinese arranged for subscriptions and we placed orders for all the Malaysian and Singapore newspapers in English and Chinese. We also received regularly *The Times* of London and *The Age*, a morning daily published in Melbourne. We read and commented on stories carried by *The Economist*, *The Far Eastern Economic Review*, *Asiaweek*, *Time* and *Pacific Affairs*.

At the outset, we broadcast in three main languages: Mandarin, Malay, and Tamil. Three announcers were attached to each section. We added English when we succeeded in recruiting a number of university students. These came in the mid-1970s from universities in Singapore and Malaysia. Despite what the Special Branches of the two countries were saying about Suara Revolusi's new recruits at the time, there were no communists among them. They were nothing more than radical or progressive leftists. A Malaysian Chinese girl named Juliet Chin was one of them. Contrary to speculation, her fellow Singapore University colleague and friend, one Tan Wha Piow, never joined us.

As much was made of the Juliet Chin saga in the Singapore press, I would like to set out a few facts for the record. Miss Chin came to us through a Hong Kong student contact who had originally gone on a scholarship to the island republic. The young man had been influenced by communist ideology during the 1967 Red Guard riots in the then Crown Colony. In Singapore he became embroiled in student activism and met Miss Chin. Hours before the local Special Branch was due to arrest him, he fled through the university campus disguised as a woman. He subsequently crossed the Causeway and entered Johore. In Johore Bahru he was apprehended and charged with illegal entry into Malaysia. His case eventually was heard in Kuala Lumpur and he was ordered deported to Hong Kong. Back in the colony, Juliet Chin approached him and offered to join our movement. But our leaders felt she was inappropriate material for jungle living and instead offered her a job with Suara Revolusi. Miss Chin gave the impression she was a Marxist socialist. We regarded her merely as a liberal socialist. She certainly never joined the Party.

As our programming settled down we began receiving numerous requests from Chinese living in different parts of South East Asia seeking enhanced Suara Revolusi coverage in various Chinese dialects. Foremost was a requirement to serve the Betong Chinese community. At first I felt things were becoming unwieldy. I was against the idea of spreading into too many dialects. My views were outweighed by popular demand and so we had to recruit more announcers.

All the families of our once Peking-based Party members were now living in a Hunan village, about three hours drive from our radio station. This had involved a movement of some forty people – including 20 children – from the national capital. Ten of these children belonged to CPM members working underground back in Malaysia. They had been shipped to China and placed under our care while their parents, living with the constant fear of arrest, undertook precarious tasks on behalf of the Party. All our children were enrolled in a rural school and my wife was assigned to care for them.

When a demand for more announcers came from our Central Committee on the Thai-Malaysia front line, it was suggested we employ our middle school teenage sons and daughters in this capacity. I was personally against disrupting their studies. The children, on the other hand, were most enthusiastic about the idea of becoming radio announcers. Eventually I had to comply with the front line request.

So we began training another set of recruits. By this stage we had some 30 announcers attached to the radio station. I remained troubled by the fact that the education of the students had been so abruptly interrupted. As the dust of the Cultural Revolution swirled about us, schools closed down all over the country and Hunan province was no exception. In desperation I again turned to the Liaison Department representatives within our station facilities. Could they assist us in establishing a night school for our young people? As it turned out, the representatives were most sympathetic. They themselves were also feeling the negative effects of the Cultural Revolution and were frustrated over the impact it was having on young lives. The matter was taken up at the provincial level. Shortly thereafter, three teachers from the Hunan teachers' training college were seconded to our radio station and night classes began.

*　　*　　*　　*　　*

Back in 1964, I had suggested to the CPM leadership it was time I returned to the front. The Central Committee disagreed with my proposal. I argued I had been away too long from the front line and as such was not qualified to lead the movement anymore. I even offered to resign as Secretary General to make my move south easier. This, too, was rejected. In fact, I had requested a transfer to the front when the CPM reverted to armed struggle under the advice of Peking in 1961. On that occasion our Central Committee accepted Siao Chang's proposal for me to remain in China for at least another three to four years to expand links to the Chinese leadership and fraternal parties.

*　　*　　*　　*　　*

In 1969, before Richard Nixon was elected president of the USA, he wrote a lengthy article in the United States quarterly, *The Diplomat*. His essay indicated he would, if elected, withdraw American forces from the land war in Vietnam. The text was translated into Chinese. I received a copy and studied it closely.

Soon after he won the election and became president, Nixon flew to Guam and there announced his *Guam Doctrine*. It set down a programme for a US military withdrawal from Vietnam. America, he said, would henceforth only support those people who had the will to fight communism. No more would she commit American fighting forces to an Asian land war. By the end of March, 1973, the last US ground force unit had been withdrawn from the Vietnam theatre.

When Cambodia and South Vietnam fell to the communists in April, 1975, I was in Hunan. Since 1968-69 we had been purchasing weapons and ammunition from blackmarket arms dealers in southern Thailand. Despite the difficulties we were encountering with the resuscitation of our armed struggle to Peking's recommendations, we were emboldened by the international scene. We felt certain the tide was turning inexorably in the communist world's favour, particularly as far as South East Asia was concerned. With the overthrow of the Phnom Penh and Saigon regimes, we accelerated our blackmarket arms and ammunition purchases. These weapons were of US manufacture and came from both Vietnam and Cambodian battlefields. Huge numbers were available and the prices were certainly right. Conveniently, we had substantial funds at our disposal.

We mainly purchased M-16 assault rifles and stocks of ammunition for our various weapon categories. Ultimately, we were hoping regional developments would continue moving to our advantage to the point where we could begin absorbing new recruits. We were looking to building up a 3,000-strong army once more. In October, 1975, there was a student revolt in Bangkok. It seemed like more good news. More than 2,000 young men and women moved from leading universities to Thai communist jungle camps. In 1979, the Vietnamese invaded Cambodia and then the Chinese attacked the northern border reaches of Vietnam.

I went to Cambodia in October, 1975 – six months after the Khmer Rouge takeover. I was on a special flight from Peking carrying Pol Pot's wife, together with Ieng Sary and his wife, back to Phnom Penh. I had asked to go in order to see for myself what was happening there. When the flight arrived at Pochentong Airport I was told to wait on the aircraft until the VIPs up front had left the cabin. I was met by a senior Khmer Rouge official and taken to a bungalow formerly occupied by one of Lon Nol's senior generals. It was located very close to the compound that formerly housed the US Embassy.

The Khmer Rouge held a welcoming dinner for me to which Pol Pot came and it was then I met him for the first time. The following day the Khmer Rouge leader came to my bungalow and gave me a lengthy analysis of the history of the Cambodian Communist Party. He explained how it had come about as an off-shoot of the Indo Chinese communist movements and was initially led by a Vietnamese. Pol Pot made no effort to mask his dislike of the Vietnamese. He recalled his student days in France where much of his time was spent in the company of Marxist members of the Communist Party of France. He then detailed how he returned to Cambodia in 1953, eventually to work as a teacher in a Buddhist temple school.

Pol Pot talked about his early days in the Khmer communist movement and spoke of how much the Geneva Agreement had worked against their interests. Rallying some of his colleagues, he had set about re-building the Cambodian communist party in the late 1950s. It finally evolved into a new clandestine movement in 1960 following an inaugural secret meeting at Phnom Penh's railway staff quarters. It was symptomatic of the suspicion in which they held the Vietnamese that the fledgling communist re-grouping agreed, from the outset, to adopt a very cautious approach to dealings with their ideological opposite numbers in Vietnam. They would establish links but never share party secrets.

As he was telling me these things, I couldn't help but be reminded that he had just come to power through strong Hanoi backing. This fact appeared in no way to have blunted his deep reservations about the Vietnamese in general and their communist movement in particular. I had difficulty in determining the political direction of his remarks. I listened without comment. The last impression I wanted to give was of a guest interfering in a fraternal party's affairs.

By 1967-68, Pol Pot went on, his party had felt strong enough to start taking action. Prince Sihanouk's response had been to seek the liquidation of the entire Khmer communist leadership. Khieu Sampan, the party's second most senior official, was arrested and sentenced to death. The night before the scheduled execution, he was sprung from detention with the help of the Chinese Embassy which also aided his escape to north-east Cambodia. Pol Pot indicated he thereafter joined his deputy. Gradually they developed a small guerrilla force. Soon the Vietnamese were offering help. When Pol Pot subsequently travelled to China, the Peking leadership also promised to give him support.

As the Khmer Rouge leader explained it to me, his party started receiving regular supplies of arms and ammunition from the Chinese. These were sent south down the Ho Chi Minh trail. On numerous occasions Chinese weapons, earmarked for his Khmer communists, had been commandeered by the North Vietnamese Army. Thus, the animosity between the Khmer Rouge and the Vietnamese communists deepened. Pol Pot confided that when they were about to liberate Phnom Penh six months earlier, he and his Central Committee had become deeply worried that their plans would be pre-empted by the North Vietnamese who appeared anxious to march on the Cambodian capital themselves.

Turning to the present, Pol Pot maintained that Sihanouk had emerged as his main problem in the immediate post-liberation period. The then prince came in from China, stayed for a while and then went back. Pol Pot was concerned about the power base that might one day rally behind the deposed royal.

I went on a tour arranged by the government and remained in Cambodia for three weeks. Phnom Penh was a ghost town. All city dwellers had been forced into rural settings. I spotted people whom I took for Khmer Chinese. But they were too frightened to speak to me. They would have been too frightened to speak openly in Chinese. I spent a few days in the southern port city of Sihanoukville and a night in Kompong Thom in central Cambodia.

*   *   *   *   *

I returned to Peking at a time when the Cambodian revolution was being warmly praised by Chinese officials. I had reservations about what I had just seen but talked about this to only a select few of the Peking-based CPM leadership. I mentioned that the Khmers were very good fighters but also voiced my concerns. Khmer Rouge policies, I said, were leading to excesses. I was particularly disturbed about the evacuation of the civilian population in the cities to work in the countryside. That seemed to me to be a recipe for disaster. In the long run, I told them, it simply wouldn't work.

Back in Hunan I suppose I should have been elated by the recent liberation of the three Indo China territories. But for all the good news we were receiving about the successes of our fraternal parties in Vietnam, Laos and Cambodia – struggles with which we were so ideologically aligned – there was always that final psychological reckoning. Where now did the CPM fit into the overall scheme of things?

Our 1959 decision to abandon armed struggle had been reversed two years later to accommodate Peking and Hanoi and their Indo China aspirations. While the military momentum of the North Vietnamese, the Viet Cong, the Pathet Lao and the Khmer Rouge had steadily expanded from 1961 onwards, the CPM had managed only intermittent strikes south of the Thai-Malaysia frontier. In the 1970s our movement was fast becoming paralysed by self-destructing rivalries and ill-conceived front line decisions. I will touch on these in the following chapter.

Meanwhile, the only project that seemed to be working for us at this time was Suara Revolusi. It was with relief – and perhaps in search of reinvigoration – that I readily immersed myself in our broadcasting functions during those brief periods I could wrench away from the ever-mounting internal CPM crises demanding my intervention. As the months passed following my return from Cambodia, however, I began feeling decidedly uneasy about the long-range prospects for even Suara Revolusi. Massive political upheavals were underway in The Middle Kingdom. The Cultural Revolution was petering out. By 1976, both Mao and Chou En Lai were dead. In October that year, the Gang of Four led by Mao's widow, Chiang Ching, had been arrested. Deng Xiao Ping, who, at the height of the Cultural Revolution had been accused of being a 'capitalist roader,' emerged from his third period in disgrace in 1977.

By the following year, Deng's rehabilitation was complete and it was both internationally and locally acknowledged that he was the real power behind Mao's anointed successor, Premier Hua Kuo Feng. It was also during 1978 that Deng launched his monumentally ambitious 'Four Modernisations' campaign which looked to stunning advances for China in agriculture, industry, science and technology and defence. The Peking propaganda machine characterised Deng's daring enterprise as 'The New Long March' designed to launch a revitalised China on the world stage.

By 1979, I learned from the deputy head of the Liaison Department that the Chinese had formally requested the fraternal Thais tone down their radio's criticism of the incumbent government of Thailand. Specifically, Peking requested that there be no more derogatory remarks made about the Thai Prime Minister, General Kriangsak Chamanand. The fraternal Thais had objected to the request and opted instead to shut down their station that had been broadcasting for several years from Chinese territory with the call-sign 'Voice of the Patriotic Front'. My informant was adamant that China had not ordered the closure of the Thai network. It had been a decision, he said, reached independently by the Communist Party of Thailand. I listened to what I was being told and made no comment.

I well appreciated Peking was supplying military equipment to the Khmer Rouge who were then at war with the Vietnamese. The Chinese supply routes ran through Thailand. Without them the Khmer Rouge could not receive the Chinese aid. Kriangsak was providing these facilities in the name of 'relief' for the Cambodians. A large part of this was flown into Thailand aboard Chinese aircraft. Some of it, I know, never reached the Khmer Rouge. The Chinese accepted this as an inevitable flaw, endemic to the arrangements. The bulk of Peking's aid, however, reached the Cambodian communists.

As Deng Xiao Ping himself personally explained to me, Thailand was the Khmer Rouge link to the outside world. If the Khmer Rouge wanted to get high-ranking officials to international meetings they had to travel from the border areas through the Kingdom to Bangkok's international airport. Similarly, all access to world organisations like the United Nations had to be coursed through Thailand. Kriangsak was very accommodating. So the Chinese had a vested interest in ensuring Kriangsak was neither antagonised nor undermined by a China-based clandestine station. Had the radio been based outside China, I'm sure that would have been acceptable.

I felt certain the Thai communists would eventually set up 'Voice of the Patriotic Front' from a location outside China. I was surprised when they did not. I never found out why and never asked. There was an element of suspicion between the CPM and the Thais. If we had probed as to why they had closed down, they would have considered it meddling in their business. They would also have suspected that we intended reporting whatever they said to the Peking authorities. By the same token, we decided it best not to explore the matter further with the Chinese.

As it turned out our clandestine station functioned without interruption until 1980. In December that year I was summoned to a meeting with Deng at the Great Hall of the People. As soon as I learned Deng wanted to see me, I immediately suspected it had something to do with Suara Revolusi. The Peking leadership had created a very friendly atmosphere for Lee Kuan Yew the previous month. It was widely noted in the Chinese capital that the Singapore leader's visit had been very successful.

I had long thought Deng held a grudge against me. Before the Cultural Revolution erupted I often saw him. He frequently briefed fraternal party leaders permanently based in Peking. He was particularly keen to inform us about the Sino/Soviet problems and China's interpretation of these. We used to speak openly then. Unfortunately, during the Cultural Revolution, we in the CPM had joined in the general anti-Deng clamour. Pointedly, he hadn't bothered to meet me since his return to power in 1978. I therefore felt, as we hadn't spoken for 14 years, there must be a very sensitive matter he wished to discuss with me on this occasion. Otherwise he would just have sent an emissary.

When I walked into Deng's office that morning he was particularly friendly. I recognised an official from the Liaison Department who was the only other person in the room. He was there to take notes. Deng motioned me to sit on his good hearing side. He explained he had become profoundly deaf in one ear. I sat down and Deng offered me tea. We sipped as we talked. He asked after my health, the CPM, our guerrillas and my committee comrades. The preliminaries over, his tone changed as he turned and said: 'I have brought you here in order to talk to you about your radio station. We would like you to close it down.'

I didn't have to ask him why. Straightaway he went into an explanation. Lee Kuan Yew had been speaking to him a few weeks earlier. The Singapore leader, he said, had come on behalf of four Association of South East Asian Nations (ASEAN) countries – Singapore, Malaysia, Thailand and Indonesia. Specifically, Lee had told him how he had taken the trouble of speaking to the leaders of the four respective governments prior to his China visit.

Lee had requested that the Chinese authorities order the closure of Suara Revolusi. Deng explained to me that unless the radio ceased operation on Chinese soil, it would be very difficult for the ASEAN bloc countries to lobby African and Latin American support for the Khmer Rouge. The Americans were working hard at blocking Khmer Rouge participation in the world body. The African and Latin American votes were essential if the Cambodian communists were to retain their presence in the General Assembly. As long as they had their UN seat, the Khmer Rouge had a legal standing in the international community and could therefore justifiably move in and out of Thailand and through to other countries.

I listened carefully to Deng's account of his meeting with the Singapore prime minister. Understandably, I was not happy. But I recognised the pointlessness of arguing. There was a long gap between the end of Deng's remarks and my response. I mentally put together my reply with great care before delivering it. I remember very clearly to this day exactly what I said. 'I thank you for informing me about this matter,' I told Deng. 'As a guest here in China I, of course, respect your decision.' The implication of what I said did not escape the Chinese leader. He knew what I felt and how much I disapproved of his request. He also knew that I had no alternative but to adhere to his remarks.

Deng's reaction was, I suppose, to be expected. For a few seconds his face remained expressionless. But soon he telegraphed his feelings and on this occasion his face looked particularly severe. I asked him when he would like us to cease broadcasting from Hunan. He replied: 'The sooner, the better.' He went on: 'Lee asked me to stop the broadcasts immediately.' Deng then claimed having informed the Singapore leader it would take time to persuade the CPM to take such action.

Lee, he said, had pressed him again for an early closure. At this point, Deng revealed, he got impatient with his guest. These were Deng's very words: 'I told Lee - I can close it right now. All I have to do is telephone Hunan and tell them to cut the power to the station. No more broadcast!' He said the Singaporean had pressed too hard. Lee had then backed down. He agreed that some time should be given for the Suara Revolusi broadcasts to wrap up. Deng then turned to me and said: 'This means we have to close down the station – not immediately – but quite quickly.'

I asked the Vice Premier what he considered would be our latest possible deadline. Deng said the UN General Assembly would convene in September the following year, 1981. 'You should,' he advised, 'be closed down some months before this in order to give ASEAN time to complete its lobbying.'

'Could you give us until August next year?' I asked.

His reply was swift. 'No. That would not give them sufficient time to lobby for the votes we need.' Deng thought for a moment and then added: 'You should have it wrapped up by the end of June.'

Deng's face relaxed and a faint smile spread across it. 'Don't worry, Chin Peng,' he said, 'now that we have reached an understanding about the radio station I can reassure you about our support for the other areas.' He went on to mention that China's financial aid to the CPM struggle would continue. Our meeting concluded in a calmer and more agreeable atmosphere than it had begun. It had lasted just an hour.

I reported in full to my Central Committee members including Siao Chang at the front. Everyone appreciated the situation and understood the workings of the Chinese. There was no point in arguing with them. I received no request for an extension of time-frames from our southern Thai headquarters.

Sometime later, the Liaison Department informed us that once Suara Revolusi ceased broadcasting from China, all its equipment would belong to the CPM. We could take everything away and do what we liked with it as long as it was not on Chinese soil. It was a generous offer but rather impractical. We were not like the Thais who, when they dismantled their station, had a convenient land route available to them for extracting the equipment. Our Hunan transmitter and associated gear amounted to a huge volume of stores. It would be impossible to carry all these along tracks, over rivers, across international borders and down through enemy territory in Thailand.

However, I told our Liaison Department contacts that I was anxious to get an alternative radio transmitter operating in our southern Thailand base area and perhaps spare parts for this could be made available. These could be smuggled through Thailand via the underground. We needed to purchase some portable radio equipment from China. Could some extra finance be found for this? The reply was quick and in the affirmative.

Unbeknown to me, while I was negotiating with the Liaison Department, my front line Central Committee men had begun exploring the possibility of purchasing a small mobile transmitter to take the place of our Hunan station. Siao Chang had called on the advice of our radio technicians in the jungles. They pronounced the project feasible. However, they had a list of components that could not be purchased on the local market. Could we supply from China? Of course we could.

Suara Revolusi closed down in Hunan on the night of June 30, 1981. Early the following morning we commenced broadcasting from our new mobile transmitter on the Thai-Malaysia border. A few days later, the Liaison people informed me that the US State Department had contacted the Chinese Embassy in Washington. The Americans had lodged a complaint with a senior diplomat about the continuing broadcasts that should have ceased. The Americans clearly knew all about the arrangements and timing of the Suara Revolusi shut down.

I was informed that the Chinese diplomat had suggested that the US complainant should check the broadcasting location of the CPM radio. It certainly wasn't coming from Chinese soil. Nothing more was said about the issue by Washington.

By then our radio station had actually changed its name. It was now transmitting as *Suara Demokrasi* – Voice of Democracy.

Chapter 28

Talk of spies and the terrible trials

Five months before Malaysia was born, Indonesia's President Sukarno began ordering guerrilla incursions of so-called 'volunteers' into the territories of British North Borneo and Sarawak – both slated to become part of the new Federation. Malaysia, he claimed, was nothing more than a neo-colonialist plot initiated by Britain. Indonesia would crush it 'before the sun rises on January 1, 1965'.

Within 12 months of Malaysia's inauguration on September 17, 1963, the whole expanded Federation concept was exhibiting very serious signs of falling apart. Destructive forces were now being directed from both without and within.

Almost from day one, observers of the Malaysia scene began chronicling the outward manifestations of personal and political rivalries between Federal leaders in Kuala Lumpur and their Singapore state counterparts. Differences in outlook and approach grew steadily irreconcilable. Tensions spread quickly down to grass-root levels. A Kuala Lumpur Malays versus Singapore Chinese political stand-off solidified.

On July 21, 1964 – Prophet Mohammed's birthday – Malay-Chinese race rioting erupted in Singapore. Security authorities quickly enforced an island-wide curfew. Despite this, violence persisted. By the time the curfew was lifted on August 2, 23 were dead and more than 400 others had sustained serious injuries.

As Federal and state politicians struggled to restore a semblance of normalcy, Sukarno substantially intensified his so-called confrontation of Malaysia by sending a sea-borne guerrilla mission to infiltrate coastal western Johore in the Pontian area. This was led by Indonesian regular troops but included radical Chinese volunteers who had earlier been recruited from the general area of the incursion. They had been among hundreds of like-minded Chinese who had secretly gone across to Indonesia from the Malayan peninsula and Singapore as Jakarta's 'crush Malaysia' programme escalated. Through a combination of Indonesian inefficiency and mixed luck and intuition on the part of security forces, the Pontian infiltrators on this occasion were swiftly routed.

Then on September 2, Indonesian paratroopers and volunteers landed in the jungle east of Labis township in central Johore. More rioting in Singapore between Malays and Chinese began on the same day and continued intermittently for the next

72 hours. A nationwide state of emergency was declared and a second Indonesian airborne incursion soon followed. The Malaysian Deputy Prime Minister, Tun Abdul Razak, flew to Singapore on September 9 where he claimed to reporters that government agents had uncovered an Indonesian-engineered plot to create chaos, confusion and communal strife on the island.

That, to me, sounded about as valid an explanation as the ploy more commonly used by politicians of blaming communists for everything that went wrong. In the CPM we wondered why we appeared to be escaping authority's finger of accusation this time. It couldn't have been our total lack of involvement in the crisis. That hadn't stopped them accusing us on previous occasions and, of course, wouldn't stop them in future.

At the United Nations in New York, Malaysia's Home Affairs Minister, Dr Ismail, claimed his nation had become the target for 'blatant and inexcusable aggression' on the part of Jakarta. In response, Dr Sudjarwo, Indonesia's permanent representative to the UN, argued his country could treat its neighbour exactly as it wished. As far as Indonesia was concerned, he said, Malaysia did not exist.

Some months earlier, Washington had equivocated on the Malaysia issue, a move from which Jakarta had gained considerable confidence. Now faced with undeniable evidence of open aggression by Jakarta, the hedging superpower was forced to take a firm position. US Ambassador Adlai Stevenson denounced the remarks of his Indonesian counterpart and told the Security Council that 'the outer reaches of restraint have been reached'.

In China, I carefully monitored press reports detailing how British Gurkhas had been rushed to contain the Labis incursions while troops of the 1st Battalion Royal New Zealand Regiment were conducting mopping up operations near Pontian. Royal Air Force Javelin fighters patrolled against further incursions while Hunters, flying from RAF bases in Singapore, targeted Indonesian intruders east of Labis. British Bloodhound missile systems had been 'activated' in Singapore and were said to be 'fully operational'. For a few days the Royal Navy seriously contemplated sending the aircraft carrier, HMS Victorious, together with two destroyer escorts, HMS Caesar and HMS Cavendish, through the Sunda Straits at the very heart of the Indonesian archipelago. It was to be a show of strength against Sukarno's repeated threats to close the long recognised international waterway to foreign shipping. At the last minute the Admiralty, doubtless directed by the British Cabinet, opted for discretion and instead dispatched the carrier force via the less controversial Lombok

Straits, still within the archipelago but some 700 miles to the east. Immediately the threat of major military action subsided.

Defence units deployed against the intruding Indonesians came from the Commonwealth Strategic Reserve that, since Malayan independence, had operated under special defence treaty arrangements with Kuala Lumpur. The treaty had recently been extended to cover Singapore and necessitated formal requests from Malaysian political leaders before it could be activated. These had certainly been forthcoming as had the Tunku's urgent request for 'immediate Commonwealth aid'. The following month, Deputy Prime Minister Razak was in Bangkok for negotiations which resulted in a signed defence agreement between Malaysia and Thailand purportedly aimed at eliminating the CPM guerrilla army in the border regions. Clearly, Malaysia was worried that we would take advantage of the general turmoil engulfing the country.

News of the new border defence arrangements left Siao Chang unfazed at our Betong headquarters. He remained confident that the understandings we had reached with the Thais would hold. Moreover, he was busy deploying to our main base camps volunteer recruits who, by now, were moving up to join us in substantial numbers from Malaysian population centres. Indonesia's confrontation policy had begun to undermine Malaysia's economy. Unemployment was growing as external trade figures for the first seven months of 1964 showed a decline of 19 per cent over those for the same period the previous year.

The mounting internal political differences within Malaysia ultimately culminated in Singapore's unceremonious ejection from the Federation in August, 1965. This and the ongoing external military threat from Jakarta saw Kuala Lumpur's attention distracted from the communist threat. The immediate result of this was a boost to our recruitment drive. In addition, we received increased financial backing from our supporters which we were able to feed back into our underground efforts. Guerrilla ranks swelled during this period from the low-point nucleus of 300 to 500, then to 800 and up to around 1,000 by 1967-68. In the aftermath of the Kuala Lumpur race riots in May, 1969, we received a flood of enthusiastic young Chinese recruits. They came in response to a word-of-mouth campaign by our underground activists. We indicated that if anyone was interested in joining the CPM guerrillas, assistance to move north was readily available. Our numbers then expanded to well over 1,600 hard-core fighters. At that stage about 50 per cent of our guerrilla army comprised recruits from Malaysia with the remainder coming from southern Thailand.

Following attacks by our guerrillas on road and bridge construction sites in the northern reaches of Perak state, the Malaysian government built a number of pillboxes to guard areas considered vulnerable to further interdiction. This one was placed to defend a major bridge carrying the east-west highway across a large man-made lake network.

By 1968, we were ready to move some of our units south of the border again. In the intervening years our base camp locations had undergone some strategic re-positioning. We still had our headquarters in the same general deep jungle area north of Betong township. Sadao camp, however, had moved to a point north-east of Sadao and a relatively safe distance in from the nearest border segment with the Malaysian state of Perlis. The two other camps, Betong East and Betong West – so named for their relationship to the main road running south and linking Betong with the frontier – were in well concealed positions some distance from the highway. All four camps had underground tunnel networks. The headquarters camp had the largest and most sophisticated of these. It spread through three storeys and contained offices, a print room with printing press, sleeping accommodation for 100, a meeting hall, a sewing room, a laundry and toilets.

Guerrillas for the 1968 forays south operated to plans drawn up by our front line Central Committee headed by Siao Chang. We started by sending groups to reconnoitre our old areas of operation. Essentially these were intelligence gathering missions with the associated requirement of creating working links to our underground network. But they were also charged with re-establishing deep jungle bases in certain areas if conditions proved favourable. Northern Perak state was our first target area. Fairly early in the operation, government security forces were alerted to these activities and began counter measures. The decision was then taken at Headquarters to push our units further south down the peninsula. Revised orders thereafter sent guerrillas into southern Perak, over to Pahang, northern Selangor and as far south as the Negri Sembilan border regions. At this point, the government side uncovered our presence in these areas and manoeuvred to cut our supply lines. While we were contemplating the recall of all units back north again, our communication lines were unfortunately severed.

*   *   *   *   *

As early as the 1968-69 infiltrations into Malaysia, Siao Chang was reporting to me that he believed a number of enemy agents were operating within our headquarters camp. The suspicion was that these agents had been seeded, either separately by Thai and Malaysian Special Branch operations, or, as the result of a coordinated intelligence gathering programme between the two neighbours.

Some of the suspected infiltrators were Thai Chinese. Others were Malaysian Chinese. Faced with what appeared a threat to the Party's very existence, senior Central Committee members appointed camp investigators to gather evidence on the suspects. Investigations continued during the following two years. A number of trials were held and these concluded with the execution of several convicted 'traitors'. For a brief period it seemed the action taken had nipped the problem in the bud and the front line Central Committee went ahead and issued instructions for a new wave of southern infiltrations.

However, in the early weeks of 1970, Siao Chang reported a second spy threat. This time a ring of traitors was supposedly plotting a coup at Headquarters. Investigators appointed by the camp Central Committee arrived at the conclusion that among the Thai Chinese recruits who had joined us over the previous decade, 90 per cent were spies. Ah Hai, my closest colleague in Peking, was never convinced of these claims. In the beginning I took a neutral stand. In any event, there was nothing I could do about the events which were to follow. In retrospect, not only was the whole issue handled very badly at Headquarters, but the means by which we had long dealt with suspected traitors was shown to be deeply flawed.

Betrayal in guerrilla ranks was regarded as the most serious of all crimes against the Party. Punishment was normally death by execution. However, if an accused admitted the error of his ways and managed to identify others involved in the plot, it was possible for him to escape the death penalty. This meant he would be immediately disarmed, held under detention and required to undergo extensive re-education. Expanding investigations resulted in alleged spy after alleged spy seeking leniency by naming more and more alleged accomplices. Under recognised procedures for handling suspected enemy agents, jungle trials had to be held promptly and sentences carried out swiftly. This, of course, led to an alarming attrition rate at Headquarters via the trial process.

Based on the reports of the investigators, the Central Committee, rather than containing the threat as on the previous occasion, informed the three other camps of the perceived danger they were facing from planted enemy agents. To make matters worse, Siao Chang forwarded to the other camps lists of suspected agents named in the numerous confessions that had been forthcoming. And so the decay spread.

Knowing full well that they would be led into the jungle and shot as soon as trial proceedings were over, petrified accused desperately rattled off names of fellow members. Inter-camp suspicions fired-up when accused from one camp started implicating guerrillas from another. Quite clearly, the numbers being framed in this way had no relevance to the true spy menace in our midst.

At jungle trials, a large number of guerrillas from Headquarters and Betong East camp were found guilty of being enemy agents. All members of the unit holding the trials were required to be present to hear the charges and evidence. Guilt or innocence was determined by a show of hands. If a camp determined a man was to be tried, it was understood he was to be found guilty. Anyone who believed the accused was innocent would himself become immediately suspect should he openly indicate his true feelings. Those who insisted on their innocence usually had to contend with three or four accusers. It was one word against three or four others, all desperate to save their skins. As a result, the man pleading innocence was pronounced 'intransigent' and deserving of the maximum penalty. Under procedures dating back to the Japanese occupation years, there was no appeal process.

These terrible trials, limited primarily to Headquarters and Betong East, took place throughout 1969 and 1970. Sadao and Betong West both rebelled. Both rejected the way Headquarters was handling the matter. Betong East, on the other hand, fell in line with Headquarters.

In 1970, the Sadao faction held what they termed a 'party meeting'. There were about 100 in attendance but only half that number were actually members of the CPM.

Significantly, there was no Central Committee member based either at Betong West or Sadao. To my mind this indicated a most serious gap in command line of control. Sadao and Betong West maintained, quite correctly, that there simply could not be so many traitors operating in their midst. To have named one or two might have been acceptable. But the numbers supposedly involved grew beyond credibility. Both Sadao and Betong West camps went on to allege that, as the spy infiltration claim was so outrageous, it indicated the Central Committee itself was now under the control of enemy agents.

They charged Siao Chang with being a 'revisionist' and stooge of the Soviets. Siao Chang, of course, had visited Moscow on several occasions. He had obviously admired Russian scientific achievements. But to say he was a Russian stooge was nonsense. Siao Chang's monumental error was his failure to appreciate the extent to which the enemy agent phenomenon had been created from outside to encourage the CPM's disintegration from within. And what a devastating ploy it was proving.

Both splinter camps set up their respective Central Committees. They termed themselves rebels and started up their own parties. The Sadao lot proclaimed themselves the Communist Party of Malaya (Revolutionary Faction). Betong West identified their party as the Communist Party of Malaya (Marxist/Leninist). Sadao went as far as to break all radio contact with Headquarters and to all intents and purposes functioned independently from then on. At Betong West, where they maintained limited radio contact, the camp Central Committee refused to follow Siao Chang's orders. Its members were equally reluctant when it came to carrying out investigations into the alleged conspirators in their midst.

An overflow of madness from the Cultural Revolution saw waves of paranoia surging through all four camps. Our guerrillas began sensing conspiracy after conspiracy. They suspected the spy trials themselves were being manipulated by enemy agents to eliminate our entire army. They perceived they were being pitted against one another to ensure eventual self-destruction. Sadao and Betong West refused to participate in our 'Second Emergency' campaign so that all guerrillas for these operations had to be deployed from Betong East. The initial rebellion involved a total of around 250 guerrillas. But the two break-away camps soon organised recruitment drives until their collective numbers had swollen to some 500-strong.

*　　*　　*　　*　　*

It was well into 1973 before I began receiving more detailed reports about the executions that had followed trials at Headquarters and Betong East. The vague and unconfirmed numbers baffled me. Someday, I knew, the Party would have to confront reality and explain the staggering extent to which the spy crisis had been taken. Devastating for me personally were the purge killings of Ah Chung, the old World War 11 veteran from Pahang, and Wu Tien Wang, with whom I could trace CPM associations going back to my teenage years in Sitiawan.

Implicated by a female friend of his wife, Ah Chung was arrested in Betong East in 1971. He inexplicably made a confession. This was a terrible error on his part. As a Central Committee member he would have had his case reconsidered if he had maintained his innocence. Ah Chung had been charged with betraying the Party. The circumstances cited at his trial had no relevance to the allegations against him. I knew that as soon as I received a report on his case. It was a shameful way to have dealt with a man who had devoted his life to the cause. I thought of all the instances when he had narrowly escaped the mass arrests of senior CPM officials plotted by Lai Te and the years he had spent in jungles fighting first the Japanese, then the British. I pondered the ignominy of his end.

Wu Tien Wang, I learned, was executed at Headquarters. I had known him well because he was one of my mentors in the Party. A Sitiawan tailor's son, he was two or three years my senior. I well knew Wu liked to talk. Indeed, he often talked too much. But when arrested, he refused to make a confession. 'If you want to kill me, just kill me,' he told his accusers, calmly, almost indifferently. As I read about his case I was bewildered. Here was a man who had the reputation of always being frightened in a firefight. Yet, faced with his imminent end, he had turned to his executioner and quietly asked for three cigarettes and a cup of samsu. Wu's last requests were granted.

Also among the reports I received was one mentioning the case of Lee An Tung's wife, Ling Ying Ting. At Headquarters she faced two charges of treason and was found guilty on both. Like Wu Tien Wang, she was also from my hometown. She had been a timid schoolgirl. One of her elder brothers and I had been best friends and we later worked together in the MPAJA. He was tortured by the Japanese, divulged information, and turned an active agent for the invaders. I got to know his sister better when she and Lee An Tung served with us in Peking. By then she had changed from the shy schoolgirl into a self-proclaimed theoretician.

The report indicated that Lee An Tung was present at his wife's trial. He heard the evidence against her as all members of the camp had done and voted in the show of hands along with everyone else. Upon Ying Ting's arrest, Lee An Tung had asked his wife to confess. She had refused. I believe he had the power to seek a reprieve on her behalf. After all, he ranked No 1 in the camp and was the CPM's propaganda chief. As far as Party hierarchy was concerned he ranked above Siao Chang. The problem was that he had isolated himself from the rest of the front line leadership when he first returned from Peking. He made several sweeping comments to the effect that nothing had changed in the ten years he had been away. His adventurist ideas which included targeting Thailand as one of our enemies and launching company-sized offensives were rejected by the North Malayan Bureau. Siao Chang thereafter emerged as de facto No 1.

Some years later Lee Ann Tung wrote me a letter. In it he declared his wife had been involved in activities against Siao Chang and the Northern Bureau. He made the point that these had not been directed against the Central Committee headed by

Chin Peng. It was a curious statement because the Northern Bureau had always consisted of a majority of Central Committee members.

*   *   *   *   *

Party financial affairs were a critical factor at this time. We were channeling funds from Peking to Headquarters as usual on a regular basis. But when the purges started, the normal disbursement of money to the other three camps was immediately interrupted. It so happened that just prior to the escalation of the rebellion, the Sadao camp had received a major injection of capital to fund the purchase of weapons. Instead of buying arms and ammunition, they used these funds to maintain themselves while they went ahead and argued with Headquarters.

After they broke away from us, the Sadao rebels drove one or two small guerrilla attacks across the Malaysian frontier into the state of Perlis. They also tried to expand and had recruitment drives in Kedah and Penang. However, the selection was lax and indiscriminate. The new recruits could not stand the pressure of life in the jungle. Eventually many of them became deserters.

On no occasion did the Sadao group attempt incursions into the Headquarters' operational area. This was partly due to the existence of a special area between the Betong West and Sadao camps controlled by a loyal Malay unit headed by Rashid Maidin, the same man who had accompanied me to the Baling talks. Later on Rashid was transferred to the Kelantan border region to strengthen the Malay presence there.

Meanwhile, Betong West was able to make contact with our underground network in Malaysia and entice quite large groups of would-be guerrillas to move north across the Thai border. These new recruits came mostly from Selangor and Johore. Because of its close proximity to Betong township, the Betong West rebels enjoyed considerable influence over the town's population. This meant greater access to funds resulting from donations and taxes imposed on merchants. So successful was the camp's tax collection that it not only became self-sufficient but actually began operating with a budget surplus.

As time passed, Betong West tried to cross the key north-south road from Betong township. In effect, they were seeking to move east and grab territory near the Perak border. This was a critical move against our interests as our routes to the south passed directly through this area. We warned them that unless they moved out of our territory we would attack. They refused. Then they targeted our food dumps. So we defended heavily and set up a number of ambush positions. Subsequently, we succeeded in ambushing Betong West patrols on at least two occasions. This resulted in a propaganda battle with Betong West claiming that the 'old CPM' were trying to kill them off.

*   *   *   *   *

At the height of all our internal problems, it was announced that Tun Abdul Razak who had assumed political leadership of Malaysia from the Tunku in September 1970, would be visiting China from May 28 to June 2, 1974. He would be flying to Peking on the invitation of Premier Chou En Lai. It had been obvious for some time that Malaysia and China were working towards establishing formal diplomatic ties. Indeed, during his visit, the Malaysian Prime Minister and Chou issued a joint communiqué normalising relations. While Razak was being feted in the Chinese capital, we struck road and dam construction sites in northern Perak. Our aim was to demonstrate the CPM's independence from China's diplomatic arrangements. This was fully consistent with Chinese communist doctrine. Fraternal parties had the freedom to work independently of Peking's direction. Some 18 months earlier, as it happened, I had been summoned by Premier Chou to Peking's Assembly Hall. He was under instructions from Mao to brief me on the CPC's intentions of working towards formal links with Malaysia. At this meeting I was assured the Chinese government would adhere strongly to Mao's teachings on the separation of state-to-state relationships and party-to-party arrangements.

All in all, we regarded our limited attacks in Perak as useful exercises. We didn't kill anyone. We targeted only construction equipment and the impression I got was that the message not only went through but was also understood. Comment was made in the West to the effect that China did not appear to be calling the shots for the CPM.

*   *   *   *   *

Betong West made its formal break with the CPM on August 1, 1974, by issuing a bombastic manifesto which, in effect, declared war on what it termed the 'Chin Peng-led revisionist clique'. Peppered with Maoist terminology, their document appealed to 'friends in the communist army and party' to choose between the 'fragrant and poisonous flowers', repudiate the old leadership and strip it of all its powers. It accused the party's 'old guard' of manipulating the aftermath of the May 13, 1969, Kuala Lumpur riots. The suggestion was that we had initiated a purge specifically to smash the communist army, dismember the Party and extinguish forever the fires of revolution.

Three months earlier, the same Betong West rebels had, on their own initiative, undertaken a most audacious mission. They succeeded in assassinating the Malaysian Inspector General of Police, Tan Sri Abdul Rahman Hashim, as he was being driven in broad daylight through the streets of Kuala Lumpur. By October, anxious to capitalise on the IGP killing and other demonstrations of their militancy, the Betong West rebels undertook a peninsula-wide flag and leaflet propaganda campaign. Boldly advertising their newly proclaimed Marxist/Leninist sobriquet, they raised red flags and distributed their pamphlets in Selangor, Negri Sembilan, Malacca, Johore, Pahang, Penang and Kedah. They even managed to hoist a flag atop a pylon at Kuala Lumpur's Merdeka Stadium and spread pamphlets in various sectors of the Federal capital.

Faced with such a flagrant challenge, the Malaysian government was forced to issue an expedient response. On November 1, a week after the first appearance of the flags and leaflets, a statement was issued in the name of Tan Sri Ghazali Shafie, then Minister for Home Affairs in the government of Prime Minister Tun Abdul Razak. It amounted to the most detailed summary of alleged communist activities issued by Federal authorities in more than a decade. It claimed that I had narrowly escaped assassination following an attempted coup within the CPM in 1967. These events, it said, had led to an initial split in party loyalties. A second rupture reportedly followed three years later when Yat Kong, commanding officer of our 8th Regiment, had allegedly refused to carry out orders to execute suspected spies.

The government statement referred to us as the 'old' Communist Party of Malaya (CPM). It identified two southern Thailand-based splinter groups – the CPM (Marxist/Leninist) and the CPM (Revolutionary Faction). It went on to reveal remarkably accurate statistics. The CPM, it claimed, had 970 armed guerrillas; the CPM (Marxist/Leninist) 150 and the CPM (Revolutionary Faction) 260. A further 200 guerrillas, the government report claimed, were operating south in Peninsular Malaysia.

Clearly, Tan Sri Ghazali had received some good statistical intelligence. I can only surmise that the Home Minister and his advisers had then gone ahead to package a propaganda exercise aimed at intensifying divisions in the communist camp, discrediting my leadership and deterring more so-called disillusioned youths from turning communists. Much of the report was devoted to a personal smear on my character.

It said I had immediately ordered the execution of 20 new recruits, considered 'government agents', when I first discovered the plot against my leadership. The Home Affairs statement also had it that I later became convinced my main guerrilla base was 'infested with spies'. To solve this, I had gone on a killing rampage. It was alleged that – around January or February, 1970 – I ordered the executions of all new recruits above 12 years of age who had joined the CPM movement after 1962.

I've never met Ghazali but I've read about him. I know he was a tough administrator and was affectionately referred to as 'Guz' by those close to him. He is about my age and I recognise his war record with Force 136, the same unit with which I was so closely associated. I judge him to have had a broad background in intelligence gathering in the war against the Japanese. With this and the intelligence data he most certainly possessed about Chin Peng, I really must question how he could truly believe I would target children for elimination in a mass extermination programme. I have since rationalised that the minister was acting on the advice of propagandists. I'm sure he was.

Wartime propaganda caters to mass audiences that can never put into proper perspective its underlying motivations and intended psychological impact. If you are authoritatively branded a mass child killer in a war situation, few will detect the campaign's realities. The overwhelming majority will accept descriptions at face value. Fling enough mud and it tends to stick. Multiply the child-killer accusations of November, 1974, by all the other occasions British colonial and Federal authorities employed similar techniques and you might appreciate how the fearsome Chin Peng image developed and took hold.

*　*　*　*　*

The Sadao rebels, despite their claim to be the 'Revolutionary Faction,' proved far less combative than Betong West's 'Marxist/Leninists'. Still, Sadao sought to drag me into their orbit in their stand against Siao Chang and Headquarters. They called an emissary from our communications and transit centre in Bangkok, briefed him about their complaints and requested he relay their sentiments to me in China.

Technically, the emissary should have reported to Siao Chang as the acting Secretary General was the regional commander-in-chief. Matters became complicated when Bangkok police raided the homes of several of our members, taking them into custody. Fearing he, too, was on the wanted list, the emissary decided to report directly to me in China. As it was obviously too dangerous to travel openly by air to Hong Kong, he opted for the overland route.

Despite their disaffections, the rebels still wanted me to recognise the bogus Central Committee they had established. I thought their request was ridiculous. I could not go against my Central Committee especially as most of its members were on the front line and I was in the rear. I discussed the crisis very fully with the Politburo members resident with me in China. Ah Hai strongly disagreed with Siao Chang's actions. Based on his experience he maintained it was outrageous to contend that so many agents had infiltrated the party. Ah Yen, the only ever female member of our Politburo, took strong issue with Ah Hai. I remained neutral. So, on the whole, Siao Chang had the backing of the Central Committee split, as it was, between Headquarters and China.

Siao Chang sent me a report setting out his side of the story. He told of how he had discovered the spy threat among the new recruits to our guerrilla ranks and how he had instituted investigations and trials to weed out the traitors. His report came via our radio link and could only be transmitted in short segments. It was a most unsatisfactory means of dealing with such a complicated crisis. I asked Siao Chang how I should reply to the Sadao group. I was in a very delicate position. I could not disregard Siao Chang and flatly oppose his view that the spy threat required such drastic corrective steps.

Prior to the rebellion the veteran leader of the Sadao guerrillas, Pai Tse Mu, had been taken suddenly ill with suspected cancer. He had been moved to China for treatment where it was discovered he was only suffering from gall bladder problems. The corrective surgery was done and the patient was convalescing by the time we were grappling with the rebellion. Siao Chang and I decided that the returning emissary should accompany the recovering Pai back to the front line. The two of them took the return journey overland.

On orders from Siao Chang, the emissary escorted Pai to Headquarters for discussions aimed at solving the rift. These were held but when Pai returned to Sadao his fellows branded him a tool in a Headquarters' plot to recapture the leadership. He was given a week to leave camp. He promptly rejoined Headquarters.

This archival photo of **Pai Tse Mu** (right), leader of the Sadao camp, was taken in May, 1946, in Kensington Gardens, London, where he went, along with the MPAJA contingent, to march in the Victory Parade. Pictured with him here is **Deng Fuk Long**. Pai was also the man sent by our Northern Bureau to make clandestine contact with Siamese communists in 1950.

As a result of the purge tactics we had earlier employed, we found ourselves in an invidious position when it came to confronting the renegade rank-and-file. We now considered they probably comprised mainly genuine revolutionary guerrillas. But, they were being led by a few disgruntled opportunists made bitter by our previous mistakes. Clearly, we couldn't regard all of them as reactionaries.

A campaign by Betong West to recruit those comrades who had been banished to China during the Emergency years soon followed. This was a fertile area. Chin Peng was portrayed among the exiles as being in the rear, enjoying the good life. On the other hand, life for the 'banishees' was harsh. The exiles were soon convinced that I had abandoned them.

I certainly understood their day-to-day problems. But, try as I might, I was simply in no position to help those living in exile. The Chinese leadership prohibited me from contacting our banished members in China. They were considered overseas Chinese. I was, to all intents and purposes, a foreign guest. They were no longer my CPM members.

Betong West agitators ignored the Peking regulations and went ahead to recruit dissatisfied Malayan-Chinese exiles in China. They found so many sympathisers that they quickly managed to form a branch of the CPM (Marxist/Leninist) party in Kwantung province. In mid-1980, acting without any invitation, the Betong West guerrillas sent a four-man delegation to Kwantung, travelling by plane via Hong Kong. From Kwantung they requested a meeting with the Liaison Department in Peking.

In the Chinese capital, Liaison officials listened to their story and then insisted that as it was all an internal party affair – what Mao would call an 'internal contradiction' – they must speak to the CPM leadership resident in China. Among the names mentioned for them to contact were Ah Yen and Chen Tien. They flatly rejected the suggested names and insisted on speaking only to Chin Peng.

This paved the way for an official meeting between us. Otherwise I would never have considered such an event as I knew it would be strongly opposed by Siao Chang and his displeasure would lead to more complications within the Party. I agreed to meet the head of the delegation, Chang Chung Min, whose name literally means 'loyal to the people'. The meeting was held in Peking and I had to travel from our radio station complex in Hunan especially for it.

Liaison officials decided to talk directly with the rebels first before I got to the Chinese capital. They told them in no uncertain terms that Siao Chang could never be regarded as a revisionist or an enemy spy. They explained Siao Chang had lived in China for many years and they knew him well. They could vouch for his revolutionary credentials. As far as Chin Peng was concerned, they said, he was blameless. He simply wasn't present in southern Thailand when the troubles occurred.

The Liaison men then asked the rebels to meet me with the objective of looking at two specific areas. Firstly, our talks should be aimed at bringing to an end internal politicking between CPM factions. Secondly, the open warfare between the groups should cease. When I got to Peking, the Liaison Department briefed me and urged that I limit my efforts to settling the issues they had already raised with Chang's delegation. The Peking officials well understood the problems. They recognised they were deep-set and appreciated that solutions could not be found overnight. They also knew of our earlier efforts to contain matters and how these had clearly failed.

Chang began by apologising for attacking my leadership. I told him there was no need for apologies. Then he zeroed in on the purge. 'What are your views of Siao Chang's order and the ensuing executions?' he asked. I reminded him of Party tradition. Even I, as Secretary General, could not speak out behind the back of the Central Committee. He eventually gave me a pledge that things would improve. However, as soon as he was back in Betong West, troubles resumed. I learned he even told his followers Chin Peng disapproved of Siao Chang's handling of the spy crisis.

Later, I requested the Liaison Department to allow members of Chang Chung Min's committee, who had been in the MPAJA, to meet me in Peking. At the same time, I asked that an equivalent group from the Sadao rebel camp be permitted to travel to China for a separate set of meetings with me.

In due course the rebels arrived. The Sadao group came first. They were very frank and I appreciated their directness. They wanted me to proclaim, once and for all, whether our Northern Bureau's 1970 decision to purge the ranks of suspected spies was just. I again referred to Party tradition. I could not voice personal opinions behind the back of the Central Committee.

The Sadao representatives made it plain that unless they received a clear-cut answer there was no point continuing the meeting with me. I was not particularly concerned by this abrupt stand. I was satisfied enough if we could just put an end to inter-factional politicking and fighting. As it was, the Sadao group had limited their moves against Headquarters to attacks via leaflets. There were no skirmishes or firefights with this rebel group.

In contrast, Betong West had launched four or five armed attacks on Siao Chang's forces. These, as it turned out, were enough to demoralise their own rank-and-file. They hadn't become members of the movement to kill one another.

Both rebel groups wanted me to give them official backing in their struggle against Siao Chang. They had failed to realise what I had earlier established – namely, that majority opinion within the CPM Central Committee stood behind Siao Chang. Even prior to the rebel delegations' arrival in China, a senior Liaison Department official had diplomatically hinted to me that I should perhaps make an open statement clarifying my stand on the purge before the situation deteriorated further. I explained then that if I were to openly support the rebels I would trigger a further split in the party. At this point the CPM would have self-destructed.

In the end, both the Marxist/Leninists and the Revolutionary faction surrendered to the Thai authorities.

In 1987, they gave up their weapons, one by one, at two special surrender ceremonies organised by the Thais. In return, each one received a red flower and photographs were taken. Those involved in the so-called 'welcome-back' programmes were mistakenly depicted as being members of the CPM headed by Chin Peng.

I find it particularly ironic that the ones who surrendered were those who had, for more than 15 years, underlined their revolutionary zeal with the bracketed adjuncts of 'Revolutionary Faction' and 'Marxist/Leninist'. They had portrayed themselves as the superior revolutionaries and had damned our leadership for being 'revisionist'. Each had its own explanations and rationalisations for capitulating. I tried to follow these for some time then, quite frankly, gave up.

To this day, I remain convinced that, by the time of the rebels' capitulation in 1987, their leaders could no longer be regarded as ideologically motivated. I felt sad for the rank-and-file. But I could not have made these observations then. I would have been accused of simply discrediting those who opposed me.

Chapter 29

The door to peace swings open

We were determined to be guided by the lessons of Baling. From 1955 onwards, the CPM vowed never to pursue peace if it meant surrendering to the enemy or, for that matter, accepting any form of settlement that smacked of capitulation. I was adamant about this as were all my fellow members in the Politburo and the Central Committee. Now, in the late 1980s, we wanted peace just as genuinely as we had wanted it at Baling. But it still had to be honourable. It had to be peace with dignity, something denied us during my talks with the Tunku and Marshall 33 years earlier. The sufferings of our comrades over four decades demanded no less.

In early 1987, our headquarters were located some 50 kilometres north of Betong by road and then some distance into the hinterland from the main highway. In the aftermath of the splinter groups' capitulations, the Thai military sent peace feelers to us there. They sought our agreement to terms that had previously been accepted by the break-away rebels. We rejected these overtures outright. The Marxist/Leninists and Revolutionary Faction followers had handed in their weapons and surrendered. We would not. Part of our post-Baling resolve included firm views on how the delicate issue of our weapons might be handled. We would never hand them across to the enemy, either publicly at an official ceremony, or privately. Either, in our view, would be a sign of capitulation. We could, however, agree to their destruction under supervision. Even then, we would demand certain conditions for this, such as the employment of a supervisory body.

When we rebuffed the Thais, their Southern Army immediately launched what would develop into a search-and-destroy campaign designed to hunt down our remaining fighting units and force us into submission. At the time, our army comprised five main guerrilla strike forces. Headquarters stayed mobile in the jungles north of Betong. Our Betong East comrades also became mobile, operating in the southern Betong Salient area. We had three Malay units to the east in Narathiwat province, one moving in deep jungle north of the Malaysian frontier. To the west, we had a Malay-Chinese joint unit operating in the Yaha area. In all, we numbered some 1,300 guerrillas.

Heavy Thai military pressure began in mid-1987 and lasted well into 1988. We were armed with modern assault rifles, had all our positions protected by booby-traps and were able to employ home-made mortars to great effect. For their part, the Thais flew air strikes against us, called in naval artillery to support ground action and even introduced their crack navy commandos. Throughout the entire year-long action we suffered four killed. The Thais, on the other hand, suffered heavier casualties.

Our guerrillas, of course, could never have emerged ultimately victorious against the Thai Army. The CPM's political leaders and field commanders alike recognised this. So did the Thais. But equally important, both sides appreciated that the CPM had the ability to maintain a protracted jungle-based struggle. If necessary, we could have continued fighting for a decade or more, inflicting further casualties, draining the Kingdom's defence budget and depriving the government of opportunities for developing its rich border provinces.

In the Peking summer of 1988, I first received reports that the Thais were again suggesting a peace initiative. I immediately sent word to Siao Chang that he was fully empowered to negotiate on behalf of the CPM. I would come into the picture only when all issues were settled. Siao Chang knew as well as I did the parameters within which we could negotiate – particularly as far as the fundamental 'no surrender' aspect was concerned.

Siao Chang and Lee An Tung considered the first Thai overtures as very much preliminary approaches. As it happened, a two-pronged peace initiative was developing. The second prong came from the Malaysians and was obviously coordinated between Bangkok and Kuala Lumpur. The government of Malaysian Prime Minister Datuk Seri Dr Mahathir Mohamad made contact with our Malay troops, but at a relatively low level. These exchanges were also exploratory in nature. We were invited to send a delegation of our Malay comrades to Penang and arrangements were finalised for a helicopter to pick them up at an agreed point on the Malaysian side of the frontier.

Our Malay guerrillas dispatched middle-ranking cadres to speak with the Kuala Lumpur representatives on this occasion. In Penang, our people met with Malaysian Special Branch officers. Some were from police headquarters in the Federal capital. Others were Penang-based. As it turned out, the Malaysians were somewhat disappointed we had sent what they considered a low-level delegation with no powers to negotiate. They had been anxious to show the CPM the progress that had taken place across the peninsula. Had our delegation been more high-powered, Penang would have been just the starting point of a rather grand tour that would have taken in other cities. It was now late 1988.

A second round of preliminary talks between our Malay comrades and the Malaysians took place in Haadyai, again without any signs of progress. Sensing the peace efforts were becoming directionless, the Thais re-entered the picture. A senior military officer suggested to our delegates that the CPM's Secretary General should, perhaps, be involved. He reinforced his advice with the offer of assistance to send a CPM emissary off to China to see me.

On receiving news of the Thai suggestion, Siao Chang immediately radioed me in Peking. I happened to be in hospital at the time undergoing my health check. I readily agreed to see whoever was tasked to meet me. By now the channel for communications was directly from the Thai military to CPM Headquarters and the initiative for negotiations was gaining momentum. Siao Chang agreed to venture from Headquarters and meet the Thai military in Haadyai. A special bungalow was arranged for our five-person delegation. As Siao Chang was ill, he was accompanied by a nurse. Also in attendance was our interpreter who could speak fluent Thai. Siao Chang brought along a radio transmitter to keep in contact with Headquarters.

The discussions proceeded smoothly enough until a point was reached when it seemed essential for Siao Chang to meet me personally and discuss the various offers being made by the Thais. Arrangements were promptly concluded for him to travel by air, first to Bangkok, then to Hong Kong and on to China. However, the Peking authorities were playing it very cautiously. They were insistent that whatever meeting took place between myself and Siao Chang be held outside Chinese territory. They wanted no part of the ongoing negotiations in case these ended in failure. Thus, Siao Chang and I arranged a secret rendezvous in Macau, details of which we even kept from the Thais. So strict was Peking's stand that they refused to issue me proper travel papers for my journey to the then Portuguese colony. I had to take the extraordinary step of procuring a genuine Filipino passport under a false name. This was accomplished through the Manila contacts of a Peking-based member of the Communist Party of the Philippines.

It was September, 1988. Siao Chang left his Thai escort, a police colonel, in a Macau hotel, giving the impression he was on his way to meet me in China. I was waiting in a private third-floor walk-up apartment in an old-styled colonial house. We hadn't seen each other for over 25 years. We hugged. It was a very emotional moment. I was shocked at how tired and sick he looked. He was pale and drawn. I first thought he was suffering from malaria. As the initial day of our discussions progressed I realised how truly ill he was. Clearly it was not just malaria. I advised him to see a local Chinese doctor the following day. Siao Chang took some persuading. He kept insisting he had his medication from a Haadyai specialist. Finally, Siao Chang took my advice. However, the Macau physician failed to give him a thorough examination. The doctor merely prescribed more medicine to control the fever.

There were so many things we could have talked about. We could have reviewed the quarter century that had slipped by since we last saw each other. But there was no time. Very briefly we exchanged notes on old comrades. Who had survived. Who had been killed. I tried to raise the issue of the purge that had taken place early in the1970s. I remembered the reports of the terrible trials and executions but knew I had to tread cautiously in confronting my frail comrade. Choosing my words carefully, I suggested our handling of the spy crisis had led to excesses. Siao Chang became visibly agitated by my remarks. I quickly dropped the subject. I also decided to save all reminiscing and small-talk for the informal moments when we were lunching or dining together. First things first. We were there to discuss prospects for peace.

Siao Chang began by briefing me on the various approaches made by the Thais and the Malaysians. He was convinced both were genuine in their separate desires to find a solution to the lingering problem of what to do with the CPM units in southern Thailand. He assured me he was talking to Thai officials fully empowered to make decisions. In particular, he mentioned a very senior Thai military officer, Major General Kitti Rattanachaya, who was then deputy commander of the Kingdom's Fourth Army based in the southern region. This man was the real driving force behind the Thai peace initiatives.

In turn, I was able to bring Siao Chang up to date with yet another avenue for peace which had opened up earlier in the year, this time in Hong Kong. Prime Minister Mahathir had given the green light to contacts made to us in China through Hong Kong business outlets with links to Chinese government agencies. The word passing through these channels was that Malaysia was keen to talk seriously.

Datuk Abdul Rahim Mohamed Noor, then Director General of Malaysia's Special Branch, brought Yau Kong Yew, one of his former deputies, out of retirement for a special assignment. The highly experienced Chinese officer would function in the Hong Kong project and act as coordinator. In relaying messages to me, the Chinese in Peking did not reveal the identities of those involved on the Malaysian side. They merely indicated that representatives of the Malaysian Prime Minister had travelled to Hong Kong to make contact with the CPM through business channels. None of the original messages passed on this way named me personally.

Siao Chang and I talked far into the night. One of the pertinent points I raised concerned the nature of previous negotiations that had been undertaken between the Burmese communists and the Ne Win government. There were lessons in these for the CPM. According to Thakin Ba Thien Tin, the BCP leader, the Burmese talks had collapsed because the Communist Party of Burma had insisted on being officially recognised by the Rangoon leadership.

I confided in Siao Chang that Deng Xiao Ping had been encouraging me since 1981 to seek avenues for a peace accord. This had been part and parcel of his policy for opening China to the world. Much later, the Liaison Department had made it clear to me there was a limit to China's ongoing financial support for the CPM's armed struggle. In fact, from that point onwards, Chinese financial assistance to us was systematically cut back.

I had, of course, been closely monitoring evolving Peking–Kuala Lumpur relations. When he visited Kuala Lumpur in November, 1978, Deng had announced in a press conference that China, henceforth, regarded her relationship with the CPM as a fact of history – something that should be left behind. In the months that followed, China underlined the Mao initiated policy of maintaining two levels of international contacts. One was at the party-to-party level with fraternal movements. The other was at the state-to-state level. The state-to-state contacts would take priority. This two-level approach was further explained by Chinese Premier Zhao Ziyang when he visited Thailand in February, 1981.

But in March, 1980, the Malaysian government headed by Prime Minister Datuk Hussein bin Onn, had chosen to demonstrate most graphically that, if China persisted in its party-to-party support of the CPM and our continuing Suara Revolusi broadcasts, then Kuala Lumpur was free to place its own interpretations on the two-level policy arrangements. Just hours before Malaysia officially welcomed visiting Chinese Foreign Minister, Huang Hwa, at the state-to-state level on March 14, she hanged three ethnic Chinese communists who had been held in detention for over three years.

Two of those executed at Kuala Lumpur's Pudu Jail on this occasion – Lim Woon Chong and Ng Foo Nam, both 23 years old – had been convicted in March, 1978, and sentenced to death for the murder of a former Perak state police chief. The retired officer had been killed in Ipoh in November, 1975. It was revealed at the time of the executions that Lim had also been awaiting trial on charges of having murdered Malaysia's Inspector General of Police, Tan Sri Abdul Rahman bin Hashim, in June, 1974. The third man sent to the gallows that day, 25 year-old Lee Hong Tay, had been convicted three years earlier of having in his possession two revolvers, a pistol and 27 rounds of ammunition. The three executed men had been members of the break-away Betong West group – the self-styled CPM Marxist/Leninists.

I told Siao Chang I felt confident this time we would arrive at a settlement as long as we negotiated carefully. Our primary preconditions to peace remained unaltered from the days of the Baling talks. No handing over of weapons. No surrender.

The word I was getting from the Chinese was that I should leave the negotiations to the front line people. I should only appear in public when all matters had been concluded and an agreement was ready for signing. I was content to go along with this advice in the light of the problems I had encountered at Baling. I therefore emphasised to Siao Chang that I should not become involved in the negotiations. He would have to handle these himself with the backing of our Central Committee front line comrades. He was in full agreement. So it was we went our separate ways on a positive note. Both of us felt the peace that had eluded us for almost 40 years was now within reach.

Although physically unwell, Siao Chang's spirits were further buoyed when, on reaching Bangkok, he was invited to be the house guest of Thai Army Chief, and acting Supreme Commander, General Chavalit Yongchaiyudh. We viewed General Chavalit's gesture in this instance as proof of Thailand's sincerity. The Kingdom's Prime Minister at the time was General Chartchai Choonhawan. After a few days in Bangkok, Siao Chang, by this stage very ill indeed, travelled as far as Haadyai where he stayed in the bungalow put at our disposal by the Thais. As he was too weak to return to our jungle headquarters, he asked a number of Central Committee members to join him. Lee An Tung was actually en route to Haadyai and had reached the jungle fringe when he heard a Radio Malaysia broadcast quoting General Chartchai, then on a visit to southern Thailand. The Thai Prime Minister was reported to have said surrender negotiations with the CPM were going well. The moment he heard the word 'surrender,' Lee An Tung and his party turned round and promptly went back to their base camp. The Thais were quick to issue a clarification of the reported remarks. They assured Siao Chang the Thai Prime Minister had made no mention of a CPM surrender.

Upon Siao Chang's return to Haadyai, Rahim Noor arrived from Kuala Lumpur for preliminary discussions. He wanted to discover whether I had given my deputy any special instructions. He was told Chin Peng was keen for the negotiations to proceed. In their discussions, Siao Chang passed on my demand that, unlike Baling, all formal negotiating sessions should be open affairs. This way the press could attend and report verbatim. Our rationale was that we had nothing to hide and were more than anxious to have our positions scrutinised publicly. This proposal was quickly rejected. It was argued that such an arrangement would not be beneficial to the smooth progression of the negotiations. We accepted this. However, there was general agreement to our second position that the final signing of any agreement reached must be done in an open place before the world press.

We were all for having the entire agreement, if and when reached, openly and publicly declared. But the Malaysians would have none of this and made strong representations to the effect that some aspects must be kept classified. They maintained there were issues far too sensitive to be placed in the public arena. With some reluctance, we eventually agreed to keep parts of the agreement secret.

Then Rahim Noor quizzed Siao Chang as to whether the CPM would be prepared to lay down their arms. Siao Chang well knew my position on this point and was ready with his answer. He assured Rahim Noor that, providing the negotiations went well, an acceptable way would be found to handle the delicate matter of weapons. Rahim Noor seemed satisfied with that reply and the door to peace talks appeared finally to have swung open. It was agreed that the negotiating sessions would take place on the Thai resort island of Phuket.

We were asked to submit the names of the CPM delegation and immediately the old communications bogey resurfaced. For some reason – aggravated by Siao Chang's illness – the Central Committee submitted my name and those of Chen Tien and Rashid Maidin. It was a repeat of our Baling panel and, as such, quite unacceptable, given my determination to remain in the background until agreement on the more sensitive issues had been reached. I quickly corrected the error. Instead, I arranged to be represented by Politburo member Madam Zainon – known within the Party as Ah Yen. Peking-based, Ah Yen would travel to Thailand for each negotiating session and return to report directly to me. In effect she would act not only as my emissary but also as an adviser to our delegation.

We purposely kept Lee An Tung out of the negotiating picture. We did not want to appear to be overloading our team and repeating the same error we made in Baling. After December, 1955, the Tunku gained propaganda mileage by claiming my very presence indicated my eagerness to seek peace. Errors notwithstanding, my chances of pulling off a reasonable arrangement in 1955 had been extremely slim. Even if I had been more flexible, I am sure the British would have found a way to block whatever it was I offered. This time, however, I sensed a genuineness of approach that was sorely lacking in the leadership I met at Baling.

*   *   *   *   *

Once again we established maximum and minimum bargaining positions. Our maximum stand was a requirement for recognition of the CPM as a legal political movement. In reality we knew this had scant hope of success. We demanded all political prisoners being held in Malaysia be released. Our estimates were that some 100 communists were in peninsular detention centres. Associated with the prisoner release issue was a demand that the Internal Security Act (ISA) be repealed. Again, this was part of our maximum position for which we held out little hope. We further asked that the Kuala Lumpur War Monument featuring representations of Malaysian and British Commonwealth troops stepping on a fallen communist guerrilla be demolished. We sought acknowledgement of the CPM's contribution to the process of independence. This was a very important issue for us. We also sought the formal demobilization of our army and a gratuity paid to all those leaving its ranks. We proposed that those desiring to move back to their homes in Malaysia be allowed to do so freely, without detention or rehabilitation.

In all, five separate rounds of peace negotiations would be held at the Thavorn Palm Beach Hotel at Karon Beach, Phuket. The Thais had chosen the venue and the tranquil surroundings seemed to provide a positive backdrop conducive to big-picture solutions.

The conference seating was U-shaped. The Malaysian and CPM delegations sat facing each other at parallel tables. The Thais, like mediators, were positioned at one end between them. A special adviser table was placed beyond the open end of the 'U' at which sat Yau Kong Yew, the Malaysian officer who had been brought out of his Special Branch retirement. Beside him was CPM liaison officer, Ah Yen.

The Thai delegation consisted of four representatives led by Major General Kitti. The Malaysians also appointed a four-man negotiating team headed by Datuk Rahim Noor. Siao Chang was our chief negotiator, assisted by Rashid Maidin.

*   *   *   *   *

There was only one major piece of advice I gave our negotiators. Through Ah Yen I told Siao Chang, before the opening session, that he must avoid the trap I had fallen into at Baling where I had allowed Marshall to dominate on several critical issues. I had held back then for fear of the talks disintegrating into a personal showdown between myself and the Singapore Chief Minister. I urged Siao Chang not to allow either the Thais or the Malaysians to insult our Party. We wanted peace, but not with denigration or insults. If, for instance, they attacked us verbally we would have to retaliate in the same vein. If they resorted to calling us 'terrorists' we would not let this pass. We would insult back with the same degree of intensity.

At the first session held from February 2 to February 4, 1989, Rahim Noor delivered the opening speech and adopted a strong stand that reminded me very much of Marshall's Baling style. The Malaysian delegation leader held us responsible for continuing to fight the legitimate government of Malaya after independence in 1957.

Despite Siao Chang's illness he was able to summon up enough strength to deliver a strong rebuttal. He rejected Rahim Noor's suggestion that we had needlessly pursued armed struggle. He told the meeting that the war had continued after the Baling talks simply because the Tunku and his government had demanded the CPM submit to the indignity of surrender, incarceration and interrogation. In fact, Siao Chang – probably because of his illness – went too far. He referred to the Malaysian government as being a 'reactionary regime'. This was uncalled for as Rahim Noor had so far refrained from calling us 'terrorists'. It was an unfortunate mistake on our part. As soon as I received a copy of Siao Chang's speech I immediately advised him to tone down his rhetoric.

Following the tough opening stand by the Malaysians and our overly robust response, it was obvious that measures had to be put in place to ensure the talks did not break down in acrimony. On a CPM initiative, it was then agreed that, henceforth, there would be two types of negotiating sessions. One would consist of the regular tripartite gathering. The other would be private one-on-one sessions allowing the CPM to meet with either the Thais or the Malaysians. The arrangement would also give the Malaysians and Thais opportunities to get together away from our scrutiny. The private sessions would be neither minuted nor recorded. On the other hand, the tri-partite sessions would be fully video-taped. Copies of the resulting video tapes would be made available to all three parties.

For the first two or three sessions, the Malaysians flatly blocked our demand for recognition of the CPM as a legitimate party. Thankfully, the Thais intervened in what was fast becoming a deadlock. They pointed out to us that not a single regional country, outside Vietnam and China, recognised a home-grown communist party. Such a demand on our part, they said, was totally unrealistic. If we wanted the talks to progress we should drop it. We acceded to the Thai urgings but countered that we should be allowed, sometime in the future, to form a political party that was not in essence a communist party. At one point it was suggested we call ourselves Scientific Socialists which, as far as we were concerned, was essentially Marxist anyhow. However, in the end, the matter of a future party for us was resolved – we would be allowed to form a political party or parties within the Federal Constitution and the laws of Malaysia.

*　*　*　*　*

At the second round of talks, from March 15 to March 17, Siao Chang collapsed shortly after delivering his opening remarks. He was first flown to Kuala Lumpur and admitted to a special VIP hospital ward usually reserved for government ministers. Doctors diagnosed terminal liver cancer.

When his condition had stabilized somewhat, Siao Chang requested he be flown to China where his two sons resided. It was just six months since our reunion in Macau. He entered the foreigners' department of a military hospital in Guangzhou.

I was in Guangzhou at the time and went to see my old friend on the day he arrived. He was in terrible shape. He flitted in and out of consciousness and was only able to mutter a few words. I made a point of visiting him on almost a daily basis and watched his life slowly ebb away. He died within two weeks.

Chapter 30

Averting a recriminatory bloodbath

As the talks progressed from session to session, Ah Yen returned to report to me in Guangzhou. The Chinese had provided me with a house there and this proved far more convenient.

In his opening remarks to the second round of the tri-partite talks, Siao Chang had informed the gathering that, as he was feeling unwell, Rashid Maidin would be taking his place as chief negotiator for the CPM. Ah Yen became empowered to handle the closed-door sessions. When it became clear Siao Chang would not be returning to the ongoing discussions, I recommended to the Central Committee that Wu Yit Shih should be appointed to take his place. Wu, another Politburo member, was the director of operations for our highly sensitive underground network that functioned in Malaysia. Wu formally began negotiating for us when the third round of peace talks got underway on May 11, 1989.

It was during this third round that much of the earlier posturing by ourselves and the Malaysians began to subside. Rahim Noor helped a great deal in setting a new tone with his opening remarks when he referred to the absence of Siao Chang. 'We wish to place on record our appreciation for his contribution in the previous proceedings,' said the Special Branch chief. The Malaysians had done all they could for our comrade in what we regarded as a truly humanitarian gesture. Rahim Noor had been fully briefed on Siao Chang's prognosis and knew, as well as we did, that the old man was dying.

Our decision to abandon the demand for legalisation of the CPM had also contributed a great deal to the improved atmosphere of the talks. We then pursued our demand that Malaysia release political prisoners of all affiliations. The Kuala Lumpur panel denied they were detaining any prisoners. During a subsequent session, however, they announced there was no need for us to argue this point any longer. All political prisoners had been released.

The Malaysians raised the issue of a 15-strong extremist Muslim group that remained incarcerated. It was alleged they had plotted an armed revolt against the Federal Government. These people had no connection whatever to the CPM but the Malaysians asked whether we included them in our demand for a general political prisoner release. We repeated our position that all political prisoners of any persuasion must be set free. We argued that if the so-called extremists were to be kept under detention, they should be formally charged and produced before a court of law. Much discussion followed and the CPM ultimately compromised by not pressing the case for the alleged Muslim extremists.

As it transpired, one of the most important issues for us centred on whether the Malaysian government would recognise the CPM's role in accelerating the independence process leading to Merdeka. Would Britain have granted independence to Malaya as early as 1957 had the military activities of our guerrillas not been a factor in the equation? This was explored at length during the private negotiating sessions. Finally, Rahim Noor, speaking in the Malay language from notes in a fully recorded meeting, made the announcement that Malaysia did not deny or dispute the CPM's contribution to the struggle for independence. As to the extent of this contribution, he went on, there was no need to argue the matter in this forum. It should rightly be an issue left for historians.

This subject was one of those considered too sensitive at the time to be made public. But it was an absolutely fundamental issue for the CPM. Otherwise, how could I assure my comrades that we had, at long last, come to an honourable settlement? Given Malaysian political sensitivities then, we had to be content in the knowledge that the CPM's contribution to the independence process was finally recognised in a document of history. It was enough for us to have had it recorded and to have heard it as we did. It was not written down. But it was most certainly video-taped. I hold a copy, as do both the Thais and the Malaysians.

There was another particularly delicate aspect we felt obliged to take into consideration. This directly concerned Prime Minister Mahathir and his political power base. We had no wish to fan the peace process into a fiery political issue for his government. It was very evident there was considerable resistance within Malaysia to the whole idea of the talks and certainly to the proposed peace settlement with us. The Tunku, well into retirement, publicly took a very disparaging view of the negotiations underway at Phuket and of me personally. 'Once a communist, always a communist,' he told the press who had sought his opinion of Chin Peng. 'That means he will make trouble if given the opportunity.' Similarly slanted rumbles of discontent came from old-guard Malayan anti-insurgency warriors who were probably feeling sidelined. I mention these issues now as the sensitivities that were worrying back then have substantially diminished. It is about time historians began exploring these areas and putting perspective – sorely lacking in documentation thus far – into the record of history.

*　　*　　*　　*　　*

The peace negotiators needed statistics on our guerrilla strength and we produced these quickly. There were 1,188 CPM members on our list. Of these, 694 were Thai-born and 494 claimed origins in Peninsular Malaysia. The latter grouping included some 15 who came from Singapore but saw little chance of ever being allowed back to their homeland. Of those claiming roots south of the border, 402 were ethnic Chinese and 77 were Malays.

The Malaysians refused, throughout the talks, to define our guerrilla force as an 'army'. After much wrangling they agreed to apply the term 'armed units'. At the same time they flatly opposed the use of the word 'demobilization'. So when it came to the demobilization of our army we had to refer to the process as the 'disbanding of our armed units'. Our representatives got upset. During the days of the MPAJA, they asserted, we had used the word 'demobilization'. Why couldn't we use it now? The matter was eventually referred back to me in Guangzhou. I had to explain to our delegates that when we wound up the MPAJA the British had actually used the English word 'disbandment'. The Chinese press had translated this as 'demobilization'. I advised them to let the issue pass.

There was a similar problem of usage when it came to discussing the 'gratuities' for our 'disbanding armed units'. The Malaysians wanted the term 'monthly allowance'. It was agreed that each disbanding guerrilla opting to return to Malaysia would receive from the Federal government a lump sum of RM8,000. This would be paid in two instalments. The first RM3,000 would be made available on their immediate return. The remaining RM5,000 would be paid after three years. At first we objected to the split payment scheme. We were well aware of the reasoning behind the measure. It was both a matter of control and a test of our sincerity and goodwill. As I understand it, all outstanding final payments of RM5,000 were settled without complication. In addition, the returning guerrillas were paid a monthly allowance of RM300 for a period of three years. These funds were allocated to help them re-establish themselves in modern Malaysian society. In the end, a total of 330 former CPM members went home to Malaysia.

The Phuket negotiations also tackled the procedure to be adopted for the documentation of returnees. At first, the Malaysian delegation insisted that those wanting to return should assemble on Malaysian soil for processing. We strongly objected and maintained that all documentation should be undertaken in Thailand. In the end they agreed to our position. Thus, when the documentation was complete, the Malaysians would provide new identity cards (ICs) and deliver these to intended returnees before they moved south. Once in Malaysia, our former guerrillas, with their new ICs, would be free to go directly to their respective towns or kampongs.

The Thai government agreed that those opting to remain in the Kingdom would each be allotted a 2.4 hectare plot of land for cultivation plus a small building block on which they could erect a residence. Furthermore, each one would be paid a 'monthly allowance' of US$22 for a period of three years. The land for cultivation would be restricted to the southern provinces of Yala and Narathiwat.

*　　*　　*　　*　　*

The Malaysians had wanted us to close down our Suara Demokrasi radio station immediately following the signing of the accords. We opposed this on the grounds that the network could provide us with a most useful means of communicating with our followers. We asked to be given three months broadcasting time in order to carry the message throughout southern Thailand, Malaysia and Singapore. The Thais and Malaysians restricted us to one month but recognised, for the record, that the rhetoric of our radio was now in keeping with the spirit of the talks.

The Malaysians had wanted us to furnish them with a list of our underground members. Rather than betray our network, we offered to contact all activists via our own channels. We would be responsible for ordering the cessation of all CPM functions.

We explained to the Malaysians the complexities of our agent network and how it might take a year or more to contact its outer reaches without the facilities of Suara Demokrasi. If they would let us use our radio to instruct our followers to stop all underground activities, problems would be greatly simplified. Kuala Lumpur was adamant that such a step should not be taken. Malaysia felt it might reflect badly on the Federal government if Suara Demokrasi was used as an ongoing channel by the CPM to reach our activists.

So we came to yet another understanding. We agreed to close down our radio within a month and start contacting our underground through other channels. The Malaysians, for their part, gave their word they would avoid arresting any underground member found operating illegally and in ignorance of our instructions. If detected, underground operatives were to be privately informed of the new arrangements and merely told to desist. In the event, these arrangements worked extremely well. There were no arrests by the Malaysians and we effected a complete shut-down of all our operations. I can state this quite categorically.

*   *   *   *   *

Our argument against the war monument in Kuala Lumpur came to naught. We were asked what sort of memorial we preferred as a replacement. Our delegates suggested one that depicted the three main races of Malaysia – Malay, Chinese and Indian – fighting together for independence. After thrashing out the issue with us, the Malaysians took time out to confer with Kuala Lumpur. When the talks resumed, they informed us that the monument had resulted from an act of Parliament and therefore required another parliamentary decision calling for its removal if the CPM's demands were to be met. Everyone realised what this would have entailed. The peace negotiations would have stalled for good. The Malaysians advised that sometime in the future it might be possible to present another parliamentary bill for consideration. If passed, the replacement could be achieved. Not likely.

In the concluding phases of the Phuket peace talks' fourth round, when all key issues appeared to be settled in principle, I received a call in Guangzhou from Wu Yit Shih. He assured me it was time for me to start making my way to Thailand. I had been invited there by Thai Army Commander-in-Chief, General Chavalit Yongchaiyudh, himself. I informed the Chinese leadership in Peking of the developments and indicated I should soon be travelling south and therefore would need travel documents. This time the Chinese arranged these expeditiously and dispatched them to me in Guangzhou. I received a new 'alien' travel document. The space assigned for nationality details had been filled in by the Chinese with the word, 'Malaysian'.

The Thais kindly sent Lt Colonel Akanit Meunsawat to China to accompany me back to the Kingdom where a visa was awaiting me. We landed in Bangkok on October 27, 1989. General Kitti was waiting to receive me in the VIP room. I was

The Kuala Kumpur war monument we were so keen to have replaced. It was an issue we pursued at the Phuket peace talks.

driven from Don Muang airport to a private house on Sukhapiban 3 road in the district of Bangkapi. It turned out that I was to be General Kitti's house guest. For the next two days the Thai general and I spent many hours exchanging opinions on how to ensure that the next round of negotiations at Karon Beach – the fifth – would be the last and that peace could be established immediately thereafter. Kitti urged that the final tripartite talks be convened from November 2 to November 4. He wanted the official peace ceremony to be held before the King's birthday, which fell on December 5. My host said that I would be invited to attend the final talks on November 3. I would appear unannounced in Phuket. At this stage the Malaysians had not been told of my presence in Thailand.

Kitti left for Phuket ahead of me. We decided it would be best if I remained in Bangkok until the last moment. That would give the Thais time to inform the Malaysians of my intended arrival at the Thavorn Palm Beach Hotel. I reached Phuket on November 3 and was invited immediately by Rahim Noor for a very private tete-a-tete. Just the two of us.

The Special Branch Inspector was surprised that I spoke quite fluent Malay. I told him I had always had Malay friends and had spoken *pasar* Malay all my life. However, after the Baling talks I had made it a point to master the language. I had spent an hour a day with Rashid Maidin until he pronounced me competent.

Small talk over, Rahim Noor was anxious to settle some very sensitive issues. He asked point blank: 'Are you still hiding some weapons, Chin Peng? I must ask you this because we don't want a repeat of what happened in the aftermath of the Japanese surrender.'

There was really no point holding back at this stage. If I withheld information now, sooner or later the Malaysians would have found out the truth. So I told Rahim Noor frankly: 'Yes, Datuk, we are.'

He countered: 'Why don't you destroy them all?' After four rounds of peace talks the overall matter of our weapons remained largely unresolved. Some progress had been made, no doubt, but there remained important details to be concluded. We had suggested the arms be privately destroyed by our guerrillas. Our proposal had been rejected by both the Thais and the Malaysians. The compromise: the private destruction of 1,188 weapons – representing one weapon for every guerrilla in our force – to be witnessed by Thai and Malaysian observers. There would be no filming or photographing of this event.

The bargaining over weapons continued. I reasoned with Rahim Noor: 'The hidden weapons are considered surplus. It will be very difficult to convince my followers to give these up. They are stored underground. They would have to be located and dug up. I need time to persuade the comrades and then more time to locate our caches. Give me some time. I would need at least two to three years. When things settle down we can then move to destroy them.'

The senior police officer was anxious to establish exact numbers. I informed him that Party records indicated we had more than 2,000 individual pieces, including pistols, hidden underground. These were in addition to the 1,188 we intended destroying ourselves under the peace agreement. Rahim Noor wanted an explanation as to why we had accumulated such a large surplus stock. Again I was very direct. 'We collected these in the early 1970s in anticipation of a major communist victory in Indo China. At the time we restricted our preparations to amassing a secret arsenal.'

I told Rahim Noor that, despite the CPM's internal problems in the first half of the 1970s, the Central Committee had still regarded the international political scene as moving very much in our favour. For this reason, our arms purchases had continued. I am sure Special Branch intelligence, two decades earlier, had reported that our Sadao camp had been a big arms purchasing centre for us. The black market weapons arrived primarily by road, having made their way across the Cambodian frontier. Some came by sea to obscure Thai fishing ports and then overland to our camps.

I was very open with Rahim Noor and felt confident enough to pursue an unconventional final solution to the arms problem. I told him: 'Datuk, the financial assistance your government intends giving the returning comrades is insufficient to sustain their resettlement needs. I am proposing that we in the CPM sell the surplus arms back to the black market dealers who sold them to us in the first place.'

Rahim Noor quickly responded: 'Why don't you sell them to the Malaysian government?'

I indicated I felt this would be unwise. One day the government might claim that the weapons I had sold comprised war booty captured from the communists.

Rahim Noor came back swiftly with an alternative. 'We could send merchants to purchase these weapons directly from you.'

That seemed reasonable. We could then never be accused of selling directly to the government. So I told him his idea was acceptable. We would settle for the best price offered by either the black marketeers or the merchants nominated by Kuala Lumpur. Rahim Noor and I thereafter agreed that within a three-year time-frame the CPM's surplus weapons would be disposed of in this manner.

At the fifth and final round of tripartite talks, the momentum for peace was such that only very minor differences were encountered. These were easily resolved. Before the sessions wound up, a secretariat had been appointed to prepare the two formal peace documents and a joint communiqué. As had been agreed during the Haadyai preliminary meetings, all documents would be signed at an official public ceremony. However, only the joint communiqué would be released to the world media. The two other peace documents – one between the Malaysian government and the CPM, the other between the Thai Internal Security Operations Command and the CPM – would remain classified. On December 2, 1989, over 300 members of the local and international media packed a conference room at the Lee Gardens Hotel in Haadyai for the signing ceremony.

I decided the occasion warranted I speak in Bahasa Malaysia. Apart from noting that I wore a business suit, there was widespread comment among the press on my fluency in the national language of my country. 'As Malaysian citizens,' I said, 'we pledge our loyalty to His Majesty the Yang di-Pertuan Agong and the country. We shall disband our armed units and destroy all weapons to show our sincerity in terminating the armed struggle.' At a follow-up press conference, I refused to answer personal questions probing my private life. When asked what China might think of the peace accords, I suggested the question be posed to the Chinese directly. I also took the opportunity to silence ludicrous press gossip that I was intending to contest political elections in Malaysia.

*　　*　　*　　*　　*

Within a few days of the signing ceremony I travelled south to the CPM Headquarters as the first stop in a general swing around our guerrilla camp locations.

I lacked first-hand background information and needed to make a personal assessment of the CPM's spy-crisis and the shocking purge that had followed. Perhaps, I decided, those at Headquarters could provide details. After all, it was from here that the purge had been directed and I knew that a number of those assigned to the camp were regarded as 'rehabilitated traitors'. At the welcoming ceremony, I made a report on the current political situation and the Haadyai Agreement. Before concluding, I said: 'What about some of you who are considered reformed enemy agents? If you consider you were unjustly accused you must come forward and speak up. We now have peace. Nobody is empowered to arrest, punish or kill you.'

The following morning the sentry guards reported that many of the so-called 'rehabilitated traitors' were crying. I told them to come and talk to me. They told me they had to confess, otherwise they would have been executed. To save themselves they had implicated others. An older woman tearfully recalled how she had met with three other female comrades in the camp's toilet to discuss how best they could escape the purge. Together they concocted a plot involving fellow comrades. They made sure their separate but coordinated accounts could withstand any interrogation. Hints from investigators helped the women piece together their stories. Investigators, I was told, were always willing to suggest whom they wished implicated. I heard even more distressing stories at our Betong East camp. By the end of my tour I discovered the purge had resulted in the executions of at least 16 comrades at Headquarters and 75 at Betong East. My worst fears were confirmed. Ah Hai had been right. There could never have been so many traitors in our midst. Siao Chang had got it terribly wrong.

By the time I returned to Haadyai I received very disturbing news. Unbeknown to either the Thais or the Malaysians I was now confronted with the horrifying prospect of the entire peace accord being suddenly blown apart by fierce and bloody fighting.

None of the participants at the tripartite negotiations had appreciated how close the expected homecoming of former CPM guerrillas would be to the traditional family reunions for the forthcoming Chinese New Year. Reports I was receiving indicated that agitation was building in the Betong area among Chinese families who were endeavouring to contact their loved ones to ensure they would be coming home in time for the important festivities. We had no answers for enquiries about comrades who had been executed during the 1970s purge. Previous efforts by relatives to establish their whereabouts had been easily fobbed off with the excuse that those absent had gone to southern battlefields. This excuse could no longer be used.

The families of those executed were threatening to invade our camps to investigate personally what had befallen their kin. Relatives were arming themselves with *parangs*, spears and shotguns. These were no match for the sophisticated weapons yet to be destroyed by our people. The danger of major clashes and extensive bloodshed was very real. I had to move fast if I was to avoid alarming recriminations.

Immediately I drafted a very urgent document to rehabilitate posthumously the majority of those who had perished during the purge. It also required that those rehabilitated in this way should be recognised as martyrs. I sent this to the yet to be disbanded Central Committee for immediate approval. I pointed out the imperative need for the measure if a catastrophe was to be averted. Among the first ones I rehabilitated were the Thai Chinese. Much later I made sure I rehabilitated my old comrades Wu Tien Wang and Ah Chung.

We well understood it would be unacceptable for many families merely to be told that their dead sons or daughters had been posthumously rehabilitated and pronounced martyrs to the cause. From our limited funds we offered and paid compensation on the basis of Thai baht 20,000 (then approximately US$800) for every member executed during the purge.

In addition, we presented each martyr's next of kin with a document formally recognising the CPM had made a grave error in taking the life of the person for whom compensation funds were being made available. It was issued in the name of the CPM's Northern Bureau. In fact, this bureau was not functioning anymore and existed in name only. But it had functioned during the purge and had been headed by Siao Chang. It was the best I could do in the circumstances. I thought at least the families now knew what had happened to those who would never be returning home. Hopefully, time would ease their grief.

These emergency measures led to disaffection among a few of the old guard. Having been viewed as excessively ruthless in the 1970s purge, we were now being accused of excessive generosity in rehabilitating so many, so quickly. One even criticised me face-to-face. I reiterated the dire circumstances with which I had been confronted. I reasoned that the measures I had undertaken were only proper and expedient.

In Chinese, Thai, Malay and English the memorial, high on a hill overlooking
Princess Chulaporn Village No 10, proclaims 'Eternal Glory to the Martyrs.'
It was dedicated on September 1, 1991.

Chapter 31

Making the peace accords work

Once the peace talks were concluded, the accords signed and the threat of a recriminatory bloodbath averted, I had to ensure that our members took personal responsibility for deciding where they wanted to live from then on.

It was infinitely more complicated than it sounds and the time-frames stipulated by the agreement posed huge challenges. Some people were in Hong Kong. Some were in Macau. Some were in China. Some were in Thailand. Many were supporting families. Some had even gone into business ventures. So we encouraged everyone to make his or her own decision without any pressure on our part.

Having set this in motion, I moved back to China, this time to Peking. There were many loose ends to tie up there. The overwhelming number of our China-based members intended moving to southern Thailand to live. There were also a number of our CPM children in Chinese educational institutions who wanted to finish their various courses. They, too, had to make up their minds where they would want to settle permanently after graduation. In the end, only two opted to stay in China. One or two chose Malaysia. The rest opted for Thailand. Adults and students alike had to be guided through the documentation processes and the responsibility for this fell on me. Those leaving required valid travel documents. Those staying needed identity cards. In order to facilitate the passage of those going to Thailand or Malaysia, I needed to compile official lists. Each person on those lists had to meet stringent deadlines. Application forms for returnees had to be submitted within a period of a year from the signing of the peace accords.

As I set about solving the China-end of the problems presented by the peace agreement, I was approached by several former CPM members who had been banished from Malaya by the British in colonial days. China was not their native land. They wanted to return to Malaysia or even to settle in Thailand and were quite willing to pay their way. Some offered to donate as much as 50,000 yuan in order to be allowed to leave or, at very least, to have their sons and daughters given a chance to get out. I felt very sorry for them but had to be firm. What they were asking for just couldn't be done.

Lee Meng's case was another complication. Originally she and Chen Tien intended moving to southern Thailand. Then, sadly, Chen Tien died. Lee Meng was caring for an ageing blind mother at the time. She couldn't make up her mind whether she should move. In one of the peace villages set aside for us by the Thai authorities, we had built a house for her. It stood empty for a year. At this point the Chinese authorities very kindly assured me they would help with her welfare. In fact, they went ahead and provided Lee Meng with a government middle-cadre residence.

*   *   *   *   *

Following the arrival of our first batch of returnees in Malaysia, a very senior Malaysian police official openly assured the press there would be no interrogation, no prosecution and no detention of any of the home-coming former guerrilla fighters. He also affirmed that, once the returnees had regained their full citizenship, they would be quite free to participate in local politics and could even be elected to parliament. He was right. But he had divulged too much. The next day an even more senior top police officer publicly rebutted what had been said by his colleague. In future, the higher-ranking officer announced, all returnees would be required to sign a document renouncing communism before Malaysia would properly accept them. If necessary, he added, this document would have to be signed in Thailand before entry to Malaysia could be permitted.

From our standpoint this was a direct violation of the peace accord understanding. Then we learned that eight of our former comrades in the first batch moving from Thailand to Malaysia, after being allowed to travel to their respective hometowns and villages, had been promptly rounded up. They had been taken to Kuala Lumpur. Reports reaching us detailed how, upon arrival in the Malaysian capital, the returnees had been instructed by Special Branch officers to sign a formal statement. They refused. After all, they had been told before leaving Thailand that everything had been ironed out and all documentation had been signed and sealed. There was no requirement for them to sign anything further once they reached home. Immediately we suspended the returnee programme while we sought clarification.

The Malaysian Special Branch operation in southern Thailand became very active trying to persuade our people intending to return south that they should sign a specially prepared document. We regarded the contents of this new form as tantamount to a confession and surrender. This, from our standpoint, was not in keeping with the peace accords either. The Special Branch endeavours met with no success. It was now mid-1991. I was in Guangzhou taking care of the myriad matters involving our people in China. At the same time, I was busy packing up my archives with the intention of moving back to southern Thailand myself.

Internationally, communism was in upheaval. Perestroika had ended. The Berlin Wall had fallen. The Russian coup to topple Boris Yeltsin failed. It meant Russia's communist party was in tatters. I felt the Malaysians regarded these international developments as a useful buttress to positions they were adopting in negotiations with us. In addition, Thai politics were going through a particularly rocky patch. There was yet another Bangkok coup followed by a series of arrests. This time General Chartchai and his colleagues were briefly detained.

As if there weren't enough complications filling my schedule, a particularly thorny issue developed around this time involving those who were taking advantage of the time-frame allowed by the peace accords for final decisions to move from southern Thailand back to Malaysia. Who would care for these people during the time it took them to make up their minds?

I travelled to Bangkok especially to confer with Yau Kong Yew, the Malaysian observer I had first met at the Phuket talks. General Kitti told me that Yau would be waiting for me at the Dusi Thani Hotel.

I began by addressing the snags encountered in the returnee programme. I told Yau I feared nobody would go home if Malaysia continued insisting on former armed communists making public confessions to their past activities. These were people who had come north to join our movement. They came from Malaysia. They did not speak Thai. They had no friends or relatives in southern Thailand. Unless we could do something for them I feared they might well take up arms and become a threat to societies on both sides of the border.

I repeated to Yau the promise I had once made to Rahim Noor in the aftermath of the peace talks. I would never again take up arms. Even if my followers urged me to do so, I would never again lead them in this direction. I wanted Yau to be quite clear about my position with the Special Branch and the Malaysian government. I explained how I had told Rahim Noor: ' I know you don't believe 100 per cent of all I have been telling you. In the same way, I don't believe 100 per cent of all you have told me over the months. You can make promises. I can make promises. What really matters is what takes place over the long term. Only then can trust be firmly established.'

Thailand's General Chavalit Yongchaiyudh (left) and Malaysian Prime Minister, Datuk Seri Dr Mahathir Mohamad, the architects of our 1989 peace accords.

Inspector General of Police, Datuk Rahim Noor, led the Malaysian government's delegation at the Phuket talks. His calm, authoritative approach did much to smooth over the countless problems we encountered with the peace process.

Norian Mai was the newly appointed Special Branch chief of Malaysia back in 1991 when I met him in Bangkok to thrash out serious complications arising from the returnee programme as stipulated in the earlier peace accords we had signed.

When the peace overtures began General Kitti Rattanachaya, then Deputy Commander of Thailand's Fourth Army, based in the Kingdom's southern region, was instrumental in establishing and maintaining contacts between all involved parties.

Rahim Noor, I have been told, accepted my word. I later heard he informed the Thais: 'That Chin Peng is an honest man. I trust him.'

Yau Kong Yew flew back to Kuala Lumpur and I stayed on in Bangkok awaiting Malaysia's next move.

Finally, a special meeting was called in the Thai capital to thrash out solutions to the new dilemmas that had arisen, many of which could never have been foreseen by any of the three parties in Phuket. Attending this gathering were General Kitti for Thailand and newly appointed Special Branch Chief, Norian Mai, on the Malaysian side. We met at the Erawan Hotel.

Here all finally agreed, even if it was tacit on the Malaysian side, that it was unfair to ask returnees for a confession statement. As to the matter of returnees' loyalty to Malaysia, to the Agong and constitution, I maintained all this had been well covered in an appendix to the accords signed at Phuket. Furthermore, I had underlined these points in my speech to the Haadyai peace ceremony. Indeed, I had been emphatic so that nobody could later claim there were any lingering doubts on loyalty. Finally I suggested to Norian Mai: 'If you want another slip of paper repeating our pledge of loyalty, you can certainly have it.' The Malaysians then accepted my point of view. The extra piece of paper was deemed superfluous. The returnee programme could slip back into gear.

*　　*　　*　　*　　*

A year after my private meeting with Rahim Noor that reached the understanding on the disposal of our 'surplus weapons', I found myself facing a most profound quandary. It threatened to undermine not only my arrangement with Rahim Noor himself, but also the very spirit of the accords and the trust placed on the pledges I had made on behalf of the CPM.

Thai newspapers published reports of a mysterious arms dump having been uncovered somewhere in the border areas by local police. The suspicion was, of course, that it was one of our secret caches. According to the press accounts some 20 weapons were recovered. Naturally the question that concerned me most was: How had the police discovered the location? I felt certain the authorities had acted on specific information and this could have come only from one of our men seeking financial reward for providing it. Indeed, my concerns would soon be confirmed.

The incident presented me with the very real possibility that other former comrades, looking for quick funds to aid their re-entry to the capitalist world, might yield to the same temptation. So I sent word to Rahim Noor suggesting we reduce drastically the two-to-three year weapons trading time-frame earlier agreed upon. I proposed we conclude the deal as soon as possible. The Malaysians, I feel, read my approach as either suspicious or a sign of weakness. They quickly dispatched Special Branch chief, Norian Mai, to meet me in Haadyai.

Like Rahim Noor before him, Norian Mai wanted me to provide exact numbers of weapons and amounts of ammunition in our hidden caches. Again, I maintained that to provide accurate figures on our arms stocks was next to impossible. Firstly, our books could not be relied upon for exact statistics. Unlike ordinary offices, we did not undertake regular inventories. I expanded on the problem to Norian Mai much as I had done on the earlier occasion with Rahim Noor. If I eventually produced more weapons and ammunition than the 'official figures' he would, no doubt, be happy enough. But, should I fall short of the stated numbers, I faced the possibility of being accused of dishonesty. Worse still, he might believe I was maintaining hidden stocks.

Norian Mai listened and said he would present my explanations to Kuala Lumpur. For some reason, it seemed, the Malaysians could not accept my reasoning. They kept delaying their formal reply. Meanwhile, my concerns mounted. Our Thai hosts were already worried about the dangers of widening banditry throughout the Kingdom's southern provinces posed by illegal arms trafficking. Before matters got out of hand, I took the problem directly to the Thais. They told me straight that they could only pay for our stockpiled weapons at the same rate they had settled for the arms surrendered previously by the Sadao and Betong West groups. To play it safe I sanctioned the sale of all our surplus arms stocks to the Thai authorities.

*   *   *   *   *

In early 1992, I officially informed the Thais that all CPM activities had ceased. Once Peking had established firm state-to-state relationships with the countries of South East Asia, I felt my continuing presence anywhere in China was likely to be an embarrassment for the CPC leadership. So, in 1994, I made a final and permanent move to southern Thailand where I currently reside. I have permanent residence as a 'stateless alien'.

Despite the disbandment of the CPM-led armed units, I still have to look after our old and disabled members. Today they number over 200. Those in the disabled category are suffering primarily the effects of booby trap blasts. We have a financial fund. Formerly when we were getting six per cent bank interest we were relatively comfortable. In recent years, following the economic crisis in the late 1990s, interest rates have fallen sharply and we find ourselves running on annual deficits. This fund has always been held in Thai baht. Unfortunately the baht was devalued back in 1998. We can last for a few more years but we are now digging into our capital. When the funds run out, that will be it.

Every month, former comrades, 60 years and above, who live in the southern Thailand peace villages, receive a personal allowance of Thai baht 540 from our community account. This sum is based on the initial monthly stipend the Thais first allocated each comrade settling in the Kingdom. The Thai payments ceased after three years as called for in the Phuket agreements. Even if financial circumstances forced us to discontinue this assistance, most recipients would manage. Only a small number of the very old and frail would be left destitute. But I would, of course, do my best to assure their well-being.

Indeed, we are most fortunate to have, as our patron, Her Royal Highness Princess Chulaporn after whom our peace villages have been renamed. They were originally known as Peace Villages 1, 2, 3 and 4. According to the Peace Agreement, they came under military administration. Through the representations of General Kitti, who was then Thailand's 4th Army Commander, and the kind agreement of the Princess herself, they have become officially designated Princess Chulaporn Villages 9, 10, 11, 12. They have now been transferred to civilian control. From time to time Her Royal Highness pays us visits and is briefed on our situation. Her continuing interest in this way serves as an important reassurance that our people will continue their integration into Thai society.

One of our four peace villages – this one Princess Chulaporn Village No 10 – in southern Thailand. The top photo shows some of the living accommodation for our re-settled former guerrilla fighters. At the centre of the lower photograph is the white dove peace symbol which stands before the village administrative area and community centre. The two buildings in the background are newly established rest houses for tourists and paying guests.

Chapter 32

A continuing exile

More and more these days, I think of Sitiawan and of the shophouse where I was born. The establishment selling Ford motor cars across the road closed down just before the Japanese invasion. It was replaced by a coffee shop which, I understand, still operates to this day. I wonder if any of my old friends meet there and, over *kaya* toast and coffee, exchange views about the world, the way our fathers had gathered in similar settings, long before the war that changed all our lives.

After meeting my end of the 1989 peace accords, I had looked forward to a homecoming. In late 1990 I made applications to settle down in Malaysia but was rejected at the end of December, 1991. Some eight years later, in early 1999, a Special Branch officer in Yala asked me whether I would like to apply for a sightseeing tour. My reply was: Of course. I indicated my wish to be allowed to visit my hometown so that I could pay homage to the graves of my grandfather, parents and my brothers in the Chinese cemetery, halfway between Sitiawan and Lumut. This duty is still uppermost in my mind.

For some reason or other, things have not worked out yet. It has been a frustrating wait. There are days when I end up thinking, if the price of my dream for a liberated Malaya extends to this continuing exile, then, so be it.

But reason always returns. I have never given consent to despair even during the gloomiest days of our armed struggle and I shall not give room to it now. I do not allow myself to fret for long. Years in isolated jungle camps have made me good at this discipline.

So I keep the trip home at the back of my mind and return to it in the quieter hours. I would start with a stay in Sitiawan. After paying respects at the family graves, I would visit the old school, trace familiar routes, rejuvenate friendships. There are images that would not leave me, of roads and trees, houses and street signs that could only belong to what I knew as Malaya. I want to see them again. It is naturally my wish to spend the last years of my life in Malaysia. It is ironic that I should be without the country for which I was more than willing to die.

It has been pointed out to me that my life — and, presumably, the lives of those closest to me — would have been more comfortable had I not taken the path I took.

The people who say this remind me of the 'bright options' I had as a young man in my twenties. I had been awarded two campaign medals, mentioned in despatches, housed in cosy bungalows, given an OBE — I could have used these early enticements to forge ahead and become what the same people like to call 'a dazzling success story'.

I find their point of view flawed. They exhibit a selfish, self-centred concept of the way one's life should be conducted.

There is a sense of inevitability that runs through life once your general attitude to it is formed. I believe in this. I recall that meeting with my mother in the rented room in Ipoh. Would it have helped had I humoured her and left her hoping I would eventually take up her offer of further studies in China? Empty promises were just not part of the equation. A lie then would have only postponed my mother's acceptance of the choices I had made and what good would that have done anybody?

When the war came, I had to be with the guerrilla forces fighting the Japanese. It seemed to be the natural progression of my childhood and teenage orientation. As a young man I saw no other route that would have sat well with me for the rest of my life. Just as I was appalled by the British colonial days before the war, I was outraged by the Japanese invasion. I had to help actively undermine the invaders. To compromise would have been more harrowing than the formidable hills and jungles we had to trudge through.

I don't think you can truly split your life in neat watertight compartments and believe that the parcels have no bearing whatsoever on one another. Good deeds, errors of judgements, miscalculations, acts of kindness and generosity, times of ill-will — they are all realities that interweave and determine the genuine quality of our lives. The sad compromises of youth will be the reality checks and the ultimate unease of old age.

We all have options — to stand our ground or to compromise, to save or to waste, to confront or to look the other way, to forget or to remember.

I had to be a liberation fighter. If you had lived in a Malayan rural population centre like Sitiawan and observed how dismissive the British colonials were of our lot in the 1930s, you would find it easier to understand how the attraction of a Communist Party of Malaya could take hold. My involvement was not born of a series of personal slights, rather it was the result of objective scrutiny and years of intellectual introspection. And if you had gone through the ghastly period of the corrupt British Military Administration immediately after the Japanese capitulation and seen the wholesale poverty that pervaded after years of Japanese atrocities, if you had watched how this administration worked in Malayan towns and villages, you would not be quick to say that I should have been cool-headed and taken an easier road. I could not compromise with the Japanese; neither could I have worked within a system that perpetrated the continuance of British colonialism.

The Communist Party of Malaya was at its strongest during the 1945-1948 period. Internal circumstances in the country were ripe for revolt. Most of the British colonials who came after the surrender of Japan were not just opportunists and corrupt; they were downright disdainful of the people they were exploiting. They shot innocent, unarmed civilians demonstrating in the countryside for food and jobs. It was Mao who first talked about power coming from the muzzle of a gun. You could say the British sought to extend political domination and economic production in Malaya through exactly the same means.

Neither the CPM Central Committee nor the Politburo ever adopted a programme that targeted civilians. The October 1, 1951, Resolution reflected my desire to pursue a war without committing excesses that might be construed as terrorism. Planters were legitimate targets. They demanded the imposition of martial law. They had histories of exploiting workers and hiring thugs to break up strikes on their plantations. Many of them were ex-servicemen, demobbed from British World War 11 units. They had broad experience in military matters. In post-war Malaya they were armed; they surrounded themselves with paid thugs; they drove in armoured cars.

To this day I maintain it was the British colonials who used terror tactics to retain their hold on Malaya. Long before the Emergency, they sowed fear and panic among plantation workers who lived under the constant threat of being transported back to India. To those who displayed anti-colonial sentiments, they dangled the horror of banishment to China which, pre-1949, meant death for the majority and prison for the rest. More thugs were brought in to silence the grievances of workers. After Japan's capitulation, the inept BMA showed no mercy. To contain the Emergency, the British burned villages, cut rations and shot civilians. More often than not these terror tactics had quite the opposite effect to that intended. The Briggs Plan was an ultimate success but its 'new villages' would never have passed today's standards of what constitutes human rights.

I make no apologies for seeking to replace such an odious system with a form of Marxist socialism. Colonial exploitation, irrespective of who were the masters, Japanese or British, was morally wrong. The CPM was blocked by the exploiters from participating in the democratic process – either we got co-opted or we took up arms. If you saw how the returning British functioned the way I did, you would know why I chose arms.

I could not have used an OBE to be the core of my life. I could not have betrayed my men the way I was being coerced to do at Baling. So many of my followers did not die, did not suffer the rigours of extreme deprivation, so that I could lead the survivors to one massive, sweeping exercise in humiliation orchestrated by the British. At Baling, trying to end a seven-year-old acrimony in two days, David Marshall had thundered that 'you're making yourselves suffer indignities and miseries in the jungle with its disease and its lack of the essentials of human life'. I'm not privy to Marshall's archives. I do not know what he advised his clients so that they may be able to escape incarceration. But basing it on his performance at Baling and what he said about 'human dignity', I challenge his interpretation of what should matter to a man.

The Emergency lasted for as long as it did precisely because I did not wish my followers to suffer indignities. Counting the time I spent fighting the Japanese, I had been in the jungle for more than ten years when I sat in that Kedah classroom. There was nothing at Baling that inspired a frank and honest exchange of ideas required in the resolution of conflict. Apart from the fact that the British were clearly calling the shots, there was also the absence of genuine motivation.

The Tunku used the occasion as a propaganda boost to enhance his political image and strengthen his bargaining position with London. Anyone who doubts this only has to read what the Tunku himself said in 1974. 'The only good thing the Emergency produced,' he wrote, 'was my meeting with Chin Peng. Because of those talks of mine in Baling we were able to wrest the initiative from the Malayan Communist Party, then sit at a conference table in London to negotiate our independence with the British, and win our freedom as a nation. Baling led straight to Merdeka.'

Baling also gave Marshall a few hours of grandstanding. Though he hardly contributed to the talks, Dato Tan Cheng Lock earned kudos as a pillar of the Chinese community.

As I see it now, the Baling talks were a doomed 'sprint to peace'. They gave no room for the re-examination of feelings and principles. I have been accused of having been 'inflexible' during those discussions. I had to be, under the circumstances. Nobody went to Baling prepared to hear what I had to say. We were blocked from

I keep in touch with old colleagues and, like anyone else looking back on long lives shared in the pursuit of dreams – realised or otherwise – there are always light moments. Rashid Maidin and I go back more than half a century.

holding a press conference. Thus, nobody else beyond the schoolhouse walls could hear CPM sentiments. The Party was evil and we were the devils and that was that. We were treated like prisoners. If that was how we were handled during 'peace talks' – and Rashid Maidin, Chen Tien and I were leaders – how would the CPM rank-and-file have been dealt with had we surrendered? We were being browbeaten to give up. Capitulate and be chastised – this was the message at Baling. And, if I may follow through Marshall's reasoning, we were expected to get the message if we wanted to sleep in comfortable beds again.

I had desired peace but it was fundamental that my men and women were not roundly humiliated. The peace initiatives of the late 1980s were different. Government representatives that the CPM dealt with listened and saw reason in why we could not accept the word 'surrender'. In turn, we listened to them and saw why our insistence on the recognition of the CPM as a legitimate party was unrealistic. The numerous sessions were characterised by a mood of 'give and take'. Sensitivities were pointed out and explained. Nobody ever thought a resolution could and must be achieved in a few hours. Everyone worked hard and long. There was respect. We were equals.

The 1989 peace accords were reached because the Malaysian government, the Thai government and the Communist Party of Malaya all genuinely wanted a resolution to hostilities. All parties looked to a bigger picture, to a future offering peace and prosperity. So the CPM got a reasonable conclusion to its struggle – peace with dignity. We failed to win the revolution but neither did we suffer the ignominy of surrender. It is the kind of peace for my people I can accept and with which I can live with some satisfaction.

I am still a socialist. I certainly still believe in the equitable distribution of wealth, though I see this could take eons to evolve. I go for the theory of each to his own ability. But, in the Malaysian context, I have definitely dropped the idea of the dictatorship of the proletariat as the central concept for an administrative blueprint.

It is good for the mind to envisage a world that is not wholly driven by greed and materialism. As I see it now, people will just go on creating and inventing needs. That proverbial ladder to success will only get steeper. People will keep on forgetting the difference between a need and a desire, a staple and a whim. Greed and materialism will continue to spread and expand. They will complicate lives further and further until a point comes – perhaps decades and decades from now – when, overwrought, people will have to question their motivations. Whole communities will be required to review their reasons for being or they will self-destruct. Greed and materialism serve only short-term objectives. They can never form the foundations of a lasting society. Any society that thinks they can, deludes itself. In the end, I think all civilisations can only return to priceless values.

The youth who have known only stable governments and live in an independent age of affluence will find the choices I made as a teenager deeply puzzling. This is understandable. The way-points I traversed as a youth are far removed from those they follow in their personal computers. They will think the Malaya I talk about in this book is another world and they will not be far off the mark. It *was* a different world. The colours of that colonial world were stark. There were no muted hues and shades of gray to provide consolations and rationalisations. I was young in a very different age that demanded very different approaches.

A revolution based on violence has no application in modern Malaysia or Singapore. None of the conditions favourable to armed struggle exist today in relation to these territories. You need complementary international and internal situations to set hearts burning for armed revolt. If the people lead reasonable lives and feel accepted in society, how can you ask them to put their lives on the line? Why would you?

I suppose I am the last of the region's old revolutionary leaders. It was my choice to lead from the shadows, away from the limelight. This was probably my undoing. My elusive approach to the struggle made it easier for British propaganda to mould the image they wanted for the CPM Secretary General – brutal, ruthless, bloodthirsty and indifferent to suffering. It was the concoction they fed town and kampong folk throughout the peninsula, during and beyond the Emergency. The shires of England and the cities of her Commonwealth nations were as vulnerable to such misinformation. The British needed to demonise Chin Peng and the CPM to explain an Emergency that proved indestructible at its core.

All that is not speculation. The declassified documents of the Emergency years prove how the British manipulated language and information lest the rest of the world got to believe the CPM was a legitimate nationalist group seeking the end of colonialism. There are exchanges of notes showing how fearful colonial officials were of having the subject of the CPM raised in international conferences and to what lengths they were prepared to go to avoid this. History has proved that earlier British assertions of Moscow and Peking directing the CPM from 1948 were totally baseless. We were never aided financially by the USSR; neither did Moscow ever order us which path to take. Medical aid for our TB patients was all we got from China until

1961 when the struggle took another form in line with Mao's reading of world revolution.

The governments with whom we signed the 1989 peace accords had the facts at their fingertips. They knew the story of the Emergency; they had their classified and their declassified files. Would they have treated me the way they did; would they have been as open and as accommodating to me had I been as callous as the British Royal Marine photographed holding two severed communist heads? Would they have given those concessions had I justified mutilation so that 'the right identification' could be made, the way Gerald Templer had done?

I think not. The men who initiated the peace accords of 1989 knew the difference between the monster created by colonial British propaganda and the man seeking fair, acceptable and humane terms for the men and women who had joined him in a just cause that was now past its expiry date.

I have read numerous books about the Emergency. Much of what has been passed on as history are well-articulated speculations and guesswork. Some historians have killed comrades long before these were actually felled in action. Propagandists have claimed I targeted innocent civilians. Untrue. I have been reported to have thrown out of the CPM people who were not even members of the Party; to have ordered the executions of those who opposed me. Again, baseless.

I thought I would relate my side of history to make the documentation of those years a little less lopsided. I waited this long because I needed to gain perspective. I was isolated in the jungles, then I was away in China. I had to gather my thoughts, pass them through a sieve and reflect on the bits that still held meaning.

I fought a liberation war. To ask whether I would do it again is idle talk. I was a young man in an entirely different setting. But the realities and the lessons I learned from that time comprise a body of values I can share with the young who may wish to look beyond their palmtops and understand how history is shaped. I would like to be involved in a forum. It is the exchange of ideas that ultimately moves the world. The barter of views still exhilarates me. You can tell me I was wrong. You can tell me I failed. But I can also tell you how it was and how I tried.

End Notes

1.   The original document signed at the Blantan meeting on December 31, 1943, is held at the Public Record Office (PRO) Kew, United Kingdom, under reference (ref.): HS 7/165.

2.   Davis' signal introducing Chin Peng to SEAC HQ was relayed to London on August 23, 1945, at 1015 hrs. A copy of this signal: PRO, ref. HS 1/114.

3.   A full English language translation of the CPM's nine-point manifesto, as first published by the Party's cyclostyled Emancipation Press in January, 1944: PRO, ref. HS 7/165

4.   Memorandum on Resistance Forces in Malaya on the Eve of Japanese capitulation, August 15, 1945, signed by Innes Tremlett as Head of Malayan Country Section: PRO, ref. HS 7/165.

5.   A copy of this eight-point programme was first obtained by the British Force 136 officer with the codename 'Humour' – Lt Colonel Claude Fenner, who was by this time functioning as a Liaison Officer with an armed MPAJA unit in Negri Sembilan. He immediately transmitted its contents to SEAC HQ in Ceylon which, in turn, radioed the information on to London where it was received at 0950 hrs on August 29, 1945. Details: PRO, ref. HS 1/115.

6.   PRO, ref. HS 1/114

7.   PRO, ref. HS 1/114

8.   PRO, ref. HS 1/114.

9.   PRO, ref. HS 1/114.

10.   'Private and personal' correspondence from the Colonial Office to Commissioner General MacDonald dated December, 1948, where London indicates how it intends to cover up MacDonald's repeated urgings that High Commissioner Gent be removed: PRO, ref. CO 967/83.

11.   Correspondence from Macdonald to Gent and Colonial Office dated July 3, 1948; correspondence from MacDonald to Colonial Office July 19 and October 7, 1948: PRO, ref. CO 967/83. Handwritten correspondence dated January 4, 1949 from the widow of Sir Edward Gent to the Colonial Office referring to relations between her late husband and Commissioner General MacDonald: PRO, ref. CO 967/83.

12.   The text of Commissioner General MacDonald's broadcast over radio Malaya, June 6, 1948: PRO, ref. FO 953/326

13.   War Office notes on the 'Military Situation in Malaya in August, 1948': PRO, ref. FO 371/69698

[14] Correspondence between Australian External Affairs Minister Evatt and British Secretary of State for Commonwealth Relations Noel-Baker dated August 17-18, 1948: PRO, ref. FO 371/69698.

[15] Memorandum of advice to Secretary of State Noel-Baker dated August 14, 1948: PRO, ref. FO 371/69698.

[16] Australian Defence Cooperation document: PRO, ref. FO 371/69698.

[17] Secretary of State for War John Strachey's May 12, 1950, report to the British Cabinet's Malaya Committee: PRO, ref. DEFE 11/36.

[18] High Commissioner Gurney's hand-written letter to the Colonial Office dated March 19, 1951, offering his resignation: PRO, ref. CO 967/145

[19] Colonial Office's April 5, 1951, response to Gurney's aggrieved resignation offer; where the High Commissioner is reassured by the Secretary of State: PRO, ref. CO 967/145.

[20] PRO, ref. CO 967/145

[21] PRO, ref CO 1022/45.

[22] General Templer's reply to Colonial Secretary Lyttleton's telegram no 82: PRO, ref. CO 1022/45.

[23] British intelligence assessment entitled 'Monthly Emergency and Political report for the period October 15 to November 15, 1953,' indicating CPM's Politburo was thought to be operating in western Pahang: PRO, ref. DEFE 11/96

[24] Notes of discussion between General Templer and Lt General Pao Sryanond held at King's House, Kuala Lumpur, April 10, 1953: PRO, ref. CO 1022/37.

[25] Outward telegram from Commonwealth Relations Office dated February 21, 1953: PRO, ref. DEFE 11/95

[26] Notes on the meeting between the British Ambassador to Siam and General Pao held in Bangkok on September 23, 1953: PRO, ref. CO 1022/37.

[27] PRO, ref. DEFE 11/118.

[28] PRO, ref. CO 1030/29

[29] Item 15 of Foreign Office Telegram No 66 Intel: PRO, ref. CO 1022/2

Additional References

In addition to official documents quoted in the End Notes, the following Public Record Office files were also researched to substantiate information recounted in this book:

AIR 10/8584
CAB 128/26
CO 537/4770
CO 537/428
CO 967/81
CO 1022/1 – 6
CO 1022/13
CO 1022/21
CO 1022/25 – 29
CO 1022/32
CO 1022/39
CO 1022/41
CO 1022/46
CO 1022/49
CO 1022/54 – 55
CO 1022/132 – 133
CO 1022/146
CO 1022/188
CO 1022/190
CO 1022/209
CO 1030/700
DEFE 11/32 – 56
DEFE 11/69
DEFE 11/74 – 75
DEFE 11/81 – 86
DEFE 11/96 – 102
DEFE 11/105

DEFE 11/107
DEFE 11/112 – 114
DEFE 11/120
DEFE 11/122 – 23
DEFE 11/158
DEFE 11/186 – 192
DEFE 11/273 – 275
DO 142/405
FO 370
FO 371/69697
FO 371/84479
HS 1/116
HS 1/120
HS 1/122 – 23
HS 7/166
WO 32/17642
WO 203/1 – 49
WO 203/1819
WO 203/4208
WO 203/5603
WO 203/5604
WO 203/5605
WO 208/1522
WO 208/1545
WO 208/3081
WO 208/3214
WO 208/3216

WO 208/3219
WO 208/3925
WO 208/3927
WO 208/3933
WO 208/3936
WO 208/3996
WO 208/4102
WO 268/46 – 50
WO 268/549
WO 268/550
WO 268/551
WO 291/1699
WO 291/1713
WO 291/1718
WO 291/1722 – 23
WO 291/1728
WO 291/1735
WO 291/1740 – 41
WO 291/1754
WO 291/1762 – 63
WO 291/1782
WO 291/1788 – 89
WO 305
WO 356/1
WO 356/6
WO 356/8
WO 357/2 – 3

Photo Credits

p.12-13, Public Record Office (Kew,UK); *p.28*, Media Masters; *p.33*, Media Masters; *p.40*, Media Masters; *p.42*, Media Masters; *p.46*, by courtesy of Mr Peter Fung Shou Yi; *p.69*, Media Masters; *p.83*, (top) Internal Security Department (ISD), Singapore; (bottom) Media Masters; *p.97*, The New Straits Times (KL, Malaysia); *p.107*, Media Masters; *p.116*, The New Straits Times; *p.120*, Chin Peng archives; *p.139*, Chin Peng archives; *p.140*, Chin Peng archives; *p.150*, Imperial War Museum (London,UK); *pp.151-152*, Imperial War Museum; *p.168*, Media Masters; *p.180*, Chin Peng archives; *p.194*, Media Masters; *pp.216-217*, Media Masters; *p.220*, Singapore National Heritage Board; *p.229*, Chin Peng archives; *p.233*, Media Masters; *p.235*, Imperial War Museum; *p.237*, The New Straits Times; *p.265*, Chin Peng archives; *p.269* (top), Singapore National Heritage Board; (bottom),The New Straits Times; *pp.281-283*, Imperial War Museum; *p.290*, The New Straits Times; *p.291* (top), The New Straits Times; (bottom) by courtesy of Mr. Jeff De Zilva; *p.293*, Media Masters; *p.296*, The New Straits Times; *p.298*, The New Straits Times; *p.303*, Public Record Office; *p.308*, The New Straits Times; *p.310*, by courtesy of Mr Daniel Loke; *p.325*, Chin Peng archives; *p.337*, Chin Peng archives; *p.340*, The New Straits Times; *p.343*, The New Straits Times; *p.349*, Ching Peng archives; *p.362*, Chin Peng archives; *p.372*, The New Straits Times; *p.374*, Media Masters; *p.378*, Media Masters; *p.399*, Imperial War Museum; *p.404*, Australian War Memorial (Canberra); *p.419*, Chin Peng archives; *p.427*, Chin Peng archives; *p.431*, Chin Peng archives; *p.443*, Chin Peng archives; *p.464*, Media Masters; *p.475*, Chin Peng archives; *p.494*, The New Straits Times; *p.500*, Media Masters; *p.504*, The New Straits Times; *p.508*, Media Masters; *p.513*, Media Masters.

Editor's Notes

The old names of places have been used and adjusted as time marched on — Malaya, of course, for Malaysia, Siam for Thailand, the Dutch East Indies for Indonesia and so on.

Some Malay terms have been included in the main text: *atap* (a semi-aquatic creeping palm used for building modest shelters, especially roofs); *kampong* (village); *lalang* (grass); *padang* (field) *parang* (knife) *pulau* (island) and *tongkang* (large wooden boat used primarily for transporting cargo).

Index

Chavalit Yongchaiyudh, General, 484.

Cheah Swee Seng, 402.

Chemor, 61, 62, 63, 64, 76, 77, 78, 104.

Chen Chin Sheng, 17.

Chen Hong, 320, 323.

Chen Jin Yun, 50.

Chen Lu, 50.

Chen Tien, 229, 299, 349, 350, 364, 365, 366, 368, 371, 375, 410, 413, 415, 416, 418, 422, 423, 429, 447, 502, 514.

Chen Yong, 155, 163, 171, 172-175, 185-186, 201, 224-5.

Chen, David Chung En, 309-311.

Chiang Kai Shek, Generalissimo, 32, 41, 48, 98, 153, 253, 441.

Chin, Juliet, 450, 451.

China Bay, 117.

China Relief Fund, 43, 44, 70.

China, 10, 31, 32, 34, 35, 37, 41, 43, 44, 45, 46, 47, 48, 49, 50, 53, 55, 57, 58, 59, 60, 64, 88, 98, 102, 109, 110, 111, 119, 126, 133, 139, 141, 146, 157, 158, 163, 176, 182, 205, 254-255, 261, 292, 327, 338, 339, 347, 350, 353, 367, 377, 380, 385, 403, 408, 411, 421, 426-432, 440, 442, 445-463, 473-478, 481-484, 488, 493, 501, 503, 507, 511, 515, 516.

Chinese Chambers of Commerce, 197.

Chou En-Lai, 43, 164, 255, 353, 447, 456, 463.

Chou Yang Pin, 229.

Christian, Ian, 214-215, 310.

Christison, Lt General Sir Philip, 133.

Chrustal, 70.

Chun Ling High School, 309-310.

Chung Cheng High School, 38.

Chung Nan Hai, 428.

Chungking, 26, 43, 98.

Chunjin School, 66.

Churchill, Winston, 295, 316, 346.

clandestine army (Mi Mi Tui), 112, 113, 118.

Coe, Frank, 444.

Coliseum Hotel, 91.

Colombo, 16, 95, 100, 115, 129,

Comintern, 57, 122, 157, 202, 449.

communist guerrillas, 14.

Communist Party of Australia (CPA), 202.

Communist Party of China (CPC), 57, 163, 177, 189, 209, 223, 351, 403, 408, 447, 449.

Communist Party of India (CPI), 202.

Communist Party of Malaya (CPM), 11, 15, 16, 17, 50, 57, 58, 64, 66, 67, 307, 309, 434-437, 439-442, 445, 489-493, 496-499, 501, 505-507, 510-511, 514-516.

Communist Party of Siam (CPS), 411.

Creech-Jones, Arthur, 234, 240, 245, 246.

Criminal Intelligence Department (CID), 57.

Cultural Revolution, 444, 445, 446, 448, 449, 450, 452, 456, 457, 468.

Czechoslovakia, 192.

D

Daily Mail, 368.

Daily Mirror, 307.

Davis, Major John L. H., 14, 15, 16, 17, 19, 22, 23, 24, 25, 30, 95, 96, 97, 99, 101, 102, 103, 106, 108, 109, 113, 114, 121, 122, 129, 130, 131, 153, 154, 155, 371-375, 387, 389-390.

de Cruz, Gerald, 192, 199, 370.

Democratic Republic of Malaya, 75, 92.

Dempsey, Lt General Miles, 153.

Deng Fuk Lung, 229, 475.

Deng Xiao Ping, 428, 429, 430, 434, 456-59, 483.

DeVries, Lt Commander W.J., 98.

Dien Bien Phu, 286, 391, 422.

Dindings Channel, 18, 22.

Dong Hoi, 418.

Du Lung San, 45, 50, 51, 55, 66.

Dutch East Indies, 127, 141, 155, 157, 203, 246.

Dyaks, 302.

E

East Africa, 26.

East Germany, 440.

eight point declaration (CPM), 119.

Elphil Estate, 213-216.

Eu Chooi Yip, 279, 436, 437.

Evatt, Dr Herbert, 249.

F

Far East Land Forces (FARELF), 316.

Federation of Trade Unions, 197, 198.

Fenner, Claude, 98, 116, 117.

Fiji, 26.

Fleet street, 306, 368.

Foot, Dingle, 344.

Force 136, 44, 103, 113, 118, 335, 364.

Ford factory, 68.

Formosa, 253.

fortress Singapore, 10.

Fraser's Hill, 287.

Fraser's Hill, 68.

Freedom News, 60.

Fuchow, 31.

Fukien province, 31.

Fung Shou Yi, 45, 46.

G

Gemas, 67.

Geneva Agreements (1954), 420, 424.

Gent, Mr G.E.J., 131, 132.

Gent, Sir Edward, 161, 196, 201, 234-236.

Georgetown, 223.

Germany, 49, 60.

Geylang, 27.

Ghazali Shafie Tan Seri, 472-473.

Gia Lam airport, 418, 439.

Giyu Gun, 125.

GLOs (General Liaison Officers), 114.

Gopeng, 78, 320, 341.

Gray, Nicol, 284.

Grik, 110, 324.

Gua Musang, 232, 233, 236, 238, 263.

Guam Doctrine, 452.

Guangzhou, 488, 489, 491, 493, 503.

Gunong Paku, 366, 368, 371.

Gurkha Rifles, (5th), 98.

Gurkha troops, 114, 117, 326, 462.

Gurney, Sir Henry, 236, 237, 284, 288-295.

Acknowledgements

Ian Ward and Norma Miraflor are indebted to the staff at the Public Record Office in Kew, United Kingdom, the Imperial War Museum on Lambeth road, London, and the Australian War Memorial in Canberra for their generous assistance.

They also wish to thank the following: Mr David Webb who read an early draft of the book, for his comments and constructive suggestions; Mr Paul Hill of the Foreign Desk, *The Daily Telegraph*, London, for arranging facilities at the newspaper's library and archives; Mr Michael Knipe of *The Times*, London, whose kind and prompt reply gave more substance to the Louis Heren-Gerald Templer episode; Dr Peter Londey of the Australian War Memorial who was always ready to advise where they might find things at the AWM; Mr Jeff De Zilva, hotelier and history buff, for the discreet enthusiasm he displayed for the work-in-progress; Mr Wong Kian Ping for the calligraphy on the front cover and Ms Ramjam Hamzah of *The New Straits Times* Resource Centre for her quiet efficiency.

This book is the result of three years' collaboration – a big collection of taped conversations, copious notes, long, long hours of analyses and arguments, interminable to-ing and fro-ing. In hindsight, would they do it again?

The co-authors take the cue from Chin Peng himself. The question is 'idle talk'. They would much rather focus on the privilege of having worked with a remarkable man who opted to live through so much strife but who now appears to be more at peace and less anguished than many men who wallow in either wealth or power . . . or both.

Ward and Miraflor would have enjoyed discussing the finished manuscript with the late Professor Michael Leifer, CMG, of the London School of Economics. It was he who initially encouraged the writing duo to undertake what he considered would be a truly worthwhile task. It was also Michael who first told them of the non-political and non-ideological links that might lead to Chin Peng.

Ward and Miraflor were in the early stages of their taped conversations with Chin Peng when Michael Leifer died on March 23, 2001. Neither Ward nor Miraflor thought the book would take another 29 months to complete. Every now and then, through the more difficult patches of the collaboration, the pair would recall Michael's incisiveness, his lack of arrogance, his intellectual generosity.

Ian Ward and Norma Miraflor wish to say, through this completed project, how much they miss Michael Leifer's friendship.